C0065 62836

D1760212

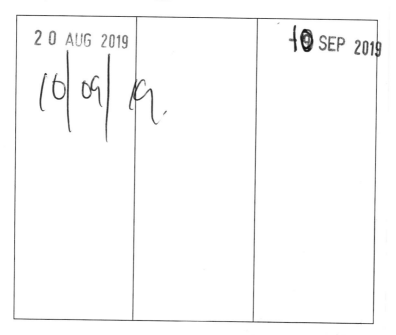

My Father Joachim von Ribbentrop

Bibliography of the Author

Charmley, John: Churchill. Das Ende einer Legende, Berlin 1995.

Ribbentrop, Annelies v.: Verschwörung gegen den Frieden. Studien zur Vorgeschichte des Zweiten Weltkrieges, Leoni am Starnberger See 1962.

——, Deutsch-Englische Geheimverbindungen. Britische Dokumente der Jahre 1938 und 1939 im Lichte der Kriegsschuldfrage, Tübingen 1967.

——, Die Kriegsschuld des Widerstandes. Aus britischen Geheimdokumenten 1938/39, Leoni am Starnberger See 1974.

Ribbentrop, Joachim v.: Zwischen London und Moskau. Erinnerungen und letzte Aufzeichnungen, Leoni am Starnberger See 1953.

Scheil, Stefan: Logik der Mächte. Europas Problem mit der Globalisierung der Politik, Berlin 1999.

——, Fünf plus Zwei. Die europäischen Nationalstaaten, die Weltmächte und die vereinte Entfesselung des Zweiten Weltkrieges, Berlin 2003.

——, 1940/41: Die Eskalation des Zweiten Weltkriegs, München 2005.

——, Ribbentrop. Oder: Die Verlockung des nationalen Aufbruchs. Eine politische Biographie, Berlin 2013.

Tansill, Charles: Die Hintertür zum Krieg. Das Drama der internationalen Diplomatie von Versailles bis Pearl Harbor, Düsseldorf 1956.

My Father Joachim von Ribbentrop

Hitler's Foreign Minister, Experiences and Memories

Rudolf von Ribbentrop

Translated by Doolie Sloman

Pen & Sword
MILITARY

First published in Great Britain in 2019 by
Pen & Sword Military
An imprint of
Pen & Sword Books Ltd
Yorkshire – Philadelphia

ISBN 978 1 52673 925 4

A CIP catalogue record for this book is
available from the British Library.

Printed and bound in the UK by TJ International Ltd,
Padstow, Cornwall.

Pen & Sword Books Limited incorporates the imprints of Atlas,
Archaeology, Aviation, Discovery, Family History, Fiction, History,
Maritime, Military, Military Classics, Politics, Select, Transport,
True Crime, Air World, Frontline Publishing, Leo Cooper, Remember
When, Seaforth Publishing, The Praetorian Press, Wharncliffe
Local History, Wharncliffe Transport, Wharncliffe True Crime
and White Owl.

For a complete list of Pen & Sword titles please contact

PEN & SWORD BOOKS LIMITED
47 Church Street, Barnsley, South Yorkshire, S70 2AS, England
E-mail: enquiries@pen-and-sword.co.uk
Website: www.pen-and-sword.co.uk

Or

PEN AND SWORD BOOKS
1950 Lawrence Rd, Havertown, PA 19083, USA
E-mail: Uspen-and-sword@casematepublishers.com
Website: www.penandswordbooks.com

Contents

Dedication

I wish to dedicate this book to the memory of my mother, who very early on in my life gave me a glimpse behind the scenes into world history; and to my beloved wife, who with endless patience has accompanied the work on this book; and to my gallant soldiers, alive or dead, whose leader I had the honour to be in the war.

Foreword

Following the Battle of the Bulge (the Ardennes Offensive), in January 1945 I was posted to the Fallingbostel military training area to arrange a 'refreshing' – the term used in those days when, after deployment, troops, weapons and equipment had to be replaced – of the armoured battalion that I had taken over after its commanding officer had been killed in action. The battalion had suffered severe losses and the division had already been transferred to Hungary again in order to take part in the imminent Lake Balaton offensive. I was in consequence directly under the command of an office which was quartered in alternative accommodation east of Berlin. The replacement troops, weapons and equipment were thence to be allocated to me.

On my way to where this office was located, it chanced that in the evening of 2 February 1945, driving my Volkswagen 'bucket' car (VW-Kübelwagen), I arrived in Berlin at the home of my parents, who would give me makeshift accommodation, as the building belonging to the Foreign Ministry housing the official ministerial residence had largely been destroyed. I was about to leave the next morning when it was announced that 'substantial bomber formations were approaching the capital'. As I was not bound to a specific time, I decided to stay on in Berlin for the opportunity to witness the effect of the notorious 'terror attacks' on the civilian population in the form of strategic 'firestorm' bombing of a populated area that one hardly experienced while in the field with the troops. Little could I foresee what lay in store for me!

The air raid's target was the quarter where the government buildings were sited: this was only too obvious because of the noise made by the impact of the strikes so close by. My Volkswagen was parked in front of the Wilhelmstrasse building. How was I to get back to my battalion in Fallingbostel should the car be wrecked? Trains had not been running for some time.

However, when the bombing abated I found that it had miraculously escaped any damage. Only then did I look down the familiar Wilhelmstrasse towards the Reichskanzlei, the Chancellery that stood a few hundred metres further away on Wilhelmplatz. Fires raged everywhere; the road was covered in heaps of rubble. My father, dressed in uniform and cap, crossed the courtyard in front of the building and asked me to accompany him on foot to the Chancellery. Because of the fires and rubble he probably considered it important to give the people gradually emerging from the basements to the daylight an example of calm demeanour.

Just down the road we suddenly saw the Japanese ambassador, General Oshima, in front of us, also in uniform. He greeted me warmly – we had known each other for many years. The two gentlemen formally acknowledged that the situation was critical but that there was no doubt one would come through it. It was a weird scene, abruptly interrupted when a woman, evidently distraught, rudely shoved her baby carriage between the two gentlemen and roughly pushed them apart, which they both took with equanimity. With a friendly smile, as the custom in his country requires even in the face of a devastating catastrophe, the general bade us goodbye.

Being in the army, after five years of war the sight of burning or destroyed cities was no longer unfamiliar, but in this case I felt the history of Germany was visibly sinking into annihilation. While still children we had been made aware that the building in front of which I now stood with my father was the residence of the president of the Reich, who in those days was Paul von Hindenburg.

The location on Wilhelmstrasse, where Bismarck had formulated Germany's policy, was a well-known address, like 10 Downing Street in London, the Quai d'Orsay in Paris, Vienna's Ballhausplatz, Washington's White House or the Kremlin in Moscow. It was here that national policies had been formed and thereby 'made history'. At the time I had no way of knowing how persistently in the years to come in the consciousness of Germans their history would be extinguished – and not only due to the destruction of historic buildings.

As we walked on, out of the blue my father asked me: 'What do you think of this? Goebbels has proposed to the Führer to repudiate the Geneva Convention with the argument that if prisoners and casualties did not have the protection of the Red Cross, combatants in the West would fight harder.' I couldn't believe my ears and entreated my father to 'prevent this madness'. Despite hopelessly inferior numbers, the army was fighting bravely on all fronts, and at no time in the front line had it come to disintegration; it would be criminal to deprive soldiers in dire straits of the protection of the Geneva Convention. I could moreover predict with certainty that it would have precisely the opposite effect of what Goebbels expected: troops would perceive it as running amok, a last-ditch act of desperation – which indeed it was; furthermore, the enemy would fight with even grimmer determination when not knowing what would befall if he were to be taken prisoner. The negative experiences with the so-called 'Commissar Order' should suffice as a warning.[1] Father completely agreed with me. When after the fact he had vigorously intervened with Hitler, in an unpleasant conversation in the garden of the Reich Chancellery, at the time it had hindered the cancellation of the Geneva Convention vis à vis the West. The Soviet Union had in any case never joined the Geneva Convention.[2]

During this conversation, which for my part had been heated, we had meanwhile arrived at the largely destroyed Reich Chancellery and encountered Otto Günsche, Hitler's adjutant (the same Günsche who was to burn Hitler and Eva Braun's bodies a few weeks later). Günsche assured us that 'nothing has happened and the Führer is well', and asked whether 'Herr Reichsminister would like to come to the bunker'? Father agreed and asked me to accompany him, which, to his surprise, I refused. With a gesture of resigned acquiescence he turned away and followed Günsche.

Today I can no longer reliably recall what had at the time spontaneously instigated me to refuse Father's invitation to accompany him to see Hitler. It may have been anger that Hitler was toying with the idea of cancelling the Geneva Convention – or was it an instinctive feeling that I would be exposing myself to a devastating impression? Instead of going with my father I strolled across Wilhelmplatz in the direction of the Kaiserhof Hotel opposite, or rather to the ruin that remained of it. I felt strangely aloof as I looked around. My thoughts suddenly sprang back to twelve years previously, when on the evening of 30 January 1933 – I was 11 – my father led me by the hand onto the wide balcony over the hotel entrance to witness the torchlight procession that the Berlin SA (the NSDAP storm troops) led past Hitler and Hindenburg. Mother had asked Father to take me with him; she would have wished her son to be able to say one day that he had been there. What was surprising on that day of 3 February 1945 was only that I was still alive and 'was there'!

Back on 30 January 1933, from Wilhelmplatz, Hindenburg and Hitler could be distinguished at the Reich Chancellery's windows lit by floodlights. Today only the burned-out holes of the windows yawned. Then, military songs had rung out from the columns, in which the enthusiastic crowd beneath us joined in every so often. Father, as well as the other gentlemen on the balcony, doffed their hats when flags went by below; in those days it was a usual way of paying respect. I remember Prince 'Auwi', as August-Wilhelm was known, a brother of the Crown Prince, with the unmistakeable 'Hohenzollern face'. At the time he ranked high in the SA. Schacht and Keppler congratulated Father on what he had personally contributed to the final successful outcome of the negotiations that had led to Hitler forming a government.

In place of the lighting effects of 30 January 1933 there were now only fires round about; above, a grey sky, with the smell of smoke, rubble and destruction everywhere. Was it a bad dream? A clicking of heels brought me out of these thoughts. In impeccable deportment, a sentry of the Reich Chancellery invited me 'to come to the bunker'. I followed him into the ruins of the Chancellery until, stepping through a fire door, I suddenly stood before Hitler. I did not even have time to present myself properly according to regulations, when he grasped my right hand with both of his – a typical gesture of Hitler's – and appreciatively talked about my division.

I stood there as if turned to stone, unable to say anything in reply; the impact of the sight of Hitler's physical deterioration was too overwhelming. What had happened to the man whom on 30 April of both 1939 and 1940 – Father's birthday – in a convivial circle, sitting at the same table, I had listened to and observed? His body was a wreck. His face was grey and puffy, his bearing bent in a way that looked as if he had a hump, holding one uncontrollably shaking hand with the other, his steps a shuffle. Only his striking blue eyes kept a certain brilliance, but without hiding an impression of great infirmity.

What he now said – we were alone with him – could not mitigate the devastating impact of his appearance; on the contrary! In 1939 he had outlined the strategy of major operative tank divisions that could potentially obviate the trench warfare of the First World War. He had then spoken with clarity and was convincing. In 1940, when there was fierce fighting at Narvik, he was holding forth in visions of mighty bridges that would one day after the war connect Scandinavia with the European continent. In those days he spoke very commendably in regard to handling traffic in Russia, that from the outset had chosen its own concept of broader railway tracks, whilst in Europe the British gauge had been adopted. After the war, he was to change over to the Russian gauge. There was no evidence of any trace of ideological antagonism towards the Soviets.

He spoke impressively in those days, with the imagination of the visionary, for the decisive Western campaign still lay ahead, and in Norway too there was still fighting. In Narvik the outcome was touch and go. The truth is that in this very intimate circle Hitler made no secret of the imminent offensive in the West and informed us about a miscalculation at the expense of the British by as much as two divisions. He appeared to be totally optimistic.

Here in the bunker – on 3 February 1945 – he said to my father and me: 'This is the turning-point, for now a new regiment goes to the front every day.' This completely unprofessional statement had no relation whatsoever to reality. He went on: 'The young Field Marshals' – the names Rendulic and

Schörner were mentioned – 'will now use the necessary relentlessness to bring the fronts to a standstill.' Then he digressed and began speaking of Manstein, of whom he attested that he was 'the best operator with large bodies of troops' but did not have the capacity to re-establish stability on a 'front in the process of fleeing'. For me, who had just come from the front line that was repeatedly exposed to a crushingly superior opposing force and had merely chanced to find myself in the Führerbunker, it was yet another eerie scene.

My impression at the time was that Hitler's mental state corresponded to his physical one. I cast a look at Father, who had been listening with an impassive expression. I knew that through Consul Möllhausen, Father was trying to sound out in Spain whether, despite Roosevelt's demand for 'unconditional surrender', talks with the West were still possible because of the altered state of things. At that moment the president of the Reichsbank, Walther Funk, greatly agitated, entered the room and told Hitler that the Reichsbank had been severely hit: 'We have no more money!' Once again Hitler showed his actor's talent as he entirely persuasively, almost amused, reassured Funk that at the moment the matter of money was not so decisive.

We said goodbye. I had not been able to utter a single word, so shattering had been the impact of that quarter of an hour during which I stood before the man who for us soldiers represented our country and in whom we believed, despite battles that were becoming ever more cruel. For more than five years, under constantly increasing heavy loss of lives, we had fought for Germany, our country, not for Hitler. But Hitler was the personification of our country. In any case we had long since not thought of 'victory' in the usual sense, we were motivated by the hope of a peace settlement. Instead, within these few minutes on the morning of 3 February 1945, I realized with absolute certainty that catastrophe was at hand. My thoughts turned around the question: what was I to say to my men in Fallingbostel? Whence would I, a 23-year-old, after this terrifying realization, draw the strength to motivate them to proceed to further action? If there were any hope at all of negotiations, a certain military force still in existence would without doubt be an advantage. To motivate the troops would in this sense count for something. The prevailing will on the Eastern Front, to protect the civilian population from the Soviet abomination, was the ever-present motive for the troops to take up the challenge. I too would have to transmit this motivation to my soldiers. To the last day of the war they were with me in this.

But Hitler was no longer able to change the situation; not even a miracle would spare him from what Providence – as he used to call destiny – had in store. The 'miracle' of the House of Brandenburg, as Frederick the Great called the death of his enemy Elizabeth the Empress of Russia that had saved him in the Seven Years' War, was not to be repeated for Hitler, although his main opponent, Roosevelt, died five weeks later on 12 April.

Upon leaving the Reich Chancellery my glance fell once more on the ruins opposite the Kaiserhof Hotel. In my mind's eye I was again the boy standing on the balcony. From Germany's great hopes and expectations at that time stemming from extraordinary early successes the pendulum had swung towards a looming and almost inevitable downfall. The question was desperately compelling: 'How could it have come to that?' An inexorable fate was about to be fulfilled. Once again I had stood eye to eye with doom. This destiny of doom bore the name of 'Hitler'.

Introduction

It was seeking an answer to the question – of desperation – 'How could it have come to that?' that finally incited me to put pen to paper about what I remembered, what I knew and had experienced in the years from 1933 to 1945. What were the exceptional circumstances that granted me the licence to chronicle those times which I lived through at first hand, as a child and as a young man, between the ages of 11 and 24, in what I may claim to have been the true sense of the word 'intimately'? It was the era of German history known variously as the Third Reich, the Thousand Year Reich or 'Hitler's Germany' that turned out to be so traumatic for the German people that as a consequence these days the subject is taboo, insofar as an objective analysis – of foreign policy at least – is concerned. For the reader to judge whether or not I have the legitimate right to express my views, let me use the English saying: 'Take it or leave it!'

In the course of the more than seventy years since Germany's collapse in 1945, the events dating from 1933 have been thoroughly scrutinized by the official German historiography, concluding, firstly, that Hitler seemed to materialize out of the 'blue' (in reference to the preceding boom years known as the Golden Twenties) and descend upon the German people, whom he then led to attack their friendly neighbours, with the ultimate objective of attaining to world rule. Germans are supposed to have followed him with unhesitating enthusiasm without a second thought, putting themselves at his disposal as 'willing executors'[3] in committing the crime. This simplistic cliché is the basis for all statements by the authoritative German historians – regrettably also the majority of German politicians – in regard to Germany's past. I shall, however, have a few things to say on this subject, based on my own knowledge, which was often obtained at first hand.

Nonetheless, it is not my aim to enter upon a comprehensive representation of the so-called Third Reich. So there is no misunderstanding, I wish emphatically to state, very clearly, that it is above all not my intention to 'rehabilitate' Hitler. It is out of the question that a politician should be exonerated, who disposed of unrestricted and uncontrolled power of the extent to which Hitler had seized it, in view of the calamity that befell Germany under his leadership. For as long as the history of Germany is at issue, in this country of ours that Hitler reduced to rubble and ashes, he will stand accused. For – and this he himself admitted, in accurate self-avowal – he bore complete responsibility for all that came about under his governance. Nonetheless, so much that occurred under Hitler's leadership, justifying the gravest of reproaches directed against him, in no way alters the initial position of desperation on which Germany's foreign policy was based, and which he found already in place to have to deal with when he came to power, obliging him to reckon with it in his conduct of foreign affairs. It is necessary to be able to make this differentiation if Hitler's foreign policy and his motives are to be analyzed with impartiality.

I have in consequence no intention of giving first place in my account to Hitler's persona, being instead much more inclined to present Germany's situation and interests that confronted Hitler and which he – as was the case for all German governments before his time and after it – had mandatorily to contend with. The plain truth is that Hitler did not simply 'drop out of the sky', neither was he an inevitable product of the German national character; he was instead caught in 'a maelstrom of coincidental circumstances'[4] and swept off to occupy a position accumulating power to an extent unprecedented in German history. Hitler was, however, not responsible for the 'coincidental circumstances' that 'made' him.

This is the start of the difficulty in making the differentiation: to what extent was Hitler's foreign policy 'forcibly' predetermined by the established political relations that preceded him, and from what point onward was it his decisions that paved the way to the culminating catastrophe? An objective analysis of world policies – from at least 1871 on – is necessary in order to answer this question. The formulation that 'Hitler has to answer for his crimes; he alone is therefore to blame for the war' is, on the one hand, rivetingly convincing and takes into account the human need to personify the blame for a fate of doom, except that it has little to do with historical fact. World history does not evolve in such an oversimplified manner. The aversion and animosity felt toward Hitler are perfectly comprehensible in view of the devastation he left behind – in no historiography is he 'innocented' from the verdict of guilt. Hitler must be condemned or, if so wished, be damned, but my plea is that it should be based on the right arguments. A comprehensive coverage of German foreign policy from 1933 to 1945 is to be achieved only when Germany's geopolitical position is the starting point, and the 'Hitler-figure' is placed in the political, economic, commercial/industrial and, not least, the intellectual interrelations of the nineteenth and twentieth centuries. Only in this manner will the prolonged shadow that was cast cease to burden the polity of Germans for a further six decades or even longer.

Thanks to the particularly close relationship I had with Grandfather Ribbentrop, who was an exceptionally cultured person – he was known in the family as the 'Walking Encyclopaedia' – as early as from the age of 10 the European political scene was gradually opened up to me, with the problem of 'the German Question' at its heart. The origins of this 'German Question', which in a way is still at issue in our day,[5] derive from the founding of the Reich in 1871, which had at one blow fundamentally altered the balance of power in Europe. In the place of two Germanic states which had to a certain degree neutralized one another – that is to say, Prussia and Austria – a structure had taken shape that due to its efficiency in all sectors increasingly gained in weightiness. '*Casca il mondo!*' ('The world is crashing down!') Cardinal Secretary General Giacomo Antonelli had exclaimed, as early as 1866, when he heard of Prussia's victory over Austro-Hungary. The failed French aggression of 1870/1871 put an end to the German wars of unification and completed this collapse of the old World Order as it had existed since the virtual annihilation of the German state by the treaties of the 1648 Peace of Westphalia. The British prime minister Disraeli had already given expression to his opinion, which was that the founding of the German state fundamentally altered Europe's constellation of political groupings.

There were from then on five Powers determining what happened in Europe: Great Britain, France, Russia, Austro-Hungary and, most recently, Germany. Bismarck had succinctly formulated the rule: when one found oneself among five, one must always make sure that three of them are of one mind. He had succeeded – despite the clashes between Austria and Russia in the Balkans – in carrying off the feat of building binding contracts, a regular league with Austria on the one hand and with Russia on the other, the famous 'Rückversicherungsvertrag' ('Reinsurance Contract' as it was known) purporting to secure protection of Germany's East from a war on two fronts, in case France were to harbour thoughts of revenge. There was no friction as far as England was concerned at that time, although 'they will not let us love them', Bismarck is said to have remarked.

This concept was abandoned in the time of Kaiser William II. The 'Rückversicherungsvertrag' with Russia was not extended. Russia, seeing itself isolated – its expansion in the direction of the Persian Gulf and India had created a tense situation with England – was induced to initiate a *rapprochement* with France. England, who anyway traditionally kept to a suspicious stance in regard to the strongest Continental power of the day –

considered then to be Germany – was irritated by Wilhelm's 'world policy' and the build-up of the German navy, to which the British attributed a hostile motivation, although there was no such intent in the naval strategy behind the plan, and the German fleet was not being expanded with a view to rivalling the British navy. However, the expansion of German interests in the Near East (the Baghdad railway) abutted British interests in a politically sensitive area, through which the 'road to India' (the Suez Canal) passed. Russian interests were also concerned by German activity in the region of the Turkish Straits. My grandfather repeatedly sharply castigated the policy of the Kaiser: challenging the British on the one hand – however unintentionally – and on the other the abandonment of the mutual 'reinsurance' with Russia. Does this sound familiar as a parallel to the situation of the Reich from 1933, that of the desperate position in the middle? In a speech in the Reichstag of 1882, Bismarck had said that 'on the whole a million bayonets are aimed mainly in the direction of the centre of Europe; that we stand at the centre of Europe so that already as a result of our geographical location, as well as moreover resulting from the entire history of Europe, we are first and foremost exposed to the effects of coalitions of other powers'. The 'nightmare of the coalitions', Bismarck said, 'will long, if not for ever, remain for a German minister a very justified one'.[6] The former French ambassador to Bonn speaks of 'a particular traditional political thought process in France, which always has an eye on Moscow whenever it is a question of Germany'.[7]

The policy of the Kaiser and his Chancellor Bülow derived from an unbridgeable opposition between Russia and England. Bülow based himself on a 'policy of the free hand' which, he assumed, would enable him at all times to opt to side either with England or Russia, until in the end the *rapprochement* between England and Russia in 1907 stranded Germany in the gap between two stools, which is to say in the resulting encirclement.

In 1905 Germany had the opportunity to break out of the 'ring' that threatened to be thrown round the Reich, by means of a preventive strike against France. Russia had lost the war with Japan and was incapable of dealing with foreign affairs because of revolutionary uprisings. The state of Germany's armament would have provided the German state with the opportunity to prevail militarily over France. In the historical phase of European national power-play, such considerations were legitimately valid, as a proper and timely preventive deterrent against possible future danger. Thus, at this time the British Admiral of the Fleet Fisher advocated that an attack should be initiated against Germany as well as the sinking of the German fleet – which would not be the first time the British acted in such a manner, nor the last.[8] The military liberating blow did not ensue in 1905, and in 1914 the Reich was therefore placed under considerably more unfavourable circumstances at the outbreak of the military conflict.

The decisive Power was England. Rival jealousy over German competition in the world markets played a serious role (such as the introduction of the 'Made in Germany' label for German goods in the British Empire). This was, however, in the end but a symptom of the growing force of Germany's weightiness. England's aeon-old principle, at all times to engender a coalition against the most powerful Continental Power, became established from the outset of the century onward as the dominant theme of British policy in regard to Germany.[9] England conducted this line of policy skilfully and successfully; there is no doubt that the erroneous estimates of world political developments and wrong judgements that the Kaiser's government arrived at played into Britain's hands. German foreign policy did not have the faintest conception of the account that needed to be taken of the consequences of the Reich's ever-perilous Central European location.

The First World War had disclosed a surprising strength on the part of the Reich. Almost the entire resources of the world had to be mobilized for the German state eventually to be brought down. The purpose of the Treaty of Versailles was the obliteration, once and for all, of this potential threat posed by the central European Power. The terms of the Treaty consequently allowed a vacuum to be created in the continent's centre. It could be foreseen that, as for every vacuum, in one way or another it would at some time be filled and therefore could not bring about a stable peace. It resulted on the contrary in a latent peril threatening Europe through the progressive consolidation of the Soviet state and its increasing military strength. The anxieties of the neighbouring states in the face of the potential strength of the European central Power, Germany, were also extant at a later date, when again in 1933 there was not the slightest inkling of any 'strength' of Germany's. It will be seen what solutions were proposed by German politics – albeit unavailingly – to solve this problem at the heart of the European political world.

Witness of the Times

'I was designated Secretary of State, but I've shifted it round instead to be posted to London!'[10] were my father's words as he came to meet my mother and me one day in August 1936 on a quiet street in the outskirts of Bayreuth. I was 15 years old at the time. That morning, for the second time, Father had been invited to visit Hitler at the Villa Wahnfried. Mother had taken the opportunity to take me to see the famous 'Eremitage', and as Father now hugged her, it was obvious that his decision had had a profound effect on him: he was beaming. But my mother's instinctive reaction was to cover her mouth with her hand, a typical gesture of hers when she heard something unexpected, surprising or portentous, whose consequences she could not at that moment appraise. Three-and-a-half years earlier, on 30 January 1933, it was what she did when she came into our living room in Berlin-Dahlem as our piano teacher Fräulein Munding was once more attempting to explain to me that when there was a '#' in front of a note, a flat instead of a sharp was to be played. At the time, all Mother said, very softly, was: 'Hitler is Chancellor of the Reich!' That characteristic gesture of the hand was expressive of the question she was doubtless asking herself: 'What will happen now?' At that moment she could not have had the slightest premonition in what a dramatic – and ultimately tragic – manner this day was destined to determine the fate of her husband and herself, indeed of the whole family.

In January 1933, Father had arranged for Hitler to make contact with Hindenburg and Papen, he himself having been brought in to take part in the decisive phases of the negotiations that led to Hitler forming a government. At the end of 1932, for my parents as well as for many Germans, the only options were that either Hitler came to power or it would be the Communists. Were it the latter, there was no doubt that a Communist takeover would signify the imposition of the rule of the Russian Bolshevik régime for Germany with the stamp of Stalinism.[11] This danger, a perfectly realistic one in those days, is today often played down or entirely overlooked.[12] At the time, Father was not contemplating a move from his profitable business into active politics, although, as shall be seen, he was already very interested in the politics of foreign affairs.[13]

In that instant, however, on Bayreuth's peaceful and sunny street, as my mother's spontaneous reaction showed what she was thinking, Father sensed her reservations. As we walked on, he explained to her in every detail what his reasons had been, when at a meeting of intensive discussion of foreign policy – triggered by Franco's request to the Reich to supply him with aircraft to transport his troops from Morocco to the Spanish mainland – Father proposed that, postponing his nomination to Secretary of State, which had already been confirmed, the Führer should send him to London as ambassador and successor to the late Leopold von Hoesch.[14] Father had explicitly and with urgency propounded that the Reich's leadership had to obtain clear knowledge of the policies adopted by the British government in regard to Germany. The British were masters of the tactics of keeping their potential opponents guessing in order to conceal their true goals.[15] A fatal consternation such as the British had in store for the Kaiser's government, when in 1914 they had declared war and Berlin was caught totally unawares, must not be repeated. In August 1914, at the farewell of the departing British ambassador Sir Edward Goschen, the then Chancellor of the Reich, von Bethmann Hollweg, had accepted that at the British declaration of war 'his entire policy collapsed like a house of cards'.[16]

We walked up and down the sleepy suburban street alone. My father always spoke to Mother openly in my presence on the most confidential subjects of German government goals in the field of foreign affairs, and this time again, to convince his wife of the correctness of his decision, he referred to the fundamental concepts of foreign policy that Hitler had adhered to with constancy since undertaking to govern three-and-a-half years earlier, namely to bring about a relatively powerful Central European bloc with the backing of Great Britain and France, as a deterrent to the Soviet threat. As far as I was concerned, this exposé of the political goals of German foreign policy constituted nothing new. In that sense, over the past three years I had been allowed greater insight and found my father's proposal to Hitler perfectly consequential. From Hitler's viewpoint, the Soviet danger at that time was acute. In the summer of 1936 he had composed his 'Four-Year Plan Memorandum', wherein he called for a German reaction to the scale of Soviet armament. Russian military preparations constituted an indisputable fact; the subsequent deployment of the Soviet Union's power in the Second World War and the confrontation between the world powers of the United States and Soviet Union during the Cold War were to prove this indubitably.[17] That the Soviet Union was eventually forced by the US to cancel their arms race does not argue against the premise.

Before the day was out, my mother told me of her objections to Father's decision, probably to weigh the risks and advantages of such a step for herself. Her essential considerations focused on three aspects: so far, Joachim von Ribbentrop's political activities had been conducted – according to Hitler's customary practice of fostering rivalries – in parallel to the Auswärtige Amt (known as the Amt – the foreign ministry). Father and his '*Dienststelle Ribbentrop*' (Ribbentrop Office) were organizationally attached to the so-called Verbindungsstab (Communications Staff) under Rudolf Hess. The assignment of this office was to maintain the communication between the NSDAP (National Socialist German Workers Party) leadership of the Reich, i.e. the 'Party', in Munich and the ministries in Berlin. Rivalry had naturally arisen between the Amt and the '*Dienststelle Ribbentrop*'; it could not have been otherwise.

It needed no great flight of the imagination to foresee that Ambassador Ribbentrop was not likely to find in the Amt the support necessary for the execution of his duties. As it turned out, as mission chief in London, my father later had occasion to appeal to Foreign Minister Neurath to be supplied with the necessary data to do his job. How right Mother's fears had been was revealed by Erich Kordt. Kordt had been seconded from the Amt to the '*Dienststelle Ribbentrop*' as liaison officer and had received instructions from Secretary of State Bülow not to correct any 'mistakes' Ribbentrop might make and not to worry about letting him commit them.[18] The 'mistakes' of a diplomat, however, whoever he might be, are inevitably damaging to the country represented, in this case Germany.

As she said, Mother would consequently have considered it of greater advantage if from this point on my father had been integrated in the Amt. If, in her opinion, he really wanted to sustain a lasting part to play in co-organizing Hitler's foreign policy, he ought to acquire inside knowledge of the instrument to use for the purpose, which was the Amt. As State Secretary he would be best placed to familiarize himself with the organization of the Amt, as well as the qualifications and mentality of the German diplomats.

At that time, however, Mother already spoke of her gravest concerns regarding the chances of success of my father's mission. She was sceptical as to whether there was truly any likelihood of bringing about a durable concordance of the policies of Great Britain and Germany, in the light of the reluctant political stance on the part of Britain for the past three-and-a-half years – since 1933 – toward Germany's proposals for the future. In her view, my father had undertaken an assignment harbouring a major innate risk of failure, should the British 'not want to be loved by us'. He risked being shouldered with the blame if an Anglo-German understanding – to which Britain also must be prepared to agree – was not to be achieved. My mother's premonition about this was quite accurate, but from Father's point of view, he was convinced that it was of prime importance for the Reich to obtain a clear insight into Britain's policies; personal considerations had to take second place in the matter.

An Anglo-German alliance was not something Hitler had conceived in the sense of a 'Germanic' quirk. A close collaboration between Germany and England at a level of world policies was in fact the key to his foreign policy. When my father said farewell to Hitler upon leaving to take up his post in London and Hitler said: 'Ribbentrop, bring me back a League with England',[19] Hitler was totally convinced at the time that this league of the two nations was also in the interest of the British. He believed in the preservation of British world dominion by the British, as he did equally in the necessity for the German Reich to be free of the threat posed by the Soviet Union's planned world revolution. Hitler considered the existence of a British world domination for the 'White Race' – which equally concerned Germany – as highly desirable.[20] However, the decisive aspect was mutually covering the back as defence against the peril looming from the East, thanks to which England too would have a free outlook over her world-wide empire, as well as ensuring its preservation.

It should be made perfectly clear to one and all, and at all times be kept in sight, that the goal targeted by Hitler's foreign policy was the Reich's 'integration with the West', to employ a modern-day term. In the conversations that took place while I was present between Father and Grandfather Ribbentrop, I often heard Father say: 'We must take an option!' I remember these discussions so well because, as I was not yet grown up, I was naturally not familiar with the distinction between the concepts of 'opting' and 'option'. Father and Grandfather were absolutely at one in the belief that the sole option for Germany was to belong to the Western world, which, as matters stood, meant taking up a position against the Soviet Union. A see-saw policy between East-West was not a consideration for either Hitler or my father. The experiences of the Kaiser's policies of the First World War, that the then Chancellor Bülow euphemistically called a 'Free Hand policy', scared one off from attempting to place the centre of gravity of German foreign policy on an ambivalent footing, playing off 'East' against 'West'. The famous British motto of 'sitting on the fence', deciding in favour of one side or the other according to circumstance, in my father's opinion was all very well for an island with naval power, but not so for a country in Germany's geopolitical location at the centre of Europe, where there was always the risk of finding herself as in

1914 between two stools, or 'trapped in the pincers' of a coalition of superior numbers.

Joachim von Ribbentrop's posting to London signified a renewed, full-scale attempt on Hitler's part to realize his concept of foreign affairs, based on which he had undertaken to govern in 1933, despite some disappointments in the foregoing three-and-a-half years: to come to an arrangement with Britain, if possible in the form of a league, to the realization of which he attributed world-wide political importance. In those days Hitler was therefore following a consistent line of a 'Western policy'. Living through these significant developments from 1933 – that is from the age of 12 – I experienced them at very close quarters. My father's posting to London in 1936 had a major, almost 'documental' significance for German foreign policy. I had the opportunity to be partially familiar at first hand with the motives of both leading players on the German side, Hitler and my father. I was privy to the most confidential cogitations on the subject of German foreign policy, once again a contemporary 'witness of the times'. This said, I state in all humility that my participation was due exclusively to my parents' conviction – in which they were not wrong – that they could absolutely rely on my keeping silent.

These insights into 'higher politics' began for me in the summer of 1932, when I was 11. We grew up as children in an explicitly political atmosphere, even though Father was not yet actively politically involved. The financial distress of the times – accompanied by the ever-present threat of Communism – was of the utmost urgency. In those days we – my schoolmates and myself – irrespective of our tender age, were much more interested in politics than is the rule today for schoolchildren. We were constantly conscious of the history of Germany, which included the country's present situation as it had been shaped by the Versailles Treaty, whether at school or in the youth organizations (the *Bündische Jugend*), and, of course, at home. In regard to domestic politics, for the young boy that I was, the question focused on the issue whether the German flag should be black-white-and-red or black-red-and-gold. I will have been about 7 or 8 when there was a heated discussion between two of my uncles and my grandmother Henkell (who was a fervent Democrat). Jokingly, I was asked which colours I would prefer, and I spontaneously opted for black-red-and-gold. Naturally, the uncles immediately wanted to know my reasons for my choice. 'If the Kaiser was deposed and we were now a republic, we ought to have a new flag,' was my reply, which left my uncles flabbergasted. Did this child's opinion manifest once again the peculiar German habit, when there was a change of national regime, of bringing in at the same time a new flag, national anthem, military uniforms, even the names of towns and streets, not forgetting history books and whatever else was representative of national identity in the way of symbols and monuments, or else to chuck them out straight away onto history's rubbish heap?

In the summer of 1932 my sister and I were struck by persistent successive infections that would not clear up for months. One sore throat, earache or pneumonia followed the other. Mother undertook to nurse us, and soon a profound bond of confidence evolved between her and me that went far beyond the usual scope of such relationships. Later, whenever Mother had something to communicate, she began what she had to say with the words: 'You must let yourself be drawn and quartered before you disclose anything of what I am about to tell you!' These communications were for instance the considerations whether compulsory military service should be reintroduced, or – which was much more controversial – that the Rheinland demilitarized zone, should the occasion arise, be suspended in a unilateral action. Although my mother was not really responsible for it, I became a first-class bearer of secrets, as well as again being a 'witness of the times'. My only role in this relationship was, as I have said, my absolute discretion, in which Mother had total confidence. In fact, I had to put up with my friends asking me rather condescendingly whether I had any interest in politics, because I never expressed any. I was careful to avoid any sort of political discussion, as an experienced listener might have been able to weed out some hint from what I said.

Fateful Negotiations

The stage of his life when for the first time my father became involved in politics was in what I remember as a fine summer in Berlin in 1932. He had secretly been invited to Berchtesgaden by Hitler, as my mother told me at the time, through the intermediary of Count Helldorff, chief of the Berliner SA, who asked Father to meet Hitler in Berchtesgaden and put the proposition to him that Hitler should make an attempt at the chancellorship, to be negotiated with Hindenburg and Papen. Wolf-Heinrich von Helldorff had served in the same regiment (the 'Torgauer Hussars') as my father in the First World War. To this day I remember him well: tall and broad-shouldered, wearing a brown uniform and with all the charm of a trooper. Later, he probably envied my father his career, for he no longer frequented our home and finally went over to the Opposition Party, in whose establishment he had cooperated.[21]

The occasion of this meeting with Hitler was the first time Mother and I spoke about politics, and I therefore remember it very well. When Father came back from Berchtesgaden, she told me that Hitler had not agreed to his suggestions. The two men differed in their approach to the strategy to be followed for Hitler to attain the nomination to the chancellorship. Father was firmly of the opinion that the interlocutors to be reckoned with were Papen and maybe Hindenburg's son, whilst Hitler thought he could achieve the chancellorship through a connection with Schleicher (who held the position during the Weimar Republic). The meeting had lasted two hours. Hitler was to say at a later date that 'Ribbentrop is stubborn; I tried for two hours to make him understand that the only way for me to form a government was through Schleicher [Hitler to Father: 'A Prussian general does not break his word.'] only to hear Ribbentrop say, at the end, that it would work only with Papen and Hindenburg.' What a noteworthy beginning to the alleged 'Yes-man' Ribbentrop's intercourse with Hitler. In the final months of 1932, after the inconclusive talks in Berchtesgaden, there was no further close contact between the two.[22]

Also in this summer of 1932, the Communists and National Socialists together started a strike of Berlin's transport services. My mother expressed her attitude to this to me, saying: 'If the Nazis get together with the Communists, as far as I'm concerned, they can get lost!' In a later conversation between my father and Grandfather Ribbentrop, while I was there, this remark took on a certain significance, as the subject was whether, if Hitler were to come to power, he would on the whole maintain the capitalist economic system. Although at the time I could not quite understand what it was about, the scene nevertheless remains vivid in my mind. It should be recalled here that there was a strong Socialist trend in the NSDAP too. When talking to my grandfather, Father said that in his opinion under Hitler the economic system would in principle remain 'capitalist'. It was meant thereby that property of the means of production would remain in the possession of the proprietors, although the state would at the same time have rights to intervene in the economy insofar as it was required. He was right on this point, although in 1932 it could not be asserted with absolute certainty.

One day in January 1933 two gentlemen came to lunch and were first taken on a short stroll round the garden by my parents. For us this was nothing out of the ordinary, as although their earlier social life had been somewhat curtailed by reason of the economic situation, we frequently had guests coming for a meal, which, as was then the custom, was often the midday meal, called 'breakfast' by Berliners. We did, however, find it noticeable that the atmosphere and tone of voice of the conversation our parents was having with the guests was quite different from their usual way: there was none of the customary light-hearted chatting that we children were accustomed to. We could have no idea what this visit would signify for our family's life. Destiny had entered the home of our childhood, inconspicuously, almost without a sound.

Both the men – they were Himmler and Keppler[23] – had been sent by Hitler and their purpose was to ask my father to undertake to set up negotiations with Papen and Oskar von Hindenburg, the President's son, and sound him out on the possibilities of undertaking to form a government, based on the ideas that he had vainly presented to Hitler at the meeting mentioned above of a few months ago.

A few days after the above-mentioned visit of Himmler and Keppler, we children were at supper when Father came into the dining room and gave the butler instructions for the visit of several gentlemen whom he was expecting. We noticed this as something unusual, for my father had never before bothered about any visit or hospitality. With Father as intermediary, discussions were resumed according to his way of thinking and took place on several occasions in our home because of the confidentiality this afforded, with the participation of Hitler, Papen, Hindenburg's son and others. They were to be held under the seal of the strictest secrecy and Hitler was introduced to the house after dark, through the garden entrance. The outcome was that, in the end, Hitler was appointed Chancellor of the Reich.

My parents kept an accurate record word for word of the happenings of those dramatic days of January 1930. I shall give these key words here again, because on the one hand between the lines they reflect my father's independent role in the framework of the negotiations, and on the other because the circumstances have repeatedly been recounted incorrectly abridged.[24] My mother noted:

'The encounters that took place at our home remained strictly secret, which was not of minor importance for the success of formation of a government. I remember particularly clearly the discussions that were held the night of 10 to 11 January 1933, because that was when I met Hitler for the first time. I greeted him in my husband's study where he was having a private talk with Mr von Papen. On 12 January we were expecting Hitler and Papen for lunch. Hitler cancelled and Papen came alone. He spoke of his worry about the Lippe elections [in a small state of the Weimar Republic]. He was afraid that the expected success of the NSDAP would have the effect of hardening Hitler's stance.

'Mr von Papen was brought to and fetched back from the talks by the chauffeur we had had for years. Hitler on the other hand took care to come in and leave from the garage area so as to approach the house unnoticed through the garden. I dictated notes on a daily basis from what data my husband gave me of how he proceeded in the last days of January ... I shall copy these below from the original I have before me:

'Tuesday 10/01/33. Discussion with Hitler and Papen. Hitler wishes no further meeting with Papen before the Lippe elections.

'Sunday 15/1. Joachim goes to Oeynhausen. Long talk alone with Hitler. Back to Berlin in the night. Appointment for a meeting between Papen and Hitler either on Monday evening at Schultze-Naumburg's or Tuesday in Halle.

'Monday 16/1. Talks did not take place in the evening as Papen was with Lersner.

'Tuesday 17/1. Papen in Halle, Hitler in Weimar. No encounter. Hitler back in Berlin in the evening.

'Wednesday 18/1, 12 noon in Dahlem: Hitler, Röhm, Himmler, Papen. Hitler persists as to the chancellorship. Papen repeats once more that it is not feasible. In order to enforce this, he might be overreaching the influence he has on Hindenburg. Hitler engages no further appointments for consultations. Joachim attempts a proposal to bring Hindenburg's son together with Hitler.

'Thursday 19/1. Lengthy negotiations between Joachim and Papen alone.

'Friday 20/1. In the evening, long consultation at Papen's. Papen says that Hindenburg's son and Meissner will come to Dahlem on Sunday.

'Saturday 21/1. Joachim advises Hitler about the planned meeting. Hitler thereupon explains why he does not want to invite Schleicher. Hitler will bring Göring and Epp with him.

'Sunday 22/1. Meeting in Dahlem at 10 pm. Papen arrives at 9 o'clock, alone. Present are: Hitler, Frick, Göring, Körner, Meissner, Hindenburg's son, Papen and Joachim. Hitler has talks with Hindenburg's son, alone, for two hours. Thereafter Papen and Hitler discuss. Papen now wants to promote Hitler's chancellorship but says that if Hitler has no trust in him he would drop the matter instantly.

'Monday 23/1. Papen sees Hindenburg in the morning. The latter turns everything down. Joachim sees Hitler to explain this to him. Long discussion as to the possibility of a Schacht cabinet. Rejection of all by Hitler.

'Tuesday 24/1. Tea at Dahlem: Frick, Göring, Papen, Joachim. Resolution to be announced to the elder Hindenburg of formation of a national front in support of Papen.

'Wednesday 25/1. Again tea at Dahlem: Joachim and Hindenburg's son talk together alone. The outcome is that chances of Hitler becoming Chancellor under the auspices of a new national front are not to be excluded. Hindenburg's son tells Joachim that he will get back to him before the elder Hindenburg's final statement.

'Thursday 26/1. Long discussion with Frick and Göring at the Reichstag. Negotiations with the Deutschnationalen (German National People's Party). Evening spent with Prince Oskar in Potsdam, letter to Hugenberg [Alfred Hugenberg, leader of the right-wing party Deutschnationale Volkspartei, a competitor to Hitler's National Socialist German Workers' Party].

'Friday 27/1. Hitler back in Berlin again. Long discussion with him [i.e. Joachim] in Göring's apartment. Hitler wishes to leave immediately. Joachim proposes to join with Hugenberg in order to establish a National Front. Another encounter with the elder Hindenburg is agreed. Hitler explains that he has told the Field Marshal everything and does not know what else he should say to him. Joachim persuades Hitler, saying that this has got to be a last-ditch attempt and that the matter is absolutely not hopeless. Joachim suggests to Hitler that a national front should be formed as soon as possible and that Hitler should meet with Papen for a finalizing discussion that evening at 10 pm in Dahlem. Hitler agrees to proceed in this sense and to discuss the matter of an agreement with Hugenberg with Papen in the evening. There followed a long talk with Göring on the subject of the further tactics to be adopted. Later in the afternoon Göring telephoned that Joachim should come to the Reich's President's residence immediately. There, meeting Hugenberg. Hitler and Göring (plus two illegible names) who differ angrily because of the unacceptable demands of the Deutschnationalen. Hitler, who is furious at this negotiation, says he will leave for Munich right away. Göring persuades him to stay a little longer or at least to go only as far as Weimar. Göring and Joachim eventually manage to calm Hitler down. But Hitler's suspicions are now all revived. The situation is critical. Hitler explains that he cannot see Papen in Dahlem in the evening because he is not in a position to speak out.'

There follows below exactly what Father dictated:[25]

'Never before have I seen Hitler in such a state. I suggest to him and Göring that in the evening I should speak to Papen alone and clarify the whole situation to him. I talk to Papen in the evening and finally convince him that only Hitler's chancellorship, to which Papen had to commit himself completely, had any meaning. Papen said that the Hugenberg question was of secondary importance, explaining that he now fully espoused Hitler's candidature to the chancellorship. This signified the decisive turning point had been reached in Papen's approach. Papen is fully aware of his responsibility in the face of three possibilities: either a *Präsidialkabinett* (presidential government) to be followed by [illegible], or reversion to Marxism under Schleicher, or Hindenburg's resignation. Against this there was really only one single clear solution: Hitler's chancellorship. It is now perfectly clear to Papen that he must henceforth at all costs conduce to Hitler's chancellorship and no longer believe, as he had done until now, that he has in every instance to be at Hindenburg's disposal. It is my opinion that this admission of Papen's is the turning point of the whole affair. Papen is to see Hindenburg on Saturday morning at 10.

'Saturday 28/1. At about 11 pm I visit Papen, who receives me with the question "Where is Hitler?" I answer that he will probably have left already and might yet be reached in Weimar. Papen explains that he must be fetched back immediately as a turning point had been reached and that after his long talk with Hindenburg, Papen thought Hitler's chancellorship was feasible. I go to Göring right away and hear that Hitler is still at the Kaiserhof. Göring telephones and is told Hitler is still in Berlin. Then there is another difficulty: the Prussian question.[26] Lengthy discussion and disagreement with Göring. I make the point that if mistrust of Papen is once again manifested I will back out on the spot. Göring gives in and declares himself entirely at one with me, promising from now on to try everything in unison with Hitler so as to bring the matter to a favourable outcome. Göring will convince Hitler to deal with the Prussian question in line with Papen's views. Göring and I go to see Hitler straight away. I spoke with Hitler alone at length, making it clear to him once again that the matter was to be handled only on the basis of trust and the chancellorship no longer seemed unattainable. I pressed Hitler to visit Papen not later than that afternoon. However, because of the Prussian question, Hitler still wants to think about it and will go and see Papen on Sunday morning. I reported this decision to Papen, who began worrying again. "I know these Prussians," he said. A meeting between Hitler and Papen is then fixed for Sunday at 11 am.

'Sunday 29/1. At 11 am, long discussion between Hitler and Papen. Hitler says that on the whole all is clear. Fresh elections would however have to be called and an Enabling Act promulgated. Papen goes straight to see Hindenburg. I have lunch with Hitler at the Kaiserhof. The question of fresh elections comes up. Since Hindenburg will not allow elections to be held, Hitler asks me to tell him that these would be the last. In the afternoon Göring and I go and see Papen. Papen assures us that all obstacles have been cleared and that Hindenburg expects Hitler tomorrow at 11.

'Monday 30/1. Hitler has been appointed Chancellor.'

The meeting of 24 January constituted a special turning point, when the 'Passing of a Resolution regarding a national front' was enacted, whereby a lever was found at the last minute to overcome Hindenburg's aversion to Hitler's becoming Chancellor. This conference of Hitler, Papen, Göring, Frick and my father may well be called the actual moment of birth of the 'Third Reich'.

I should like to insert here a relevant and amusing little story: Goebbels wrote a book about 'Hitler's *Regierungsbildung*' ('formation of a government') as it was known in those days, entitled *Vom Kaiserhof zur Reichskanzlei* (From the Kaiserhof to the Chancellorship of the Reich), wherein he purports to give the authentic account of the events that transpired up to 30 January 1933. The role my father played, which appears clearly from the foregoing account, is not even mentioned by Goebbels, who did not himself in fact participate at all, nor was he even informed in detail. Laughing, Father commented on this one day at lunch in Dahlem, saying: 'There is one thing I have already learned from my political activity: that distortion of history is not committed a hundred years later; it is done at the very moment it is made!' He could not foresee how aptly his comment would one day apply to the record of his acts and his own political involvement. At the time, at any rate, he could still laugh about such things and at the actors of the falsification. For me, what Father said – and I remember it precisely – was a 'little revelation', the foundation for a growing conviction: that there is no such thing as absolute historical truth. This knowledge has helped me enormously to 'overcome' the past unperturbedly and, above all, to judge it without prejudice and with an open mind.

It is understandable that, I being an 11-year-old boy, Mother at first told me nothing of what was going on. She had not yet had the opportunity to test my discretion and confidentiality, but this was soon to change. When Hitler took office he asked my father to initiate private soundings in England and France as to German-British as well as German-French relations and to report back. Father's reports, as his position was initially quite unofficial – that is to say only answerable to Hitler personally – went directly to Hitler himself. In no circumstances could he dictate them to his company secretaries: this would have offended all the rules of confidentiality. This is why one day Mother asked me whether I would be able to type a most secret letter 'addressed to the Chancellor of the Reich'. (When I was 7 or 8, my parents, who had a very modern outlook, had given me for Christmas a small American Underwood portable typewriter. They thought it was never too early to learn to use one.) My mother very seriously made me promise never to breathe a word about the contents of the letter: it was a case of a state secret. I continued therefore to type all the various confidential reports. Nonetheless, my father often had no other option but to write his reports by hand.[27]

On one occasion I had to type a letter that I remember concerned an unpleasant disagreement between Father and Rosenberg. Rosenberg was head of the so-called 'Außenpolitischen Amtes der NSDAP' (Office for Foreign Affairs of the NSDAP). Mother told me about the background story of the letter I was to type: it had to do with Rosenberg's jealousy of my father as a newcomer, Hitler's interlocutor, who had Hitler's ear in matters of foreign policy. This was my first glimpse behind the scenes of the corridors of power. At a later date Father – who was then still amused by it – told me how he and Rosenberg had eventually divided their competencies between themselves. When he informed Hitler about this, the latter seemed hardly to want to know anything about it. From early on, Father had seen through Hitler's system of keeping on several tracks at a time. He had to come to terms with it if he wanted to exert influence on decisions regarding foreign policy. An instance is his proposing to Hitler in April 1935 that the NSDAP's 'Foreign Office' be renamed 'Kulturpolitisches Amt' (Cultural Political Office) whereby, as he wrote, '[it should be] clearly documented that Rosenberg's Eastern Programme does not belong within the Reich's official foreign policy'. An interesting example of the interior difficulties with which German foreign policy had to contend within Hitler's system. It need not be said that such a proposition was hardly likely to make a friend of the person it affected – in this case Rosenberg. Since in a dictatorship everything published is at the very least of an unofficial nature, Father had to try to eliminate interference factors. I shall in due course revert to what are considerably more problematic observations that Hitler makes in his book *Mein Kampf* concerning Germany's policy in regard to France and, above all, with reference to the '*Ostpolitik*' (toward Eastern Europe).

I was now often the recipient of Mother's warnings that: 'You must let yourself be drawn and quartered before you ...', as when in early 1935 she told me that Hitler and my father were considering unilaterally re-establishing German military emancipation, since so little progress had been made during the endless negotiations with Britain and France over the implementation of Germany's military equal rights [Papen's government had already been pledged this *de jure* by the Geneva Decree of 12 December 1932.].[28] Then in the following year (1936) Mother shared with me information of the plans being considered to implement the emancipation of the demilitarized Rheinland unilaterally. At the time, Mother explained why it was thought this step should be taken and in this way firmly established in me the conviction that it was necessary to recover the sovereignty of the Reich in its entire territory. In Hitler's and Father's eyes, this is where the prerequisite lay in order once more to attain unrestricted freedom to negotiate foreign affairs; without it, the capability of the Reich to form alliances was not self-evident, which was thought in turn indispensable so as to break out of the isolation from foreign politics wherein the Reich still found itself since the end of the

First World War. Reinstating German sovereignty in the Rhineland would not be considered by British public opinion as a provocation to retaliate militarily against the Reich. However, without British backing, France would not make a move, nor, it was certain, would Poland dare to go it alone. On the other hand, Mother did not confide in me that such action naturally contained a grave risk since, because rearmament had only just begun, only minimal German forces could be deployed in the Rhineland. As a reward for the little things I had done to help, above all for my discretion, she had engaged Father to take me with him to the session of the Reichstag in the Krolloper, where Hitler was to announce the Resolution.

My excitement can be imagined as I entered the spectators' gallery of the Krolloper's auditorium, where the Reichstag sessions were held, which stands opposite the old Reichstag building that had been gutted by fire. Hardly any one of the people present – delegates, foreign diplomats, high dignitaries of the state and the Party amongst whom I was seated – knew why they had been convoked. When Hitler proclaimed that the Reich government had resolved to reinstate full sovereignty in the Rhineland demilitarized zone, a sustained storm of applause of course broke out. The gathering then seemed ready positively to erupt when he went on to say that 'at this very moment, when German troops are moving into their peacetime garrisons in the Rhineland'. Before the war, with regard to Versailles, the point of honour did not play an insignificant role and there is no doubt that it had substantially contributed to Hitler's success in the elections. I remained in a state of great excitement for the next few days. Would it come to the Versailles Signatory Powers resorting to military action?

This is how from 1933 I was living in 'two worlds'. One of them was 'idyllic' in relation to the other. The description of my 'normal life' in my parental home, which looking back was as wonderful as it was stimulating, stood in sharp contrast to the world of 'high politics' into which my mother lent me insight to an ever-growing degree, whether of the 'heights' where the momentous foreign policy decisions were made as well as of the 'lows' of intrigue and dubious human motives. In my parents' conversations, in which Grandfather Ribbentrop often took part – with me as a silent but thrilled listener – the most confidential aspects of Germany's foreign policy were discussed. The core of the deliberations was always the goal of a 'West-Arrangement' as the foundation of German foreign policy. At one time or another, however, in the ensuing years a question kept coming back as to what alternatives were feasible if it were to transpire that the goal aimed at was perhaps for some reason unattainable.

For my age I was unusually passionate about history and military history, which consequently enabled me to put the 'West-Arrangement' in context from the past and, with the keenest interest, comprehend the concept as it evolved in the years from 1933 to 1941. To whom is it granted to be a witness to world politics in one of their most dramatic phases from very young adulthood onwards and at such close quarters? I think I may justifiably name myself as a 'Witness of the Times', from which the obligation also arises to record what I know about what was going on in those days.

Versailles and the Central European Power Vacuum

In the First World War, Germany and her allies, Austro-Hungary, Bulgaria and Turkey, were known as the 'Central Powers'. This was an apt designation of the four countries that were surrounded on all borders by superior allied powers – of the 'Alliance' – which is to say they were 'encircled'. In 1933, Germany's situation as a European 'Central Power' was much more inauspicious than in 1914.

From its founding in 1871, the European central power, the German Reich, saw itself increasingly exposed to a dilemma: nobody wanted a powerful – hence a potentially 'threatening' – Germany. This was re-experienced once more by us Germans on the occasion of the unification of the Federal Republic and the German Democratic Republic (West and East Germany). One should not be blind to the fact that both the British and the French governments, by intervening with the Russian government, attempted to prevent the unification of the two German states. That an overly powerful Germany constitutes a problem for Britain and France is today still, beneath the surface, not a negligible factor in European politics.[29] As a German too, one can have absolute comprehension for this anxiety: all politicians, looking ahead, have to identify possible hazards and take them into account. The French writer Mauriac is said to have commented on the reunification with wit, albeit caustically, with the *bon mot*: 'I am so fond of Germany that I would rather have two of them than one!'

Every German government since Bismarck was confronted by this quandary. The latter's scornful reaction to the highly praised advantages represented to him of the acquisition of African colonies is well known: 'Here lies Russia and over there lies France, and we are in the middle; that is my map of Africa.'[30] The result was on the one hand the realization of the need to maintain a substantial military force in order to be able to assert oneself in Central Europe (it was necessary to be able to prevent a repetition of a 'Thirty Years' War' among the European Powers on German territory, so as to preserve the substance of the German people), a fact that in the

1930s acquired a specific gravity because of the Soviet display of power. On the other hand, the traditional foreign policies the British and French governments and their allies clung to, that wished to see Germany as weak as possible for fear of her hegemony, had to be taken into account. The problem had after all led to the outbreak of the First World War, spawned Versailles and from 1933 onward had to be faced by Hitler and the German policy-makers once again. The Federal Government too had to grapple with it to some extent, whereby the military reason against the economic one was happily no longer to be a given. In 1966, the French Conservative politician Maurice Couve de Murville said to the Polish Foreign Minister, Adam Rapacki: 'Germany has once again become a problem … Were there no Germany, did we have no problem in Europe, it is our problem and also yours.'[31] Henry Kissinger put this question to the point (in free translation):

'President Clinton's notion of partnership in leadership of the United States and Germany was not exactly wise … It is indeed a notion that drives everybody to the barricades, for two world wars have been fought precisely for a German dominating role to be prevented.[32]

It was a vicious circle that could be broken only through cooperation between Britain, France and the Reich. Father's activities in the years from 1933 to 1937 were defined by his efforts to bring this about. German foreign policy had not attained its goal. Hitler, who was aware of Germany's imperilment, deduced from this that the comprehensible sequence to follow might, as in 1914, conceivably be a renewed formation of a major coalition against Germany.

The formula for British policies in Europe had ever been to preserve the 'Balance of Power' among the states of Europe; or, to be more precise, Great Britain had at all times to place herself alongside the second weakest Continental Power against the strongest. This was for centuries the line taken in British politics. In this manner Britain had won freedom of action to establish the British Empire and herself as the foremost World Power. Whether British policy was directed against Spain or against Louis XIV, against Austria or against the two Napoleons and eventually against Wilhelm's Germany, in every instance the axiom was recognizable that dictated the blocking or overmastering of the strongest Continental Power with the help of the second strongest and other allies. As early as March 1936, Churchill had declared thus to the Foreign Affairs Committee of his Conservative Party with brazen openness.[33] Speaking in the House of Commons he had then said:

'The question is not whether it is Spain, or the French Monarchy, or the French Empire, or the German Empire, or the Hitler regime. It has nothing to do with rulers or nations; it is concerned solely with whoever is the strongest or the potentially dominating tyrant … The question therefore arises which is to-day the Power in Europe which is the strongest?'[34]

Would it be feasible to communicate the German point of view, as assessed by Hitler and by my father in regard to the relations of power in Europe, to the decision makers in England? Both saw the European balance of power as safeguarded if the Reich were once more to rise to be the European Central Power, and were indeed of the opinion that the Reich's military weight was necessary in order to neutralize the Russian deployment of power. The existence and the weight of the Soviet Union would prevent any unchecked hegemony of the German Reich. In 1936, Germany still hoped that these estimations of world politics would be promoted in London too.

A few weeks after his appointment as Reich Chancellor, Hitler had visited my parents in Dahlem. They gave a dinner for him with very few guests. After dinner, Hitler brought up the subject of foreign policy and said that 'his main goal was to come to a lasting and clear relationship with England'. Harking back to this first initial talk with Hitler on foreign affairs, Father wrote:

'On that evening, it was discovering our common inner attitude of mind in regard to England that planted the first seed of trust between Adolf Hitler and myself. I could not then foresee that from it one day a close collaboration in the field of foreign policy would come about, as it turned out in later years.'[35]

As ambassador to the Court of St James's – despite some disappointments experienced in the intervening three-and-a-half years – he was still entrusted with the assignment to try to achieve this personal objective of Hitler's, which was also his own.

To analyze and judge Hitler's foreign policy properly, one must put oneself in the place where the German Reich found itself at the beginning of 1933, that is at the outset of his governance. In all fields, this place is determined by the Treaty of Versailles. Since the Allies refused any negotiation whatsoever as to its provisions, the Germans' designation of this 'Peace treaty' as the '*Versailler Diktat*' [a diktat is a harsh penalty or settlement imposed upon a defeated party] is hardly surprising. It is very useful and instructive to have an historical atlas to hand and open it at the page with the political map of Europe as it was upon conclusion of the treaty.

In substance, among other things the Versailles Treaty grievously slammed Germany on four counts:

1. As shown above, the complete and unilateral demilitarization as well as the dichotomy of German territory constituted – in the age of national statehood – an extraordinary imperilment for the Reich.
2. The so-called 'Reparations' imposed upon Germany were contrary to any economic rationality and would lead perforce to the pauperization of the population, quite irrespective of the deleterious repercussions it would unleash on the world economies.[36]
3. The territorial cessions encompassed about 13 per cent of the Reich's area, with corresponding losses in population, investments and resources, etc.
4. Additionally, there was the loss of all Germany's foreign assets, the forced surrender of countless industrial assets, such as patents, steam engines, cattle and internationalization of rivers and so on. The whole text of the treaty should really be read for the fine print in the so-called 'Versailles Peace Treaty'.

It should be retained as especially noteworthy that at the 1946 Nürnberg so-called 'War Criminals' trial – and therefore also the German Foreign Minister's trial – any mention of the Versailles Treaty by the defence was expressly prohibited.[37] The indictment virtually submitted the treaty as 'exhibit number one', charging the accused with its violation, without permitting the defence any contrary argument. '[T]he Tribunal will not listen to your contending either that the Versailles Treaty was not a legal document or that it was in any way unjust,' the presiding judge pronounced.[38] Let it be mentioned here as amusing posturing in the spirit of the times [familiar in English as *Zeitgeist*] – in the sense of 'political correctness' – that the voice, ever more loudly heard, of a contemporary German historian should express the staggering assertion that the reason the terms of the Versailles Treaty were non-negotiable with the Allies was entirely attributable to the arrogant personal stance of the German Foreign Minister, Count Brockdorff-Rantzau.[39]

It could be foreseen, in view of what was said above, that for decades to come European policy would be determined by the painstaking endeavour of the German government to amend the treaty's unfulfillable financial and military sanctions. To what extent these claims for amendment were justified is proved by the fact alone that already in 1932 (11 December 1932) – i.e. before Hitler's

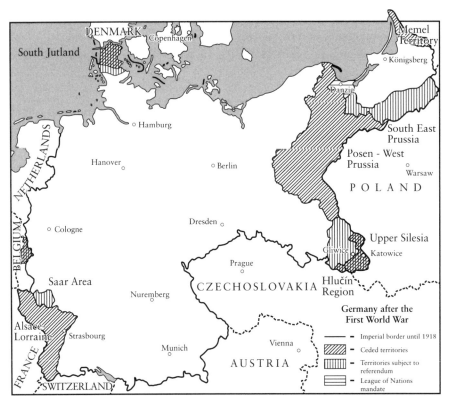

The German Empire after the First World War.

time – military equal rights had also been pledged. A line should moreover have been drawn under the reparations.

The Versailles Treaty has long been a part of history. Besides, from an early date Anglo-Saxon politicians and scientists criticized it pragmatically and sharply. At the very time of finalization of the treaty, the renowned British economist John Maynard Keynes, whose ideas on the politics of the economy and finance are still the object of discussion, said that:

> 'There are few episodes in history which posterity will have less reason to condone, – a war ostensibly waged in defence of the sanctity of international engagements ending in a definite breach of one of the most sacred possible of such engagements on the part of the victorious champions of these ideals.'[40]

Keynes, who attended the Versailles Conference as a delegate of the British Treasury, knew what he was saying. And he was referring least of all to the breach of promises made to the German people for a 'just peace' by Woodrow Wilson in 1918 in his 'Fourteen Points', wherein for instance there was mention of the 'right to self-determination of peoples'. At any rate, putting its faith in the 'Fourteen Points', following an abundant exchange of memoranda with US President Wilson, the German Reich had laid down its arms, thus putting the country in the hands of the Allies. Wilson had stated expressly that the acceptance of his terms would open the way to a negotiated peace. However, on the other hand simultaneously what was formulated for the first time, and that was later to turn out to be so calamitous, was that he compelled the 'unconditional capitulation' of Germany. The German government signed the Armistice in view of these expectations and awaited a negotiated peace. In this they were to be 'cruelly disillusioned', as my father wrote.

The centre of Europe, the German Reich in two parts, was disarmed over its total extent and thereby deprived of power, in the perspective of the military strength of its neighbours. The 'Reichswehr', the armed forces, consisted of 100,000 troops. They had no heavy artillery, no tanks, and all of what was known at the time as 'heavy weapons' were prohibited. Any air force was absolutely forbidden. Naval forces were not to exceed 15,000 men, with additional broad restrictions. They could have no heavy-duty ships, no submarines, no naval air arm, and so on.

According to the Versailles Treaty, the Western border of the Reich was completely demilitarized. In a zone whose boundary ran 50km east of the Rhine, no garrisons of any sort or other installations could be maintained, let alone fortifications. It should be remembered that the Ruhr had been occupied in 1923 for spurious reasons, on the pretext that a delivery of timber had failed to be made. On this occasion, the British diplomat John Bradbury, who was outvoted by his Belgian and French colleagues, said that 'wood had never been so misused since the Trojan horse'.[41] But even in East Prussia, which had been cut off from the Reich by the so-called 'Polish Corridor', no border fortifications were permitted, whereby this province was exposed, defenceless against any Polish aggression. In other words, there persisted in Central Europe a 'perfected power vacuum' that under the circumstances of those days represented a latent threat to Europe's political stability. Renewed French military pressurization of the Reich was a possibility at any time. Even after the 1920 plebiscite, every Weimar government had to take the Polish aspirations concerning further inroads into the Reich's territory into account.[42]

When the political map of Europe in 1933 is scrutinized and the military relations of power visualized as they were in the 1930s, the only conclusion to be drawn is that the Reich's defence position was desperate. Not only were Germany's two biggest industrial areas, the Ruhr in the West and Upper Silesia in the East, open to and unprotected against aggression from France, Poland and Czechoslovakia and unable to defend themselves, but the Reich had absolutely no possibility of fending off any military action by these countries.

Of especial gravity in this situation of – literally – 'impotence', was the isolation of the Reich, or rather, to express it more appropriately, that the Reich's isolation was the inescapable result of its military 'impotence'. Father quoted Hitler from the first conversation of political content he had with him, when Hitler had said: 'Germany must once again become a factor of power or else she will never have any friends.'

This statement of Hitler's conveys the dilemma traditionally portrayed that German foreign policy had to contend with. It was not invented by Hitler but is found in Germany's geopolitical situation and pre-determined importance. A specific power potential is on the one hand the precondition in order to be 'alliance-capable' and able to hold one's own in the centre of Europe, while on the other hand the concern over this very potential upsets the desired partner-allies. This is the problem that the Soviet Union presented for Europe's stability and security as early as the 1930s – at the very least as a world power, ruled by an outright aggressive ideology – which as yet has not been resolved.

It was an eye-opener for Germany in 1931, when French politics exposed the weakness and isolation of the Reich emphatically and strikingly as France forcefully intervened in the plans forged by the German Reich's Chancellor, Brüning, and the Austrian government to establish a customs union between them in view of the looming worldwide economic crisis. I was 10 years old when in the summer of 1931 a German diplomat stayed with us in Dahlem for a few weeks. He was a relative by marriage of my father's sister.[43] The German–Austrian negotiations were taking place at that time, and as my parents were following them with interest, this relative kept them informed of developments. When, after the plan had to be scrapped because of the interventions of the French, I asked him and my parents why it was not simply carried out despite the objection of the French, the answer was that it was for fear of eventual reprisals such as a renewed occupation of the Rhineland or the Ruhr, which could not have been prevented. In 1918 already, in the Austrian constitution the intent had been formulated to become part of the German Reich.[44] For us children, the occupation of the Rhineland by the Allies –

albeit dating back ten years, to the end of the war – was absolutely omnipresent. In Wiesbaden at every turn one came across a representative of the occupying forces in uniform, and our grandparents had French military personnel billeted in their home. When the Reich's government envisaged a so-called 'auxiliary police force' to prevent the constant street fighting among Communists, the Reichsbanner (Social Democratic paramilitary) and the Sturmabteilung (pseudo-military branch of the NSDAP), the French government protested. At lunch one day, Father, furious, told us that the French ambassador in a press interview had given as grounds for the *démarche*: 'When a child plays with fire, it has to be knocked out of its hand!'

Taking another look at the map with the political borders of 1931, the completely disarmed Reich was surrounded by strongly armed states, linked together by treaties, who, under the leadership of France, were in a position to decisively restrict the freedom of action of the Reich's government and, if need be, to enforce decisions favourable to them by exerting military pressure. This pact, put together by France, included Belgium, Poland, Czechoslovakia and Yugoslavia. These countries had in some cases aspirations over wider areas of the Reich, or were hostile to it for very diverse reasons, not least because of the attraction these regions exerted on the millions of German 'minorities' living in them.

Whilst the countries of the so-called 'Little Entente' – named thus to emphasize the contrast to the 'Entente Cordiale', the alliance between France and Great Britain – were heavily armed, Great Britain had somewhat reduced the numbers of its strike force, although in quality maintenance it was up to date. Keep this situation in regard to Germany's foreign policy, that Hitler found when he came to power, clearly before you. The Weimar governments had already been obliged to grapple with this extremely endangered position – of itself alone – meaning it was critically weak.

Hitler, however, seeing beyond this very real menace to Germany from the 'Little Entente', also saw that a martial danger threatened not only the Reich but the whole of Europe in the display of power of the Soviet Union. He cannot be said to have seen spectres. The Soviet leadership had long been preoccupied with thoughts of 'snapping the handcuffs' on the states on its western borders.[45] It was a constantly growing potentiality. At a later date, after the Second World War, the independence of Western Europe was preserved only through the participation of the United States within NATO, which is to say through the American nuclear potential, thus averting a Soviet hegemony with the well-known consequences thereof.

With an eye on the Soviet Union, the power relations in Europe presented as follows: Central Europe was a complete power vacuum; France, entrenched behind her Maginot Line, had her eyes fixed on this picture of powerlessness called the 'German Reich'; the Eastern European countries of some weight such as Poland and Czechoslovakia bent a malevolent, if not covetous eye on this Central Europe devoid of power; the United States had firmly withdrawn into isolation from foreign affairs. Roosevelt's election campaign propaganda in 1932 insisted on non-involvement in Europe. Admittedly already in 1933 his action, recognized by international law, of the formal recognition of the Soviet Union was a step that also had an impact on European politics. All the American governments preceding him had strictly eschewed this.

The question Hitler asked himself was: who was actually going to halt the 'Russian steamroller' if Stalin was one day going to have the bright idea of letting it roll on? The countries known as the 'Buffer States' – Poland, Czechoslovakia and Romania – did not come into consideration for the purpose. The concept of the 'Russian steamroller' had been coined at the beginning of the 1914-18 war as a vivid image characterizing the quantitively superior military potential of the huge Russian state.[46]

A German head of government, whoever he was, who was conscientious about his responsibilities had to take into account that in certain circumstances Soviet Russia would not shrink from expanding her power sphere – possibly by force – in Europe. The 'power vacuum' in Central Europe deriving from the total demilitarization of the sole country that would be in a position to oppose the Soviet Union challenged such expansionist policies, if only to choose the right moment. One need think only of Molotov's claims relating to the Dardanelles and the Balkans, not to mention the outlets to the Baltic Sea, that is to say the Straits of Sund and Belt, which he raised when he visited Hitler and his Foreign Minister in Berlin in November 1940, at a time when the Reich was after all at the high point of its power. It should be mentioned in this context that in both the principal European states – France and Germany – strong, militant Communist parties were established, controlled from Moscow by the 'Comintern bureau'. Soviet Russia had incorporated the motto of 'World Revolution' on her flags, which underlined, in terms of *Realpolitik*, Moscow's aspiration to world domination. 'Whoever has Berlin has Europe' was a well-known statement of Lenin's.

From the angle of these relations of power and their risks, to tackle the armaments question was hence also a given for Hitler's government. A general disarmament would either be achieved through the Geneva Disarmament Conference or the armament of Germany would be an imperative necessity, as to the extent of which Hitler wanted to come to an agreement with Great Britain and France.

It must be pointed out here that according to the wording of the Versailles Treaty, the disarmament of Germany was supposed to be the premise for a general disarmament. As stated in Part V of the Treaty:

'In order to render possible the initiation of a general limitation of the armaments of all nations, Germany undertakes strictly to observe the ... military, naval and air clauses.'[47]

However, for their part the signatory powers of the Versailles Treaty had not complied with the obligation to disarm – the 'basis of the transaction' of the Treaty's armament clauses. Further down there is the statement:[48]

'[The requirements] are also the first steps towards that general reduction and limitation of armaments which they seek to bring about as one of the most fruitful preventives of war, and which it will be one of the first duties of the League of Nations to promote.'

On 18 May 1926, the Preparatory Commission for the Disarmament Conference foregathered for the first time. The German delegate, Johann Heinrich Count von Bernstorff, explained to the delegates:

'The Allies forced an army limited to 100,000 troops on the Reich. The Peace Treaty, the League of Nations Statutes and now moreover the Locarno communiqués, however, all agree to recognize that German disarmament should pave the way to a general disarmament. This may be attained through three ways only: either you reduce your armed forces to the level conceded to Germany or you allow Germany to raise her armaments to your level, or you combine both, reducing your own armaments.'[49]

The Foreign Minister of a later date in Hitler's Cabinet, Neurath, who had already served in the same post in the governments before Hitler, had formulated the situation very aptly at the time: 'Germany continues to be the creditor in the disarmament question.'[50]

The Reich's claim to equal military status can be denied neither politically nor juridically; its entitlement to it had been categorically confirmed to the Papen government already in December 1932, and furthermore arose from the League of Nations Statutes, whose Article 8 obligated every member of the Statute to maintain their armaments to only the minimum required in order to safeguard their national security.[51] The modalities of either disarmament of the highly armed states, rearmament of the disarmed states or a combination of the two were to be negotiated. It was with good reason that Father's first official post should bear the title 'Special Commissioner for Disarmament Issues'.

A solution to the 'Armaments Question' – in whatever sense – was of vital importance for the Reich on two counts: it had on the one hand to restore the Reich's government's freedom of action, thus restituting its unification capacity, and on the other to enable the creation of a counterweight – from Hitler's and Father's point of view a 'European counterweight' – against the expansion of the Soviet Union's power. One could speak of a European concept. It will be my task in what is to follow to present the endeavours on the part of Germany, undertaken from 1933 to 1936, with a view to reach a settlement with England and France along these lines.

In March 1933 the Reich's Minister of Defence, Werner von Blomberg, asked for a memorandum on the Reich's military situation to be drawn up.[52] The chief of the Troop Office of the Reichswehr, Lieutenant General Wilhelm Adam, was assigned its compilation and had to grapple with the eventuality of the Reich having to defend itself against a simultaneous attack by France and Poland, possibly with the participation of Czechoslovakia.[53] Adam came to the following conclusions in the memorandum:

'France cannot be hindered from conducting a war on German territory as she pleases.

'The defence of the Line of the [river] Oder against Poland is feasible for as long as munitions last. The currently available equipment suffices for 14 days …

'Even so, a successful defence against Poland from the Line would be questionable were Czechoslovakia to enter the war.'

In this context, the concerns confronting German Reich Chancellor Brüning in 1931 are interesting. Poland threatened to advance on Silesia, Pomerania and East Prussia.[54] In 1928, the Reich's Defence Minister of the day, Wilhelm Groener, had already spoken in the Reichstag of the danger of a Polish advance against these provinces. And as early as 1923, during the French-Belgian occupation of the Ruhr region – five years after the end of the war – the

French Marshal Foch had gone to Warsaw, where his so-called 'Foch-Plan' was agreed with Piłsudski which envisaged a simultaneous operation of Polish forces against East Prussia, Pomerania and Upper Silesia.[55]

In Paris in 1933, after Hitler had undertaken the government, Piłsudski had sounded the French out as to whether they were inclined to advance against the Reich.[56] Clearly, it was not the case, most probably because Great Britain was not prepared to commit herself. Lord Vansittart, the anti-German 'hawk' in the British Foreign Office, acknowledged in his memoirs that in the Weimar days Piłsudski had in fact asked France 'twice a year' to cover Poland's rear in the event of an attack on Germany.[57] Vansittart, who will be mentioned again, would probably have seized upon this suggestion. The fact of Piłsudski's venturing a probe of this nature shows only too clearly the threat to the Reich already in domestic policy processes which could possibly allow a certain consolidation of relations in Germany to appear. At this point in the context, the intervention of the French government to stop the customs treaty with Austria should once more be brought to mind.

If in those days any hope had been entertained on the part of Germany for adherence as a member to the League of Nations, and consequently the military planning for 'delayed resistance' adjusted until the mechanism of the League of Nations began functioning, it would soon have been revealed as an illusion. When Japan invaded Manchuria in 1931, the action taken by the League of Nations was limited to the appointment of a Commission (the Lytton Commission) to investigate the conflict.

The concerns of the then Chancellor Brüning can be imagined. What line could be taken by the League of Nations against a possible aggression from France, Poland and Czechoslovakia? Who would impose sanctions – if they were at all resolved – on the aggressors? It is unlikely that Britain or even Italy would instantly trigger economic or yet military sanctions against the 'Little Entente'. The fate of Abyssinia is one more example of the 'protection' afforded to victim states by the League of Nations' trumpeted so-called 'collective security'. The United States were in any case not a member of the League of Nations, and were at this time keeping to an enlightened isolation.

And in this description of Germany's situation a possibly envisageable aggression by the Soviet Union is not as yet even taken into consideration. The political power *'horror vacui'* caused my father sleepless nights, as I could so frequently infer from talking to him and from the conversations between my parents and Grandfather Ribbentrop where I was allowed to be present. The phrase that as I have said my father uttered before me on various occasions, 'We have to take an option!', was an exclamation of sheer desperation. Whoever cannot understand – or will not – that Hitler's politics had to be conducted *a priori* from a situation of extreme weakness will not know the true motivations behind his actions in foreign policy.

The Dilemma

Let us now revert to the assessment of the defence-political situation found at the time of Hitler's taking on the mantle of government. Lieutenant General Adam states literally in his memorandum:

'At this moment we are unable to wage a war. We have to do everything to avert it, even at the price of being defeated diplomatically ...

'We have to reinforce our defence force by working with more tenacity, more patience and more care, at the same time preparing the population for the harsh moment.

'However, even if we do everything to avert war, also depriving the enemy of any pretext to declare it, we cannot avoid war if others decide to do it preventively. It would be folly to make plans for operations and troop concentration just for an eventuality.'[58]

In this 'situation of desperation' – may I be permitted the repetition – everything conduced to Hitler's intention to restore the Reich's capacity to defend itself by means of a politico-diplomatic agreement with both the Western Powers.

We shall follow the endeavours of the successive German governments to attain equal status in the armaments question from 1932 on, the opening of the so-called Disarmament Conference. It convened in Geneva, at last, on 2 February 1932 – twelve years after Versailles. Germany demanded 'a general disarmament to follow after her compliance'. The French government blocked the conference with security demands before any general disarmament could be possible. The conference broke up with nothing resolved.[59]

In a Note dated August 1932, the Reich's government under Chancellor von Papen once again called for complete equal military status. The Note was sent back by the French government couched in sharply worded form. The government under Papen finally delivered a 'Declaration of Dissociation'. This signified that no further participation in the deliberations of the Geneva Conference was wanted until some progress was achieved in direct negotiations.

British Prime Minister Ramsay MacDonald, in a 'Five-Powers-Declaration' in December 1932 between Germany, France, Italy, Britain and the USA, finally granted the Reich equal military status.[60] However, its practical implementation was not achieved at the disarmament conference which became locked in something of a 'vicious circle' in part due to the French government's blocking of negotiations. From the juridical point of view the German position was improved, although no *de facto* equal status had yet been reached.

On 16 March 1933, MacDonald presented a plan that came to be known as the 'MacDonald Plan'. Although in regard to the status quo it may have meant a certain improvement, it did not touch at all upon the Reich's right to equal status, not even as to adequate defence capacity, as emerges from the most important points raised in the Plan, summarized as follows:

According to the Plan, Germany would be entitled to 200,000 troops; France to 400,000; Poland 200,000; Czechoslovakia 100,000; Soviet Russia 500,000; Belgium 75,000; Italy 250,000. Britain was not mentioned in the Plan and therefore retained a completely free hand in the adjustment of her armed forces.

No air force whatsoever was to be permitted to the disarmed states, whereas France was authorized 500 aeroplanes; Poland 200; Czechoslovakia 200; Soviet Russia 500; Belgium 150; Italy 500; and the United States 500. Again, no limitation of air forces was foreseen for Britain.

As to artillery weapons, the Plan made the following provisions: Germany was allowed to add guns of 11.5cm calibre only, while states which already possessed arms of greater calibre were allowed to retain them. This signified a considerable inferiority in weaponry for Germany.

Military service was to be limited to eight months and professional armies to be disbanded within a specific time span. This clause too was primarily aimed against Germany. It should have commuted the highly qualified Reichswehr into a short-lived army, without however having the within fifteen years' born age group reservists at its disposal, as had all its neighbours. These details allow it to be clearly seen that both victorious countries had no intention of granting Germany an adequate defence capacity, let alone complete military equal status. Nevertheless, Germany accepted the 'MacDonald Plan' as a valid basis for negotiation. On 17 May, Hitler made a placatory speech in the Reichstag, which was 'honoured' on 11 June by the British Minister of War, Lord Douglas Hailsham, in an intransigent speech in the form of an ultimatum.

In September 1933, France and Great Britain seriously 'spoiled' their own – that is the MacDonald – plan. The new proposal foresaw two stages: in the first four years standing armies were to be made into militias; only for the second stage were the armed states to commence disarmament according to the British plan. As far as Germany was concerned, the plan was henceforth no longer acceptable as a basis for negotiation. It placed the realization of the Reich's equal status as well as the restoration of its defence capacity at the discretion of the Conference's decisions – which was not to reconvene before another four years, and thus at one stroke postponed the final decision for eight years. The proposal was furthermore once again directed unilaterally against the highly qualified professional German army, the Reichswehr, and did not take the lack of reservists' age groups into consideration, which the armed states had at their disposition for the last fifteen years. It was clearly not feasible to turn them into speedily trained militiamen.

A component of domestic politics may have played a role therein. It should be mentioned here that from the outset of his collaboration with Hitler, my father exerted himself to alter the former's negative attitude toward France to a positive one. Father used to speak of the War Minister of the day, Blomberg, who always warmly supported him in his 'French policy', and Blomberg's unfortunate dismissal was a blow for Father too. A particular problem often underlay the relation of the management of foreign policy to that of the armed forces. French politician Georges Clemenceau once said: 'War is too serious a matter to entrust to military men!' Blücher spoke of 'pen-pushers'. In this context, Father wrote from Nürnberg: 'I must mention here that SA Chief of Staff Ernst Röhm ... substantially contributed to Adolf Hitler's gradually revising his negative conception regarding France.'[61]

Röhm's efforts to turn the army into a militia in close connection to the SA are well known. I remember very well that after the events of 30 June 1934 (the purging of Röhm's SA, known as the Night of the Long Knives), my father said: 'Röhm is supposed to have admitted to a connection with a foreign power.' A connection of Röhm with French circles seemed all the more likely since both pursued the same goal of making a militia out of the army. In any case, Röhm met with François-Poncet, the French ambassador in Berlin, whatever they may then have discussed.

The Finance Minister of the day, Schwerin von Krosigk, says: 'The French President of the Council Barthou had been informed in the spring of 1934 that a change of the system was imminent in Germany. Whence he got this information is not known, nor is its content in detail.'[62] In his memoirs, Churchill leaves no doubt that the SA constituted a powerful potential threat to

Hitler's dominance, perhaps even a current one. He says that 'he [Schleicher] was imprudent enough to drop hints to the French Ambassador in Berlin that the fall of Hitler was not far off. This repeated the action he had taken in the case of Bruening.'[63] Schleicher was aware of the rumours going around, and only a few days before he died he denied having spoken with François-Poncet about anything but private matters.[64]

To deprive Röhm of power may have been necessary for the consolidation of domestic policy relations in the Reich from Hitler's point of view, and possibly also in the above-mentioned sense. The form and the manner of Hitler's handling of the row with Röhm and finally putting an end to it had without doubt in its brutality – neither justified by rights nor necessity – disastrous repercussions in the long term. It broke with the traditional concept of what is just. This appearance of arbitrariness, unprecedented by an autocrat in ordering executions by firing squad at his discretion – in some cases of his oldest comrades at arms – without giving the person concerned a fair chance of vindicating himself, was all but suited to conduce the broad domestic policies consensus that the country needed. The unpredictability thus revealed could prove a serious handicap in the field of foreign policy, in the sense of my father's efforts to win over confidence in the German concept thereof on the part of his interlocutors in other countries.

Did the governments of Britain and France perhaps entertain hopes of a change of government in Germany? Did the view that a 'diplomatic defeat of the Reich' (General Adam) constitute a contributory factor – envisaging for instance being outvoted in the Steering Committee of the Disarmament Conference – that might further this change or even bring it about? One can only venture a guess in this case, but it is not entirely to be excluded out of hand. In any case, Hitler was resolved not to let himself be outvoted in Geneva and thereby be shouldered with the blame for the breakdown of the 'MacDonald Plan' or the Disarmament Conference. Germany quit the League of Nations and the Conference on 14 October 1933.

Hitler gave two stars of journalism of international fame, the Englishman George Ward Price of the Rothermere Press (*Daily Mail*) and the Frenchman Fernand de Brinon for the Paris *Le Matin*,[65] each an interview, in which he once more expressed his wish to come to an understanding with both nations as to Germany's entitlement to equal status. At the time, both interviews attracted a great deal of attention. Both had been arranged by my father and contributed considerably to appease the temporary agitation aroused by Germany's quitting the League of Nations and the Conference.

After 1933, both journalists visited us in Dahlem on various occasions, de Brinon more often than Ward Price. The latter was a versatile man, with an easy approach to his interlocutor, not the typical Englishman apart from the dark blue pin-stripe suit he usually wore; de Brinon gave an impression of greater intimacy, also with us children, whose knowledge of French he praised. As Father constantly criticized our French – as is well known, he himself spoke it fluently – this did us a lot of good. In one of his books de Brinon mentions me as a 'Jungvolkjunge' (Hitler Youth boy scout) and gives a description of me.[66]

Both journalists were in favour of a major arrangement between their countries and Germany, and the atmosphere of their visits was one of open-mindedness, indeed it was genial. The interview Hitler granted de Brinon was particularly noteworthy because in it Hitler expressly showed himself to be disinterested in Alsace-Lorraine. Here Father's 'French policy' requires an explanation and I shall turn to his activities, conducted initially in an unofficial capacity and from 1934 officially, as 'Special Commissioner for Disarmament Issues'.

In the first discussion of foreign policy, mentioned above, between Hitler as Chancellor and my father at our home in Dahlem in February 1933,[67] Father had expressed his conviction that 'for a German-British rapprochement a compromise between Germany and France … would be a precondition'. At the time, as Father wrote, Hitler was 'not responsive'.

Father's argument set out from the premise of the validity of the British principle of 'Balance of Power', the European equilibrium so often quoted, characteristic of current British politics. Britain would not allow herself to be separated from her ally France in order to take an isolated stand against Germany or even to accept Germany's taking steps against France. The Reich was viewed by Britain as the strongest Continental Power – it should actually be formulated as 'potentially' the strongest – not that it was yet at the present moment. At the discussion with Father on the occasion of this visit to Dahlem, Hitler had closed with a request that Father should use a business trip to Paris and London to investigate the state of mind reigning in the political circles of the two capitals. Father wrote on the subject:

'After having sojourned in Paris and London for a fairly long time I reported to him [Hitler] again that according to my estimate only a gesture of reassurance toward France would bring about a relaxation in the international state of affairs that would be favourable to us. Everyone in Paris asked me what Adolf Hitler thought about France. What he wrote in his book *Mein Kampf* about the ancestral enmity between Germany and France was constantly quoted and put an end to any political discussion.'[68]

At the time when Hitler was writing his book (1924-25) in the Festung Landsberg prison, the Ruhr had been occupied by the French and the Belgians, where they maintained a rule of terror of a sort.[69] The book was of course supposed to prepare his comeback to politics, and in those days he could therefore express only anti-French sentiments. In the book, he had already 'stuck his neck out', as we would say today, when he sharply rejected a policy that aimed at repossessing the German regions lost to Versailles.[70] It should be remembered when the time comes, to speak of his offer to Poland in the autumn of 1938, that characteristically included the guaranteeing of the Polish borders, consequently also of the Corridor through the Reich.

The head of the delegation of French combatants whom Father had brought to Hitler as one of his 'confidence-building actions', Scapini, who had been blinded in war, mentioned to Hitler the anti-French chapters in *Mein Kampf* and asked the Führer whether he was now going to write another book. Hitler retorted promptly and with emphasis: 'I shall refute my book by my policies!' Father told my mother about this in front of me with delight. He could attribute Hitler's turn-about to a 'pro-French' political stance to a personal success of Father's own, since from the start he had sustained the opinion that 'the way to London led through Paris', in the sense, in fact, that it would be impossible to separate France and Great Britain. Meanwhile Hitler had realized that he had to bring France in, were it only for the reason that by their own choice, the policies of the French depended on London, even though he saw London as the heavyweight. Thereby territorial problems on the Reich's western border were eliminated, the referendum in the Saar region having been established in the Treaty of Versailles. It might at most temporarily have led to tensions.

On 26 January 1934, Hitler concluded a Non-Aggression Pact with Poland. The year before, the aged Marshal Piłsudski had found no support from the Western Powers for his planned attack on Germany; he was 'an exponent of "one thing or the other"', as Robert Vansittart, regretting the missed opportunity, wrote in his memoirs.[71] He was aware of the state of his country, that in a certain way was comparable to Germany's. Poland, wedged between two powerful neighbours, was in rather greater danger. Polish policy was based on an alliance with France and in the first instance was directed against her Western neighbour, the German Reich. According to circumstance, combined with the Little Entente, this alliance with France purported to neutralize the

Reich. The second cornerstone of Polish policy rested on the assumption – in 1934 in no way unjustified – that the opposition between National-Socialist Germany and Bolshevik Russia was unbridgeable. In this way, in the eyes of the Polish government a state of equilibrium came about in Eastern Europe that signified security for the Poles and which was bolstered by a Polish-Soviet Non-Aggression Pact in 1932. A further such pact with the Reich could only reinforce this security and moreover cost nothing, since for years Piłsudski had anyway experienced the political inability to launch an attack against Germany. Hitler, for his part, may have hoped that such an arrangement would make it easier to concede a favourable climate for the French government in the issue of equal status. At this point mention should not be omitted that Conservative circles, the entourage of State Secretary of the Auswärtiges Amt Bülow, were opposed to such an accord with Poland.[72] This will have to be borne in mind when judging the later activities of the 'Conservative' conspiracy against a pro-Polish policy of the German government in 1938-39.

We children spent the summer holidays in Büsum, where Mother visited us. There was an event of particular interest for me while she was there, as she learned that on his way back from London Father would fly into Hamburg. He wanted to be met so as to join us for a few days in Büsum, and my mother took me in the car to meet him at the Atlantic hotel in Hamburg. She briefed me during the drive about the mainly political grounds for Father's trip to France and England. He was unofficially charged with sounding out what possibilities existed for bringing about an arrangement in the issue of equal status entitlement between Germany on the one hand, and Britain and France on the other.

This was the return trip of the journey about which Father had spoken to Hitler in Dahlem in February 1933. In any case, during the drive from Hamburg to Büsum – which in those days was a matter of a few hours – he spoke with optimism about the talks he had held in both countries insofar as he thought he would be able to achieve putting the equal status issue on the path to a deal with Britain – thereby perhaps also with France. For me, the problem at the core of the German desire for equal status very gradually began to be clear. A genuine reconciliation based on equal status was the political goal. This meant that I – all of 12 years old – had to rethink certain things, for in my books about the First World War and the Treaty of Versailles, France and England were naturally always the 'enemies'.

However, in our life as children the will to reach an understanding with England and France was nothing new. We had a French governess for three years. Her mother was a Sudeten German and she felt herself connected to both peoples; she was basically a pacifist and in favour of understanding between nations. Many foreigners and diplomats frequented our home in the 1920s; both our parents had a distinct affinity with France as well as England. Father spoke the two languages faultlessly, and his English at least was without an accent. He had lived in Switzerland before the First World War, had studied at Grenoble and had been commercially active in the United Kingdom and Canada, with an interval in the United States. The French as well as the British way of life suited both my parents. In Wiesbaden, Mother had had an English governess for many years, of whom she was very fond and who remained faithful to our family through all the ups and downs until her death in the 1950s. In both countries, Father's business connections, which he had built up after the First World War, belonged to the circles that also determined the politics of their countries. It was inevitable that, being someone who had already always been highly interested in politics, he should have expert knowledge of the political scene in Paris and London. The experience acquired through his close business connections, that he was able to accumulate over ten years, was exactly the right qualification for his assignment to conduct sounding out talks.

I shall insert here a minor personal memory that may illustrate the ever-present political atmosphere of our Dahlem home. It will have been in 1930 that a French friend who was of the same mind as they, made my parents a present of a board game played with dice, to introduce children to an awareness of the economic absurdity of European customs barriers. It was played with a quantity of fake money and the winner was the one who came out of the customs labyrinth to best advantage, that is who at the end still had the most money left over. The customs duties payable each time disappeared into a big jar. We often played this game with our 'Mademoiselle', as we called our French governess. It was not until seventy years later that this 'game' became reality!

I can say, looking back, that the political atmosphere at home was characterized by the insight into the necessity for a good understanding with both Western European Powers. Intelligence demanded it, sentiments wished it. It was precisely for this understanding to survive that the 'entitlement to equal status' was conditional.

Father's unofficial activity corresponded to the unofficial status of his visitors. Two Englishmen are before my mental eye as vividly as though I had last seen them but yesterday. They were often our guests, one a Mr Tennant and the other Professor Conwell-Evans.

We gazed with awe at Ernest Tennant, the big, heavily built Scotsman, in secret admiration, for he had told Father his story, that he must be one of the few people who had been lying severely injured underneath a lion, and yet had been rescued. Dogs had drawn the predator away and his life had been saved. However, he was far from having escaped death. What is dangerous in wounds from the paws of huge felines – they had torn up his chest – is the ptomaine putrefaction that sets in from the traces of rotting flesh caught in the animal's claws that are left in the skin of its prey at the final laceration. He escaped this life-threatening danger thanks to crystals or salts that a native medicine man had pressed into the wounds. Tennant being a Scotsman, Father was rather amused by his thriftiness – if in doubt, Tennant let Father pay the bill – which seemed somehow to confirm the commonplace reputation of Scots for stinginess.

Tennant roamed the world, collecting butterflies. He was well off and financially independent. Like many British people with connections abroad, he placed himself at the disposal of the Secret Service – in this case as contact man with my father. My parents explained to me that many British people abroad cooperated with the Secret Service, seeing it as a self-evident duty to their country, an attitude found only rarely in Germany. My parents regretted – although they did not quarrel with it – that German career diplomats did not encourage their compatriots with international connections to provide the '*Dienst*' (trans., to serve the foreign policy of the home country) with such knowledge, observations and connections. It was Father's opinion that businessmen, journalists, scientists etc. were often better informed about the country where they were guests, as well as its relations with others, than career diplomats who, moreover, only ever stayed for a limited time in their post in the country they were accredited to. Already then, financial representatives were complaining of the lack of support in their efforts in the sector of exports on the part of the Reich's diplomatic missions.

The other Briton, Thomas P. Conwell-Evans, called himself 'Professor' because he had a visiting lecturer's chair at Königsberg University in East Prussia. He presented himself as a cheerful, energetic and amiable chap who was fluent in German. As far as I remember, his field of scholarship was English literature. This 'cover', as professional camouflage is known in the intelligence services, enabled him to make use of the most diverse contacts all over the world and to be active in the interests of his country. Father rated Conwell-Evans as fairly high-ranking in the Secret Service.[73] We children made contact with Conwell-Evans more easily than with the reserved Scot. He was a frequent visitor to our embassy in London.

But we got on best with de Brinon, who was friendly to and spent time with us. After 1940 he was the Vichy government's ambassador to Germany. This was a good choice on the part of France, for his longstanding close contact with my father meant that de Brinon had the best prerequisites to represent his country's interests effectively to the German government. His life ended after the liberation in his homeland in front of a firing squad. About him, Father wrote:

'On the day of Montoire [24 October 1940, when Hitler famously shook hands with Marechal Petain, signifying the beginning of organized French collaboration with Germany], Ambassador de Brinon made a remark to me typical of him: "We have not lost the war. We just did not want to fight!"'

When my father was appointed 'Special Commissioner for Disarmament Issues', we had ever more visitors. I have already mentioned the star lead-article writer for the Rothermere Press, Ward Price. Now Lord Rothermere himself appeared. He was a calm and worthy representative of the Empire. Lord Rothermere and Lord Lothian – both of whom I remember well – were on various occasions Father's interlocutors during the long-drawn-out efforts to place German-English relations on a footing of mutual trust. The Rothermere Press committed itself to this end. Someone who gave a quite different impression, of being lean, tough and energetic, however, was, as I remember him, Lord Lloyd, who at the time was not necessarily seen to be the militant opponent of Germany that he later turned out to be. One might ask oneself what Lord Lothian, as British ambassador in Washington during the war, will have thought when at Churchill's behest he had himself to get the sell-off of the British Empire underway. What will the feelings have been of the British hardliner Lord Lloyd – who had propagandized for a military conflict with Germany – when during the war he had protested to Churchill about the ruthlessness with which the Roosevelt government was forcing the British to relinquish their investments abroad so as to be able to pay for American supplies?[74]

Our numerous foreign guests in Dahlem sought to have contact with my father as having newly appeared on the diplomatic scene, news of which had swiftly made the rounds with the adjunct that to a certain extent he had Hitler's ear. They wanted to find out what he had to offer and how Hitler's policies were to be assessed. Father was aware of his role and was tireless in proffering the important arrangement he had in mind. The many talks held in Dahlem confirmed the German desire to come to terms with Britain and France in the broadest sense.

The person who made the greatest impression on us children when he came to Dahlem was the Frenchman Georges Scapini, who had been blinded in the war and was President of the French League of Frontline Fighters. The dignity with which this man endured his harsh fate was striking. He genuinely aspired to prevent a repetition of the events that had cost him the sight of an eye. He was charming to us children, and there is the amusing story of how my sister Bettina tried to describe a grouse's mating call to him. Her knowledge of French was inadequate for the purpose, so she said: '*C'est un oiseau qui crie toujours je t'aime, je t'aime.*' ('It's a bird who is always calling out I love you, I love you'). Scapini was royally entertained because he had of course immediately understood what bird the 13-year-old girl meant. At Father's instigation, after the 1940 campaign on the Western front, Scapini was appointed with diplomatic status and a staff to take care of the camps of the French prisoners of war. After the victory over France, Father also represented the policy of reconciliation, albeit finding himself exposed to strenuous opposition in its execution, added to by the bickering over competencies in the Third Reich, which went one step further and also had an extremely negative impact within occupied France.

Father's position as 'Special Commissioner for Disarmament Issues' was a structure typical of the Third Reich, or rather of Hitler. As has already been said, my father was not subordinate to the Auswärtige Amt. This signified for him that on the one hand he had greater freedom of movement, although on the other the ministry's facilities were not at his disposal. He was also obliged to set up an organization of his own – known as the '*Dienststelle Ribbentrop*'. On instruction of the Führer, Father had agreed to draw a budget for the Dienststelle from the Reich's Ministry of Finance Government. The adventurous account of Reinhard Spitzy[75] about the financing of the '*Dienststelle Ribbentrop*' is as undeserving of belief as his account of political events during the short period of his employment by my father.

With his small organization Father developed an intensive activity of 'trust-building measures', as they would be called today. Associations, one German-English and the other German-French, were founded, together with friends from those countries and to which significant personalities from all three belonged, such as Sir Robert Vansittart to the German-English one. With hindsight, one may be justified in doubting whether when Sir Robert joined it his intentions were of the best in the sense of the objectives set by the association; however, as Permanent Undersecretary of the Foreign Office he could not be overlooked. The '*Dienststelle Ribbentrop*' organized meetings of front-line fighters from the three countries, which was not greatly to the liking of the French ambassador François-Poncet.

The work carried out by the '*Dienststelle Ribbentrop*' was nevertheless not restricted to 'creating an atmosphere'; it was a matter of reaching concrete results. The armaments problem, included in the formulation 'German right to equal status', had to find a solution in view of the Reich's endangered situation, whether it was through general disarmament or acceptance of the restoration of its defence capacity. Father's Paris contacts were to bring about a meeting between Hitler and French Prime Minister Édouard Daladier. Father had this to write about it:

'To take advantage of the favourable atmosphere on both sides [following the famous Hitler-de Brinon interview with the declared relinquishment of Alsace-Lorraine], shortly afterwards I asked Hitler if he were prepared to meet the French Prime Minister Daladier. I had heard from friends in Paris that M. Daladier would not be averse to such a meeting. The Führer gave his agreement to an informal, private and confidential get-together. For the purpose, a hunting lodge in the Odenwald was chosen. I went to Paris in the firm hope of bringing the visit to fulfilment and thereby for a further step to be taken to a better understanding and rapprochement between the two countries – a goal toward which I had worked in the framework of my opportunities from as early as 1919.

'In Paris I met M. Daladier for breakfast [luncheon] in a friend's apartment ... As soon as we said our greetings, the President of the Council said: "I cannot come. I am situated in a system that does not permit me such freedom of movement as Herr Hitler has."'[76]

For Hitler and my father, this negative reply was more than a disappointment; it was one more symptom of the lack of willingness to tackle the problems, proof of the desire for reconciliation on the part of Germany countered by intransigence on the part of the French.

The German government did not let itself be disheartened, and more efforts were exerted to achieve progress in the negotiations. The problem of the Reich's defence capacity had sooner or later to be solved. A discussion my father had with Stanley Baldwin, then Lord President of the Council, John Simon, Foreign Secretary, and Prime Minister Ramsay MacDonald triggered a speech by Baldwin in the Commons in which he proposed a middle way compromise between the armed and the disarmed nations. Father wrote that at the time it was more than he could have hoped for, albeit in Paris the speech was received with less satisfaction.[77]

Those were the days when Paris blocked all progress in the armaments issue, which was of such vital importance for Germany. The advocate for this policy was the French Foreign Minister Louis Barthou. It was he who in 1913 had introduced three-year military service in France, in 1921 prepared the French-Polish alliance and finally, in 1923, when he was Minister of Justice in the Poincaré cabinet had voted in favour of invasion of the Ruhr.[78] In his talks with my father, Barthou kept to the line adopted so far by his government and diplomatically evaded discussion of armament matters, while basing the discussion wholly on existing French connections to Eastern Europe. On the subject Father said:

'Shortly after, I saw Barthou again in the fine Chateau d'Orsay of old M. Buneau-Varilla, owner of the *Matin*, at a dinner party with ladies present – this time my wife too had come with me. Barthou sparkled with wit and good cheer and it was an extremely interesting and delightful evening. Although I already feared that Barthou would again avoid discussing politics – for which reason I was there – he asked me to come into the garden. There we then had a long and this time very serious conversation. The French Foreign Minister was about to set out on his trip to Eastern Europe: he intended to forge a fresh ring of alliances round Germany. In vain I entreated him, instead of Warsaw, Prague, Bucharest and Belgrade to come first to Berlin … The French Foreign Minister was not to be persuaded otherwise. His standard reply every time was that before he could negotiate armaments issues with us he had to put his Eastern alliances in order.'

A few weeks after departing from the Disarmament Conference, the Reich's government recorded their wishes in a Note dated 18 December 1933. Quite rightly, the Note assumed that disarmament in Europe was unthinkable without a framework of worldwide disarmament, which at that present moment would not be very realistic. Hence, the highly armed states should freeze their arms situation. For Germany, the Note demanded 'equal status', which included 'defensive arms', the 'equivalent of the normal arms equipment of a modern defence force'.

In the Note the German government accepted an international, periodic and automatically functioning and general control, that could also be extended over the so-called 'Wehrverbände' (trans., unarmed paramilitary units);

meaning also the Sturmabteilung SA, the Schutzstaffel SS, Labour Service etc. The German government held out the prospect of converting the armed forces of the Weimar Republic, the Reichswehr, into an army with a short military service, whereby an original French postulation was met. The total strength required was of 300,000 troops. Lastly, non-aggression pacts were to underpin the accords.[79]

Once again, bitingly couched, the French government turned down the German Note, whilst the British government submitted a proposal of mediation which did nonetheless postpone the outset of German air armament by at least two years in that a general air-arm disarmament was not applied. This was, however, but an illusion as, remarkably, at the same time the American President Roosevelt had introduced a draft Bill to Congress that was thought out as the basis for a substantial reinforcement of the American air force. Take good note of the date: it was January 1934.[80]

Anthony Eden, who arrived in Berlin on 19 February 1934 to confer with Germany about the British proposal, found himself before a Hitler who was open to discussion and who had a counter-proposal only in the question of the air force. He was prepared to fix the strength of the German air arm at 30 per cent of the combined air strike forces of his neighbours, but not to exceed 50 per cent of the French air force. He would entirely renounce bombers. Nevertheless, Germany must be entitled to begin the appropriate preparations immediately, which was plausible in view of the necessary delays for development of airplanes.[81] On 17 March 1934, the French government also rejected the British compromise solution. French policy was incomprehensible in its inflexibility, which repeatedly thwarted every reasonable concession to the Reich. It was firmly bound to the dogma of the Treaty of Versailles and missed the opportunity to tie Hitler down to a specific, controllable state of armament. If he had then not adhered to the terms agreed, his contractual partners would accordingly have had the time for and the possibility of an appropriate reaction, since they were far ahead in their armament, which meant that at any time the prerequisites existed to force Germany by ultimatum to conform to the terms agreed. Furthermore, since Hitler had declared he was prepared to admit controls to cover also the SA, SS and Labour Service, no secret armament could be possible. It was not difficult for Hitler to accept such controls, for as a matter of fact up until the war there had been no pre-military training through the organizations that the French referred to as '*formations militaire*'. It may be that Röhm had plans to merge the SA and the Reichswehr into a militia army; but such plans nowhere near reached realization. After Röhm's execution·the SA dwindled to become a group of 'pub-night regulars'.

That the potential of the SA and, to a certain extent, of the Hitler-Jugend was not utilized for the purposes of premilitary training and development was symptomatic of a failure to construct a consistent armament policy. If anything it is Hitler that is to be reproached for this. The same omission may however also be brought in as evidence that he had not counted on a military conflict. It is difficult, in view of the geopolitical situation of the Reich described above, to bypass labelling this readiness for compromise as having been far-reaching. The repeated rejections of these proposals triggered Hitler's doubts as to the realizability of Germany's claim to equal status by the means of negotiation of an agreement with Britain and France.

On 16 April 1934, the Reich's government had orally submitted these proposals to Eden on his visit to Berlin in a Memorandum destined for the British government. It is of sufficient importance for part of it to be quoted here word for word:[82]

'The German Government find it impossible to wait two years for appropriate means of aerial defence. They wish to possess a defensive air force of short-range machines, not including bombing planes, from the beginning of the convention, the numerical strength of which would not exceed 30 per cent of the combined air forces of Germany's neighbours or 50 per cent of the military aircraft possessed by France (in France itself and in the French North African territories), whichever figure was the less ...

'The German Government would be prepared to agree ... to ensure the non-military character of the S.A. and S.S., such character to be verified by a system of supervision. These regulations would provide that the S.A. ... would

1. possess no arms;
2. receive no instruction in arms;
3. not be concentrated or trained in military camps;
4. not be, directly or indirectly, commanded or instructed by officers of the regular army;
5. not engage in or take part in field exercises.

'The German Government are also prepared to agree to the postponement of the reductions of armaments of other Powers until the end of the fifth year of the convention, the measure of disarmament laid down in the United Kingdom Memorandum being carried out during the second five years of the convention. All the other proposals made in the United Kingdom Memorandum, which would be unaffected by these modifications, such as for example, a supervision, are accepted by the German Government.'

Lord Lothian called the rejection by France of this basis for negotiation (in free translation from the German) 'a No of ominous historic consequences'! He was not alone in this assessment. As he says in his memoirs, it was said that on 9 April the French ambassador to Berlin, André François-Poncet, made an approach to his government to tie Hitler down to the latter's proposals:

'It was clear as day: if no agreement were to be reached conceding the Reich a limited rearmament also supervised by international controls, Hitler regarded himself acquitted of all obligations toward the Versailles Treaty and free to arm at will with no restrictions and no controls, borne up by the enthusiastic approval of his people.'[83]

Notable in this ascertainment is that François-Poncet therewith confirmed the obligation on the part of the signatory powers of the Versailles Treaty to disarm. From Barthou he was to find comprehension, but a cutting rejection by André Tardieu, formerly Georges Clemenceau's adviser, as well as by President of the Council Gaston Doumergue. Besides, the Belgian Foreign Minister, Émile Vandervelde, had already declared at the 1931 League of Nations Conference:

'The other Powers must either reduce their armies in relation to the Reichswehr or the Peace Treaty will be invalid and Germany arrogates herself the right to claim to have armed forces capable of defending her territory's invulnerability.'

Father had once said in my presence that he considered François-Poncet the most intelligent French politician – albeit no friend of Germany's – whom Hitler liked nonetheless; the two of them occasionally indulged in friendly word-play. I heard after the Western campaign from Mother, that Hitler had had his eye on François-Poncet as the Vichy government's ambassador to Berlin but that Father had his reservations in view of François-Poncet's fundamental attitude to Germany. Who knows, maybe François-Poncet was thereby spared difficulties after the war. Mother had also told me then that my father had suggested to Hitler that a son of François-Poncet's who was in a German prisoner of war camp should be freed.

On 7 March 1934, Charles de Broqueville, Belgium's Head of Government, made a noteworthy speech in the Belgian Senate, saying that (translated from German):

'I feel so very much, as you all do, the bitterness of the situation. It is the result of the great illusion harboured by those people who in the Versailles Treaty overlooked historical teaching and truth and believed it is possible to keep a great nation in a condition of disarmament for an indefinite length of time. We have to say goodbye to this illusion. It is the immutable Law of History that the defeated will sooner or later rise again.'

There had been by now, since the formal pledge for German entitlement to equal military status by Britain, France, Italy and the USA on 11 December 1932, almost one-and-a-half years of unavailing negotiations. No concrete outcome was in view; on the contrary the stance of the French government in refusing any concession to the Reich had hardened even more. Beyond that, a policy of alliance on the part of France loomed ahead whose goal was the integration of the Soviet Union in her system of pacts, thus even constituting a considerably greater threat to the Reich. The inevitable conclusion was gradually reached that both Western Powers were not in the least concerned with really granting the Reich a true right to equal status.

The Reich's government took a noteworthy step in this state of affairs. The Reich's 1934/35 Budget was published, wherein substantially higher amounts for the army, navy and air force than in foregoing years were scheduled. A query from the British government was answered by the German Foreign Minister, von Neurath, with the explanation that the disbursements for the army were necessary in order to prepare for the changeover of the professional army to a force with a shortened time of service, those for the navy were determined by the need for replacements of antiquated ships, while the Air Ministry's budget had to be increased due to the extension of winter- and night-flights, and that this was in consequence not part of a defence budget.[84]

It is perfectly clear that the Reich's government wished to push forward the negotiations over a disarmament agreement. If it had wished to proceed to arm secretly, such a public announcement would be incomprehensible. There should be no doubt that it had no way of concealing rearming had that been what it wished. This publication of the clauses of the Budget is a further indication that Hitler wanted the talks with the two Western European Powers to continue so as to solve the armament issue in concert with them. On 16

April 1934,[85] the Reich's government again officially declared its readiness to conclude an Armaments Convention. It was based on the British Plan of 29 January and repeated Hitler's proposals to Eden in February with regard to the air force.[86]

It cannot be clarified too often: on Germany's part it was categorically desired to come to an agreement with both Western Powers as to arms equalization. It was seen as the prerequisite for an arrangement in principle with Britain, to which France would probably then adhere. In order to bring this 'West-Arrangement' about, Hitler was prepared to make concessions in advance. It cannot be said that his propositions for agreement as to an air force were exorbitant, for he conceded a considerable inferiority of his air force, so as to achieve the desired accord. Over the agreement concerning the Navy, a year later he was similarly low-key, submitting German forces at sea to be limited to 35 per cent of the British, thereby also rendering its maximum strength dependent on a decision from London.

On 17 April 1934, the French government rejected negotiations over the British Plan of 29 January. It seems absurd: Hitler was attempting time and again to come to an arrangement that would restrict his armaments and submit them to international control, whilst the French government regularly thwarted every such attempt. There are and have been the most diverse explanatory interpretations of this incomprehensible policy on the part of the French government. Stresemann is said to have declared in the 1920s that: 'The fear of seeing Germany back on her feet paralyses the will of the French politicians and prevents them from thinking objectively.' No proof need be given that for a country of the size and importance of Germany a certain minimum military power was conditional to her acquiring partners in an alliance. This was equally valid for the Federal Republic of Germany, and it was not for nothing that Adenauer strove for Germany's rearmament. A neutralized Federal Republic, even reunited, would hardly have found partners to form an alliance with.

To revert to negotiations on disarmament in respect of arms equalization among the European states, more than two years had passed since the Geneva Five-Powers-Declaration in regard to the right to equal military status of the German Reich, without the slightest material progress having been made. The French government was on the contrary preparing a Bill according to which military service in France was to be prolonged to two years. This would lead *de facto* to a substantial increase in the armed forces. In no way is a prolongation of military service an indication that successive governments seriously concerned themselves with considerations of disarmament.

At the beginning of 1935, common French and British proposals were addressed to Germany, on the basis of the so-called 'London Communiqué' elaborated by the French and British ministers, dated 3 January 1935. Yet again the Reich's right to rearm was contested, although it was declared that negotiation of the issue was desired. 'Collective security' was now brought back into the game through the proposition of an 'Eastern Pact', which would have meant recognition of Germany's eastern borders (including the Corridor). Even Stresemann himself had unequivocally rejected this recognition (of the Corridor), correctly assessing that 'any German government that was prepared to accept this would be ousted'.[87] We shall have to bear this in mind when we come to 1938, when Hitler offered Poland a guarantee of her borders, including the Corridor, thus effecting a settling of German-Polish relations once and for all.

A convention was suggested in the Anglo–French proposals to be negotiated among Italy, Belgium and Germany, according to which 'the undersigned pledge themselves to accord the support of their air force to each among them who would be the victim of an unprovoked air attack by one of the parties hereby contractually bound'.

It is today presented in such a manner as to imply that it was Hitler himself who wrote the German Note of reply. It was in fact a draft written by my father. I remember very clearly how Father recounted that while the German reply Note was being prepared, Hitler took Father's draft 'out of his pocket' and presented it for discussion, but without revealing that the original author was my father. In his draft, Father had audaciously formulated that the Reich's government was 'basically prepared to utilize its air force to act as a deterrent against disturbances of the peace'. My mother, with a somewhat malicious smile, had pointed out the passage in the text to me.

On 4 March 1935, the British government had introduced a White Paper to the Commons whose content concerned a substantial reinforcement of the Royal Air Force. On 10 March, as said above, the French government presented the Bill extending the French armed forces' service to two years. The conclusion arrived at from the military plans of the British and French governments can be only that they had no intention of sorting out the armament issue by reducing their armed forces to the level of the disarmed nations. In consequence, all the disarmed states had left to do was to rearm. For Britain and France the order of the day would henceforth be to bring the increase of the Reich's armed forces to a contractual framework. Father's activities, unofficial until 1934 and thereafter official, were primarily directed toward an agreement with the Western Powers along those lines.

Did the German government not come to the conclusion that they were held off because the readiness of the armed states to grant Germany an effective equal military status or else to go ahead with a general disarmament did not exist? In the face of these facts the head of the German government proceeded to do what François-Poncet had foreseen as the logical outcome, which was unilaterally to rearm, possibly 'swept along by the enthusiastic approval of his people',[88] but in any case at least with the consent of the majority thereof.

Another reason for Father's advocating the step taken on 16 March 1935 (the reintroduction of generalized military service) was that he had information regarding the endeavours of the French government to strike an alliance with the Soviet Union directed against Germany. The initiator was the French minister Edouard Herriot. The goals Herriot had set harboured the risk of bringing about a 'situation of ultimatum' which would become ever more acute as the negotiations dragged on without resulting in a material right to equal status. The role of the time factor increased in importance in view of the general tendency of Britain, France and not least the United States to rearm, let alone Soviet Russia. Some four weeks after general military service had been reintroduced in Germany, the representatives of Britain, France and Italy met in Stresa and resolved 'to resist with all suitable means any unilateral cancellation of contracts'. And there the matter rested.

'Stresa' once again strikingly demonstrated one thing: the Reich's isolation in the politics of foreign affairs. This had been the situation since the end of the First World War. It would not be wrong to assume that at the moment of the Stresa Conference, Mussolini will have already been contemplating expansionist plans for Abyssinia. Who would assist him, or at least not knife him in the back? In the preceding years Britain and France had brought 'collective security' to the foreground, guaranteed by the League of Nations that was under their control. At this point in time – that is April 1935 – however, Mussolini was convinced he could neglect ties of friendship with the Reich to such an extent as to align himself with those Powers that thought they could deny Germany the right to equal military status.

As to myself, the days leading to 16 March were filled with great suspense. My mother's stereotyped use of the figure of speech of my being 'drawn and quartered' rather than betray a confidence at this time had an unusually intense and forceful impact, as during the preceding period she had been imparting to me Father's and Hitler's thoughts on the reintroduction of general military service if necessary – in case it was not to be attained within an armaments agreement – as an action to be taken unilaterally. Mother justified the step on the grounds of the 'phase of risk' which had now been entered into. The German government had registered its wishes for minimum defence armament and was making preparations for actualizing them one day. As an occasion for the reintroduction of general military service, there was a parade on Berlin's avenue Unter den Linden. For the first time in my life I was to have the experience of a German military parade. (At that time it was still saluted by Hitler in front of the Zeughaus Museum.) Then the famous Prussian-German military march music resounded, matchless in its verve and musicality. To my mind the Strauss waltzes are as unique for dancing as is German military music for marching, in which I count not least the (in)famous *Badenweiler* March. Because of its thrilling beat, Hitler – the political performer – had ordained it as 'his' march and decreed it was to be played only when he was present. The directive, which was not rescinded, after the war occasioned a Bavarian judge, who evidently had a sense of humour, to base his prohibition of playing the march on it. He was probably not aware that the *Badenweiler* March was composed in 1914 by the conductor, Georg Fürst, of the Bavarian Guard regiment to commemorate the fighting at Badenweiler (Badonviller in France) in which the regiment had distinguished itself. Similarly, few Austrians are probably aware that the derogatory nickname of 'Piefke' for Prussians is the name of Johann Gottfried Piefke, whom the Viennese had cheered enthusiastically. In 1865 the Prussian king, accompanied by Bismarck, had paid Austria an official state visit. The story goes that in the course of this visit the military band of a Prussian Guard regiment gave concerts in the squares of Vienna. The conductor's name was Piefke.

Featured as the leader of the military band was the drum major, whose special accomplishment was to strut with his leg stretched straight out in the air (this made him a sort of ballerina in military uniform). This parade stride of the drum major was the sole unnatural movement in the parade – and extraordinarily strenuous it was too. I still remember an English weekly newsreel from May 1938 showing in close-up a German drum major practising this parade step, which of course gave a strained and somewhat martial impression. It was filmed from an unflattering angle and seemed to symbolize Germanic militarism – no doubt the desired effect. The British propaganda mechanism directed against Germany toured in 1938.

An entire mounted regiment made a thrilling picture – they were all riding chestnuts – as they trotted past to the sound of light parade-marching music. We were no strangers to the world of horses. Father and Grandfather were both passionate riders, and we children had riding lessons from an early age and did horseback acrobatics. Father owned a few racehorses and sometimes took us along, even when we were very little, to the races at Hoppegarten and Karlshorst. Hitler would not have been particularly impressed by this magnificent performance of cavalry. He had no rapport with horses, nor with hunting. A few months earlier, the French Foreign Minister, Barthou, and the king of Yugoslavia had been shot in their car in Marseille, despite mounted police protection. A photograph circulated in the press of the time showing a mounted police officer at the moment when he struck the assassin down with his sabre. At the time Hitler had said to my father that if he ever saw the 'backside' of a horse as escort in front of him he would have the police officer responsible punished. The divergent perceptions of Hitler and the army leadership with regard to the importance of motorization may subconsciously have played a part. There is incidentally to be added on the subject a personal memory of mine of something Hitler said at our house in Dahlem on the occasion of my father's birthday on 30 April 1939, concerning the use of major motorized units. For some reason the conversation turned to the material battles of the First World War. Hitler observed that the advantage had always then been with the defender, since the attackers had a gruelling struggle to get across the expanse of craters that had been created by their own artillery in preparation for the engagement. This in turn gave the defenders the time necessary to block incursions by bringing up reserves, since contrary to the attackers they possessed an intact network of roads and railway.[89] (As for the entire duration of the First World War Hitler's regiment had been deployed only on the Western front, these were his experiences at first hand.) However, major motorized units would swiftly be able to extend an incursion into an operational breakthrough without giving the defenders the time to take countermeasures. Of course the mobility of these motorized units would demand a high standard of training and first-class ability to lead. I knew something about the theories regarding the operational deployment of major motorized units from my reading of military books. It was to be assumed from what Hitler said that they would already be applied in the German army. He went on to say that in Austria the deployment of motorized troop formations had in a way led to utter disorder, but that a lot had been learned. On this splendid day of April 1939, I could not guess that a totally new strategic concept had been quite openly brought about that would enable the sensational military successes of the German Army in the years from 1939 to 1941. A year later, almost to the day, I myself would be a soldier rolling towards the English Channel through Northern France in a similar personnel carrier in the framework of just such a motorized mass muster.

Back on 16 March 1935, here on Unter den Linden Avenue none of this was as yet conceivable. In any case the whole parade actually demonstrated only the

Reich's military deficiency, although the general enthusiasm was unchecked. In my parents' conversations, however, the tension and strain caused by running the risk of rearmament were apparent. The German weaponry on display that day of the parade in Berlin's Lustgarten was not really anything very exciting: small 10.5cm cannon – naturally they were harnessed to horses – no tanks, no heavy-duty weapons, no anti-aircraft or other type of gun, nor were there any airplanes accompanying the parade. But there were of course horses.

Remembering this, Father wrote:

'Unfortunately, however, during the winter of 1934/35 these efforts had no results and we had to conclude that the way to negotiation of revision of the Versailles armaments stipulations was hard and without end. This whole state of affairs was the reason behind Hitler's announcement in March 1935 of generalized military service and establishment of the Wehrmacht forces.'[90]

The opportunity to put Hitler on a leash by means of an armaments agreement, and moreover under a commonly agreed control mechanism, had been lost by the Western Powers.

It is said that in view of this decision to reintroduce generalized military service, the army commander-in-chief, Colonel General Freiherr (Baron) von Fritsch, advised Hitler 'not to be precipitate in next proceeding to rearmament'. If Fritsch did indeed express himself to Hitler in this sense, he must surely be agreed with, for one must never be precipitate in anything. It should, however, not be forgotten that in this phase what mattered was to attain – or to show – as swiftly as possible, a specific standard of armament so that the Versailles signatory powers should be aware that taking a line of deterrent action against Germany would also signify a risk for them.

What Fritsch is quoted as having said to Hitler, however, also reveals that at that point the 'black' – secret – rearmament cannot have been far advanced. This is important, for it cancels any plausible grounds for furthering rearmament, above all on the part of France. The alarmist figures submitted to the French cabinet by Herriot and Pétain as to secret German rearmament were devoid of substance. For the sake of simplification, however, the political organizations – like the SA, SS etc. – had simply been added onto the German troop formations.[91]

In a memorandum dated 3 April 1935 – that is three weeks after reintroduction of generalized military service – Ribbentrop recommended to Hitler a re-entry into the League of Nations, under condition that article V of the Versailles Treaty, wherein the restrictions of armament for Germany stood, was unconditionally deleted. He ought at the same time to bring an air force pact into play.[92] The memorandum says further:

'The duty to prove to British politicians and British public opinion that National Socialism is not expansionist hence acquires even greater significance. [underlined by hand]
  'I therefore recommend the following:

1) not to release the Parteitag (Nazi Party Rally) film[93] abroad *at present* as it would foster agitation.
2) …
3) Avoidance of every radical solution to the question of the Church and instead containment of the conflict … Avoidance of pointless arrests of pastors, *since at the moment they cannot anyway all be arrested*, because of the retroactive effect on the Archbishop of Canterbury whose voice counts with the King and in the Cabinet.
4) Our wishes for the military … are now known abroad and consequently, in order to prevent sensationalism in the world Press, avoidance as far as possible of too much public showing off in military matters.'[94]

Also apparent in this memorandum, irrespective of the problems of foreign policy, is the ideological problem that Father confronted during his entire activity in the politics of foreign affairs, namely the domestic controversy in Germany over the Church. Father took a firm stand on the issue of the Christian religion. If he took up a position against the arrests of pastors, he had to produce arguments that could have an effect on Hitler; in dealings with Hitler it was an instant always to be on the alert for, when reactions contrary to what was desirable were to be avoided. Whoever can place himself mentally in the circumstances of those times must see that it was an unmistakable criticism by the foreign affairs adviser of the arrests of pastors. Hitler's ideology, which he believed had to be forced upon the German people, burdened German foreign policy like a latent heavy mortgage. Incidentally, our parents had my sister and me christened in 1932. It was their opinion that baptism had more substance if it was consciously experienced. As we were living in Dahlem at the time, the well-known pastor Martin Niemöller, formerly a submarine commander and later a known opponent of the regime, officiated at the christening. Our parents had no qualms whatsoever when in 1936 I said I wished to receive instruction for my Confirmation.

The question might arise why it is that no Weimar government was capable of restoring a particular military potential to the Reich, the inalienable precondition for it to be able to conduct an alliance policy, thus breaking out of isolation. Asking the question requires a reply: in the given conditions of the domestic politics of the Weimar Republic, no parliamentary government had the opportunity of taking anything more than minor steps in the direction of strengthening the defence potential at its disposal. One must think of the hopeless parliamentary fragmentation of the process of formation of political objectives; the considerable and very militant bloc of the Communists; the partly deficient state of readiness of the military; and the pacifist disposition of the parties of the centre; as well, finally, as the totally shattered economy. In the atmosphere in the Weimar Republic of clashes among the classes, it was impossible to ensure the resolve of the people for which, in order to get through the phase of risk, some rearmament was an essential prerequisite. Quite to the contrary, in 1927/28 the construction of a single armoured cruiser of the size authorized by the Versailles Treaty led to a months-long blocking of the Budget by the parties of the left, under the catchy slogan 'Food Aid for Children instead of Armoured Cruisers' (in German, 'Kinderspeisung statt Panzerkreuzer').

Hitler's bluster about the achievements of his regime, the constant stressing of 'defence-willingness', the emphasizing of the bravery of German soldiery in the First World War, the forms of militancy that the regime demonstrated on numerous occasions, in combination with the impressive and indisputable work done by his government of rebuilding the economy – one need think only of the eradication of unemployment[95] – all evoked a strength of the Reich that was materially non-existent. It did, however, enable the survival of the phase of risk. Against a background of Hitler's rhetoric, his theatrically sinister decisiveness was a sort of 'frightened barking' combined with a certain showmanship in a weak and therefore extremely vulnerable position. The huge, constantly repeated demonstrations of the people's determination under his leadership were to make it quite clear that any action against the Reich would be no stroll in the park.[96] Mother had then explained the outlays spent on the Nuremberg Party Rally in this sense. In the 'Memorandum for the Führer' mentioned above there is also the statement:

'It is meanwhile our duty to do everything to avoid the inception of a ...
crisis and without fail, first and foremost to reach the year 1936.'

The debility of the German position could not be expressed more clearly. The recommendations already mentioned follow on after this, that is, that the early stages of the gradually emerging military strengthening of the Reich ought not to be overly stressed when brought to the foreground.

Naval Agreement with Britain

Politically, the outcome resulting from the reintroduction of generalized military service was favourable. The British State Secretaries Simon and Eden paid Hitler a visit in Berlin. Father recorded Britain's reaction as follows:

> 'Adolf Hitler clarified the necessity for introduction of generalized military service to the British ministers, saying he had undertaken this step in order finally to establish clear conditions of relations. As he had always maintained, again he stated his readiness to come to terms with the other countries in the issue of retrenchment of naval and air armed forces. Furthermore, he stressed his sincere wish to come to a generous accommodation with Britain. It was agreed to keep in touch through diplomatic channels in regard to the matter of an understanding on the issue of the navy. Diverse feelers were put out in the ensuing weeks and at the end of May 1935 an invitation was received to send an envoy with full powers to negotiate the naval question to London.
>
> 'It was the Führer's wish that I should undertake these negotiations and he appointed me to the post of ambassador "for special purpose".'[97]

A picture of the days of June 1935 has remained clearly distinct in my memory. With a leg in plaster, I was lying in the sun on the balcony of our house in Dahlem. Late in the morning, both my parents came out to sit with me for a moment. Father asked after the progress of my leg affectionately if a trifle absent-mindedly. My mother, deep in thought, was looking out to the sunny garden and hardly took part in the brief conversation. I was perfectly conscious of my parents' somewhat preoccupied mood, and I thought it odd that Mother should herself drive Father to the Tempelhof airfield, Berlin's airport of the time, notwithstanding that she was a first-rate and enthusiastic car driver.

When she came back, Mother sat next to me again and told me that Father was flying to London so as to work out an accord as to the reciprocal strength of naval forces. Hitler and he hoped a long-term agreement with Britain would be reached through a voluntary restriction of Germany's naval force. I was 14 at the time, the age when one opens up to the world. The historic perspective unfolding before me made a profound impression on me. I could feel, literally, the wafting of the frequently evoked 'Breath of History'. A German–British connection signified security for my country in its continuing precarious situation in the centre of Europe. The foundations of the German foreign affairs concept for forging a common policy with Britain were once again in the foreground.

Among other things about the negotiations Father wrote:

'Sir John Simon chaired the opening session. In view of the experience to date of negotiations with Britain, I thought it right to establish from the outset the ratio desired by the Führer of 100:35 for the British-German naval force as a "*conditio sine qua non*". I also thought it necessary to reach an immediate valid and solid accord with England …

'Sir John Simon replied that it might be envisaged that a demand of the sort could perhaps be conceded, but not before the end of the talks and that it was hardly possible it could be accepted as a fundamental clause for negotiation right from the start.

'The conference continued in the Admiralty House boardroom where the famous wind clock is. The clock was brought in, in Nelson's time, to show the admiral in command the direction of the wind so that at every moment he could know whether the French fleet could sail out of the harbour of Boulogne or not.

'After some difficulties my claims were accepted by the British side.'[98]

A German journalist and biographer (Joachim Fest), in his biography of Hitler, gives this account of the negotiation tactics employed: 'Arrogant and limited as he was, he [Ribbentrop] obviously lacked any sense of how to handle the matter,' only to say, a few lines further on: 'Two days later, however, the British asked for another meeting; their opening statement declared that the British government had decided to accept the Chancellor's demand as the basis for further naval discussions between the two countries.'[99]

Now, the problems in conducting negotiations and the tactics required are well known to everyone who in their life has to broker difficult deals. It is often the stand of the initial position that was taken that clinches the success of the negotiations. There are many variations possible, from standing firmly on one's own demands, to giving way on the leading of negotiations by drawing a veil over one's own goals. What decides matters is the success thereof, and here it was unequivocal. There can be no doubt that Fest never led negotiations in the field of high politics and he clearly lacks experience therein, but one can give him no credit for his capacity – so decisively essential for an historian – to think himself into historical situations and, above all, to be able to present them with impartiality. The clear and solid agreements in this case helped to overcome precisely those obstacles that had stood in the way of any accord for so many years in Geneva.[100]

The *fait accompli* of reintroduction of compulsory military service constituted a major triumph for a foreign policy that brought about a concrete armaments agreement with England, whereby the arms restrictions of the Versailles Treaty were cancelled *de facto* and *de jure*. Father, who as he said was very pleased with the result of his negotiations – Hitler had moreover called the day of the finalization 'the happiest day of his life'[101] – could see beyond them that a significant prerequisite had been put in place to establish a long-lasting good relationship with England, the objective of German foreign policy. At the time it was clearly a not unreasonable hope that a step toward a major accord with Britain had been accomplished that gave both men so much satisfaction. Hitler viewed the Reich as a Continental Power without great maritime ambitions, whence resulted the contractual relinquishing of any competition with the British naval power. It was not surprising that on Germany's part hopes were entertained that further progress could be made in that direction. Father thought of an air force pact.

Father valued the British as sober-minded 'merchants'. It is no coincidence that in their favoured understatement, with which they could cleverly be coquettish, the British spoke of themselves as a 'nation of shopkeepers'. In Father's opinion, he himself was a successful merchant, which self-description he considered to be very positive. If he wrote to Hitler two-and-a-half years later that he had never thought the term for the British as a 'nation of shopkeepers' was correct, he had meant something completely different. He wanted to emphasize that these 'shopkeepers' were also prepared to fight fiercely – as far as going to war – for their world trade interests. He hoped, after conclusion of the naval agreement, that having weighed up the pros and cons of an alliance with Germany, the British would prefer it to a renewed dispute. In the clash of arms with the Reich in the First World War they had already forfeited their world supremacy. A fresh global conflict – in my father's estimate – would cost them their Empire, even as victors.

There had been accomplished in a little more than two years what for so long the Weimar Republic had vainly striven for, namely, equal military status. Whoever denies the necessity that at this point of time the Central European power vacuum had to be filled would also have to spurn the need for provision by the United States of protection for Europe against the Soviet Russian threat after the Second World War. The dissolution in the 1980s of the perilous Soviet deployment of power would not have come about without the ascendancy of the American military potential, and most certainly not by 'speeches and parliamentary resolutions', as Bismarck would have expressed it.[102] An attempt by the 'Little Entente' to take action against the Reich was to be averted only by a particular military minimal potential; the Soviet threat, however, was to be defused only with a militarily powerful Central European bloc. One year later, Hitler delineated this threat in detail in his 'Memorandum for a Four Year Plan'.

In view of this development, the question arises once more why England and France did not make use of the phase of risk in which the military build-up of the Reich found itself, to try to bring the Reich's armament into a contractual framework. Clearly, at that point there was already a trend within certain British political circles that adopted Sir Eyre Crowe's theory, dating to 1907, that never should there be any affiliation with Germany nor even a pact entered into with her. (The British Foreign Secretary of the day, Edward Grey – who was in the same post at the outbreak of war in 1914 – had described Crowe's memorandum as 'most helpful as a guide for policy'[103] and saw to it that it was made known to the Cabinet.) One of the most eminent supporters of this 'guide' was the Under-Secretary for Foreign Affairs already mentioned, Vansittart. Father had visited him on the occasion of the conclusion of the naval agreement. Vansittart had been evasive as to his true opinion and was noticeably reserved. Father then learned from friends that Vansittart had raised objections to the immediate validation of the agreement and that the difficulties that arose on the day before the signature derived from him.

Father knew what he was up against with Crowe, in whose memorandum of 1907, with many convolutions in the subjunctive, it is imputed to the Reich that it is consciously aiming at the 'establishment of a hegemony, at first in Europe, and eventually in the world', next to a possible maritime supremacy and the establishment of a 'German India in Asia Minor'. Crowe foresaw that the world would unite to counter such a 'nightmare'. My father had another tête à tête encounter with Vansittart a year later, about the outcome of which more will be said later.

Father had plans to follow after the conclusion of the naval agreement: he was thinking of an air force pact. In this intended pact too, the German conception and readiness is evident to recognize the British need for a guaranteed security, thus automatically including France as well. Advances in aeronautic technology had rendered the insular state vulnerable from the air as well as from the sea. Any potential alarm on the part of the British about an air threat from Continental Germany should be done away with in the same way as had been for the sea. As early as 1936, by the intermediary of Erhard Milch,[104] Hitler had afforded the British a glimpse into the moderate plans for Germany's air force, since at the time Churchill had already been writing on the wall in the form of the spectre of a surprise air attack by Germany against London.[105] In the German files captured at war's end, for the British, Milch's figures were confirmed.

A meeting between Hitler and the British head of government Baldwin now presented as the next step. Based on the naval agreement, from such an encounter Father expected further stimulation in his endeavours to reach a fundamental German-British accord. Father wrote that Hitler had 'instantly agreed' and goes on to say:

'But it was difficult to win Baldwin over to the idea. I had at the time the support of all my English friends to bring the meeting about. Mr. Baldwin was hesitant. Thereupon Hitler proposed to meet on a ship in the North Sea and said he was even willing to fly to England to see the British Prime Minister at Chequers. I heard that Mr. Baldwin had no objection but that he was just slow to make up his mind. Then I learned that Baldwin had said he had to talk to "Van" first – meaning Vansittart. This worried me, for I did not expect any positive response from Vansittart. Finally, Baldwin let me know through his friend Mr. T.J. Jones that such a meeting "needed further preparation", which was practically a refusal. Later I heard Baldwin said he did not know "how to talk to dictators".'[106]

Baldwin's refusal to meet Hitler was, for both my father and for Hitler, not only a disappointment, but above all once again a symptom. I can only state that the Reich Chancellor's attempts to discuss the possibility of a general agreement with the heads of the French as with the British heads of government were not accepted by either. Father said of this:

'As had been the case with previous German governments, the Third Reich also was faced with the irrefutable fact that a revision of the road to an amicable negotiation with the states of the League of Nations was quite simply an impossibility. That had been the reason for Germany's quitting the Geneva Conference and choosing to follow the path of direct negotiations with the Great Powers – principally Britain and France. The naval agreement was the only accord through which a revision of

Versailles was on the way to an amicable renegotiation with at least one of the Powers. Unfortunately it remained the exception … In those days I kept hearing that on the part of the British professional diplomacy under Sir Robert Vansittart, strong pressure had been exercised upon the British Cabinet obstructing any development tending to free negotiations outside of the Versailles system.'[107]

Baldwin's refusal to conduct discussions with Hitler was maybe a warning signal that British politics could move along the same lines as before the First World War, indicating a murky and in the end anti-German position. German policy for its part had settled on integration with the West. As early as 1933, Hitler had rejected the pursuit of a Russian option proposed to the German ambassador to Moscow, Rudolf Nadolny, who had in a memorandum advised the Reich government to take it up and had discussed it with Hitler. This time it was France that fetched the USSR back into the European game.

The Franco-Russian Pact of 1935, ratified in the spring of 1936, represented a *de facto* military alliance unilaterally directed against the Reich. The military alliance between France and the Soviet Union, including the 'air force mother-ship' Czechoslovakia, constituted a serious threat to the Reich. The important industrial regions in central and eastern Germany were within reach of air strikes from Czechoslovakia, while those in western Germany, as a result of the total demilitarization up to 50km east of the Rhine, were thrown wide open to and unprotected from any Franco-Belgian occupation. In this situation, every German government had the duty and the right to orientate their political planning to these realities. Furthermore, the inclusion of the Soviet Union was a real culture shock. This was known in France to those in responsible positions. Herriot had even compared an alliance with the USSR to the Turkish policy of King François I, who had allied himself with the Turks against the Christian Habsburgs.[108]

Even if rearmament had materially progressed farther in Germany – which in so little time could not have been the case – the situation of the German Reich was clearly worse than at the outbreak of the First World War. France's system of pacts, the so-called Little Entente (Poland, Czechoslovakia, Yugoslavia, Romania, Belgium), had encircled the Reich and now, with the addition of the Soviet Union, had become a huge threat. There had been no further progress in the efforts to come to a foundational arrangement with Britain since the conclusion of the naval agreement. As to the stance held by President Roosevelt of the United States toward Germany, the German side could have no illusions in that quarter. As has been said, the US had already diplomatically acknowledged the Soviet Union in November 1933, after evading the issue for sixteen years. Recognition of the Soviet Union was to be seen as a warning flash, since even at this early date it represented no positive element in regard to Germany's consistently anti-Soviet policy. The Bolshevik danger was after all much farther away from the West than it was for Germany, which is why it was underestimated and a Germany powerful again was considered to be a greater danger than Soviet imperialism. This imperium first had to approach a thousand kilometres closer before Germany's usefulness as a defence against it was discovered.

However, at this point – the turn of the year 1935 to 1936 – the significance of the German Reich as a political power factor was not to be rated too highly: the eastern part split by the Corridor; the western part, up to 50km east of the Rhine totally demilitarized, lay completely open to any Western military initiative. At the same time, a major portion of German industrial might was exposed to an inimical attack. The German government was not the master of its own house. Moreover, after the conclusion of the Franco-Russian military pact not so much as a glimmer existed of a prospect of changing this state of affairs through the path of negotiation. If the Reich's government was to regain a completely free hand, thereby becoming an interesting partner for other states, it could only be by its own initiative – and on Germany's part Britain continued to hold the preferred place in the field as partner. No reciprocity was to be expected from a France that was largely dominated by parties of the Left (including the Communists) and that was excluded by a pact with the Soviet Union unilaterally directed against the Reich, to agree to alter the status of the German Rhineland in the sense of reinstating normality, signifying the unrestricted sovereignty of the German government.

On this phase in German foreign policy, finalized with the reinstatement of the Reich government's sovereign right in the so-called 'demilitarized zone' of the Rhineland, Father wrote:

'Both for Adolf Hitler and myself one thing was a certainty: if military sovereignty [in the Rhineland] was to be reinstated – and following the Franco-Soviet alliance Hitler was of this mind – it was not to be through the way of negotiation. On the contrary, there was a risk that in case of long-drawn-out discussion about the problem a situation of ultimatum might arise which could perhaps more easily lead to a real crisis and a clash than if the counter-party countries were faced with a fait accompli. These were our preoccupations at the time and which eventually led Adolf Hitler to undertake the measure.'[109]

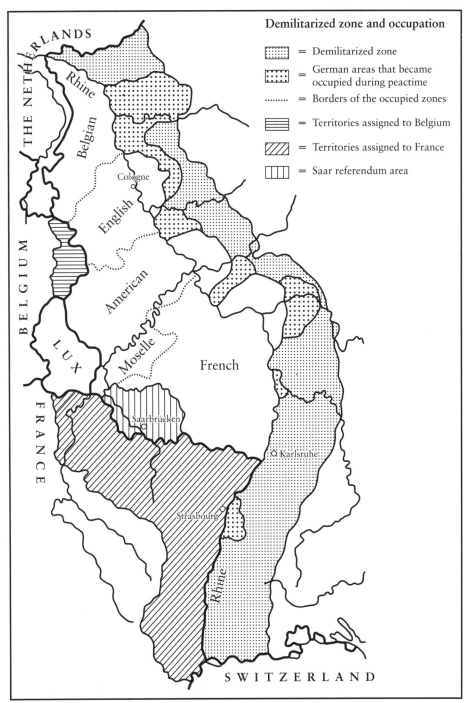

The borders redrawn following the Versailles Treaty; the Allied occupation of the Rhineland and the demilitarized areas of the Right Bank of the Rhine.

The ratification by France of the Franco-Russian mutual assistance pact ensued on 27 February 1936, having been signed on 2 May 1935. It was followed immediately by a military alliance between France and Czechoslovakia, subsequently extended by a treaty between the Soviet Union and Czechoslovakia, the coming into effect of which was, however – interestingly – made dependent upon the precedence of France.

In the face of the ratification of this treaty, the military sovereignty proclaimed by Hitler in 1935 – the previous year – was extended over the entire territory of the Reich. This meant the abrogation of the demilitarized zone in the west of the Reich and installation of garrisons in the heretofore demilitarized Rhineland, a step that had been announced. Father commented:

> 'He [Hitler] later often told me that had been one of the most serious decisions he had taken but that in view of the signing of the Franco-Russian military alliance he could not have acted otherwise.
>
> 'During the winter of 1935/36 I had made contact in Paris and London with a number of influential figures. I frankly and expressly made it clear in these discussions that there would have to be either an understanding between the Western powers and Germany through a commonly agreed revisionary programme or Germany would take the measures necessary for protection of her country into her own hands which meant that the Locarno Treaty would have to be amended.'[110]

The risk was correspondingly great that Germany for her part was prepared to take on responsibility for putting an end to a state of affairs arising from an attack by France against the Reich's western region, and hence a vital part of German industry potential. The so-called Rhineland occupation had resulted from a predicament imposed by foreign policies, the gravity of which is barely conceivable.

Father said the following to this:

> 'The hours preceding the occupation were thrilling. It was reported that from the French side a motorized army of some 250,000 troops were on the march, and it was obvious that given the small size of our forces[111] the occupation could in fact have only a symbolic effect. They were tense hours for me too, since it was I who had advised the Führer that in the end England would come to an accommodation with the reinstatement of German military sovereignty in the Rhineland.'[112]

When the German government had re-established full sovereignty of the Reich in the Rhineland it received the injunction to represent the German position before the League of Nations. Father writes that originally Hitler had wanted to speak in person to the League of Nations assembly. The Reich Foreign Minister, von Neurath, and my father had been able to dissuade him. Father was appointed to represent Germany at the League of Nations assembly. A date was fixed in London and ultimately, with one abstention (by Brazil) Germany was found 'guilty' of a breach of the Locarno Pact – also voted for by Italy. This verdict was reached unanimously, which will not have quite suited the Italian representative – as Father could tell 'from his expression'.[113]

The atmosphere stayed dichotomous, there was no break with Germany and the verdict regarding the alleged violation of the treaty had no effective consequence. Father also had occasion for another exchange with Robert Vansittart:

'Before my departure I received another invitation from Vansittart, whom I visited together with the German ambassador von Hoesch. Vansittart lived in a solidly built old English country house, well cared for, in a rare harmony with the tasteful modern interior decoration, which will have been due to his American wife. Little was said about politics at table. I particularly welcomed this invitation and was glad to accept, because I still considered it my most important assignment to find a way to forging a definitive amity with England, and because Sir Robert Vansittart – about that there was not a shadow of doubt – had always held a key – if not the key – to the solution of the German-British question. On the road back, I discussed the subject at length with Herr von Hoesch. He too stressed Vansittart's weighty importance, describing him as someone with a very sceptical stance towards Germany, coming across as rather opaque, and who could be won over only with difficulty. Hoesch also confirmed that Vansittart exercised a strong influence on the other Cabinet members. Herr von Hoesch, whose thorough knowledge of London was not in doubt, had not always been favourably disposed toward me. On the way back from the visit to Vansittart we entered into something like a first friendship and we undertook a common engagement to do everything possible to further good German-British relations. We agreed to keep in close contact in the future.

'Shortly after, I flew back, to report to Adolf Hitler, who was staying at the Dreesen Hotel near Godesberg. There, the next day I got the news of Herr v. Hoesch's sudden death from a heart attack. I truly regretted the passing away of this able ambassador.'[114]

To an unprejudiced observer it is evident from what has been set out that both of what were called faits accomplis, that is the reintroduction of generalized military service and reinstatement of full German sovereignty in the Rhineland, were notable and significant steps on the road for Germany's foreign policy to embark upon a peaceable track so as to win back its freedom to negotiate. At the time of his opening the Olympic Games in Berlin in 1936, three-and-a-half years after his accession to government, Hitler had constructed a completely new foundation for German foreign policy.

The choice of Britain had from the outset been Hitler's and my father's highest priority. Consolidation of circumstances in Germany had to generate reflection by the British government – or so it was hoped – whether ultimately coming to an arrangement with Germany was preferable to a renewed confrontation. Germany's improved circumstances now permitted the 'attempts at convergence' of the German government to appear no longer as supplication but as the offer from a partner on a basis of equality. It was not least from this viewpoint that Father suggested to Hitler that he should be sent to London as ambassador. That Hitler welcomed the suggestion evidenced the renewed, large-scale attempt to enter into sincere negotiations for an alliance in the European political world.

A certain alteration in the relations of power in Europe now came into the picture when Italy, as indicated earlier, came into opposition to Britain and France due to her Abyssinian venture. The League of Nations had resolved to sanction Italy, although Mussolini had thought he would have the acquiescence of the Western powers in his proceeding. A rapprochement was consequently in sight between Germany and Italy, whereby the Fascist anti-Bolshevik facet constituted but a component part of the general interest.

In no way was a cooperation with Italy (the treaty of 26 October 1936) seen in Berlin as an alternative to the efforts being made to reach an accord with Britain. For one thing there was no intention of playing Italy against Britain. This is attested by a confidential missive that my father as German ambassador in London addressed to Hassell, the German ambassador in Rome. The incentive for this letter was that it had come to Father's ears that the Italians were maintaining Father was conducting an 'anti-Italian' policy in London. Hassell had seemingly done nothing to dispute these allegations.

In his letter, Father outlined German policy regarding England and Italy as follows:

'As far as the existing foreign policy of Germany is concerned, it is clear that the contrast between National Socialism-Fascism on the one hand and Bolshevism on the other takes on a paramount significance in every calculation of foreign policy. Collaboration between National Socialism and Fascism is correspondingly compulsory, through which the relation of Germany to Italy is in turn fundamentally determined.

'I have never left the British in any doubt about this conception of mine and I see it as one of the main tasks for our diplomacy in London to enlighten them as to the very real danger presented by Bolshevism, to restrain them from any affiliation with a Bolshevik front and to foster the thought that *à la longue* [in the end] their world empire is under a considerably greater threat from a further expansion of Bolshevism than from a divergence from Italy in the Mediterranean.'[115]

The base lines of German policy are once more apparent in this entirely personal letter for internal consumption, to wit that a rapprochement with Italy should on no account be deleterious to the possibility of reaching an arrangement with Britain. In the German view, an anti-Bolshevik platform was acceptable to both Britain and Italy. The same was assumed in Berlin regarding cooperation with Japan. In this case, the first step was to form an anti-Comintern pact.

Father reiterated that, 'we have to take an option, meaning we must find partners even if Britain cold-shoulders us, "will not allow us to love them".' The Reich's ever-precarious situation in Central Europe obliged it 'to intervene actively in world politics'. An anti-Comintern policy was the path for cautiously emerging from isolation, without losing sight of an arrangement with England.

Whilst high politics were evolving in a way that was to alter our family life completely, there was no dearth of other worries. In the early summer of 1936 I had quarrelled with my fate – in the way, mark you, that it happens in the everyday destiny of a youth who perhaps grew up too fast – when a careful intern forbad me to take part in a Hitler Youth excursion as he had diagnosed an 'athlete's heart' condition. My parents offered to take me with them to Bad Wildungen, where Father was to undergo treatment for his remaining kidney. The other had already been removed before the First World War as he had been infected by a tubercular cow in the Canadian backwoods. Understandably, I was none too happy at the prospect of spending my long holidays 'taking the waters' instead of going on excursion. On the other hand, to be in close contact with my parents for three weeks was very attractive. In the remoteness of Bad Wildungen I could count on very interesting political discussions. In those days I absorbed everything I heard about politics – fascinated as I was by history – and it all remained locked in my inner self. At the same time, however, I was also learning a lot about the human and personal problems of politicians.

We went for long walks in Wildungen, usually just the three of us but often my father and I alone. We spoke mostly about the state of the Reich's foreign policy in regard to the centre of Europe. Father was not at all reticent about his worries. The Reich was still isolated. What foreign statesman conscious of his responsibilities could envisage associating the fate of his country with the powerless entity that at that point the German Reich still represented? German rearmament, promulgated only one year earlier, cut through all sectors of the 'risk phase'. Germany would have little to set against action taken against the Reich by the 'Little Entente' (France, Belgium, Poland, Czechoslovakia and Yugoslavia), which was ever an eventuality. Britain's stance in such an event was not clearly distinguishable and, in the end, the Soviet Union, weapons at the ready, stood in the background, by now a declared antagonist. It was certainly a situation worthy of causing anxiety to the government of the Reich. I remember being deeply impressed at the time by the weakness of the German position that Father outlined to me on our walks. He spoke incidentally of problems of strategy, for example whether a flank attack cutting off French strike forces advancing over the Rhine would be feasible.

It was not, however, only the extreme military debility that had to be remedied, it was also a matter of breaking out of the isolation in foreign affairs. England was the declared preferred partner, but what could the outcome be if the German solicitations were further to fail? The question was hard to answer. The time had not yet come, but it was time to direct a thought to such an eventuality. It will be seen what way out Hitler and Father sought, indeed were obliged to tread. I was consequently not surprised to see Oshima, the Japanese military attaché of those days, occasionally visit us in Dahlem.

During these walks Father also confided to me the problems that he had with his status towards Hitler and the leading circles of the State and the Party, as well as the Auswärtiges Amt. To all he was the outsider, whose remit was to Hitler directly as to his activity, and he was consequently seen as 'being in competition' and was to be fought. Hitler's mode of leadership, which was not one to favour clear-cut responsibilities and competencies, signified an additional complication for the work of the chief of the '*Dienststelle Ribbentrop*', not taking into account that far from frowning on antagonism among his collaborators Hitler frequently downright fomented it. This most interesting time spent with my parents was brought to a sudden end when they received an invitation from 'the Führer and Reich Chancellor' to attend the Richard Wagner Bayreuth Festival as his guests. To my great delight my parents wanted to take me with them if tickets and lodging could be found for me. Fortunately, they were. We drove to Bayreuth in a convertible with the top down, in brilliant midsummer weather across the beautiful countryside. Thanks to Fräulein Munding, who had done her best, we had been to see and hear a great part of the Wagner operas in Berlin. I was therefore not completely unprepared for this musical treat. The well-known quotation from Goethe 'One sees only what one knows' is also valid for what one hears. One hears therefore only what one knows (unless one is a musical genius), and it is incidentally an important factor for enjoyment.

For the time being, however, high politics were in the foreground. General Franco's military coup was already known before we left Bad Wildungen. We were having breakfast, and Father said he was of the opinion we should stay out of it. In the sense of German conception of policy there would be nothing gained from an intervention in the Iberian Peninsula, a classic field of British interests. The most important nerve fibres of the British Empire ran through the Mediterranean, so that only negative repercussions on the German-British relationship could ensue from intervention in that sphere. The same went for French foreign policy, which was anyway closely linked to the British. In this one need hardly bring the foregoing history of the 1870 German-French War to mind.[116] As far as my father was concerned, at that time the foundation of a German-British accord was of top priority in foreign policy. Already before leaving Wildungen he had sought to have a talk with Hitler, but on reaching Bayreuth he was informed that Hitler had not yet arrived at the Villa Wahnfried. Having good reason to want to know whether this was true, my father asked me to try to find out. I was able to tell him that Hitler had just driven up to the villa when I got there. Father was promptly granted a meeting, which pleased me as much as it interested me, for I was aware, to its full extent, of the significance that this rapid fulfilment of Father's wish for a meeting was a good sign for his standing with Hitler, thus offering him the opportunity to discuss with Hitler his view of the matter at hand – which I knew: in this case, the Spanish question. If historians of today often disparagingly say that Father frequently sought Hitler out, all they actually prove is their deficient sensitivity as to the circumstances of the times about which they are writing. Whoever wanted their political vision to be adopted had to have the ear of the all-powerful dictator, meaning that they had to be present when he made his decisions.

That this 'talk' in Bayreuth was in fact a 'discussion' appears from Father's notes. He wrote:

'When he [Hitler] received me, he seemed preoccupied and came directly to the point about Spain, telling me that Franco had requested a number of airplanes for an airlift of troops from Africa to Spain in order to deploy them against the Communists. My spontaneous reaction was to say we would better stay out of Spanish affairs … I feared fresh complications with England, as there was no doubt that they would view a German intervention with great distaste. Hitler emphatically insisted on his contrary opinion.'[117]

Despite his misgivings about possible complications with England, because of the Soviet infiltration of the Spanish government Hitler decided to go ahead regardless. He said:

'If it is really feasible to create a Communist Spain, then the way things stand in France at the moment, the Bolshevization of that country too is but a matter of time, in which case Germany can "pack her bags". Wedged in between the powerful Soviet bloc in the East and a strong Communist French-Spanish bloc in the West there is hardly anything we could do if it should please Moscow to make a move against Germany.'[118]

This once more corresponded to the thoughts Hitler had formulated at this time in his Four Year Plan memorandum. To this Father wrote:

'I saw things another way. Regarding France in particular, the French bourgeoisie seemed to me surely to be a firm guarantee against a definitive Bolshevization of that country. I told the Führer this, but it was incredibly hard for me to obtain any decision from him that went against his ideological principles, which in his opinion I did not understand. He reacted rather irritably to my objections and cut our conversation short, saying he had already made up his mind. He said that this was absolutely a matter of principle where my purely Real-foreign policy thinking was insufficient. Ever since the emergence of the major social questions of our century, day-to-day politics had to be subordinated to that fundamental problem, else one day our foreign policy will be scotched at a dead end after all. Here was once more manifested the recurring divergence of my views on foreign policy with those of Hitler. It was later expressed in its most typical form when in a memorandum in 1943 once again I advised an immediate peace with Stalin, to which Hitler in reply informed me through Ambassador Hewel that "in the war against Bolshevism there is no compromise. I cannot endorse Ribbentrop's shopkeeper-politics. This war cannot be decided by diplomatic means!"'[119]

But years were to pass before Hitler adopted this extreme stance and a number of further attempts at making contact with Britain were to follow. The very next day Hitler took the first step and called Father in to see him again to inform him of his appointment as State Secretary in the Auswärtiges Amt:

'He then brought the conversation round to filling the post of ambassador to Britain anew, which had been unoccupied since the death of Herr von Hoesch, and asked me whom I thought should be sent to London. This evolved into a lengthy discussion about German-British relations. The Führer wanted to know how I judged the chances of yet coming to an understanding with England; I replied that there was no doubt many opportunities had not been seized by Britain. I therefore saw the outlook, based on quite sober estimates, as not particularly favourable for the time being. However, at least, from all I had heard, King Edward VIII was not prejudiced against Germany. As he was very much beloved by his people it could be envisaged that an understanding might still be reached if the king supported the idea of German-British friendship, albeit a British sovereign normally has little influence on the policies of his government.'[120]

As a scenario, this sounded rather lame. Hitler too expressed his similar scepticism as to whether the project of an alliance with Britain could be realized. Thereupon my father came to a decision:

'I therefore proposed that the best thing might be to send me to London instead of making me State Secretary. Hitler was so pleased with the idea that he immediately seized upon it and said he was quite agreed ... I told Adolf Hitler at the time once again, very clearly, that the chances of an alliance with Britain were not great, rather the contrary should be expected but that I would nevertheless do my utmost. I know the English well enough to have been able to brief him perfectly soberly and objectively about the British state of mind. For the rest, obviously a great deal depended on Germany's further policy. At that same time I also stated unequivocally that – at least from experience heretofore – England would insist on her thesis of equilibrium and would oppose us if it was feared that Germany would become too powerful.'[121]

Two standpoints are particularly noteworthy:

Firstly, Hitler's repeated statements confirmed that his unequivocal concern in the face of the latent threat from the Bolsheviks was what defined his foreign policy. He saw the necessity to keep his back free – the prevention of a Spanish-French combination under a Communist label – even at risk of disrupting his declared policy of rapprochement with Great Britain. Whether, with hindsight, in this context he may have overestimated the danger of a Bolshevized France is of lesser importance. The eventuality of the Reich being threatened also from the West by a French-Spanish combination under Communist ideological pressure was, the way things stood in 1936, not to be discounted.

However, also noteworthy is the gradually sensed scepticism on the part of Hitler and his future ambassador as to whether the desired major arrangement with Britain was still feasible. I myself could sense through my parents the slowly altering judgement for the future in contrast to their hopes of 1933 and 1934, and especially following the conclusion of the naval treaty in June 1935. The nightmarish prospect of a renewed encirclement of the Reich was a constant theme of talks with my parents, and also Grandfather Ribbentrop when he was there. There was no doubt that it was an option open to both Western powers, since the Eastern and South-Eastern states that had newly emerged in 1919, Germany's neighbours, were indebted to the gracious favour of the British and the French, almost for existing at all.

London

The announcement of my father's appointment to the post of ambassador to London in August 1936[122] was made public in the week before the Olympic Games. The *Agrément* (official approval) from the host country was swiftly forthcoming. Since before the visit to Bayreuth, my parents had planned a garden party at our house in Dahlem, on the occasion of the Olympic Games. It was for Father to greet the many foreign friends and connections he had invited to the Games at his home, to enlarge the personal and establish new contacts.

Father writes:

> 'From London alone I expected a minor invasion of friends. Lord Monsell, with whom we had concluded the naval treaty, had accepted, Lord Rothermere, Lord Beaverbrook and other personalities of the Press wanted to come, all personal friends were invited as well as from Paris, Italy, Spain, all the European countries and America, whence I expected personal guests. The sporting event was very opportune to sound out the politicians and influential personalities from the most diverse countries. I was very pleased that Sir Robert Vansittart and his wife accepted … The party lasted until the early morning hours. Of the last to leave were Sir Robert Vansittart and his wife, who danced a lot and seemed to have a very good time. Was this a good omen? … Sadly, it was to be otherwise.'[123]

Would the significance – indeed the opportunity offered – be recognized in Britain of Hitler's solicitations of friendship? And if they were recognized, would they be taken up? Before departing for London, once again Father sought out a meeting with the person who was best suited to answer those questions. He met Robert Vansittart for lunch at the Kaiserhof Hotel in Berlin and submitted Hitler's proposals for an alliance of our two countries to him:

> 'Unfortunately, it was mostly I who spoke, and from the start I had the feeling of speaking to a wall. Although Vansittart listened quietly, he

stayed completely tight-lipped, evading every attempt of mine to come to an open exchange of views. In my life I have had hundreds of talks with Englishmen on the subject but never had one been so fruitless, so lacking in any response and outspokenness, without the slightest receptivity from the interlocutor as to what it was about. When I asked Sir Robert to give me his opinion, his calm and frank criticism of my statements, or to tell me on what basic points or details our opinion diverged, I got no reply whatsoever except commonplace generalities. I often thought back to this talk in the years to come ...

'I could see I would have a tough task in London.'[124]

The fact was that for the longest time Vansittart had harboured immutable prejudices about Germany and Germans that superseded any political rationale. This derived originally from his personal relationship with Crowe – we have already come across him above – who was the mentor of an entire generation of anti-German convictions and with whom Vansittart remained close until Crowe's death in 1925, whose views had virulently influenced Vansittart and others in the Foreign Office. A cooperation with Germany did not even enter into their conception, from whatever side it may be offered. Vansittart was an opponent of any pact with Germany and against any aspirations Germany may have, frankly expressed in his memoirs.[125] This had not been grasped by the Conservative 'Conspiracy' in the Auswärtiges Amt even after the war was over. In 1948, Erich Kordt maintained that Vansittart had 'wantonly annihilated the chance to avert a world catastrophe through an alliance with German patriots'. Looking back, it seems clear that it was less a case of wantonness than of a decades-long persistence with the same attitude toward Germany; a persistence that entailed an acceptance of the risk of a war with Germany, and with that a major European war, as a means of achieving its desired ends, thereby putting the very existence of the Empire at risk, as history was to demonstrate.

It was besides noteworthy that Göring and Hess – Hitler's two deputies – were at my parents' reception on that evening. Father's position at the time was anything but top-ranking in the state and the Party. His status rested upon his nomination to the post of 'Ambassador to the Court of St James's', the official title, designated as 'Ambassador Extraordinary and Plenipotentiary of the German Reich', and furthermore he headed his '*Dienststelle*', but his standing was nowhere comparable to that of Göring and Hess. Since Father's appointment as ambassador to London had been made public the day before the reception and many prominent guests from London were present, the attendance of Göring and Hess underlined the importance ascribed on the part of Germany to Father's mission.

There is a photograph that was taken at this reception of Mother talking to Göring. At the time, she had told me what they talked about. Father had once again had a dispute with Hitler. These disputes rested either on a genuine difference of opinion or were sparked off by intrigues. On that occasion Mother had openly broached the subject of the problematic relations between my father and Hitler to Göring. The latter, really quite nicely, had reassured her, saying that such phases of differences occurred every so often in collaboration with Hitler, as they had all of them experienced. All would soon be put right. In Mother's opinion, Father ought to have made himself more connections in the state and Party hierarchy and won over some 'friends' so as to broaden and consolidate his narrow base of influence – in the sense of putting across his political views and judgement – on Hitler. As will be seen later, Father took this advice only from time to time and conditionally. It cannot be repeated too often, that influence is the presupposition to realize one's own political concepts. This is valid for all political systems, and a democracy in particular. Father was perfectly aware that by his own suggestion of being sent to London he was running a major risk in distancing himself from the centre of decision-making, i.e. Hitler. Father believed it his duty to take that risk, in the interests of the issue at hand.

How seriously Hitler meant this fresh attempt at a fundamental alliance with Britain to succeed is evidenced by his directive to get the German embassy in London on the right footing and properly readapted without stinting. This gesture also underlines the degree of political significance the new posting to London had for him. There have been attempts to suggest that for a passionate, manic master architect such as Hitler, there could be no greater 'profession of love' toward England. The interest Hitler took in the task in hand is demonstrated by the fact that he once sent Albert Speer to London to make an assessment. With her refinement of style and elegant taste, Mother, who had exerted much influence on many things, could be satisfied with his verdict: Speer had said 'Well done!' A house in Eaton Square was leased as a temporary abode for my parents. Funnily enough the owner was the future prime minister Neville Chamberlain.

There is in the context a little detail: Father directed that all works for the renovation of the embassy should as far as was feasible be assigned to German companies and craftsmen so as to save on foreign currency exchange. New furniture, installation items and so on were ordered from the Munich firm Vereinigte Werkstätten. A Mr Paepke was in charge there for customer relations with the higher officials of the Reich and the Party. I happened to be sitting with Father in the Eaton Square house when he had a phone call from Göring, who was exasperated and had sent Father a handwritten letter containing reproaches about the alleged foreign currency expenditure caused by the alterations to the embassy (which had anyway been approved by Hitler). He ardently begged Father to destroy the letter unopened. He had, he said, been misinformed and had only just learnt from Mr Paepke that everything imaginable had been done to manage with the least possible outlay of foreign currency. Göring's letter, which had indeed arrived in London on the same day by courier, had been delivered to my father. It seemed it had been written in a spontaneous first reaction of agitation, without giving concrete figures or modifying his offensive remarks in any way. A strong personal aversion to my father emanated from it. Father only muttered 'what insolence' and, as he had assured Göring on the phone, did not use his knowledge of the letter. He could perhaps have used the episode to ease his relations with Göring, who was after all second man from the top in the state. Göring's main preoccupation may well have been that Father could damage him by speaking to Hitler about the letter, since it was Hitler who had ordered the works in London. This sort of conduct, however – which in the warfare for Hitler's favour was not rare – did not belong in Father's preferred style of behaviour.

When my parents told me that I too would be affected by the move to London, I had at first taken the news very calmly. Following the magnificent experience for a 15-year-old boy of the Olympic Games, that had ended with the Great Tattoo in the stadium as their crowning impact, a realization was nevertheless becoming ever clearer to me: Father's assuming the post of ambassador to London signified a profoundly decisive event in the life of us all. My parents thought it best that I enrol in one of the major English boarding schools, not only to improve my English but above all to become familiar with the principles of education of the renowned public schools, of which my parents always spoke with esteem. In those days it was their view that ultimately the roots that made the British Empire were to be traced to these principles. Because of a letter of complaint from my school in Dahlem, the Arndt-Gymnasium, about some prank, my father said how much he regretted that a teacher in Germany did not enjoy the same highly regarded status in public opinion as in England. I wish not to be misunderstood on this point: I have had the good fortune in my time at school to have had teachers who were exceptional both professionally and as human beings. This goes for both the well-known Arndt-Gymnasium in Berlin-Dahlem as well as the National Political Institute of Education (Napola) in Ilfeld. My teachers were often avowed eccentrics and did not restrict themselves to inculcating the material of the syllabus, laying great value instead on transmission of general knowledge, also keeping character development in mind. In Ilfeld naturally much more was devoted to that aspect of education.

My parents would most have wished to see me at Eton, the most famous of English public schools. This was not feasible as at the time a pupil was enrolled at birth, on condition his father too had been an Etonian. It was naturally not possible to ascertain whether political reasons had played a role in my being unable to enter Eton College. I was, however, admitted to London's Westminster School without difficulty – with the intermediary being Conwell-Evans. Westminster School, where I spent three terms – almost a year – lays claim to being England's oldest public school. English public schools were in those days most exclusive, accessible only to a particular class of society, at any rate as far as the best known and those of traditional repute were concerned.

In what follows I shall recount the experiences and impressions I garnered from my time at Westminster School. My parents were most interested to hear them. A great part of the families of the Westminster schoolboys were from the circles that largely determined political life. The Head of House I was in was an Asquith. He will appear again in this account, together with his mother.

In 1937 Westminster and Eton were the only schools in Britain whose uniform still consisted of morning coat, top hat and umbrella. It was scrapped after the war, no doubt as being too expensive. For me it was altogether surprising to notice that actually all schools had a sort of uniform which all pupils wore. The reference to wearing a uniform by all British schoolchildren was an argument used from time to time when Germany's use of uniforms came up in discussion.

My somewhat ambivalent feelings – to express it mildly – will be imagined when on a trip to London to get ready, a very sweet and aged tailor in an ancient tailors' shop measured me for my school uniform. This tailors' workshop must have been making Westminster School's uniforms for centuries – or so it seemed from its installations – so strict conformity was guaranteed. Was I to go to school every day through the London streets in this get-up? To my surprise, nobody even noticed, as morning and evening I trod the crowded Victoria Street and crossed St James's Park on my way to school. Londoners knew the Westminster boys and were used to the sight of them.

After the war my attendance at Westminster School was given a little more 'publicity' by the actor Peter Ustinov, who says he was there at the same time. I have to say I do not remember him, although he says he sat between me and the son of a petrol magnate sheikh, which is not true – there were no such pupils at the school in those days. I should be grateful to him for attributing to me capabilities that unfortunately I do not possess; according to him I painted a triptych depicting 'Ancient Germans with flaxen-haired wives equipped with breast plates and gleaming with loathsome optimism'! I am sorry to say that in drawing I have never progressed beyond stick-men. Ustinov will have heard something the famous Irish writer Oscar Wilde once said, quite correctly observing that people did not want to be 'informed' but 'entertained'. Also, my 'red hair' he described was never seen, to my mother's chagrin, who loved a reddish hair colour. A man as witty as Oscar Wilde will, however, perhaps also have avoided the conventional cliché of an ambassador's sonny-boy being driven to school in a large Mercedes – and white to boot – by a chauffeur, naturally, who on departing would click heels and, performing the raised arm salute with a loud 'Heil Hitler', take his leave. It may have all been a little name-dropping to prove that Ustinov – an Eastern European – had been to this school of great repute. Funnily enough, years later in a film[126] Ustinov acted the part of a Russian con-man who used invented 'common' memories of this sort to establish new contacts.

A few days before I started at Westminster School, a line of press photographers appeared in front of the house to take pictures of the son of the new German Ambassador. The preoccupation with the private life of prominent persons, which always includes the family sphere, has ever been – as it still is – very prevalent in the British press.

I would have to get used to it, that the children of VIPs would not be left out. So, albeit reluctantly, I let myself be roped in and 'posed' (as Father said on the telephone a few days later) for the gentlemen of the press. Of course I did everything wrong that could be done wrong, as I planted myself with a cross expression on my face and arms crossed over my chest, on the steps of the house. What did I, at the tender age of 15, know about dealings with the international press? When my likeness appeared in the papers the next day, I was shocked at how unfriendly the photo was. Right away I realized that if one were to be presented to press photographers, the least you could do was to offer a favourable and pleasant aspect for publication. I was soon to have the opportunity to put this realization into practice.

Naturally, I walked to school. There was never any question of my being driven in the ambassadorial car, and nor was I ever. In any case, at the time when my parents had first moved to London there was only an English driver assigned to the embassy, an old and wizened little fellow who allegedly understood not a word of German. (My parents had a rather higher opinion of the British Secret Service, and later when they were living there brought a German driver with them.)

The English driver remained at the embassy, because he had been at the service of Father's predecessor Herr von Hoesch for many years. It goes without saying that never would it have been expected of him, nor was it likely he would have acquiesced, to execute the 'German salute', although he did – as was customary in those days all over the world – doff his cap when the master and mistress got into the car.

To return to my way to school, when I left the house in Eaton Square in the morning, a herd of reporters descended upon me, cameras flashing away incessantly. I am, however, able to report, from a photograph I was given for my 70th birthday from a press archive, that I had quickly learnt my lesson. With the photograph as evidence, it can be seen that from now on I smiled amiably into the clicking cameras.

In the end I thought I had done rather well, because at the entrance to the school in Little Dean's Yard, another barrage of photo-reporters had been set up. At first they did not discover me at all. Perhaps they were waiting for Ustinov's 'white Mercedes' and therefore did not notice me walking round the corner without attracting any attention. With a few grinning schoolboys who were also waiting there looking on, the lightning flashes of the cameras started up again, but I was quickly able to escape them.

But my self-satisfaction did not last long. A couple of days later I got a phone call from my father from Berlin, who very irritably asked me 'what did I think I was doing, posing for the press?' He seemed to be under the impression his sonny-boy fancied himself in some self-appointed public relations post, as it would be called today. I was indignant, as I thought I had come out of it rather well. I could only defend myself with the question, 'what then should I have done?'

What had spurred Father's anger? It is probably safe to guess that the Propaganda Ministry – 'friend' Goebbels no doubt – had launched the photo, complete with morning coat, top hat and umbrella, in the German press, where it appeared in various papers. The ensuing whispered gossip can be imagined, of the sort 'for the Ribbentrops our German schools are not good enough'. This interpretation will certainly also have been carried to Hitler. Such ingeniously administered blows below the belt sometimes did not miss their objective and did have an effect on him.[127]

I had in this way unwittingly become the nucleus of a minor intrigue directed against my father. I realized that everything I did could from now on play a role in the political sphere. It was now no longer enough to be restrained, it also mattered to do the right thing. The Berlin days of my childhood and early teens were over, irrevocably. I was now challenged in a completely different way from what I had to confront at home in Dahlem, at school at the Arndt-Gymnasium or in the 'Jungvolk'. I could not know at the time that in the rest of my life I would be in my beautiful Berlin again only as a visitor in school holidays, a casualty of war or on business after the war. From time to time it can happen in life that one learns truly to value and love something only once it has been lost. This was the case with the Berlin of my childhood and early youth. I was able to breathe the famous Berlin air (still proverbial today because of the surrounding forests and lakes) again at the end of 1941 as I was recovering from a serious injury I had suffered in the war, in a military hospital adjacent to the city, before Berlin gradually sank into dust and ashes. The fatal intensity of the government quarter buildings in flames following the air raid of 3 February 1945 and the macabre encounter with Hitler in his bunker on the same day could not have had a stronger impact, putting a final end to my relationship with Berlin as 'home'.

Getting back to Little Dean's Yard and the entrance to Westminster School, there were five 'houses' where the school's life really took place, aside from classes. These were conducted in 'forms'. The school buildings – some of them 'period' and therefore very old and some in the modern style – stood round a square laid with large paving stones. Certain of these could be trodden by particular pupils only, evidently an ancient rite, but one that was strictly observed. Everything rather emanated tradition, enhanced by the appearance of the pupils dressed in severe black – that morning coat. Teachers wore 'civilian' clothes, but were marked out in school by the gown they wore slung across their shoulders in a picturesque manner.

I was assigned to Ashburnham House. Each house had sections according to age groups – upper, middle and under – and each had its own space. The boys of the upper house, the oldest, elected the Head of House, who had wide-ranging functions and rights in the area of discipline, extending to punishment by caning. I, however, was spared this during my time there. Only on one occasion, caused by the lack of discipline among the 'unders' and some misconduct that had to be castigated, did the Head Boy shake the cane in my direction with a wicked grin, saying: 'If things in the house don't work democratically, we can try dictatorship!'

The first impression was immediately the Spartan simplicity of the accommodation in the three common rooms: on the well-worn tiled floor there were some rough wooden benches round a ping-pong table. On the wall there were lockers where we could keep our school materials. The room for the 'middles' was barely any better equipped, whilst as I remember, the 'uppers' benefited from a threadbare carpet and a few chairs. The head boy had a rickety old armchair at his disposal. I do not know what the present living conditions in Westminster School are like, but for those days to call them Spartan is more an understatement than an exaggeration.

If one wanted to withdraw, there was a comfortably furnished comprehensive library available for all pupils, where there could be no talking. It had been donated by a wealthy former pupil. This large and warm space was eagerly used in the winter because the usual common rooms were often rather chilly.

When I told my parents about the living conditions at Westminster School, Father found his conception of the English ruling classes confirmed: that they were in no way effeminate and decadent, and were instead sporting, hardened and tough. My mother told of something said to her by a Foreign Office official who belonged to the 'Establishment' as his son was at Eton, which made her speechless. He had received a letter from Eton, this man said, that he should forbid his son from playing football because the boy had a heart defect and the exertion could be harmful. The man had disregarded it, because the status of a boy among his schoolmates largely depended on his sporting performance and the father did not want to do his son any harm in that regard. Sadly, the boy had dropped dead on the football field. As can be imagined, Mother was very struck by this father's account. For Father, who was always very interested in my reports about school life at Westminster School, this was further proof that public schools, where the Empire's ruling elite was educated, did not exactly produce weaklings. I was able to confirm this impression from my experience at school.

Less than two years later, Mother was asked by Mussolini (at a banquet on the occasion of Hitler's state visit to Italy in 1938 she was seated at Mussolini's right hand, as abroad – because Hitler was not married – she was Germany's First Lady; at home it was Mme Göring) what she thought of the English. Spontaneously, she told the Duce the story of the death of the boy on the football field, thereby implying the toughness of the English upper class. After some reflection, when the dinner was over, she told my father about this, wondering whether her reply to Mussolini's question with this story had been opportune. Father reassured her, saying it was basically always preferable to overestimate rather than underestimate an opponent, as propaganda tricks often backfired in the long run.

As I have said, life at school unfolded mainly in the framework of the 'houses'. Sports, above all, were exercised entirely within the house system. Team games such as football and cricket were the main field sports and held an exceptionally high place in school life, whether they were inter-house matches or against other schools. Organization of sports – as with so much else at the school – was entirely in the hands of the pupils.

A teacher was housemaster of each house, but many duties were undertaken by 'upper' pupils who, without too much formality, occupied positions almost of 'superiors' over the other denizens of the house and had a corresponding authority, which was however in general applied rather gently. Everything was hallowed by long-standing tradition, and therefore in solidly established form.

Some of the pupils consisted of day-boys, as I was, who went home in the evening. Boarders were housed in the previously described Spartan style. Lunch was eaten by all together. Ancient Sparta would not have been ashamed of the meal, which was surpassed only by the food at Ilfeld – that in this regard may be named Super-Sparta – in simplicity and tastelessness. Older generations always believe they had a worse time than the younger, but I would really like to see the reaction of today's boarders – nevermind their parents – if they were offered the cuisine of my time at Westminster or Ilfeld.

Frugality was certainly cultivated in both establishments. It is to my mind a very important pedagogic practice to prepare young people for life ahead which, as is well known, is not all whipped cream.

Life at Westminster School was extremely multifaceted and rich in variety, if the opportunities offered were appreciated. There was every sort of facility available to take advantage of, whether in the artistic, sporting or scientific fields, even a Debating Club. Taking part in these activities was always voluntary. They were conducted by elected pupils. The Debating Club once organized a rhetorical disputation on a theme that will have been chosen in my honour: 'Should Germany have colonies again or not?' For the date, 1936, it was a most topical subject! The discussion-meeting was conducted as follows: two 'proposers' and two 'opposers' from the group of pupils acted as representatives to support either side of the motion. They could speak for five minutes and, naturally, extemporaneously. Then anyone could ask to be heard, and under the same conditions claim two minutes' time of free speech; after that a vote was taken.

Because I too was present, and since the possibility of giving the German point of view was availed of, the result was a very kind majority of votes in favour of a restitution to Germany. It would be a good idea to institute Debating Clubs in German schools, to acquire and to exercise the capacity to exchange divergent opinions calmly and factually.

At the time I had been highly impressed by the session. I was tempted to smile when a 10-year-old Lilliputian stuck his thumbs into his waistcoat's armholes and addressed his schoolmates as 'Gentlemen' when giving them the benefit of his opinion on the issue under discussion. Yet I was fully aware of the educative worth of this training in public speaking. The whole meeting had the form of a sort of parliamentary debate, providing an excellent learning process in discipline and repartee, not least to be open to acceptance of different views, but also to take an eventual defeat in good temper. The English preference to conduct a discussion with humour and quick-wittedness was evident in my schoolmates. The British admonition 'don't argue',[128] to avoid acerbic and obdurate – and in the end fruitless – debate, has a lot to be said for it.

In Westminster School's everyday life politics were generally not a particularly important issue. For my part I did not provoke any political discussions nor initiate any unless I was directly addressed on a political matter, which very rarely occurred. Despite my difficulties with the language, I managed to integrate quite satisfactorily in my House, and as I won some successes in various competitions in light track and field athletics – also against other schools – I was considered to 'belong'. However, as the son of the German Ambassador, in those politically agitated times, I naturally had to be on the alert to be careful of what I said. In this sense I once had an amusing experience:

One day some friends drew my attention to a very interesting talk that was to be given by a member of parliament[129] on the League of Nations, that I should not fail to hear. It turned out that this MP – a Mr Garnett – was President of what was called the League of Nations Union, a sort of association that purported to promote the ideas of the League of Nations. The event was, exceptionally, to be conducted by one of the teachers, Mr Blake, probably because the speaker was an MP. My friends had warned me in diverse ways that Mr Blake was not very fond of my country. The occasion of the talk could be an exciting subject for me, since Germany had after all quit the League of Nations three years earlier, so as not to be voted down in the question of Germany's claim to equal status. Following the departure of more states, the League of Nations had sunk into meaninglessness, no pleasing situation for an official of a League of Nations Union.

Added to this was the fact that Hitler had only recently announced the Four Year Plan that was supposed to solve the problems of Germany's provisions in raw materials. The goal was to achieve the greatest possible self-sufficiency. There were two reasons for the desired economy in the matter of raw materials and foodstuffs: the shortage of foreign exchange and the experiences undergone by the German Reich in the First World War of the British naval blockade, that is the strangulation of routes of supply of imports necessary for

Germany, which was deficient in natural resources whether in war or peace, a situation opening a door to blackmail.

It was only in 1936 that Hitler had taken the decision to organize a solution to the problem of the Reich's provisioning in the sector of raw materials (including foodstuffs), which took the form of the Four Year Plan. The date is a further indication of his initial concept of foreign affairs as an alliance with both Western European powers. If this were to come about, that is in a close international world-political cooperation in Europe, the provisioning of the Reich would fairly easily be ensured, also in the case of crisis in Eastern Europe. The uncertainty about Britain's policies resulted in the Four Year Plan, three-and-a-half years after Hitler's access to governance.

Participation in an event of the sort of this talk was, as always, voluntary. As, however, I had been alerted by my friends, I had no other choice but to attend. It was besides also politically correct not to evade a representative of the 'ideas of the League of Nations', since German policy too desired a Western European cooperation. Germany's rejection of the League of Nations was only as an instrument for perpetuating the Versailles Treaty by outvoting Germany. The talk took place in the school library, and by pure coincidence I had been manoeuvred into the front row, right in front of the lecture stand. The big room was packed.

Taking the speaker's attitude into account, I had not expected any friendly comments about Germany and her government, but what the speaker expressed, in aggressive one-sided bias surpassed the usual rules of the game – toward a foreigner – of tact and politeness. Very soon I saw from Mr Garnett's remarks that I would be obliged to request to speak, if I could, at the end of the talk. There was no way I could remain silent in the face of such massive attacks against my country. It would have disappointed my friends, who were in suspense as to my reaction. The greatest difficulty lay in my still very limited knowledge of the language, clearly insufficient for a discussion such as might ensue.

When the speaker finished, Mr Blake did indeed call for questions from the audience. I let a few others put their questions and then took my turn, to point out that the origins of the Four Year Plan and the current German aspirations to be self-sufficient – which had been acrimoniously attacked by the speaker as evidence of Germany's reluctance to cooperate – were in the end to be found based in the terms of the Versailles Treaty, according to which, as everyone knew, Germany had lost all her colonies. The deficiency in raw materials that had resulted from the loss of overseas sources was what had forced my country to find ways of gaining – or economizing on – provisions of raw materials. It was for this purpose alone that the Four Year Plan had been drawn up.

Mr Garnett's reply was not very satisfactory, nor clever, because it was unadulteratedly hostile. Without touching on my points factually, he told me I should not bring the Versailles Treaty into it, for, he said, 'if Germany had won the war the Germans would have imposed much heavier terms on their opponents, as was proved by the treaty of Brest-Litovsk that the Reich had contracted with the Russians'.

The answer he gave revealed some pangs of a bad conscience in regard to Versailles. This was where my knowledge of history came to my assistance, as I was able to counter Garnett, correcting him that the treaty of Brest-Litovsk had after all given Eastern European peoples such as Poles, Latvians, Estonians, Lithuanians, Finns, etc. their freedom and autonomy, which he could not dispute. Besides which, the founding of these states had corresponded to the ideas of the American President Wilson's 14 Points Plan.

Instead of replying, Mr Garnett turned to Mr Blake and whispered something to him, upon which Mr Blake stood up and said: 'We don't want to hear speeches, we want to hear questions.' As I have said, at that time my English was anything but perfect, but I understood this much: that I was not to say anything more.

At this point something strange happened behind my back. I heard a lot of chairs being pushed back and when I turned around, to my amazement I saw that nearly everybody in the audience had left the room; the rest were preparing to do the same, leaving Mr Garnett and Mr Blake alone with some three or four listeners only. There being no reason for me to stay either, I left to fetch my things and go home.

When I reached Ashburnham, the Head of House was waiting for me in front of the door. He looked typically British: tall and thin, with bright red hair. His name was Asquith. He came from a family involved in politics for generations. (An Asquith, namely Herbert Henry Asquith, had been British Prime Minister at the outbreak of the First World War in 1914.) Now on the doorstep a very good-looking lady stood next to our Head, waiting for me. He introduced me: it was his mother, who had apparently been among the audience at the lecture. She did not beat about the bush and spoke to me in the kindest terms about the discussion that Mr Blake had suppressed, saying his conduct had been 'unforgivable'. It was unbelievable, she said, that such an interesting discussion had been broken off, irrespective of the fact that it was my right and my duty to stand up for my country when it was under attack. Aside from all that, I had been quite right. I should in no way think Mr Blake's behaviour was usual in England – it was on the contrary most un-English. I was very impressed by the fairness with which I was treated, although at the same time I was surprised how seriously the matter was taken. It seems the minor incident was quickly made known in London, because soon after, my father's age-long interlocutor Professor Conwell-Evans spoke to me about it and said that I had given Mr Garnett's 'silly speech' the right reply. However, what had at the time made the greatest impression on me was the fundamental hostility against Germany that transpired from what this Member of Parliament said. It had basically nothing to do with German autonomous aspirations, which could at any time have been reversed by a foundational settlement with the Western powers. What stood behind such an outlook was the traditional principle of British policy to be intransigently opposed to the strongest Continental Power. This was already how Germany was rated by prominent circles in Britain at the turn of 1936 to 1937, although this alleged 'power' was far from the reality. My schoolmates' spontaneous reaction was noteworthy though, when they left the room for the sake of fairness because the teacher had deprived me of the right to argue for my country that had been attacked. As if on a word of command, they had stood up at once and quit the room. In the days that followed various schoolmates spoke to me in the same spirit as Asquith's mother.

The major public schools were completely integrated in the political system and had their place in public life. The pupils' consciousness that to some degree they stood in the public spotlight gave them poise and self-assurance. Major London newspapers reported occurrences in these schools, sometimes in detail, and to my astonishment my victory in bowling was related, even accompanied by a picture. Regularly held competitions were an important part of character-building. For one thing, it was training for the nerves; one learned to lose with serenity and to congratulate the victorious opponent, and not to take either victory or defeat too seriously.

One morning, when I came to school at the beginning of term, I thought I must have lost my way and strayed into one of the nearby Guards barracks. Soldiers were running around all over the place, dressed in impeccable khaki uniforms, who nevertheless on closer inspection turned out to be Westminster boys in British officer uniform. When in my amazement I asked whether war had broken out somewhere in the empire, I was told laughingly that they were pupils who had enrolled for the OTC. This was the Officer Training Corps, in which the participants received preliminary military training and were destined to serve as officers in an emergency.

The same day, a very nice younger teacher, now dressed as a captain of the British Army, spoke to me to ask whether I wanted to take part. Not surprisingly, I was flabbergasted. In 1936, as the son of the German ambassador in London, to be invited to take part in British preliminary military training whose objective was to provide the army with officers in case of war, was extraordinary!

It would of course have greatly tempted me to acquaint myself with this training, as there was nothing comparable in Germany. As far as I could make out in the Square, it consisted of exercises in handling light infantry weapons. There were therefore no secrets to be revealed; however, after the experience with Goebbels and the photos in the press of me in morning coat and top hat, I thought it advisable to have my father's previous consent before I was engaged in His Majesty's Army. One thing was clear in any case: the British press would not forgo the joke of publishing a spread in enlargement of the son of the German ambassador in British infantry uniform.

Father was just as astonished as I was, and also thought how interesting it would be to take a look. Neither did he think of military secrets that I might find out; what interested him was the idea in principle, for in Germany until well into the war there had been no preliminary military training of youths. That was in my opinion a great omission. Training of our recruits could have progressed much faster and more intensively if they were already familiar with certain basics of weapon-handling techniques and 'conduct on the battlefield' when they were called up. Even in the 'Napola' (National Political Institutes of Education), not the slightest instruction was provided in this respect. After he had given the matter some thought – no doubt in view of complications 'at home' – my father advised me to 'ask the school if they agree to your taking part in the training in German uniform'. The captain-teacher could, however, not accept this, so that alas the prospect of acting as 'His Majesty's soldier' at the age of 15 did not materialize.

Britain had begun intensive arming a while before. An extremely important factor – I can say from my own experience perhaps the most important – for effective and successful armament preparations is the availability of well-trained officers. Officer training takes the longest, yet it is the indispensable prerequisite for forming efficient troop units: as are the officers, so are the troops! In Britain they went about this more consistently than we did in Germany. In Germany only in the last part of the war was there preliminary military training for the Hitler Youth (Hitler-Jugend). After the war its leader Baldur von Schirach made it clear that he had repudiated the Wehrmacht through Rommel (the general of subsequent renown), in his role as liaison officer between the Wehrmacht and the Reichsjugend leadership, any preliminary military training of the Hitler-Jugend because it did not correspond to his perception of a National Socialist youth – whatever that perception might have been. In 1934 Schirach wrote a book entitled *Die Hitler-Jugend, Idee und*

Gestalt (The Hitler Youth, Idea and Structure). None of us read the book, which was slightly flippantly spoken of as 'the Idea without Structure'. Hitler had of course finally to make a decision and take responsibility on an issue of such fundamental importance as the preliminary military training of the youth organization. I maintain that we would have been spared so much blood-letting in the war if the military training of young men had begun in peacetime. Time and again we officers had to hammer the precept into our recruits, as well as the soldiers experienced in warfare, that 'training spares bleeding'. This example too shows how non-belligerent Hitler was; he can in fact on the contrary be accused of not having considered the inescapable risks his foreign policies were running with a corresponding comprehensive armament programme. I shall revert to this in due course.

There was a school- and house-mate of mine I have to mention in my account of Westminster School, Michael Wedgwood Benn. His younger brother Anthony (Tony) Neil Wedgwood Benn became well known as a 'far-left' member of the Labour Party, and his father was William Wedgwood Benn MP, later made a peer as Lord Stansgate. Michael was my class- and house-mate. As recorded in the school register, he was a fighter pilot killed in the war. This sibling was, however, just as remarkable a figure in our 'under' category at school, and I am convinced that he would have had a political career before him after the war, had he wished to engage in it. At the age of 15 he was a born politician, a talented orator, quick-witted and audacious, as well as thoroughly skilful and intelligent, and he occupied a prominent position within our 'under' group. Nothing took place without him; Wedgwood Benn had a finger in whatever was arranged and he influenced a great deal of what went on. If he were seen standing to address the classroom, thumbs hooked into his waistcoat armholes, calling his classmates 'Gentlemen' – which by the way nobody found odd – he could be pictured in the House of Commons, making statements or speeches. I am not very surprised that his brother Tony evolved at the far left of the Labour Party, for the atmosphere at Westminster School as I remember it in my day had a certain Leftist-Liberal touch. The reaction brought about by the point I had made to Mr Garnett about the liberation of Eastern European peoples resulting from the German-Russian Brest-Litovsk treaty was in harmony with this attitude. Certainly the Wedgwood Benn who was in my 'under' group seemed to me to be most pragmatic and to have a lot of common sense. This somewhat Leftist-Liberal or even partially Socialist tendency of the school in no way impeded the schoolboys from volunteering to fight for their country, proved by the large number of casualties.

Actually, the Fatherland (slash Empire) was never spoken of. The great allegiance to Crown and King as personifying this world empire was so self-evident that there was no need to say a word about it. When tradition is truly ingrained it gives a great deal of inner self-confidence. The occasion of the crowning of King George VI in the summer of 1937 strikingly demonstrated this bond to the monarchy – and not only by the denizens of Westminster School. What I experienced at the school was very clearly imprinted on my memory, and my consciousness of it sharpened and consolidated in the many conversations I had with my parents on the subject. They listened attentively to me when I was telling them about school. They found their opinion fully confirmed that in the final analysis one of the roots of British world domination lay in the public schools – at any rate the old and famous ones. Personalities of the entrepreneurial and political world were recruited from them, as well as in the broader sector of education, from Oxford and Cambridge, who had initially generated the empire and had maintained it for more than three centuries. Would the institutions, laden with tradition, also bring forth major figures with equal far-sightedness, or in other words grand vision and boldness, in the twenty-first century in a world so rapidly changing, who would ensure that Britain could still play the role it wished in the political world today?

The leadership of the British Empire always grew out of a small but power-conscious ruling elite, highly disciplined as well as ruthless and unscrupulous when necessary in representing the empire's interests. Their education was not left to chance but evolved out of these universities and public schools of age-long tradition, one of which was Westminster School. The well-known English writer and diplomat Harold George Nicolson once described the principles of selection for the British ruling class: he begins with the premise that the British people's basic attitude is one of fairness. The cultivation of fairness is fundamental to the education they receive for their character-building in the famous schools and universities. This entailed solid rules of the game and hence imposed an obligatory conformism. However, fairness does not conquer and keep an empire. In consequence only those were suitable who were able to overcome the limitations of the education and its conformism. Only those were able to rule the empire with the requisite adroitness and, when needed, lack of scruple.

I had the good fortune to spend my school years in three outstanding establishments. One of them was Westminster School. The impact on me of the year I spent there was less in the knowledge that was inculcated than my experiences in significant principles of education that were in the end the best preparation for a life of politics, in the broadest sense. For me, at the age of

15 to 16, the experience brought a great broadening of my horizons, above all because the time of the opportunity I was granted was against the background of the dramatic emerging developments in the political world.

The headmaster wrote 'Good ambassador for his country!' on my leaving certificate, which pleased my parents and that I found rather an amusing and friendly comment. Mind you, in the war a communiqué circulated in the British press in connection with an award I received that spoke of the 'British-educated son of the German Foreign Minister', which was of course an exaggeration. Dedication to one's country was as self-evident in England as it was in those days in Germany. In this sense, in the school's pupils' list I was sent after the war I appear with my military rank and awards.

Nevertheless, after the war, my status of Old Westminster boy did not inhibit my schoolmates' compatriots from locking me up in what was called a 'murder cage' in Hamburg Fischbek to stew for months without a hearing, let alone so much as an indictment. In Dachau I had been brought before a Canadian parachutist captain who asked me if I knew why I was standing in front of him. I could only say I had hoped he would tell me. I was supposed to have shot two Canadian war prisoners because they had refused to make a statement. To my question regarding the circumstances, he told me the following cock-and-bull story: that I was alleged to have interrogated the two prisoners in a French house and, as they would not make any statement, had shot them with a pistol, one of them fatally, the other I had wounded in the hip. This one had feigned death and escaped under the cover of night to get back to the Canadian lines.

Hearing this rubbish, I became cheeky and told him plainly that he himself couldn't possibly believe what he was saying. I then asked him precisely when and where this incident was purported to have occurred. To this he replied he would not tell me. I would first have to make him a detailed list of exactly where and when at any given time I found myself on the invasion front. I laughed in his face. These were the practices adopted by the American prosecutors in Dachau too. They kept the poor prisoners rotting in Dachau for two years or more without charging them. Then, a friendly interrogator would outline the prospect of his case being reviewed if the accused gave a precise schedule of where and when he had been stationed. Had the prisoner hoped that it would indeed result in some relief in his case, instead the well-known 'professional witnesses' were called in, who swore on oath to have seen him at such and such a time in this or that place, and sure enough the verdict of death by hanging ensued. We had had occasion to observe these practices at Dachau in the course of the trials conducted there.[130] In the summer of 1947 it was exactly ten years since I left Westminster School, when in this British concentration camp I recalled this kindly headmaster and decided to inform him of my fate in the hands of his compatriots. This was technically not so simple, for the prisoners' mail – although in the legal sense they were in any case 'prisoners under interrogation' – was very strictly censored in Hamburg-Rahlstedt and it required no stretch of the imagination to foresee that such a letter of complaint may have unpleasant consequences, aside from the fact that he would certainly never receive it. The letter would have to be smuggled out.

The so-called 'murder cage' was a sort of special sub-camp within the main camp. It was elaborately fenced with barbed wire and electric fencing, guarded by a swarm of what were known as 'Polish (or Yugoslav) sentries', that is, manned by Poles and Yugoslavs who did not want to go back to their country. The denizens of this 'special camp' were completely cut off from the outside world, with one exception: visits were allowed. These visits, however, took place in conditions that did not permit an exchange of letters, for communication was through a wire mesh and both prisoner and visitor had a 'Polish guard' sitting next to them who nearly always spoke German, or at least understood it. A new camp officer, a captain (his predecessor, a certain Captain Carter, had been dismissed for mistreatment of prisoners), had allowed as a concession that after inspection by the 'Polish guard' of parcels that the visitor brought to the prisoner, the packaging could be returned to the visitor for re-use. That was the way to do it. I prepared a little corrugated-cardboard packet, carefully loosening the corrugated cardboard and slipping the letter to my headmaster into the back part.

I described my situation to him in detail in the letter, stressing above all that I had so far not even found out what crime I was supposed to have committed, although my lawyer had repeatedly appeared before the examining authorities. I asked him if he could see his way to being of assistance to me, or at the least if he could find out what I was accused of. I finally begged him not to send a reply, as our mail was censored and his answer – if he wanted to reply – would naturally reveal that I had transgressed by writing to him without the letter going through the censor. It would signify my being severely punished by the camp officers. He could give my mother some information. My letter did in fact reach the headmaster and he wrote, quite soon, to my mother, to tell her he had initiated 'inquiries'; there was nothing pending against me.

It seemed at first as though the headmaster's intervention had helped me, for I was transferred from the 'murder cage' to the ordinary camp. There, the problem of my detention 'by kinship association' was solved by the approved method: after a few weeks I was handed over to the French. An analogous case occurred at the same time, albeit with fatal consequences. A certain

Count Bassewitz was incarcerated with us, a former high-placed police officer. The British submitted him to a war criminals' trial for alleged shooting of '*Ostarbeiter*' (workers from occupied Eastern countries). There was nothing the British could do but set him free because there was no charge against him. So, immediately after his acquittal, they simply handed him over to the Russians. He was never heard of again. His attorney was the renowned Hamburg lawyer Dr Grimm, who also acted on my behalf in exemplary fashion, which is why I was able to follow the affair closely.

Not to get too far ahead in the course of events and to return to my London days: not only my London school made demands on me, there was also my parents' ambassadorial life. One evening shortly after enrolling at Westminster School, when I came home, Mother told me to change my clothes as quickly as possible: I was invited to a cocktail party at the king's personal physician's daughter's, who was coming out as a debutante that season. Mother's request that I should go to a cocktail party left me aghast. Until a few weeks ago my free time had been spent in camping trips and scouting games.

I mention this incidentally, just as a minor instance of the warmth of interest evinced toward my parents in their reception in London,[131] where Father's posting was very popular, causing a stir in his wide circle of acquaintances and friends. The calumnies that at that time already were deliberately and systematically being spread by the 'circles with vested interests' (opposition) in Germany were saying that my father had developed resentment against England because he had failed to be welcomed by 'Society' there.[132] Not only were they untrue, they are in any case irrelevant. When will it be understood in Germany that an ambassador's task is to represent the interests of his country and to send objective reports, but not necessarily to be beloved by the host country, meaning to be successful in high society? The British Secretary of State for the Colonies, Joseph Chamberlain,[133] had the occasion to say in a speech, before the First World War, that 'no British Minister has ever served his country faithfully and at the same time been popular abroad'.[134] What a masterful attitude Chamberlain demonstrates here in the interest of his country. It ought to be taken to heart by every German diplomat.

From time to time I had to 'make up the numbers', as long as it did not interfere with school duties, if Mother needed a 'man' at a table, and was thus present at some dinner parties. I remember one of them particularly well, when unknowingly I owed my 'board' to the famous Aga Khan. My mother used to instruct that courses should be served once only, which I greatly regretted for at the age of about 16 one is always hungry. As is well known, every year the Aga Khan received his weight in gold from his sect. I don't know if it was only for this reason that he was a 'gourmet gourmand', or if he just liked to eat. Possibly both. Anyway, he asked for a second helping and then a third more of the main course which, naturally – what housewife would not be? – flattered Mother for the excellence of her kitchen.

What, however, had the greatest importance for me in that year spent in London was the special closeness to my parents due to the circumstances. How could I have predicted it, but it was to be the last year of my life when I would live 'at home', that is to say, with my parents. Sometimes Mother would come into my room unexpectedly to ask me whether I would like to go out to dinner with her and Father. I didn't need to be asked twice to accompany them to some smart venue.

We did, however, also drive through the slums of London and other cities, which made a sad impression with their bleakness and dirt. The 'social question' in Britain in those days did not play a role comparable to Germany's approach, where it had become prominent in the public domain. The Communist Party in England was feeble and had only one representative in the House of Commons. This MP, his name was Gallacher, offended Father on his arrival in London by saying that Father had workers' blood on his hands. As is usual in such an event, the German Embassy initiated a routine *démarche*, or diplomatic 'move'.[135]

King Edward VIII was considered to be very receptive to social issues. On his first visit to Wales as king, it was said that on his own initiative he had changed the route to be followed, in order to see the living conditions of the coal miners for himself. It was also said that from this point of view he had developed a certain liking for Germany, where the improvement of such conditions was programmed. However, such arbitrariness did not suit the concept of the British Establishment. Father once said, as we drove through areas of slum housing: 'The British rule the world, but they have to pay for it!' He was referring to the undemanding discipline of the British masses of those days, who were directed by a skilful leadership, as being a condition for their bearing a responsibility in common with British Empire politics since they were willing to accommodate it. By this statement Father meant, indirectly, that the British people would follow suit if their leaders perhaps decided to engage in renewing a conflict with the Reich. What direction would British policy pursue, however? That was the constant uncertainty during our stay in London.

At his first press conference upon arriving in London, Father had stressed and explained the anti-Bolshevik policy of the German government. The offensive remark about him by the Communist MP was the revenge for this.

Nevertheless, therein lay the essential question between German and British politics: would the British government recognize the threat from Bolshevik Russia and not only tolerate but actually promote a shift of its Balance of Power policy eastward, where the core of such a European balance could only be in a Germany capable of defending herself?

As Father had written to the German ambassador in Rome, Ulrich von Hassell, German policy had to attempt to enlighten the British as to the very real danger presented by Bolshevism, to restrain them from any affiliation with a Bolshevik front and to foster the thought that *à la longue* their world empire was under a considerably greater threat from a further expansion of Bolshevism.

What could be meant by this threat was observable at the time in Spain, where during the civil war the Leftist government had been overthrown by the Communists. In London, the political summer of 1937 was defined for the German ambassador by the ongoing sessions of a 'non-involvement committee' on the Spanish Civil War issue. This symbolized the wavering state of international relations and their fruitless debates just as well as the earlier disarmament conferences had done, whilst in reality several of the states represented actively interfered in Spain, which was no secret. Father repeatedly regretted the German military engagement in the Iberian Peninsula, whereby, together with Italian and Russian campaigning, the situation there was naturally escalating. He did nevertheless ask himself whether a German abstention would have been honoured by the British government in the sense of a German-British arrangement, since the naval agreement – much more important for Britain – had not effected any fundamental alteration of British policy.

A Coronation and a Report

As much as Edward VIII's abdication was a pity for Germany's policies, it gave me the opportunity during my time in London to witness the coronation of King George VI. I did of course not have a place in Westminster Abbey, where the ceremony took place, but I experienced the procedure, days-long, with intensity, on the one hand from school (the school buildings had direct access to Westminster Abbey) and on the other through the embassy's obviously inescapable involvement in the festivities for the coronation. In those days the embassy building lay on the Mall, the road leading from Buckingham Palace to the Admiralty, which the coronation procession would take on its way to the abbey. My father saw the occasion as an opportunity to further his endeavours to attain a German-British friendship, giving it a fresh impetus. The forced participation in the 'non-involvement committee' sessions on the Spanish Civil War in London was certainly not ideal for the facilitation of his task. From what my mother told me, I knew about Hitler's indecisiveness as to whether he should send someone – or who this should be – as his personal representative to the celebrations. In view of the events in Spain that concerned German seagoing military forces[136] and the British attitude to them in the non-involvement committee, there was talk of not choosing anyone and leaving the business to the ambassador, my father. Father had used all his arguments to persuade Hitler to send a special envoy to the coronation. Anything said to suggest something else is slanderous. Father had to concede to all to lighten the load of his duties in England.

The greatest social event in which I could take part was without any doubt the party given by the embassy in honour of the representative of Germany at the coronation of George VI, the then Minister for War, Blomberg. It was a very special experience. The Duchess of Kent – the ducal couple represented the British court that evening at the German Embassy – seemed to me to be the most beautiful woman in the world. There could be no words too superlative to use of the impression made on me by the appearance of this lovely as well as – which was not the case for all the members of the royal family – elegant lady. I was permitted to kiss her hand! She and her husband were one of the best-looking couples of those days. They stayed on at the party long past the time foreseen. The embassy's reception rooms were crammed. There had been far fewer refusals than is usually expected for such functions. The very next day the comment of French Chief of Staff Gamelin, whom the French government had delegated to the celebrations and who was naturally also invited, that 'this gala is too wonderful for me to be able to be happy about it!', made the rounds in London.

After the day of the party at the German Embassy there was the grand fleet review at Spithead, which I and many of our embassy's guests could attend; it was another high point of those days. The embassy's protocol department had chartered a steamboat for us, in which we set off together with the magnificent display of the British fleet and the battleships from all the countries in the world. It was forty years to the day since 26 June 1897, when the world's most powerful fleet of the times had appeared at Spithead. The occasion then had been the celebration of the aged Queen Victoria's Jubilee. Based on that potential, before the First World War British politics embarked on a collision course with the German Reich which, as the greatest continental power, had to be curbed, according to their traditional rules. That this Continental Power had furthermore become an extremely successful and therefore bothersome competitor in the world markets, added to which it was itself equipped with a strong navy – albeit in no way comparable to the British – gave the policy directed against the German Reich more impulse and arguments.

The resulting conflict of the First World War that ultimately arose from this had obliged the British fleet to share its position as first among the world's navies with the USA. Nor could the whole of the British Empire, despite its victory, resume its status of world hegemony. The ever-recurring query in 1937, which once again obtruded in view of this demonstration of strength, was whether Britain would again utilize this power potential against what was for the British the strongest continental power, i.e. Germany? Were the thought processes of the leading British-empirical politicians aligned with those that Lord Balfour, leader of the Conservatives in 1910, is said to have expressed in a discussion with Henry White, American ambassador in London, that:

'We are probably fools not to find a reason for declaring war on Germany before she builds too many ships and takes away our trade.'

White: 'You are a very high-minded man in private life. How can you possibly contemplate anything so politically immoral as provoking a war against a harmless nation which has as good a right to a navy as you have? If you wish to compete with German trade, work harder.'

Balfour: 'That would mean lowering our standard of living. Perhaps it would be simpler for us to have a war.'

White: 'I am shocked that you of all men should enunciate such principles.

Balfour: 'Is it a question of right or wrong? Maybe it is just a question of keeping our supremacy.'[137]

Returning to the review at Spithead, the ships were anchored in four rows, the fourth being reserved for the foreign vessels. There was a pensioned British naval officer on board our excursion boat who gave details over a loudspeaker on the ships as we passed them. The battleship *Warspite*, at the time the most powerful in the world, headed the Royal Navy's lines. In the row of foreign ships, somewhat maliciously, the German and Soviet-Russian ships had been juxtaposed, doubtless considered by the organizers as a touch of irony. The irony was reversed when two years later Father signed a German-Russian pact in Moscow.

No longer standing at attention on deck, as the king and queen had already inspected the ships anchored in parade formation, the crews were cheerfully waving at us. Only from the Russian ship did nobody reciprocate our waving, the sailors staring at us without moving. This caused our guide to comment that the crew was at the moment probably busy voting for next week's captain. What arrogance! The man was echoing the attitude typical of many British politicians, that Soviet Russia did not constitute a danger for Europe. It was for this reason that these circles targeted Germany and refused to count the Eurasian superpower of Soviet Russia in the European balance of power.

Germany was represented by the armoured cruiser *Deutschland*, which despite all the previously mentioned commotion about the '*Kinderspeisung*' slogan (for free school meals) had in the end been built (in the Weimar Republic) according to the provisions of the Versailles Treaty, with a displacement of not more than 10,000 tons. The large ships of Britain and other countries displaced many times the multiple thereof. Nevertheless the commentator pointed out the *Deutschland*, and not merely to be polite, as a wonder of warship technology, for what had been fitted into this light ship in weaponry and armour plating was extraordinary, combined with considerable speed. At the time, the *Deutschland* was still the German navy's mightiest ship, albeit in relation to the great battleships assembled in Spithead she was but a 'boat'. In international maritime circles it was called a 'waistcoat-pocket-armoured-ship'. It symbolized Germany's policy, which was to avoid a maritime competitive situation with Britain.

Father drew up a report (the 'Report on the Coronation') for Hitler, to include the empire conference convened in London.[138] The report manifests his very positive estimate of Blomberg and of his presence in London. The main points of the report, however, regard the prospects of success of achieving a lasting rapport with Britain. This is Father's report, summarizing the main points:

'For the time being there is the firm impression that the structure of the British Empire, despite much loosening in the last few years, is at present still firmly anchored in London and that the British are determined to tie the bonds in the Empire more firmly again by means of rearmament, the national defence plan, the Defence Committee that was formed today, and other organizational measures. In the next few years, therefore, it will be necessary to expect a strengthening rather than a weakening of the structure of the British Empire.

' … I, too, had numerous discussions with influential British personalities. They were mostly very friendly, and with Eden and Vansittart, too, with whom the Embassy, on the purely personal level, has established a pleasant relationship. There has, according to my latest information, been but little real change in the well-known attitude of these gentlemen towards German affairs. According to strictly confidential information, Neville [*sic*] Henderson is said not to have been very edified by his first discussions at the Foreign Office about his future activity in Germany.

' … It must be noted from the conversation with Eden that it was not so very productive as regards the furtherance of the question of the Western Pact or the Belgian question.

' … Britain does not wish to commit herself with regard to the East. In reality, however, through her guarantee to France and through the French guarantee to Russia, she is nevertheless greatly entangled in the French system of alliances, i.e., she is nevertheless indirectly linked with the East. This is further underlined by her constant moral support of the Franco–Russian Pact, i.e., by her supporting the French wish for hegemony in Europe which finds expression in the French Alliance with Russia. As things are today, there is a danger that in the event of a Russian–German conflict Britain will somehow be drawn through France into war against Germany. (There are, of course, plenty of methods of doing this: false reports by Havas, false allegations of aggression, sabotage actions, and so on and so forth.) The only clear way of preventing this would be an unambiguous assurance of British neutrality in the event of a German-Russian war. We would thus, in all probability, be altogether safeguarded in the West, since, without armed assistance from Britain, France would doubtless hardly attack the German fortifications in the West. The key to the situation therefore lies solely in Britain, and confronted with the alternatives – on the one hand, friendship with Germany, British interests being fully secured (Naval Agreement, and readiness to assure the integrity of those countries, including France, that lie between Germany and Britain), and, on the other hand, a fresh life and death struggle between the two great Germanic nations for interests that are really foreign to them, a struggle which Britain might have to take up within a much more unfavourable constellation than in 1914 and which in any event would hazard the existence of the British Empire – the British statesmen ought surely to make the correct choice.

' … Meanwhile, despite the friendly Coronation atmosphere, we shall do well to preserve a good measure of scepticism [Father spoke of 'constant attacks' against Germany 'in the Press'] and leave nothing undone in the course we have adopted to strengthen our other friendships without finally blocking our path to Britain. I myself believe that there will only be a change when the British signature appears beneath a treaty instrument acceptable to us, whether it concerns the questions: Belgium, the Western Pact or the colonies, or even a large-scale, general, direct British-German agreement. The Embassy will continue to work by every available means in the direction of German-British friendship, although our friendships with Italy and Japan will naturally be borne in mind in every way. This work must certainly not be described as being devoid of prospects, for British public opinion is well disposed to Germany on the whole, and it is therefore a question of winning over the governing stratum.'

It was in this sense that in the days when the 'Report on the Coronation' was made Father invited Winston Churchill to a luncheon at the embassy. During the tête à tête conversation, Churchill had stated, brutally but frankly: 'An over-powerful Germany will once again be destroyed!' When Father retorted that this time Germany did not stand alone but had allies, Churchill imperturbably replied: 'We are pretty good at getting them around at the end!' In his memoirs, Churchill gives a certainly more amusing version, but not the true one, of his answer: 'In the First World War we [the British] had the Italians as allies, so it's only fair that this time you [the Germans] have them with you!' What happens when the victors sit in judgement over the defeated is demonstrated in this example too: the Nuremberg Trial ruled that what Churchill did or did not say at this discussion was irrelevant.[139]

The report's political passages soberly analyze the state of German-British relations at the moment of the coronation festivities. It reflects in plain language the world-political predicament in which Germany's central location placed her; the necessary German forces in order to neutralize Soviet Russia were felt to be a threat by both Western European powers, not so however the enormous potential threat of Bolshevism.[140] Father pinpoints the problem at the core of European politics, namely the concern of Germany's neighbours about a possible German strength that could in their view lead to hegemony. He states that Eden, the British Foreign Secretary, had raised 'not so very productively' the question of a Western Pact. The report is unequivocal that should it come to a dispute with Soviet Russia, the German wish for a secure 'rear cover' in the West was expressed in the sense of the desired declared neutral stance of Britain. At the same time he sees the risk of war on two fronts in the case of Britain being drawn into the confrontation by France because of the automatic consequence arising from the Franco-Russian pact. To avert a possible conflict with Soviet Russia did not lie exclusively in the hands of Germany if the Soviet side wanted to bring one about, when France, and potentially Britain, would be on their side.

What my father writes in the report, that Germany would 'necessarily have the greatest interest in the maintenance of the British Empire, whose heir, after all, she could never become', corresponds entirely to Hitler's conception. Note that this report was of the highest confidentiality, addressed to the head of state, and therefore reflects the most intimate and confidential and in consequence most genuine considerations of the German leadership. One may ask oneself whether at this juncture of world politics Britain missed an opportunity to secure her empire through an alliance with the Reich.

In order to deal with the above-mentioned predicament, there was no choice for German politics but, without abandoning the chance of an agreement with Britain, to seek friends wherever they were to be found. The most significant motivation for contracting the Anti-Comintern Pact with Japan was the threat looming from the Soviet Union. It faced Japan just as much as Europe. There was, however, a further aspect, which was to break out of isolation in general.

Hitler saw the Soviet Union as the cardinal opponent, an opponent of Germany as well as of European culture. In the already-mentioned Four Year Plan Memorandum of the summer of 1936 he says that a victorious incursion by the USSR would to his mind be the greatest calamity to befall humanity since the dissolution of the Roman Empire. It was his opinion that the credibility of the arguments employed toward Britain rested on this fact. Germany's view was that in the 'new' European balance of power Germany should be in the balance together with France and Britain on the one side and the Soviet Union on the other. In order not to run the risk of being completely dependent on Britain's good will, Germany had to 'take an option', as Father had repeatedly postulated. To this end, as things stood, Italy and Japan were predominantly the options so long as Britain did not 'declare' herself and continued in certain circles to speak of only a 'Bolshevik bogey' which Hitler was allegedly propagandizing purely so as to extort Britain's good will. Father encountered this attitude when he elucidated the recently signed Anti-Comintern Pact to Foreign Secretary Eden:

'I pointed out that the Pact was directed against nobody except world Communism and open to Britain to join. I met with total incomprehension on Eden's part ...] Britain would not see the Communist danger.'[141]

The Anti-Comintern Pact naturally contained a political element, which was first of all anti-Russian, since Moscow was the bearer of Comintern thinking. Adolf Hitler and Father hoped to create a certain counterweight against Russia, for at the time the Soviet Union stood in opposition to Germany both politically and ideologically. Father writes:

'There was for us no other way to go also in regard to England but to pursue the anti-Comintern policy. Only by becoming as powerful an ally as possible could we assist those circles in England, who viewed their country's future as best secured by an affiliation with Germany, to exert a decisive influence. A form as loose as possible for the anti-Comintern pact had been chosen ... so as to have a free hand diplomatically for an eventual alliance with England.

'The goal of German foreign policy was to convince Britain that between the choices of a possible grouping of alliance [on the part of Germany] directed against Britain and a German-British alliance, the latter was the most preferable option [for Britain].'[142]

At this point, with hindsight, may the question be asked: would it not indeed have been the latter that was the most preferable option, in the sense of preserving the British Empire? I can testify to this as a witness of the times, for during my time in London I had gathered on various occasions from what

Father said that at that moment the anti-Comintern policy also had as its ultimate goal to arrive at a major agreement with Britain. The vain endeavours in that direction through the years 1933 to 1936 had by now led to another emphasis being given to the ways of attaining an alliance with Britain; the aim, however, remained the same. In consequence the pact contained only consultation clauses and no obligations of assistance. German politics had little choice but to reinforce the German position by alliances and to demonstrate a self-confident desire to acquire Britain's amity as a partner of value without cutting into British vested interests. It was on these precepts that Father had undertaken his post in London.

When, looking back, Father writes that 'Britain would not see the Communist danger', the statement concerns the Soviet Union and the potential threat it constituted to Europe. It is a fact that the Communist Party did not play a role in Britain.

It must be seen that up until that moment Hitler cannot be reproached with any action in foreign policy that exceeded the usual framework. To put aside the discriminating provisions of the Versailles Treaty had been a juridically correct move, as well as a politico-military imperative that had for instance also been seen in Britain. The introduction by the French government of two-year military service – instead of the disarmament foreseen by the treaty – as well as the military alliance of France with the Soviet Union, were additionally, on the part of the 'other side', steps that had gone beyond the Versailles Treaty system. In Hitler's view this considerably increased the Russian menace, most particularly by the inclusion of Czechoslovakia in the treaties.

Upon the conclusion of the French-Russian military alliance in 1934/35 – that, as Father wrote, 'was constantly morally supported' by Britain – the encirclement of the Reich was practically complete in that England, having rearmed, was to join this concourse formed against Germany. Until that time, to determine that Britain had a free hand, the Reich would possibly be left in the dark. As a scenario this was grim, but it was to be envisaged that it would not come to the common establishment of a European policy and that instead there would be a confrontation of blocs directed against one another, with the inclusion of the USSR. In this Father saw as his second most important task in London to cast the light of clarification on Germany's policy.

A further factor of world politics of those days, of the greatest significance, has to be mentioned at this point, namely the hostile stance in regard to Germany of the President of the United States, Franklin Delano Roosevelt. One day at school my friends came up to me with grave expressions and very kindly told me their sympathy for my country at a time when it had been struck by such great misfortune. Their regrets concerned the catastrophe that had destroyed the *Hindenburg* airship at New York's Lakehurst airship landing field on 6 May 1937. The accident had cost many lives. One of its causes was the earlier refusal of the American government to supply Germany with the non-flammable helium gas that in those days was available only from the United States. Since airships had long lost any military significance, in 1936 such an act on the part of the US government demonstrated an expressed unfriendly stance toward Germany.

Here I shall relate one more personal experience I had, with direct relation to the attitude of the American president toward Germany and that also happened in 1937. A few years ago my wife and I were invited to a big reception given by friends of ours in the USA, in the state of New York. A son of the president's, Elliott Roosevelt, was placed at the right of my wife. I happened to join them after we had dined, and to my surprise heard him speak of my parents in the friendliest way. He said my father spoke better English than an Englishman and that both my parents had been charming to him. When I asked how he came to meet them, he told me he had gone to Europe with his wife on their honeymoon in 1937. When they were in Bavaria they had met my parents, who invited them to dinner in a magnificent hotel in the environs of Munich.[143]

Father rang him up the next day to ask if he would be interested to meet Hitler. Hitler would be glad to receive him on the Obersalzberg. He was, however, reluctant to accept the invitation without the approval of his father, the president, whom he telephoned. President Roosevelt said it would certainly be a most interesting experience in the young man's life to have met Hitler, but it was quite unsuitable for his – the president's – policy and he should instantly remove himself to England, whereupon he promptly followed his father's wishes.

Please bear in mind this is the summer of 1937. On Germany's part there were intensive efforts to reach a lasting settlement with Britain: Hitler had dispensed with Alsace-Lorraine in every way and acknowledged Britain's supremacy at sea in the Naval Agreement. In November 1937 Roosevelt made his famous 'Quarantine' speech, in which he attacked not only Japan and Italy but Germany as well. This speech made it clear that Roosevelt, president of the world's greatest power, was determined to pursue a policy directed against Germany. For no reason, Roosevelt placed Germany on a par with the two powers that had indeed recently altered the world's territorial status quo, Italy and Japan. I shall revert to President Roosevelt's role in detail, in due course.

Thereby the two most powerful nations of the earth, *viz.* the United States and the Soviet Union, with France and her alliances with the 'Little Entente' added, were blatantly declared to be against Germany. True, the Reich entertained loose friendly relations with Italy and Japan. It was in any case no longer completely isolated. In such a situation, to attribute 'stage-by-stage plans' to Hitler with a view to attain a sort of 'world hegemony', as German historians tirelessly maintain, is a propagandist interpretation of history and has nothing to do with the reality.[144] The truth was the opposite. Hitler's policies were determined by the Reich's vulnerable position of marked weakness in its location in the centre of Europe. This is the key to Hitler's politics from 1938.

At the time of the coronation, Britain's policies had not yet been openly declared. There is no doubt that a portion of the ruling elite saw a renewed clash with the Reich as a life-threatening danger to the British Empire. The others, however, saw in a rekindling of the First World War, and the defeat of the Reich, a sort of future securing of the empire. In that period, England kept the German leadership in the dark as to her intentions. Germany could, however, not assume Britain's neutrality as a sure thing in case the situation in Eastern Europe came to embroilment. However, if preparations for defence against Soviet Russia were to promise to be successful, political relations in Eastern Europe had to be rearranged from that point of view. In that case the Reich had to lay claim to being the strongest, or even the sole power that could resist the Russians, and be at the head of an anti-Soviet grouping.

Czechoslovakia presented a particular danger, being at the time already the 'air force mother-ship' for the air forces to be set against the Reich, first and foremost out of the Soviet Union.[145] The Czech government under Benesch attempted to involve France in a military imbroglio with the Reich in May 1938, hoping to rope in Britain and the Soviet Union on their side. Their policy in regard to the Sudeten German population group in Czech national territory brought up considerable problems that the Reich could not leave unnoticed for ever. Instead of the pledged 'second Switzerland', as the Czech leadership had put it to the Allies in 1918, a centralized state had arisen, ruled by Prague. Neither the Slovaks, the other half of the nation's name, nor the second largest national population, the Germans, actually had any of the influence that had been promised them.

Since a European settlement was not to be reached with Britain, the question arose of what policy the British government would pursue in regard to the Reich if the latter were to undertake a certain reordering of Eastern European relations. Father's posing of this question runs like a red thread through his reports. An Eastern European organization in the sense of the German policy for neutralizing the Soviet expansion of power was imperative. It cannot be doubted that Hitler's concern in the face of the Russian colossus, in view of later developments, was neither an empty scare nor a false delusion.[146]

Be Warned about England – The Bottom Line

Father answered the fateful – and the word is appropriate here – question as to the future policies of Britain in his Embassy Report dated 28 December 1937, to be followed five days later by his Conclusions (in German '*Schlussfolgerungen*') to the Main Report ('*Hauptbericht*').[147] Therein he arrives at the clear conclusion that the Reich must count on opposition from Britain in the new order to be established in Eastern Europe. It would be an antagonism that did not exclude war: there was a possibility Britain would not shy away from another war against Germany. It is to be surmised from this that the 'leading elite' is in no way decadent and weak, and is on the contrary hard and bellicose; in fact Father added the word 'heroic' by hand so as to remain in Hitler's way of speaking. The report should be read most attentively, as in it he analyses Britain's policy in regard to Germany with great clarity, at a time when all Hitler had done was to restore the defence apparatus of the Reich, in combination with repeated offers for a general disarmament restriction or a pact of friendship with Britain, but had undertaken no steps of aggression in shaping his foreign policy.

The quandary for Britain was in the choice between triggering a renewed armed conflict with the gradually strengthening Reich or the acceptance of Germany as the strongest power on the Continent, with the risks to the British Isles this implied. This choice, in this form, was not enforced by German policies. It was the outcome of the inner dispositions of the British elite. Father's report made an exposé of this standpoint adopted by the British opponents of an understanding with Germany, found above all in the Foreign Office. The display of the expanding Bolshevik power as a counterweight to the German Reich was not properly assessed by England. British politics were firmly fixed in the narrow concept of the 'balance of power' of the preceding centuries and refused to take into account that the global power blocs were in the process of shifting to other continents.

The Embassy Report that my father addressed to Hitler after a year-and-a-half's work as German ambassador in London basically set out what my father had observed in the train of thought of the British leadership:[148]

'The principal issue for England, who of course sees in the maintenance of peace the best guarantee for the safeguarding of the Empire, remains ever whether it will after all be possible to come to an arrangement with Germany that would secure world peace and keep the European balance of power. It is conceivable that there are men in the British government (that Chamberlain and Halifax belong among them I doubt, by reason of my experience and observations) who even today believe in a friendly arrangement with Germany, to wit on the following basis:

'Restitution of a few German colonies and leaving the matter of a solution to the Austrian question open that might lead to a peaceful affiliation, as well as improvement of the situation of the Sudeten Germans, possibly as far as their obtaining cultural autonomy, additionally as to the rest a repeat of Germany's obligation to refrain from attacking neighbouring states and the obligation to solve any problems with them only through peaceful negotiation; moreover a clear convention as to at least a qualitative restriction of an air armed force on the model of the German-British Naval Agreement, for instance through bombing prohibition, limitation of bombers and potentially in quantitative relevance through disclosure and possible reduction of the budget.

'In my estimate, this would be approximately the maximum of what these men, who basically believe in an amicable relationship with Germany (that is to say, therefore, those who do not at all see an insuperable obstacle to an arrangement with Germany in the continuing existence of a Germany that has a so-called expansionist National Socialist '*Weltanschauung*' [trans., view of the world] in itself) would be able to picture in an arrangement with Germany ...

'The typical characteristic of the British leading class is today as it has always been, their materialistic selfishness, consciousness of power and, most importantly, the will to rule as well as the basic enduring heroic[149] conception of life – that we have too – which is what in the final analysis created the British Empire and preserved it for centuries. Slogans such as "nation of shopkeepers" were basically never apt, in my opinion, as to the character of the English ruling class. Today just as previously the English ruling class will adopt a course favouring their important material interests as well as their position of power in the world, as long as there is any chance of their being victorious, in the final analysis to go to extremes, i.e. war.[150] England will never dare to make such a wager thoughtlessly. She will always carefully weigh up the relations of power and if need be, delay any decision. When the best chances favour the side of England, she will go to war …

'To sum up on the subject of further developments in German–English relations, we ought not to allow ourselves to harbour illusions, for as demonstrated by the Report, there still remain significant difficulties of a basic nature in the way of a lasting understanding between the two nations as matters stand. The special amity and warmth with which my colleagues and I have always been treated so far by the British should to my mind not hide the fact that for the time being there is no indication of a turn-about of real significance in English politics in the direction of an understanding – as we see it – to be ascertained. Should England then attempt in the future to block Germany, there can be no doubt that the two nations will in the end be driven apart. Notwithstanding, it appears to me to be right to keep our future policy regarding England on the path of reaching a compromise. The Embassy will therefore also strive with constancy in the direction of a German-English understanding. Such a task must however not lead our other friendships to suffer. In this sense, with their approval, this year also the Embassy has ever handled the Berlin-Rome axis as well as our anti-Comintern relations with Japan as constant factors of our foreign policy, while we continue to work on England.'

This was a clear warning. The British elite is described here as being tough, power-conscious, coolly calculating and ready for a fight. It is particularly that cliché, current in Germany at the time of the First World War about the English 'nation of shopkeepers' competing with the 'heroism' of the Germans, that Father refuted. In those days, a number of German observers had drawn a comparison to the wars between Rome and Carthage, in which the role of Rome was given to Germany. In view of his own observations, the German ambassador was now advising the greatest prudence, indeed in virtually prophetic terms:

'It will not be impossible for the English government, both toward the British people and the Dominions, to present the progression to war in such a manner as though the British vital interests were at stake. Some length of time is naturally necessary before such propaganda can be effective. A special role is played therein by the spectre of a potential bombing of the British Isles from the air.'

Five days after the drafting of this report, 'Deutsche Botschaft, London A 5522' ('German Embassy, London A 5522'), Ribbentrop wrote the appertaining Conclusions under the date of 2 January 1938, and, from his country house in Sonnenburg near Bad Freienwalde sent the whole memorandum to Hitler in Berlin. In contrast to the previously mentioned unpublished ambassadorial reports from Ribbentrop and the Main Report – concealed until 1968 – these Conclusions, which will presently be referred to, were produced as 'evidence' against him at the Nuremberg tribunal. Nevertheless, only point five from page nine of the ten-page report was read to Ribbentrop as an alleged 'surprise' document. The complete document, the 'Conclusions to A 5522', was published in 1949 in the documentation of the International Court of Justice and in 1950 in the Acts of German Foreign Policy I.

In these Conclusions, destined for Hitler's eyes alone and not – as was the ambassadorial report A 5522 just mentioned and the other ambassadorial reports from London – dispatched to Foreign Minister Neurath at the same time, Ribbentrop underlines with even greater stress the British will to encircle Germany. He here expounds in detail the reasons that induced Chamberlain to send his Foreign Minister, Halifax, to Germany in November 1937. In contrast to Report A 5522, the Conclusions are not found in the original or original carbon copies, but only in the transcript of the Berlin Auswärtiges Amt's Political Archive. They proceed on the assumption that a settlement with England should continue to be sought:[151]

'As to England, our policy ought in my opinion to continue to be aimed at compromise while fully safeguarding the interests of our friends. We must also continue to foster England's belief that a settlement and an understanding between Germany and England are still possible eventually. Such a prospect might, for example, have a restraining effect on any possible intention to intervene on the part of the British Government, should Germany become involved in a local conflict in Central Europe which does not vitally concern England … I believe that the question whether a German-British settlement can then still be achieved at all, may be answered as follows:

'If England with her alliances is stronger than Germany and her friends, she will in my opinion fight sooner or later.[152] Should Germany, however, be so successful in her alliance policy that a German coalition would be stronger than its British counterpart, or perhaps as strong, it is quite possible that England would prefer to try for a settlement after all …

'An unequivocal British concession regarding the Austrian-Czech question in accordance with our views could clear the political atmosphere in Europe. Judging from my previous experience, however, I consider such a turn unlikely and believe that at best only the force of circumstances could compel England some day to tolerate such a solution. My opinion that this problem cannot be solved by official negotiations with England is strengthened by the fact that Chamberlain is enmeshed in a system of domestic as well as foreign policy (together with France) that makes important decisions exceedingly difficult.

'Once the fronts have become rigid, only distinctly abnormal changes in the balance of power or events in Europe or the world (France going Bolshevist, collapse of Russia, serious changes affecting our friends) could force political developments to take a different turn. However, a policy cannot be based on such possibilities. Therefore, in my opinion it is proper to continue the course we have taken in our foreign policy.

'In conclusion I should like to sum up my views in the following sentences:

1. England is <u>behind in her armaments</u>[153] – therefore, what she is playing for is to gain time.
2. England believes that in a race with Germany <u>time is on England's side</u> – exploitation of her greater economic resources for armament – time for extending her alliances (e.g., the United States).
3. The visit of Halifax, therefore, is to be considered as a <u>manoeuvre to obtain information and as a camouflage</u> – even Germanophiles in England frequently play only a role that has been assigned to them.
4. <u>England and her Prime Minister</u>, after the Halifax visit, in my opinion see <u>no possible basis for an agreement</u> with Germany (they consider National Socialist Germany capable of anything, just as we consider the British capable of anything); therefore, they fear that some day they might be forced by a strong Germany to accept solutions that are not agreeable to them. In order to meet this contingency <u>England</u> is at all events <u>preparing</u> by military and political measures <u>for a conflict with Germany</u>.
5. Therefore, we must draw the following conclusions:
   a. *Outwardly, continued understanding with England* while simultaneously protecting the interests of our friends.
   b. *Quiet but determined establishment of*[154] *alliances a g a i n s t England,* i.e., in practice, strengthening our friendship with Italy and Japan

and in addition winning over all countries whose interests conform directly or indirectly with ours. For this purpose the diplomats of the three great powers are to cooperate closely and intimately. *Only in this manner can we meet England, whether it be for a settlement someday or in conflict.* England will be a tough and keen foe in this diplomatic game.

6. The special problem as to whether France and thereby England would intervene if Germany should become involved in a conflict in Central Europe depends upon circumstances and the time when such a conflict were to break out and end and upon military considerations which cannot be evaluated here. I should like to present personally some views on that subject to the Führer.

'This is my evaluation of the situation after having carefully weighed all the circumstances. I have worked for friendship with England for years, and nothing would make me happier than the possibility of its achievement. When I asked the Führer to send me to London[155] I was sceptical about the likelihood of success, but, because of Edward VIII, it seemed that a final attempt should be made. Today I no longer have faith in any understanding. England does not desire in close proximity a paramount Germany, which would be a constant menace to the British Isles. On this she will fight ... Henceforth – regardless of what tactical interludes of conciliation may be attempted with regard to us – every day that our political calculations are not actuated by the fundamental idea that England is our most dangerous enemy <u>would be a gain for our enemies</u>.[156, 157] sgd. R.'[158]

It must be said once again that the above is a totally confidential report from the German ambassador in London directly to the head of state (not even under copy to the Foreign Minister), or in other words it contained the most secret thoughts about German policy. The German government's wish to place relations with Britain on a long-term, solid and amicable base without impairing British interests is quite clearly demonstrated from the document.

At the centre of this major England-memorandum is the ascertainment that Father had stressed to Hitler already in the summer of 1936, namely that the concept of a balance of political power in Europe was now and as ever remained the fundamental principle of British politics. Any shift of the balance to the detriment of the insular nation would lead the English leading class to a diplomatic and finally military intervention. There is an interesting phenomenon to bring to attention at this point: to an impartial reader the report would make it perfectly obvious that Hitler had been put in the picture by his ambassador in London unequivocally as to British policy and had to be aware of the risks he would be running. The German ambassador in London in his report maintains unmistakably that in bringing about a new order in Eastern Europe, German policy had to assume that it would come up against a bitter opposition from Britain – and France too – who would potentially confront the Reich with the force of arms.

The German ambassador in London bases his conviction on explicit detail, beginning with the age-old principle of balance of power that had dominated in internal European clashes for at least three centuries and that purported to ensure Britain's role as referee in Europe. It was Britain's abidance by this that had led to the outbreak of the First World War. He showed the 'ruling elite' as hard as steel and power-conscious, ready to fight for their status in the world and their material vested interests. He consciously employs Hitler's use of words so as to be clearly understood, as when characterizing the English leading class he puts in the word 'heroic' by hand. In the awareness that a people will behave like its leaders, the British group of leaders' approach was a subject frequently broached between my parents and me, and they were very interested to hear of my experiences and what I lived through at Westminster School. This is why Father's formulation in his Report that it should be counted upon that England will 'fight' and the leading class 'will go to extremes, i.e. war' bear no misunderstanding and are completely explicit.

It is astonishing and should be examined that even before the war it was said of my father that he had erroneously advised Hitler regarding British politics in the sense that he characterized the British leading class as weak, decadent and degenerate, and therefore in no position nor having the will to fight for their empire and place in the world. In the meantime, the misrepresentation is firmly entrenched in the repertory of numerous writers of memoirs and judgemental historians – in the German Federal Republic above all – with no foundation, and is reiterated and hammered into the public as established fact.

At Nuremberg Father took a stand against this in writing:

'When I had been in London for a few months I supplied him [Hitler] with a detailed report of my impressions. My Report expressed my conviction that England was strong, the leading class heroic and that the basic direction of British foreign policy was as always the "balance of power" in Europe. All my subsequent reports addressed to Adolf Hitler during my posting bore this state of things out as fact. My Memorandum dated 2 January 1938 produced by the prosecution in Nuremberg summarises this coverage and confirms it. It is obviously the duty of an ambassador in a post as important as London to take all possibilities into account in a report required by the head of state concerning England's future stance; to draw the conclusions therefrom was the Führer's affair.

'I bring this up because of the propaganda directed against me both at home and abroad, during and after the war, that I had wrongly informed the Führer as to England's strength and stance. I am told among other things that the former Reich Finance Minister Count Schwerin von Krosigk will have drafted a memorandum stating that I had not briefed the Führer correctly with the truth and comprehensively about England. It is a case of the contrary and I am all the more surprised at the Count's statements since I had told him too about my conviction that England would fight and that I had already reported to the Führer in this sense from London.'[159]

I remember Schwerin von Krosigk very well. I came to know him at a shoot in the Sudetenland. He was the sole minister Father had invited to this meet. The hunting grounds had been leased by the Auswärtiges Amt so as to be able on the occasion of a state visit to proffer a guest a shooting treat. This is why this shoot remains in my memory – it must have been in November 1939 – because the quarters of my regiment were in Pilsen in the Protectorate (of Bohemia and Moravia), near the meet. Some 'high-placed' good soul wanted to do my parents – probably my mother mainly – a good turn and granted me two days' leave. I did not particularly value this sort of intervention 'from above' in my ordinary soldier's life, because there was always the risk that some superior – and quite rightly too – would object to it, which could turn out to make things uncomfortable for me in my duties.

Father and Schwerin von Krosigk were evidently on good terms, or Schwerin von Krosigk would not have been invited to this purely private meet. No state shoots took place during the war, but the grounds had to be controlled if for no other reason than that agriculture suffered damage from an unchecked wildlife population. Schwerin von Krosigk, who was not at all a poor shot, had naturally accepted the invitation with pleasure. But it is true a friend in need is a friend indeed, and it is certainly not fairness that was uppermost in the minds of writers of memoirs following the last war, most particularly not in those who had been implicated in the regime and had but one thought: to exculpate themselves, by means of blaming those who could no longer defend themselves. Hitler's Finance Minister Schwerin von Krosigk is but one of many instances of this.

Besides, in a speech to the European heads of state gathered in Berlin on 26 November 1941, Father had calmly said that:

> 'whether the ... English propagandists are right in saying that I, in ignorance of the essence of the British nature and misjudgement of their true character reported to the Führer that England would never come to fight, I shall be pleased to leave to the judgement of the future.'[160]

Upon closing his notes, a few days before his death, Father could not anticipate that the claim that he had misinformed Hitler as to the English readiness to fight a war had been supplied to the English propaganda from the German side. Aside from other considerations, let it be said only that from the part of the German conspiracy, the British were repeatedly requested to remain 'obdurate' in the face of the German proposals. If it came to war, the psychological climate for a coup d'état was already prepared, because the German people did not want a war. The group of conspirators in the circle of the State Secretary in the Auswärtiges Amt, Ernst von Weizsäcker, again and again assured their British interlocutors – they were of all people just such as Vansittart, Churchill and other 'friends of Germany' – that Ribbentrop was reporting to and influencing Hitler in the sense that England would not fight because it was decadent and weak. In order to show that the opposite was the case, England should strike an attitude of toughness. The conspirators hoped the tactic would lead to a collision course from which the outcome would be a war, which is what they saw as setting the stage for a military coup against Hitler. This traducement against the German Foreign Minister consequently had a clearly political background. It may be remarked only as an aside that most of the political discussions held between Hitler and Father – due to Hitler's custom of not convening sessions to discuss current problems – took place in tête à têtes so that there was nobody present to witness the true exchanges of the 'consultations' between them. All I can produce, unfortunately, as proof is that the actual ambassadorial report leaves no doubt as to Joachim von Ribbentrop's judgement of British politics. He is sceptical, not to say pessimistic, about Hitler's wish for establishment of a lasting cooperation with Britain. He describes England as a mighty, tough and possibly bellicose opponent of Germany, maybe according to the intra-British decision-making process, even <u>the</u> opponent par excellence.

It is the preferential practice of today's writers of memoirs and historians simply to reproduce clichés and assertions regarding the 'man in the forefront' without checking them – or indeed instead of knowing better. Here is a prominent example: the Reich's former Chancellor von Papen, a well-known 'Münchhausen of memoir literature' as they call him,[161] in his memoirs[162] reproduces five lines of the around 290 pages of the Report, in such form, with the date, the address and the signature as to intimate that it is the original document, i.e. the entire report. When my mother pointed out this incorrectness to Mr von Papen, he replied imperturbably that he was not aware of the original report. When Mother was able to direct him to the entry in the English edition of his memoirs that had come out a few months before the German edition, where the exact source was given, he merely remarked:

'It had slipped my memory that I had already quoted sentences from the Report in the English edition and I regret this lapse ... It is undeniable that I had read the report, as it is printed in the "Documents of German Foreign Policy, London 1949".'[163]

It cannot be said with certainty that Spitzy is purported to have made an error, since at the time of the Report's drafting he was Father's Aide de Camp. He insists today that at that time he already belonged to the Weizsäcker and Kordt conspiracy. Spitzy reproduces the three sentences verbatim from Papen's book, also as 'Memorandum for the Führer' (furthermore with a different print image). He too postulates that to Hitler Father presented the British as decadent, weak and, for the sake of the final word, even as 'Judaized', coming to the conclusion that England would not fight. On the basis of the Report given here, readers can now draw their own conclusions as to how my father assessed the British and at the same time form a judgement as to Spitzy's credibility, since he states in writing that he had known the Report.[164]

I explain these two examples in order to show how ruthlessly authors of memoirs have treated historical truth, especially when they themselves were actively involved in the forging of history. To find this traducement again in Spitzy is interesting only because he says he belonged to the circles that diffused the calumnies[165] with a clear political objective in mind.

To come back to the assessment of the world political situation as it is condensed in the Report, until far into the war Hitler did not cease his wishful thinking of reaching an agreement with Britain:

'F (Führer): All are alliances of convenience. For instance, the people know that the alliance with Italy is only an alliance between Mussolini and me. We Germans only have sympathies for Finland, could have them for Sweden and, naturally, for *England*. A German-English alliance would be one of a people with a people. All the British need to do is get their hands off the Continent. They can keep their Empire and the world!'[166]

In 1937 his ambassador in London saw the situation more soberly. To his mind, one could not force one's partner or opponent to their good fortune. If the British government did not share Hitler's opinion, one would have to make the best of it. Father drew the conclusion from it that nothing further could be done but to pursue the policy of alliance, which had been initiated under the label of an Anti-Comintern Pact, meaning to look for partners in alliance. This he recommended explicitly.

Hitler's pro-West – in other words anti-Soviet – policy had determined the Reich on a course that was to come to an arrangement with the Western powers, England and France. This could signify falling between all the stools in the end, but a see-saw policy between West and East would have been an even greater risk, as the outbreak of the First World War demonstrated.

Up to this moment, Hitler's 'Western connection' had not so far been achievable. Hitler had aligned his policy in that direction and had not followed in the Russian policies of Bismarck, since in contrast to the Bismarck era he saw Russia as the greatest threat. 'With caution', one could say, on the German side they began to look around. From the point of view of underlining the anti-Bolshevik component, initially only loose ties to Italy and Japan could be established. Naturally, there was a highly political component in the Anti-Comintern Pact. It could be expanded, in case the two Western powers should abstain in the long run. In any case, it was in the state of affairs in 1936 better than nothing. For, viewed objectively, 1936 had still been a case of mere survival, so to speak. The ambassadorial reports expressed it unequivocally. Britain would move against Germany, in order, as Churchill put it, once more to smash a Germany that was too powerful for the European balance. Hitler had to take this into account. Time was beginning to run out for him. Hitler's subsequent moves have to be seen in this light.

Let it be said at this point that Father's Report from London does not mention the Soviet Union. For him, questions of ideology had no role to play in foreign policy. He had gone along with the early and one-sided commitment of German policy opposing the Soviet Union, because the Reich's pro-Western option was thereby clearly accentuated. However, the more reservations with which one was obliged to assess British policies, the more pressing was the reflection that Germany's position vis à vis Russia had to be rethought.

Although it was too soon, Father may have had one or the other thought in the back of his mind. It is noticeable that in the main Report from London, which is really a drafted conception of German foreign policy, Soviet Russia is not mentioned, seeing that opposition to the Soviet Union was the starting point for the Hitlerian foreign policy. In the collection of papers Father left, there is a Note of his:[167]

'The anti-Comintern Pact naturally also harboured a political factor ... Even while bearing England in mind, we had no choice but to follow through with the anti-Comintern policy. It was only if we were as strong as possible a partner that we could help those circles in England to exert a decisive influence that saw the future of their country best secured by a common course with Germany. A formulation as loose as possible for the anti-Comintern Pact was chosen, and its aspect of the world outlook placed in the foreground, in order to keep a free hand in diplomatic negotiations for a possible alliance with Britain.'

When it came to a rapprochement with the Soviet Union in 1939, both contracting sides were clear that the Comintern would also in the future not be permitted any sort of activity in the countries that had joined the pact. In the negotiations, from the Soviet side no such corresponding stipulation was raised. In fact my father was able to jest, in Moscow, that the USSR itself could join the pact.

Hitler saw himself once again on the horns of a dilemma. From 1933 to 1936 he was confronted with the necessity to rearm so as to fill the power vacuum in Central Europe, not only in view of the 'Little Entente' but above all because of the powerful Soviet Union. However, in the eyes of the British this rearmament tipped the scales of the balance of power. Hitler now faced the problem of having placed himself one-sidedly in the position of favouring the West – that is to say in an anti-Soviet one – only to find that Britain rejected him (to say nothing of the French government's stance of hostility towards Germany and amity to Soviet Russia). He had fallen between two stools, with Italy his sole support in Europe.

At the turn of the year 1937 to 1938 it is possible that through the purges in the Party and the army Hitler may have seen Russia's threat as temporarily somewhat moderated. But time, as has already been said, began running out. British (as well as American) military build-up was in full spate, and Russia would recover from the blood-letting of high-ranking officers. All that remained to be done was to make the position of Germany as strong as possible. This meant rearmament of Germany on the one hand, and on the other a consolidation of the situation on the eastern German border, in Eastern Europe and the Balkans, therefore in the Soviets' 'front yard'. It will be seen to what extent Hitler took this situation into account.

I should like to refer here to a minor personal incident. I remember the days of Christmas 1937, during which the ambassadorial reports were drafted.[168] We were celebrating the holy days in Sonnenburg near Bad Freienwalde, a farmhouse of my parents' amid the beautiful natural surroundings of the Oderbruch. Our Ribbentrop grandparents were with us from Naumburg for the Christmas holiday, as they always were. I had come from Ilfeld, a German boarding school to which I had meanwhile transferred, a day before the holiday. After the austerity of boarding school life I was eagerly looking forward to being spoiled by my mother and the usual joyful atmosphere that always made Christmas at home so enjoyable.

Father was, however, preoccupied during those days, deep in thought and talking to Grandfather for hours at a time; he was certainly not as relaxed as he had been the previous year, when once more we had all foregathered in Sonnenburg. The responsibility of drawing up his reports must have weighed heavily on him, and even we children felt it. On Christmas Eve Father would usually play *Silent Night* on the violin, accompanied on the piano by Grandmother, and we would sing it. This year there was no violin – it had stayed in London. Something very significant happened to me in those Christmas days, that was also quite unexpected. I must say first of all that I had grown up with Mother's motto that 'as long as I am alive you will not get a motorbike!'. She considered motorbike riding too dangerous – and she was not entirely wrong. Now there I was, stuck in Ilfeld, a tiny spot in the Südharz, with only a bicycle with which to get around. As the slopes in these lovely central uplands are fairly steep, one can hardly ride around very far. Ilfeld permitted possession of a motorbike, so I began feeling Mother out as to her thoughts about it, while of course stressing the harmlessness of the BMW 200cc machine I had my eye on. To my surprise Mother did not react with the severity of a flat refusal to give permission and the usual formula of 'as long as I am alive … ' etc.; all she said was 'is it really necessary?' and 'but it's so dangerous', finally referring me to Father. Understandably, she did not want to have sole responsibility. I started on Father, trying to convince him, but naturally he too was basically reluctant. What parents are delighted when their son wants to have a motorbike? In the end, Father retreated to the position of saying I would have to chip in on the purchase price from my savings account, since after all it was a pretty expensive present.

In 1925 my savings account had been opened with a deposit of five Reichsmarks. Since I was particularly thrifty as a boy, my credit was now a few hundred Reichsmarks. I could therefore be very correct and contribute half the purchase price to my father, who accepted it without demur. Mother's grounds for tolerating the motorbike – 'You never know what might happen' – as she told me at some later date, had to do with the uncertainty of Father's political future after he had clearly and unequivocally informed Hitler that as things stood he was unable to fulfil the latter's wish for a British alliance nor, consequently, to carry out his mission to London. The reaction of a dictator is in the final analysis always unpredictable, to say nothing of the entourage eternally plotting intrigues. Nonetheless, Hitler was now fully briefed as to British policies and had been warned.

That brief conversation must have taken place between 28 December 1937 and 2 January 1938, the date on which Father had transmitted his major Report together with the Conclusions to Hitler. After the fact, it turned out to be the final report from Father's posting as ambassador to London (not that he knew this at the time).

As I have said, I had meanwhile transferred back to a German school. I have described how the year I spent at Westminster School had broadened my mind. I was now a pupil at a National Political Educational Institution, popularly known as a 'Napola', this one being at Ilfeld in the Harz region. The academy had grown out of an Evangelical monastic school; the high level of education demanded was upheld. The curriculum corresponded to a German humanist high school. I was at this boarding school from September 1937 to March 1939, and I owe to it my well-grounded schooling in the two upper forms. National Political Educational Institutions were elite establishments. Pupils were recruited from gifted primary school children, who if necessary were exempt from payment of school fees. Their motto was 'Be more than you appear to be'.

It was during this phase of my life, that is between September 1937 and March 1939, that occurred my father's nomination to Foreign Minister; the *Anschluß* (link-up) with Austria; the so-called 'May Crisis' – during an exchange visit of my form with an English public school in the spring of 1938; the Sudeten Crisis; and finally – after I had written my *Abitur* (secondary school leaving exam) essay on the subject *'Völkisches und politisches Denken in der Politik der Gegenwart'* (National and Political Thought in the Politics of the Present), which was set in the sense of a national foreign policy – the establishment of the Protectorate of Bohemia and Moravia. (What was expected of the treatment of the subject was that it should be a repudiation of imperialist expansion politics, an irony of which I was at the time completely aware!) I shall come back to the establishment of the Protectorate.

My written correspondence and personal contact with Mother – since my parents had returned to Berlin – was now much easier and closer than when they were in London. I was once again receiving much more detailed glimpses of political developments. It culminated on that day of March 1939 when – just a little bit craving their praise – I was to announce I had obtained my *Abitur*, with the mention 'Good'. However, the impact of my news was lessened when my breath was taken away by Mother's information that Father was intensively endeavouring to persuade Hitler to conclude a pact with Russia.

Some four weeks after the end of the 1937 Christmas holidays, from which despite the cold winter weather I had gone back to school on my motorbike, one night at 11.00 pm I was called to the Duty Master, our English teacher Stolte, fetched out of the dormitory to be told what had been broadcast from the people's receiver in his room: 'Your father was made Foreign Affairs Minister!'

Half asleep as I was, I did not see any particular reason to be pleased. I would now attract even more attention. I could not at the time foresee that such attention was to pursue me for the rest of my life, under the most diverse auspices and the most contradictory circumstances. In one way or another I would for ever, to this day, be seen as 'his father's son'. I did, however, learn fairly quickly how to adapt to this, to react accordingly and find out whether my interlocutor was speaking to me or to 'my father's son'.

I was given two days' leave from school to go and congratulate my father, and met my parents at the Kaiserhof Hotel, where they were living since they returned to Berlin from London, as our Dahlem house was locked up. It had not been foreseen when Father would return to Germany. I would have been wrong to think I would find Father ecstatic about his appointment. Rather, he was pensive. About his appointment, he wrote:

'My appointment to Foreign Minister of the Reich came as a complete surprise. On 30 January 1938 I was present in Berlin at the celebration of the anniversary of the accession to power, when Hitler asked me to stay on for a few days. It was the week of the so-called Blomberg crisis. On 4 February the Führer called me to him and disclosed that he wanted to make changes in various higher government posts in the framework of a reshuffle, among which was that of the foreign minister. The Reich's present Foreign Minister Neurath would be nominated President of the Secret Cabinet Council. I was to step into his shoes.

'When I took over the post, Adolf Hitler briefly put me in the picture of the general political situation. He said Germany had placed herself in a new position due to the Wehrmacht build-up and the occupation of the Rhineland. We were back in the circles of the nations of equal status and it was now the moment to find solutions to certain problems – problems that could be solved only with a strong army, not that it was in any way by its deployment but by the mere fact of its existence. "A country" – he said – "that is not also militarily strong cannot have any sort of foreign policy." We had sufficient evidence of that in the past years. It must now be our goal to come to clarified relations with our neighbours. The four problems he enumerated were Austria and the Sudetenland, Memel and Danzig with the Corridor. It would be my task to assist him in finding the diplomatic solution to these problems.'[169]

It was certainly not a coincidence – even if the so-called Blomberg-Fritsch crisis[170] was the ostensible cause – that Father was appointed Foreign Minister four weeks after depositing his ambassadorial Report, which could in fact be called a Memorandum on the situation of the Reich in foreign affairs. The Report makes Father's conclusions – in Hitler's sense – of the failure of the efforts undertaken at the Court of St James's eminently clear and soberly depicts the consequences for the future conduct of German foreign policy. Its concept, of a secure position of defence in Eastern Europe vis à vis the Soviet Union, thereby achieving the containment of Bolshevism, with the rear covered by Britain, appeared, at the time of Father's appointment, difficult to achieve. The only thing left to be done at present was to build up the German Central European position further, in the hope that the British leadership could finally still be persuaded that their Empire's future was indeed better secured in the long run by an alliance with the Reich than in a renewed confrontation.

Once again quoting my father:

> The goal of German foreign policy was to convince Britain that between the choices of a possible grouping of alliance [on the part of Germany] directed against Britain and a German-British alliance, the latter was the most preferable option [for Britain].'[171]

One could, as said before, add 'the most preferable option in Britain's situation would have been', and complete with 'as has been proved by history'! It will be shown that this concept definitely had a chance of being a reality. It will further be shown which Power – and its leading statesman – was responsible for foiling it, to the calamitous detriment of the British Empire.

It was not Hitler's wish to use the supposed, factitious armaments advance to wage war – it was mere propaganda, of which he had taken advantage, as he had of the temporary crippling of the Soviet Union from Stalin's 'purges' – but, on the contrary, to effect the amendments he aspired to without resorting to arms. It was feasible, which was how he had expressed himself in November of the previous year in the instances of Austria and Czechoslovakia. The way to do it, which he now had to put on the table, resulted from the British policy which evidently rejected any German courtship.

In business administration, in order to reach a decision, there is the so-called 'worst-case scenario' method. It means that all potential adverse consequences must be rehearsed in advance. It is to be applied for every important decision to be taken. If the German leadership had adopted this method to assess the situation of the Reich at the beginning of 1938, they would in all probability have come to the following result:

– Britain is playing to gain time so as to complete her rearmament and, unavoidable in a democracy, by propaganda to create the prerequisites of a domestic-policy psychological climate of envisaging an eventual confrontational course with the Reich.
– The same is valid for the French government, extended by the endeavour to mobilize their alliances in the 'Little Entente' against the Reich.
– The French alliance with the Soviet Union (concluded as early as 1935) constituted a serious threat to the Reich, accentuated by the participation of Czechoslovakia in the pact and the innate automatic triggering of anti-German sequences to follow.
– The Soviet Union is so to speak 'by definition' the declared enemy of the Reich. The government of the Reich may be sure that at any suitable opportunity it can be trusted to take the side of Germany's opponent, so as to expand its influence in Europe – eventually even by the use of force – westward.
– The United States will assume an ever-growing role in world politics. The 'Quarantine' speech of November 1937 leaves no leeway for doubt against whom the activities of the USA in foreign affairs will be directed.

All this being taken into consideration, Hitler should have proceeded from the danger that possibly at a given time he might be forced to solutions not agreeable to him and endangering the Reich, through a superior, overpowering coalition of those powers. This 'worst-case scenario' had an absolutely realistic basis – *nota bene* – albeit until the outset of 1938 Hitler had undertaken nothing that could have disturbed the famous balance of power in Europe.

The End of the 'Second German Partition'

Once again I was woken in the night by the Duty Master and fetched in to listen to his radio. He probably thought I knew more. We heard that 'in any case' – which is how the announcer expressed it – the German Army would invade Austria. I did not in fact know anything, and Father too, who was at the time in London for his farewell visit, was in a way taken by surprise. It is an interesting example of how Hitler worked, always keeping the end decision to himself and sometimes springing it at a moment when even in his entourage nobody expected it. There was frequently no systematic preparatory groundwork when steps were taken in foreign affairs. *Ad hoc* decisions were made instead, with which Hitler felt he had to react to unexpected developments, as in this case, the declaration by the Austrian Chancellor Schuschnigg of the separation of Austria from Germany to be made permanent as the result of a manipulated plebiscite.

Nevertheless, this swift move, which in the end was to lead to the *Anschluss* or union with Germany amid the jubilation of the Austrian population, was, in view of the current situation, only logical. At that time, particularly from the angle of the armaments build-up of the Western nations, there could be no other policy for Germany to follow but to reinforce the German position and hurriedly find a solution to the present problems in Eastern Europe. Irrespective, Austrian enthusiasm over the *Anschluss* was genuine. It is absurd nowadays to want to maintain anything else. There will certainly have been circles which were not against the *Anschluss* as such, but rejected the National Socialist regime. The matter of Austria's claim for *Anschluss* with Germany was raised at the German-Austrian National Assembly in November 1918. From its founding, the alpine republic had expressly seen itself as part of Germany. Referendums in the federal states (Bundesländer) of Salzburg and Tyrol had given consent for union with the German Reich of respectively 99 and 97 per cent. The Allies had thereupon prohibited further referenda. Karl Renner, the Foreign Minister, Austria's first federal president after 1945, had said in 1922 that Germany was the nation 'to which we belong by nature'. From 1918 Austria named herself 'German-Austria'. The name German-

Austria was prohibited in the peace treaty of Saint-Germain. Renner spoke of the 'second German partition' after 1867, when Austria first parted from the German federation, to which she had belonged for close to a thousand years since its foundation. The union of Austria with the Reich was without doubt a substantial reinforcement of Germany's position. Czechoslovakia, the 'air force mother-ship' of the French-Soviet alliance, was now better in hand. The relation to Italy, Germany's allied partner, had not been burdened, which was for Hitler a reason to feel he was henceforth personally bound to Mussolini – not always to the advantage of the German position. The full dimensions of the problem surrounding Hitler's dictatorship were now also imposed on a unified Austria. At the Ilfeld Napola we had from time to time posed ourselves the question how in fact the Reich would be constituted after Hitler. Basically, we were clear that an absolute dictatorship such as Hitler's could never be anything but an exception, and were perfectly prepared to acknowledge the extraordinary full powers Hitler had lain claim to based on his successes so far in regard to the position of the Reich. Our projections for the future were, to tell the truth, not very precise concerning a corporatively organized polity in common.

An English teacher of our form had arranged an exchange relationship with an English public school in Bath. Every year Ilfeld's seventh form was invited to Bath for a few weeks, and in return a group from Bath came to stay at Ilfeld. This is how it came about that in May 1938 our form was to travel to Bath. I was excited to see what a 'normal' public school, not as deeply entrenched in tradition as was Westminster School, would be like. Moreover, I was particularly interested to see the political ambience I would find. I had left England in July 1937; ten months had since passed. The map of Europe's states had altered through the inclusion of Austria in the German Reich. How would that be reflected in English public opinion?

Before going to Bath we briefly stopped over in London. The form of course had to know the Empire's capital city. Only too soon, to my profound dismay, I registered the altered political atmosphere in the capital. The British propaganda mechanism had toured in Germany. Films inflaming hostility against Germany were announced shortly to be shown in the major cinemas, with huge posters where the colour red intimated flowing blood; I have already spoken of the film with the martial drum major. The British establishment has always been very competent in manipulation of propaganda. The German Reich had already felt its effect in the First World War, when Lord Northcliffe and his news agency Reuters supplied the whole world with horror stories about Germany; for instance the notorious story of amputated children's hands in Belgium which the British ambassador in the United States, Lord Bryce, shared with the world. The Belgian Cardinal Mercier, and in 1922 a Belgian investigation committee, were not able to verify a single case of the alleged atrocities.[172] The appellation 'Huns' had unfortunately already been provided to British propaganda by Kaiser Wilhelm II in an unsuitable expression formulated on the occasion of a farewell speech addressed to the marine battalion departing for China to crush the Boxer Rebellion. In 1936/37, propaganda had still been moderate and was restricted to some sheets that were known to represent the anti-German coterie. A slanderous propaganda attack against potential or declared enemies is a standard constituent in politics, and in consequence legitimate. What is, however, astonishing is that the machinations of propaganda of our opponents were frequently sown on fertile ground in Germany and their contents believed.

We were nevertheless received in Bath in the friendliest way and integrated in the scholastic operation. At Bath there were none of Westminster School's rituals of ancient traditions, that had sometimes verged on the bizarre. However, in Bath the principle was also cultivated in the pupils of the greatest possible self-responsibility. As at Westminster, they were entrusted with the organization of games and sport, as well as many secondary activities, and also for free time. We were integrated in the curriculum and sports, as well as regular attendance at church, which plays a role of considerable importance in English schools.

The 1938 'May Crisis'

While I was in Bath I experienced the beginning of what was called the 'May Crisis' of 1938. Following the *Anschluss* of Austria in March of that year, Germany's position vis à vis Czechoslovakia was considerably improved. Many observers consequently expected a German attempt to take advantage of these new possibilities. The British press was working on the announcement of a sensational rumour that the German Wehrmacht was marching up to the Czech border to campaign against Czechoslovakia at any moment. Naturally, the rumour was taken up by the world's press, so in a very short time a particularly tense situation arose in world politics. The suspense was exacerbated when the head of the Czech government, Benesch, ordered mobilization of their armed forces, based on the alleged German troop movements. Benesch's goal was to expedite the developments to an ultimative situation, in the hope that it would bring about a direct confrontation of the Reich with France and hence with Britain. He hoped the Soviet Union would then stand by him as was provided for by the framework of the French-Russian military pact.

It must be said, however, that the 1938 'May Crisis' was not caused by German troop movements, for there had been none. I shall go so far as to say that at that moment a march of German armed forces to the Czech border was quite unfeasible for military reasons. The unexpected transfer of units of considerable numbers to Austria in the aftermath of the *Anschluss* had taken place only a few weeks ago. The Austrian federal army was to be integrated into the German Wehrmacht. In these circumstances it was unimaginable, even had it been desired, that a deployment against Czechoslovakia was possible from, so to speak, a standing start. There was no time to forge a plan. It must be borne in mind that on the Czech side, the Czech-German border was well fortified in places. What's more, it is worth restating that the entry of motorized German units into Austria had resulted in considerable difficulties.

Another minor indication that at that moment there was no plan on the part of Germany to invade Czechoslovakia is that the exchange trip of our class to the school in Bath went ahead. We had started out just a few days before the 'May Crisis'. It could of course not have taken place without the express permission of the parents for every pupil, if only for the reason of the extra expense. My parents too had not hesitated to agree to this trip to England.

In the English press, to which we had access at school, we followed political events a little. When the teacher who had organized the journey spoke to me about it, I assured him that I could not envisage that Germany had really planned a military incursion against Czechoslovakia, since in that case my parents would not only have forbidden my participation but would have dissuaded the establishment at Ilfeld from undertaking such a trip at that moment..

It is now no longer a matter for discussion among serious historians that in May 1938 on the German side there could have been any preparations of a military nature that could have been taken as a threat by Czechoslovakia. The British military attaché in Berlin could see for himself by taking a trip to the border area that there was no foundation to the rumours. Nevile Henderson, the British ambassador to Berlin, writes in his memoirs: 'The Germans had never mobilised, nor ... had they actually any intention at that time of a "coup" ... We had cried "Wolf, wolf" prematurely.'[173] He had advised London that 'There is no evidence here of any abnormal military preparation' by Germany against Prague.[174] On this point after the war the Nuremberg Tribunal found itself obliged to execute massive manipulation and did not admit the defence's submission of Henderson's final report as evidence, based on the argument that it did not contain historical facts![175]

The end of the Nuremberg trials unfortunately for a long time did not mark the end of such methods. May an amusing anecdote be allowed at this point, to show how today in Germany its recent history is presented? For any person interested in history, the book known as '*Ploetz*', the full title being *Ploetz, Auszug aus der Geschichte* (Digest of History), is a household name. It gives an overview and many details of world events, and therefore serves as a reference book. In Germany generations have grown up with it. It is arguable that what is formulated in *Ploetz* stands as the last word in historical research. My parents had given me *Ploetz* to read at a very early age, and it has accompanied me through my life, every newest volume as it is issued.

But I now have reason to doubt *Ploetz*'s reliability, for whereas in the 1951 issue on page 728 the entry for 20 May 1938 is (translated from the German) 'Mobilization of Czechoslovakia *due to alleged German troop concentration*', in the 1991 issue for the same date, on page 866 the entry is 'Mobilization of Czechoslovakia *due to German troop concentration*'.[176]

I contacted the *Ploetz* publishers (owned by Herder Publishers/Freiburg i. Br.) with a request for information as to the corresponding source, as the wording in 1991 gave a totally different and new statement of fact. The answer was quite astounding from a house that presents as being of scholarly accuracy, that the author of this excerpt (Professor Werner Conze) had died and that the sources were no longer available. It was only after I insisted, with reference to the standard historical authorities on the 'Sudeten Crisis', that the publishing house eventually 'thanked me for having drawn their attention to the matter, that it would be taken into account and corrected for the next issue'.[177] In the 1998 issue of *Ploetz*, on page 748 under the date 20 May 1938, it is noteworthy to see again 'Mobilization of Czechoslovakia due to German troop concentration'. It shows that distortion of pre-war history is not only a matter of the immediate post-war period or the attitude of the Allies, but is actually for a good part a home-made German product. What is the Herder house intending by this systematic concoction of history?

When in the spring of 1938 there was no reaction on the part of Germany to the allegations in the British press, it was triumphantly explained that Hitler had drawn back in the face of world opinion and cancelled his plans. In post-war literature it is sometimes claimed that this version had 'annoyed' Hitler by attributing weakness to him, and is what motivated him to provoke the 'Sudeten Crisis'.[178] Now, Hitler may very well have been annoyed by one or other foreign press release. There was occasion for it every so often. Father always regretted that he had no say in the *Pressevorlage* (trans., 'presentation of the press') to Hitler. He saw it in the sense of an adequate appraisal of the diverse newspapers in view of their importance. In order correctly to sort the publications of the foreign press and evaluate their pertinence in the sense of practical politics, there has to be a subtle perception of the press scene in each country and the background for it. Father quite rightly considered that only the Auswärtiges Amt could possess such knowledge, in all ramifications thereof. However, the Press Department of the Auswärtiges Amt was competing in this with what was called the 'Reich Press Chief', as well as with the Propaganda Ministry – they saw each other as competitors. It was to be expected that, above all for collaboration with the foreign press, it would lead to grave problems of competence. As a result, Hitler was sometimes unnecessarily informed about polemical headlines of insignificant provincial papers.

To revert to Hitler's 'annoyance' in 1938, which out of anger or even vengeance is supposed to have instigated the 'Sudeten Crisis', this picturesque image of the bad monster Hitler furiously hitting out may well be suitable for the purpose of 'educating' the population. But for an understanding of political events as they evolved in the summer of 1938 and were concluded at the Munich Conference, it is not helpful.

The 'May Crisis' unleashed by the British press, from which Benesch hoped that an automatic response of the French-British mutual defence alliance would be called forth, as well as the inclusion of the Soviet Union, had disappointed Hitler in the sense of what he hoped for and, understandably, made him thoughtful. Austria's *Anschluss* to the Reich had taken place amid the jubilation of the Austrian population, which can hardly be disputed even today. Nevertheless, just a few weeks later a campaign was launched from Britain that could easily have led to a real crisis. Germany could have the impression that in the UK a psychological mobilization was fabricated, with an unambiguous direction of impact against Germany. Viscount Halifax, the new British Foreign Minister following Anthony Eden's resignation, informed the German ambassador in London, Herbert von Dirksen, that Britain could be drawn into a conflict, for the French, 'in whatever circumstances, even in the event of serious acts of provocation by the Czechs', would march against Germany.

This was meant to be a diplomatically discreetly formulated threat, but on the other hand Viscount Halifax signalled clearly at the same time that he would be 'grateful for any suggestion and any proposal from the German Government'. The decisive point of view in this obvious poker game between Britain and the Reich was, in view of subsequent German policy, the situation of world politics. The '*tour d'horizon*' depicted above does not show a strong position of Germany in Central Europe. The armaments programme of the Western democracies was going ahead at full speed, so the time factor became ever more crucial. Hitler's directive for military preparations against Czechoslovakia is to be seen in this perspective. In the poker game over the Sudeten question, Hitler did not want to leave the initiative to the opposing side. In view of the commencing pressure of time, he had hardly any other choice and had to give the impression of vigorous decisiveness. He formulated it with the words: 'It is my unalterable decision to smash Czechoslovakia by military action in the near future.'[179] Father's statement to the representative of the French news agency Havas at a function during the crisis for the foreign press in Berlin was in line with this: 'We will solve the Sudeten problem in one way or another.' The chief of the Press Department of the Auswärtiges Amt, the envoy Dr Paul Schmidt,[180] who attended the discussion, asked on the spot for authorization to release the Foreign Minister's formulation to the press. He was given it.[181]

In this context an observation of my mother's about which she spoke to me after the Munich Agreement has great significance. She described the order of events of the crisis, coming to Hitler's well-known speech at the Sports Palace of 26 September 1938, at which point she said: 'When you know him you can tell he did not want to!' Mother's formulation 'did *not* want to'

'Czechoslovakia between the two World Wars'.

referred explicitly to military action. Her words were moreover couched in an unmistakeably critical tone, with the meaning that when one played poker one must also do it consistently. That is, that it should not in the least be allowed to be seen that one in reality 'did not want to', as she had expressed it. This comment of Mother's, which was even something of a criticism, demonstrates that on the part of Germany there was manifestly no wish to go to war over the Sudetenland. Why would there be? The matter was one of consolidating the German position in Central Europe by peaceful means to enable Germany to assert itself in the unfortunate situation of being between the Western Powers and the Soviet Union.

Conspiracy

Neither Hitler nor my father could have suspected that fellow players in high places were standing behind them with a view of their cards, and were actually signalling to the opponent on an ongoing basis in order to sabotage Germany's game. During the Sudeten Crisis, the group of conspirators around the State Secretary in the Auswärtiges Amt, Ernst von Weizsäcker, the former Chief of General Staff Ludwig Beck and the Chief of Counterintelligence Wilhelm Canaris were actively at work, through the most diverse channels, to induce the British government to take a hard line and keep to a stance of imperviousness towards German wishes. The grounds for such an approach to the British government, as has already been said, were based on the premise that German Foreign Minister Ribbentrop was consciously feeding Hitler with false information as to Britain's preparedness to go to war. On this basis Hitler believed he could push his demands through without Britain resorting to arms to counter him.

In fact, Father's reports from London, which have been given above, leave nothing to be desired in regard to the unambiguity of his evaluation of British politics. England was dangerous, and a dissolution of Czechoslovakia would most probably mean war with Prague and Paris, into which London could also be drawn; this was what Father had written in his Final Report. The conspirators were now suggesting that the British should send to Hitler a 'General with a riding crop' with which to bash the table. This was language he would understand. This had been thought out with subtlety, for – and this was naturally known to the conspirators – with Hitler's mentality such behaviour would call forth just the opposite reaction, namely a break-off of negotiations. This was precisely what the conspiracy desired and hoped for.

To encourage the British to run the risk of starting an armed conflict with Germany, which was then to unleash the military coup, through the emissaries of the German conspiracy – Ewald von Kleist-Schmenzin, Rittmeister a. D. Viktor von Koerber, Carl Goerdeler, Hjalmar Schacht, Erich Kordt and others – the domestic German situation was always depicted as one of desperation, divulging military secrets revealing the state of armament as miserable and the psychological state of the country as being ripe for an overthrow. It would be going beyond the framework of these personal memories to describe the activities of the conspiracy in detail. There exists a comprehensive literature on the subject.[182]

I shall therefore only refer here to two actions that were initiated in the summer of 1938, in close accord between General Staff Chief Ludwig Beck, Chief of Counterintelligence Admiral Wilhelm Canaris and his deputy Hans Oster, and above all State Secretary Weizsäcker.

On 18 and 19 August 1938 a certain Ewald von Kleist-Schmenzin visited Churchill and Vansittart in London. Kleist owned a manor in Farther Pomerania. He described himself as a monarchist, a Conservative and an enemy of Hitler. By his own account, throughout the 1920s he made a name for himself among his comrades of his class in intensive wage disputes with the Pomeranian rural workers. Shortly after the *Anschluss* of Austria, Kleist had urged the British journalist in Berlin, Ian Colvin, to induce the journalist's friends in London to counter Hitler's future claims with a categorical 'No'. Colvin was a high-ranking undercover agent of the Secret Service, posing as a journalist, who had maintained contact with the conspiracy in Berlin. Kleist imparted the most confidential military information to Colvin, such as the stocks of reservists and raw materials, the state of the fortifications in the west and so on. The Nazis were merely bluffing, he was always asserting to the British.[183]

He was not entirely wrong about this last assertion. Of course there was bluffing on the part of Germany, but it only goes to prove that there was no will to initiate military action. However, a precondition for such bluffing is that no 'mole', as such secret informants are called in espionage circles, betrays the cards in one's hand to the opponent. This, however, is exactly what Kleist-Schmenzin did, in agreement with Weizsäcker, Beck and others.

On 18 August he assured Vansittart that Hitler had decided on war and that it was up to 'Britain to stop him'. The date was already said to have been fixed. Chamberlain indeed maintained he knew the presumed date from Lord Lloyd, who had in turn been informed by a friend in army circles. On 19 August Kleist-Schmenzin had a meeting with Churchill, when he promised the latter that with the help of the generals a new system of government would be constituted within 48 hours, probably of a 'monarchist character': 'H. [Hitler] … wanted war.' Churchill indicated concessions in the colonial question and in economic relations. At this point Kleist-Schmenzin mentioned that 'his friends were not greatly concerned about the colonies, but that the Polish Corridor was the matter that affected them most'. This fetched a rebuff from

Churchill, to wit that 'it [the Corridor question] had been officially dropped by Germany, and this is certainly not the moment to discuss it'.[184]

In 1938 Churchill and Vansittart were both the most radical exponents of a policy in Britain inimical to Germany. This was known in political circles in Germany. Such knowledge may be imputed to the State Secretary in the Auswärtiges Amt, the Chief of the General Staff of the Army and the Chief of Counterintelligence Canaris, but also people such as Kleist-Schmenzin who were intruding into politics by conspiracy and who should have obtained that sort of information. All these gentlemen had experienced in the First World War that England's main concern was not to 'liberate' the poor Germans from their nasty Kaiser but to eliminate the Reich's position of power.

Once again, as so often in history, the classic 'Coriolanus Problem' arises. Coriolanus, a patrician and outstanding warrior in Rome's struggle with their Volscian neighbours, went over to the Volscian enemy in the course of the 'Scores fight' between patricians and plebeians – that is, therefore, on domestic political grounds – and led them in an assault on his native city. According to legend his mother and his wife succeeded in dissuading him from destroying it. This in turn led to the Volscians killing him as a traitor. In our case the question is posed as follows: is one allowed, on domestic political grounds – in other words to be rid of a dictator – to summon one's declared enemies to submit one's country to a war, when for the conspirators, albeit possibly by risking the participant's life, the potential definitely exists for them to remove this dictator?[185] Coming from me, it may seem somewhat amazing when at this point I decidedly regret that the attempted assassination of Hitler should have failed – as for our family it would, to say the least, have had quite uncomfortable repercussions – but the German people would have been spared terrible catastrophes.

When the conspiracy now demanded the restitution of the Corridor concurrently with their promise of a coup, it evidently saw it as a national issue. Their claim, almost as a reward for the promised coup, goes much farther than the later proposal addressed to Poland by Hitler, who would have been satisfied with Danzig and ex-territorial access to East Prussia; and note, with a guarantee for existing Polish borders, therefore also of the Corridor!

It is interesting that after Kleist's visit to London, Colvin remarked that in a meeting with Chamberlain, Halifax, Simon, Vansittart and Wilson, 'Sir Nevile was quite emphatic that there was no use in hoping for any opposition to Hitler.'[186] The ambassador in Berlin evidently knew his stuff.

However, the most significant activity – in the sense of influencing the British government to present an adamant front with no readiness to come to a compromise in negotiations with the Reich's government as to the future of the Sudeten Germans – was the work of Weizsäcker. Where Kleist-Schmenzin was concerned, from the British viewpoint he had merely been an unknown Pomeranian landowner. Churchill had nevertheless given him a letter – on the occasion of Kleist's visit – which the latter was to show all the personalities of consequence in Germany. The letter expressed the interest of Britain in the activities of the conspirators. After the bomb plot of 20 July 1944, the letter was found in Kleist's possession and led to his condemnation for treason. Koerber, as a retired officer, was attributed as belonging to 'reactionary' circles. The action of Weizsäcker, who was after all the second highest German official in the domain of foreign policy, had an entirely different dimension.

On 7 September 1938, the time that is when the Sudeten Crisis loomed, through Theo Kordt, the German chargé d'affaires in London, Weizsäcker had sent British Foreign Secretary Halifax a secret message in the name of the German conspirators. A cousin of the Kordt brothers (Erich Kordt was head of Father's ministerial office), Susanne Simonis, had learnt the content of the memorandum by heart and had transmitted it to Theo Kordt on a trip to London. On the night of 7 September Kordt went to No. 10 Downing Street, entering by a back door, and presented it to Halifax.

Kordt then clarified that he had not come in his capacity as German chargé d'affaires but as spokesman for the conspiracy. The message handed to Halifax professed that Hitler was planning an attack against Czechoslovakia. Weizsäcker was speaking on behalf of political and military circles which were forcibly against such a policy. He requested a statement from the British government that 'could not be unambiguous and strongly couched enough for the purpose we have in mind'. Weizsäcker furthermore said that the prospect of a war was unpopular in German public opinion. After Weizsäcker attributed the blame for the outbreak of the First World War to the then imperial German government, there follows the decisive passage:[187]

> 'If the requested statement is forthcoming, the army's leaders are prepared to act against Hitler's policy with resort to arms. A diplomatic defeat would be a setback for Hitler in Germany to be taken most seriously and would literally bring about the end of the National Socialist regime.'

In other words, Weizsäcker promises the British a coup if they come out with a strongly worded statement which places them in a situation of ultimatum from which they could not escape except with the gravest loss of prestige. That signified they would fight if necessary. It was what the conspiracy came down to. While Hitler was playing the negotiation poker game, his compatriot conspirators were signalling what cards were in his hand to the opponent, presenting them moreover as weaker than they actually were – which was already weak – to provoke a showdown. When the news was made known that the Munich Agreement would release 3.2 million Sudeten Germans from Czech overlordship by peaceful means and lead them into the Reich, one of the conspirators expressed his disappointment, saying that was the 'second best solution'. The 'best' would have been war![188]

It is hardly surprising that the British hesitated to satisfy the wishes of the conspirators. Britain's armament was still lagging behind, although the passage of time was in her favour. There would nonetheless also be time gained in the field of diplomacy. Roosevelt needed an interval in order to prepare American public opinion for an intervention in Europe and Asia. The 'bending' of the Axis at the Roman end was also not something to be accomplished in a day. The decisive point was indeed armament. Britain had eventually to consider having to enter into a war with the Reich if the conspiracy did not abide by its pledge to engineer a coup. It is well known that when war with Poland broke out a year later, the promise was in fact not kept and no coup was attempted.

There were furthermore two currents in Britain: one would rather ultimately come to an arrangement with Germany, in the correct acknowledgement that renewed armed conflict would signify the end of the Empire. The British ambassador in Berlin, Henderson, was probably of this view, however much he had always loyally represented his government's policy. The exponents in the other direction who wished to see, as Churchill had brutally formulated it, that an over-powerful Germany would once again be destroyed, were Winston Churchill, Robert Vansittart, Alfred Duff Cooper, Anthony Eden, Lord Lloyd and others. At this point in time, because of the Sudeten problem it was not desired to run the risk of war breaking out but most probably first to scrutinize in depth what was actually concealed behind the sensational offer made by the highest-placed German state officials. After the conclusion of the Munich Agreement, British Foreign Secretary Halifax told Theo Kordt, a German diplomat who coming through a back door in the dead of night had brought him Weizsäcker's message:

'We were not able to be as frank with you as you were with us. At the time that you gave us your message we were already considering sending Chamberlain to Germany.'[189]

Poland's Decision

When I was at Ilfeld we had a rather unclear perception of the 'Polish Corridor' issue, directed more towards a truly effective minority status than to radical solutions. We were well aware of the antagonism between Russia and Poland, and for me of course the German-Polish Pact of Non-aggression – spectacular in its day – of 1934 was absolutely of the present day. We did, however, also know that after the Great War, at the beginning of the 1920s, all Germans who did not want to become Polish had been expelled. That had been the first major expulsion of Germans from Poland. The offer made by Germany to Poland, in return for the unification of Danzig to the Reich and an ex-territorial railway and motor highway through the Corridor, to guarantee the entire Polish territory including the Corridor, was very far-reaching and comprehensible only in the framework of the Reich's anti-Soviet policy. It may definitely be taken as a fact that the German people at that time took the border's regulation with Poland as provisional. No German politician would have dared to offer the Poles a guarantee of the Corridor ... except Hitler!

I shall deal with events in order. The solution to the Sudeten Germans question had considerably alleviated the strategic and political danger of the Czechoslovakian position near the centre of German national territory. The threat was constituted not only by Czechoslovakia's geographical location, but also by the political possibilities of a government inimical to Germany that could, via automatic alliance, unleash the action of the French-Russian-British coalition against the Reich, which had been Benesch's aim. In any case Czechoslovakia, albeit reduced, continued to exist and still possessed a well-armed military force.

The year 1938 had therefore brought about a substantial reinforcement of the German position. The German dilemma could be considered as more or less solved. If the relationship with its eastern neighbour Poland could now be freed of all ambiguity and possible flashpoints of dispute, Germany's position would be secure. Poland was the last stone in the wall that Hitler wanted to raise against Bolshevik Russia. It was, however, also a hornet's nest. The Polish Republic had remained constantly active over recent years. First of all an attack on Germany was contemplated after the abrogation of the demilitarization of the Rhineland, they then utilized Austria's *Anschluss* to the Reich to force Lithuania to finally formally acknowledge the annexation of Vilnius – dating from 1920 – and then set out to batten on Czech territory, the so-called 'Olsagebiet', during the 'Sudeten Crisis'. At the time, British newspapers spoke openly of 'plundering of corpses'. There were no objections on the part of Germany, who did not intervene in Polish-Czech relations, as neither did the other powers of the Munich Agreement. As I remember it, after occupying the Olsagebiet, the Poles began taking action against the German population there too.

Nevertheless, Hitler consistently continued his anti-Bolshevik policy, still – regardless of the experience of 1938 – oriented in a pro-Western direction. Hitler saw in Poland the 'born' federal ally against Russia. In the German concept, the traditional good relations between Poland and France should be no obstacle to a basic agreement with Poland. On the contrary, an arrangement with Poland might perhaps yet still achieve a prospect of fundamental points of agreement about Europe with both Western powers or the obtaining of a covering of Germany's rear against the Soviet Union. In order to win Poland over, Hitler was prepared to go to the most generous lengths to find solutions acceptable to Poland. He offered Poland an accommodation that every Weimar government would have overthrown, had anything comparable even been thought of. In the Reichstag on 18 May 1925, Stresemann had declared:

> 'There is no-one in Germany who could admit that the borders drawn in the East in flagrant contradiction to the right to self-determination of the people were forever an unalterable fact. No regulation of the question of security can therefore be taken into consideration that included a renewed acknowledgement of these frontiers.'

On 7 September 1925, Stresemann wrote to Crown Prince Wilhelm as follows:

> 'The third great task is the readjustment of our eastern frontiers; the recovery of Danzig, the Polish Corridor, and a correction of the frontier in Upper Silesia.'[190]

On 24 October 1938, the day on which Father had his first meeting with Lipski, the Polish ambassador, a phase in world politics began which, in its drama and tragedy, led to such intensification of events as is rarely recorded in history. The proposals put forward to the Poles were to open the path for formation of an alliance in the sense of the German–Italian settlement (South Tyrol to remain Italian, in exchange for which Italy would accept the *Anschluss* of Austria). The rendering of Father's discussions with Lipski follow below, according to the notes he dictated to the then Legation Councillor Hewel:[191]

'Adolf Hitler wanted to reach a finalized clarification with Poland and had charged me already in October 1938 to negotiate with the Polish ambassador for settlement of the questions pending between Germany and Poland.

'Thereupon I asked the Polish ambassador to Berchtesgaden where we had our first discussion on 24 October 1938 about Danzig and the Corridor complex issue ...

'Then I expounded to the Polish ambassador that it was time to make a clean sweep of all existing possibilities of friction between Germany and Poland – as the crowning of the work inaugurated by Marshal Piłsudski and the Führer. I instanced our relations with Italy as an example. In that case also with deep insight for the sake of a general settlement the Führer had renounced all claims to South Tyrol once and for all. A similar agreement was worth attempting with Poland and would be useful for Poland; and it accorded with our policy of establishing amicable relations with all our neighbours. I mentioned in this context that there also existed a possibility that with France – beyond the German renunciation of Alsace-Lorraine – even clearer accommodations might be achieved ...

'I then sketched out my thoughts to Lipski as to how I broadly saw a solution:

1. The Free City of Danzig to return to the German Reich. Danzig was German – it always had been German, and would remain German.
2. An extra-territorial motor-road belonging to Germany to be built across the Corridor, and likewise an extra-territorial railway with several tracks.
3. Poland likewise to obtain in the territory of Danzig an extra-territorial road or motor-road, a railway, and a free port.
4. Poland to obtain a guarantee for the sale of her goods in Danzig territory.
5. The two nations to recognize their common frontiers, and it could eventually come to a territorial guarantee.
6. The German-Polish treaty to be extended to 25 years. The two countries to add to the treaty a stipulation providing for consultation.

'Lipski kept a very reticent stance and replied that he had first to speak to Mr Beck, but pointed out that Danzig was in no way a product of Versailles, like the Saar Territory, for instance. One must follow the growth of Danzig historically and geographically to get a correct angle.

'I asked the Polish ambassador not to give me an answer now to my proposals but to brief Mr Beck as soon as possible. I pointed out to Lipski that it must not be overlooked that for reasons of home politics a final renunciation as to the Corridor was not easy for the Führer too; one must think in terms of centuries: Danzig after all was German and would remain so. In the course of our talk I extended an invitation to the Polish Foreign Minister Beck at a date to be fixed.'

Lipski's reaction was reticent, although he had been asked to think things over and await his instructions. The decisions were after all of great moment. A further discussion followed on 19 November 1938 between my father and Lipski, who meanwhile had received his instructions from Warsaw:

'Lipski then read portions of his instructions aloud from a slip of paper: The Minister for Foreign Affairs Beck was of opinion that German-Polish relations had in general stood the test. During the Czech crisis it had been shown that German-Polish relations stood on a durable foundation. Foreign Minister Beck considered that Poland's policy had been of use to Germany when the latter acquired possession of the Sudeten German Territory, and had contributed materially to the attainment of a solution of this question in accordance with German views. During the critical days the Polish Government had turned a deaf ear to all lures coming from a certain quarter. (This was correct, for Poland had territorial claims in regard to Czechoslovakia. Furthermore the British attempt to include Russia in the Munich negotiations had met with Poland's reticence.)

'I answered Mr Lipski that in my opinion too the German-Polish Agreement had shown itself capable of withstanding considerable strain. The Führer's action against Czechoslovakia had enabled Poland to gain possession of the Olsa territory, and to satisfy a number of other wishes with regard to frontiers. For the rest I agreed with him that the Polish attitude had made things easier for Germany.

'Lipski then made a lengthy speech to prove the importance and value which Danzig had as a Free City. For reasons of home politics too it was difficult for Foreign Minister Beck to assent to the incorporation of Danzig in the Reich. Beck had been revolving the question in his mind how all friction about Danzig which might possibly arise between Germany and Poland could be done away with once and for all. His idea was that the League of Nations' Danzig Statute might be replaced by a German-Polish treaty dealing with all Danzig questions. This treaty might be based, thought Beck, on the recognition of Danzig as a purely German town with all rights resulting from this, whilst on the other hand Poland and the Polish minority should likewise have all economic rights assured to them, whereby the character of Danzig as a Free State and the customs union with Poland would be preserved.

'I answered Mr Lipski that I regretted Foreign Minister Beck's attitude. The suggestion for a permanent solution of the German-Polish problem by which Danzig fell to Germany might increase Mr Beck's burden in home politics, but on the other hand it was obvious that it would also be no easy matter for the Führer to tell the German people that he was guaranteeing the Polish Corridor. The purpose underlying my suggestion was to establish German-Polish relations on a lasting foundation, and to do away with all possible points of friction. It had not been my intention to have a diplomatic chat. As Lipski could perceive from the Führer's speeches, the latter had always taken a long view in dealing with the German-Polish question. In his presence, at a recent meeting of international press representatives, I had made it clear that good German-Polish relations were fundamental to German policy.

'Lipski thanked me for these remarks, and returned to the proposal for a bilateral treaty about Danzig. I explained to him that I could not give a final decision on this, but to me the proposal did not seem easy of accomplishment, and on my side was asking what Beck thought about the question of an extra-territorial motor-road and of a double-track railway through the Corridor. Lipski could not make any official pronouncement. For his own person he could say that such a wish might conceivably not fall on barren ground, and that perhaps opportunities might occur for finding a solution in this direction.

'After I had spoken to Lipski about the Polish postage stamps just issued, which were intended for Danzig use and which represented Danzig as if it were a Polish town, in closing I said:

'It was my opinion that it would repay trouble to give serious consideration to German proposals dealing with the whole complex of German-Polish relations. It was desired here to create something lasting on both sides and to bring about a real stabilization. Naturally that could not be done in a day. If Mr Beck would think over our proposals quietly, he might perhaps see his way to adopting a positive attitude.'

Apparently the Polish government no longer considered the matter required by them for many years of recognition of the existing German-Polish borders as important as previously. As to this aspect of the German proposition Lipski did not say a word. Thereupon Father had held out the prospect of a 'Guarantee of the Territories', a guarantee that would also have been valid for Poland vis à vis the Soviet Union. The Reich could not condone an aggression by the Soviet Union against Poland. How seriously, on the other hand, the proposals addressed to Poland were taken in Berlin was manifested by the invitation to Polish Foreign Minister Beck to a meeting with Hitler in Berchtesgaden, or in Munich. In the documents Father left he gives a summary account of the discussions that took place between Hitler and Beck on 5 January on the Obersalzberg and between Father and Beck in Munich on 6 January 1939:

'The continuation of the negotiations followed in the course of the visit that the Polish Foreign Minister Beck paid to Germany on my invitation at the beginning of January 1939. On 5 January a lengthy discussion took place between Adolf Hitler and Beck in Berchtesgaden. I subsequently then had another talk with the Polish Foreign Minister in Munich. The outcome of these negotiations was not particularly encouraging. Beck was not however totally non-cooperative. He explained that the problem was very difficult but that he would work on his fellow members of the government so as to find a solution. The thread was consequently not severed and Beck invited me to Warsaw, which visit took place but a few weeks later on 25 January 1939. Neither at these discussions in Warsaw did negotiations advance much: Beck confined himself to repeating the difficulties he faced. Once again I pointed out that the German populations in Poland were in an unendurable situation, and the derogatory state the Corridor signified for Germany. Beck promised his favourable response in the population question and wished to submit the other issues to "further examination".

'On conclusion of our talks in Warsaw I invited the Polish Foreign Minister to an official visit to Berlin. On 21 March I reiterated the invitation to Ambassador Lipski, assuring him once again that upon settlement of the Danzig and motor highway question the Führer was prepared to give Poland his guarantee of the Polish borders. I stressed the fact that no previous German government had been in a position to give such a guarantee. However, Beck did not go to Berlin and instead went to London.'[192]

Hitler had made his proposals to Poland known to world public opinion in his well-known speech to the Reichstag on 28 April 1939, stating explicitly how he regretted that – 'to him incomprehensibly' – they had been rejected by the Polish government. He had further extended his offer by being prepared, jointly with Poland and Hungary, to safeguard the new Slovak state, which, as he formulated it, meant 'in practice the renunciation of any unilateral German hegemony in this territory'.

On 4 May 1939, Henderson, the British ambassador in Berlin, in a letter to Foreign Secretary Halifax took up a position in regard to Hitler's rejected offer to Poland:

British Embassy, Berlin, May 4, 1939

Dear Secretary of State,

... Once again the German case on the immediate issue is very far from being either unjustifiable or immoral. If an impartial Martian were to act as arbitrator I cannot believe that he would give judgment otherwise than more or less in accordance with Hitler's offer. Did he count on its being refused?

My thesis has always been that Germany cannot revert to normalcy ... until her legitimate (in German eyes) aspirations have been satisfied. The Danzig-Corridor question was, with Memel, one of these ... It must be borne in mind that Danzig and the Corridor was the big question prior to 1933. One of the most unpopular actions which Hitler ever did was his 1934 Treaty with Piłsudski ... Today all the most moderate Germans, who are opposed to a world war, are behind him in his present offer to Poland ... According to my Belgian colleague, practically all the diplomatic representatives here regard the German offer in itself as a surprisingly favourable one. The Dutch Minister, the United States Chargé d'Affaires and my South African colleague have themselves spoken to me in that sense. I consequently ask myself whether, if we are going to fight Germany, is it well-advised to do so on a ground on which the world will not be united as to the immorality of Germany's case? Will even our Empire be united? *Of course the underlying motive of war will be something far deeper and more important than just Danzig itself*[193] ... Even so I am appalled at the thought of Danzig being even the ostensible cause, and I am even more appalled at our fate being in the hands of the Poles.

Heroic no doubt but foolhardy and ask anyone who knows them whether they can be trusted. Did Beck even play fair in London over the German offer? Ribbentrop asked me yesterday whether Beck had informed His Majesty's Government when he was in London of the German offer. I was obliged to say that I honestly did not know: to which Ribbentrop replied that his information from London was to the effect that he did not ...

The German people are sick of adventure but Poland and the Corridor with the spectre of 'encirclement' and 'Soviet Russia' in the background is a battle cry which would be more likely than any other to rally the whole nation.'[194]

One may well ask oneself exactly why the British government, and above all the American President Roosevelt, did not stringently advise the Polish government to accept the German proposition, whereby the Reich would have had fixed borders as they currently stood. The letter shows that Henderson is 'appalled' by the thought of war. He knows that Danzig is but an 'ostensible cause'; something that is much 'deeper and more important' lies at the heart of the motives for war than 'just Danzig itself'. Henderson unveils here the true fundamental trends of British policy: decisive for Britain is – as in 1914 – the demolition of the Reich's position of power in Central Europe. He explicitly characterizes the German question itself as 'very far from being either unjustifiable or immoral'.

Henderson seems to be against a war with Germany. As a reminder, I refer to Father's Ambassadorial Report (the Report on the Coronation) reproduced above, in which he transmits a confidential item of information according to which Henderson had been 'not very edified' by his first discussion with the Foreign Office before undertaking his posting to Berlin. This is not surprising, since his briefing as to the duties that he was to fulfill had without doubt been by Vansittart.

Beck mentions among other things, from the discussion between Father and Lipski on 21 March 1939:

'Ribbentrop touched on all questions that had been tabled by Germany since October 24th 1938: the question of a broad-based Polish-German settlement, also of an anti-Russian collaboration, the threat of Germany reverting to the Rapallo policy.'[195]

Beck confirms the anti-Bolshevik goal set by the German policy. However, his final statement cannot be cross-checked: it is unlikely that at this point

Father should have threatened Poland with a reversion to the 'Rapallo policy'. The matter had not yet progressed that far, although Father had pondered the issue. In this context a report by Karl Julius Schnurre, an envoy in those days, is interesting. Schnurre was chief of the Auswärtiges Amt's commercial policy department and, among other issues, dealt with the discussions on trade with the Soviet Union that had never been entirely broken off. He writes:

'In the weeks following the conclusion of the Munich Conference my talks were intensified with the then Chief of the Soviet commercial representation Skossyrew about a new contract of credit for 200 million Reichsmark for a 6 year duration. The contract hinged on the condition that militarily necessary raw materials should be delivered for ¾ of the amount.

'These efforts had the support of a *démarche* on the part of the ambassador in those days Merekalov, who came to the Auswärtiges Amt with Skossyrew and declared his government's preparedness to conduct negotiations on this basis.

'Merekalov suggested Moscow as the place for the negotiations. The deliveries of militarily necessary raw material were of great interest to the German side but there was reluctance at this time to introduce commercial negotiations with the Soviet Union of more substantial dimensions. Instead, Ribbentrop called me in and asked me if I could not travel to Moscow to visit my friend the ambassador Count von der Schulenburg and on the occasion undertake to introduce the subject of economic negotiations with the People's Commissar Mikoyan. My reply to Ribbentrop was that it was perfectly feasible since I was in constant contact with Mikoyan about the commercial representation, especially as I had an appointment with the Polish governmental committee in Warsaw for mid-January, so that I could go on from there to Moscow without arousing curiosity. Ribbentrop then charged me with a corresponding assignment and I arranged with our Embassy Counsellor in Moscow Hilger for a meeting with Mikoyan on 31 January 1939.

'It was agreed with Count von der Schulenburg, who at the time was in Berlin, that we would travel together from Warsaw to Moscow. I therefore set out in mid-January, first to Warsaw where I would conduct my discussions with the Polish governmental committee. At the same time however, Ribbentrop was in negotiation with the Polish Foreign Minister Colonel Beck in Warsaw over the questions of the Corridor and Danzig and Poland's stance toward the Soviet Union. Unfortunately, through some indiscretion, probably from the Polish side, my planned trip was leaked to the Western Press. [The] *Daily Mail* and a few French and Polish papers published information – sensationally couched – of a large German delegation under my direction travelling to Moscow allegedly for economic negotiations. An abundance of cartoons about this trip appeared in the Western press. The familiar Western spectre of a renewed German-Russian Rapallo contract was painted in all colours.

'Ribbentrop was shocked and took the publicity as a disruption of his talks with Colonel Beck. He notified me that I was to cut my visit short and return to Berlin immediately. My remonstrances that I did already have a fixed date for a meeting with Mikoyan made no difference in his order to annul my Moscow trip. I informed Hilger and cancelled the meeting with Mikoyan of 31 January 1939. I went back to Berlin, and Count von der Schulenburg, who was going to accompany me from Warsaw on the journey to Moscow, went there alone.'[196]

How did the world political situation present itself after Munich in regard to Germany, and what were the prospects of success for the German government in the acceptance by Poland of their propositions?

Polish Foreign Minister Beck is said to have stated to the French Foreign Minister, Laval, in Geneva in January 1935:

'History teaches us, firstly, that the greatest catastrophe to which our country fell victim was the outcome of the joint action of the two states [Germany and Russia] and secondly that in this desperate situation no power in the world came to our support.'[197]

The lesson he and his 'teacher' Piłsudski should have learned from this ascertainment was the obvious and correct conclusion that in doubtful circumstances one could have no confidence in the Western Powers. Taking advantage of the momentary weakness of both its neighbours in 1917/18, Poland had snatched major parts of the abutting states. It was another case of lack of gratitude, as is usual in politics, for Poland had the imperial German policy to thank for her resurrection, which policy wanted to see a buffer erected between Germany and the giant country of the East. Furthermore, Germany was under the illusion that she could count on the support of Poland because of this stance. Poland also had the problem of being in the 'middle place', which for that country was even more difficult to solve than it was for the German Reich, that found itself in a similar position. Poland was not even close to reaching a level of military force comparable to the Reich's to defend her existence between two superpowers: namely Germany and Russia.

Nevertheless, in this precarious situation Poland did not opt for one of her neighbour states, and instead relied on the alliance with France. Since Versailles, Poland now had nothing to fear from Germany; on the contrary, it occasionally occurred to them that they could squeeze more territory from a defenceless Reich. With regard to the Soviet Union, they tried to ensure security through non-aggression pacts, after Piłsudski's campaign of conquest in the Ukraine failed to have the desired success and a compromise had been reached by the Peace of Riga that did not fulfil Polish expectations.

The German Reich's regaining of strength gradually began to fundamentally alter these premises of Polish foreign policy. Already in 1936, in Paris, the Polish government had put out feelers for a common action to be taken against Germany, based on the reinstatement of full German sovereignty in the still demilitarized Rhineland. Hitler had not begrudged the Poles these considerations. He is said to have stated:

'The Rhine bridges were even more important for Beck than they were for the French, for whoever wants to speed to the assistance of Poland out of France must speedily cross the Rhine. Only an idiot could consequently be horrified or offended that nothing was more fervently desired by the Polish General Staff than that the Rhine bridges should remain in the hands of their French ally.'[198]

Poland had not exactly made itself popular in British public opinion during the Sudeten Crisis because of the annexation of the Olsa region. From the German viewpoint, there was a lot to be said for Poland's quitting her 'balancing act' and making a choice under the altered relations of power politics in Central and thereby also Eastern Europe. Since in the opinion of the League of Nations Commissioner Burckhardt the Poles were more afraid of the Russians than of the Germans, it was thought in Berlin that there was a chance of coming to terms with Poland. The unification of Danzig with the Reich – Danzig being in any case, as has already been said, under National Socialist administration – and an ex-territorial connection between the two parts of the German Reich providing the guarantee of the Polish borders – not of the Corridor alone but also of the industrial region of Upper Silesia – must after all have been extraordinarily attractive to Poland. It must not be overlooked in this context that thereby a guarantee of the Polish eastern border against Soviet aggression would *de facto* also be given, for Hitler could not condone a Russian attack on Poland.

The German policy was still consistent. The starting point was the formation of a defensive front against the Bolshevik Soviet state and the securing of a cover for its back in the West, i.e. through Britain and France, at least in the sense of political neutrality; in other words a free hand in Eastern Europe, meaning the tolerance of an Eastern European, anti-Bolshevik system of alliance under German leadership.

It has been shown here that in view of the refusal of Britain and France to be fundamentally of one mind as to Germany's position in Central Europe, Germany had no other choice initially but to build up that position as swiftly as possible, in the hope that in the end there would come about an insight from both Western governments into the necessity and obviousness of a strong German presence in Eastern Europe.

This hope had foundation, as is for example demonstrated by an interesting document from the British archives: a letter from the British Foreign Secretary, Halifax, to the British ambassador in Paris, Sir Eric Phipps, dated 1 November 1938.[199] Excerpts from this letter, which may absolutely be seen as a memorandum regarding future British policy, are reproduced below:

'My dear Phipps,
'In your despatch No. 1120 of October 4 you referred to the view which is sometimes expressed that the French Government might be tempted by German intrigue to drift apart from His Majesty's Government. Like you, I have never lent much credence to this theory, which does not to my mind take into sufficient account fundamental facts which underlie Franco-German relations.

'The position, as I see it, is rather as follows: there can be no assured peace in Europe unless genuine agreement can be reached between Germany, Great Britain and France.

'One of the chief difficulties of the past has been the unreal position which France was occupying in Central and Eastern Europe. She claimed great influence in the policies of the Central European States in virtue of her system of alliances, but owing to the rising strength of Germany, and France's neglect of her own defences, she could no longer count upon being able to make her claims effective. At the same time, the fact of France making these claims was a continual irritant to Germany. With the conclusion of the Munich Agreement and the drastic change in French policy in Central Europe which that involves, Franco-German relations should have a fresh start.

'Henceforward we must count on German predominance in Central Europe. Incidentally I have always felt myself that, once Germany recovered her normal strength, this predominance was inevitable for obvious geographical and economic reasons.

'In these conditions it seems to me that Great Britain and France have to uphold their predominant position in Western Europe by the maintenance of such armed strength as would render any attack upon them hazardous. They should also firmly maintain their hold on the Mediterranean and the Near East. They should also keep a tight hold on their Colonial Empires and maintain the closest possible ties with the United States of America.

'The greatest lesson of the crisis has been the unwisdom of basing a foreign policy on insufficient armed strength. In my letter to you of October 28 I spoke of the efforts which we are making to fill up the gaps in our own defences and the importance we attach to France doing likewise. It is one thing to allow German expansion in Central Europe, which to my mind is a normal and natural thing, but we must be able to resist German expansion in Western Europe or else our whole position is undermined. It would be fatal to us to be caught again with insufficient strength.

'But provided this "lay-out" is clearly grasped and its requirements in terms of adequate armed strength are adopted, I see no harm, indeed the reverse, in any direct Franco-German discussions which may improve the atmosphere ...

'The immediate future must necessarily be a time of more or less painful readjustments to the new realities in Europe. While my broad conclusion is that we shall see Germany consolidate herself in Central Europe, with Great Britain and France doing the same in Western Europe, the Mediterranean and overseas, certain factors remain obscure. What is to be the role of Poland and of Soviet Russia? If the Poland of Beck, as I take to be the case, can never ally herself with Soviet Russia, and if France, having once burnt her fingers with Czechoslovakia, relaxes her alliance with Poland the latter can presumably only fall more and more into the German orbit. Soviet Russia, on the other hand, can scarcely become the ally of Germany so long as Hitler lives, although there are obvious economic reasons for bringing them together; she may choose to go into isolation or else she may prefer to maintain contact with the Western Powers through the French alliance.

'There is also the problem raised by possible German expansion into the Ukraine. Subject only to the consideration that I should hope France would protect herself – and us – from being entangled by Russia in war with Germany, I should hesitate to advise the French Government to denounce the Franco-Soviet pact as the future is still far too uncertain!

…

'Finally, we hope that the bringing into force of the Anglo-Italian Agreement will improve our relations with Italy and that France will succeed in doing likewise. Although we do not expect to detach Italy from the Axis, we believe the Agreement will increase Mussolini's power of manœuvre and so make him less dependent on Hitler, and therefore freer to resume the classic Italian role of balancing between Germany and the Western Powers.'

This 'lay-out' of a possible British policy, as Halifax formulated it in his letter to Phipps, corresponds very broadly to the German concept of the political new order in Eastern Europe as it appeared to become a reality at the end of 1938. Halifax's starting point is from an unambiguous division of interests in Western Europe. This had already been acknowledged, in advance, by the formal renunciation on the part of Germany of Alsace-Lorraine and the recognition of British supremacy at sea. He starts out from the corresponding positions of France and Britain in the Mediterranean and in the Middle East. Here Father's dissent over a German intervention favouring Franco in Spain should be brought to mind.[200] It should in any case be emphasized that after the termination of the Spanish Civil War Germany again withdrew entirely out of Spain. Halifax considers German supremacy in Central and Eastern Europe as normal and natural. He sets out the immutable opposition between Germany and the Soviet Union that Hitler had repeatedly expressed as fundamental to his policy. He realizes the possibility of a *de facto* gain of equilibrium thereby, which is why he advises France not to abandon the pact with Russia. In the entire concept he explicitly sees the possibility of concentration on retention of the colonial empires as heretofore.

He assesses entirely correctly the position, so far unclarified, of Poland, which, however, he sees as sooner or later within the German field of influence. In other words this indicates the 'free hand' desired by Germany in Eastern Europe in order to organize it against Bolshevism. The wish and the hope of the British Foreign Secretary not to become involved in any eventual Eastern

European quarrels should actually have led to a declaration of neutrality by the West in the eventuality of a state of war developing in Eastern Europe. Intensive efforts in rearmament by Britain and France were militarily to underpin such a policy.

The British Foreign Secretary sees a way for additional securement of his policy when he writes 'and maintain the closest possible ties with the United States of America'. It was because of this that an unprecedented drama in world politics unfolded, that led in the end to Britain's complete dependence on the United States. However, by then the executor of the policy was no longer Halifax, but Churchill, who was to shift Halifax from the post of Foreign Secretary in his cabinet to that of British ambassador in Washington.

On 20 November 1938, Father received the French ambassador in Berlin, Robert Coulondre, who followed François-Poncet when the latter was transferred to Rome (in order to 'bend' the Berlin-Rome axis at the weaker end). The notes recording the discussion include the following:

'Ribbentrop: "[an] agreement ... would be much easier ... [if] the European states ... confine themselves to their own actual interests – France to her great colonial territories, Britain to her Empire, and Germany to her particular sphere of interest, namely, southeast Europe." M. Coulondre ... said that he regarded the question in precisely the same light.'[201]

In December 1938 Father went on an official visit to Paris in order to sign a German-French declaration stating that both countries had no territorial questions pending between them and that they mutually guaranteed their borders.

In the course of this visit to Paris two lengthy discussions took place between French Foreign Minister Bonnet and Father. What Bonnet had to say could only be taken by Father as being in the sense of a French statement of abstinence with a view to Eastern Europe. A very detailed investigation in 1963 by the chief at that time of the Auswärtiges Amt's Press and Information department, the envoy Dr Paul Schmidt, a member of the German delegation, confirmed this.[202] A report by the British ambassador, Phipps, addressed to Sir Orme Sargent in the Foreign Office even mentions rumours from 'well informed circles' in Paris that Bonnet had told the German Foreign Minister that in the case of German action in the Ukraine, France would not react.[203]

In this context, the account as given in his memoirs[204] by the French ambassador in Warsaw at that time, Léon Noël, of a discussion with Bonnet that took place before Father's visit to Paris, in November 1938, is of interest. Noël says (in translation from the German edition):

> 'M. Bonnet interrupted my very first words to prove to me that our treaties with Poland allowed us sufficient elbow space to permit our country to stay out of a war whatever happened. He scrutinized them under a microscope, took pleasure in a juridical analysis and saw himself secured thereby. I warned him against that sort of consideration, remarking that we were no longer as in the days of our long-ago youth in a courtroom, with the task to administer justice and were instead face to face with international conditions that were in fact of the most brutal. He told me upon this that he had decided to disregard my suggestion. To hear him speak this way showed that he had decided – simply and completely – without hesitation to cancel all treaties concluded by France. He also meant thereby – aside from the French-Polish treaty – the French-Soviet pact of mutual assistance. To this I countered that it would make more sense not to break up with Poland entirely nor to abstain from the support that our army could expect from the Polish army, which was famous for its bravery. I emphatically insisted that the issue should be restricted to stripping the French-Polish alliance of its automatic character.
>
> 'Our lengthy discussion ended on the most formal of notes. I was to be instructed to commence negotiations with Joseph Beck with the purpose of revising our treaties.'[205]

In a report dated 17 December 1938[206] addressed to the Polish Foreign Minister, the Polish ambassador in Paris quotes the French Foreign Minister. Bonnet had told him quite spontaneously that he had pointed out to Father the 'abnormality' of the French alliance with Poland and the pact with Soviet Russia.[207] Although Bonnet may be of a vacillating nature he had given Ribbentrop his assurance that 'France would not oppose German economic expansion in the Danube basin'. Furthermore, Juliusz Łukasiewicz, at that time Polish ambassador to France, thinks that Ribbentrop 'could not have failed to leave Paris with the impression that also a political expansion in this direction would not meet with any determined action on the part of the French'.[208]

That Bonnet was in fact harbouring considerations in such a direction is confirmed by the indication in the letter already quoted from British Foreign Secretary Halifax to Phipps, the ambassador in Paris: '[He hesitates] to advise the French Government to denounce the Franco-Soviet pact as the future is still far too uncertain!'

In rounding off, the London *Times* correspondent was quoted as having said on 16 March 1939:

'There is no doubt, that after Munich the leaders of the French Government believed and hoped that Germany would continue her eastward drive, and, as a price of French complacence [(interposition in the German text) complaisance is probably meant], leave this country in peace.'[209]

The German government cannot be reproached with having neglected to prepare their policy for the reorganization of Eastern Europe with an anti-Bolshevik objective systematically and carefully. In the discussions with Hitler and Father, Beck had repeatedly pointed out that the restitution of Danzig to the Reich made for great difficulties in domestic policy. On the German side it was hoped that a recognizable distancing on the part of France from its previous policy dictated by the 'Little Entente', which was directed against Germany, would reduce the influence of the circles inimical to Germany in Poland in a natural way and possibly free the path to a major arrangement with Poland. Such an agreement, which would guarantee Poland her borders, must be agreeable to France too because, according to the reasoning, it would also hinder an expansion of the Reich in Eastern Europe so that with a view to Poland, who was still her ally, France would not lose face in this respect.

Consequently the German Foreign Minister could by all means travel to Warsaw armed with a certain optimism. In his investigation, Schmidt (Press) quotes him as saying:

'Beck tends toward a *folie de grandeur* and would like to conduct world politics the British way: "Balance of Power"! [author's note: between Germany and Russia is meant here.] However, Mr Beck learned in 1936 that the French would not so readily be prepared to facilitate his "Balance of Power" with French blood at the river Weichsel!'[210]

This closes the circle. The declarations of the French Foreign Minister to Father that France was not interested in Eastern Europe should in theory have had the effect on the Polish government of coming to an arrangement with the Reich, above all because at the same time exceptionally favourable terms were being offered. Without the support, reticence of the French alliance and the so-called 'Little Entente', Beck's conception of the 'balance' between Germany on the one side and Russia on the other could not be sustained. Since the Poles feared the Bolsheviks even more than the Germans – as was the opinion in Berlin – they would incline towards the German propositions, for in German eyes they had no other sensible choice. At a later date Bonnet denied that he had intimated a 'distancing' in the sense of the above. In the meantime some events had occurred that were to swing French as well as British policy away from disinterest in Eastern Europe back to an anti-German trend.

Taking a look at European politics in the span between the end of January 1933 to the end of January 1939, the date of Joachim von Ribbentrop's visit to Warsaw, German foreign policy appeared close to its goal. The reinvigoration of the Reich and the new organization of Eastern Europe with an anti-Bolshevik objective were near to reaching their conclusion if a final settlement of the German-Polish relationship was to be sealed in Warsaw on the basis of the German proposals. What could cause Poland still to hesitate in accepting the German offer of guarantees in regard to the German-Polish borders[211] (Father had actually intimated a territorial guarantee) in return for the restitution of Danzig to the Reich and an ex-territorial railway and highway?

In the first preliminary talks with the Polish ambassador in Berlin, Father had said that it had not been his 'intention to have a diplomatic chat'. The fundamental significance of the negotiations to be initiated should thereby have been made clear to the Polish representative. Would the Polish government recognize the fateful moment (the hackneyed formulation is once again actually apt here) or would they try to manoeuvre through in accordance with the motto of Count Lubienski, Foreign Minister Beck's Cabinet Chief? He replied to the question how Edward Rydz-Smigly, the Polish commander-in-chief, could feel comfortable in his anti-German and anti-Soviet stance – i.e. between two great powers both of whom he treated as enemies:

'He [Rydz-Smigly] compensates for his fears of both the neighbouring
  enemies by his hope of the distant friends.'[212]

By these 'distant friends' he meant France and Britain, but also, as seen in the dossiers of the Polish Foreign Ministry found in Warsaw, the United States!

Would European history open at a new page because the Reich, with its Eastern European allies, would act as in a position, from now on consolidated, of a *pièce de résistance* against the threat constituted by Soviet Russia, that is in concord with both Western European powers, who would be able for their part to dedicate themselves to their overseas possessions in order to maintain their importance for the European economy under the altered circumstances of world politics, for as long and as efficiently as possible?

Envoy Schmidt (Press) told of the thrilling circumstances under which Father's visit to Warsaw took place:

'Colonel Beck had extended an invitation for the first evening to a festive banquet in the Palais Brühl. A dinner was served first, followed by a big reception for a couple of hundred guests. Everything was dazzling and splendid.

'The interior of the fine Palais Brühl however was highly over-ornamental. The reception rooms were decorated in the style of the turn of the century, with green marble columns, massive *portieres*, marble statues and floodlit oil paintings from Polish history. The impression was rather of being in an indoor swimming pool building or at the Foro Mussolini than behind the façade of a Saxon Baroque palace in Poland's spiritual centre.

'Before the dinner began Ribbentrop had already given me his and Beck's speeches for the toast so that I could transmit the texts to the German news agency in time for the Berlin newspapers to receive them before copy deadline. I came back to the hall just as dinner was announced.

'Beck escorted Mme von Ribbentrop to the table with a plaintive expression on his face. From time to time a spasm of pain giving a very histrionic impression contracted his features. Dörnberg saw my astonishment and as he passed whispered "Ischias!" If there is an illness that can break out unexpectedly and all of a sudden and is grave enough considerably to be a serious hindrance and to take away the appropriate friendliness but not so dangerous that one has to take to one's bed, that is sciatica. An ideal diplomatic illness.

'We had just finished the soup when Ribbentrop waved me over and quietly asked if the speeches had already been given to the Press. I said they had. And then Beck stood up, already with pointedly laborious effort, spoke the first sentence of his speech, appended a couple of clichés, excused himself for his sudden malaise and lifted his glass. An icy shiver of discomfiture ran along the festive table. Ribbentrop, to whom a poor diplomatic manner is so gladly attributed, behaved with flawless correctness and did not at all betray his astonishment. He stood up, thanked the Pole and regretted the unfortunate contretemps to the latter's health, referred to the exchanged speeches in a clever turn of phrase and refrained on his part also from speaking the whole text, instead raising his glass for the closing formula according to protocol. This astute behaviour of Ribbentrop's and the fact that neither he nor his wife had given the slightest indication of anger or offence made even the distrustful guests think that Beck might possibly be really gravely indisposed so that the whole incident would have no political significance.

'Beck was of course not ill, or at any rate not so ill that he could not have read his 42-line toast. It was a case of eliminating the speeches, already exchanged, with a trick.'

What had happened? What had triggered the Poles to throw a 'rebuff' at the German Foreign Minister in an almost rudely abrupt form? The externally recognizable motive was a speech by French Foreign Minister Bonnet to the Chamber in Paris on 26 January 1939. In this speech Bonnet had distanced himself from the declarations he had made to Father in the sense of France's political disinterest in Eastern Europe:

'Bonnet spoke of the friendship with England as the cornerstone of French policy. Never had the Entente been more intimate. In case of the outbreak of a war – which was wholeheartedly hopefully to be avoided – into which both countries were to be drawn, all Britain's forces would be at the disposal of France, as would France's be for Britain. There was consequently a mutual interest in a build-up of military force to the maximum …

'Depiction of relations with the Soviet Union was characterized by France's repeated contacts with Moscow during the September crisis in the sense of the aid pact. In regard to relations with Poland, it sufficed to remind that the Polish Foreign Minister Beck had declared that the Polish-French friendship remained unaltered as one of the fundaments of Polish policies. France stood by the treaties concluded with the Soviet Union and the countries of Central and Eastern Europe. Then Bonnet spoke of his concord with Roosevelt's statements of foreign policy.

'President of the Council Daladier directed an appeal to the Chambers to place themselves solidly behind the government … It was however valid to oppose a categorical "No" to the claims of certain neighbours. France could not engage in any sort of policy of surrender and had to be on the alert in every sector where French interests were at stake.'[213]

Envoy Schmidt, a member of the German delegation, reported that the offence by some Polish officers in civilian clothing in order to ascertain the effect of the French '*volte-face*' on Poland had not been necessary. In a nightclub that had been designated by the Polish Foreign Ministry as a venue for meetings of the German delegation members they had handed over to the German guests pieces of paper on which there was, in German, 'Before ordering *Danzig Goldwasser* [liquer] please read the declaration of guarantee by the French Chamber'.[214]

With the rear covered by Paris and thereby London too, Beck thought he could continue his 'balance of power' policy between the Reich and the Soviet Union. This signified dispensing with German wishes for a close cooperation and refusing German offers. Whether it was a good idea to aggravate the 'No' by couching it in offensive accompanying circumstances is more a question of Beck's qualification than of the broader policies, as was the occasion when the representatives of the Polish War Ministry had made the German Foreign Minister wait for twenty-five minutes – without apologizing – at the wreath-laying ceremony at the Tomb of the Unknown Soldier, as well as more such slights.

If on the part of Germany any hopes had been entertained from the outcome of Father's visit to Warsaw, that through a generous land reparcelling with Poland the consolidation of Germany's position in Central Europe could be finalized and concluded, following the parliamentary speeches of Daladier and Bonnet, the situation was totally different. The 'Great Entente Cordiale' explicitly exerted the greatest possible efforts to bring their armaments up to the highest level. France's Eastern European alliances were characterized as the fundamentals of French policy. It may be assumed that this was thereby also valid for the British. Bonnet had re-established France's 'presence' in Eastern Europe. The hope that both the Western powers' abstention from Eastern Europe would open Poland, in her own interest, to the German proposals had been dashed by the about-turn of French-British policy. The renewed gravity of the threat to the Reich through encirclement by the system of alliances could not be overlooked. The announcement by the French chief of government of exceptional efforts in armament did not bode well.

For Father and his closest colleagues already then in Warsaw the question was posed of what the effect had been of the French turn-about. In Bonnet's speech Father saw an unmistakeable change of course in French policy from the stance the French Foreign Minister had taken in the talks with Father in Paris. According to his colleagues, already while in Warsaw Father was of the opinion that it must have been interventions by Roosevelt through his Paris ambassador, William Bullitt, that were the principal lever in the reversal of French and thereby also Polish policy.

In the winter of 1939/40 I was stationed in Würzburg in the military. Mother paid me a visit. As an ordinary soldier, such visits were enjoyed to the full. The bathtub in Mother's hotel room was at my disposal every evening. She spoiled her first-born, given the amenities available in those days, not least with the relish of *Bocksbeutel* (fine Franconian) wines. It goes without saying that Mother briefed me in what was going on in the current political and military fields. She recounted to me that the files of the Polish Foreign Ministry safeguarded in Warsaw (Operation 'von Künsberg') had caused a certain surprise to the German side as to how broadly and intensively American President Roosevelt had become involved in European politics so as to obviate a peaceful outcome in German-Polish negotiations. It could be concluded from all records and documentation meanwhile available that it was the massive intervention of the American president that had brought about the reversal of French and British policy. The layout of British policy, as it had been set out by Halifax in the letter quoted above to his ambassador in Paris, was evidently no longer valid, as neither was Bonnet's intention to reduce French engagement in Eastern Europe that the French Foreign Minister had expressed to Noël, his ambassador in Warsaw.[215] True, Noël also later denied that Bonnet had formally renounced a French influence in Eastern Europe, although he did admit that:

'it is undeniable that the personal attitude of M. Bonnet at the time of Munich … and in the subsequent months had given the German statesmen the impression that from now on their country would have a free hand in the East, despite the treaties still in force and the solemn declaration.'[216]

On 21 November 1938, the Polish ambassador in Washington wrote thus to the Polish Foreign Ministry after a conversation with Bullitt, the American ambassador in Paris, at that time still Roosevelt's close confidant and whom the former met on the occasion of Bullitt's stay on leave in the United States:

'Bullitt replied that the democratic countries absolutely needed another two years until they were fully armed. In the meantime, Germany would probably have advanced with its expansion in an easterly direction. It would be the wish of the democratic countries that armed conflict would break out there, in the East between the German Reich and Russia. As the Soviet Union's potential strength is not yet known, it might happen that Germany would have moved too far away from its base, and would be condemned to wage a long and weakening war. Only then would the democratic countries attack Germany, Bullitt declared, and force her to capitulate.'[217]

Bullitt had returned to Paris on 21 January, that is a few days before Father's trip to Warsaw,[218] from a stay of several months in the United States with a 'suitcase full of instructions'.[219] Between 21 January and 25 January – still before Bonnet's speech in the Chamber – Bullitt had had two discussions with him. He also spoke twice with the Polish ambassador.

It may be taken nowadays as a confirmed realization – although all the documentation is as yet by no means available – that during these months American diplomacy was intensively active to prevent an agreement between the Reich and Poland. There were naturally no doubts among the members of the German government as to Roosevelt's stance in regard to the German Reich and his anti-German policy, however the extent of the high-pressure efforts of American diplomacy to obstruct a German-Polish arrangement became known to the German side only from Polish documents found in Warsaw.

On the other hand, Father was absolutely aware of the negative impact of American policies; the Polish documents were only a confirmation of his opinion. Envoy Schmidt (Press) had this to say on the matter:

'For this much was made clear in the discussion with Ribbentrop on the way back from Warsaw: the Foreign Minister saw that in Roosevelt and the USA lay the true reason for the change of mind in Paris ...

'On what grounds Ribbentrop based his suspicions that Roosevelt was the initiator of the Paris turn-about was not talked about in the saloon car. What I found interesting was that upon arrival in Berlin ... Ribbentrop immediately took Rudolf Likus aside ... and asked him "Is there any news from Sofia, Likus?" [Likus] nodded eagerly and replied: "Very interesting news, Herr Reichsminister!"

'In Sofia Likus had access to a particular source of information who always delivered very good material from the American Legation: reports from the American envoy addressed to the State Department, directives from Washington, even very confidential messages to the envoy personally were part of the material. The source Likus had tapped was excellent, albeit also very expensive. Not only information was obtained from it but analyses of American policy as well.'

There follows the decisive question from Schmidt (Press):

'The question posed today is whether it is verifiable that Roosevelt … was responsible for the French rejection of the Paris agreement? That therefore it was Roosevelt who triggered Bonnet's speech in the Chamber of 26 January, thus decisively steeling the resistance of Poland?

'In my opinion the answer is Yes …

'Bullitt said to the Polish ambassador: "Should war break out we shall certainly not take part in it at the beginning, but we shall end it." To the question whether the USA would possibly enter into a war on Germany, he replied:

'"Undoubtedly, yes, but only after Great Britain and France had made the first move."'[220]

At this point the President of the United States had already been pursuing the return of the States to world politics for years. However, since the great potential of America could only be deployed effectively in the sense of active world politics in a worldwide conflict, he did not shy away from utilizing the possibilities of such a conflict breaking out. It was not for the purpose of preserving the British Empire or the French, Belgian and Dutch colonial empires; it was also not about Poland's independence, for later, in his negotiations with Stalin he unhesitatingly sacrificed it, as, incidentally, did Churchill. It was all about expanding the American power potential. Through the agency of his trusted Bullitt he exerted a latent pressure on the British and French governments not to enter into any sort of compromise with Germany.

Almost overnight Germany's situation had altered dramatically to her detriment. At the beginning of 1939 there was hope that the Reich's status could be conclusively consolidated by means of a generous regulation with Poland, whereas following Poland's declared refusal it was clearly confronted by an open preparedness to intervene on the part of the two Western powers, who had additionally declared their intention of escalating their armament efforts to the highest possible point. The latent hostility of the United States and Soviet Russia rounded the picture off to an extraordinary imperilment of the Reich.

The well-known American historian Tansill quotes the American journalist Verne Marshall:

'President Roosevelt wrote a note to William Bullitt [in the summer of 1939], then Ambassador to France, directing him to advise the French Government that if, in the event of a Nazi attack upon Poland, France and England did not go to Poland's aid, those countries could expect no help from America if a general war developed. On the other hand, if France and England immediately declared war on Germany [in the event of a Nazi attack upon Poland], they could expect "all aid" from the United States.

'F.D.R.'s instructions to Bullitt were to send this word along to "Joe" and "Tony", meaning Ambassadors Kennedy, in London, and Biddle, in Warsaw, respectively. F.D.R. wanted Daladier, Chamberlain and Josef Beck to know of these instructions to Bullitt. Bullitt merely sent his note from F.D.R. to Kennedy in the diplomatic pouch from Paris. Kennedy followed Bullitt's idea and forwarded it to Biddle. When the Nazis grabbed Warsaw and Beck disappeared, they must have come into possession of the F.D.R. note. The man who wrote the report I sent you, saw it in Berlin in October, 1939.'[221]

In a report that Łukasiewicz, Polish Ambassador in Paris, sent to Polish Foreign Minister Beck regarding a discussion with the American ambassador in Paris, Bullitt, there is the following:

'The United States has several immensely important means of compelling England. The mere threat to employ them might suffice to hold Britain back from a policy of compromise at the expense of France.'[222]

An entry in the diary of the later US Secretary of Defense, James V. Forrestal, records a discussion with the American ambassador in London, Kennedy, when he learnt from what Chamberlain had said to Kennedy that 'America … had forced England into the war [against Germany]'.[223] Roosevelt had been the determining figure. He wanted to set world politics in motion, knowing perfectly well that with the enormous potential of the United States he held the best cards in his hand for a global 'power play'.

In a report dated 12 January 1939,[224] the Polish ambassador in Washington, Count Potocki, revealed Roosevelt's and his fellow-campaigners' game to Beck. According to this report, domestic American propaganda was directed entirely one-sidedly against Hitler and National Socialism, whereby Soviet Russia was almost completely eliminated: '[I]f mentioned at all, [Russia] is mentioned in a friendly manner and things are presented in such a way that it would seem that the Soviet Union were cooperating with the bloc of democratic states.' Potocki goes into detail in representation of the influence exerted by the media that were in Jewish hands. By generating a war psychosis, says Potocki, the president was serving a double purpose: for one thing 'he wanted to divert the attention of the American people from ... domestic problems' by creating a war psychosis and by spreading rumours concerning dangers threatening Europe; for another, the American people should be induced to accept an enormous armament programme which far exceeded United States defence requirements. Potocki continues:

'The entire issue is worked out in a mysterious manner. Roosevelt has been forcing the foundation for vitalizing American foreign policy, and simultaneously has been procuring enormous stocks for the coming war, for which the Jews are striving consciously. With regard to domestic policy, it is extremely convenient to divert public attention from anti-semitism which is ever growing in the United States, by talking about the necessity of defending faith and individual liberty against the onslaught of Fascism.'[225]

Had liberty truly been Roosevelt's concern, he would actually have had to exert influence on Poland to accept the extraordinarily favourable German terms. But he held back. It was in exactly the same way that he later managed Japan into the position of 'firing the first shot'.[226] It was not a matter of Polish independence, which was under no threat – as Allied propaganda maintained it was – but to incite Germany to fire the first shot. England hoped that would trigger a military coup, and Roosevelt in that case reckoned on a global conflict that would bring the exceptional might of the United States to full advantage. In the British-Polish alliance by which Poland definitely aligned with the anti-German line, thereby tying herself for better or worse to the British and consequently to the United States, it is noteworthy that the mutual defence clause applied only in case of a German advance against Poland, but not if Poland came into conflict with Russia.[227]

In Poland it was noted with satisfaction that the 'West', and the USA in particular, had adjusted to the inimical concept of Germany. In Beck's eyes, the decisive prerequisite was thereby ensured to be able to enter into a conflict with Germany. After the Warsaw talks it was now manifest that no settlement in German-Polish relations would be reached in the foreseeable future, let alone an amicable relationship in the sense of a common preparedness for defence against Soviet Russia. Poland based herself on the alliance with France, and on the German-Russian antagonism which the Polish government regarded as insuperable. In these circumstances the strategically unfortunate German-Polish border and the Czech army still extant constituted an additional problem, since it was possibly necessary to take the enmity of the remainder of the divided state of Czechoslovakia into account just as much as Poland's antagonism.

Irrespective of the negative outcome of Father's visit to Warsaw, hopes in Berlin that a settlement with Poland could be achieved were not abandoned. On 21 March 1939, Father reissued the invitation to Beck in a discussion he had with the Polish ambassador, Lipski. But Beck went to London, where apparently he received the initially oral promise of a guarantee from the British government, which then permitted him to reject the German propositions to Poland in all formality and to proceed to the mobilization of the Polish Army.[228]

The miscarriage of the German-Polish negotiations were proof of the impossibility of organizing Eastern Europe through corresponding treaties in the anti-Bolshevik sense. Since the Western powers did not condone it, German policy had to find a new concept. The consequences of the Polish behaviour became clear to Father on the return trip from Warsaw. He told his collaborators that 'the only way out left to us is to come to terms with Russia if we do not want to be conclusively ringed in'.[229]

The 'Castling'

Following the negative experience of Warsaw Father did not hesitate long over his deliberations in an entirely different direction. Envoy Schmidt (Press) recounts the scene in the special train of the return trip in detail:[230]

'On 27 January Ribbentrop was in no way convinced that the negotiations were to be seen as having definitively failed, although he was very pessimistic about them …

'I was all the more surprised when during the return trip the Foreign Minister called me into his saloon car to deliver the press report and after some brief introductory words, in the presence of Mme Ribbentrop asked me the precise question:

'"Do you believe there is a possibility of reaching a German-Soviet cooperation?"

'I must have looked very nonplussed, for Mme von Ribbentrop laughed and said to her husband: "Dr Schmidt is quite scared", whereupon the Minister quickly added: "In politics, as in a General Staff, one has to examine all the possibilities, also this one which is naturally a purely theoretical question. And you have after all often told me that you have occupied yourself intensively with the history of the German-Russian cooperation after World War One."

'Ribbentrop was thereby alluding to my penchant, well known to him, for the chapter in history of German-Soviet relations between 1918 and 1933 …

'I therefore joked about his question in the saloon car, saying: "It might be difficult for Stalin to associate himself with the anti-Comintern pact." I was left almost speechless when the quick-witted Mme von Ribbentrop retorted: "Why not, if it is renamed?"

'It was instantly clear to me that Ribbentrop was evidently very seriously occupied with the question of a German-Soviet settlement …

'Walter Hewel also came into the saloon car and joined in the discussion. In the course of it Ribbentrop's train of thought became fairly clear: he had evidently been convinced by the last talks with Moltke [German ambassador in Warsaw] that the resistance of the Poles to a close collaboration with Germany was indeed greater that he had thought and no longer saw a real chance of a solution for Danzig or a greater bonding of Poland to the Reich to build up the deployment area[231] against the Soviet Union. The consequence of this realization presented itself as an urgency for ... [the] Foreign Minister.

'If Poland could not be drawn into the German sphere of interest with the tacit consent of France, then Warsaw would have to be manoeuvred back into its old German-Russian dilemma on the horns of which Piłsudski had always evinced such panic and fear that he had made the undertaking of preventing a German-Russian collaboration in some way a political testament for the Polish diplomacy.'

Hewel's inclusion in this discussion is noteworthy. Hewel was an old comrade-in-arms of Hitler's, having taken part in the 'March on the Feldherrnhalle' in the putsch in Munich in 1923 and then spent many years in South-East Asia. I was there in London to see how Hewel cleaved to Father, to become in the end Father's or the Auswärtiges Amt's permanent representative to Hitler. Presumably Hewel was now brought in for him to be made aware from the start of the thoughts with which Father now had to attempt to 'turn around' Hitler from his anti-Bolshevik stance to a 'pro-Russian' line, something that without any doubt would be extraordinarily difficult. Hitler had entered politics with the maxim: War on Marxism, Communism, Bolshevism. I have depicted his concept of foreign policy – which he had consistently pursued since his access to Government – step by step. The fundamental principle of the German policy was the organization of Eastern Europe for defence against the aggressive Russian Bolshevism. Now his Foreign Minister was attributing to him a 180-degree *volte-face* and his associating with the Devil. In 1933, shortly after his access to government, Hitler had said to Nadolny, the German ambassador in Moscow: 'I will have nothing to do with these people.'[232]

Had his Foreign Minister, this very Ribbentrop, ever taken part in the fierce street and demonstration battles against the Communists? Had he not, as he himself had declared to Hitler, been a party-supporter of Stresemann's for many years? Did he not, accordingly, come from that bourgeois milieu to which Hitler did not attribute the capacity and above all the preparedness to acknowledge the worldview dimension of his fight against Bolshevism, not to speak of endowing the fight with the necessary harshness? In these circumstances it could occasionally be beneficial if a 'veteran' such as Hewel were to drop an appropriate word at the right moment, here in the sense of a – in Father's eyes – necessary 'turnaround' in German policy.

I first heard about these fundamental new concepts regarding German foreign policy in the few days I was able to spend at home between obtaining my *Abitur* and commencing Labour Service. Mother had had another operation on her frontal sinus, this time in Kiel. For some reason of protocol she had to be present in Berlin shortly after the operation, to be on hand, and was therefore fetched from Kiel by air. I took the opportunity to be on the flight with her so as to report on my having successfully passed my *Abitur*. I was received with the words 'if we crash, you'll still beforehand have your ears boxed!' (In the slight Mainz accent Mother sometimes adopted when she was agitated.) She was joking, of course, but it displeased her very much if family members were in the same airplane without sufficient reason.

The flight was an opportunity for a thorough discussion of the political situation; my parents' visit to Warsaw was just a few weeks since. The first thing Mother spoke about was Stalin's 'Chestnut Speech'. On 10 March 1939, in a speech to the Party Congress, Stalin had said that certain 'powers' should not think that the Soviet Union would 'pull the chestnuts out of the fire' for them. Stalin could unmistakably be interpreted as meaning that the Soviet Union would not permit itself to be embroiled in direct confrontation with Germany for the sake of the Western powers. The formulation could be a signal sent to Germany, but not necessarily so and could instead be a tactical move in the direction of the Western Allies. I gathered from Mother's report that Father was ready to put the Russians to the test. The possibility seemed to present itself here to break the deadlock and thereby avoid the mistakes of imperial policy before the First World War. Mother, however, also pointed out the difficulties there would be in moving Hitler to approve such a policy. I was impressed beyond all measure.

I had – sometimes in close proximity – experienced the efforts made over so many years to obtain Britain's amity. During the weekend excursions with my parents I have described, Father used to speak of the liability burdening his efforts resulting from the calamitous Spanish 'non-involvement committee'. German-English relations were the pivot around which everything turned. I had registered in my inner self the disappointments of the German side. Not to be forgotten was the article written by the London correspondent of the *Berliner Lokalanzeiger*, von Kries, under the headline 'Test-run Mobilization' on British policy during the 'May Crisis', that came to the unequivocal conclusion that Britain was preparing for war with the Reich. The altered atmosphere in England that I had already sensed at the time of our exchange visit to Bath could not be overlooked. Bismarck's policy of 'reinsurance' through an agreement with Russia was familiar to me. Its non-renewal by German Reich Chancellor Caprivi in 1890 was almost a 'hobbyhorse' of Grandfather Ribbentrop's. However, the Pan-Slavic movement had also existed in tsarist Russia, directing a particularly aggressive impact against the West, that was widely supported by circles in Moscow and St Petersburg. But it was precisely because of the Soviet Union's potential that it was worth striving for – indeed necessary – so as to take the pressure off in that direction. Germany had to opt for the West, and if such an option was not open, then it would have to be for the East. Some time later I heard from Mother that the Russian government was said to have been absolutely cooperative in the technical processing of Russian diplomatic representations in Czechoslovakia following the establishment of the Protectorate of Bohemia and Moravia. According to Father's estimate this detail could signify a renewed signal.

Naturally, Mother and I also talked about the establishment of the Protectorate. Mother seemed to me to be very thoughtful on this point and said nothing when I told her about the subject of my *Abitur* essay. Father too remained very serious and silent when this subject came up. After Munich the circumstances in Resttschechei (remainder of Czechoslovakia) had in no way been consolidated, quite to the contrary. The various populations now also wanted their independence; they were diverging from one another or respectively turning to their mother countries. The Slovaks did not want to live in a country determined as Czech. Czechoslovakia was a fabrication of the policy of the allied Great Powers and would fall apart into its separate components without their constant protection – which is indeed what happened immediately after 1989. In the situation of 1939, support was sought from Germany. Vojtech Tuka, later Slovak Prime Minister, said to Hitler:

'I lay the destiny of my people in your hands, my Führer; my people await their complete liberation by you.'[233]

The Slovaks wanted to be liberated, that is, to obtain their national independence; the Hungarians to be annexed to their mother country. Poland had already, without much ado, annexed the territories she claimed – among others the Olsa region already mentioned – without treaties nor negotiations. Czechoslovakia's disintegration in 1938 was not unleashed through German intrigues, it was a consequence of dissent in the interior of that country.

In his brief accounts, Father describes the events and their consequences as follows:

'In the course of the past months I had had various talks with the Foreign Minister Chvalkovsky and after an entirely new situation had arisen following the Hungarian invasion of Carpatho-Ukraine and the declaration of independence of Slovakia, by the intermediary of our Chargé d'Affaires in Prague he now enquired of me whether the Führer would grant State President Hácha the opportunity of a personal interview. Adolf Hitler agreed and told me he wished to take the matter in hand himself. I had an exchange of cables with Prague in this sense and instructed our legation to stay out of it. It was replied to President Hácha that the Führer wished to receive him.

'Up to this point, so far neither the Auswärtiges Amt nor I were aware of military preparations from our side. Shortly before the arrival of President Hácha I asked Hitler whether a state treaty should be prepared. He answered that he wanted "to go much further".'[234]

Hácha's visit to Berlin on 15 March ended with the well-known establishment of the Protectorate of Bohemia and Moravia. Father goes on to say:

'The next day I travelled to Prague with Hitler, where, as he had charged me, I had to read a proclamation out loud that had been handed to me, wherein the states of Bohemia and Moravia were declared a Protectorate of the Reich.

'Following upon this state ceremonial, I had a long, very serious discussion with Adolf Hitler at Prague's Castle. I pointed out to him that the occupation of Bohemia and Moravia would have unavoidable considerable repercussions from the British and French sides. Since this discussion in Prague I have always stressed my conviction to him that further territorial changes would no longer be tolerated by England, whose armament and alliance policies were in every way intensified, without a war. Until the day war broke out my stance was opposed to the Führer's opinion …

'Adolf Hitler answered my objections, which concerned the possible reaction in England with the postulation that the Czech question was totally unimportant to England, whereas it was of vital importance to Germany …

'At the time I said to the Führer that England would view the occupation of Bohemia and Moravia purely from the angle of the increase of Germany's power … – but Adolf Hitler stuck to his opinion.'

These words, addressed openly to the head of government of the German Reich, once again struck a somewhat sour note with the 'veteran fighters'. On 13 March 1939, Goebbels noted in his diary about these scenes:

'Until three in the morning foreign policy debates at the Führer's. Ribbentrop was also there. He advocates the point of view that it would unavoidably come to a conflict with England later. The Führer is preparing for this, but he does not consider it unavoidable. On this point Ribbentrop has no tactical flexibility. He is intransigent and therefore not quite in the right. However, the Führer will correct him.'[235]

In the light of these words, first of all what is to be corrected is the slander of Joachim von Ribbentrop disseminated by Weizsäcker and the other conspirators, in which it is stated that he had wrongly advised Hitler, telling him England was degenerate and would not fight.[236] In England the truth could be known. On 4 May the British ambassador in Berlin, Henderson, wrote to Alexander Cadogan at the Foreign Office, who had replaced Vansittart:

'certainly Ribbentrop did not give me the impression that he thought we were averse to war. Quite the contrary: he seemed to think we were seeking it.'[237]

Furthermore, Goebbels, the Foreign Minister's enemy, accuses Ribbentrop of 'intransigent' behaviour toward Hitler, with no 'flexibility', as he puts it. In clear language this means that Father stood by his point of view although Hitler was evidently of a different opinion. In such a situation, there is no doubt Goebbels would have struck what was to his mind a 'cleverer' attitude. In government circles at the time he was considered the master of the art of gathering information, through middle-men, about Hitler's thoughts and statements so that he could utter them as being his own, either directly to Hitler or in his presence, thus placing himself in a favourable light or to have a particular effect on Hitler. Father once recounted that Hitler had on occasion seen through this ploy and had told Father that he would henceforth refuse to tolerate the manner in which Goebbels, with the gentlemen of his entourage, 'passed the ball' so as to influence him.

Goebbels' diaries disclose the constant controversies with Father over foreign propaganda, for the chief of propaganda erroneously thought he could consider this area as a specialized field for himself. In a dictatorship especially, press releases are naturally an exceptionally important instrument of foreign policy. Goebbels, as well as Hitler himself, however, often handled foreign propaganda on the basis of the experiences they had garnered from the domestic propaganda of the fighting days and gave too little consideration to the completely altered present circumstances under which the public abroad, which had to be addressed, was living.

Meanwhile, with the march into Prague Hitler seemed to have once again proved his political instinct. Father said:

'The initial English reaction to what happened with Prague appeared at first to justify him [Hitler]; from the German standpoint it could be marked down as positive: on 15 March, in the House of Commons, Chamberlain stated, factually correctly, that no breach of the Munich Agreement had been constituted. The British government was no longer bound to their obligation vis à vis Czechoslovakia, since "the State whose frontiers we had proposed to guarantee [were] put an end to by internal disruption" …

'In contrast, the English Foreign Secretary Lord Halifax, however, from the start adopted a stance of rejection when notification of the Prague Agreement was given by the German ambassador von Dirksen.

'Two days after his speech in the Commons, under the influence of the Opposition Chamberlain too abandoned his earlier tranquil attitude of "wait and see" and had completely modified his approach. This was clearly expressed in his well known Birmingham speech.'[238]

The British change of mind, which my father had expected as a consequence, was encouraged by American intervention. The journalists Drew Pearson and Robert S. Allen, who were close to Roosevelt, published an article in the *Washington Times Herald* on 14 April 1939, in which they confirmed that on 16 March of that year Roosevelt had requested of the British government, in the form of an ultimatum, that no concessions whatsoever should be made to the Reich and that they should pursue an anti-German policy.[239] These reactions were not unforeseen. If my father expresses himself in the sense that following the Munich agreement he had repeatedly tried to maintain a friendly contact with the new government in Prague, then that is entirely plausible. In view of the German exertions to reach a fundamental agreement with Poland, any suspense or even a situation of ultimatum in Prague was clearly unwanted by him. If an arrangement with Poland were to be reached, then the Czech problem would anyway have lost its potentially explosive nature and a close collaboration would most probably have been achieved without spectacular steps being taken.

In view of the way things were, it was advisable to neutralize the Czech armed forces. There is no doubt that marching in with 'drums and trumpets' played into the hands of opponents' propaganda. What mattered, however, was to wind up the action swiftly and without incident, which, with the agreement of the Czech government, was also achieved. Furthermore, already on the night of 14 March, British ambassador Henderson had, as instructed by Chamberlain, declared in the Auswärtiges Amt that the British government 'have no desire to interfere unnecessarily in matters with which other Governments may be more directly concerned than this country'.[240] This signalled official disinterest.

It is nowadays frequently presented in such a way that the establishment of the Protectorate of Bohemia and Moravia had been the turning point in the politics of the West – of the British above all – in regard to Germany, and had triggered the rejection by Poland of the particularly favourable German proposals for the solution of the Corridor question, for one could no longer put any trust in German policy. It is overlooked – it must be said unfortunately often intentionally – that the German proposals had been put to the Polish government as early as November 1938. They had been offered by Hitler himself to the Polish Foreign Minister on the Obersalzberg and through the German Foreign Minister again to the Polish government in Warsaw, with Polish Foreign Minister Beck, as late as March 1939, also having been invited, via my father, to come to Berlin for negotiations on the issue. Beck, however 'went to London', as Father put it. Thereby Poland had gone over to the Western side and became a potential opponent. Neutralizing the well-equipped Czech forces became a compelling necessity.

It must therefore be borne in mind that the establishment of the Protectorate of Bohemia and Moravia was the consequence of British and Polish policy directed against the Reich, and not the other way round. The very wide-ranging settlement offered to Poland by Germany would have substantially relieved the tension of the threat that the Czech army still undeniably constituted to the Reich. It must not be forgotten – I say it again – the Polish ambassador in Berlin, Lipski, had already in March 1939 confronted Father with a threat of war if the efforts on the part of Germany were pursued to unite Danzig with the Reich. Against this background it was evidently Hitler's belief that for overriding aspects of foreign policy he would have to repudiate his own ethnic principles.

Father's fears, that he expressed to Hitler, must also be taken against the background of his efforts to stir Hitler to accept a sounding out of the Soviet government so as to explore the possibilities of an agreement. Contrary to Hitler, Father assumed that Britain, and France with them, were now determined to obstruct any further strengthening of German influence in Eastern Europe. To his mind, it had to be attempted to keep Russia out of this grouping and to reach a positive policy towards the Soviet Union itself. It was a vital matter for Germany to keep her back protected, which meant to come to an arrangement with the Soviet Union. But Hitler hesitated; it was only on 10 May that the Reich's relation with the Soviet Union was discussed in his presence.

Commercial relations with the Soviet Union had never been abrogated after 1933, but were overshadowed by the profound ideological antagonism between the two powers. The chief of the Auswärtiges Amt's commercial policy department, Envoy Schnurre, at the time – that is, in January 1939 – as has been said, was conducting negotiations over a credit agreement of 200 million Reichsmarks. Father wanted Schnurre's trip from Warsaw to Moscow to coincide with a meeting of Schnurre with Mikoyan, the Russian Minister of Foreign Trade; the journey was, however, cancelled then so as not to disturb the important negotiations with the Poles. It should also be mentioned that a vivid interest had been evinced on the part of Russia in the negotiations over the credit agreement, stressed by a *démarche* on the part of the then Russian ambassador Merekalov, who, as Schnurre writes, 'came to the Auswärtiges Amt … and declared his government's preparedness to conduct negotiations on this basis'.

Envoy Schnurre, who upon assignment by my father undertook the first steps in the task of exploring the possibilities of a fundamental new orientation of German foreign policy under the duress of the circumstances, has this to say on the subject:

'The next startling step taken by the Russians was Stalin's speech [the "Chestnut Speech"] pronounced on 10 March 1939 before the Party Congress XVIII. In it he accused the English, French and American press releases of intending to incite the Soviet Union against Germany and underscoring alleged German claims to the Ukraine. The speech concluded with the remark that the Soviet Union was not prepared to pull the chestnuts out of the fire for others, i.e. Western democracies. This declaration of Stalin's signified that he was keeping the way open for a German–Soviet understanding.

'Despite this, shortly after negotiations were opened with an English and a French delegation with the purpose of forming a common front of defence against a German aggression …

'Commencing talks with England and France demonstrated that Stalin, as before, still had two irons in the fire …

'The English-French efforts were further reinforced at the beginning of August 1939 by a military mission, working towards a military alliance. The English and French efforts were wrecked from the outset by the refusal of the governments involved to concede to the right of the Soviet Union to march through Poland and Romania in the event of a German attack. Despite all the efforts it was impossible to put aside the categorical refusal of the Polish and Romanian governments.

'A further signal was the removal of the long-standing Soviet Commissar for Foreign Affairs Litvinov, who retired on May 3rd 1939.

'The Commissariat for Foreign Affairs was taken over by Molotov, Chairman of the Council of People's Commissars, who thus stepped more forcefully into the public limelight and became a central figure of German-Soviet politics.'[241]

I have already mentioned that an initial discussion took place on 10 May 1939 in Hitler's presence, with the inclusion of two experts on Russia from the Auswärtiges Amt. The timing of the discussion is interesting insofar as it was only a few days after Litvinov's departure. Until then Litvinov had been mentioned in the German press only under his double-barrelled name Litvinov-Finkelstein. He was Jewish, and was besides also an exponent of the anti-German policy of the Soviets, which he conducted under the postulation of 'collective security'. This renewed signal may have triggered in Hitler a growing preparedness to occupy himself henceforth more intensively with the 'Russian question'. Stalin had evidently intended the dismissal of the Jewish Foreign Minister as a further signal addressed to Germany.

Whatever the case, the visible haste with which the discussion with Hitler was now scheduled is noteworthy, for both the German ambassador in Moscow, Schulenburg, as well as the German military attaché there, General Ernst A. Köstring, were prevented from participating; Schulenburg was attending the wedding of the Persian Crown Prince in Teheran and Köstring was on a tour of duty in East Asia.

Would Hitler gradually become aware of the Reich's perilous situation, that was to cause him to make a 180 degree turnabout of German policy? It did not as yet appear to be so, but reading in Schnurre, who after the war drew up a detailed account of developments in German-Russian relations from 1939 to 1941, there stands the following:

'At the beginning of May Count von der Schulenburg [who was not present for the reason given above], Embassy Counsellor Hilger and I were invited to the Berghof to take part in a detailed discussion on the current situation of the Soviet Union … this led to the conference on Russia at the Berghof on 10 May 1939 as had been arranged.

'Following corresponding preliminary talks with Ribbentrop, we arrived at the Berghof on 10 May 1939. We convened in the vast, spacious room of the Berghof, whose narrow end was fitted with a huge window giving a view over the alpine landscape. After a brief greeting by Hitler we sat down at the large round table. Besides Hitler and Ribbentrop, present were General Field Marshal Keitel, Chief of the Supreme Command of the Armed Forces, Colonel General Jodl, Chief of the Operations Staff of the Armed Forces High Command, as well as Walter Hewel, the liaison of the Foreign Minister to Hitler. Hewel belonged among Hitler's comrades-at-arms of old. He had been imprisoned in Landsberg with Hitler, had worked in the domain of the economy of Indonesia for many years and was admirably distinguished by his open-mindedness and amiability as a man of the world.

'Although we were prepared for Hitler on this occasion to lead the discussion and expand into one of his usual lengthy monologues, it was not the case at all. Hitler let Hilger and myself brief him in every detail concerning the situation in the Soviet Union and the state of our relations.

'He began the discussion with a question on the reasons for Litvinov's dismissal. Hilger answered that Litvinov had been dismissed because he constantly insisted on reaching an understanding with England and France and he pursued the thought of a consensus for the disablement of Germany. Hitler's next question as to whether under certain circumstances Stalin would be prepared to come to an understanding with Germany, gave rise to a detailed description of the various efforts on Russia's part to reach an understanding with Germany. We particularly noted Stalin's speech of 10 March and it was somewhat surprising that none of the participants was familiar with the wording of the speech, although the embassy as well as the Auswärtiges Amt had reported on it in detail.

'The discussion subsequently turned to the Red Army, that had on the one hand been weakened by the purges of 1937/1938 but on the other had become a power to be reckoned with through reorganization and a steely discipline. Stalin was striving to restore the strength of Russian national consciousness. The great personalities of the tsarist past were strongly brought to the fore in literature and the theatre, such as for instance Kutuzov as the victorious opponent of Napoleon, Peter the Great, and others. In economic matters we pointed out the major possibilities that the Soviet Union's wealth in raw materials could offer us and the close contacts which had already been made.

'Hitler listened attentively to our remarks, interrupting nobody. He asked more questions, so as to extend the discussion, without revealing his own stance toward the issue of an understanding of ours with the Soviet Union. We thought he would tell us how the talks with the Russians should proceed but were disappointed in this expectation. He thanked us – and the meeting was over.'[242]

Schnurre's statement that none of the participants was familiar with the wording of Stalin's speech (the 'Chestnut Speech') is of course not true, for it was precisely this signal transmitted by Stalin in the speech that Father had employed so as to persuade Hitler to rethink Germany's Russian policy. How else would it have come to a discussion with Schnurre and Hilger? It is, however, a well-known routine for leading figures to let collaborators make statements once again of facts already known, for interesting shades of meaning may be distinguished from the gist of the presentation, not only in view of what is actually happening but also as to the stance of the speaker to the problem at hand, which in each case has to be taken into consideration when assessing the presentation. Schnurre will probably have meant the military men, who quite probably, as was Hitler's wont, had not been comprehensively informed.

Hitler's overt distancing from the Soviet Union since 1933 does not seem comprehensible, for a power such as the Soviet Union then represented could not be ignored as if it did not exist. It is slightly reminiscent of the fatal instructions given by Hitler at the beginning of the war with Russia, denying the Auswärtiges Amt any competence in the sector of Soviet Russia, as if this international power no longer existed.

When following Schnurre's account it may be seen that the meeting on 10 May 1939 on the Obersalzberg had been a matter of a purely informative discussion. I assume it was as a result of Father's insistence on again using Litvinov's dismissal as motivation that had brought Hitler once more to discuss the 'Russian question'. From Hitler's point of view, playing the meeting down, and the absence of the ambassador and the military attaché, could also have been intended to cloak his intentions. It was evidently still difficult for him to reach a decision about an understanding with the Soviet Union, although the encirclement of the Reich, in view of the negotiations of the Anglo–French delegations in Moscow, seemed possibly to be close to a conclusion.

However, even regardless of the hostility of the USSR, the situation in which Germany found herself in the spring of 1939 was extremely grave. This is why following the conclusion of the pact with the Soviet Union, Father spoke of a great relief of tension in the foreign policy sector. Whereas nowadays German historians think they can detect the first signs and prerequisites for Hitler's alleged plans for world domination, this is not comprehensible, in view of the facts. Basically, Hitler still hoped for an agreement with Poland, thereby for an arrangement with Britain. This was in the end what was also accomplished by the pact of non-aggression with the USSR. He could not know what powers had wrought influence on the decisions made by the British and French governments, in order to prevent such an arrangement on the basis of the German offer to Poland; an arrangement that in Hitler's opinion could only be in the interests of Poland.

For six years he had directed his foreign policy with the objective of a limitation of the Soviet Union, for which he had sought a partnership with both Western European powers, and now he was supposed to have bonds with 'these people' – the Soviets? For a pragmatist such as Father that presented no fundamental problem, but for Hitler the road to Moscow signified a rough path to tread. One may nonetheless also comprehend Hitler's wavering out of factual causes, quite irrespective of his basically anti-Bolshevik policy so far. It was perfectly reasonable to think that Stalin was making these advances to the Reich solely to present himself to the Western powers in the light of a more valuable player, thus demonstrating that he had other irons in the fire. It may perhaps be possible one day to deduce from Russian documents – insofar as they will not, nor have been, manipulated – what Stalin's true thoughts were when he introduced a rapprochement with the Reich. There is today a widespread theory that Stalin's final decision to take up the option of Germany had been triggered by the strict refusal of the Polish and Romanian governments to condone the right of Russian troops to march through their national territory in case of war (*casus foederis*). To my mind this explanation does not extend far enough. At the back of Stalin's policy the hope must have existed to see the Central European and Western power blocs embroiled in a conflict, as Litvinov had allegedly said to Goldmann. The weight and position of the Soviet Union could only be reinforced in such an eventuality, since all options would be open to it.

The Polish and Romanian governments were doubtless right to start from the premise that once they were there they would be unable ever again to be rid of Russian troops who would come to their 'assistance'. The Polish and Romanian governments quite rightly saw no chance of the two Western powers protecting them from the Russians once these were in the country, a perception that was to become a bloody reality five years later. Such thoughts must have nourished Hitler's hopes of at last coming to an agreement with Poland and Britain in the Danzig and Corridor question, for unlike Stalin he did not think of demanding the right to march through.

Schnurre reports that at Pentecost 1939 a session with Father took place at our farmhouse near Bad Freienwalde for consultation as to further proceedings vis à vis the Soviet Union. Participants were State Secretary Weizsäcker, the lawyer and expert in international law Ambassador Gaus, Undersecretary of State Woermann and Schnurre himself.

They had judged the chances of an understanding with Russia with pessimism and conceded that endeavours toward England and France had better prospects. This opinion, expressed by Weizsäcker, is not surprising since behind the back of the German government he had warned Britain against a German-Russian understanding. Schnurre will have pressed for reinforced resumption of politico-commercial efforts, which seems perfectly plausible. Since this is also what was decided, Father's wish to continue the talks is obvious.

It was already somewhat awkward to put the discussion with the Soviets in train at all without mutual loss of face after one had for years 'covered' each other 'with pails of manure', as Stalin later expressed it to Father in Moscow. It was no less difficult for Father to convince Hitler, who had followed the banner of anti-Communism, of the necessity of a rapprochement with the Soviet Union. Father says of this:

> 'To seek a settlement with Russia was originally purely my very inherent[243] idea; I had represented it to the Führer because I wanted on the one hand to bring relief to German foreign policy, in view of the attitude of the West, and on the other, however, also to ensure Russian neutrality for Germany in the event of a German-Polish conflict.
>
> 'In March 1939 I thought I read into a speech of Stalin's a wish of his for improvement of the Soviet-German relations. He had said then that Russia did not intend to "pull the chestnuts out of the fire" for certain capitalist powers.
>
> 'I showed the Führer the text of Stalin's speech and urged for authorization to take the necessary steps so as to ascertain whether a genuine wish on Stalin's part was in fact behind this speech. At first Adolf Hitler's response was temporizing and reluctant.'[244]

Even on 29 June 1939, following a recording and presentation of the above-mentioned by Legation Councillor Hewel, Hitler made public that the German government was 'not interested in a resumption of the economic discussions with Russia at present'.[245] There was still a lot of persuasion to be done on Hitler in the sense of a German-Russian understanding. Father, however, was not discouraged and charged Schnurre with the task of undertaking a more greatly in depth sounding–out of Russian intent from the current negotiations over the credit treaty, as the latter reported:[246]

'At the end of July, Hitler decided to take the initiative vis à vis the Soviet Union.[247] On 26 July 1939 I received from Ribbentrop instructions to invite the Chargé d'Affaires of the Soviet Union's diplomatic mission Astakhov, and the Head of the Trade Delegation Babarin to dinner, and to conduct a wide-ranging political discussion. This discussion took place on 26 July 1939. I had asked them to Ewest, the old wine restaurant in the centre of Berlin … The Russians took up the conversation about the political and economic problems of interest to us in a very lively and interested manner so that an informal and thorough discussion of the various topics mentioned to me by the Reich Foreign Minister was possible.'

Schnurre then sketched out three stages in which the German-Soviet collaboration could be realized, on the premise that 'the Soviet Government attached importance to it'. In his opinion, 'controversial problems of foreign policy, which would exclude … an arrangement between the two countries, did not … exist anywhere along the line from the Baltic Sea to the Black Sea.' Schnurre then went on to describe Astakhov's reaction:

'With the warm approval of Babarin, Astakhov designated the way of rapprochement with Germany as the one that corresponded to the vital interests of the two countries. However, he emphasized that the tempo might well be only slow and gradual.'[248]

Here the time factor comes once more to the fore, a card cleverly played by the Russians and uncomfortable for the German side, for time was pressing. Through Astakhov, Molotov let Schnurre know that confirmation of the discussion was however awaited from an authorized German source. Thereupon the German ambassador, Schulenberg, was instructed to have a corresponding discussion with Molotov. The sounding-out resulted in the ascertainment of an evinced Russian interest, but Molotov designated the conclusion of a merchandise and credit agreement as an essential prerequisite and the touchstone for undertaking political talks. The Russians bid the full value of their trump card, that contrary to the German side they did not have any time problems, and let the Germans know this.

On 2 August Father himself had a discussion with Astakhov, the Russian chargé d'affaires. He briefed Count von Schulenburg in Moscow in a cabled decree that is reproduced here verbatim because of the importance of the discussion:[249]

'Last night I received the Russian Chargé d'Affaires, who had previously called at the Ministry on other matters. I intended to continue with him the conversations with which you are familiar and which had been previously conducted with Astakhov by members of the Foreign Ministry with my permission. I started with the trade treaty discussions which are at present progressing satisfactorily, and described such a trade agreement as a good step on the way toward the normalization of German-Russian relations, if this were desired. It was well known that the tone of our press with regard to Russia had for more than six months been substantially different. I considered that, insofar as the Russians so desired, a remoulding of our relations would be possible on two conditions:

a) Non-interference in the internal affairs of the other State (M. Astakhov believes that he can promise this forthwith).
b) Abandonment of a policy directed against our vital interests. To this Astakhov was unable to give an entirely clear-cut answer, but he thought his Government had the desire to pursue a policy of understanding with Germany.

'I continued that our policy was an unswerving and long-range one; we were in no hurry. We were favourably disposed towards Moscow; it was, therefore, a question of what direction the rulers there wished to take. If Moscow took a negative attitude, we should know where we stood and how to act. If the reverse were the case, there was no problem from the Baltic to the Black Sea that could not be solved between the two of us. I said that there was room for the two of us on the Baltic and that Russian interests by no means needed to clash with ours there. As far as Poland was concerned, we were watching further developments attentively and ice cold. In case of Polish provocation we would settle accounts with Poland in the space of a week. For this contingency, I dropped a gentle hint at our coming to an understanding with Russia on the fate of Poland. I described German-Japanese relations as good and friendly; these relations were lasting ones. As to Russian-Japanese relations, however, I had my own special ideas (by which I meant a long-term *modus vivendi* between the two countries).

'I conducted the whole discussion in a tone of composure and in conclusion again made it clear to the Chargé d'Affaires that in high policy we pursued no such tactics as did the democratic Powers. We were accustomed to building on solid ground, did not need to pay heed to vacillating public opinion, and did not desire any sensations. If conversations such as ours were not handled with the discretion they deserved, they would have to be discontinued. We were making no fuss about it; the choice lay, as had been said, with Moscow. If they were interested there in our ideas, then M. Molotov could, when convenient, pick up the threads again with Count Schulenburg.

'Addition for Count Schulenburg:

'I conducted the conversation without showing any haste. The Chargé d'Affaires, who seemed interested, tried several times to pin the conversation down to more concrete terms, whereupon I gave him to understand that I would be prepared to make it more concrete as soon as the Soviet Government officially communicated their fundamental desire for remoulding our relations. Should Astakhov be instructed in this sense, we for our part should be interested in coming to more concrete terms at an early date. This exclusively for your personal information.'

It is easy to see that there was great interest on the part of Germany in a speedy progress in the negotiations. However, Father wished to cloak this interest as much as possible and expressly stated that there was no hurry and that no sensationalisms were desired. Hitler had long vacillated to abandon his anti-Russian policy. Now he was gradually coming under pressure by the passage of time.

Hitler was not a skilled negotiator. He did not have the patience for a long-drawn-out negotiation that would elicit the opponent to take a stand and to let discussions reach the decisive point of maturity, with all the necessary finesse. This is why at the hotel on the Petersberg mountain Father's intervention in the negotiations during the Sudeten crisis had had to save the situation when news of the Czech mobilization had exploded into the discussion, and which but for a hair's breadth would have caused Hitler to break off the negotiations. On this, Father writes:

'In order to judge Hitler's personality, there is another aspect of importance: he was hot-tempered and could not always control himself. This was sometimes also apparent in diplomatic occasions. He had been about to break off the conference with Chamberlain in Godesberg, when the news of the Czech mobilization came and he spontaneously jumped up, red in the face, a sure sign. I intervened to calm him down and Hitler later thanked me for having thereby rescued the conference.'[250]

It is incidentally further proof that Hitler clearly did not want to precipitate a showdown in the Sudeten crisis. This trait of Hitler's personality was to have a fateful effect on German policy when in 1940 Molotov's wishes to exert a wide-ranging influence in Europe irritated him to such an extent that he cut short any further negotiations with the Russian government.

The wire addressed to Schulenberg discloses that despite the externally apparent equanimity reigning in the German side, it was vital to come to an understanding with the Soviet government as soon as possible before a situation of ultimatum were to arise in relations with Poland. On the German side it was calculated, with some justification, that an understanding between Germany and Russia would induce Poland to back down. In any case there were two options opened by an understanding with Russia: either a peaceful solution, which according to the German estimate had a good chance of succeeding if there were an agreement with Russia, or the last resort: military action, in other words.

Father's words, that nowadays sound rather grandiose, about German policy being 'unswerving' and built on 'solid ground', in contrast to the 'tactics' of the Western democracies, absolutely make sense in the context. It was a matter of making it clear to the Russian government that it was a case of a fundamental turn-about in German foreign policy and not a mere tactical dodge with a short-term expiration date, with the objective to pressurize Poland to back down in the Danzig issue or to induce the Western powers to influence Poland in that sense. Father's formulations are justified when seen in this light. Since Hitler had come to power, German policy had been geared to come to an arrangement with Britain, by eschewing any 'see-saw' policy between East and West. In the more than six years that Hitler had determined German foreign policy he had remained consistently anti-Bolshevik, and had never been tempted to flirt with the Soviet Union for tactical reasons by resuming what had been designated as a 'Rapallo policy' since 1922. It was therefore already absolutely of significance for the Russian side if the German Foreign Minister spoke of an 'historic turning-point' arrived at in German policy. Mutual mistrust was naturally not to be dissipated overnight. Neither side wished to 'play the joker', as we say, for the other side, but Father could in all confidence point to a consistent German policy.

If nowadays – I wish unhesitatingly to call it a cliché – it is maintained, with no further reflection, that the alliance with Russia now placed Hitler in the position of at last being able to wage 'his war', it simply does not correspond to the facts, for on the contrary there was hope in Berlin that the conclusion of a German-Russian treaty would have brought about a diplomatic constellation who could be seen as the requisite for a peaceful settlement of the Danzig-Corridor problem. There were others who backed a war in this situation. Just at the beginning of August, the Polish government had again openly threatened to take up arms if the government of the German Reich further pursued the Danzig problem.[251]

The Russians had declared that the conclusion of the merchandise and credit agreement, under negotiation since the spring, was a pre-condition for political discussions. Schnurre received instructions from Father to speed up the negotiations as much as possible. Delays cropped up every so often, as Babarin had to obtain the approval of Moscow for every detail. According to Schnurre, Father asked him 'not to come to grief over a trifle'; it was urgent to conclude, so as to enable the opening of the 'political talks'. On the German side there was no option left but to exert pressure. In a cable to Schulenburg of 14 August, Father said approximately the following: differing philosophies would not prohibit 'a reasonable relationship between the two States, and the restoration of new, friendly cooperation'. There existed no 'real conflicts of interests between Germany and Russia': there would be no question 'between the Baltic and the Black Sea which cannot be settled to the complete satisfaction of both countries'. The German-Russian policy had come 'to an historic turning-point'. The 'natural sympathy of the Germans for the Russians' had never disappeared. 'The policy of both States' could be 'built … on that basis'. That was an optimistic prognosis, but sincerely meant by Father. Later, in the winter of 1940/41, he tried everything to dissuade Hitler from his decision to attack Russia, and after the outbreak of the German-Russian war he pressed Hitler again and again or an authorization to extend feelers for peace in the direction of the Soviet Union. The decisive paragraph then read as follows:

'As we have been informed, the Soviet Government also feel the desire for a clarification of German-Russian relations. Since, however, according to previous experience this clarification can be achieved only slowly through the usual diplomatic channels, Foreign Minister Ribbentrop is prepared to make a short visit to Moscow in order, in the name of the Führer, to set forth the Führer's views to M. Stalin. In his, Herr von Ribbentrop's, view, only through such a direct discussion can a change be brought about, and it should not be impossible thereby to lay the foundations for a final settlement of German-Russian relations.

'Annex: I request that you do not give M. Molotov these instructions in writing, but that you read them to him verbatim. I consider it important that they reach M. Stalin in as exact a form as possible and I authorize you, if occasion arises, to request from M. Molotov on my behalf an audience with M. Stalin, so that you may be able to make this important communication directly to him also. In addition to a conference with Molotov, a detailed discussion with Stalin would be a condition for my making the trip.'[252]

The Russians played a game of gaining time so that in the end Hitler personally telegraphed Stalin to obtain for the German Foreign Minister an early date for a visit to Moscow. In Hitler's telegram the pressure that time was gradually exerting on Berlin is shown, because of the Polish threats of war and the automatic effects from their alliance with the Western powers if the Danzig-Corridor problem was still to be solved by 1939 'in one way or another' in the German sense.

In his telegram to Stalin, Hitler expressed his satisfaction at the conclusion of the commercial agreement and accepted the draft of a non-aggression pact handed to Schulenburg by Molotov, but considered 'it urgently necessary' to clarify the questions connected with it as soon as possible. Hitler wired:

'The substance of the supplementary protocol desired by the Government of the Soviet Union can, I am convinced, be clarified in the shortest possible time if a responsible German statesman can come to Moscow himself to negotiate … In my opinion, it is desirable, in view of the intentions of the two States to enter into a new relationship to each other, not to lose any time. Consequently, I therefore again propose that you receive my Foreign Minister on Tuesday, August 22, but at the latest on Wednesday, August 23. The Reich Foreign Minister has the fullest powers to draw up and sign the non-aggression pact as well as the protocol. A longer stay by the Reich Foreign Minister in Moscow than one to two days at most is impossible in view of the international situation. I should be glad to receive your early answer.'[253]

Father added as instruction to Schulenburg: 'Please hand to M. Molotov the above telegram of the Führer to Stalin in writing, on a sheet of paper without letterhead.' Finally, on the next day, that is 21 August 1939, Father sent Schulenburg a further telegram in which the urgency of the German wish for negotiations was underlined: 'Please do your utmost to ensure that the journey materializes. Date as in telegram.'

At 3.00 pm on 21 August Schulenburg handed Hitler's message addressed to Stalin to the People's Commissar for foreign affairs, Molotov, and subsequently telegraphed Berlin that Molotov had evidently been 'deeply impressed'. Schulenburg was asked to see Molotov again as early as 5.00 pm, when Stalin's answer to Hitler was given to him. It states:

'I thank you for the letter.

'I hope that the German-Soviet non-aggression pact will bring about a decided turn for the better in the political relations between our countries.

'The peoples of our countries need peaceful relations with each other. The assent of the German Government to the conclusion of a non-aggression pact provides the foundation for eliminating the political tension and for the establishment of peace and collaboration between our countries.

'The Soviet Government have instructed me to inform you that they agree to Herr von Ribbentrop's arriving in Moscow on August 23.'[254]

Father considered the non-aggression pact foreseen to be concluded with the Soviet Union as of such significance that, without regard for his personal self, he wanted its conclusion in no way to be jeopardized. He wrote on the subject:

'I had initially suggested that not I but another plenipotentiary – I had Göring in mind – should be sent to Moscow. Because of my activity as ambassador in England, my Japanese connections and my entire foreign policy so far I thought I was all too firmly established as anti-Communist for a mission to Moscow. But the Führer insisted on my being sent because he thought that I "understood it better".'[255]

Father had two goals in sight when he constantly urged Hitler to speedy and broad-based discussions with Russia. For Father the most important aspect was breaking the encirclement of the Reich. Beyond this it did, however, not seem to be a mistake to assume that if there were a successful agreement reached with the Russians the prerequisites were there for the Danzig-Corridor problem to be solved by peaceful means. The German side could reasonably expect that under the impact of a German-Russian collaboration Poland would accept the proposals, of further benefit, from the German government.

For one reason or another, the labour service camp in which I served in August 1939 had been given a long weekend's leave, so I took the opportunity to visit my parents in Fuschl,[256] where they were staying when Hitler was on the Obersalzberg. As soon as I arrived, Mother took me aside and briefed me as to how things stood. Father was to fly to Moscow to try to conclude a pact of non-aggression with the Russians. I was most profoundly impressed and – this is not in retrospect – extraordinarily relieved. Since for years I had been able to follow the unavailing German efforts for the realization of the 'Western option' at first hand, I could see the peril of a renewed encirclement of the Reich, that in 1914 had had such a fateful impact, looming clearly once again. It was going to be countered by Father's journey.

Once again Mother recounted the diverse phases of the developments that had now finally led to Father's mission to Moscow. There was of course no certainty that his visit would have a successful outcome. In this sense the instruction to Schulenburg is without any doubt also to be understood, namely that Hitler's telegram should be delivered to Molotov on paper 'without letterhead'.

Father's notes confirm the uncertainty with which he anticipated his journey:[257]

'It was with mixed feelings that I stepped on the soil of Moscow for the first time. We had stood against the Soviet Union with hostility for many years and had given battle ideologically to the utmost ... Above all, for us Stalin was a kind of mystic personality.

'I was aware of my particular responsibility in this mission, since it was I myself who had proposed an attempt for an understanding with Stalin to the Führer ... At the same time the English and French military missions were still negotiating in Moscow with the Kremlin over the projected military pact ... We arrived at Moscow airport in the Führer's aeroplane on 23 August in the afternoon between 4 and 5 o'clock where the flags of the Soviet Union and the Reich blew next to one another. We were received by our ambassador Count von der Schulenburg and the Russian ambassador Potemkin. Following the march past of a guard of honour of the Soviet airforce, which undoubtedly made a good impression as to appearance and military bearing, accompanied by a Russian colonel we went to the former Austrian embassy, where I was to stay for the duration of my visit.

... and received there the information that I was expected at the Kremlin at 6 pm. Who would be negotiating with me, Molotov or Stalin himself, was not to be elicited. "Odd Muscovite customs" I thought to myself. Shortly before the appointed time we were fetched once again by the broad-shouldered Russian colonel – I heard he was in command of Stalin's bodyguard – and soon drove into the Kremlin ... then we stopped at a small portal and were taken up a short flight of tower steps. At the top we were led by an official into a long study at the end of which Stalin stood awaiting us, with Molotov next to him. Count Schulenburg could not repress an exclamation of surprise. Although he had been serving as ambassador in Moscow for several years now, he had never spoken to Stalin himself!'[258]

It must be mentioned at this point that at the time Stalin did not occupy a fixed position of state, but was simply General Secretary of the Party. One can imagine his personality and the authority he must have emanated to have ruled that gigantic country, as was the case, so absolutely from an indirect position. Only shortly before the German-Russian war did Stalin undertake the offices of head of state and Generalissimus of the Soviet Union.

Father carries on:

'After a brief formal greeting, the four of us sat down at a table: Stalin, Molotov, Count Schulenburg and I. There were present besides our interpreter, Embassy Counsellor Hilger who was an excellent connoisseur of Russian relations and the young blond Russian interpreter Pavlov who apparently had Stalin's special confidence.

'At the outset of the discussion I expressed Germany's wish to place the German-Soviet relationship on a fresh footing and to bring about an equalization of interests in all sectors; we desired an understanding as far-seeing as possible with Russia. I thereby referred to Stalin's speech in the spring wherein in our opinion he had expressed similar thoughts. Stalin turned to Molotov and asked him whether he wished to answer first. Molotov however asked Stalin to take over since he alone was competent to do so.

'Stalin then spoke – briefly and succinctly, without too many words, but what he said was clear and unmistakeable and, it seemed to me, demonstrated the same wish for a settlement and understanding with Germany. Stalin utilized the distinctive expression: we may have "covered" each other "with pails of manure" for many years, but that was no reason not to be able to get on well together again. He had made his speech in the spring fully consciously so as to indicate his willingness for an understanding with Germany. We for our part had apparently understood this correctly. Stalin's answer was so positive that after the first basic utterances in which the preparedness of both sides to conclude a pact of non-aggression had been established, it was possible immediately to go into the issues of the material side of the demarcation of mutual interests and the German–Polish crisis in particular. There was a favourable atmosphere at the negotiations although the Russians are known to be tough diplomats. The spheres of influence in the countries interjacent to Germany and the Soviet Union were demarcated. Finland, the greater portion of the Baltic States and Bessarabia were declared as belonging within the Soviet sphere. In case of the outbreak of a German-Polish conflict, which in the current state of affairs could not be excluded, a "line of demarcation" was agreed.

'Stalin had declared already in the course of the first part of the negotiations that he wished to have certain spheres of influence. As is known, by "sphere of influence" it is understood that the interested state conducts negotiations that concern the said state only, with the governments of the countries belonging to its sphere of influence, while the other state explicitly [shows itself to be] disinterested.

'As to this, Stalin assured me he did not want to touch the domestic structure of these states. I had replied to Stalin's claim for spheres of influence by pointing to Poland: the Poles were becoming ever more aggressive and it would be desirable, in case they brought matters to a war, to fix a line so that the German and Russian interests would not clash. This line of demarcation would be along the courses of the rivers Vistula, San and Bug. I indicated to Stalin on this point that on the part of Germany every effort would be made to solve the issues in a diplomatic-peaceful form.

'It is self-evident that agreements touching upon other countries are not committed to treaties destined to be made public and that instead secret contracts are concluded for this purpose. There was a further reason for the agreement to be secretly contracted: the German-Russian agreement contravened an agreement between Russia and Poland and the treaty concluded in 1936 between France and Russia foreseeing a consultative procedure in the case of treaties with other countries.

'The relentlessness of Soviet diplomacy showed in the issue of the Baltic and especially in regard to the port of Libau which the Russians laid claim to for their sphere of influence. Although I had plenipotentiary powers for conclusion of a treaty, in view of the import of the Russian claims I thought it right to consult Adolf Hitler. The negotiations were therefore interrupted and resumed at 10 pm when I had Hitler's agreement.'

a) The annexation and division of the Polish state territory after the end of the German-Polish and respectively Polish-Soviet military action. (Capitulation of the last Polish field troops on 6 October 1939.)

b) German-Soviet Boundary and Friendship Treaty dating to 28 September 1939: Map bearing the signatures of Stalin and Ribbentrop.]

It must be said here that it is a well-known trick of negotiations to play up the weight of concessions one is prepared to make under certain circumstances, by means of appearing to delegate the decision thereon back to a higher level. This is what Father resorted to here when he referred the decision whether to relinquish the port of Libau to the Russians back to Hitler. Father continues:

'There being no more difficulties, the pact of non-aggression and the secret supplementary protocol were initialled and signed already before midnight. A light and simple dinner was then served to the four of us in the same room, which was Molotov's study. Right at the beginning there was a surprise: Stalin stood up to say a few words, in which he spoke of Adolf Hitler as the man whom he had always extraordinarily revered. In strong terms of friendship, Stalin expressed the hope that a new phase in German-Soviet relations had been introduced by the treaties just concluded. Molotov also stood up and expressed himself similarly. I replied to our Russian hosts with an address in equally amicable words. In this way, but a few hours after my arrival in Moscow an understanding had been established such as I had thought unthinkable when I had departed from Berlin and that moreover fanned my greatest hopes for the future evolution of German-Soviet relations.

'From the first moment of our meeting, Stalin had made a profound impression on me – he was a man of unusual stature. His sober, almost dry and yet so apt manner of speaking and the hardness as well as however his generosity in negotiation showed that he rightly bore his name [trans., Stalin = 'Man of Steel']. The content of my talks and conversations with Stalin gave me a clear understanding of the strength and power of this man who had but to nod for it to be a command obeyed as far as the most distant village of Russia's enormous vastnesses and who had succeeded in blending together the two hundred million people of his nation more strongly than

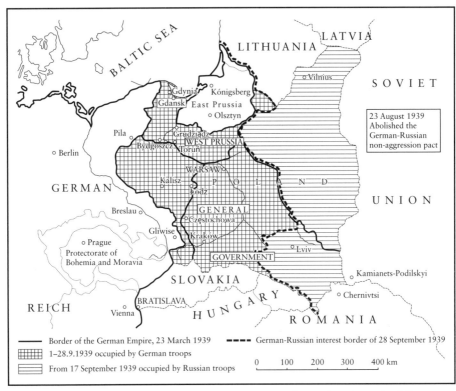

The annexation and partitioning of Polish national territory after the end of German–Polish and Polish–Soviet conflicts. [The last Polish field troops on 6 October 1939].

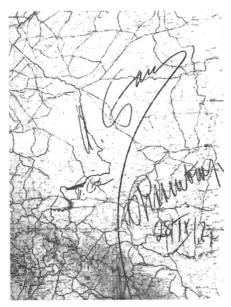

German–Soviet Frontier Treaty from 28 September 1939: Map with the signatures of Stalin and Ribbentrop.

any Tsar before had been capable of. A minor indicative occurrence that came about at the end of this evening seems to me worth mentioning: I asked Stalin whether the Führer's photographer accompanying me could take a few pictures. Stalin agreed and it was probably the first time he permitted this to a foreigner in the Kremlin. When however among other shots Stalin and we the guests were photographed with glasses of the Crimean sparkling wine we had been offered, Stalin did not allow it – he did not want it made public. As I asked, the photographer removed the film from the camera and handed it over to Stalin; he gave the little roll back however, remarking that he trusted that the picture would not be published. Trivial as the episode may have been, it was nevertheless illuminating of the generous attitude of our hosts and of the atmosphere in which my first visit to Moscow was concluded.'

On the conclusion of the treaty, Father writes:

'Rescinding Bismarck's Russian policy had introduced the encirclement of Germany that led to the First World War. In the situation the year 1939 was in, resuming the historical relations for realistic reasons signified a political security factor of the first order.

'For me personally, who had proposed this settlement with Russia to the Führer, in detail my hopes were raised for:

1) Gradual elimination of one of the most dangerous causes for dispute that could threaten the peace in Europe by a foreign policy bridging the oppositions in the world views between National Socialism and Bolshevism;

2) Establishment of a truly amicable German-Russian relationship as one of the foundations of German foreign policy in Bismarck's sense;

3) For the particular state of affairs as they stood in August 1939: the possibility of a diplomatic solution to the Danzig-Corridor problem in the sense of Hitler's proposals.

'On 24 August I flew back to Germany with our delegation. It was foreseen I was to go by air from Moscow to Berchtesgaden so as to report to Adolf Hitler at the Berghof. I was thinking about proposing to him that a European conference should be held for pacification of the Polish question.

'Surprisingly, by radio message our aeroplane was re-routed to Berlin where Hitler had flown the same day. For security reasons our machine had to make a wide detour over the Baltic.'[259]

Father speaks of a 'security factor of the first order'; the relief may almost be sensed that as a first step, due to the Moscow treaty the build-up of the ring of encirclement around the Reich had been broken. By the conclusion of the German-Russian treaty, world political-power relations had once again been fundamentally altered. For Germany the European equilibrium had been restored in a positive sense. Henceforth the Reich entertained friendly relations with Russia, Japan, Italy and Spain, as well as several smaller states in Eastern and South-eastern Europe. The strangulating encirclement of the Reich that was beginning to show had been prevented.

Furthermore, it had been succeeded in manoeuvring Poland, who had played the card of the West, into a situation whereby actually only a friendly settlement with Germany remained as a possibility, so as not to bring about the fateful situation that in 1935 Beck had set out so strikingly before Laval. It was Piłsudski's insight that Beck had transmitted to Laval. For Piłsudski too lost sleep over the *cauchemar des coalitions* (nightmare of coalitions) and he had tried to soften the nightmare through a wise policy – his successors evidently slept better. It will be seen what sort of 'comfortable pillow' it was on which the Polish politicians thought to endure their country's perilous situation.

However, from the German side it had to be assumed that Poland was now ready to negotiate under the present completely altered circumstances. A glance at the map in fact makes it clear even for military laymen that 'no power in the world' (as Beck had expressed it to Laval) could give Poland, wedged in between Germany and Russia, the requisite support if a military confrontation was indeed ventured.

It could of course now become rather more 'costly'! As has been seen, Hitler would have gone to considerable expense to ensure Poland's entry into the Continental-European-anti-Soviet bloc. It had been in no way a matter of 'so to speak' that Father had declared to Beck as well as Lipski that nobody but Hitler could guarantee the Corridor borders.[260] At present too, despite the pact of non-aggression with Stalin, it was not demanded of Poland to give up parts of her state territory. However, now, in the negotiations of the last week of August 1939, Hitler did demand a national referendum in the Corridor under international supervision, on the basis of the 1920 population structure. It can hardly be claimed that it was an unreasonable demand, and the British ambassador Henderson was also of the same opinion. I have already pointed out that after the First World War Poland had demanded that the populations of the regions ceded to Poland should opt for Poland if they did not want to be expelled. This referendum Hitler now demanded only for a restricted part of the Corridor.

Poland therefore remained the way out for the negotiations. Basically, Hitler had no antipathy toward Poland. A remark of his has been quoted: 'Every

Polish division at the Russian border spares me a German one!' Although the comparison can certainly not be qualitatively interpreted, it does make sense, if countered by the fact that a Poland hostile towards the Reich would necessitate a substantial military expense to secure the unfortunate borders of the Reich against Poland. Even if Poland's tendency to overestimate her own potential is assumed and taken into account, and that the Poles had taken the propaganda slogans 'the German tanks are made of cardboard' at face value – which would not be speaking for the qualification of the Polish General Staff – it would after all have been realized in Warsaw that they had no chance against an active German-Russian alliance.

It shows clearly from what has been said before how hard it had been for Hitler to accomplish a 'turn-about' – as proposed by Father – of German foreign policy from the anti-Soviet Central European bloc with the integration of Poland to a pro-Russian and thereby anti-Polish policy. As a matter of fact he had vacillated much too long. Hitler and my father – it cannot be said too emphatically – had accomplished this turn under duress, since, influenced by the British and the Americans, Poland had rejected them and had opted for the anti-German side. And yet Poland could still have reached a solution that did not place either their national substance nor honour in question.

It should not be forgotten that until a few days before the German-Russian pact it had still been unclear to the German side whether the Russians would decide on an alliance with the Reich or with the Western allies. Hitler's hesitation, next to his inhibitions, to come to an arrangement with the Bolsheviks is to be explained only by reason of his hopes that he could after all settle with Poland, and in the broader sense also with England, thereby avoiding both the war and ideological compromise by an agreement with the USSR.

His diplomatic *démarches*, just before the outbreak of war, are also proof that it was important to him not to let things reach the point of a military confrontation. Other than the official channels, he also utilized unofficial ways, such as for instance calling in the Swede Birger Dahlerus. Decisive is, however, the abrogation on the afternoon of 25 August of the order to advance, on Father's instigation, after the ratification of the new British-Polish treaty was made known, which gave more precision to the mutual guarantee offered by both countries in March: that is limiting it to a conflict with Germany.[261] If Hitler had only been concerned with the Russian cover of the rear to 'pick a quarrel so as to have his war', there would have been no cause to rescind the marching order for the Wehrmacht on 25 August at the last possible moment and under considerable technical difficulties. The countermand definitely harboured great military, and above all political, risks.

Poland and the Outbreak of War

'We Germans should also learn to put up with the truth, even if it is favourable to us!' (Heinrich von Brentano)

It was in the treaty with Russia that the German government saw the chance of finally reaching an arrangement with Poland. The Soviet Union's demand to maintain the right of marching through Poland and Romania in the case of an alliance formed against Germany should have made the real goals of the Soviet Union clear to the Polish leadership. The sudden interest of the British following the conclusion of the German-Soviet non-aggression pact in restricting their hitherto sweeping wholesale guarantee of Poland now only to the case of a war with Germany should also have given Beck and his colleagues particular food for thought. In the situation reigning in 1939 the Reich alone could protect both countries from Soviet aggression. No power in the world could have induced the Russian leadership to withdraw their troops from both countries again. An irony of world history is that just a few years later this was proved to be the case! A sensible Polish policy would even have given Poland, as a potential ally for Germany against the Soviet Union, a relatively strong position also vis à vis the Reich.

At this point two pressing issues impose upon an unbiased historian:

1) What were the motivations of the Polish government and what were their goals when they rejected or did not act on the renewed negotiations proposed by Germany after conclusion of the German-Russian treaty?

2) What was the objective of the British government by the ratification of the Polish-British treaty that came about in the clear acknowledgement that there was no possibility at all of coming to Poland's assistance militarily? Through this treaty Poland was induced into taking a stance, suicidal and totally intransigent, vis à vis the Reich.

Curiously, these decisive issues have so far not been raised by official historical research. To begin with the first question: was the already cited remark by the Polish Foreign Minister Beck to the French Minister Laval no longer valid, i.e. that the greatest catastrophe for the Polish nation always occurred when 'Germany and Russia jointly' acted? Should this totally evident truth, historically confirmed, after the passing of four years in which Germany had once more become a power factor, all of a sudden be obsolete? Even if one attributed to Beck a tendency to overestimate the Polish position that allowed him to dream of a Polish domain of power and influence extending from the Baltic to the Black Sea, it can after all not be assumed that he believed it could prevail between the Reich and the Soviet Union. In any case there existed a Polish–Soviet pact of non–aggression.[262]

The American endeavours have been depicted whose objective was to extract the Poles from German influence, thus forcing them on a course of confrontation with the Reich. The assumed certainty of the backing of the Western powers, including the USA, and the supposed unbridgeable opposition between Germany and Russia may have initially prompted the Polish Foreign Minister to reject the German propositions. The negotiations conducted with Britain and France on the one hand, and the Soviet Union on the other, concerning a military alliance may have reinforced his opinion that his back was covered should he let it come to a confrontation with Germany over Danzig.

Even with all this being assumed, Poland's policy after conclusion of the German-Russian treaty from now on remains incomprehensible. Does another key exist that could solve the riddle for us of the train of thought of the Polish government? They were thoughts that finally, transposed to reality, once again brought about the self-immolating end of Poland's national independence, and therewith its national catastrophe.

Ever since 1938, hidden opposition groups in Germany – albeit holding the highest posts – through the most diverse channels had time and again incited the British government to keep to a 'hard' stand and threaten Hitler so as to thwart his policies. Those who initiated these incitements are already known, as was depicted on the occasion of the Sudeten crisis. They were State Secretary von Weizsäcker, General Staff Chief Beck, Chief of Counterintelligence Admiral Canaris as well as, among others, Schacht and Goerdeler, Kleist-Schmenzin, Count Schwerin von Krosigk and Koerber. The tenor of their activities was always the same: The situation in Germany was depicted as miserable, so a military putsch was seen as having good prospects of success. The precondition would, however, be either the diplomatic defeat of Hitler, or war. In my opinion this is where the decisive explanation lies for Beck's incomprehensible policy which then became Poland's catastrophe. Beck, and probably also the British General Staff, hoped that an emergency, in view of the British declaration of guarantee to Poland, would not even arise. It must in any case have been clear to both that military assistance for Poland would not be possible. This was particularly so for the British General Staff, which had not even theoretically envisaged such assistance.

The British ambassador in Berlin, Nevile Henderson, had at the last moment seen to it that the Polish ambassador, Lipski, was urgently requested at least to take delivery of the German proposals, and on the morning of 31 August had them read to him by Dahlerus and British diplomat George Ogilvie-Forbes, receiving the answer from Lipski (as Dahlerus writes):

> 'that he had no cause in any way to be interested in Notes or offers from the German side. He knew the situation in German well after his five-and-a-half-year posting as ambassador ... ; he [Lipski] declared himself convinced that in case of war unrest would break out in that country and the Polish troops would successfully march against Berlin.'[263]

The events leading up to this were as follows: on the morning of 30 August Kleist-Schmenzin, whose activities in 1938 have already been mentioned, called in at the British Embassy. Kleist, who 'was in close touch with [the] War Ministry', gave the British military attaché a detailed report on military plans and the situation in Germany as he saw it. Henderson passed on this report to British Foreign Secretary Halifax in a cable by telephone. Kleist-Schmenzin gave the British military attaché the following information, including detailed strategic plans, which were contained in the telegram. Brauchitsch is said to have stated that war on two fronts was out of the question, since it could not bring about a quick decision.[264] The West Wall was strong only in places, but weak at Freiburg, Saarbrücken and Aachen, where the German General Staff feared a breakthrough. Hitler was having a nervous breakdown. The General Staff wished to make use of Hitler's nervous condition in order to enable a military coup (putsch), but he had to be certain that England would not give way. If the General Staff was persuaded that Ribbentrop's reports on England were wrong, this would be favourable for the dissident elements. It also contains the phrase: 'Repeated to Warsaw'.

In a marginal note on the report, Sir Ivone Kirkpatrick says:

> 'I cannot identify this officer from the description, but I think he is a retired officer in touch with the reactionary elements of the General Staff. He gave us a lot of fairly correct information last September, when

his line was to urge us to stand up to Hitler. This note was read to the Prime Minister on the morning of August 31.'[265]

It may clearly be seen from this information too that the conspiracy wished to suggest to the British that Hitler was on the brink of a breakdown. Through a 'coup', as Kleist-Schmenzin expressed it, the whole regime was to collapse. Not the least noteworthy about the report is that Chamberlain promptly passed it on to Warsaw and as appears from Lipski's words, once there, determined the completely unapproachable attitude of the Polish government – even after the German-Russian Pact. In this instance as well, to introduce a personal remark, once more the allegation being used as an incitement for the British is that Joachim von Ribbentrop was giving false reports, in the sense that England would not fight. What the conspiracy thus maintained is proof that their intention was to employ every means to lure the British government to a military confrontation with Germany, thereby triggering the outbreak of war. Once more the ulterior motives behind the systematic slander of Father and his reports to Hitler are clearly seen.

However, returning to the motivations of the Polish and in the end of British policy, these two countries were also on the horns of a weighty dilemma. The Polish dilemma was defined by Poland's geopolitical situation between two superpowers, the German Reich and the Soviet Union. Piłsudski had seen it correctly, that it was up to Poland to reach a *modus vivendi* with both neighbours and sustain it. Poland ought as far as possible avoid to have to take one side or another. Thus it was first of all understandable when Poland was hesitating to allow herself to be hitched to the anti-Soviet, Central European bloc.

One has to put oneself in Beck's place. He was naturally aware of the plans of the German conspiracy. We have seen that Kleist-Schmenzin's report, with the projected German deployment, military tips and the promise of a military putsch, had immediately been passed on to Warsaw by Chamberlain. Most probably, therefore, Beck had already been put in the picture of the plans of the German conspiracy earlier. It was this view that will have constituted a fundament of his policy, for even Beck – who entitled himself 'colonel' – for all the overestimating there may have been of Polish potential, could not count on effective assistance from Britain and France if it should come to a military confrontation with the Reich.

Not only did Beck have knowledge of the plans of the German conspiracy, he was also under the massive pressure exerted on him by the USA and Britain not to come to an agreement with the Reich. Since he did not wish to set his stakes on the German card and because, due to the support from the United

States, he considered the position of the Western powers as the stronger in the long run, he remained adamant towards the German propositions, although he must have thought to himself that an extremely perilous situation could arise out of it for Poland. It was here that the prospect of a putsch in Germany was the lifeline Poland needed. At the same time, Beck could probably not know that Kleist-Schmenzin – somebody therefore who purported to represent a voice of the German conspiracy – had himself demanded the Corridor from the British; a claim that went incomparably farther than Hitler's.

A highly interesting detail is to be noted here: in 1939, Legation Secretary Hans Herwarth von Bittenfeld belonged to the German Embassy in Moscow. Although not entirely Aryan – as the expression was at the time – he had no sort of difficulties nor even persecution to endure, and occupied instead a secure position as a German diplomat of the 'higher service' in Father's Auswärtiges Amt. Herwarth had kept the American diplomat Charles Bohlen currently informed as to the state of the German-Russian discussions and had finally given him access to all the details of the treaty (copies of the telegrams to Berlin that he had to encode), including the secret supplementary agreement. Bohlen had naturally immediately put the State Department in the picture.

It emerged from this secret supplementary agreement that if it came to a conflict, Poland should once more be 'partitioned', in any case into spheres of interest, whatever one wished to conclude from that. These intentions of the Soviet Union and the Reich were therefore known to Roosevelt and the British government. Neither Roosevelt nor Chamberlain considered it expedient to communicate them to the Polish government, the country directly concerned. It is possible that this lethal danger arising for Poland out of the German-Russian accord might yet after all have led the Polish government to negotiations and perhaps to giving in. But the information, provided by an unknown conspirator promising a military putsch, was however promptly forwarded by the British government to Warsaw. It is also surprising that Herwarth did not also let the Poles know of the information he had about the German-Russian treaty. It would probably have been – and one would expect a diplomat to be aware of this – the surest way to avoid a war; this was how Herwarth justified his action.

There was consequently evidently no interest on the part of the British or Americans to appease the Polish crisis peacefully. This crisis had not arisen because Hitler wanted to 'pick a quarrel' so as to have a war but because stringent national and – as far as the German population of Poland was concerned – equally humanitarian issues were at stake. The situation was that in fact the conspiracy did not want to avoid war, but wanted on the contrary to cause one so as to be able to realize their goals. Had Kordt not labelled the peaceful Munich solution to the Sudeten problem as the 'second best solution', meaning thereby that the 'best' solution was the outbreak of war?[266]

The question therefore remains open, why England did not force an understanding between Poland and Germany? What could the British world-empire gain from a fresh passage at arms with Germany? The First World War had brought Britain to its position as the greatest power in the world. In the late 1930s, however, the United States, as well as Japan and Russia, due to their size, geopolitical situation and, other than Japan, their vast raw material base, were the rising powers. It must always be borne in mind that in this circle Germany was the weakest power, determined by her geographical position and lack of resources. But it was against precisely such a power that the British Empire thought it should turn, despite the experience of the First World War and above all under complete disregard for the German offers of lasting cooperation that the German leadership had addressed to London ever since 1933.

At the time British policy had decided against a worldly-wise solution, giving precedence to the centuries-old policy of a tight 'European balance', as the Foreign Office, Sir Eyre Crowe and his spiritual pupil Vansittart conceived it. For the British leadership therefore, the dilemma lay in the major probability of once again having to engage in a life-or-death armed encounter with the Reich. Once again the British Empire was gambling with its world-wide position. The strength of Germany was still remembered from the First World War: it determined England's wariness of the strongest Continental power.

The balancing weight of the Soviet Union could not be seen – or did not wish to be seen – as widely putting German power in perspective, and could possibly have yet still left Britain's choice open to opt for one or the other side, together with her 'mainland rapier' France. The British dilemma was therefore self-made, but for the British government absolutely presented itself as a real one. History has confirmed this dilemma, as the British leadership saw it, insofar as precisely what the British leadership feared did occur. The English statesmen of the first half of the twentieth century 'succeeded' in what their clever predecessors for over three centuries were successfully able to avoid, which was to make England politically on a world scale a small island situated off the coast of the Continent, more or less dependent on Europe, after the USA moved in to occupy the position the Empire once held as the most important power on earth.

From 1938 onward, a 'patent remedy' was apparently now offered to the British that would liberate them from the dilemma depicted. This remedy was the offer from the German conspiracy to overthrow Hitler through a military putsch. It needs little imagination to conceive that a putsch by the military after the outbreak of war would have decisively weakened the Reich. It would no longer, in the foreseeable future, be in a position to take major action in foreign policy.

However, Hitler's moderate demands on Poland harboured the risk that Poland would in the end finally come to an arrangement with Hitler. Here lies the key to the incomprehensible policy of Poland and the British government. Britain and France declared war on Germany at a moment when, through the accord with Russia, German foreign policy had succeeded in setting up the strongest imaginable grouping after the Western powers had rejected an understanding with the Reich.

The British government ran the risk of a war in the hope that the German conspiracy would in the end remove the risk and overthrow Hitler, which would thereby again decisively weaken the strengthened Reich. Through this, Britain would have restored her narrow European balance – in defiance of the global shifts of the seats of power. In 1938 the risk for England was still too great and she had not yet progressed sufficiently in her armament to be able to run it.[267] The Polish ambassador in Paris, Łukasiewicz, wrote in a report addressed to the Polish Foreign Minister on 29 March 1939:

> 'that the ultimate aim in the pursuit of its [England's] actions is not peace but to bring about the downfall of Germany.'[268]

Henderson, however, did not believe in the 'patent remedy' of the putsch as the solution to the British dilemma, and he was right. It is apparent from British documents how intensively the British government had clearly counted a putsch into their calculations. Already following Kleist-Schmenzin's secret visit to Vansittart in 1938, in a conference with Chamberlain, Halifax, Simon, Vansittart and Wilson, Henderson issued a warning that there was no use in hoping for any opposition to Hitler.[269] As the British ambassador reported to Halifax in February 1939:

> 'My definite impression since my return here is that Herr Hitler does not contemplate any adventures at the moment and that all stories and rumours to the contrary are completely without real foundation ... I regard and always have regarded it as a bad mistake to attribute excessive importance to stories spread generally with intention ... by those who regard war as the only weapon with which [the] Nazi regime can be overthrown.'[270]

Henderson's estimate of the situation is correct if at this point he does not believe in an 'adventure' of Hitler's, for on 21 March, once again Father was to renew Hitler's offer of November 1938 (in which a guarantee of Polish territory including the Corridor was foreseen) to the Polish ambassador, and invite Beck to Berlin.[271] Only when Beck abruptly (threatening war) rejected the offer and instead went to London did a fresh state of affairs arise for Hitler to which he had to adjust.

The role of the inner-German conspiracy is nowadays taboo, contrary to the early years after the war; nothing is heard any more about their fateful activities. This is why at this at this point a few quotations will be inserted, from statesmen who had then played a decisive role, who must after all have known upon what premises they conducted the policy that led to the declaration of war on Germany.

French Foreign Minister Georges Bonnet writes in his memoirs (translated from German):[272]

> 'An easy and swift victory was reckoned with … in the hope of an imminent assassination attempt that had already been prepared and was to topple National Socialism. As in 1938, we had been told about it constantly already in the last week before the war. Were it all summed up, the words were: "Hold out, and the German generals will overthrow Hitler!"'

At another point in his memoirs, Bonnet underscores that following the declaration of war on Germany by Britain and France on 3 September 1939:

> 'the way was consequently open for the "military coup d'état" that had so generally binding been announced to us.'

He later continues:

> '[In the Nuremberg trials] they [the German generals] depicted with an unheard-of wealth of detail the preparations they had made to topple the Führer yet they never – and one must ask oneself why – carried these into effect …
>
> ' … planned military conspiracies against Hitler had been announced to us in similar detail in 1939 and 1940, before and after our defeat, yet Hitler still lived until 1945.'

Somebody who is not familiar with the history of the last world war may take the depiction given here as a fabricated political thriller or espionage fiction. Unfortunately it is not so, as is proved by the following quotations, which must for that reason be given at this point.

In what was called the Wilhelmstrasse Trial at Nuremberg, which saw the indictment of high-ranking officials, among them the State Secretary of the Auswärtiges Amt, von Weizsäcker, a letter from the then Embassy Counsellor – and brother of Erich Kordt of Father's ministerial bureau – Theo Kordt (the same Kordt who had brought Weizsäcker's memorandum to Halifax at night by the back entrance) was produced and expressly corroborated by a sworn statement by the British Foreign Minister of the time, Lord Halifax, which states:

'In 1938 and 1939 I was in close (sometimes daily) contact with the Chief Diplomatic Adviser to H. M. Government, Sir Robert Vansittart. My brother [the Erich Kordt of Father's ministerial bureau] came several times personally to London, notwithstanding the obvious risks for his safety, in order to inform Sir Robert personally of the impending danger on the international horizon. Sir Robert assured me that he would pass this information to you [Lord Halifax] at once, for example, of Hitler's plans to come to an agreement with the Soviet Union, the negotiations between Hitler and Mussolini for an alliance, and the advice from the German opposition to put pressure on Mussolini.'

This letter of Kordt's to Lord Halifax, dated 29 July 1947,[273] was confirmed as genuine in a sworn statement. The statement by the chief at that time of the Central European sector of British Intelligence, Sigismund Payne Best, may also be placed on record about the information that was communicated to the British Cabinet in those days:

'At the outbreak of war our Intelligence Service had reliable information that Hitler was faced with the opposition of many men holding the highest appointments in his armed forces and civil service ... According to our information this opposition movement had assumed such proportions that it might even have led to revolt and the downfall of the Nazis.'[274]

The South African Minister of Defence, Oswald Pirow, reports on the 'warmongering [British] chauvinists in London, emboldened by German traitors' and that 'if war were to break out between England and Germany, a rising against Hitler should be reckoned with'.[275] The French writer Paul Morand says in his memoirs (translated from German):

'The French historians of *France Libre* may tell the French what they will. I was in London before they were, since July 1939, and was able to follow the efforts of a small warmongering minority who, with Churchill, attained their objective step by step.'[276]

British Prime Minister Neville Chamberlain, finally, confided the following to his diary on 10 September 1939, a few days after war broke out:

'what I hope for is not a military victory – I very much doubt the feasibility of that – but a collapse of the German home front.'[277]

The true motivations for the British declaration of war could not be expressed more clearly. Chamberlain was the statesman who was in the end responsible for the war with Germany, so he is thereby the most important witness.

The German conspiracy did not only contribute to embroil Germany in a fateful war, but then did not actually draw the consequences from it and strike a coup. The conspiracy also tricked Germany's opponent Poland with the promised putsch; she suffered one of the gravest catastrophes of her history. Finally, England lost her world empire and prestige status in the world because of having relied on the promise of a putsch by the German conspirators, and later did not want to alter her own course.

It was the hope of a 'patent remedy'[278] that led Britain to declare war on Germany, a solution spelling 'collapse of the home front', by which the military coup is to be understood, which, as French Foreign Minister Bonnet writes, they 'had repeatedly been assured was to happen'. But no putsch ensued, and the 'patent remedy' remained unobtainable for Poland and Britain. The conspiracy had enticed Poland and Britain into war with their promises, but at the decisive moment stayed inactive.

Why then was Hitler not in fact eliminated when war did break out? Did the foxy old diplomat Vansittart have afterthoughts when at the Nuremberg trials he closed an affidavit requested by Father's defence with the words:

'I have never agreed to treaties with the Germans, because Germans rarely kept to them.'

Had Vansittart been thinking of the accords with the German conspiracy who had not kept their word to the British government, and thereby also to Poland? Perhaps in this basically anti-German resentment that was here expressed, the embittered 'betrayed betrayer' played its role and recognized the consequences of his error in having relied on small-time conspirators at a decisive, vital time for the British Empire. Vansittart will have realized already in the course of the war that the era of British world rule was coming to an end, and that he had played a part in the swift decline at a decisive point. His bitterness is understandable.

As I heard after the war, he also adopted this negative attitude toward the Kordt brothers when they are said to have turned to him to have their above-mentioned role confirmed. They will have then finally addressed Halifax on the subject of the requested statement. Old man Adenauer knew why he refused the reinstatement of this very Erich Kordt in the Auswärtiges Amt:

> 'That man betrayed Ribbentrop and thwarted his policy. What is to give me the assurance that he will not treat me the same way?'[279]

The European powers participating in the outbreak of the Second World War – Britain, France, Poland and the German Reich – all hoped without any doubt to be able to avert the war, which, however, finally did break out. The British, French and Polish governments hoped for the collapse of the home front in Germany. The German government, in turn, could not believe that under the given circumstances Poland would allow matters to reach a military confrontation.

How does the current cliché that Hitler wanted to have 'his war' with Poland square with his proposals, which he repeatedly offered Poland for almost half a year? Against this, the Polish ambassador had declared already on 26 March 1939 in his discussion with Father that pursuit of the German desire to reunite Danzig with Germany would 'mean war with Poland'.[280] It should be held in mind that Danzig had a freely chosen (under the supervision of the League of Nations) German government. Hitler reacted calmly and instructed Father simply to let the Polish ambassador know 'that naturally a solution could not be found if there is talk of war here'. It was the end of March 1939. He evidently still hoped for an arrangement with Poland.

The same is valid for Britain. Even if Chamberlain's entry in his diary that he hoped for 'a collapse of the home front in Germany' were not known, this conclusion would arise from the policy actually pursued by Britain. When has Britain ever entrusted her fate – in this instance the decision between war and peace – to a second-rate power? The ratification of Britain's 'blank cheque' to Poland through the House of Commons after the conclusion of the German-Russian pact shows clearly that in Britain it was believed that real war could be avoided by formally unleashing it. The goal was obvious: thereby to attain the desired weakening of the Reich without surrendering completely to dependence on the United States. Poland was the 'sacrificial lamb', and willingly undertook this role in order to bring about the outbreak of a war – for Britain – who hoped for a 'collapse of the home front' to ensue from it. The Polish ambassador in Paris had comprehended this, for the following stands in his report, already mentioned, to Polish Foreign Minister Beck:

'It is childishly ingenious, and at the same time disloyal, to propose to a state that finds itself in Poland's situation that it should jeopardize its relations with a strong neighbor like Germany and hurl a catastrophe on the world, such as a war.'[281]

To sum up: Britain, France and Poland undertook the military confrontation with Germany in the hope of a putsch, that is the collapse of the home front in Germany.

After the concluding of his case in Nuremberg, Father drew up a paper in which the course of events that led to the actual outbreak of the war is stated. These statements were consequently not for the purpose of his defence; it mattered to him to record his view of things for history, for he reckoned with being 'eliminated', as we called the expected death sentence in our last conversations. He said:[282]

'The situation I found before me upon my return was considerably more tense than before my flight out … On the day after my arrival in Berlin the crisis reached its first peak. Only then did I learn that during my absence Adolf Hitler had had on Mt Obersalzberg a very serious discussion with the British ambassador Henderson who handed over a letter from the British Prime Minister. It stood therein that a warlike conflict between Germany and Poland would bring Britain into the arena. In his talk with Henderson and in a letter to Chamberlain that followed on 23 August, Adolf Hitler stated that he was determined to solve the Danzig-Corridor question and would tolerate no further Polish provocations. He was obliged to see in military measures taken by England an act of threat against the Reich and would in that cases [*sic*] order the immediate mobilization of the German armed forces. The situation was at a total stalemate, the Führer had come to Berlin.

'In the morning after my return from Moscow, that is before noon on the dramatic day of August 25th, I discussed the letter to Chamberlain with Hitler and proposed that I should once again make an attempt with England. I learned shortly after this talk that on our part military measures had already commenced being taken. At this point, Hitler will not have counted on it that England would intervene and start a war because of Poland. Early in the afternoon, through an employee of the Auswärtiges Amt, I received the news of the ratification of the British-Polish treaty that had been only informally concluded on 6 April. I immediately hastened to the Reich Chancellery with the announcement so as to urge the Führer as to his cancellation of the military measures taken – with the words that the ratification of the English-Polish treaty of guarantee signified "the war with England" if he made a move against Poland, and that therefore the "marching order must be rescinded immediately".'[283]

Hitler accepted Father's communication without argument and at once put his proposal to cease the military movements in motion through Keitel. Only then did Father hear from Hitler that 'Italy did not consider the mutual defence clause valid in the case of a military conflict with Poland'. It is once more indicative of Hitler's working method that for example my father, as foreign minister, was not immediately informed about Hitler's discussion with Henderson on 23 August, the introduction of military measures on 25 August or the communication from the Italian ambassador on the same day. Hitler's personal Luftwaffe Adjutant, Nicolaus von Below,[284] had noted that Father had never taken part in military conferences. Even in the situation of acute crisis of the last days of August there were no discussions in common under Hitler's chairmanship. The Foreign Minister was brought in, as he writes, only on 28 August, after Henderson had flown to London in the Führer's airplane to discuss the situation with the British government:

'Henderson flew back to Berlin at 5pm of the afternoon of 28 August, bringing with him the Memorandum that had been elaborated by the British Government. Therewith the decisive phase of the crisis began. Three hours before Henderson's departure for Berlin on 28 August at 2 pm, the British government had telegraphed Warsaw to ask whether the Polish government authorized them to communicate to the German government that Poland was prepared to enter at once into direct discussion with Germany.

'The Memorandum from the British government handed to Hitler contains the corresponding ascertainment: "They [His Majesty's Government] have already received a definite assurance from the

Polish Government that they are prepared to enter into discussions on this basis." The basis mentioned immediately preceding was to be that Poland's essential interests should be safeguarded and a still to be finalized German–Polish agreement internationally guaranteed.

'In the "Blue Book" made public by the British government after war broke out, this reassurance as mentioned of the Polish government is noticeably missing. Since the enquiry was made at 2 pm, and Henderson had departed from London at 5 pm, it must have reached London within this span of time. The wording of the reply from the Polish government, kept secret to this day, is of the most decisive importance for judging the further development of subsequent events.

'On 1 September the British Prime Minister Chamberlain trumpeted that "all the relevant documents had been made public" – whereas this particular important document is missing … My defence in the Nuremberg trial made an application requesting the submission of Poland's reply of 28th August to the British government. The court did not comply with this request!'[285]

At 10.30 pm on 28 August, Henderson handed the British Memorandum to Hitler.[286] Father gives the content of the Memorandum as meaning that the British government agreed with Hitler as to the dangers at the present moment being in the reports of the treatment of the German minorities by the Poles. In their view, direct negotiations between Germany and Poland ought to be initiated, in which it should be clear from the outset that an agreement achieved would be guaranteed by other powers. Father continues:

'In the afternoon of the next day (29.8) Henderson was summoned to the Reich Chancellery at 6:45 pm. In the course of this discussion the British ambassador became very fierce and even permitted himself to pound the table with his fist, a behaviour that would have caused the Führer, as he later told Hess, to break off the meeting had I not managed to calm tempers by a deflecting intervention, thus preventing the foundering of the negotiation.'[287]

One may be reminded in this context of the advice given by the German conspiracy to the British in 1938 that a general should be sent to Hitler to bash the table with his riding crop, this being language Hitler understood. Had Henderson thought of this idea from the German side? Whatever the case, Adolf Hitler finally gave Henderson his answer in writing. Father says it arose from it that the German government of the Reich:[288]

1. though sceptical as to the prospects of a successful outcome of such direct discussions with the Polish Government, they are prepared to accept the English proposal;
2. accept the British Government's offer of their good offices in securing the despatch to Berlin of a Polish Emissary with powers, and count on the arrival of this Emissary on Wednesday, the 30th August;
3. in making these proposals had never had any intention of touching Poland's vital interests or questioning the existence of an independent Polish State;
4. would immediately draw up proposals for an acceptable solution and would, if possible, place these at the disposal of the British Government before the arrival of the Polish negotiator.

'By this statement Adolf Hitler had unequivocally accepted the British proposal for immediate, direct and equitable negotiations with Poland. To judge subsequent developments the fateful question arises: when and in what form did the British government fulfil the duty they had themselves undertaken to transmit this proposal to the Polish government?

'Ambassador Henderson duly passed the German reply on to his government by telegram in the evening of 29 August. As the British Blue Book shows, Henderson's report reached London at 0:15 a.m. The first immediate reaction from the British government was to cable Berlin saying it was "unreasonable" to expect a Polish representative to undertake negotiations within 24 hours. Thereupon Henderson reported to Lord Halifax by telegram on 30 August as to the transmission of this communication he had received. In it he quotes a remark of Adolf Hitler's that one could fly from Warsaw to Berlin in one and a half hours. Henderson added his own comment in his telegram, he would recommend "that the Polish Government should swallow this eleventh-hour effort to establish direct contact with Hitler, even if it be only to convince the world that they were prepared to make their own sacrifice for preservation of peace ... "

'The British government did not follow through with this suggestion from their ambassador in Berlin at least not to reject Adolf Hitler's proposal outright. They did not at once transmit Germany's Note in reply to the Polish government, thereby consciously delaying the transfer of the German invitation to negotiations. Although they did straight away inform the British ambassador in Warsaw Sir Kennard they gave him instructions not to communicate Hitler's answer to the Polish government before he received further instructions from London.[289]

'The instruction given by the British government to their ambassador in Warsaw does not appear in the English Blue Book and is not known of until this day. In this case too, the attempt by my defence counsel in Nuremberg to acquire the missing document from the British government had no success.

'It is of the highest historical interest to find out what connection there is between the instructions of the British government to their ambassador in Warsaw and the fact that in the course of the same 30th of August the order was given for Polish general mobilization, albeit not yet made known. The timing of this mobilization – of which we were confidentially informed the same day – is of the greatest significance for an overall judgement of the crisis. It stands in blatant contradiction to the alleged assurance of Poland that they were ready to negotiate directly with Germany.'

It was but in the afternoon of 30 August that the British ambassador in Warsaw was authorized by his government to inform the Polish government of the text of the German Note in which the readiness of the German government to negotiate direct with Poland is declared. At the same time the Polish government was given the advice 'to be prepared', under certain conditions, 'without delay' for direct discussions. This advice was, however, not given for instance for the purpose of the early clearing up of the crisis but instead rather, as is revealingly stated, 'from the point of view of the Internal situation in Germany and of world opinion'. The mention of the 'Internal situation in Germany' may be expressing the intention to portray Hitler as usual as the warmonger – as a precondition of mass psychology for the planned and promised military putsch.

Interestingly, it was not until midnight on 30 August that Henderson handed in a further Memorandum from the British government, therefore after expiration of the deadline set by the German side for the arrival of a Polish negotiator. Although on the 28th the British government had demanded immediate direct discussions as the 'logical next step', they now proposed a German–Polish discussion on the 'method of contact and the arrangements for discussions'.

Father describes these dramatic hours as follows:

'On handing over the British Note, Ambassador Henderson informed me according to his instructions that the British Government was not in a position to advise the Polish Government to accept this procedure

Friedrich v. Ribbentrop, *Generalintendant* in the Prussian Army, President of the Royal Prussian audit office (1768-1841).

Ferdinand Ribbentrop, Joachim v. Ribbentrop's grandfather, in the uniform of major and *Braunschweigischer Artillerist*.

Karl v. Ribbentrop (1822-1893), decorated with the 1864 Pour le Mérite Medal. In 1925 his daughter Gertrud adopted Joachim v. Ribbentrop.

Joachim v. Ribbentrop's parents: Richard and his wife Sophie, née Hertwig.

Arosa, *ca.* 1910/11. Steering the sleigh is Joachim Ribbentrop. As brakeman, his father, Major Richard Ribbentrop.

Centre front: Lieutenant Joachim Ribbentrop, Hussar Regiment 12, in a Baltic country, 1915.

Richard Ribbentrop in his major's uniform, 1915.

Hitler greets Ribbentrop following the conclusion of the Naval Agreement with Britain, 1935.

Ribbentrop with the journalist from the Paris newspaper *Le Matin* and the *Journal des débats*, Fernand de Brinon, Dahlem, 1935/36.

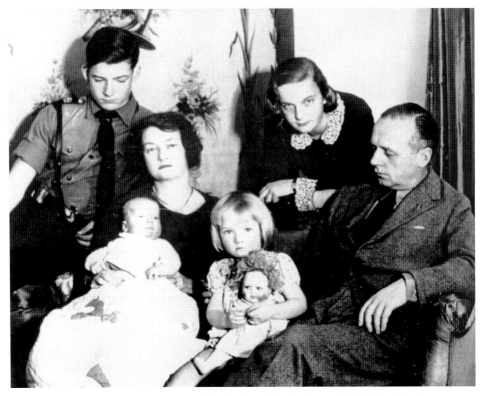

The Reich Foreign Minister's family, 1936. Left to right, back row: Rudolf and Bettina, centre: Annelies and Joachim v. Ribbentrop, bottom: Adolf and Ursula.

Rudolf v. Ribbentrop in London, 1936.

In front of the Embassy in London, 1936. In the middle of the photograph from left to right: Annelies, Ribbentrop and Ernst Woermann.

Arrival of Chamberlain to the Munich Agreement on 29 September 1938.

German-French Declaration, Paris, December 1938.

Ribbentrop with Hitler and the children, Adolf and Ursula, having a coffee in the Auswärtiges Amt, 1939.

British historian Thomas Conwell-Evans, pictured in 1939 in Germany.

Annelies v. Ribbentrop with her father-in-law, Richard Ribbentrop *ca*. 1939.

Left to right: the Ribbentrop parents, Hitler, the two children Ursula and Adolf, Joachim and Annelies v. Ribbentrop, Julius Schaub and Walther Hewel in front of the Ribbentrops' Dahlem house, 1939.

Left to right: Hewel, Ribbentrop, Franz v. Papen and Ribbentrop's sister, Inge Jenke, after April 1939.

Signature of the Pact of Steel between Italy and Germany, 22 May 1939. Sitting: Ciano, Hitler and Ribbentrop. Standing behind: Keitel and Weizsäcker.

Signature of the German-Soviet Pact of Non-Aggression on 23 August 1939 in Moscow. In the background are Gustav Adolph v. Halem, Deputy Protocol Chief of the Auswärtiges Amt (left) and Richard Schulze [-Kossens], Ribbentrop's temporary adjutant (right).

Ribbentrop and Schulenburg with an unknown Soviet official. Moscow Airport, 1939.

Molotov greeted by Ribbentrop in Berlin, 1940.

Ribbentrop greeted in 1939 at Moscow Airport by the German Ambassador, Count v. der Schulenburg.

In the Auswärtiges Amt in Berlin (*ca*. 1940); standing, from left: Schweimer, Halem, Gottfriedsen; front row, from left: Dörnberg, Gaus, Schmidt (press secretary); right: Erich Kordt.

Joachim v. Ribbentrop with his son Rudolf, May 1940, in the Artois.

Reception of the Corps Diplomatique in the new Reich Chancellery before 1941. In front: Ribbentrop, Hitler, Meißner.

Hitler and Ribbentrop standing in front of the Special Train, *ca*. 1941. To their left is Max Wünsche (Adjutant) and Schulze [-Kossens].

Ribbentrop, Hewel (centre) and Mme Pappritz, Legation counsellor in the Auswärtiges Amt's Protocol Department, after 1941.

Renthe-Fink, Ribbentrop, Hewel, Steengracht, after 1941.

Parade in Paris, summer 1942.

With the Lehndorffs in East Prussia, *ca*. 1942/43. Proprietor of the East Prussian accomodation of Joachim von Ribbentrop.

Rudolf v. Ribbentrop, Commander 7th Company, Panzer Regiment 1, Leibstandarte SS Adolf Hitler Division, March 1943 in Kharkov.

Rudolf v. Ribbentrop in street fighting in Kharkov, March 1943.

Rudolf v. Ribbentrop (1943). Wearer of the Knight's Cross of the Iron Cross and the Wound Badge in gold.

Ribbentrop with magnifying glass and violin in Fuschl, *ca*. 1943/44.

Rots near Caen (9 June 1944): Max Wünsche, Regiment Commander Panzer Regiment 12, with bandaged head. In sidecar: Rudolf v. Ribbentrop.

Jochen Peiper (1915–1976). Peiper was one of my most esteemed superiors. This photograph was taken in autumn 1944.

Schmidt (head interpreter), Mussolini, Alfieri (Italian Ambassador to Berlin), Ciano, Ribbentrop and Schmidt (press secretary).

Hitler, Ribbentrop and Mussolini.

Rudolf von Ribbentrop in the 1960s.

Rudolf von Ribbentrop, 2016.

proposed by the German Government. They recommend to adopt the normal diplomatic way i.e. by handing their proposals to the Polish Ambassador in order to set matters going ...

'In case the German Government would also communicate these proposals to the British Government and the latter would come to the opinion that the proposals constituted a reasonable basis for a settlement of the problems to be discussed, they would use their influence in Warsaw to achieve a settlement.

'I for my part pointed out to Henderson that as per confidential information which reached us, during the day the Polish general mobilization had already been ordered. Furthermore I had to draw his attention to the fact that on the German side a Polish negotiator had been awaited in vain, therefore the question of a possible proposal could no longer exist. However, in order yet to make one more attempt at a solution, I read out to the ambassador the prepared German proposals that Adolf Hitler had dictated quite alone and had handed to me with precise instructions, and I elucidated them in detail.

'In his speech of 1 September 1939 in the House of Commons, Prime Minister Chamberlain maintained that this reading out had ensued "at top speed". The contrary is correct.[290] Chamberlain's statement is all the more curious as Henderson's report on this discussion later published in the British Blue Book places on record that Henderson had absolutely correctly grasped all the essential points of the German proposals and transmitted them to his government. On this, Henderson reports in his book of memoirs *Failure of a Mission* (page 273) that following upon his discussion with me, at 2 a.m. he himself had mentioned the cession of Danzig to the Reich and the plebiscite in the Corridor as the main points in the German proposals to the Polish ambassador Lipski. Henderson remarks thereto that he had stated them as not too unreasonable and had suggested to Lipski that his Government should propose at once a meeting between Field-Marshals Smigly-Rydz and Göring ...

'Upon my return to the Reich Chancellery at the end of the discussion I reported to the Führer that Henderson had been very serious and that my conviction that the English guarantee for Poland would be implemented had been reinforced anew. I recommended that the German proposals that I had set out to him should be communicated to Ambassador Henderson also in writing. Hitler rejected this suggestion, although in the course of the morning of 31 August he did after all send the text to the British ambassador through Göring–Dahlerus. On that day Adolf Hitler had again awaited an intervention by England and/or the appearance of a Polish plenipotentiary, and finally, in the evening of 31 August had the German proposals made public also on radio. The immediate response from Warsaw radio was a clear provocation.'[291]

The content of the German proposals was in essence:

- Return of Danzig to the German Reich.
- Plebiscite in the Corridor on the basis of the Baltic Sea and a line running from Marienwerder-Graudenz-Kulm-Bromberg-Schönlanke. Entitled to vote are all Poles and Germans living in this area on 1 January 1918. (If the line given on the map is traced it will be noted that only a relatively minor part of the northern 'Corridor' would underlie the referendum.)
- Gdingen stays exempt and remains with Poland.
- The rest of the proposals regard free lines of communication for Germany and for Poland, minority rights for the respective minorities, demilitarization of Danzig and Gdingen, international controls, etc.[292]

Father's notes from Nuremberg continue:

'The English Blue Book records that the British Government was in possession of the Henderson Report in the morning of 31 August at 9:30 a.m. Since Henderson had informed Ambassador Lipski already at two in the morning it is not to be assumed that he briefed his own government as to the content and outcome of the discussion conducted with me only at such a late hour. It is also proven that on the morning of 31 August the *Daily Telegraph* contained a mention of a night-time session of the English Cabinets at which the German proposals had been debated. Remarkably, this issue of the major London newspaper was taken out of circulation and another issue was substituted wherein that item was not contained.[293]

'The fact is in any case that the German proposals were known both in London and in Warsaw in the morning of 31 August, and it is also a fact that in the course of this decisive day the English Government made no further serious attempts to overcome the crisis. It could yet have been remedied even on the 31st of August without further ado by an intervention from England. All that was needed was for Warsaw to authorize Ambassador Lipski to receive the German proposals, but not even that was done …

'The Polish ambassador Lipski called on me at 6:30 pm on 31 August. He explained that the Polish Government "was in favour of the British Government's proposal"; a formal reply to it would "soon" reach the German Government. As Lipski expressly stressed to me, he had no authorization to receive German proposals nor indeed for any effective negotiation or even mere discussion. On the same day the Polish Foreign Minister had orally assured the British ambassador Kennard the Polish ambassador in Berlin would not be authorised to accept German proposals … [294]

'By making their proposals public, the German government had once more opened the door for Poland to agree to the promised negotiations. What transpired could have yet been corrected if the Polish government had picked up the ball now publicly thrown to them and over their radio network declared a positive attitude. The Warsaw broadcast had in fact given a reply already on 31 August at 11 pm. But this reply – missing in the British Blue Book – spoke only of an "impudent proposal" and indignantly rebuffed negotiations. Germany, it was cynically underlined, had waited in vain for a Polish delegate. The Warsaw government's answer exists in military orders.[295]

'The Polish stance is comprehensible only if one takes two facts into account, that were partly made public only at the Nuremberg trials:

1. Not only had the British Government not done anything decisive in Warsaw to solve the German-Polish problem, but had instead said a possible visit of the Polish Foreign Minister Beck to Berlin was "undesirable". Evidently, it was feared that in discussion with Adolf Hitler Beck would yet decide to settle peacefully.
2. Ambassador Lipski, obviously informed about the plans of the German opposition circles, was of the opinion that "were war to begin, a military putsch would break out in Germany", "Hitler removed" and that "the Polish army be in Berlin in 6 weeks at the latest" … [296]

'On 2 September Mussolini again attempted a solution to the crisis. He proposed an international conference to convene on 5 September with the objective of "reviewing clauses of the Treaty of Versailles which are cause of the present disturbance in life in Europe." The Duce let it be known that he could bring about such a conference "if the armies were to be at a halt".

'We accepted this proposition and, as France also gave a positive reply, for a few hours on 2 September it appeared that peace might still be rescued. Only the British Government, through Lord Halifax, in the House of Lords in the afternoon of 2 September rejected this last proposal for peace.'

For 10 September Chamberlain enters in his diary:

'the final-long-drawn-out agonies that preceded the actual declaration of war were as nearly unendurable as could be. We were anxious to bring things to a head, but there were three complications, – the secret communications that were going on with Goering and Hitler through a neutral intermediary, the conference proposal of Mussolini, and the French anxiety to postpone the actual declaration as long as possible, until they could evacuate their women and children, and mobilise their armies. There was very little of this that we could say in public.'

He follows up on this entry on the same date with:

'I believe he [Hitler] did seriously contemplate an agreement with us, and that he worked seriously at proposals (subsequently broadcast) which to his ... mind seemed ... generous.'[297]

Father wrote:

'There is today no longer any doubt at all that in the last two days of August England would have had the possibility to avert the crisis and therewith the risk of war with a signal to Warsaw. That the British Government consciously did not do it signifies that they had decided to go to war.

... It goes without saying that in these days of crisis ... I maintained toward my Office and the diplomatic corps an unequivocal stance, for therein lay the only chance to bring the opponent to a compromise. With an uncertain or ambiguous stance of the Foreign Minister a readiness for peace on the opponent's part could in this situation in no way be targeted.'[298]

In those days of September 1939 he could indeed not have had the knowledge that he put to paper in 1946 in his Nuremberg prison cell shortly before his execution:

'We of course did not know in those days that in London they were counting on the conspiratorial group already mentioned of most authoritative German military personnel and political figures, whereby they had arrived at hoping for an easy victory over Germany. These circles of conspirators consequently played a decisive part in the outbreak of war. In the last days of August they thwarted all our efforts to reach an amicable solution and probably tipped the balance in the English decision for war.'[299]

There is no doubt that Hitler did not want a war with Poland. I shall not forget Father's very thoughtful mood as I said goodbye to him so as to join the Deutschland Regiment as a recruit in Munich-Freimann. It did not derive from his alleged wrong advice to Hitler about Britain's willingness for war, quite the contrary: he regretted having been right in his estimate of England since the beginning of 1938.

Hitler wanted to attain the consolidated position of the Reich in Central Europe without a war. This thesis is absolutely plausible if the facts are objectively evaluated. The question must again be posed: '*Cui bono?*' Of what real use would the war be to him? For Germany, desperate in her central location and deficient in resources, war always signified an exceptionally grave risk. In order to achieve a partly secure position in this sense, German policies had to run risks, but do everything possible to avert a military conflict. This was, however, not in the hands of the Reich Government alone.

After a front against the Reich had been put up, the Polish problem had become so acute that it had now to be solved when Germany had the strongest possible alliance grouping at its disposal. To hedge any longer in case Poland remained unapproachable would have spawned much greater political risks, irrespective of the fact that time was henceforth running against the Reich, in view of the American support given to Britain's and France's striving for armaments.

However, the most important aspect for judging German policy was, as repeatedly mentioned before, the possible threat from the Soviet Union.[300] As a far-seeing politician, Hitler had to organize Eastern Europe under German leadership to prevent a possible expansion of Soviet Russia. He could not simply stand by and see how matters would evolve. One need only take as an example that the Soviet Union would have managed to seize the Romanian oil wells by exertion of massive pressure, whatever form it may have taken. The Reich would have been cut off from its natural hinterland in the Balkans, thereby also from the sole oil wells that were accessible to it by land. Czechoslovakia was tied by alliance to the Soviet Union, by tradition maintaining good relations also with Yugoslavia. It will be seen that Moscow's demands, as presented to Hitler and Ribbentrop in Berlin in 1940 by Molotov, are couched in clear language in view of the objectives that Moscow had in mind. The grouping of alliance with the Soviet Union brought to fruition in the summer of 1939 had to be utilized to solve the Polish problem so as to be able to occupy a halfway tenable position in the centre of Europe.

If I firmly state, with the knowledge of the information – that at the time I received from my parents – that on the part of Germany there was no desire to wage war, it was nevertheless necessary to reckon with the possibility that one would be forced to it. It may serve as further proof that Hitler did not want a war if it is ascertained that Germany was in no way in the optimum state of readiness for a military conflict. This, however, in view of the Reich's situation signifies a reproach to Hitler that cannot be put more sharply,[301] for he should have reckoned with being embroiled in a military dispute. His Foreign Minister had repeatedly put the danger before his eyes since the beginning of 1938. To this I shall revert later.

The sensational military successes in Poland and the West were due to the novel strategies of motorized major military units that took the opponent totally by surprise, and not to the quality of the German weapons, to say nothing of the planning and organization of the German armament. German arms production reached its peak only in the latter course of 1944 – despite the Allied bombing: proof of how unprepared the Reich was for warfare and what the Reich's leadership had neglected.

A personal memory at this point: in the winter of 1939/40, when she visited me in Würzburg where my regiment was quartered, Mother asked me how many German U-boats I thought were permanently operating in British waters. I knew that at the conclusion of the 1935 naval agreement Father had negotiated an agreed relative strength between the British and the German fleets of 35 per cent. The agreement concerned the total tonnage and could therefore be varied in the diverse sort of vessel. It was in other words, for example, permitted to build more U-boats at the expense of heavy shipping, according to the agreement up to 100 per cent of the English tonnage. I therefore estimated some thirty submarines, to be told by mother there were two! Numbers may have varied but it could evidently be seen that there had been failure to place the focus of the marine armament on the weapon that promised the greatest chances of success against Britain. These omissions once more contradict the claim that Hitler had wanted 'his war', planned and consciously unleashed long before. The war was nevertheless now a reality and had to be waged – I was soon to be involved in it.

In summary, we can say the following: because of the hostile policy of the West (Britain, France and the USA), with which Poland had entirely sided, the consolidation of the German position in Eastern Europe had to be effected as long as the rear was safe, through the treaty with the Soviet Union. On the German side it was perfectly clear that a limitless, unconditionally friendly policy toward Germany on the part of the Soviet Union could not be reckoned with.

Roosevelt

Following the successfully conducted campaigns in Poland and France, the question for the Reich's leadership was with which strategic goals the war was henceforth to be waged, since the British government under Churchill was not prepared to treat with German offers for peace. However, before I come to the cogitations and planning on the German side for the continuation of the war, I have to dwell on the particular power and its leading personality that world politics initially cloaked, then ever more openly defined in the war's first phase, finally to define it as the greatest power waging war: the United States of America under their president, Roosevelt.

In the First World War the USA had played the decisive role in the outcome being favourable to the Entente and against the Reich. The prospect of a fair peace proclaimed in American President Woodrow Wilson's 'Fourteen Points' had motivated the Kaiser's Imperial government to lay down their arms. In the First World War the United States had come down on the side of the British-French Entente, although there was then in Germany neither a Hitler nor persecutions of Jews. President Wilson had declared the 'end of isolation':

> 'The isolation of the United States is at an end, not because we chose to go into the politics of the world, but because, by the sheer genius of this people and the growth of our power, we have become a determining factor in the history of mankind and after you have become a determining factor you cannot remain isolated whether you want to or not. Isolation ended by the processes of history, not by the processes of our independent choice.'[302]

The disappointments of the Americans in Versailles and the tensions in Europe resulting from the treaty had given rise in the American public opinion to a trend to isolation. They did not want to be embroiled in European quarrels. The United States did not sign the Versailles Treaty and stayed out of the League of Nations. They were nonetheless involved in the economic and political relations of Europe, as they occupied a key position in the reparations issue. The debts of the Allies were to be erased by the German reparation payments. The looming global economic crisis was in the first place certainly not helpful in arousing the readiness of Americans to engage in international politics.

Roosevelt had conducted his election campaign with the domestic political-economic slogans of the so-called New Deal, and had been elected to the presidency of the United States in 1932. Already in 1933 the American delegate at the Geneva Disarmament Conference, Norman Davis, had declared:

> 'it would neither have been just or wise, nor was it intended, that the Central Powers should be subject for all times to a special treatment in armaments. There is and has been a corresponding duty on the part of the other Powers, parties to the peace treaties, that by successive stages they too would bring their armaments down to a level strictly determined by the needs of self-defence.'[303]

However, on 6 May 1933, Roosevelt stated to Hjalmar Schacht who was visiting him, that in the matter of German armament the United States insisted on the status quo being maintained, and at the end of the conversation stressed 'as strongly as possible' to Schacht that he considered 'Germany as the only possible obstacle to a Disarmament Treaty', as the American Secretary of State informed the American ambassador in London on 8 May that year.[304]

Roosevelt had first of all to consolidate and expand his position as the newly-elected president of the United States. He nevertheless undertook his first steps in world politics as early as 1933. In November 1933 the United States formally acknowledged the Soviet Government. The negotiation took place in Washington between Roosevelt and Soviet Foreign Minister Litvinov. For sixteen years the United States had refused to acknowledge the Soviet Union. German policy was avowedly determined by a position of defence against the Soviet Union, whose recognition by the USA at this time could mean nothing positive for the Reich.

As early as 1936, Roosevelt attacked the 'have-not' nations in a speech to Congress, that they had lacked the 'necessary patience' to attain sensible and legitimate goals through peaceful negotiations or an appeal to the world's 'sensitive sense of the notion of justice'. The notion of the 'have-nots' – at that time in the first place Italy and Japan were meant, but Germany too was named as a third nation in this context – was a term also used by the German press. I remember my parents talking about it in London, and my father considering the term unfortunate. To present one's self as a 'have-not' insinuated on the one hand the existence of a deficiency in material resources and, on the other, aggressiveness. As ambassador to England, he however had absolutely no influence on the terminology of the German press, as also later as Foreign Minister he attained no unequivocal authority over German foreign propaganda. It was a permanent apple of discord between the Auswärtiges Amt and the Propaganda Ministry, evidently not regarded by Hitler with disfavour.

Roosevelt had remained firm in his foreign policy in regard to Japan, Italy and also the Reich since his famous 'Quarantine' speech of 5 October 1937, at the latest. At the same time, the aggressive wording recommended a stance that was, simply, 'against dictators'. Another memory from London: my parents had then ascertained that this was 'the new form of propaganda against Germany', since the slogan 'against dictators' was first of all directed against Germany. The Soviet Union was almost totally left out before it attacked Finland, whereupon, on a surge of American domestic indignation at this, Roosevelt declared publicly – or in the 1940 election year was obliged to declare – that it was 'a dictatorship like every other'. In general, Italy was not treated roughly as it was hoped that she could again be distanced from the 'Axis'. There was no mention of the numerous dictatorships or quasi-dictatorships in Europe and the world, to speak here only of Spain, Portugal, Turkey, Poland, Hungary, Austria, Jugoslavia, China and Japan, as well as a number of South and Central American states.

In Japan, the United States saw their opponent in East Asia and, insofar as the policy of improvement of relations with the Soviet Union was plausible, the Soviet state nonetheless stood in direct contradiction to the principles of 'liberty' and 'democracy', the banner under which the Americans were shortly to conduct their political and, in the end military, 'crusades'.[305] Whilst in regard to the most radical and brutal dictatorial regime Roosevelt embarked upon 'appeasement', he challenged Germany and Japan, in an increasingly brusque manner. Roosevelt had need of Japan so as to let the concern of Americans regarding the security of their country grow little by little. Japan had expanded onto the Chinese mainland and was thus calling the traditional American 'Open Door in China' policy into question.

American policy had as far as possible been to obstruct an 'Ostpolitik' of the Reich, thereby meaning that understanding with the Soviet Union that came to be known as the Rapallo policy. Hence Roosevelt opened his arms to the Soviet Union, albeit between 1933 and 1939 there was little actual inducement for such a step. Roosevelt's opting for the Soviet Union signified setting a course for world politics of the first order, in the sense of the position the United States intended to take up in the future in global politics.

Two great powers decisively influenced the political events of the world in the twentieth century. They were not the traditional European 'Great Powers', i.e. Britain, France or the German Reich. They were the United States and the Soviet Union, the two determining decisive powers in world politics.

Both great powers utilized attractive ideologies. Russia proclaimed the 'Promised Land of Socialism' for the future, the Unites States a perfected democracy and 'anti-colonialism'. When I say 'utilized' these ideologies, it means that for the leadership of both powers these ideologies were not only instruments in order to motivate their masses to espouse the furthering of unequivocal imperial goals (in whatever form these goals may have manifested themselves, whether in economic or military fashion), but also so as to find partners, above all in the Third World.

What, in the end, does 'imperialism' mean, once it is scrubbed of all clichés of ideology or propaganda? In the broadest sense, imperialism means extending one's own sphere of influence so far that the greatest security and the greatest possible well-being (possibly at the expense of other countries) of one's own body politic against a possible competitor for power is attained. 'Security' is to be understood in its widest sense, and not infrequently amounted to an express demand for influence to be exerted on the affairs of foreign countries. For England, for instance, security could, according to Prime Minister Baldwin, signify the preservation of a 'border on the Rhine'. In the political arena, the loss of an independent position always contains the risk that foreign powers might attempt to play a role co-determining the fate of one's own commonwealth.

Roosevelt and Stalin realized that, due to their size and potential, the United States and the Soviet Union would emerge victorious from a war in Europe or the Far East in which the traditional powers of Europe (Britain, France and Germany) let themselves become involved. I have already quoted from the US ambassador in Paris, an intimate of President Roosevelt's, Bullitt, as saying in 1939 that the United States 'in a coming war would at any rate take part, not begin it but to end it'. The US would 'with certainty enter into a war', but only if Great Britain and France would make the first move.

The materially strongest world power, as the United States had already proved themselves to be in the First World War, found in President Roosevelt, a man almost entirely confined to a wheelchair, a politician whose will it was to use the movement emerging in world politics in 1932 to turn the United States into the world's hegemonic power. Great efforts of propaganda were, however, to be needed for him to win American public opinion over to be prepared to intervene or indeed to go to war.

To revert once more to the time of the 'Quarantine' speech, uttered in October 1937, until then Hitler had done nothing but procure the right to equality for the Reich in the world of international states. It could not even be maintained that Germany had armed to a greater strength than was required for her self-defence. Roosevelt was perfectly aware why he did not permit his son to accept the invitation to visit Hitler proposed by Father, as he did not 'fit into his political concept'.

Many historians have held the recession that reappeared in the United States in 1934 responsible for Roosevelt's reinforced activation in foreign policies, so as to distract the American people. It is a procedure that certainly has parallels in world history. Roosevelt's early commitments to the goals for a foreign policy and the consistency with which he pursued his path – a path that in the end led to war – militate against this however. Roosevelt did not need to lead the United States into a war in order to solve his economic problems. The formula employed of 'short of war', with which already before Pearl Harbor he had manoeuvred the reluctant Americans *de facto* into a sort of state of war, could have sufficed for him to solve the United States' problems by the shipments to Britain and finally – after Hitler's offensive against the Soviet Union – to Russia. As early as 1937 he was sketching the spectre of war in lurid colours, when in his 'Quarantine' speech he said: 'let no one imagine that America will escape … that this Western Hemisphere will not be attacked.'

With this and many more warnings, Roosevelt whipped up massive panic-mongering. Three years later the Germans could still not even risk an amphibious assault across the few kilometres of the English Channel due to a lack of air supremacy, meaning the idea of an attack on the USA across the Atlantic was even more illusory. Japan also, although disposing of comparatively much better naval equipment, had no opportunity to attack the American continent, but left it to a single blow against the American fleet advanced several thousand kilometres into the Pacific Ocean in order to obstruct American amphibious operations in East Asia, which at a later date did in fact lead to Japan's defeat. The two atomic bombs were not a militarily necessity, although they did speed the defeat of Japan and spared 'more sacrifices' on the part of Americans, as the official version of the United States government states. It acknowledges thereby of itself that the nuclear mass annihilation of hundreds of thousand of civilians was caused so as to avoid waging war against regular Japanese troops in accordance with the valid laws of war. It was literally a blatant bottom line after a century of propagandizing the threat to the 'Western hemisphere'.

Anglo-Saxons are well aware of the meaning of a 'self-fulfilling prophecy', whose realization is actively achieved by the very proclamation of the prophecy.

Churchill was one such prophet who, with the assertion that 'Hitler is fomenting war', did everything to bring about a war with Germany. The same goes for Roosevelt, who finally managed to drive the Japanese into a corner through economic strangulation so that only a pre-emptive strike was left open to them.[306] It is comparably as valid for the conspiracy against Hitler which, with the assertion that 'Hitler wants war', did everything to induce the British to risk a war, so as then themselves to be able to 'putsch' Hitler out of the way. Roosevelt was cleverer, maybe also shiftier than Hitler. Slyness is absolutely the right of a statesman who is conducting world politics, as Roosevelt had decided to do from 1933, regardless of the strong isolationist attitude of the American people.

When the French ambassador in Washington at the time, Georges Bonnet, the future Minister for Foreign Affairs, asked American Secretary of State Cordell Hull in March 1937 to brief him on the plans of the United States Government as to how the 'chief international problems' were to be solved, Hull answered that the American government was 'keenly aware of the numerous problems of an international character which in many respects were now growing more acute and dangerous'. It should, however, not be forgotten that the 'definite, concrete steps' that the President may be contemplating were his affair alone, and that the Secretary of State was not able to impart the slightest information about them.[307]

Concurrently, American diplomat Norman Davis explained to Anthony Eden, the British Foreign Secretary, upon the latter's proposing that the United States 'should take the lead', that the President 'had no desire or intention of interjecting himself in the European political situation' as long as 'Europe makes up its mind that it wants peace', and as long as 'the British ... are prepared to get behind any efforts that may be made by anyone to achieve such a result'. He urged that the British Government should at once take steps in the direction of close 'economic collaboration' with the United States. When Eden expressed the view that Chamberlain wished to achieve this objective, Davis remarked he hoped they would not wait 'until they missed the boat'.[308]

Is the massive pressure exerted upon Britain by Roosevelt to engage actively against the Reich – together with her giving up her independence – recognizable in Davis's 'diplomatic' language? It could be seen as a tragic irony of world history that Britain, which centuries-long, in an almost genial manner, had deployed her 'mainland rapiers' – Austria, Prussia and France – in order to obstruct the hegemony of a single state in Europe, should now be pushed into the role of the American 'Europe rapier' through the policies of Churchill and his friends, so as to bring about a conflict at the end of which there stood the loss of the British Empire. What had happened to Britain, even at this early date? Leadership is offered to the United States and the reply is that 'one should hasten to place oneself in economic independence from the United States, so as not to "miss the boat" at the right moment!' To study Roosevelt's foreign policy is to come to the breathtaking ascertainment of what game on a global scale this man, chained to his wheelchair, played. Bullitt's statement to the Polish ambassador is redundant in order to see this. He categorically declared that Washington's attitude would result entirely from the realistic interests of the United States, but not by ideological elements.[309] In the same way as the Americans had given the Japanese a free hand in East Asia before the First World War against Russian expansion, Roosevelt was now embarking on a systematic, albeit concealed and sly course of confrontation with Japan, knowing well that the Japanese were not beloved in the United States.

Roosevelt appeared on the scene with the world's strongest economic power, a power that could not be reached with the weapons systems of that time, still less endangered. He was, however, determined to play his card of strength to the fullest. In order to do this he had to convince the American people that they were in danger which at the time – unlike the subsequent rocket and nuclear age – was a totally unrealistic claim.

'Liberty' stood written large on Roosevelt's banners. The concept of liberty was acceptable to all nations. It spoke to the political intellect of colonial populations, who wished to shake off the tutelage of the colonist powers. To this extent, in reality this American motto was directed against Britain, France, the Netherlands, Belgium and Portugal. Later generations were stunned as the great colonial powers fell into the arms of the United States of America, personified by Roosevelt the 'anti-colonialist', thus disempowering a Germany which had an ideologist as her leading figure who wished to maintain the colonial supremacy of the white race. In his speech in the Reichstag on 28 April 1939, Hitler explicitly stated:

'During the whole of my political activity I have always stood for the idea of close friendship and collaboration between Germany and Britain. In my movement I found innumerable others of like mind. Perhaps they joined me because of my attitude in this matter. This desire for Anglo-German friendship and co-operation conforms not merely to my sentiments, which result from the origins of our two peoples, but also to my realization of the importance of the existence of the British Empire for the whole of mankind. I have never left room for any doubt of my belief that the existence of this Empire is an inestimable factor of value for the whole of human cultural and economic life.'[310]

Difficile est satiram non scribere![311] In 1956 the American Mediterranean fleet blocked the way to the Anglo–French forces who wanted to reoccupy the Suez Canal which had been nationalized by Nasser.

A skilled statesman – that is, one who is not an ideologist – will take care not to disclose his ultimate intentions. It is thus difficult to prove the proposition, in strict, empirical terms, that Roosevelt's ultimate motivation was to succeed the British Empire as the world's foremost power. Very cleverly, he made no statements in this sense.[312] It would hardly have succeeded in generating in the American people the readiness for war that he needed for his policy. On the other hand, in the issues of human rights, democracy, freedom of the seas, anti-colonialism, liberating populations from dictatorships, religious liberties, anti-racism etc., the Americans could indeed be galvanized, above all when the propaganda-media were on one's side.

It was Roosevelt's goal to obtain a worldwide supremacy for the United States. To be the sole advocate championing democracy, human rights and a market economy is most deeply ingrained in the American consciousness, as was represented in numerous later appraisals of the American rise to sole superpower – '*Novus ordo seclorum*'.[313] A New Order of the Ages was how that aspiration was announced, as willed by Roosevelt, on every single dollar note from 1935, when after the war – in vain – every German document had been searched through. Roosevelt expressed it openly, whether he delivered a 'World Peace Plan' to Chamberlain, demanded of Hitler and Mussolini that they should deposit documentation of commitment to 'good behaviour' in Washington or, soon after war broke out, invited the neutrals to a conference to establish the fundamentals of the post-war order. He always proceeded as though it were up to him to define what the world order should look like. Is it possible to think that their President's efforts to get the Americans ready to go to war were exerted so as to save the world or the British Empire from Hitler? Furthermore, from a Hitler who had made a friendship with Britain the motto of his foreign policy?

The British Empire had already lost its place as the leading world power in the First World War. By now the great political weight of the British was due only to routine and experience, as well as their centuries-old reputation. It was this supposed potential that seduced Poland to rely on Britain as an ally – which was her undoing – and caused Hitler time and again to nurture the hope that there could after all be a collaboration with Britain. It was indeed in a partnership with Germany that Hitler saw a future for the Empire.

Roosevelt was aware of the independence of England, and France with her, from the United States, and played his hand coolly and 'in his own interests only', as Bullitt had expressed it. Churchill, the 'half American' (his mother was American) who offered Roosevelt his services, did everything he could to play into his hands. Churchill, which meant Britain as well, had long ago become Roosevelt's junior partner. Chamberlain may have tried yet to conduct a policy belonging to Britain. It is a moot point whether he wanted to avoid completely a renewed conflict with the Reich or was only playing to gain time. He probably wished to leave both options open, finally choosing the third option, which was to trigger the hoped-for military putsch in Germany by means of a declaration of war by the British.

However, the policies of the West were determined by Roosevelt. He had decided against Germany and Japan. He was unable to fix the entry of the United States into the war at will to a particular moment – he was dependent on US public opinion – but he was a virtuoso at playing the instruments that were to bring him ever closer to his objective. Although he concentrated entirely on Japan, a country unloved in the United States, he had Europe at all times in his sights. Barely had Hitler done him the favour, under the impact of the Japanese attack on Pearl Harbor as well as the intention Roosevelt had announced shortly before of launching an invasion of Europe in 1943, of declaring war on the United States, than he gave priority to the European war theatre. We have seen how Roosevelt drove England into war, let himself be well paid for giving aid and eventually took over the position in power that the British Empire had occupied for 300 years.

There lay the great dilemma for British policy. Britain had two options, which were either to come to an accommodation with Germany, thereby accepting that the Reich was established as the Continental hegemonic power – bringing equilibrium in the balance of power between the Reich and the Soviet Union – or pursuing, with the sole goal of disarming the German Reich again, to join forces with the United States, thereby risking selling the Empire out and its dissolution. It looks as if Chamberlain was aware of this alternative: his stance of reluctance toward the United States and his tactics of temporization, often ambiguous, toward the German revisionist wishes permit this to be assumed.

It was just this ambivalent stance of the British government, however, (Vansittart: 'We must keep Germany guessing as to our attitude'[314]) that provoked Hitler's mistrust and, in his opinion, forced a speedier course of action so as to consolidate the German position. The anti-German attitude taken by the British government in the 1938 'May Crisis' already mentioned had without doubt considerably contributed to a speedier course of action. At the beginning of April 1939, speaking to the American ambassador in London, Chamberlain was enough of a realist to admit that Hitler was 'definitely aware that the longer he permits England and France to arm the less likely he is to win with one decisive blow'. This was reported by Joseph Kennedy, US ambassador in London, to the American Secretary of State, Hull.[315]

Here – as expounded above – lies the key to Hitler's decision to establish the 'Protectorate of Bohemia and Moravia', following Poland's rejection of the German proposals. Lipski, the Polish ambassador in Berlin, had added fuel to the fire when he declared to Father that the furthering of the plan to incorporate Danzig into the Reich again would lead to war. Polish Foreign Minister Beck had, as we know, entirely oriented himself toward England. He too had succumbed to the fascination of the British Empire and had greatly overestimated its strength and potential. Churchill had no qualms about letting himself in for a renewed conflict with Germany, and nor did the group who had stood against a German-English understanding for years.

Roosevelt now had the British dig deep into their own resources. They first had to transfer bases in the Caribbean to the Americans ('without valuable consideration', as Lord Beaverbrook expressed it), and were assigned in exchange fifty destroyers, of which apparently at first thirty-nine could not be used. In December 1940, and again in March 1941, the United States sent a warship to Cape Town to collect gold in payment of the American deliveries to Britain. The deliveries had to be paid to the Americans in order to keep them happy. Churchill had put all his eggs in one basket, which is to say entirely put himself in Roosevelt's hands, and he had to pay the price, which was fixed by Roosevelt. Morgenthau, the American Treasury Secretary, demanded from the representative of the British Treasury, Frederick Phillips, a complete statement of the sum of British capital deposits in the Western Hemisphere, breaking them down into separate units of their convertibility into cash. One wonders how Morgenthau's words to Phillips must have sounded to Churchill's ears:

'It gets down to a question of Mr Churchill putting himself in Mr Roosevelt's hands with complete confidence. Then it is up to Mr Roosevelt to say what he will do!'[316]

The British ambassador in Washington, Lord Lothian, suggested to Churchill that he should put his cards on the table and give Roosevelt a complete statement of the needs of Britain and the limited means at disposal to meet them.[317] Upon his return to the United States on 23 November 1940, he is said to have called out to the journalists in attendance: 'Well, boys, Britain is broke; it's your money we want.'[318] In the course of a 'Lend and Lease' debate in Congress, Roosevelt callously formulated it to a Cabinet member as follows:

'We have been milking the British financial cow, which had plenty of milk at one time but which has now about become dry.'[319] On 10 March 1941, the gun was put to British Ambassador Halifax's head with the demand that Britain must part very swiftly with a major company as evidence of her good will. Thus, as is always the case in a forced sale, a subsidiary of Courtaulds' was sold off at an unfavourable rate.[320] Lord Beaverbrook complained bitterly:[321]

'They have conceded nothing. They have exacted payment to the uttermost for all they have done for us. They have taken our bases without valuable consideration. They have taken our gold.'

At the end of 2006, the final instalment to be paid of the contract fell due, with which the United States had charged Britain, their ally, for deliveries of matériel and services rendered during the war.[322]

Lord Lloyd, a Cabinet member and one of the most radical representatives of the anti-German British policy, suspected that a plan may lie behind the American actions to force Britain's world supremacy out of its place. Does it not mean that the scales had fallen from his eyes as to where Churchill's policy – which he too underscored – was leading, when he declared that the Americans were 'gangsters and there is only one way to deal with gangsters'? It can only be concluded that such a path is no longer open when one has put oneself in their hands. Furthermore, Roosevelt had but proceeded with the very same political maxims with which the British themselves had established their Empire. For the 'Anglo-Saxon brotherhood', the word 'gangster' only underlines Lord Lloyd's bitter acknowledgement that in the sense of the preservation of British supremacy in the world, an erroneous policy had been initiated.[323]

Lord Lloyd's words bring to mind a memory from the early, as yet unofficial days of Father's political activities when Lord Lloyd was guest in our Dahlem home. I can still see his wiry figure before me. At the time he will not have been strictly entrenched in the anti-German approach, for he was one of Father's interlocutors. However, Father already described him as one of the extremely power-conscious representatives of the imperial greatness of British world power. In that sense Lloyd had said, somewhat arrogantly, to Father that the one thing England detested was when a great nation tyrannized a smaller one (he meant Austria). Father, in turn, asked him whether he meant Ireland?

At the time of the inspection of the list of British capital monies, Roosevelt had said: 'Well, they aren't bust – there's lots of money there!' Churchill now considered Roosevelt something like a sheriff 'collecting the last assets of a helpless debtor'.[324] The Foreign Office, which gave the appearance of being obliged to protect Europe from Hitler, as once it had been from the Kaiser, trembled at the notion that Churchill would stubbornly assert his independence from Roosevelt.

Roosevelt had successfully manoeuvred Japan into a corner, step by step, by means of economic strangulation, from which Japan could liberate herself only through a pre-emptive strike or declaration of bankruptcy. The practically desperate efforts of the Japanese government to avoid a military confrontation with the States may be seen on perusal of the documentation. They were possibly even prepared to sacrifice the tripartite alliance with Germany and Italy. Roosevelt remained adamant; neither on the part of the United States nor the Dutch East Indies was the oil embargo lifted, nor were there any other concessions; on the contrary, Japanese bank accounts in the US were frozen.[325]

On 25 November 1941, American Secretary of War Stimson confided in his diary that at a conference with Hull, Stimson and Knox, as well as General Marshall and Admiral Stark, Roosevelt had said that the main question was: 'how we should maneuver them [the Japanese] into the position of firing the first shot without allowing too much danger to ourselves'. Having deciphered the Japanese code, the United States could read the instructions of the Tokyo Foreign Ministry to the Japanese ambassador in Washington, Nomura.[326] Roosevelt consequently knew of the Japanese deadline of 25 November, by which date an arrangement had to be reached with the United States. Otherwise, only a pre-emptive strike remained in the Japanese view. The date was then postponed to 29 November. That too was known to the American government. Their reaction was to manoeuvre them into the situation of firing the first shot.

The renowned American historian Tansill ends his well-known book *Back Door to War* with the following remarks:[327]

'The unaccountable failure of high naval officers to convey a warning to Honolulu about the imminence of war was given additional highlights on the evening of December 6 when the Japanese reply to the American note of November 26 was sent secretly to Ambassador Nomura. It was intercepted by Navy receiving stations and decoded. When the President read this message to Nomura he at once exclaimed: "This means war!"

...

'It would ordinarily be assumed that the President, after reading this intercepted Japanese message, would hurriedly call a conference of the more important Army and Navy officers to concert plans to meet the anticipated attack. The testimony of General Marshall and Admiral Stark would indicate that the Chief Executive took the ominous news so calmly that he made no effort to consult with them …

'At 9:00 A.M. on December 7, Lieutenant Commander Kramer delivered to Admiral Stark the final installment of the Japanese instruction to Nomura. Its meaning was now so obvious that Stark cried out in great alarm: "My God! This means war. I must get word to Kimmel at once." But he made no effort to contact Honolulu. Instead he tried to get in touch with General Marshall, who, for some strange reason, suddenly decided to go on a long horseback ride. It was a history-making ride …

'It was 11:25 A.M. when General Marshall returned to his office. If he carefully read the reports on the threatened Japanese attack (on Pearl Harbor) he still had plenty of time to contact Honolulu by means of the scrambler telephone on his desk, or by the Navy radio or the FBI radio. For some reason best known to himself he chose to send the alert to Honolulu by RCA and did not even take the precaution to have it stamped, "priority" …

'Was the General under Presidential orders to break military regulations with regard to the transmission of important military information? Did he think that the President's political objectives outweighed considerations of national safety? …

'In the quiet atmosphere of the oval study in the White House, with all incoming telephone calls shut off, the Chief Executive calmly studied his well-filled stamp albums while Hopkins fondled Fala, the White House scottie. At one o'clock, Death stood in the doorway. The Japanese had bombed Pearl Harbor. America had suddenly been thrust into a war she is still fighting.'

Roosevelt had attained his objective: the United States were now a war-waging power. From now on the policies and military operations in the Western Hemisphere would be determined by him. The United States of America were on the way to acquire the foremost position on Earth.

Whoever does not acknowledge or will not comprehend that the extraordinary dynamics of world politics which led to the Second World War were determined in the first place by the American President Roosevelt and in the second place by the Russian dictator Stalin, will never be able correctly to analyze and understand this significant period of world history. In the attempt to consolidate the Reich's weak position, Hitler played the role of catalyst. He was basically desperately trying to keep its head above water between Scylla and Charybdis.

It is Europe's tragedy that the British and French statesmen, trapped in imperialistic and nationalistic prejudice, did not take up Hitler's offers for 'European' cooperation. It is further tragic that on the other hand Hitler, having achieved the halfway consolidated position of the Reich, could not be prevailed upon to conceive a generous European Charter that would have guaranteed the European states a self-sufficient existence and in which the Reich too would have had to be integrated.

German Planning for the Continuation of the War – 'Options'

It is now the moment to scrutinize what considerations there were on the part of Germany, following the successful campaign in the West for the continuation of the war. First of all Hitler addressed the well-known offer of peace to Britain, rejected on Churchill's instigation. It is once more the place to quote here: '*difficile est satiram non scribere*'! What is written about it must surely appear as satire to anybody who is not familiar with this fascinating material.

In the conditions of a peace treaty Hitler had approached the British as far as it could possibly be done. The visionary in him was still hoping for an understanding with Britain. Only at the last minute had he agreed with Father's proposals to come to an agreement with the Russians, but he had basically not completely abandoned hope that the British would be brought to see reason by this move and that an arrangement could be reached with them. At that time Hitler would still have gone to great lengths to come to such an arrangement. I gathered from what was said by my parents that there was a possible eventuality for the re-establishment of Poland to a certain extent.

The offer of peace to Britain in his speech to the Reichstag of July 1940 was without any doubt sincerely meant, particularly as at the same time the precise conditions for it were transmitted to Lord Lothian, the British ambassador in Washington, as described in detail by the historian Stefan Scheil.[328] Lothian found the German conditions 'more than satisfactory', but nobody in London took any notice. Once again Britain had been given the chance to maintain her independence and her world supremacy intact. Churchill bears the responsibility for this opportunity having been missed. The end of their world supremacy was thus rung in.[329] The picture formed in the meantime of Churchill and the English policy in regard to the German Reich was published in a long article in *The Times* in 1993 by a clear-thinking and unprejudiced observer, the historian and at one time Defence Minister in Margaret Thatcher's Cabinet, Alan Clark. It is most illuminating to peruse his thoughts.[330]

Following Clark's depiction of the tensions in the Conservative Party which could have erupted as a result of the defeat looming in France in 1940, but which, however, Churchill dealt with harshly and in a manner that was far from objective, he continues:

'The defeat of Hitler was his [Churchill's] raison d'être. It was this which had brought him, stage by stage, against all prediction, the whole way from the political wilderness to the premiership ...

'There were several occasions when a rational leader could have got, first reasonable, then excellent, terms from Germany. Hitler actually offered peace in July 1940 before the Battle of Britain started. After the RAF victory the German terms were still available, now weighted more in Britain's favour. In spring 1941, following the total defeat of the Italians in Africa, Britain had recovered its military poise and not yet paid over all its gold reserves to America. Hitler wanted to secure his flank before he turned to Russia. Hess, his deputy, flew uninvited to Britain with terms. Churchill, who saw the domestic dangers [for his policy], would not talk to him, and repressed (in conspiracy with the whole establishment) the documents.

'This was the real watershed, because if Britain had made peace in April 1941 the fleet and the Spitfires could have been moved to Singapore. The Japanese would never have attacked and the Far Eastern empire would have endured. But Churchill did not attach as much importance to this as to defeating Hitler; and he realised that total defeat was only possible if the United States entered the war. Only the Japanese could cause this to happen. Why deter them?

'Churchill's abasement of Britain before the United States has its origins in the same obsession. The West Indian bases were handed over; the closed markets for British exports were to be dismantled, the entire portfolio of (largely private) holdings in America was liquidated. "A very nice little list," was Roosevelt's comment when the British ambassador offered it. "You guys aren't broke yet." ...

'Anyone in the Tory party who realised what was happening was horrified. Even Beaverbrook and Bracken, ... were uneasy, and complained to him [Winston Churchill] ...

'The war went on far too long, and when Britain emerged the country was bust. Nothing remained of assets overseas. Without immense and punitive borrowings ... we would have starved ... The Empire was terminally damaged. The Commonwealth countries had seen their trust betrayed and their soldiers wasted.'

Not much need be added to this article in the renowned *Times*. It was composed by a prominent member of the party that Churchill also belonged to. As a historian and Defence Minister in Margaret Thatcher's Cabinet, Clark can certainly not be accused of treating British interests lightly or of being over-friendly to Germany. To stay with the satire: Churchill sacrificed the Empire in order to annihilate Germany as a power factor. Hitler for his part admired that Empire and would have done everything to preserve it if a reasonable arrangement between Germany and the British Empire had been achievable.

I have already recounted Father's State Secretary Weizsäcker's whispering propaganda campaign that he spread both in Germany and abroad, saying that Father was falsely instructing and advising Hitler that Britain would not fight for her interests. Father knew of these rumours, without being able to locate their source. Already in 1941 (26 November) he had taken up his position, in a talk to European state leaders convened in Berlin: he had dwelt therein also on British policy toward the Reich. Having described the attempts to find an understanding on common ground on the part of Germany, he elucidated:

'Whoever rejects such uniquely favourable offers has decided on war! That was our conviction. I shall be pleased to allow the judgement to the future whether the know-all English propagandists are right to say afterwards that while ignorant of and misrepresenting the British character I had briefed the Führer to believe that England would never fight. However, the future will also have to pass judgement on something else, much more important, to wit whether or not the British statesmen of the day conducted a wise policy. I for my part believe it has already done so.'

With regard to the British Empire, these words may be said to be prophetic. Further on in the talk he said:

'In continuing the war, England will lose one position after another and her world supremacy will forcibly instead become an ever increasing dependence.'

In his discussions with Hitler on the subject of the English policy, Father had every so often stressed that 'we [cannot] force the British to do what's best for them'. After seizure of the documents of the Polish Foreign Ministry, it was known in Germany what an active role Roosevelt had played in preventing a German-Polish settlement. No illusions were harboured as to the political objectives of the American President. Under these circumstances Father regarded a good relationship with the Soviet Union as a cornerstone of German policy. There was naturally a certain dependence of Germany on supplies from the Soviet Union of raw materials and foodstuffs. The German side was often in default of the counter-supplies, but that was ever and again dealt with. However, German dependence on the Soviet Union did not go half as far as Britain's on the Unites States. The picture is remarkable. Both European opponents were respectively supported by one of the great powers outside of Europe ('flank powers', as Oswald Spengler called them), namely the USA and the Soviet Union. Whilst Britain threw herself completely into the arms of the United States and proceeded in the conflict as a second-rate power, Germany tried to protect her independence, or to attain it, and also foundered.

But to revert to the situation of the Reich following the successfully conducted Western campaign: Hitler had achieved a strong Central European position. The Reich's situation was considerably improved in comparison to the start of the war. On analyzing the position of Germany after the campaign, beginning from the north, the first thing to be noticed is that in the occupation of Norway the British had just been beaten to it, despite the substantial superiority of the British Navy. Ore supplies from the Swedish Kiruna district via the Norwegian harbour of Narvik were first of all secured. It should also be noted that after lengthy preparations the British had landed almost at the same time at Andalsnes and Namsos, of which Hitler was informed in time. What has become part of history that was valid in Germany at that time as an alleged German 'invasion' of Norway turns out on closer inspection to be a defensive step against British strategies.

In the east, the hazardous borders drawn by the Versailles Treaty were disposed of, and the same went for the security risk of the remnants of the Czech state. German influence in the Balkans had strengthened in a normal way, despite the situation that arose from Italy's advance into Greece and the unclear situation that resulted from those unfortunate military operations, which called for a revision. It is unnecessary to point out that the Italian incursion had taken place without the accord of the German leadership, and was regarded with utmost displeasure by Hitler and by Father.

In the area of the Mediterranean, when Italy finally came in on the German side it signified on the one hand an extension of the operative possibilities in the fight against England, although it was also, regarding Italy's military inefficiency, a not inconsiderable liability. Following the victory in the West, it appeared that the entry of Spain into the war on the side of the Axis powers was but a matter of time and negotiation. The Reich's operational potential in the Mediterranean region would be decisively extended thereby. The occupation of the entire Atlantic coast from Spain to Holland offered Germany options such as a landing in England, a U-boat war waged from a much broader base than in the First World War and an effective war from the air against the British Isles.

This Central European position was made secure by the treaties with the Soviet Union, although it was clear to the Germans that the border demarcation between the so-called 'spheres of interest' certainly did not have to be the last word in German-Russian relations. The swift progression of the Russians, even during the Western campaign, was a clear indication that on the part of Stalin the development of the conflict between the two Western powers had been seen somewhat differently. A certain exertion of pressure from Russia was perceptible; at least, Hitler said he felt it. The Russians had demanded Bessarabia from Romania, which had been lost in the First World War, by ultimatum, and South Bukovina was occupied. Both regions fell into the Russian 'sphere of influence', according to the Moscow Treaty. However, Russia also occupied and annexed North Bukovina – formerly Austrian territory – which did not. On the other hand, the connection to Soviet Russia for the supply of raw materials for the German army had worked very well.

Hitler had attained the German position of strength in Central Europe he strove for and considered a necessity, albeit it did not coincide with his original conception of it being in concord with both Western European powers. It was also not achieved without a war. Indeed he had, in the eleventh hour and after much hesitation, performed a radical about-face turn by joining with his declared enemy, the Soviet Union, so as to keep his back free in order to solve the problem of the Corridor, while still nurturing the hope of achieving a peaceful settlement with Poland.

Both of Britain's current 'mainland rapiers' – or should France and Poland be designated as the European 'rapiers' of the United States? – had been disabled. In the case of the latter, it can safely be said that she had been sacrificed. For the German side, four options now stood open.

Closest at hand, but without doubt the most difficult and riskiest, was a direct attack on the British Isles. The planning of a landing in Britain was code-named '*Seelöwe*' (Sealion).

The second option was to drive the British away from the Mediterranean. The British Empire's main artery would in this way be blocked and at the same time Europe's 'soft underbelly' would be protected.

The third alternative was entrenchment in Europe, possibly with the establishment there of a political New Order[331] and the organization of armament with the aid of the broadened potential offered by the occupied areas and a simultaneous U-boat warfare.

As for the fourth option, to bring down the Soviet Union, it has to be mentioned even though it will be demonstrated that at first there was no thought of taking such a decision. If Hitler did in fact, as is postulated, give an order in the summer of 1940 for drawing up a plan for a campaign against Russia, it may have been as a precaution under the impact of the Russian westward drive. It has already been said that the occupation of North Bukovina did not correspond to what had been agreed between Germany and Russia. It is nonetheless a truism that irrespective of that, all general staffs have to make theoretical plans for every eventuality, without thus in any way influencing the country's policies or even being able to define them. The political points of view are always decisive.

- The first option – Operation *Seelöwe*, the invasion of the British Isles – was tackled immediately after ending of the Western campaign. It was revenge for having let a major part of the BEF get away from Dunkirk. An indispensable precondition for the undertaking of Operation *Seelöwe* to succeed was, however, to win air supremacy over the Channel. This could not be done.
- For the second option, to drive the British out of the Mediterranean an important prerequisite was the elimination of Gibraltar.
- The third option, the build-up of the German position with simultaneous U-boat warfare against the British Isles, would doubtless have afforded the States the time to advance in their armaments efforts. This option would be helped through maintaining amicable relations with the Soviet Union. But it was upon this that Hitler felt he could not rely, at latest following Molotov's visit to Berlin in November 1940.
- As we know, Hitler had recently, after lengthy hesitation, decided to attack the last – as he saw it – 'mainland rapier' of Britain, the Soviet Union, so as to fight to secure the back of the Reich once and for all. It must be expressly noted that this decision was taken only when it became clear that the premise for Operation *Seelöwe*, namely air supremacy over the Channel, was not feasible and that a decisive strike against the British Empire in the Mediterranean could not be effected. To this end, the removal of Gibraltar

would have been indispensable, which, because of Franco's refusal to join the Reich in this objective, could not be realized.

On investigating the course of the Second World War objectively from the German point of view, the acknowledgement keeps coming to the fore that the pre-emptive war on Soviet Russia – pre-emptive is here to be taken in its broadest sense – represented for Germany the most decisive unfavourable turning point. This brings up the question of what motivated Hitler consciously to initiate a war on two fronts? Had it not been he who had reproached the Imperial Government of Germany for not having avoided a war on two fronts in the First World War? Hitler himself had repeated this in his most recent dictations:[332]

> 'I had always maintained that we ought at all costs to avoid waging war on two fronts, and you may rest assured that I pondered long and anxiously over Napoleon and his experiences in Russia.'

Nevertheless, he goes on to say that there was a whole list of reasons that rendered the attack on Russia unavoidable: Soviet blackmail, indispensable raw materials, ideological antithesis and Soviet preparations for an offensive. Already, this sounds rather like a 'rationalization' for the decision.

The most plausible support of theories for the reasons of motivation for weighty decisions are first of all the 'given facts'. Yet of course 'facts' too are open to interpretation when one considers their historical catalysts. It will therefore be necessary to examine whether the diverse theories propounded correspond or contradict. Contemporary historical research offers a variegated bunch of explanations and motives for Hitler's decision to attack the Soviet Union. They are partly in contradiction. It cannot be up to me to give a full overview of the current scholarship on Hitler's motives for the Russian war. I shall deal briefly with the generally maintained theories and thereafter give what I see as the facts that for me derive principally from what I learned personally from my parents or from the documents at my disposal. I shall finally say a little about my experience as a 'minor troop officer' in the vastness of Russia.

If one ignores the slanderous postulations of propaganda – which are admittedly constantly broadcast by German historians themselves – such as war-lust, power-trip, megalomania and so on, we have to tackle the following questions that arise as to Hitler's motives for the pre-emptive strike against the Soviet Union, and examine them as to their plausibility.

We will begin with the long-known and celebrated argument that Hitler had wished to realize the gaining of the necessary – in his opinion – *'Lebensraum'* (space to live) for the German people, a thesis he had stated in his book *Mein Kampf*. The *'Lebensraum'* theory is probably the most widespread and most generally believed as the grounds for Hitler's attack on the Soviet Union. It is true he does expound this issue vehemently in the book he wrote in 1928. He speaks of a 'land policy' in contrast to a 'commercial and colonial policy', championing the opinion that the German Reich should seek its required *'Lebensraum'* 'in the East' – that is, at the expense of Russia.

At first sight, and seen superficially, the arguments in his book and the war on Russia seem to correspond. Certain aspects of the German policy of occupation seem additionally to underline the *'Lebensraum'* thesis. Himmler's romantic image of a military frontier deep within Russia that would be secured by 'soldier peasants' was only one of its facets. The elimination of the Auswärtiges Amt commanded by Hitler in relation to all questions relevant to Russia is also in line with this. When Father wanted to hand the buildings of the Soviet Embassy in Berlin over to a protective power, Hitler refused and disposed of them to Rosenberg's Ostministerium (Reich Ministry for the Occupied Eastern Territories).

There are, nevertheless, serious doubts about the *'Lebensraum'* thesis. Firstly, as to Hitler's book itself, it may not contradict the *'Lebensraum'* thesis that he himself told my father that it had been a bad mistake to write the foreign policy chapters of the book himself.[333] It does, however, address the point of time at which Hitler wrote it, as well as its contents, against the postulation that in 1941 he wished to realize the principles of foreign policy he had externalized in 1925. Hitler wrote *Mein Kampf* when he was a prisoner in the Festung Landsberg fort after his failed attempted coup of 1923. His party had been prohibited and his political prospects were uncertain. There is no doubt the book was meant to prepare his return to the political scene, or he would not have written it. The man was 35 years old at the time. He could not really count on the chance to influence German policies in the foreseeable future, so he would not therefore have given much consideration to what he wrote. He wanted above all to have himself stand out and acquire supporters from amongst the national-minded Germans.

Quite irrespective of this, it is always overlooked – or not taken into consideration – that for his 'Eastern or Land policy' Hitler claimed a perfectly clear precondition, namely an alliance with England. But in 1941 this particular precondition did not exist, indeed to the contrary. England was at war with the Reich, and was also – after the defeat in France – not prepared to initiate peace talks. England was as implacable as ever toward Germany and was enjoying massive support from the USA. She moreover endeavoured to achieve a rapprochement with the Soviet Union.

It is furthermore not considered that at the time when Hitler was committing his concept of a possible 'Ostpolitik' to paper in the Festung Landsberg, the Soviet Union did not constitute a power factor. Weakened by the revolution and the previous war, internally ripped by civil war and the recent defeat by Poland, the Soviet Union did not yet represent the power that was later to turn into a massive threat to Europe. In 1941, however, this position had been reached. The Soviet Union was a highly armed state, strictly organized, with an expressly aggressive political ideology, led by a man – one may think what one wishes about him morally – who held the vast country firmly in hand and had made it clear by his earlier actions that he was at any time prepared to exert influence on world policy.

Although in 1940 Hitler had after all managed to achieve a halfway consolidated position for the Reich through the successful outcome of the campaign in the West, it cannot nevertheless be overlooked that it was emerging increasingly that the United States would become the Reich's real opponents. Churchill was basically naught but Roosevelt's agent, actually waging the war on his behalf, since, due to broad swathes of American public opinion that were against participation in the European war, Roosevelt had at least to seem reluctant. That to a certain extent the German war budget was undoubtedly dependent on Soviet supplies was furthermore a point of weakness for the Germans. Taking all these factors into account, Hitler was in no way in a situation – without having secured his rear – to launch an attack against, in the truest sense of the word, a giant country in order to gain *'Lebensraum'*.

There must consequently have been other reasons for his fateful decision. Hitler's arguments were frequently ambivalent, geared to address his interlocutor so as to make an impression, in order to motivate or to obtain something. He stated after the campaign in the West that he was 'saturated' and that it would require time – centuries – for the acquisition of land in the East to be digested.

The theory of a deliberately planned acquisition of *'Lebensraum'*[334] moreover does not fit in with the partial demobilization of the German army after the Western campaign. I remember how, at lunch in the summer of 1940, Father, beaming, said: 'The Führer has already ordered the suspension of armament production in many sectors.' The reason this little scene is so memorable for me is that I realized, rather disappointed, that for me there would be no opportunity to gain the Iron Cross First Class. A 19-year-old youth does tend to have his own 'war goals', irrespective of the fact that I did not want to be unworthy compared with the foregoing three generations of my family, who wore or had worn that medal.

Father's statement was exactly aligned with instructions that went out to the army after the Western campaign. Fromm, the commander of the reserve army, signed the relevant directives on 20 June 1940, wherein it is succinctly stated that: 'The reserve army will be disbanded at the earliest moment.' On 25 June 1940, on the order from Hitler from 7 June, Keitel commanded the beginning of demobilization to the extent permitted by warfare and 'the securing of occupied territories'. This order says as to materiel equipment: 'Capacities, means of production, raw material and workforces instituted heretofore for fitting out of the Wehrmacht and no longer required in future, are, by the Defence Industry and Armaments Office, with the accord of the supreme authorities of the Reich in charge, to be reinstated in their peacetime destinations.'[335]

In July and August 1940, seventeen infantry divisions were disbanded and a further eighteen sent on leave.[336] The reduction of the strength of the army to 120 divisions was ordered, with a reinforcement of the tank divisions. However, monthly tank production was determined to an output of only 213, which meant that the 'rebuilding' of the army – to the augmented numbers of the tank division – was attained only in 1944. In accordance, 'medium-term planning' signified no land warfare in view.[337] This partial demobilization of the German army following the Western campaign is unequivocal proof that at that time Hitler was not considering a war against the Soviet Union, and thus also had no intention of gaining '*Lebensraum*'.

'Mediterranean'

Convincing evidence of Hitler's stance at this time is provided by an examination of the Situation Conferences of the Commander-in-Chief of the German Navy to Hitler, which have been preserved in their entirety and are available in book form with commentary. The study of these protocols, in the context of the demobilization measures undertaken, gives a clearly recognizable profile of Hitler's plans for engaging in further warfare. After the Minutes of the Situation Conferences dated 21 May 1940 – that is during the Western campaign – to Raeder's question, Hitler declares himself for long-term planning of U-boat warfare. He elaborates: 'following the conclusion of the main operations in France, to shift the focus of emphasis [of armament] to the U-boat and Ju-88 Programme.'[338]

On 4 June, Raeder notes:

> 'Führer shows his objective: after defeat of France, reduction of the army, dismissal of all the older skilled workers. Focus of emphasis on air force and navy.'[339]

It is noteworthy in this context that the existing armaments capacities were not to be extended. These insuperable facts, and the documents, are proof that the claim that Hitler had a stage-by-stage plan to conquer Russia for '*Lebensraum*' is unsustainable.[340] Hitler had no plan at all, unless the objective of gaining a position as unassailable as possible for the Reich in Central Europe may be designates a 'plan'. It is precisely in regard to this objective, which – it must be said again – he wanted to attain by peaceful means, that he would have had to prepare a clear plan and coordination of the Reich's material capacity. This he neglected to do.

On 6 September 1940, a discussion between Hitler, Raeder and Jodl took place. It is minuted in detail and is substantiated by a memo from the Maritime Warfare Command on 'warfare against England in case of cancellation of Operation *Seelöwe*'. The decisive passage of this protocol, composed and signed by Raeder, is given here (in English by the translator) word for word by reason of its significance:

'Considerations of the Maritime Warfare Command about further possibilities of warfare against England next to or in place of Operation *Seelöwe*:

'Decisive strategic significance for the German-Italian warfare in the Mediterranean region: GIBRALTAR – SUEZ CANAL.

'Elimination of England from the Mediterranean – determining significant domination in the Mediterranean area for emplacement of Central Powers in South-Eastern Europe, Asia Minor, Arabia, Egypt and in the African area. Securing of unlimited raw materials sources – disposition of fresh strategically more favourable base of operations for further action against the British Empire – decisive difficulties for British supplies traffic from the South Atlantic through neutralization of Gibraltar.

'Preparations for these actions, that do not have the character of an "intermediary action" but of a MAIN ACTION AGAINST ENGLAND must ensue immediately so as to be implemented BEFORE AN INTERVENTION by the U.S.A. Führer gives the order.'[341]

The Maritime Warfare Command's memorandum, which convincingly presents the significance of domination in the Mediterranean for the 'Central Powers' – as attested to by a handwritten note on the document – was read aloud by Raeder.

In the protocol of the 6 September Situation Conference, 'The S Problem' is mentioned for the first time (S = Soviet Union). However, the decisive passage is, as minuted by Raeder, that Hitler orders preparations for the taking of Gibraltar as a *main action*. It must be judged improbable that Hitler should have wished to conduct both actions – Gibraltar/Mediterranean and Soviet Union – simultaneously, added to which it followed that the reduction of the army by thirty-five divisions, as it is expressly stated that he agreed, meant that *Seelöwe* and the 'S Problem' could not be tackled at the same time. Preparations for war with the Soviet Union on the part of the General Staff did not, above all by consideration of the army's partial demobilization, signify that at this point in time Hitler had made the decision to attack the Soviet Union.[342] In the Situation Report of 14 September 1940, from a discussion between Hitler and Raeder about air raids on London that are not thought of as terror measures, Raeder says:

'Air raids on London are to be continued, with extension once more of the assault areas with targets significant for the war and of vital importance for the capital. Terror attacks are expressly held in abeyance as a last resort.'[343]

This last resort of pressure was to be utilized only as retaliation for English attacks of that sort, as was noted by Raeder. On 4 November 1940,[344] a discussion took place between the chief of the 'Maritime Warfare Command' (Operations department), Rear Admiral Fricke, and the chief of the Wehrmacht's High Command, General Alfred Jodl. In the minutes of the discussion, under Point 4 it is stated, word for word:

'GIBRALTAR: Führer is decided to proceed to possession of Gibraltar as soon as possible. Franco appears to be ready soon to enter the war on the side of Germany – the army (Gen. Staff) has already made preparations for the expedition of the troop units required. Führer has ordered: Immediate initiation of expedition of a reconnaissance troop of a force of some 50 officers to Spain. Immediate deployment of troops for the Gibraltar-operation at the French-Spanish border. Spain will be summoned to provide a road for German troop movements.'[345]

This is followed by further detailed stipulations for the advance on Gibraltar and the consequences arising from it. It is further to be noted that in the protocol of the discussion, Jodl's allusion is retained to the fact that on Hitler's instruction the preparations for an *Ostfall* as well as for a 'Spring *Seelöwe* Operation' were to proceed. This proves the fact that the *Ostfall*, meaning the Russian war, presented only one of several possibilities of how the war was to be further conducted, and therewith given no priority.

If from Raeder's Situation Conferences it is taken into account to what extent the preparations for *Seelöwe* availed themselves of the capacity in materiel and personnel of the German war economy, it will readily be recognized that in the preparations for the invasion it was not a case of mere camouflage. Hitler wanted to keep all possibilities open in the fight against the British Empire. Moreover, on 3 December 1940[346] after a Situation Conference to Hitler, in the protocol Raeder notes verbatim:

'Further steps against England must have the objective of relieving Italy and the cleaning out of the Mediterranean:

a) Removal of Gibraltar, which would mean a great loss of prestige for England; at the same time, taking control of the Western

Mediterranean; then, if still necessary, an advance in the Eastern Mediterranean. Führer agrees.'

It is also to be noted that at the conference between Jodl and Admiral Fricke on 4 November, the need for an offensive on the part of Germany with Italy against Greece was spoken of. In the minutes of the session it is explicitly stated:

'Neutrality of Russia expected. In the coming days, discussions with Molotov on the questions arising from this.'

The notes unequivocally show the primacy for Hitler of waging war against England. Another order from the Führer on 20 December 1940 demands that henceforth all personnel measures are to be subordinated to the navy and air force as a precondition for the war against England, disregarding the army's requirements. Hitler was still following the plan to take Gibraltar, although talks with Franco in Hendaye had not been satisfactory. It was only on 27 December that Hitler allowed it to be seen that at the time he no longer believed in Spain entering the war on Germany's side. After the decisive deterioration of the Italian position in the Mediterranean had been ascertained – Hitler speaks of a 'total deficiency of leadership' in Italy – renewed mention is made of the significance of Gibraltar in the war effort against England:

'CONCLUSION THEREFROM: possession of Gibraltar of great importance for Germany's further warfare. MILITARY DEMAND FOR A SWIFT IMPLEMENTATION OF "FELIX" [code name for the Gibraltar undertaking] IS MAINTAINED. Answer from the Führer: exactly the same view regarding significance of occupation of Gibraltar. At present however Franco not ready as he cannot make the decision and still allows himself to be held up by England's promises of supplies … Führer tries once more via Foreign Minister to gain influence on Franco through Spanish ambassador.'[347]

Hitler did not insist on a Russian campaign but on political cooperation with the USSR, as Stefan Scheil stresses, quoting him:

'If England wants to continue the war, it will be attempted to rope in everything politically against England: Spain, Italy, Russia.'[348]

The establishment of the 'Continental block' suggested by Father was the leitmotif of German policy in the second half of 1940. I could now again more closely follow the efforts made, having been ordered to the War Academy in Braunschweig. Our training time in Braunschweig extended from May 1940 to March 1941. I was enabled through this to visit my parents in Berlin on various occasions—it took only two hours by express train. We were given leave over Christmas and the New Year. I was thus able to keep abreast of political developments. I remember Mother's descriptions of the relations with Spain very well. Hitler's meeting with Franco at Hendaye on the French-Spanish border had not gone well from the German angle. In his memoirs, Father describes how Hitler sprang up excitedly during the discussion with Franco and Serrano Súñer – the Spanish Interior Minister and Franco's brother-in-law, later to be Foreign Minister – when Serrano Súñer 'cut in to Hitler's conversation with Franco somewhat awkwardly'.

During my visits to Berlin Mother recounted that the Spanish position being confronted was a riddle. The preliminary talks with Serrano Súñer had been very promising and the trip to Hendaye had actually been undertaken in order to conclude a pact with Franco, which was to set the seal on the 'Axis'. The pact had, however, not subsequently been concluded, due to Franco's demands. He had required supplies to an extent and under specifications that could not be provided from the German side. What or who had brought about this change of mind in Franco? Father would never learn the answer to the riddle of why Franco changed his mind in 1940; he was executed before the reason was revealed in 1948 (see below).

On 16 April 1940, even before the Western campaign, Serrano Súñer had officially declared to the German ambassador in Madrid that Franco and he placed their entire confidence in a German victory, as a guarantee for an 'in itself already self-evident alliance' with Germany. Therein the hope of driving the British out of Gibraltar played a particular role. The acquisition of Tangier was also hoped for.[349] On 12 June 1940, Spain abandoned the order given by Franco on 5 September 1939 for 'maintenance of the strictest neutrality' and declared herself as 'not engaging in warfare'. On 14 June Tangier was occupied by Spanish troops under the slogans 'Long live Spanish Tangier' and 'Gibraltar for Spain'. In December 1940 Franco suddenly made the final decision not to enter the war on the side of the Axis, after having declared in July 1940 in a public speech that:

'Two million soldiers are ready to create a nation, to weld an empire together: the dominance over Gibraltar and the extension in Africa remain Spain's duty and mission!'[350]

Plans of this sort were naturally to be pursued and realized only by being on the side of the Axis powers.

There was in Berlin in the five years preceding the war an English correspondent by the name of Ian Colvin, of the London paper the *News Chronicle*. I have already said that Britons working abroad or who have foreign connections were in those days frequently employed by the Secret Service, if not actually full-time, albeit of course secretly. This was the case in Colvin's instance. He was probably relatively high-ranking, for he was heard by Churchill personally when the latter was already prime minister. Churchill mentions him in his memoirs as 'deeply in German affairs and making contacts of a secret nature with the German Generals'.

After the war Colvin wrote up biographical material on Admiral Canaris. He entitled one book *Master Spy* and in it presents Canaris as the English master spy. The sub-title is 'The incredible Story of Admiral Wilhelm Canaris, who, while Hitler's Chief of Intelligence, was a secret ally of the British.' Colvin gives a detailed account of the Admiral's activities and those of his deputy, Oster, to the extent of ongoing transmission of military secrets to the enemy during the war. What is of interest here is the role Canaris played in German-Spanish relations and to what extent he influenced the Spanish policy against the Reich. Colvin recounts that an item of news from Canaris reached Serrano Súñer in Rome, brought by Josef Müller (code name 'Ochsensepp').[351] It said:

> 'The Admiral [Canaris] asks you to tell Franco to hold Spain out of this game at all costs. It may seem to you now that our position is the stronger. It is in reality desperate, and we have little hope of winning this war. Franco may be assured that Hitler will not use the force of arms to enter Spain.'[352]

In his memoirs, Serrano Súñer did not describe in detail Spain's initial declaration of readiness to enter the war on the side of the Axis powers and its subsequent retraction. He did, however, make Canaris responsible for the 'confusion' that in those days reigned in Berlin in regard to all questions relating to Spain, and calls him a 'singular and disquieting personality'. He describes the role played by Canaris as follows:

> 'Admiral Canaris, Chief of the German Secret Intelligence Service, played a very peculiar role in these affairs. He frequently travelled to Spain and conducted significant and highly secret discussion with us of which the Foreign Ministry had no inkling.'[353]

According to Colvin, in the negotiations with the Germans, Serrano Súñer will have demanded ten 38-cm guns, which he knew from information could not be supplied by Germany. Jodl will have told Franco in Madrid about the German plan for acquisition of Gibraltar on 11 December, wherein it was stipulated, as wished by Spain, that Spanish forces would take part in the operation. It was then, however, proposed to Hitler to entrust Canaris with the task, due to his good connections with Spain.[354] In his memoirs, Serrano Súñer ponders the possible consequences of an entry of Spain into the war at that moment:

'It is more than probable that such a decision by Spain at that moment signified the end of the war. At that time the United States were unable to act. Roosevelt himself, who was much more realistic than many people there thought, would then have altogether altered his foreign policy, because it was not in vain that isolationism ruled the sentiments of the overwhelming majority of the American people.'[355]

Churchill was best able to know and judge what Spain's neutrality signified for Britain and the Axis powers, writing in his memoirs:

'Spain held the key to all British enterprises in the Mediterranean, and never in the darkest hours did she turn the lock against us.'[356]

It is tempting at first sight to rate Colvin's account as a journalist's spy thriller, had he not been legitimized by Churchill himself as an important agent of the British Secret Service. Confirmation, however, of the activities of the British 'master spy' – as Colvin calls him – Canaris comes from a much more competent source. In the so-called 'Wilhelmstrasse Trial' at Nuremberg, in which Weizsäcker too was accused in the course of the latter's questioning, he admitted the following (excerpt from the official court records):

Military tribunal No. IV, Case XI
Nuremberg, Germany, 9 June 1948
1:30 – 4:45 pm Session

Page 7989 of the German protocol
The accused, Weizsäcker, is in the witness stand:

Q: How were you placed toward the plan of attack against Gibraltar tabled at this time?

A: In any case in such a way that a reconciliation with France could not be envisaged at the same time as an attack on Gibraltar. This Gibraltar plan was after all meant now to embroil Spain too in the maelstrom. One could think either of winning over Spain as partner in war or to make a decent peace with France; the two could however not go together.

Q: For this reason you therefore did not adhere to the plan?

A: That was the reason why I did not adhere, but not the only one.

Q: You had other reasons?

A: I had in fact nothing but reasons against it: military, financial and moral too. Militarily we would not have the superior strength to defend the extended coast of Spain even in the least effectively. We would have had just the same fate as Napoleon's in his Spanish campaign. Financially, we were totally incapable of making sure of Spain's even merely modest claims, which we knew, for ensuring the country's sustenance. And Spain would have served no purpose for us but as ballast, not to speak of the moral responsibility for a country just emerging from civil war.

Q: Did the Spanish government itself then want the war?

A: I was unable myself to ascertain the will of the Spanish government to enter the war at that time, albeit I too had the opportunity to speak to the Spanish Foreign Minister once. However, so as to make sure, I resorted at that time again to an extravagant method of action with Canaris. For, in order to incite the Spaniards to war, Hitler sent Admiral Canaris to Spain, as it was known that he had good connections there. And Canaris and I agreed that he would instead tell the Spaniards the plain truth and make the certain disaster clear to them to which they would come, inevitably and inexorably.

Q: Is it your view that Canaris' advice contributed to keeping Spain out of the war?

A: That I do not know. But I have heard that 'Yes!' What is more, I will say 'the advice he gave was certainly right'.

Certification

I, Attorney Alfred Seidl, certify the accordance of the excerpt above from the Minutes of the session of the military tribunal No. IV, Case XI, on 9 June 1948, signed, Dr. Alfred Seidl.[357]

Weizsäcker's statements during the 'Wihelmstrasse Trial' confirm those of the Secret Service agent Colvin. Colvin's book came out only in 1951; when giving his testimony in Nuremberg, Weizsäcker therefore did not know it.

It emerges with the greatest clarity from the available papers and documents that the anti-Russian component was ever more strongly forthcoming in Hitler's considerations as the hope faded of being able to induce Britain to conclude a peace. One of the preconditions for it would have been the blocking of the Straits of Gibraltar, which, again, without the cooperation of Spain, or at least her positive tolerance, was not feasible. However, no responsible statesman will tie the fate of his country to an ally whose highest executives and officers conspired behind his back to counter the policies of their government. As things stood, therefore, Franco acted absolutely sensibly when he finally withdrew from the German courtship for him to join in the war on the side of the Axis powers.

What role was played by Spain in Hitler's considerations regarding the continuation of the war also emerges from a diary entry by Hewel, the liaison between Hitler and his Foreign Minister. Under the date of 14 February 1941, Hewel notes: 'Telegram from Rome regarding Mussolini-Franco meeting. Negative, as expected.'

The discussion between Mussolini and Franco was yet another attempt to sound out Franco's intentions so as to ascertain whether there was still a chance of bringing him over to join the Axis. That would have still enabled undertaking Operation Felix, the acquisition of Gibraltar. Under the dates of 29 and 30 May, Hewel makes another note regarding Spain: "'F" [Führer]: "… Gibraltar is not on today any more."' Although by this time it was too late, Hitler continued to preoccupy himself with the option of taking Gibraltar. His verbal outbreaks against Spain recorded by Hewel clearly give the impression that as far as he was concerned he gave the 'Mediterranean option' priority over a strike against the Soviet Union.[358]

Raeder had repeatedly presented the potential that the acquisition of Gibraltar meant for the German war effort in the diverse Situation Conferences to Hitler, and had obtained Hitler's complete agreement. The possibility of blocking the Straits of Gibraltar would have solved the question of supplies for a subsequent operation against the Suez Canal. A landing operation against the Spanish coasts, as Weizsäcker exaggerated in his interrogation in Nuremberg, would have had no chance against an intact German force that was not tied up in Russia and had the support of Spanish armed forces. Weizsäcker's statement to the contrary shows a thin justification of his 'extravagant' actions – as he called them – behind the back of his government.

The domination of the Mediterranean by the Axis would have become a grave threat to the British Empire and might have incited the British to give in, since Hitler would have been broadly accommodating to them. The position of the Axis powers would have in any case been considerably reinforced, not least from the angle of operational potential that had arisen from the matter of the Near-Eastern oil wells. It thus came only to a weak movement of uprising in Iraq that could not be sufficiently supported by the Axis and petered out.

If on the threshold of 1941 the question arose once more for Hitler as to how to pursue the war, then the altered situation in Spain signified the decisive turning-point in his plans. Father always wracked his brains as to the reasons that could have caused Spain's joining the Axis to fall through. He could not conceive that the conspiracy around his own State Secretary, that together with Canaris had spawned the fateful outcome, was what finally drove Hitler to the decision to attack the Soviet Union. Delegate Dr Paul Schmidt (A.A. Press and Information Dpt) remembers a little scene in Hitler's special train following the failed talks with Franco in Hendaye. Hitler had abruptly demanded 'maps of Russia' from Keitel and Jodl, and had intensive consultation with them in the train.

A word more as to the significance of historic sources. Next to memoirs and factual reports, contemporary sources of written material, that will have in any case been accessible to all the participants, are of the greatest importance. Next to the Minutes of the Situation Conferences that both Navy Commanders-in-Chief, Raeder and later Dönitz, presented to Hitler, it is Walter Hewel's diary for 1941, already quoted from, to which we have access. The diary is therefore of the utmost value, as it was kept only occasionally and with entries of verbatim references, meaning that they were clearly quite spontaneously handwritten and have no apparent recognizable bias.

The Minutes of the Situation Conferences were filed among the official documents of the Maritime Warfare Command. They were thus at any moment also at the disposal of Hitler and others taking part in the meetings. This restricted any possible 'bias' of the Minutes. Naturally, they were composed from the point of view of the Navy, but it is the personal misgivings of Raeder about Hitler – already mentioned – that render the statements very valuable, above all in places where Raeder – as in the case of Gibraltar – repeatedly notes Hitler's agreement.

Both sources repeatedly point out how Hitler's train of thought turns only on the war with Britain. Whether he is referring to the 'Felix' undertaking, i.e. Gibraltar, or 'S' ('Barbarossa') from the turn of the year 1940/41, his considerations are ever running on how to get England prepared to make peace.

How little the decision on war with the Soviet Union was determined from the '*Lebensraum*' perspective is once more evidenced by a Note of Raeder's about a report to Hitler of 26 September 1940 that took place tête à tête.[359] To begin with, Raeder asks Hitler if he may 'tell him his own perception of the conduct of the warfare – also going beyond his own competency'. After he described the Mediterranean 'as centre of the [British] general position', mentioning the strong positions of the English in the Eastern Mediterranean, he requests that the 'Mediterranean issue be cleared up by mid-winter'. According to Raeder, this means that:

'"GIBRALTAR" must be taken … SUEZ CANAL must be taken; doubtful that the Italians on their own alone will manage it; therefore support by German troops necessary. From Suez, an advance through Palestine, Syria as far as Turkey necessary. If we get that far, Turkey is in our power. The Russia problem then takes on another aspect. Russia is basically afraid of Germany. Query, whether then an advance on R. from the north will still be necessary. Dardanelles question.'

There follows more from Raeder on the Italian position in East Africa, strong emphasis on the significance of North-West Africa for the German and Italian conduct of the war, and a warning about a United States-supported advance of England against Dakar, with de Gaulle's backing. Raeder then tells of Hitler's attitude to these statements:

'Führer basically agrees with train of thought. Following conclusion of the alliance with Japan he will immediately undertake consultation with the Duce and poss. also with Franco …

'England-U.S.A. have to be thrown out of North-West Africa. If Spain came along, Canaries, poss. also Azores and Cape Verde first to be secured by Luftwaffe.

'An action through Syria would also depend on stance of France, but should be quite feasible. Italy was OPPOSED to the surrender of the Dardanelles to Russia. He would however try to incite the Russians to advance energetically against the south – Persia, India – to reach an outlet to the ocean from there, that is more important to Russia than the positions in the Baltic Sea.

'The Führer too is of the opinion that Russia greatly fears the German power; he believes that Russia, e.g. Finland, would not attack this year.'

Raeder's remarks are more unequivocal proof of two observations:

- All Hitler's strategic considerations come from the standpoint of forcing England to make peace and/or to bring the Reich to so strong a position that the British Government would realize that a conclusion of peace with the Reich under acceptable conditions was preferable to continuing the war.
- The relations to the Soviet Union are seen exclusively under politico-strategic criteria, and once more above all from the point of view of the British 'mainland rapier', that is of the Continental power that could be allied with the British against Germany.

The extent of Hitler's accord with Raeder's concepts in their discussions is interesting. All statements and, above all, all orders given by Hitler until the end of December 1940 unequivocally demonstrate the priority of warfare against England and his preparedness – according to Raeder – to transfer the focus of operations to the Mediterranean. The reduction of the army, the withdrawal of which was effected in October, is plausible if it is taken into account that both Hitler and Raeder, as well as the army high command, had previously hesitated whether *Seelöwe* should actually be set in motion. Possibly decisive for this was that aerial domination was still not yet achieved, at least not in the planned invasion areas, and the undoubted inferiority of the German *Kriegsmarine* to the Royal Navy. The remobilization of the army was imperative for realization of the ambitious plans for North Africa and the Near East, as discussed by Hitler and Raeder on 26 September, which would have to include operations in North-West Africa, to say nothing of an operational reserve in order eventually to enable prevention of a landing of English-American forces on the French-Spanish-Portuguese coast.

Hitler was of the opinion that all three options were open to him: *Seelöwe*, *Felix* (Gibraltar) and *Barbarossa*. He was reluctant about *Seelöwe* because of the lack of air superiority, and the *Felix* option had been taken from him by the German conspiracy – which he did not yet know. He consequently charged Franco with wrongful submission to England. Thus his cogitations concentrated ever more on a pre-emptive strike against the Soviet Union.

There is no doubt at all that the actions of the conspirators Weizsäcker and Canaris against Hitler's plans to concentrate completely on warfare against

England in the Mediterranean and North Africa do not justify Hitler's 'risky game'; the war on Russia, as will be seen, cannot be characterized differently. Canaris and Weizsäcker will, however, be reproached by history for having forced Hitler's hand through their 'extravagant' (as Weizsäcker called them) interference with the Spanish leadership in such a direction and in consequence having their share of responsibility for the ensuing disaster. Keitel confirms this in his estate of written material. He could not have known of Weizsäcker's testimony, for by that time he had already been executed.[360]

The Attack on the Soviet Union

The war with Russia was waged pre-emptively, and was justified, but in my view was not inevitable, at least not as things stood in 1941. Had the Soviet Union in fact attacked, Germany's political and probably military position would have been more favourable. In 1940, in a much-quoted study, a German general[361] formulated it: '[T]he Russians will not do us the favour of attacking us!'

I have already mentioned that in the winter of 1940/41 I was occasionally able to travel from Braunschweig to Berlin on weekend leave, and was thus in closer touch with what was going on politically. One day Father surprised me by telling me about the Congress of Berlin, in which Bismarck had played his well-known role of 'honest broker' and mediated between Britain and Russia in the Balkan question. There ensued an interesting conversation on the Congress of Berlin and its great and in the end – in Father's opinion – ominous effect on the relations of the Reich with Russia.

Father wondered why Bismarck would have risked his reputation to defuse relations between Russia and England, particularly since the Reich had no direct interests to safeguard regarding the Straits (Bosphorus and Dardanelles). Bismarck himself had expressed it in the famous adage that 'The whole of the Balkans is not worth the bones of a single Pomeranian grenadier.' A certain criticism of Bismarck's role during the Congress of Berlin resonated in what Father said, or I at any rate thought I detected it and instantly pricked up my ears. The good relationship with Russia that Bismarck ever sought had always been considered the key part of his policy by my father, and in particular also by Grandfather Ribbentrop. In our conversation, the reflections expressed and its tenor ran unequivocally on the question why Germany would have had an interest in holding up or indeed in thwarting the Russian pressure on the Straits. Father and I were aware that we were making historical observations after the fact, but here, as it became increasingly clear to me, it was a means to an end.

That England was the pivotal point of Hitler's considerations was proven to me by the conversation with my parents about the Congress of Berlin and

Bismarck's role. Both my parents said repeatedly that with hindsight it would probably have been better if in 1878 the German government had stayed away from the problems of the Straits and the Russian-British confrontation. The result in prestige gained from the Congress of Berlin and the alienation of Russia from the Reich that came of it had not been worth it. True, Bismarck later let the Russian government know that the Reich was 'totally' indifferent to Constantinople and Bulgaria.[362] So in 1940 it was equally Father's concern not to trouble Russia's ambitions in the Near East.

As far as I was concerned, the perplexities lying behind Father's querying were at that moment not yet clear in their enormous implications. That conversation with Father took place before Christmas 1940, but after Molotov's visit to Berlin. I did, however, have an inkling of what Father's questioning was about. It was confirmed two days before Grandfather Ribbentrop's death. He died on 1 January 1941. He had previously suffered a stroke which left him barely able to make himself understood. When we came out of his sickroom on 30 December, my parents talked about what Grandfather might have wanted to say, for it had seemed as if he wished to speak about something. Father thought he must have once more wanted to entrust the care of Grandmother to them. Mother, on the contrary, was almost vehemently of the opinion that he had wanted to say: 'On no account against Russia!' Yet again, I noticed this and it took my breath away. Was the danger of a conflict with Russia already a concrete reality? Mother's tone of voice was indubitably exceptionally worried. She told me about a recent talk with Grandfather, when he had finished with the words: '[I]f he [Hitler] wants to lose the war, all he needs do is to go to war with Russia!'

Perhaps in that case his influence – together with Mother's – over Father might have sufficed to convince Father to resign. Without any doubt Grandfather would have argued that Father ought not to go along with a decision of such dire consequences, against his convictions. The Russian interpreter who had been in attendance when the declaration of war had been transmitted through Father to the Russian ambassador attested that even upon taking his leave of the Russian ambassador, Father had spoken out against the attack on the Soviet Union.[363] According to the report of other eyewitnesses, this was disputed as a fabrication,[364] and would of course have been contrary to his ministerial sense of duty – the obligation outwardly to represent the policy Hitler was resolved on – without in any way intimating a rift in the German leadership. It would, however, have absolutely corresponded to his political convictions. In his life, Grandfather's threshold of compromise over which he was not prepared to step had undoubtedly been set too low and had been the reason – albeit having been judged as an outstanding quality – for his not having pursued a military career. This will without doubt have diminished how he influenced Father in comparable situations. It might in this instance have turned out otherwise.

Then, however, all was still open and the struggle of the decision as to Russia continued. In the Minutes of the Situation Report of 27 November 1940, Raeder ascertained that the Führer wanted to 'gain influence on Franco by Spanish ambassador through Foreign Minister'. Hewel's diary entry then followed, of 14 February 1941, that Mussolini too could not get to Franco in the sense of wooing him to accede to the Axis. Even if the often quoted 'delusion of grandeur' is ascribed to Hitler, it is not feasible to assume that he had in mind to embark upon a major operation in North Africa simultaneously with *Barbarossa*. *Felix*, that is the abstraction of Gibraltar, made sense only if it was followed by a major operation in North Africa, which, in both Hitler's and Raeder's opinion, could well lead as far as the Near East. Had Hitler had the confidence to entrust to himself, or rather to the German Wehrmacht, to allow both operations to be conducted at the same time, he would not have had to postpone *Barbarossa* – for the necessitation of a Balkan operation due to Italian setbacks and the British attempt to put up a major Balkan front – which turned out to have so fateful an effect on the time factor in the late autumn of 1941.

On reading Hewel's diary one has the feeling almost that until well into 1941 Hitler entertained the hope of yet avoiding *Barbarossa*. In any case, he was aware of the risk, as evidenced by the entry for 29/30 May:[365]

'H [Hitler]: [that] Barbarossa were also a risk like everything else, in that if it misfired everything would be over. If it succeeded, a situation would have been brought about that may well force a peace on England.'

Once again we have Hitler's setting of the goal to 'force a peace on England'. Not a word about '*Lebensraum*', but instead – evidently in Hitler's view– an exceptionally risky enterprise. It may be called an irresponsibly great risk if Hitler is to embark upon a campaign about which he himself said that if it failed 'everything would be over'. Even now, more than sixty years later, it sends a chill down the spine to read, in the original, this low-key handwritten comment by Hewel. And again we can read for 8 June 1941:

'Long talk alone w. t. F. [with the Führer] about Russia. "A difficult enterprise" but has confidence in the Wehrmacht. Air force: fighter and bomber aircraft in superior numbers. Some anxiety about Berlin and

Vienna ... Their entire force on the Western border. Greatest deployment in history. If it goes wrong, all is lost anyway ... It is just the miserable time of waiting that makes everybody so nervous!'

For 13 June 1941 Hewel writes:

'Discussion on Russia with F. Believes this signifies the end of Engl. resistance. I do not think so as yet, since for a while Engl. will see a weakening of G in this.'

Once again, the argument is propounded that England must be brought to make peace. Finally, on 20 June 1941, that is just two days before the attack, is written:

'Long talk with F.: Great hopes for the R-campaign. Wishes it were 10 weeks further on. It was still a major risk. One stood before a locked door. Secret weapons? Toughness of the fanatic? Now sleeps with sleeping pills. Dictating. Said to me that this morning he had played it all through to the tiniest detail – saw as yet no possibility for the enemy to crush Germany. Believes Engl. has to give in, hopefully within this year.'

These entries, together with Raeder's Situation Reports – in both cases the documentation is first-hand – clearly demonstrate Hitler's motivations in proceeding against the Soviet Union, particularly if one considers that Hewel had a very personal relationship with Hitler. What Hitler said to Hewel was in circumstances of the strictest confidence. Hewel stayed with Hitler in Berlin until the latter's suicide, and took his own life shortly after.

All these remarks of Hitler's do not give the impression of a head of state, certain of victory, setting out on a campaign of conquest, instead painting the picture of a man wanting to extricate himself from a predicament by means of a *coup de force*. These entries – as well as the partial demobilization of the army after the Western campaign, the emphasis on the navy and air force, and other indications – counter the theory that Hitler attacked Russia in order, finally, to attain the goal he had set himself in 1925, to gain '*Lebensraum*'.

Hitler was perfectly aware of the risk; he was concerned about the superiority, at least numerically, of the Russian air force. In view of the superiority of the German air force at the outset, this concern was not justified, since a large part of the Russian air force stationed near the border was quickly destroyed. Nonetheless, the Romanian oil wells, on which the German conduct of the war was extensively dependent, were unquestionably within reach of Russian air strikes. At the time Hitler had also spoken to Father of gaining access to the 'gate to the East', which he had to kick open and behind which nobody knew what was hidden.

Hewel correctly remarks in his diary that 'at the outset England would see in the German-Russian war a weakening of Germany'. As we know, Hewel was Father's representative to Hitler and remained faithful to Hitler; it is therefore probable that in this entry he is speaking in the Foreign Minister's voice, for at no other point in the diary does Hewel express his personal considerations or concepts that do not coincide with Hitler's.

Not to get ahead of the subject, a hard match was still being played between Hitler and his Foreign Minister, disputing the final decision whether to attack the Soviet Union or not.[366] On 10 January 1941, Delegate Schnurre, who had conducted commercial relations negotiations with Russia for years, had, as he writes, negotiated a far-reaching commercial agreement with the Russians. Of the briefing he gave Father after his return to Berlin, Schnurre gives the following account:

'After my departure [from Moscow] to Berlin I called on Reichsaussenminister Ribbentrop and reported in detail in a written analysis on the outcome of the Moscow negotiations. His opinion, akin to mine, was that through the economic agreement of 10 January 1941 the road to the East was wide open and that by reason of this fact the attempt should be made to reach a peace. Ribbentrop paid the closest attention to my report.'[367]

Schnurre told me before he died (in 1990) that his first words to Father had been: 'Mr Reichsminister, I congratulate you: you have won the war!' Schnurre thought that thanks to the commercial agreement the German problems of foodstuffs and raw materials supplies for the needs of military production had been solved. The war against the 'sea powers' of the United States and Britain could thus last out; naturally, on the assumption of the USSR fulfilling the contract. In his *Erinnerungsnotizen* (Reminiscence Notes) completed after the war, Schnurre describes the agreement as follows:

'The commercial agreement of 10 January 1941 was in its breadth considerably greater than the first made with the Russians and, based on reciprocity, its terms substantially ensured the Soviet Union's supplies to us in foodstuffs and raw materials for the long term. Fodder, crude oils, cotton, phosphates, iron and scrap, chrome ores, precious metal (platinum) – non-ferrous metals, and more, to a worth of 640 million Gold-Marks, with additional supplies from expired contracts. Of especial importance was the regulation of the transit question. These terms enabled us to transport raw materials purchased with the intermediary of the Soviets in the Far East and the Pacific Rim region to the Reich through Siberia along the speediest route. In the very last hours before the outbreak of war a train was on the way to Berlin from the Chinese border with a load of rubber. Purchases in the Far East and the Pacific Rim region were transacted on the basis of gold and concerned rubber, non-ferrous metals, silks and more raw materials indispensable to the German war economy ...

'It would of course be under the condition that we for our part also complied with our obligations in industrial equipment supplies. For this I required his – Ribbentrop's – support and the corresponding instructions from the Führer that the supplies would be effectuated on priority or *pari passu* basis of military specifications. Ribbentrop listened very attentively and made it clear in diverse ways that he was opting for fulfilment of this agreement. When I said: "Mr. Reichsminister, this is now the foundation for Germany to conclude a successful peace," this too he took in without disputing it.'

Further on, Schnurre writes that when he said goodbye to them when the negotiations were over, Molotov and Mikoyan had 'expressed the hope that based on this agreement a further broadening and consolidation of mutual relations would ensue'. On these grounds Schnurre asked that an end be made to the war; he was later to repeat this to Hitler, without, however, taking into consideration that a conclusion of peace was in no way up to the German leadership alone. There had been a wealth of overtures for peace addressed to the British since 1 September 1939.[368] If under their Prime Minister Churchill that government wanted to pursue the war under any circumstances, there was no way to force them to make peace. However, was this 'constellation' not calling for a relaxed atmosphere of negotiation from now on and on all sides? Was it not at last an opportunity to organize one's own armament calmly, taking into account the potential that was now within the German sphere of interest and bring it to a satisfactory state? The stocking of reserves of raw materials was not the least of the significant tasks to be prepared for any eventuality that may crop up. Raeder's Situation Conferences repeatedly point to the major difficulties of supplies of raw materials. To draw upon Schnurre's further account of the endeavours undertaken by Father to prevent a war with Russia, the former says:

'Herr von Ribbentrop said he was thankful for the successful conclusion of the Russian negotiations. He would arrange for me to visit the Führer in the days to come and – this was his request – I should present the content and scope of the commercial agreement in just the same way. He himself would accompany me and by his presence set the seal of his approval of my perception.

'…As soon as the following day, 25 January 1941, Ribbentrop went with me by air to Salzburg, and the next, 26 January 1941 we travelled together to the Berghof, where the task fell to me of presenting the matter to Hitler in the same tenor as I had previously done to Ribbentrop before. Hitler received us first alone in a small study in the Berghof. I placed the treaty on his table, once again with an explicatory analysis and – as I had done before with Ribbentrop – told him the content of the agreement. He listened attentively, asking a few questions here and there about personalities and the state of the Red Army, and manifested his interest in the details of the agreement. I repeated to him that henceforth the gate to the East was wide open, that we ourselves could purchase our raw materials from the Pacific Rim through the intermediary of the Russians. They had indisputably proved all the pessimistic forecasts wrong as to the problem of transport in bulk of mass commodities. Transit traffic from the Far East via Siberia was also operating well. The English blockade had been fruitless … I closed with these words:

'"Mein Führer, this is the solid foundation for Germany for an honourable and great peace."

'He made no reply to this daring remark of mine. When I mentioned to him that both in Moscow as also in Berlin it was rumoured that Germany was preparing for a war with Soviet Russia he sprang up and vehemently denied in hefty terms that he was planning a war with Russia. I – and everyone else – should most vigorously contradict such rumours. He was not about to wage war with Russia. When I then asked Hitler to give instructions for the economic and military positions ahead to be established so that also the supplies destined for the Soviet Union contracted by the agreement could be executed in due time, he became very hesitant and said that this he could not do. Moreover at this stage military production was a priority. He had to give thought to the situation in Africa, in Albania and Greece and was unable to take any chances with delays that might be taken into account because of Russian supplies.

'Therewith it was clear to me, despite his protests that no war with the Soviet Union was planned, that the opportunity I had indicated would not be made use of and that fate would take its course.

'Herr von Ribbentrop gave me support several times during my presentation of several hours. His stance in this exchange was, for the moment anyway, that he was unequivocally opposed to a Russian war. That he was not able to prevail lay in Hitler's final decision to rush into the Russian venture, whose far-reaching consequences both he and his counsellors largely underestimated.'[369]

Father writes:

'I had a great deal of trouble, indeed it required serious disputation, in order to obtain his [Hitler's] consent to conclude the German-Soviet commercial agreement. He had been strongly influenced by others against this projected treaty. Even then I already had the feeling of standing alone with my Russian policy.'[370]

That Schnurre in his above remarks about 'counsellors' meant Hitler's military counsellors emerges from his further remarks:[371]

'I should like in addition to mention my subsequent visit to General Field Marshal Keitel and Colonel General Jodl.[372] I described the result of the Moscow negotiations and the great advantages that arose for Germany from them: securing the raw materials supply and foodstuff reserves, and a broad commercial free hand in trade in the East.

'Unfortunately, the rumours of an imminent war with Russia had thickened and I do after all wish – just as I had with Hitler, Ribbentrop and Göring – to emphasize my arguments against it as strongly as I could […] [Schnurre adopts the arguments of the size of Russia, the severity of the winter, the muddy season and almost inexhaustible reserves in men, and mentions Coulaincourt's arguments[373] to Napoleon.] Sadly, my formulations fell on deaf ears. Jodl replied that everything had been foreseen in the planning. According to all prospective signs it would be a matter of a short-lived war. It was however the unique historical opportunity to eliminate the perpetual Russian threat in the back.'

Father had, however, succeeded – as he had agreed with Schnurre – in that Hitler received the German ambassador in Moscow, Schulenburg, once more. The meeting took place on 28 April 1941. It was unsuccessful in the sense of Father's efforts. About Schulenburg's report to Hitler, Hewel writes:[374] 'F: Reception of Schulenburg.[375] Cursory discussion about Russia [...] Chief ill.'

For psychological reasons, Father will not have taken part in the discussion. Hitler would hear from Schulenburg all the arguments against the war with Russia once more and in private. It is not clear from the diary entry whether Hewel was present at the discussion and whether the characterization as a 'cursory' discussion is his own comment or derives from Hitler.

Meanwhile, as Hewel mentions in his diary, Mussolini had also had a fruitless talk with Franco that signified the end of planning for the *Felix* enterprise against Gibraltar. Hitler was now definitely decided to wage the pre-emptive – as he saw it – war against Russia. In his diary, Hewel mentions that Father did not participate in the discussion between Hitler and Schulenburg because he had been 'ill'. It seems to me to be ruled out that Father did not take part in what would be a decisive course-setting of the German policy he supported for health reasons: the reasons that led him to stay out of the discussion were most probably psychological. He was expressly placed in opposition to Hitler as to preventing the war planned with Russia; he would therefore, in view of Hitler's mentality, not have wished to encumber the meeting with Schulenburg by his participation. Hitler would have the discussion with Schulenburg uninhibited – alone, without Ribbentrop witnessing it – so that once again all the arguments against a war with Russia could be expounded. It was well known that Hitler had developed a prickly sensitivity against having witnesses. Schulenburg's note on the half-hour's dialogue with Hitler indicates that he had tried to nullify Hitler's mistrust of the Soviet Union. Why else would Father have sent him to see Hitler – anyway an unusual procedure – all the more so since Father remained absent from the meeting? As inferred from the note, Hitler was unimpressed by Schulenburg's arguments.

On the same date, 28 April, as the discussion between Schulenburg and Hitler took place, a telegram from Weizsäcker reached Father, who had requested from him a summary of the arguments employed in the Hitler-Schulenburg discussion against a German-Russian war. Weizsäcker closes with the words: 'The opinion is summed up in brief, since the Reich Foreign Minister wished to receive it in the shortest possible space of time.'

The findings of the German intelligence service concerning Russia were minimal, or no longer corresponding to the facts. Above all, there was no comprehensive, accurate picture of Russian armaments. Only thus can the hair-raising underestimate of the Red Army be explained. General Paulus, assigned the plotting for a possible 'Eastern campaign' as Halder's deputy, believed on 17 September 1940 that the campaign could be undertaken with 128 divisions, estimating the Russian forces at 180 divisions. Irrespective of these numerical miscalculations, it should here be said that these presumed 180 divisions represented a threat of major dimensions. After the war, at the Nuremberg trials, Paulus was forced by the Soviets to make a statement, learned off by heart, that no Soviet threat existed in 1941. Recordings published from prison wire-tapping, however, demonstrate that Paulus admitted in discussions with other prisoners to have presumed at the time of his drafting it, that the onslaught was in the nature of a 'pre-emptive strike'.[376] The German officers were in any case confident of victory over the Red Army. Major General Marcks, who, as Chief-of-Staff of the 18th Army that secured the Russian border during the Western campaign, had initially been entrusted with drafting a study as to the possibility of a campaign in the east, believed it was possible to conclude the campaign in nine to seventeen weeks. In his memoirs, General Guderian states that: 'Halder will overthrow Russia in 8–10 weeks!' The German military attaché in Moscow, General Köstring, wrote to Halder that following the purges, the Russians would need four years for their army to recover their 'earlier magnitude'. Hans Krebs, deputizing for Köstring during an illness of the latter, shares his judgement of the Red Army: 'On the face of it, negative'; 'Officer corps poor'; 'It will be twenty years before earlier magnitudes are recovered.'

On 20 May 1941, that is a good four weeks before the outbreak of the war with the Soviet Union, Halder adjudges that 'the risk of just standing there in October without trained substitutes can be borne'. In his chronicle, Nicolaus von Below noted that there had not been the slightest objection from the army chiefs to plans for a war with Russia. Hitler naturally remembered the sceptical restraint of his army leadership as to a campaign in the West. However, Hitler had implemented the Manstein Plan and had been proved right. Now, at last, following the astonishing success in the West, the generals as a body were of a mind that they were facing an opponent to whom they felt far superior and that consequently they need have no qualms as to an offensive against them. What was it that Köstring had written from Moscow on 8 August 1940? That he was of the opinion 'that we are soon to be far superior to the Russians'. The reality was to be different. To mention here a characteristic episode I remember, in the Hohenlychen military hospital in September 1941, when came the 'special announcement' of the successful conclusion of the Kiev battle of encirclement; in an undertone, Mother had whispered to me: 'Now the mood will get better again "up there" [in Hitler's Wolf's Lair headquarters in East Prussia]. They [Hitler and his military advisors] were after all very nervous about how well the Russian fights.'

Following the military successes attained heretofore, in Germany the feeling of superiority of the Wehrmacht had obviously been considerably increased. It was very tempting to judge the Russians from experiences from the First World War; there had as yet been nothing to show that these yardsticks had shifted considerably. The difficulties encountered by the Red Army in the 1939/40 winter war in Finland added to this attitude. Delegate Dr Paul Schmidt (head of the Auswärtiges Amt's Press and Information Department) heard with his own ears what Guderian said to Hitler: 'Mein Führer, only in the vastness of Russia will the German tank force be able to show what it is capable of doing!'[377]

The troops shared this sense of superiority, from which I do not declare myself personally exempt. Prior to the Western campaign, we all had before us the picture from the First World War, not least the Allied artillery superiority which had enabled their infamous 'barrage'. We thought the Russian would be an easier opponent to face. We had learned our lesson from one much better, or rather, far worse! How Hitler felt about his military strength against the Soviet Union is shown in a note Father wrote down in Nuremberg, which says:[378]

'Following the outbreak of the German–Russian war in the summer of 1941 I attempted to win Japan over to entering the war against Russia, while inducing that the intentions regarding Singapore were abandoned. It seemed of importance to me that in this way Japan would be committed and would not for instance make a move against the American Philippines, which might set the United States against us as a fresh opponent before Russia had been crushed.'

Father writes that Hitler 'seriously reproached him for having sent a telegram to Tokyo in this tenor', for he hoped 'to be done with Russia by himself'. What had he said to Hewel already on 20 June 1941? 'He wished things were ten weeks further on', which could only mean that he hoped in ten weeks' time to witness the success of the campaign. There is no doubt that he was to a certain extent aware of the risk, as emerges from the above-mentioned notes made by Hewel.[379] There is a remarkable entry under the date of 23 June: 'Russia as yet a question mark.' Are Father's misgivings about a war with Russia – which as the Foreign Minister's representative to Hitler, Hewel would naturally share — reflected in this entry?

I should like at this point to touch upon a query often made: why did Hess get on a plane to England? Up to the end it was not clear to Father whether Hitler had known of it. He once said to Mother: 'Had I been sure that Hitler knew of it I would have resigned, for no foreign policy can be conducted in such a way.'

It is of course possible that Hitler had suggested the idea to Hess, without giving him direct instructions. Whatever the case, it is odd that the documents of his hearings are still embargoed. Hess had overtly made concrete negotiation propositions, with the objective in fact of putting an end to the war. It is furthermore confirmed from new documented sources that from English signals he received he had also been brought to consider such a trip as promising.[380] Besides, the Hess family has always maintained that it had been the British government and not the Russians who had prevented the liberation of the old man, quite aside from the mysterious concomitant circumstances surrounding the death of the 93-year-old on 17 August 1987 in Spandau prison when it was under a phase of British administration.

As has been mentioned, I could already at that time deduce from what my parents said, that in order to make peace with England, the Germans may have been prepared, should the situation arise, to re-establish Poland to a certain extent. This was the alleged reason for Britain to have declared war, albeit this was forgotten in the further evolution of the war when Churchill and Roosevelt handed Poland to the Soviets.

It is noted in the OKW (Supreme Command of the Armed Forces) war diary for 21 January 1941 that it was not known 'whether the Führer still adhered to execution of the Barbarossa enterprise', since on 18 November 1940, therefore after Molotov's visit to Berlin, Halder had noted that 'it seems that the Russian operation [will be] postponed'.

One more observation of Hitler's work method. The great figures of world history have often kept their real plans and intentions to themselves, or cloaked them. In our times this was valid for both Roosevelt and Stalin. Hitler may be permitted to have this right. That is where the crucial difficulty lies in investigating his motives with hindsight. Bismarck too is said once to have admitted that he allowed nobody to see into the most recondite corners of his brain. As no in-depth systematic discussion of the Russian problem among Hitler's circle of leadership took place, it is particularly hard to clarify what his motivations were. The capacity to listen to predominantly controversial opinions from competent counsellors – indeed, to work out differing concepts by conferring in common – so as to calculate all aspects of a problem, thus enabling convincing and patient motivation of those bearing the responsibilities following a once-and-for-all decision, was not a part of Hitler's personality structure; nor, at the time of the crucial decision-making at the turn of the years 1940/41, was it diminished. It is beyond any question of doubt that one of the reasons for the disaster that he unleashed lay in this personal trait of Hitler's.

Naturally, a further reason always brought out for the attack on the Soviet Union is the so called *Weltanschauung* motivation. This argument too is supported, not only by the tenor of his book, *Mein Kampf*, but also in the statements he made in his speeches during the political fighting days as well as when he was head of government. Hitler's rigidly anti-Bolshevik attitude had domestic and foreign policy components. On the domestic scene, the Communist organization had swiftly been eradicated following Hitler's access to power in government. In foreign policy, the Soviet Union represented one of the components of the new balance of power wherein – according to the German perception – the cooperation of the three Western European Powers – England, France and, as the *pièce de résistance*, Germany – should ensure a balance of power in regard to the Soviets' might.

Even after the successful Western campaign, the Reich's situation was not consolidated to such a degree that for ideological reasons Hitler would have rushed into a war on two fronts. That he let the ideological factor be exploited when the Russian war had begun does not confute the realization that it was not ideological motives which triggered his decision to attack Russia. As early as 8 March 1940, Hitler wrote to Mussolini:

> 'Since Stalin's final victory, Russia has without doubt experienced a modification of the Bolshevist principle in the direction of a nationalist Russian way of life ... There can be no doubt that the conditions for establishing a reasonable relationship between the two countries [Germany and Russia] exist today ...
>
> 'But if Bolshevism in Russia is developing into a Russian national state ideology and economy, it constitutes a reality which we have neither interest nor reason to combat.'[381]

The words reflect Father's conviction following his negotiations with Stalin, that in Moscow traditional imperialist Russian policies were conducted and that the so-called 'world revolution' was submitted to such a policy as a welcome instrument. In Nuremberg Father wrote:

'The Führer's great concern consisted in the fear of being embroiled, in the further course of the war, in an east-west pincer, in a war on two fronts shattering men and materiel to a gigantic degree. He hoped to be able to gain a breathing space in the East until the moment when the British-American potential in the West would be deployed.

'These were Adolf Hitler's most important considerations, as he expounded to me after the start of the Russian war in 1941. He had decided on the assault in the hope that in just a few months the Soviet Union could be nullified. His error as to Russia's potential and America's aid was fateful. He was however not entirely certain himself, for at the time he stated to me expressly that: "We do not know what strength lies at the back of it if we truly do have to break open the door in the East."

...

'I repeat: against the risk of an attack from two sides, the Führer saw that the only way out was a prior elimination of the Soviet Union. Above all, he had struck so as not to be tackled himself from east and west simultaneously, as later was the case. In a common strike by the three world powers Adolf Hitler foresaw defeat in the war.'[382]

Once again, Father ascertains that it was the fatal underestimating of the Russian military force that was the real cause of the defeat in the war.

Again and again the question arises nowadays whether Stalin would in fact have attacked the Reich in 1941 or 1942. The most daring versions maintain that the German strike pre-empted the Russian only by days or weeks. This postulation,[383] which is by now put forward even from the Russian side[384] and supported, seems to me conditionally plausible, in the sense that a Russian strike, or at least very strong pressure on the German position, could have been expected at any time, had the German army been tied up in operations elsewhere. The statement of fact is totally correct, that agreements with Stalin were in no way a guarantee against a surprise aggression. This is proven among other things by the declaration of war on Japan in 1945, with whom in 1941 the Soviet Union had concluded a pact of non-aggression, as well as that countries such as Finland, Estonia, Latvia, Lithuania – as well as Poland – despite their valid non-aggression pacts with the USSR were invaded by the Red Army. In any case, Hitler had declared the pact of non-aggression with Poland as null and void in every form by reason of the Polish-British pact of April 1939, since its intents against Germany were hardly consistent with the German-Polish non-aggression pact. This was primarily meant to constitute a warning in the poker game of negotiations with Poland, and is proved by the German propositions for negotiation with Poland before the outbreak of war. It is nevertheless true that Hitler too marched against Russia with no corresponding abrogation of the agreements.

To me, the point seems much more important that if in 1941 the Russians had attacked the Reich while its position was intact, they would have done precisely what in 1939 Stalin had rejected in the 'Chestnut' speech, namely to 'pull the chestnuts out of the fire for certain powers'. Stalin too must have taken into account that an assault against a Wehrmacht tried and tested and experienced in warfare must constitute an exceptionally grave military risk. Even had he succeeded in inflicting severe losses on the Wehrmacht, both armies would have weakened one another so greatly that the United States, with their armed forces as yet untouched, would have been promoted to the world's arbiter. Precisely that would therefore have occurred which Stalin wished to avert by the 1939 agreements with the Reich.

The argument against this is that there is no doubt that in 1941 the Red Army had marched to the western border to take up a position for an offensive. The 'Russian steamroller' was indeed under steam, but the question of if and possibly when it would have started rolling is not thereby answered. Stalin must have expected developments to evolve differently from what actually happened. The German successes in the West had surprised him. The role of an arbiter which he may have had in mind had, at least for now, receded a long way back. A series of wishes, or rather demands, had thus been foreseen in the negotiation schedule that Molotov had brought with him to Berlin in November 1940, over which there would have been hard bargaining with the Soviet Union. Stalin would also never have had any scruples about exerting pressure. However, pressure cannot be exerted if one retires hundreds of miles behind the border to a reinforced defence line (the 'Stalin Line); pressure is exerted by assault forces whose front line is the border. In any case, in Berlin the Russians did not want to discuss Finland alone – which already anyway belonged within their sphere of influence – but the Dardanelles as well as Bulgaria, Yugoslavia, the 'Danube Commission' and, finally, the entrances of the Baltic Sea. This last is said to have most particularly irritated Hitler. On the other hand, a commercial agreement was negotiated with the Russians in January 1941 which would have enabled a certain consolidation of the German armaments industry, despite ever-recurring arrears in German deliveries to the Soviet Union. 'Speaking terms' in the best sense were thus established with the Russians.

What objection was there on the German side to the installation of Russian bases on the Dardanelles? Contrary to the case of the First World War, Turkey had declared herself neutral. Germany had no obligation to defend Turkish interests, not even morally. The sole argument, admittedly of itself a weighty one, was *coûte que coûte* (at all costs) to keep the Russians as far as possible out of the Balkans, securing supply from the Romanian oil wells upon which German warfare was dependent. They were situated relatively close to the Russian and thereby – according to Hitler's fears – also the British air forces.

Did, however, such a concern justify staking a risky game of such gigantic proportions? To my mind, only the complete military underestimate of the Soviet opponent's – and over-estimate of one's own – potential can explain this fateful decision. Was Hitler unaware of the deficiencies of German armament? The facts alone, which I personally experienced at very first-hand, are most indicative. Speaking of my personal experiences, I shall revert to this later.

Hitler was wagering on a great risk by pressing on political developments in Eastern Europe, in the sense of a defensive front against the Soviet Union for as long as he still had a supposed advantage in armament. He has to be credited with the fact that he had no choice. He had now carved out a strong Central European position, having separately beaten one opponent after another, thus keeping his rear free, employing the diplomatic route. He had indeed gained the time to organize his present broadened base of resources and his armament efficiently and, above all, to bring them to a necessary state, therefore recuperating what had been reprehensibly neglected. There was a possibility that the war in Europe would have fizzled out. The 'Anglo-Saxon sea-powers' had hardly had a chance to undertake effective invasion operations against intact military positions of the Reich in Europe, their rear being covered by Russia. It is questionable whether under these circumstances Stalin would have 'pulled the chestnuts out of the fire' for them. In the latter case, however, Hitler would truly have found himself before the psychological prerequisites for herding the greater portion of Europe together behind him, since in the end the Russians had become more feared by the European peoples than had the Germans.

The tones of aggression with which Stalin expressed himself in speeches to the officers of the Red Army need not be evidence of pre-ordained Soviet Union military action against the Reich. An army such as that of Russia which had undergone severe 'purges' had first to have its morale boosted and the necessary self-confidence restored to it. That may be achieved only through adoption of an assault doctrine. A fighting spirit entails a sense of superiority, taking the initiative in negotiation, for in the end, a war can only be won in an attack, an effective defence enabling the proper pre-conditions for it; at the crunch, however, the enemy must be attacked if they are to be defeated. If

Stalin desired Russia to take part in the major decisions of world politics, he had to have an army at his disposal that had adopted such an assault doctrine as its own. Even if Stalin reckoned with a German attack, he had to bolster the Red Army with a mentality of attack, for in the decisive phases, for the defence of the gigantic Russian land, the question was the capacity of attack of the Red Army. That in the winter of 1940-41 Stalin marched for his western border in an offensive grouping therefore does not necessarily signify that an attack from the Soviet side was imminent: it could have been possible at any moment. As has been stated, Stalin would not have had the slightest hesitation to take advantage of a difficult situation for the Reich. It is certain he would not have been plagued by moral scruples.

Russians have always shown themselves to be hard and skillful bargainers. The deployment of the Red Army on the eve of the German attack, as well as Stalin's protestations of friendship and much more, were 'part of the game' and were to be taken as such. As he himself admitted, Hitler did not have the tenacity nor the patience to try to distill a deal satisfactory to both sides. He feared the Russians would make ever more demands without nonetheless desisting from following up by launching an offensive, as Father, quoted above, wrote after the event.

Father's conception of the way out, from this point of departure, was to conduct tough negotiations with the Russians so as to place a dividing line between the interests of Germany and Russia. He wanted the fusion of the 'Continental Bloc', as it is called nowadays, with the incorporation of Soviet Russia. In a worst case scenario it would still have been preferable – for political and military reasons – to have the Russians attack a well-prepared German defensive position rather than be exposed to play the role of aggressor against the vastness of Russian. Would Stalin, however, have staked all in order henceforth to 'pull the chestnuts out of the fire' for the West?

A further point of view should not be omitted here: it was to have a role to play again in 1943, when it was a case of grappling with ostensible Russian peace feelers. Stalin had made a noteworthy statement to my father in the course of the negotiations in Moscow: 'I shall never stand for it that Germany should become weak.' To this Father writes:

> 'That unequivocally demonstrated the consciousness of the military strength of the Soviet Union and their intention to intervene in the case of an evolution of the war unfavourable to Germany. The statement, which I recall exactly, was brought out by Stalin so spontaneously that it certainly corresponded to his conviction at that time. I was especially

surprised by the self-confidence in regard to the Red Army that emerged from Stalin's words.'[385]

If a particular political significance is indeed to be attributed to the remark – and Father's assessment that it sounded spontaneous and credible is indicative that it was – it can in the end only have meant that Stalin wished to express that he appreciated the existence of Germany as a power factor, so as not to find Russia standing alone against the two Anglo-Saxon world powers.

If it is taken from the starting point that Stalin was better informed than Hitler and the German chiefs of the military and the economy as to America's potential, the remark sounds plausible, since he would have assumed that if the worst came to the worst the United States, joined with Britain, had the advantage over him. This is the development that barely fifty years later President Reagan brought to its conclusion, resulting in Russia losing out as a superpower. The purchase of the large cruiser the *Lützow* from Germany in 1940, when Stalin made a condition that German engineers be placed at his disposal to show his people how to build large ships and manufacture vital armouring and ballistic equipment,[386] fits the scenario. These considerations – a certain interest on the part of the Soviet Union not only in the technological but also political potential of the Reich – played a role for Father in 1943 when he fought with Hitler over the issue of introducing peace feelers with the Russians. Recent history, with the spectacular changes that took place in Soviet Russia, have confirmed these considerations, beginning with what Stalin said to my father. The Soviet Union was in the long term not up to coping with the purposefully deployed American potential.

In Nuremberg, Father expressed himself as follows regarding Stalin's possible considerations upon conclusion of the pact with Germany:

'My personal opinion tends to seeing Stalin as having initially taken the agreement with Germany as a particularly good deal, as indeed it truly was. He may possibly also further have been convinced that in a war between Germany and the Western powers Russia had nothing to lose. Perhaps he foresaw a war in the west lasting years, in trenches, as in 1914-18. Should the war last longer, and Germany's position [be] weakened through it, then would the Reich be all the more dependent on Russian aid in her economy and food supplies …

' … The speedy German victory in the west will certainly have been a surprise for Stalin. Already at the time of our advance into France a new tendency could be felt in the Soviet policy toward us and this was the outset of the tragic developments that ... led to the outbreak of the German-Russian war.'[387]

To clarify the relations with Russia as to the further course of the war and place the matter on a broader base, on 13 October 1940 Father wrote a detailed letter to Stalin. Its most important paragraph is as follows:

'In summing up, I should like to state that, in the opinion of the Führer, also, it appears to be the historic mission of the four Powers – the Soviet Union, Italy, Japan, and Germany – to adopt a long-range policy and to direct the future development of their peoples into the right channels by delimitation of their interests for the ages.'[388]

The letter bore an invitation to Molotov for a reciprocal visit to Berlin. The invitation was accepted. Father anticipated a great deal from this visit but later wrote, with resignation, that:

'Unfortunately things turned out differently. Molotov's visit to Berlin was not to be under such a lucky star as I had wished.'[389]

As has been said, Father's conceptions ran along the lines of building a 'Continental Bloc' that would have resulted from Russia's joining in the Three-Power pact alongside Germany, Japan and Italy. Hitler had initially adopted the concept and expounded it to Molotov in lengthy discussions. He had said to Raeder on 26 September – only a few weeks earlier – that:

'He would attempt to induce Russia to act forcefully against the south – Persia, India – so as to open the route to the Ocean there which was of greater importance to Russia than the positions on the Baltic Sea.'[390]

Molotov, however, barely gave these considerations any thought. He always brought the discussion back to Finland, Bulgaria, the Dardanelles, the exits from the Baltic Sea and, finally, to the Danube Commission. However, as is stressed by Stefan Scheil, Molotov went substantially beyond these points, describing the agreement signed the previous year in regard to the spheres of interest as 'outdated and exhausted', in essence abrogating it, on Stalin's instruction.[391] Molotov and Hitler became somewhat bogged down over the Finnish question, wherein, as Father notes in his comments, following the secret agreement concluded in Moscow concerning the 'spheres of interest',

Molotov was quite 'in the right'. In his notes, Father described the Führer's approach as 'in Foreign Affairs, downright uncomfortable'. Further on, Father remarks that 'to those of his circle Hitler was accustomed to speak almost ostentatiously of the "brave Finns"'.

Father tried to bring the discussion between Hitler and Molotov, that had come to a dead end, back onto the floor. The obstacle was the supply of nickel for the German armaments industry, that was entirely dependent upon the Finnish nickel mines at Petsamo. Reading between the lines of the commentary, Father's concern over the development of the discussion can be sensed. He knew from experience that Hitler was not a patient negotiator. Everything therefore came down to him to avoid a serious split in relations with Russia and to maintain a close connection with the Russians in regard to the further conduct of the war.

Let us hear Father once more on events prior to the Russian war:

'Finally, Molotov promised me [on the occasion of a tête à tête in the Auswärtiges Amt's air raid shelter during Molotov's Berlin visit] to talk to Stalin about a Russian entry into the Three-Power Pact. At the same time I promised Molotov that I would bring up the subject of the whole question of German–Soviet relations with the Führer in order to find a way out of the present difficulties.

'As Molotov had to return home the next day already there was no opportunity to hold further talks … After his departure, by diplomatic route through the German embassy in Moscow discussions resumed about the project of Russia's entering the Three-Power Pact. The Soviet government informed us that they did not wish to exclude such an eventuality completely, but, as well as a free hand in Finland, also demanded as a prerogative for – that is a guarantee of – certain military rights in Bulgaria, and furthermore desired the installation of military bases in the Turkish Straits.

'In December 1940 I had an in-depth discussion of these Russian wishes and conditions with Adolf Hitler. On the occasion I recommended to him a most urgently required accommodation in regard to the Soviet Union and proposed a sort of accord more or less on the basis of Stalin's demand. The Balkan questions would – with the Italians also – be further clarified and an attempt made for a four-power pact to include Russia to be substituted for the Three-Powers. If this were to succeed, it would put us in a favourable position: such a grouping would neutralize the United States and also isolate England while threatening her in the East.

Through a strong system of alliance of that sort – albeit certainly not without one – a swift diplomatic end to the war with England could yet be envisaged. A fresh peace-offering approach to England for which we would also then have a free hand would in such case be more promising of success than after Dunkirk. Nevertheless, there would have to be sacrificial offerings to Russia.

'At this meeting Hitler gave me the impression of maybe being more yielding than before in the Finnish issue, but he considered the Russian demand vis à vis Bulgaria, for one thing because of King Boris – who would never allow himself to be involved in it – not feasible. Adolf Hitler expressed the view that upon the Soviets assuming a military influence in Bulgaria the whole of the Balkans, particularly also Romania with its oil wells, would ineluctably come under Russian influence. Consequently, he judged allowing Russia military bases on the Dardanelles therefore an impossibility, for Mussolini too would hardly agree. At the time, however, his stance toward my emphatic presentation was not yet absolutely one of rejection, in fact, at the end of the lengthy meeting, which took place in the Reich Chancellery's air raid shelter, saying the hopeful words: "Ribbentrop, we have already achieved a great deal together, perhaps we will bring this off too."'[392]

In Stettin, shortly after 20 April 1941 (the date when I became an officer), when Mother visited me in our port of embarkation for Norway, she did not deny it when I asked her whether there could possibly be a war with Russia. She looked pale and worn out, which I attributed to her constant headaches due to the chronic sinusitis she suffered from. On that day, 28 April 1941, Count Schulenburg's visit to Hitler had taken place, mentioned by Hewel in his diary as a 'superficial conversation'. The die had been well and truly cast; it would come to war with Russia.

Father would have been prepared to make concessions to the Russians; Hitler was not. Thus did doom take its course. In his notes, Father reports on a discussion with Hitler in his special train near Vienna after the Balkan campaign began on 6 April 1941, which had been triggered by the putsch in Yugoslavia abetted by Russia and England. Father had quoted to Hitler Bismarck's famous remark – Mother told me about it with concern – that 'in the case of a pre-emptive war the good Lord does not let himself be seen in the cards'.

After six months of German 'Pyrrhic' victories in Russia, Hewel was to write in his diary on 24 December 1941: 'Gloomy Christmas. F. [Führer] elsewhere in his thoughts. No candles lit.' On 31 December 1941, Hewel added:

'Bad news from the front. Kaluga-Kertsch. Dinner too late. Evening with the Führer. Sleeps; low mood. 11:40 [23:40] Field Marshal Kluge telephones – Führer on the phone for 3 hours. End of year [celebration] cancelled!! … 2:30 Tea with the Führer. F.: "I am happy to be able to solve quite big difficulties. I hope 1942 brings me as much good luck as 1941. Worries can stay. It has always been thus, that really bad times were the forerunners to truly great events." …

'Bruckner's Seventh Symphony. Moody atmosphere.'[393]

This sounds different from the 'ten weeks' Hitler had spoken about to Hewel just before the campaign against the Soviet Union. These remarks express the surprise caused to Hitler by the Red Army's fighting spirit and will to resist. The content of the aforementioned conversation with Kluge had been about holding on to territory conquered, on which Hitler was fixated. As strategy, in the first Russian winter this had even been more or less correct, in the main at least. As yet, maintaining one's presence in an area already captured did not lead to the great crisis of confidence in the military leadership as occurred a year later, after Stalingrad. It was, however, without question a grave error on Hitler's part, in the first Russian winter to dismiss a tried and tested commander such as Guderian on the grounds that, being better informed as to the situation at the front, the orders 'to hold position' from the Führer's headquarters had been ignored.

Looking back, this was the turning point for Germany, the sudden reversal in fortune (the *peripeteia* of ancient tragedy). How was Hitler to cope with this realization? Would he, in this grave situation in which he had placed himself, react reasonably and soberly? Would he still try to utilize the negotiation space which, at the turn of the year 1941/42, he without doubt still possessed to some degree. Hitler was well aware of the enmity of the president of the United States toward the Reich. Well-known Republican Senator Robert A. Taft had as early as late spring 1941 explicitly declared that it was Roosevelt's goal 'to push' the development 'further and further toward war without consulting the people'.[394] Hitler was without doubt the 'driven' one in the world political game. For 11 July 1941, Hewel's diary entry mentions that Hitler had spoken to him – addressing him personally – of 'this battle, to which I was forced, stage by stage'.

In the winter of 1941/42, when I was in a military hospital near Berlin, I suddenly realized that my mother no longer believed there would be a satisfactory end to the war. Looking grey and worn out, she had not denied it when I had asked her in Stettin several months before whether war was now to be aimed against Russia; that silence had been the first hint. From her very serious mien, when in the hospital she remarked that 'up there' (in the Führer's headquarters) they were extremely nervous about the Russians' capacity to resist, up to the unmistakeable criticism of German foreign policy in general, there was a noticeable chain of hints. It was not Father she was critical of. Mother had, of course, intimate knowledge of Father's fight against a war with Russia. When Hitler now also declared war on the United States, she found her worst fears confirmed.

After Roosevelt, through economic strangulation, had brought Japan to strike first, Hitler inexplicably did him the favour of declaring war on the United States. It was a decision that will have occurred spontaneously to Hitler, and his motivations thereto have to this day not been conclusively clarified. When the news came of the Japanese attack on Pearl Harbor, Hitler is said to have shouted spontaneously: 'Germany is saved now!' Mother told me about this, profoundly worried. Father makes the claim that he had advised against initiating a war against America.[395] This seems plausible. A foreign minister who had always taken a stance against the war with Russia would not approve a war on two fronts.

Sooner than a year later, when the Allies landed in North Africa, this same foreign minister proposed to Hitler to enter into negotiations with the Russians. It was a proposal he had made even before Stalingrad. I had already witnessed a discussion between Father and Himmler over Christmas 1941. As Father did not come to Berlin for Christmas, I had visited him in his East Prussian headquarters, having been given leave before being posted to the unit. For some reason or other Himmler turned up for a talk with my father and stayed for a meal. In the course of the conversation at table – we were the three of us – Father declared very seriously and emphatically to Himmler that the Russian problem had to be solved by the coming summer. The insinuation was: if not by military means, then by diplomacy. Himmler made no response.

As Mother told me at the time, Himmler will surely have sounded Father out in the course of 1942 as to whether Father could be persuaded to carry out certain activities behind Hitler's back. Father had not succumbed; he considered Himmler the most unsuitable personality to initiate a policy in parallel to the official one, in the state the situation was in at that time. In all probability, Father would have run into Himmler's open knife. There was no foundation of trust at all for undertaking such a difficult venture. However, he also did not utilize Himmler's approaches to foment an intrigue against Himmler. Mother was always convinced that Himmler was in contact with the plotters of the 20 July assassination attempt in 1944 and that he had broken off immediately after its failure. A definitive clarification of these rumours, that are ever cropping up, is still lacking to this day. It does, however, make it understandable that Himmler from then on endeavoured to checkmate Father, so as to save his own skin.

The declaration of war on the United States was the second fatal error committed by Hitler in 1941. It facilitated Roosevelt to henceforth instantly prioritize the American war effort to the European theatre. Hitler, furthermore, had no kind of inducement to immediately join with the Japanese, nor, in view of their pact of non-aggression, would they have acted in a similar fashion upon his war against Russia. The declaration of war on the United States in essence signified the cessation of German foreign policy, at least insofar as it could be defined in cooperation with the Foreign Minister. The efforts of the Foreign Minister were now restricted to tough attempts to obtain Hitler's agreement to put out peace feelers toward the Soviet Union, which, without Hitler's consent, would have had no sense. After the demand for 'unconditional surrender' announced by Roosevelt in Casablanca, in my father's opinion the only chance lay in the attempted approach to the Russians.

Hitler had abruptly rejected Father's proposition the first time, to undertake talks with the Russians after the Allied landing in North-West Africa. Father recounted the discussion, which took place when he joined Hitler's special train, as follows:

'In the discussion that ensued, I briefly said the following: The English-American landing was a serious matter. It showed that we had made a fundamental error in our estimate of the enemy's tonnage figures and thereby in the possibility of waging our U-boat war. If the Anglo-Americans could not successfully be driven out of Africa again which, in view of our experience of transport in the Mediterranean, seemed to me to be most doubtful, Africa, together with the Axis forces, would be lost, the Mediterranean [left] in the hands of the enemy and Italy – already weak – in the worst of situations. It was my opinion that the Führer was in need of some effective decisive relief in order to further the conduct of the war, and I was therefore hereby requesting immediate plenipotentiary powers to connect with Stalin through the Soviet ambassador in Stockholm, Mme. Kollontay, regarding a peace treaty, indeed – if it had to be, under surrender of the greater portion of the area conquered in the East.

'The minute I mentioned the surrender of the Eastern regions, there was a violent reaction from the Führer. Bright red in the face, Adolf Hitler sprang to his feet, interrupted me, and said – with unprecedented sharpness – that he wished to speak with me solely about Africa and about nothing else. The manner in which he said this made it impossible for me to repeat my proposal at that moment ...

'At the time – it was before the Stalingrad disaster – we would still have been in a more favourable position for negotiations with Moscow than shortly after. The Russian assault came eight days later, the collapse of our allies at the river Don and then the catastrophe that struck the 6th Army at Stalingrad.'[396]

Father later continues:

'After the betrayal by the Badoglio Government in September 1943, I entered upon a fresh, very dynamic venture. This time Hitler was not so dismissive. We went over to a map together, and Hitler himself drew a line of demarcation upon which we could come to terms with the Russians. When once again I requested plenipotentiary powers, he said he would think it over until the next morning. Next day, however, again nothing came of it ... I sensed there were forces at work that constantly reinforced Hitler in his unyielding stance against an agreement with Stalin.

'When after his liberation Mussolini came to the Führer's headquarters, to my surprise Hitler mentioned his wish to come to an agreement with Russia. As to my request for instructions that I thereupon repeated, I received no precise reply and as soon as the next day he again refused any sort of feelers being put out. He obviously noticed my great disappointment, for shortly afterward he came to my quarters, and on leaving, suddenly said: "You know, Ribbentrop, if I come to an arrangement with Russia today, I shall tackle it tomorrow – I cannot do otherwise." Bewildered, I answered: "Foreign policy cannot be conducted in this way, because it means total loss of confidence in us." In my inability to be able to do anything about it, I was gripped by a dread of what lay ahead.'[397]

After Stalingrad, Hitler appeared to be more inclined to receive vague Russian signals. However, again and again he brought up the reservation that he had first to have a military success as a basis for negotiation. Was *Unternehmen Zitadelle* (Operation Citadel; the Battle of Kursk), initiated in the summer of 1943, too late and with too weak forces, an attempt at targeting a limited military success so as to bring about the preconditions demanded by Hitler so as to be able to take up negotiations with the Russians?

'Operation Citadel' ('*Unternehmen Zitadelle*') – Battle of Kursk

I should at this point briefly describe my experiences from February to July 1943 as a low-ranking Panzer officer in a famous tank division that was deployed at all critical flash-points, because they illustrate – mirroring, if you like, the Reich's political state – the dramatic military situation most vividly. In this span of time the Stalingrad disaster occurred, the reconquest of Kharkov and *Unternehmen Zitadelle*, which must have been anticipated by Hitler as promising the military success that was already in sight from the retaking of Kharkov.

As has already been said, when the Eastern Front appeared to be stable once more, Father again initiated an approach to Hitler. He wanted to obtain Hitler's assent to a sounding out whether a prospect existed of the possibility of talks with the Russians regarding a ceasefire. As in Father's opinion the spectacular reconquest of Kharkov had once again bolstered the German negotiating position, the opportunity should be utilized. I knew of my father's hopes of success for the military operations; we, the soldiery, would have done everything possible to achieve success.

Horst Groepper, later the German Federal Republic's ambassador in Moscow, confirmed to me how Father had endeavoured to persuade Hitler to put out feelers for peace. Groepper had been designated to initiate the first such moves in Stockholm. During a mission to the Balkans he had a meeting with Schulenburg and Hilger on a train, when they had declared that 'we had hoped to see you travel in a different direction'. Groepper expressly confirmed that Father had initiated the action, but that it had been aborted by Hitler.

In the summer of 1942 I was transferred from Sennelager military training camp to the staging area for the southern Russian summer offensive, only to be transposed a few days later all the way to the area west of Paris. We were somewhat puzzled, without suspecting that we were the passive witnesses to a grave contravention of an elementary strategic rule, which in this case obligated a presence as strong as possible at the decisive crucial points, accepting that risks may be run at another point. Thus, among other lapses, the three SS divisions for the summer offensive were absent; ensuring the long flank of the River Don was left to the allied troops and German forces were massed in front of Stalingrad, thus creating a classic 'Cannae' precedent[398] favouring the enemy. After I was wounded a second time, which necessitated several months' stay in a military hospital, at the beginning of 1942 I was seconded to the newly instituted tank column of the *Leibstandarte* (Bodyguard), now given the status of a Panzer-Grenadier division, and only near the end of 1942 refitted to a tank division. So much for the alleged better arming of the SS divisions. We were equipped with the old Panzer IV, inferior in every way to the Russian T-34. Only in late 1942 were we supplied with vehicles with a longer tank gun, occasioned by the appearance of the T-34, which was a nasty surprise for the German tank force. True, the disadvantage of the Panzer IV in regard to motors, armour plating and cross-country terrain mobility was somewhat compensated by the tank commander, whom the T-34 did not have, which offered an advantage in the handling of the tank.

In the course of 1942 the I SS-Panzer Corps was formed out of the 1st, 2nd and 3rd SS-Panzer Divisions. SS-Senior group leader and Waffen-SS General Paul Hausser was nominated Commanding General. Hausser had been a General Staff officer in the First World War and retired in 1931 as commandant of the Reichswehr Military Academy in Dresden. In 1934 he became Inspector of the SS-Verfügungstruppe (Dispositional troops), and was finally the oldest serving general of the Waffen-SS. Hausser played a decisive role in the shaping of the high quality of the Waffen-SS.

At the outbreak of the war the Waffen-SS consisted of four infantry regiments (motorized), one artillery regiment and divisional units (Pioneer Battalion, Reconnaissance, Signals and Panzer Abwehr [Anti-tank unit] detachments). Two infantry divisions (motorized) were formed after the Poland campaign. In the Russian war the Waffen-SS already had five infantry divisions. They were constituted exclusively of volunteers and were in consequence highly motivated – which always represents the prerequisite for exceptional military performance – acknowledged over and over throughout the war.

In the course of the war, the Waffen-SS was constantly enlarged. We members of the Waffen-SS observed developments with increasing scepticism. There were finally so to speak two armies (a large regular one and a smaller Waffen-SS one), which without doubt did not meet the need to knit all the Reich's forces closely together. This had an additional psychological aspect. The regular army had to question whether they were perhaps no longer good enough. I have always harboured a certain comprehension for the resentments felt by the army against the Waffen-SS – even though it was not justified –

which is recurringly brought up again as stemming from the assertion that they were better equipped than the army divisions. From the point of view of an infantry division whose transport was horse-drawn, all motorized units were better outfitted. There is, however, one thing I am in a position to assert: all the regular army divisions were pleased to have us as neighbours in difficult situations. When, therefore, former army officers express defamatory remarks regarding the Waffen-SS, they are offending the unspoken camaraderie among all soldiery at the front that has always existed, of men willing to lay down their life for their country, irrespective of the 'colours' under which they are fighting.[399]

Only in January 1943 – probably much too late – was the I SS-Panzer Corps deployed by express transport from France to Russia, to the Kharkov region, to counter the surging Russian offensive. I had been given leave over the Christmas period, as we were still encamped in France. I had only just arrived in Berlin when I was recalled to the unit, to be sent to Russia as the advance party for the tank regiment. I chanced to meet our divisional commander, Sepp Dietrich, on the Wilhelmstrasse; I reported to him that I was about to return to the troop. 'You are first to go to your father in East Prussia!' was his clear and kindly order. Thus, I travelled, standing up in crammed trains, to Steinort, to Father's headquarters in the environs of the Führer's headquarters. Father appeared hours later, coming from the 'Wolf's Lair', in a very serious mood, saying: 'The Führer has now decided that the Sixth Army holds Stalingrad, Göring has guaranteed air supply!'

In freezing weather, we unloaded our tanks in Lyubotin, a Kharkov suburb, and were immediately directed to Merefa, south of Kharkov, marching by night. The wildest rumours circulated about how far the Russians had already advanced. The poor railwaymen who had to shunt our rail transport kept asking us if their safety was ensured, because they had no way of defending themselves. We were already observing some unpleasant signs of dissolution. Scattered Italian soldiers wandered, frequently helplessly, around streets covered in snow. The poor fellows were not equipped for the Russian winter and were hopelessly inferior to the Soviet army in arms and equipment. But the German army too did not always look its best when in retreat; it was not something that had been practised. In this way the story made the rounds of the ranks of the chief of an army catering supply depot who refused to give out rations on the grounds that 'everything had already been foreseen to be blown up'.

Circumvented to the north and south by the Russians, the 1st and 2nd SS-Panzer Divisions were trapped in Kharkov for the next few days; 3rd SS-

Panzer Division was still on its way. The Führer's orders for I SS-Panzer Corps were that Kharkov was to be held 'to the last man'. The order was repeatedly confirmed by the command authority of the army (Army Detachment Lanz) – despite forceful objections from our commanding general, Hausser – which would shortly have led to the destruction of both the fully equipped, superbly trained and unspent divisions.[400] In the end Hausser overrode the Führer's order, and gave the order to abandon the city and break up the enclosing noose. The first thrust was to be led by the Reconnaissance Battalion of the Leibstandarte, under their commander Meyer – already legendary at the time, the famous 'Panzer-Meyer'. The tank company to which I belonged as a platoon leader was subordinated to 'Panzer-Meyer' for breaching the encirclement.

On a clear and frosty morning we stood on the snow-covered village street of Merefa, ready to march to the south-east. The commanding general stepped out of the wooden hut, in front of which I stood in the turret of my tank with the motor running, the map board under his arm – to the troop he was always 'Papa Hausser' due to the unbounded confidence they had in his leadership – and shook Meyer's hand once again. It was the order for the breakthrough. When I saluted he called up to me in the turret to wish me 'good luck'. We would be needing it, as our task was to deeply penetrate the flank of the Russian advance, so as to bring the Corps relief to be able to extricate themselves from the encircled area. Just before, Hausser's intelligence officer – in rather an excited state – had brought him yet another order from Lanz, confirming, once again, the Führer's order to 'hold to the last man'. Hausser had calmed him down with the words: 'It is not a pity for my old head, but for yours, young man!' He was thereby alluding to the risk of being hauled before a court martial for the offence of not obeying a repeated order from the Führer. It is reminiscent of the situation that arose at the Battle of Zorndorf between the famous cavalry general, Friedrich Wilhelm von Seydlitz, and Frederick the Great's adjutant when – after the order to attack had been given repeatedly but in vain – the latter delivered the king's threat that the general would pay for it with his head if he did not as of that instant send his squadrons in to attack. Comparable to Hausser's response is General Seydlitz's: 'After the battle my head is at His Majesty's disposal, during the battle I need it still for the benefit of His Majesty!' Seydlitz correctly waited to launch the cavalry charge until, in pursuit of the defeated Prussians, the Russian infantry had dispersed on the battlefield, and only then to confront them with a surprise cavalry charge which destroyed them. Thereby Seydlitz turned Frederick's looming defeat into a brilliant victory.

To go back to the Kharkov encirclement, 'Meyer's wild chase' was let loose. We had to break through a sprawling village in front of us, occupied by the enemy. Meyer's orders were to make our drive through, taking no notice of enemy fire; what mattered was to 'gain space' so as to free the way for the Corps as rapidly as possible. This was less of a problem for us tank crews than it was for the *Schwimmwagen* (floating car) vehicles of the reconnaissance battalion. The leading tank was nevertheless instantly taken out by a direct hit. It fell to me to take over the tank in the lead, 'Panzer-Meyer' going just behind me in an open *VW-Kübelwagen*. As quickly as our unwieldy Panzer IVs were able to, we proceeded in the thick snow – whereas for the Russian T-34s the snow presented no problem thanks to their broader tracks and more powerful diesel engines – and advanced deep into the Russian hinterland. After breaking through the Russian lines, at first we came across hardly any enemy action.

At dusk we reached the location of Jefremovka. Meyer called out to me: 'Drive through and secure the other edge of the location!' As it was not occupied by the enemy, I left the tank at the location's exit. As I was directing the vehicle traffic, my gunner called out that a vehicle was approaching. As far as it could be made out in the twilight, it was a single horse-drawn sleigh. Assuming it was just a peasant from the village returning home, I sauntered to meet it and grabbed the reins with a loud shout of 'Stoj!' (Stand!). To my horror I saw heavily armed Russian soldiers sitting on the sleigh, probably a scouting patrol.

In such situations it is amazing what quick thinking can be done. Like lightning I remembered an account of my father's from the First World War of a similar situation. His Squadron Chief, a Cavalry Captain von Asseburg, in the course of a long-distance patrol happened to open a barn door and found himself face to face with Russians. He slapped the nearest Russian in the face. I did the same, and struck the sleigh's coachman in the face as hard as I could, so that he fell back onto his companions, bringing about the desired pandemonium, while at the same time I shouted 'Achtung, Russen!' (Watch out, Russians!), beating my arms around wildly. My men were only a few metres away in their tanks. For them to be able to shoot, I had to get out of the tumult, so I flung myself into the snow. Just as astonished as I, the Russians ran off into the dark. Only one of them went for me. He stood there with his machine gun, 2 metres away, shooting single shots at me, to the right into the snow, left into the snow, as I twisted around like an eel until I felt a hit between the shoulder blades which left me unable to breathe. Then that Russian too ran away. The medic found a point of entry in my right shoulder blade and a bullet hole in the upper left arm near the shoulder, both evidently gunshot wounds with the bullets still lodged. The injection of a shot of S.E.E. (a mixture of morphine and a cardio-vascular agent) sent me into a deep sleep. Other than myself, another wounded soldier, of the reconnaissance unit, lay in the dressing station hut.

The next morning I had an altercation with the doctor, the importance of which I realized by accident only months later. I had a fever and consequently had a somewhat reduced consciousness of reality, to which the above injection contributed. I had thus not been conscious of the sound of an airplane engine. The doctor rushed into the room in a hurry and told me that a Fieseler-Storch had landed on the village street, bringing petrol, as we had long been cut off and trapped. This plane was now to take me off to a military hospital. I indicated to the doctor that it was not seemly that I, an officer, should be flown out before a serviceman. Tersely, he let me know that he as the troop doctor determined the gravity of the injury, and consequently the order of departure by transport. There was no doubt he was right in this. To my arguments to the contrary he gave me in the end the 'official order' to be on that plane, for which he had the authority. Most amicably, I then pointed out to him that I would unfortunately be obliged to refuse to obey the order. It seemed to me that for a second I caught an expression of profound comprehension in the doctor's professional medical bearing, as he turned away with the words 'You are stubborn as a mule!' and gave the order to have the wounded soldier carried onto the plane.[401] No more aeroplanes landed in our sector in the days that followed. Only aerial delivery bombs were dropped, but when any could at all be salvaged they too were but a drop in the ocean.

On the fifth day we ran out of fuel, and munitions were running out. 'Panzer Meyer' gave every casualty that was no longer ambulatory – they had meanwhile greatly increased again in the day-long fighting – a pistol each. Every wounded man should be able to shoot himself before being massacred by the Red Army soldiers. There were examples of it. He wanted to try to break through to our own lines in the night with the combat group, on foot and in thick snow; it was a desperate venture.

As at the dressing station all my outer clothing had been cut off, I now wore nothing but a coat and was frightfully cold if I had to go out of doors, so I spent most of time in the command post's wooden hut. Under the circumstances, my injury did not even give me much discomfort; my torso was indeed blue and green, but I did not really have a lot to complain about other than the local pain of the bullet entry holes. My tank, which could by now shoot only with the machine gun because its cannon had become inoperative, stood guarding the command post's security in front of Meyer's hut, as the 'Boleros' – as we the soldiers called the Russians for some inexplicable reason, possibly in irony of the designation 'Bolsheviks' – were forcing their way into the location. We could as yet keep them down with our Turm-MG (turret machine gun) until the courageous Grenadiers had thrown them out. Late in the afternoon I heard Meyer call into the radio: 'Max, the division is at stake!' He was speaking over the radio-telephone to Max Wünsche, commanding the 1st Division of our Panzer regiment that was fighting its way through to us. He did in fact reach us just in time in the growing evening twilight, and fought off the Russian noose choking us so that Meyer's combat unit could reach their own lines in the night with all their vehicles and wounded.

Both bullet holes in my shoulders had meanwhile closed, so I stayed with the Company. The bullets lodged in my chest would have to be taken care of later. Weeks later, at the termination of the fighting around Kharkov, our doctor sent me to military hospital to 'have a look' where those bullets could actually be. There I was stood on my head and then back onto my feet, but the bullets could not be found. The shot – at close range, that is from less than 2 metres away – must have traversed the whole torso diagonally, apparently hitting the soft parts only. This is probably what caused the abnormal haematoma which had painted my entire upper body in many colours for weeks. Once the Storch had flown from the 'kettle', as an area encircled by the opponent was called in those days, my Company Commander, Astheger, had said to me: 'Your men were pleased that you stayed with them!' In those days, such conduct on the part of an officer, comparable to that of the captain of a sinking ship who according to his code of honour will be the last to quit it, was actually taken for granted; nowadays it would hardly meet with any comprehension.

A few days later we lost a company commander, and I took over the 7th Company at the very moment when the counter-offensive against Kharkov began. I knew them well, having been their platoon leader for half a year. We achieved some successes. The Detachment Commander told me that when the fighting was over he had wanted to recommend me for the 'German Cross in Gold' medal. The regimental commander had, however, thought that in my case it should not be so readily awarded. Whatever the outcome, one simply stood out as 'special'. It was soon to happen to me once more. At a boozy evening in the company of a Luftwaffe close reconnaissance group when the fighting around Kharkov had ended, I heard the air commodore behind me ask our General Staff officer: 'How is he then?' The question immediately caught my full attention. How often may it have been asked behind my back? Our 1a – as in the Wehrmacht a General Staff officer was called – answered: 'We wanted to fly him out of the encirclement with a stork [Fieseler-Storch] as a casualty but he didn't fly!' I sprang up as if I had been stung by a tarantula and, admittedly in a most unmilitary manner, bitterly reproached our General Staff officer. I would have been placed in an untenable situation if I had not resisted a flight out of an encircled area. This superior man just said, in a very calm and friendly manner: 'No need to get so uptight. You didn't fly out. That makes you thoroughly one of us and not the son of your father!' But one still had to prove precisely that! As the Russians often utilized their 'prominent' prisoners as a propaganda tool against their will, the division wanted to prevent my falling into Russian hands, dead or alive.

There followed weeks of fierce defensive fighting. Hausser's decision to give up Kharkov had brought about the conditions to cut off the Russian attacking spearheads, which, aiming at the Black Sea, were to stage a 'super-Stalingrad' at the River Donets, and to annihilate them. In his memoirs, Manstein does not do justice to Hausser's performance and that of the SS-Panzer Corps, although it was the decision Hausser took, against the Führer's orders, to give up Kharkov and salvage the two divisions that gave the preconditions for Manstein's operation to intercept and destroy the Russian advance movement already at Dnipropetrovsk. Our division was assigned to cover the back of this operation. There were by now but infantry screens representing our own lines, since the heavy losses of the fighting over many weeks could not so far be replaced. The poor infantrymen had not had a roof over their heads for weeks at a time, in freezing temperatures.

At the beginning of March it was to be our turn to counter-attack. Marching to the marshalling area in a blizzard was extremely arduous. Despite the difficulties, the narrow track of our Panzer IV in relation to the T-34 tanks only just enabled us to get through the snowdrifts, but this was not the case for our wheeled vehicles. There was no other solution but to have them towed by the tanks; the picture was grotesque but alas no exception. We pushed forward to Walki. This is where, as mentioned before, detached as the leading company, we surprised a withdrawing Russian infantry regiment in a hollow. Our MGs caused havoc among the Russians. The roles were at last reversed. The next morning we were positioned at Lyubotin. Again my company, now in possession of only three Panzer IVs, was at the head. We came across a Russian anti-tank gun front which we were surprisingly able to fight off with no losses. In the afternoon there was another one at Lyubotin's outskirts. We also defeated this one speedily and with no losses, so the three tanks were still at my disposal. However, we had no more high explosive fragmentation shells, which are essential for attacking targets without armour plating such as anti-tank guns. Lyubotin lay before us, seething with Russians, in the snow easily distinguishable everywhere. While I pondered what should be done – at that moment we were not in radio communication with the commander and were in a hollow – the vehicle behind me came on to the radio with a message that I should open a hatch, as the commander of 1 Grenadier Regiment, Witt, was next to my tank.

Witt, already decorated with the Knight's Cross with Oak Leaves, was one of the best infantry regimental commanders I had to deal with, of great personal bravery combined with outstanding strategic skills. Witt's leadership radiated inspirational confidence, one of the most important qualities for leadership in war. He had driven ahead to the first tank in an open motor car, and called out to me: 'Ribbentrop, we must have that place!'

Witt was highly esteemed in the division. I was not at that time under his orders, but as the place had to be taken, the opportunity of a thrust into the Russians' retreat had to be taken advantage of. This signified moving in with no high explosive fragmentation shells, however, and without relevant orders from my commander. With the laconic radio signal to the two other vehicles to 'Follow!', we set off. I knew they would follow, unquestioningly, even if it were to Hell. I could depend on that, and it was going to be a trip to Hell. The sprawling village was crammed with Russians and we drove straight into its centre with three lonely tanks, with the machine guns firing in every direction. From the tanks of those days there was no chance of hitting any target with machine-gun fire while speeding along bumpy village streets. The psychological effect of three tanks hurtling ahead, shooting wildly around, would have to suffice. A courageous Grenadier engineer had clambered on to my tank and was now riding with us amidst the Russians, on a 'one-way ticket'. He probably saved his own life and ours as, when we went around a bend in the middle of the village we found ourselves 10 metres from a heavy-duty Russian anti-tank gun ready to fire, whose crew were no doubt as taken by surprise as we were. They had manifestly not calculated that we would already be so far into the village. My gunner immediately fired the gun, although it had only just been loaded with a tank shell, hoping for a psychological effect or a chance hit; his shot may well have succeeded, we could not make sure. With great presence of mind, the Grenadier jumped off the tank and flung a hand grenade at the feet of the Russians; they fled. That could easily have gone wrong! There was now no longer any time to stop, we could not be held up any more; to keep moving was our only chance. At a break-neck pace our three tanks dashed straight through the kilometre-long village and the middle of Russian columns, scattering them as we went. Finally Stollmeyer, commanding the tank behind me, standing in the turret of his vehicle, was still firing his pistol into the Russians when his vehicle suffered a direct hit. It was, thank goodness, only a high explosive shell that could not damage the tank, but a small splinter did pierce his cheek, a wound that may not have been serious but was still extremely painful. He stayed with the company, however. Sadly, this brave officer was to fall a few days later. We spared the Grenadiers the arduous effort of fighting their way through the length of the village. None of our tanks were disabled; all three were still operational.

When we reached the exit from the village, we were stopped; we turned to the north, from where Kharkov was to be surrounded. It became a horrific march. It had meanwhile become pitch dark, it was snowing and the maps were worthless. We had to reach the village of Derhachi north of Kharkov that night, as it was to be attacked in the morning. We managed, 'following our noses' and with a lot of luck.

Because of flooding, the attack had to take place along a narrow village lane. Once again my company was installed as company ahead, with myself at the head. This is not in itself the duty of a company commander but, as 'newly-appointed Chief', a strong incentive for the company if in hairy situations is for the 'old man' (aged 21!) to drive the lead vehicle himself. There were after all only three Panzer IV left. Here once more we experienced how ineffective tanks can be against infantry, especially in built-up areas. To right and left of the street, through the gaps in the boarding, we could see the Russian soldiers close enough to touch, without being able to do much about it. They threw hand grenades over the fences and fired rounds against the observation slits with their anti tank rifles. One of the Russians shot with admirable accuracy, directly into my front observation slit. The safety glass of the Panzer IV's vision hatch (*Kinonblock*) saved my life, but it shattered and my forward vision was suddenly blind. The *Kinonblock* had to be replaced right away as it is impossible to drive a tank without being able to see ahead. That was done, thanks to the skilled personnel. Suddenly, with a frightful crash, the tank received a tremendous blow. I thought to myself that there must be an enemy tank or anti-tank gun nearby that would make short shrift of us on the narrow street. My second vehicle then came on the air to announce that with a high explosive shell they had killed a Russian who was about to jump onto my tank with a 'Molotov cocktail' ('petrol bomb' incendiary weapon). The damn MG 34 had jammed again, so only the main gun remained. The high explosive shell with its highly sensitive fuse could do no damage to the tank itself.

I now decided to drive through the location at top speed, despite the danger of falling into an ambush. There was nothing else we could do. Once again, all went well. At the exit of the village we scattered the withdrawing

Russian infantry and immediately after, swiftly gaining access, attacked the next location, Cherkasskoye. We could not allow the Russians time to entrench themselves once more. In view of our ludicrously weak force we had to keep them on the run. Our only chance was to break through the major route from Kharkov to the north and then turn in the direction of Kharkov. We dashed through the village, again at top speed. We then turned on to the Belgorod-Kharkov road to the south towards Kharkov. At the airfield we caught one more Russian tank that was trying to escape. Borgsmüller, my gunner, got it from behind with a clean shot.

The next morning we proceeded no further than the Kharkov city limits. We could not wipe out dug-in T-34 tanks, as because of the terrain we had to stick to the streets. A Tiger from our regiment now drove ahead and, in a burst of firing from close range, shot up six of these T-34s, until it received an unfortunate hit to the optics in the tank turret which disabled it. The Russians gave up towards evening. With the infantry ahead, we drove into the town. In front of 'Red Square' we found a barrier closed with an abandoned KW-1 (heavy Russian tank). As I was in the lead, I had to pull the Russian out of the way, so as to clear the way for us. My second tank with Stollmeyer drove through the barrier to accompany the infantry further on. I had time to call to him to be careful, for everywhere in the streets a concealed anti-tank gun or indeed a tank could be lurking. Seconds later armour-piercing shells were streaking along the street. I feared the worst. Sure enough, a few hundred metres further on Stollmeyer had met with a second barrier where there was a T-34 still manned. Stollmeyer was hit in his turret and killed, together with his gunner and loader. The driver and radio operator were able to save themselves and escape the tank. It may be said that once again fate was kind to me. Had my position been second tank, which as company commander would have been quite proper, and if instead of myself Stollmeyer had pulled the Russian tank out of the barrier, I would then most probably have fallen victim to the lurking T-34. Through the night I stayed with my vehicles – three again as one had come from the workshop to the front – between the tower-like buildings of heavy industry at the northern edge of 'Red Square'. The strictly purist-functional architecture of the grandly conceived square was extremely impressive in the moonlight, indeed surrealistic, but at the same time oppressive. We were frightfully cold, and hungry too, for no provisions had followed; added to this I had lost one of my best officers. His 'iron grave', as it is so aptly called in a Panzerlied song, stood charred and black some 150m in front of us. The major achievement of being on 'Red Square' was at that moment honestly not much of a consolation. It was depressing. However, just six weeks after Hausser's disobeying of an order repeatedly issued by the Führer, at the cost for us of heavy albeit successful fighting, the city was in German hands once again. Other parts of the division had entered from the west and pushed into the centre.

We were granted a short day's rest. I used it to look in on the wounded of my company at a main dressing station north of Kharkov. The dressing station was housed in wooden huts, the wounded often not even lying on straw, one man next to the other, all of them gravely injured. The stench was indescribable. The doctors and paramedics were on the brink of breaking down physically because of the countless injured from the heavy fighting. Here, the wretched misery of war was depressingly only too apparent. Whoever speaks of war should have seen a casualty clearing station or, even better, have been in one as a casualty himself. The impact that again and again throughout the war these sites of suffering had on me were some of the most keenly felt as well as the most dismal.

In the spring I visited the Kharkov North military cemetery near the airport at the entrance to the city, looking for the graves of my men. I arrived just as the division's war graves officer was trying to identify some 120 soldiers killed in action whose bodies were lying there in rows. They were a company of Grenadiers who had been trapped in a '*balka*' (ravine) by the Russians in the course of the turbulent defensive fighting when the city had been abandoned. They had put up a desperate resistance – countless cartridge cases were scattered around each man – before being overcome by the Russians. The Russians had stripped the Grenadiers naked, some had been tied up and finally shot dead. They were found like that by a search party. The winter fighting for Kharkov was particularly bitter.

Just a few days after taking the city, we advanced northward and were placed under the orders of the APC (armoured personnel carrier) battalion commanded by the later to become legendary Jochen Peiper. The 'APC men' took good note of the welcome fire cover we were able to provide them with when late in the afternoon once again we came across an anti-tank gun front which we were able to overcome speedily and, happily, once more with no losses. The longer 7.5cm cannon which had been incorporated into the old and cumbersome Panzer IV proved itself a first-rate weapon. The commanders and gunners of the tanks had by now become experienced tank personnel. The emplacements of the Russian anti-tank guns, lit by the setting sun, were clearly distinguishable. Through deep snow, we topped a rise, when in front of us from the edge of a village there were a lot of flashes of shooting, and grenades burst next to an APC in front of us, by the grace of God missing it.

In a few seconds, my tried and tested gunner Borgsmüller had put two Russian pieces out of action. The remainder were dealt with equally swiftly by the two other tanks. Upon this the APC men waved at us gratefully. We were unable to communicate by radio; throughout the entire war the German arms industry was not able to make it work.

On the next morning, in brilliant sunshine – for once, at last, accompanied from the air by three Me 110 ground attack aircraft – again with Peiper we advanced on Belgorod. We swiftly broke through the Russian fortified lines and pressed on in a northerly direction at full speed. On the way our 'wild chase' took a Russian tank formation by surprise in a village, which we wiped out. This did not hold us up very long, true to the maxim 'What you have reached by moving fast you do not need to fight for any more!' What counted was to reach Belgorod.

In his memoirs, General Field Marshal Erich von Manstein erroneously attributes the taking of Belgorod to the *Grossdeutschland* Panzer Division. I myself drove the lead tank, which, together with the APCs of our *Leibstandarte* Division was the first to enter Belgorod, whilst underway we destroyed a few more Russian vehicles whose crews were taken by surprise. In the afternoon we launched a minor assault westward so as to give the *Grossdeutschland* Division emplaced to our left, which evidently had greater resistance to overcome, some air.

It was, however, obvious that the force was not adequate to further bolster the success and drive through to Kursk. An advance by our armoured group under Peiper met with stronger resistance the next morning and was cut off, in the course of which an APC received a direct hit and went up in flames. The driver of this APC was one of Peiper's most tried and tested NCOs. As at the withdrawal the fate of the crew could not clearly be determined, Peiper called for volunteers to drive ahead again in a tank to see what had happened to the crew of the burning APC. It had to be assumed that the Russians would again strafe the attempt with artillery fire, as they had before. The expedition could turn out to be tantamount to a suicide mission. Under the circumstances it was awkward for me as company leader to appoint another of our three vehicles for the task, and I therefore took it upon myself and, from the remnants of uniforms collected, was able to confirm that the entire crew had been killed. Surprisingly, the Russians did not disturb my search with more firing. Peiper was very grateful.

During 'Operation Citadel' there was another opportunity to earn Peiper's acknowledgement, which was worth more than any distinction. With my company, I was part of Peiper's APC battalion when very shortly after we came across an extended Russian anti-tank front which Peiper, unhesitatingly, attacked and put out of action in true hussar fashion. An attack against a front of heavy-duty anti-tank guns is a long-remembered experience. It is a charge – so to speak – straight into the muzzles of the enemy cannon. A hit could be absolutely fatal. There was no point in oneself firing, and with the tank's armament technology of that day and age it would have only had an effect on the opponent's morale. The only chance was to keep moving. One developed a slight distance from one's self when exposed to such an extraordinary risk. Peiper's rapid attack had surprised the Russians. They were overrun and their guns destroyed. Peiper possessed what Frederick the Great called the *coup d'œil* of a commander, by which he meant a quick eye for appraising a situation and the tactical possibilities arising from it. Peiper said to us after the attack, standing amongst the destroyed Russian 'crash-bang' guns,[402] 'Ribbentrop, we would be happy to take you on [in his APC battalion]', by which naturally he meant the whole company. Coming from Peiper, that was grand appreciation indeed.

It must be borne in mind that this counter-offensive of March 1943, which restored Kharkov once more into our possession and led to a considerable gain of territory, was executed by a division which was burned out, with the heaviest of defensive fighting, lasting weeks, behind them, and moreover with no replacement supply of personnel crews, weapon and equipment. The quality of the troops and their leadership was yet still a factor to be reckoned with, set against the numerical superiority of the Russians. Even with our antiquated old Panzer IVs we felt ourselves to be superior to the Russians: we moved more skilfully and were better shots. Without doubt, however, because of their readiness to fight the troops had gradually 'spoiled' the leadership. Ever more was therefore demanded of us, until finally it could no longer be satisfied. In some respects, in the day-by-day life at the front, the motorized and tank divisions were now somewhat better off than the horse-drawn infantry divisions that had to march as far as the Caucasus and back again in the heat and the cold. With his APC battalion, in February 1943 Peiper pushed through as far as the River Donets in an almost foolhardy strike, in order to give an infantry division (the 320th), in a struggling march on foot, a helping hand. Its commander, Lieutenant General Georg Postel, could not quite repress his resentment against the Waffen-SS, his saviours; his 'thanks' to Peiper consisted of rather provocatively asked questions about provisions.

I remember a depressing experience in the course of *Unternehmen Zitadelle* so well that I can still give the place and date exactly. On 11 July 1943 – it was one day before the major tank battle of Prokhorovka, to which I shall come later –a prisoner Russian lieutenant was brought to our command post positioned in the culvert[403] under a railway embankment that played a role in the following day's events. He looked, by the way, just like a 'last Teuton', tall and blue-eyed, and his attitude throughout was that of an officer. A cigarette and a shot of schnapps relaxed the ambience, which turned into a discussion that was no longer in the nature of an interrogation, between him and us as to the prospects of this war. Suddenly, he said (in broken German): 'Russian soldier poor rations and good morale, German soldier good rations and poor morale.' Naturally we did not take the remark as reference to ourselves, but we were profoundly affected. Subconsciously we felt that Stalingrad signified the beginning of a crisis of confidence in the highest command. Were it not for the threat of Bolshevism and Roosevelt's and Churchill's demand for 'unconditional surrender', the war may possibly have ended earlier.

Was not the stopping of the Russian offensive, as well as the German counter-attack which led to the recapture of Kharkov, already the criterion of success which in Hitler's eyes could signify the prerequisite for the possibility of now being able to put out feelers in the direction of Russian leadership without too much loss of face? In Father's opinion the successful consolidation of the Eastern Front and the retaking of Kharkov provided the occasion. Hitler, however, insisted upon embarking on *Unternehmen Zitadelle*.

The highest command thus would not take the time calmly to restore the experienced divisions of the army and the Waffen-SS, to provide reserves and to give thought to strategic options so as to institute them where and how was best. One of the essential maxims of German military theory, valid at all levels, was the principle, if feasible, never to allow the initiative to be taken out of one's hands. It may quite be said to be a 'dogma'. In this way the preparations for *Unternehmen Zitadelle* were soon undertaken. The objective was to pincer off the 'Kursk Bulge' which had deeply penetrated the German front, intending to cut off and destroy the Russian troops positioned in it, and subsequently to realign the front. So much for the operational objectives established.

This offensive, of 'limited objective' as it is called in the jargon of the profession, which means that no targets decisive for the war were connected to it, was under intensive preparation in our division. The terrain foreseen for the division's offensive was reproduced in big sandboxes. Dispositions for the attack in all possible variations were again and again talked through with all commanders, including the company commanders. The maxim of the German leadership, that familiarity with the position and the objectives of the high command are the prerequisites for an adequate action, undertaken if necessary under one's own responsibility, to be taken at all levels of command, was entirely corresponded with. The two jaws of the pincer which was to cut off the Kursk salient were positioned to the north of Belgorod and south of Oryol, both points at which every last ordinary unimaginative ensign would first expect or launch an attack. Under Hitler's orders, the German military command had lost its imagination.

Even we company commanders were given a look at the maps of how the enemy was situated. They boded no good. The red captions marking Russian defence works and troop deployment on the map were ever more numerous and dense, the longer the start of the assault was put off. It was said that Hitler absolutely wanted to bring into action the newly constructed tank, the Panther.[404] It was a novelty that had not yet got over its teething problems.

On the eve of the attack, Hitler had as usual addressed a rather pathetic Order of the Day to the troops, in which if I remember correctly the extraordinary significance of this battle was pointed out, although it was clearly no longer a question of an operation decisive for the war. This might be an indication that he anticipated from this limited operation the military success which at the time he had described to Father as the precondition for an attempted approach to the Russians to engage in negotiations. In this way, it was only on 5 July 1943 that we moved against an opponent who had had the time to be fully armed defensively and prepared for the German offensive. The SS-Panzer Corps was to attack the Russians at their strongest position, the focal point of the southern front, precisely at the spot where they expected it. For days at a time we fought through ever more defensive works, minefields, tank trenches. Time and again we defeated counter-attacks led by tanks. The German strategic concept foresaw that the front-line divisions of infantry would actually break through the enemy lines of defence, through which the intact tank divisions were then to thrust into the enemy hinterland. There was no hope that these purely infantry divisions would succeed against the Russian defensive positions that had been constantly reinforced by dug-in T-34s. The tank divisions therefore had to fight their way free by themselves, sustaining heavy losses.

On 11 July, in the fighting before the little town of Prokhorovka, at last we overcame yet another long, deep anti-tank ditch, having thereby broken through the opponent's numerous lines of defence. We were in our vehicles, awaiting the order to attack Prokhorovka, which lay within our sight. Meanwhile, through our powerful binoculars, looking beyond the small River Pschel we were already observing fierce counter-assaults by Russian tanks on our left-hand tank division. This was the reason why the order to take Prokhorovka could not yet be given and, impatiently, we stayed on a rise between the Pschel valley and the Kharkov-Kursk railway line. What had happened to the order to attack? There is nothing more disturbing than to be standing exposed to enemy fire without being able to do anything. Sometimes, at such moments I would say to my loader: 'Fix me a sandwich.' He kept the crew's provisions in a cartridge box at his feet, under the cartridge case bag containing the cases of grenades that had been fired. The crew consisted of five men. The commander – in this case I myself – was in the turret, and to my left, below and in front of me, was the gunner. The commander had to guide him to each target as quickly as possible, with a precisely directed approach, as the gunner had only a limited field of view at his disposal through his optical periscope. This teamwork between the commander, the gunner and the driver was often a matter of survival. The driver had to be given continuous directions, while at the same time he had to utilize every slightest protective cover and, above all, not get us bogged down. Basically, he was the most important member of the crew as he was responsible for the mobility of the vehicle. The commander was connected to the gunner, driver and radio operator by the on-board intercom. The loader could neither see nor hear anything, but had to see to it that at any time the gun was loaded with the correct shell (explosive or incendiary) and the machine gun, if possible, was always operational. The radio operator had to switch the transmitter over each time, depending on whether I wanted to talk to the company vehicles or to the commander, while at the same time if the situation arose he had to fight off enemy infantrymen with his machine gun. Life or death could depend on each single member of the crew. It can be imagined how closely these circumstances welded us together.

The loader had bent over to get to his box with the provisions, when at that very moment there was a sharp report inside the tank. The loader straightened up and stretched out his arm, which was bleeding, to me. He in particular – indeed all of us – had once again been very lucky. A light-weight Russian anti-tank gun had fired at us from the flank and pierced the right-hand side of the turret. The ammunition had splintered against our gun and grievously wounded the loader. If he had not bent down at that moment he would have been killed by a direct hit.

The days when we had been attacking, that lay behind us, had already cost us heavy losses. Of the twenty-two vehicles in my company, with which I had reported for duty on 5 July, on the morning of 12 July I had but seven left that were operational and at my disposal. The remainder had either been blown up or were in the workshop for repairs. Besides myself there was one other officer left in the company.

The Russians were very well prepared for the German offensive. Moreover, the German leadership also did the Soviets the favour of attacking at precisely the expected flashpoints. The attack lacked the surprise factor, and in the end did what the opponent expected. Had the lessons of military history been forgotten by the Germans, that against a superior enemy only the out of the ordinary, or rather the surprising, could achieve success? Had the success of the Western campaign not been the best proof of this tenet?

Additionally, the Russians furthermore had the advantage of the interior line, meaning that over short distances they could rapidly bring up their reserves to whatever sectors of the front were under threat. Their interventions reserve, the Fifth Guards Tank Army, had been positioned exactly on the arc of the 'Kursk Bulge' at Stary Oskol. On the German side, on the other hand, there were no notable operational reserves at our disposal for use following the breakthrough of the Russian defensive positions.

Up until 11 July, the SS Panzer Corps, put into the centre of the assault front, had succeeded in advancing deep into the Russian front. It was at the tip of this wedge where on the evening of 11 July stood the 'armoured group' of the 1st SS Tank Division, the so-called *Leibstandarte*, to which my company belonged. We had gone for a rest over to an elongated slope at the back of a Russian anti-tank trench to wait for the two neighbouring divisions to catch up. On the next day Prokhorovka – a significant step on the way to Kursk – was to be taken.

Very early on the morning of 12 July the irregular clatter of the two-stroke DKW motorcycle of the messenger was heard by the unit; it always heralded a fresh assignment. I lay fast asleep underneath the tank with my crew, but at the annoying noise of the motor was, as usual, immediately wide awake. As I crawled out from under the tank I was subconsciously aware that there was restlessness at the front. I could hear infantry and artillery fire; aircraft from both sides flew above. There came the call: 'Company leader to the commander!' My commander – who had obviously just been woken from the deep sleep of exhaustion – instructed me that as the infantry thought they heard what was supposedly the sound of tanks from the enemy ranks, I should take a look. I ordered my company to prepare for battle. Taking the motorcycle with side-car (*B-Krad*), I found the commander of the infantry battalion positioned in front of us on the rise. Our consultation did not produce any fresh information; he too had not received any precise messages. I left a reliable NCO behind with the motorcycle at the infantry command post for him to be able to contact me immediately when necessary.

It was a beautiful summer's morning, and I walked down the hill to my tanks. The company-grade officer announced that battle preparation had meanwhile been completed. My loader handed me a sandwich and a mug of hot ersatz coffee. The sergeant major had brought breakfast up just in time, as it turned out. I swore a little to myself, because actually my company had been classed as a reserve company when the commander had issued his orders the evening before and we had hoped for a couple of hours of sleep. Instead we were now exposed to this unclear situation requiring permanent battle stations.

It was going to be another warm day; the sun was already hot. How hot the day would be was something I was to see like a flash of lightning a few seconds later, when in front of us on the hill there rose a purple smokescreen. It was sent up by the flare cartridges, the signal designated for that day as a tank warning. The considerable number of such purple smoke clusters rising into the air indicated that evidently a major tank attack by the Russians was underway. Then I caught sight of my assistant hurtling down the slope on the motorcycle, in a dense cloud of dust, constantly punching his fist in the air as he went – the signal for 'Fall in!' Was it the Fifth Guards Tank Army which was joining in the battle, and of whose positioning near Stary Oskol we knew? We were soon to be informed!

I had long given the necessary orders. This was the moment to take immediate action – without waiting for orders. We young officers were trained in the fundamental German principle of leadership, if necessary to be resourceful, relying on one's own initiative in the framework of the general order given and the situation as it presented itself. Nowadays this precept is called 'mission-type tactics'. In our officer training, time and again we were confronted with new situations and told to make a 'situation assessment' and immediately to come up with the corresponding 'decision'. 'Situation assessment and decision' were the actual secret of the German army's success.

I called out to my company officer, Malchow, a man as brave as he was nice: 'We deploy on the slope at the back and shoot the Russians off. Spread out [with your platoon] a bit to the left!'' We did not have a direct connection to the division next to us; it was a lucky opportunity for the Russians to outflank us, but one which amazingly they did not respond to with the necessary vigour.

As trained on the military exercise campus, at the greatest possible speed the company deployed upward on the hill. These young soldiers, in the tanks they were in or driving, took their place in the battle formation as expertly as seasoned combatants – it made one's heart beat a little faster! We drove over a small hump in the terrain. The slope at the back where I wanted to position myself with my vehicle was about 100m in front of us. At that moment in a hollow to the left at 800m we saw Russian tanks surrounding us. For our skilled gunners it was the ideal distance, and very soon several T-34s went up in flames.

In that instant there appeared at less than 100m in front of us, overtaking their own infantry lines, some ten, twenty, thirty and more T-34 tanks – at full speed and carrying infantry, coming directly at us. 'That's it!' I muttered to myself. We no longer had a chance! Sure enough, both tanks to my immediate right side straight away took direct hits and were ablaze.[405] I was able to see one of my best commanders just have time to jump out of the turret. We never saw a trace of him again. This must be what it felt like for foot soldiers in former centuries when a cavalry charge thundered up to them. I had already long given the gunner sitting below me to the left a kick to his right hand, which meant 'turn the gun to the right as soon as possible. Maximum danger!' – an almost automatic reaction. I already heard Schüle, my driver, shouting over the intercom: 'Can you see them, First Lieutenant? On the right! The right! Here they come!' I could see them, only too well, and the gunner had already fired the first shot, properly blowing up a T-34. From the minimum distance, 20–30m, we shot up another two or three T-34s. They were then passing right and left, close enough to reach out and touch: we could see the faces of the Russian infantrymen sitting on them, and more and more stormed over the hump of terrain in front of us. Our rescue was that at that time the T-34s did not have a commander in the turret. The T-34 was driven by a gunner, who did not have the panoramic view that we had. He therefore could see only a small portion of the battlefield, at which he aimed – with his view restricted at that moment. It appeared therefore that the Russians had not yet discovered us, although we stood in bright sunlight on an open field.

However, the next split second the situation changed dramatically. A T-34 had seen us and stopped still about 30m to our right, suspension slightly seesawing. The gun swivelled on us so that I was looking directly into its mouth, but not before having immediately shouted 'Full acceleration! Step on it! Go! Go!' into the throat microphone to the driver. Our only chance was to disappear from the field of vision of the Russian right away. As I have said before, even in moments of fatal danger it is possible to think fast as lightning. The thought that streaked through my mind was: the last thing you will take with you from this earth is a ball of fire, the shot from the Russian's gun, fired from a distance of 30m which means certain death! My driver, Schüle – one of the best in the regiment – straight away started our cumbersome Panzer IV moving. He had of course engaged a gear just in case, and at full speed we then drove straight for the Russian tank group. We passed a few metres from the Russian while he was frantically trying to turn his gun at the same time. We managed, however, to disappear from his field of vision. Whilst constantly more Russian tanks drove past us on the right and left a few metres away, close behind our 'adversary' we swivelled round and fired a tank shell into its turret from 5m, which literally exploded the T-34. The turret nearly fell on our gun. I murmured into the intercom: 'That one isn't going to try to shoot us up any more.' Grinning, my gunner nodded. At such moments one does not have consciousness that four Russian armoured soldiers, who also were fighting for their country, had just been sent to kingdom come: all that counts then is the pitiless 'you or me', meaning 'if one of us two is going to the devil, it had better be you!'. Both my other two tanks were burning right next to us.

I knew with absolute clarity, with a probability verging on certainty, that it was our turn next. Our sole chance lay henceforth in keeping moving at all costs, since with its poor field of vision the single Russian tank could not survey its surroundings. In this way, amidst the pack of Russian tanks, we drove up to our own unit,[406] positioned at the anti-tank ditch previously mentioned, some 800m behind, and which now began shooting on the Russians coming down the slope. Using my rather ridiculous cover name for that day of 'Kunibert', I kept a constant flow of communication over the wireless with the other companies, asking them not to fire at us as we were among the Russian group. In the meantime, every so often we shot one Russian tank after another when they overtook us: they were much faster and more mobile than our old Panzer IV. Then the loader called out: 'I need tank grenades [shells].' In the cramped space of the operational interior of the tank, the loader had about eighteen to twenty grenades within immediate reach, some of which were, however, what were known as explosive shells, to be used only against our non-armoured targets. The remaining stock of the tank's grenades was distributed all over the vehicle. Now, under the most extreme conditions, from every corner of the vehicle time after time tank grenades had to be handed to the loader. This anti-tank ammunition was approximately a metre long, and in the narrowness of the tank very cumbersome. While moving, the driver had to remove it from its halter and hand it over backward, and the gunner leave his observation post, which, in that instant, meant that the crew in the vehicle was entirely without protection. As soon as another grenade was in the barrel we stood still and shot the next T-34 down. Only I as commander had a view in the round and espied the 'comrades of the opposite side' as they drove alongside us for the length of a few metres or overtook us. If one of them were to recognize us, it would have meant a final 'goodnight'. We did not have the slightest chance of survival. At one point a Russian tank overtook us a few metres away, carrying an anti-tank gun and with infantry men sitting on it. The Red Army men recognized us and, horrified, stared straight into the mouth of our gun. 'Hold still!' was the order to the driver and the shot was already out, from

20m at most, a devastating direct hit. My new gunner, Hoppe (Felden, my tried and tested gunner, had been taken behind the lines a few days earlier due to illness and Borgsmüller had been transferred to the military academy at the end of the fighting for Kharkov), fired with excellent accuracy, aided by Schüle, the driver, who, with amazing dexterity, manoeuvred the ponderous tank amidst the chaos of burning Russian tanks and our own vehicles. Bergner, the radio operator, wrought havoc among the Russian foot soldiers with his machine gun,[407] whilst the loader, Trautmann, who could see nothing, with the greatest *sang-froid* grabbed grenades from the most remote corners of the vehicle so as to reload the cannon as quickly as possible; our life depended on it. There were more than enough targets at a short distance around us. This was when our youngsters' rigorous battle training came to the fore. Firing drill, often mocked, was the prerequisite, even in utmost danger and the most extreme circumstances, every movement to be carried out with exactitude. Who nowadays can understand how fascinating it was at that time to have successfully lived through the most alarming situations such as this one with a highly practised crew, when that grain of good luck remained true to one and allowed one to survive! The thanks of the crew on the evening of that day, for the leadership of their vehicle in this furious battle, was the best recognition to be had.

The battlefield, measuring about 800m by 400m, was the scene of a proper inferno. The Russians, if they had been able to get so far, drove into their own anti-tank trenches, where they were naturally easy targets for our counter-defence action. Russian tanks were in flames all over the place, partially having run over one another, emitting a thick black miasma from the burning diesel fuel, in amongst them the Russian foot soldiers who had jumped off the tanks, desperately trying to find their way and easy prey for our Grenadiers and artillery men, who were also present on the field. We sometimes simply drove over the poor fellows who had jumped off their tanks from behind, because of course they had not reckoned with a German tank being part of their tank pack. The whole scene had an aspect of the Apocalypse such as is very rarely seen in the course of war. The attacking Russian tanks – at an estimate more than a hundred of them – were all destroyed. In the ZDF film mentioned, a Russian tank officer who had taken part in the fighting also said that 'They went to their death!' 'Papa Hausser', our commanding general, is said on one of the ensuing days to have counted the Russian tanks shot out, marking them with a piece of chalk, because he could not believe the number that was reported to him. However, since the Russian hulks were all behind the front line he was able to make sure. Reports of tanks having been hit were always something of a problem when there were several different army services taking part (tanks, anti-tank defence, artillery, etc.). Each one liked to claim a hit for themselves, so some could occasionally be counted twice.

At the end we had taken up position with our vehicle behind a shot-out T-34, and from there saw to the destruction of the remaining Russian tanks. Then the gunner cried out: 'I've had it in the eye!' We had been hit by an unlucky strike in the opening of the front armour plating, which was important for the gunner's optical periscope. It was pushed backward with great force and grievously injured the gunner, who was taking aim at that moment. This disabled us operationally. I got the vehicle out of the line of attack and drove it back a few hundred metres to the rear for cover. Coincidentally, there a vehicle of my company's came toward me which had just come out of the repair shop. All I had to do was change over, but I had to take my trained crew – with the exception of the gunner – with me, which caused protest among the men to be left behind. This is how great the readiness for action was prevalent in those days, including the men transferred from the Luftwaffe, who had not volunteered to come to us (but who are nowadays calumnied just as are the volunteers). This has to be clearly perceived: from where we were, those youngsters had an overview of the battlefield – an inferno – and yet wanted to stay with their comrades and join in.

An impressively successful feat of defensive fighting was to prove victorious. The counter-attack immediately launched, in which I could participate with the substitute tank, by noon had almost entirely restored our former positions into our hands, with surprisingly few casualties for us. The unit had but three or four totally eliminated tanks, among them the two vehicles right next to mine that had been hit at the start of the Russian assault. We had good reason to be proud, looking out at the battlefield which was strewn with countless burned-out wrecks of Russian tanks. The surprise attack on the head of the German attacking force that had advanced furthest – with parts of the Fifth Guards Tank Army which had been brought up overnight – had been launched quite inexplicably by the Russian leadership. The Russians were forced to drive into their own anti-tank trench, which was as a matter of fact clearly marked on the maps we had captured.

Nevertheless, significant as the destruction of more than a hundred Russian tanks had been, the fighting of that day marked the turning-point of the battle. The massive tank force the Russians could put together made us very thoughtful. Our tank unit, which was able to claim the major part of the destroyed Russian tanks – although the Grenadiers by means of close combat and the artillery with direct hits had most bravely contributed – on this day now disposed of about twenty-five battle vehicles. The famous tank battle of Prokhorovka of 12 July 1943 was the greatest concentration of armoured vehicles in the most restricted space in the entire war. Stalin had allegedly wanted the commanding officer of the Fifth Guards Tank Army that attacked us, General Rotmistrov, court-martialled. In our view he would have had good reason to do so. The Russians' depictions of the battle as 'the grave of the German tank force' have no relation to reality. We did, however, have the unmistakable feeling that the offensive was at a standstill. We could no longer see any chance for us to gain more ground against our opponents' superiority, unless fresh, strong forces were made available. Such forces were, however, not at our disposal.

Looking back, *Unternehmen Zitadelle* was a mistake. It was the wrong moment, which is to say too late, and equipped with insufficient forces. The tank divisions that had just been reconditioned were depleted in segments of the battlefield where the opponent was expecting the attack, so they were consequently not available to fend off the Russian counter-offensive which was executed with great might. The major tactical successes that the SS-Panzer Corps, as the main focus group of the offensive, had carried off could not compensate for the fact that 'Citadel' resulted in a heavy defeat. The Russians' counter-offensive pushed the German front far back and led again to the brink of collapse. The prerequisite for putting out peace feelers as seen by Hitler could not be achieved. The lack of imagination with which *Unternehmen Zitadelle* had been planned was henceforth to characterize the German leadership's course of action in the war until the final catastrophe ensued.

From 1941 on there was no longer any German foreign policy worthy of the designation. Time and again Hitler forbad any sounding out of the possibility of negotiations with the Russians, despite the Foreign Minister's insistent pressing. From 1942 he had become a man rigified and basically broken, who at that point could no longer summon the necessary flexibility to seek ways out of the looming calamity. Hitler did not block only sensible military decisions, but also shut out his Foreign Minister, who constantly pressed for exploration of political solutions; they were steps that could have had no prospect of succeeding without Hitler's consent.

I should mention at this point an incident which from the point of view of contact with the Soviet side might have acquired some significance. Stalin's son, a lieutenant, had been taken prisoner by the German army in 1941. He ran into the barbed wire fence of a prisoner of war camp and was shot by a sentry guard. When telling me about it at the time, my mother had called the occurrence a 'grave mishap' and said that Father was beside himself.

She held Himmler responsible for it, not in the sense that he had wished the prisoner dead, but that he had not taken sufficient measures for the safety of the 'hostage'. Father had of course been thinking of the possibilities of a potential later contact with the Soviets. It was said that Himmler had Stalin's son incarcerated together with British officer prisoners of war who had purposefully made sure that he did not exactly have an easy time of it. He would in the end have been driven into the fence by sheer desperation. Stalin's grandson Yevgeny Dzhugashvili, the lieutenant prisoner's son, confirmed this to me in a telephone conversation.

There are today two diametrically opposite views on the attack against the Soviet Union. The 'politically correct' view sees in the assault on the 'pacific' Soviet Union an attempt to bring Hitler's arrogant aspiration of world domination to fruition. The opposite side sees the attack as a necessary 'pre-emptive strike' in order to forestall a Soviet attack.

Therefore the initial question arises: would Russia actually have attacked us? Some are of the opinion that it was a matter of but a few weeks that the German offensive anticipated that of the Soviets. They can irrefutably put forward in support of their argument that, as has already been stated, there had been Russian troop concentration in offensive formation, or that they were close to being complete. Stalin wanted to play an active part in European politics, whether by applying pressure or by the threat of force. For the latter, in view of the distances to be covered in a march, he had to position his forces in place in good time. From this alone it is not possible to draw an accurate conclusion of intent to attack. It would after all have been feasible to attack Western Europe at any given moment after troop deployment had been completed.

The second question should be: would the Reich's military situation in an offensive by the Red Army against a German Wehrmacht that was intact, with defences already installed, and being experienced in warfare, have really been so much more unfavourable than in a pre-emptive strike eastward? Admittedly, there is no doubt the potential endangering of the Romanian oil wells played a role in Hitler's deliberations.

In the event of an attack by the Soviet Union, the Reich's political situation in Europe would, however, have changed to a positive mode in a flash. It would then have been revealed to the European peoples that their real danger did not lie from the direction of Germany but from the 'Red' power in the East. On the basis of a European statute that would have guaranteed the European peoples self-determination, they could probably have been induced to undertake major war efforts. It would have become apparent at a stroke that the Reich alone could protect Europe against the Soviet Union. This fact would have diminished the weight of the feared German 'hegemonic power'.

If it is thought that the military strength of the Soviet Union may be estimated so low, maintaining the judgement that its defeat could possibly be a matter of short shrift, there would not really have been any cause to fear such an attack; there would instead have been the latitude to negotiate with toughness and patience before embarking on the risk of a war on two fronts. The astonishing successes of the Wehrmacht in the campaigns against Poland and France obviously nurtured the erroneous judgement of Hitler and the General Staff, as much as the difficulties of the Red Army in the Finnish-Russian war.

It is beyond any doubt that by the attack on the Soviet Union, Hitler played into the hands of Roosevelt and the United States, because he encumbered their future rival – Russia – with the major burden of the fight against Germany and thereby substantially weakened them. This is precisely what Stalin – and I refer again to the 'Chestnut Speech' of 3 March 1939 – had wished to avoid. Following the consolidation of the front in the spring of 1943, the moment had arrived to tackle the Soviets on the issue of a peace initiative. Hitler was, however, not ready for this, nor possibly in a condition to do it. Did Stalin's statement to Father, that 'I shall never stand for it that Germany should become weak', have some other concealed meaning? It is certainly questionable whether the political scene could have been restarted in the sense of resuming proper negotiations with the Soviet Union. However, perchance the agony of the almost two years until the downfall of the Reich might have been avoided. It could not have been any worse.

Hitler

A chapter of this book must be devoted to the man behind Germany's downfall, namely Hitler. Who was he, this man who determined the fate of my father, Joachim von Ribbentrop, and the entire German people? The spectrum may perhaps be further enlarged and the question asked whether his appearance on the stage of world history also initiated a turn in the fate of the Soviet version of Marxism, which therewith lost its real political power base.

One would need to ask about the indications, that must have already been discernible in his youth, of the role that this man would play one day in world politics. It ought to be possible to depict the extraordinary development in his life, which should have been recognized as the preparatory phase for his later ascent. In the exceptional circumstances prevalent in the First World War, the calibre of the man should also have been apparent.

There is nothing to be ascertained that could until the end of the First World War have allowed any insight into the role Hitler was later to play. He was without doubt an exceptionally brave soldier and dispatch runner, and in early 1917, as a simple private, was decorated – which was a very rare occurrence – with the Iron Cross First Class. His regiment was fighting exclusively in the heavy defensive battles of the Western Front, where losses were very high. Nevertheless, to his superiors Hitler did not seem suited to be the leader of a group of even ten men, the position in general held by an NCO, but due to a lack of NCOs, privates were often entrusted with the leadership of a group. The great Führer, the leader who according to Goebbels' propaganda was the 'Greatest Military Commander of all Time', with a following of millions, was not, despite an elevated distinction for a lowly soldier, deemed suitable to lead a group of ten men on the battlefield.

Every officer at the front knows – the same was valid for the Second World War – how frequently, due to heavy losses, a company commander was forced to appoint any man, even the youngest who seemed only partially qualified, to the position of leader, because nobody better suited was at hand any more. In my company I had tank commanders who were barely 18 and who – what's more at great risk – handled their tanks like seasoned warriors.

The course of Hitler's life until the outbreak of war – he was 25 in 1914 – is, except for his solitary nature, characterized by nothing that would have corresponded to his future role as Führer of the Reich. In his writing, he says that he was a great reader during that time, but what actor of the historical scene has been impelled by reading books to penetrate the mechanism of world history?

It must be made clear what a phenomenon Hitler presents. A man who despite earning high distinction in the heaviest of fighting is rejected as leader of a group – the smallest unit of an infantry formation – five years later initiates a putsch against the Reich's government and, as a former private, alongside the celebrated General Ludendorff marches towards the *Feldherrnhalle*. Less than ten years later he is Chancellor of Germany, and in a very short space of time assumes the role of absolute ruler.

There exists a class photo from Hitler's schooldays in Linz. He stands in the middle of five pupils in the top row, arms crossed over his chest. When one knows something of his subsequent life, a foretaste of the aspiration to power to come may be detected in the pose he struck. However, until the end of the First World War there is nothing externally apparent in this sense.

It could, in the case of a man whose great bravery cannot be denied, whatever aversion to his persona there may be, have been a bespoke challenge for him to take the combative events into his hands to prove himself as a 'Führer'. German military training had the specific goal of developing individual initiative as far down as NCO, indeed down to the individual fighter. This lone fighter should have the capacity to adjust to every situation that presents itself and if necessary, within the framework of the order given, to be self-sufficient in dealing with it. The notion of 'blind obedience' derives from Early Christian monasticism, not from the Prussian-German army!

It is certain that the most stupid soldiers were not chosen as dispatch riders. It was expected that some helpful thought would be contributed in every situation that arose; it could be that the real meaning of messages or orders transmitted on occasion had to be interpreted. These soldiers had to be able to find their way under all circumstances, even when subjected to heavy gunfire. They therefore had to be especially well-tested soldiers. Often, however, they were soon made group leaders, by reason of the abilities demonstrated, so Hitler's persistence in the role of lone fighter is puzzling. It is in situations of existential extreme danger that the charisma of someone born to be a leader is manifested. It was a charisma that Hitler had, as a speaker in the political arena, to the highest degree, and that he consciously utilized; it was this gift of rhetoric that was the basis for his political existence. It can obviously not have been out of fear that he did not earlier stand out as a leader of men.

What sort of personality transformation took place in Hitler following his release from military hospital at the end of the war following injury from a gas attack? This 'ordinary soldier' attaches himself to a handful of men from a small Munich suburb who want to change the conditions reigning in the Reich. In a very short space of time he places himself at the head of this so-called 'Party'; in 1921 he was already its leader with full dictatorial powers. With the tenacity of a terrier, henceforth this man took on at the same time both organized international Marxism and the victorious powers of Versailles, armed with nothing but a visionary conviction that he was 'right' and a speedily evolving gift for public speaking. With the self-confidence and pertinacity of a prophet, Hitler hammered into his ever-growing droves of audiences the premises which were supposed to 'rescue' Germany. His speeches should not be dismissed as the clamouring of a demagogue. They may not be in today's style, but in those days millions of people in Germany were carried away by them, as they seemed to proffer a way out of the Reich's desperate situation in the face of clueless democratic parties and the overlordship of the victorious states. They brought Hitler to the leadership of the most powerful party within a few years. The rapidly deteriorating political and economic conditions provided him with a sounding board for his speeches.

An experience repeatedly recurring in life is that what is said is often not as important as how it is said. This is valid to a quite extraordinary degree for Hitler's speeches. Their achievement can only be understood when taking into account the political situation in Germany at this point of time. Words were at Hitler's disposal and, as he writes himself, he quickly mastered the emotionalism needed for public speaking. The personal traits that were most in evidence were his decisiveness and ability to communicate to his audiences. The passion of the tenor of his speech, that could on occasion – seen from today – border upon hysteria, was no mere acting. Those listening to him sensed it. What Hitler said was sincerely meant – at particular moments at any rate. Passion of such intensity is the attribute only of a person who has the inner certainty of the visionary, and is consequently so convincingly effective on his audience. We are today no longer accustomed to hearing speakers with that sort of charisma and power to convince.

Hitler must only at that point have discovered his exceptional talent as a public speaker. There is no doubt that it contributed decisively in his journey to power; his talent as an orator appears as a derivative of a visionary personality. Hitler was a rhetorician: this fact must be acknowledged. His gift had lifted him out of the shadow of a humble existence into the glitter of public life and politics. There is no doubt that he owed to it the first taste of success in his life. He sensed how his speeches gave him power over people; they followed along with him and in return provided him with the confidence in his public appearances that success bestows. In the 1920s he is said to have still called himself 'the Drummer'. In Hitler's sense, a speech signified the wish to convince, to induce the audience to accept the speaker's point of view and react to it accordingly. That was his strategy for success.

The SA (Sturmabteilung) was the instrument appropriate to the times, in order – if necessary – to stand up in the face of Communist street terrorism. The best rhetoric is useless if the orator is chased off by Communist thugs. The SA was to make the platform secure for his voice to be heard. That was its primary task. After 30 June 1934 (known as 'The Night of the Long Knives', when the SA was forcibly disbanded), Hitler no longer assigned any motivating activity to this major organization of men ready to do their bit, who during the fighting days had fought the streets clear of the Communists for him. This was a lapse on the part of the state and party leader.

When Hitler came to politics he was a nobody and knew nothing – in the middle-class professional sense. He had nothing to lose, only to gain. He could therefore risk all, and so he did. He ran great risks time and again throughout his political career. To begin with he had to take risks, and was successful until he finally placed everything at stake by attacking the Soviet Union and foundered.

The fascination Hitler exerted on the masses and his intuition in regard to what the electorate's concerns were, combined with a marked instinct for power, enabled him to traverse unscathed through all the leadership crises and intra-party attempted coups of the fighting days. He was nevertheless completely aware of the perilous position in which he constantly found himself. He was the leader of the party with dictatorial power, which was, however, not the outcome of an internal party consensus reached through a democratic process. Notwithstanding, dictators can be overthrown by a 'Fronde' (rebellion or uprising). To avert this was a decisive if often overlooked precept of his domestic – and above all his personal – policies, from the outset of the party's fighting days up until his end in the rubble of Berlin.

On his course to power, he constantly had to renew his established position as Führer of the party. He owed it to his personality, his charisma, gift of oratory and tactical skill. To bind to himself figures such as Röhm and Strasser and have them under his control presumed a pronounced sense of power. Röhm had organized the SA for him, Strasser had constructed the Party's organization. Both knew that Hitler was the 'crowd puller'; it is possible, however, that both were also prepared to go their own way.

There is a personal observation I made during those days, of how strongly conscious he was of the interaction between his persona and his audience of the masses, how he registered their reactions and maybe felt confirmed by them. I heard a radio broadcast by Hitler – as far as I remember it was from Stuttgart. In this speech, to the sound of spontaneous and impressively loud approval from the audience, Hitler reinforced his renunciation of Alsace-Lorraine. Knowing Father's efforts, which I have mentioned, I did not only take in this part of the speech with satisfaction but also noted the astonishingly vigorous agreement of the audience; it was, mind you, an organized mass event. Shortly after, Father – who had attended the event – told me that after the speech Hitler had said to him: 'Did you notice how they [the audience] were with me?' It is certain that it was this intercourse with the masses and consideration of their wishes and hopes that upon the outbreak of the war restrained Hitler from actually proclaiming 'total war',[408] which for instance would have comprised women's military service.[409] In dealing with the masses he was basically a lifelong populist.

To what extent Hitler relied on his gift for public speech is proved by his intention in 1936 to go in person to the session of the League of Nations that had been convened in London following the restitution of full German sovereignty in the Rhineland. There, Germany was to 'assume responsibility'. Hitler thought he should personally represent the German point of view. Had he carried it out it would have been a resounding failure, for, as Father ascertained, the condemnation of Germany was a foregone conclusion and it would have signified a grave loss of prestige for Hitler himself and for the Reich. As an orator, however, Hitler had confidence in the powers of conviction of his speeches, even before a body such as the League of Nations. At this point it should be noted again that it was Hitler's intention – after he had come to power – to meet both the British (Baldwin) as well as the French (Daladier) heads of government. He hoped to be able to exercise his powers of persuasion in the sense of an arrangement with the West. Father also had difficulty in dissuading Hitler from initiating a 'battle of words' with Roosevelt in the spring of 1941.[410] In his diary for 28 May 1941, Hewel notes:

'Roosevelt speech. Weak, but dangerous propaganda-wise. The man must be restrained from always proceeding onward unpunished. Chief [Ribbentrop] to Führer. Long discussion on this subject. Führer would really like to speak, for no other reason than because he finds it fun.[411]

RAM [Reich Foreign Affairs Minister] fears it might degenerate into a war of words + that the Führer's speech may not go down well in the USA. To pull to and fro.'

It could be said this is not the behaviour of a 'Yes-man'! Once again Hitler would have liked to transfer his recipe for success from the domestic fight to the diplomatic field, to the despair of his foreign minister, as can be read between the lines. As much as he believed in his capacity to persuade or to be convincing, and thereby be able to motivate, he also become impatient when he felt that the effect on his interlocutor he aspired to was lacking. Talks with Franco and Molotov are fateful examples.[412]

The Hitler of the so-called 'fighting days', that is up to 1933, may be called a party-political publicity expert of the first order. One need think only of the party colour, brown, which in its aesthetic ugliness cannot be overlooked as a shock colour; of the symbol, as simple as it was memorable, of the swastika and of the brilliant red of his flags which he himself had thought of. He was a very competent manipulator of propaganda, for his times of course, and under the prevailing circumstances, but with extraordinary success. Catchphrases such as 'The Common Good comes before individual good', *Volksgemeinschaft* (trans., 'people's community'; a form of racial soul uniting all Germans) or 'Workers of the mind and of the fist' were appealing and plausible. They could be adopted by anybody.

Naturally, Hitler was a demagogue. In ancient Athens the word meant 'leader of the people'. The negative sense of the notion was given it in the nineteenth century by the 'Reactionaries', embodied by Metternich, thereby slandering the exponents of the middle class with liberal tendencies. Nowadays one says 'populism' and it means the same thing. The 'People's Führer' naturally knew very well what people wanted to hear and to know, that is, 'which side their bread is buttered on'. They needed a prospect for the future that would show how everything could get better in the end. Hitler had the necessary imagination to formulate visions. Think of his vision of the German people, as a nation of car drivers in vehicles affordable to everybody, for whom the most modern road network should be at their disposal. The statement repeatedly brought forward nowadays, that the motorways of the Reich were built for strategic reasons, is totally deceptive. Every armoured soldier knows the degree of attrition undergone by armoured vehicles of those days if they were exposed to a lengthy overland progress, and especially on concrete paved roads. Hitler should on the contrary be reproached for having devoted the Reich's meagre resources to the 'luxury' of highways, etc. instead of a logical military build-up. When he came to power, Hitler proceeded to realize his vision of the car-driving German nation, which does not correspond to a lust for war. Besides, the *VW-Kübelwagen* made its first appearance in the army only in the course of the war with Russia. The Volkswagen industry was not conceived from the angle of armament technology – it might almost be said, inexplicably. The 'Lance-Corporal' Hitler had anyway expounded the vision of a future war conducted under extensive utilization of motorized troops in 1924 in his book *Mein Kampf*. It was not Hitler who invented the four-lane motorway, which was an idea dating back to the Weimar days, albeit it had then remained in a drawer due to lack of funds and determination, neither was it his original idea to use self-sufficiently operating pure-blooded motorized troops in a future war. He did, however, go on to institute both.[413] He never lacked futuristic ideas: the difficulty always lay in realizing them.

Spontaneous actions, doubtless well prepared for and consistently carried out, were Hitler's field. The subtle and thought-through – and planned – coordination of a modern state and government apparatus, on the other hand, was not. He often withdrew from that sort of laborious detailed work by means of monologues in a futuristically couched attitude; it was a serious handicap for the leadership of the German Reich in a foreign policy situation of extreme gravity. However, he eschewed delegating this task to a 'chief of government', a way that for instance Franco and de Gaulle chose to give themselves relief. He probably feared for his position of dominance since, being a completely unsystematic worker, he lacked any system capable of supplying an autonomously functioning government with methodical guidelines and regularly to oversee their implementation, so as to integrate himself into the systems necessary for it.

Expressing his visionary ideas, he could occasionally 'talk himself into trouble', in particular since often, even in close circles and at most significant events, no authorized minutes were kept of his utterances. Consequently, the misunderstood and frequently purposely misconstrued representations and interpretations of his statements were given every facilitation, of which the so-called Hossbach Memorandum is a particularly good example. This document occupies a key position in post-war historical writing under the inappropriate designation '*Hoßbach-Protokoll*' and is central to the 'evidence' against Hitler in the sense that he had the intention of bringing things to the point of war. It is by Hitler's military adjutant at that time, Friedrich Hossbach, dated to five days after a session of 5 November 1937 – attended by, besides Hitler and Hossbach, Göring, Blomberg, Neurath, Fritsch and Raeder. He did not compose it at the Reich Chancellery but at the War Ministry. There is no indication of when notes started to be taken, nor when they were finished. According to this, it is not a *Protokoll* (or official record) but a memorandum Note drawn up subsequently. It was not initialled by any of the participants in confirmation of its contents.

According to this 'document', Hitler is supposed to have declared to those present that the '*Lebensraum*' necessary in the long term for obtaining the racial substance of the German people was to be achieved only by force. Following long-winded statements in the same sense, he is said to have been more concrete:

> 'For the improvement of our ... military position our first objective, in the event of our being embroiled in war, must be to overthrow Czechoslovakia and Austria simultaneously in order to remove the threat to our flank in any possible operation against the West.'

This is not the place to undertake a detailed analysis of the so-called Hossbach Memorandum; suffice it to ascertain that neither the original nor a copy of what Hossbach had written are extant. The American prosecution counsel at Nuremberg merely submitted the photocopy of a microfilm. The microfilm is also not to be found. On the other hand, diverse versions of the photocopy have been published, differing among themselves. None of the participants has unconditionally verified the wording of the text submitted at Nuremberg. A Colonel Count Kirchbach is said to have discovered the Hossbach memo in the winter of 1943/44 in the files of the General Staff. He had a copy made and handed it to a relative, Mr von Martin, who routed it to the British during the Nuremberg trials. Neither Kirchbach nor Martin have indisputably verified the text submitted at Nuremberg. They both describe themselves as sympathisers of the conspiracy, which is also to be gathered from the fact that they placed the memo at the disposal of the Allies.[414]

A further aspect should be considered, or at any rate mentioned. Hossbach was a confidant of Beck's. It is known that Beck was opposed to Hitler's policies, and less than half a year later, together with the state secretary in the Auswärtiges Amt, von Weizsäcker, made contact with the declared enemies of Germany, Winston Churchill and Robert Vansittart, to induce them to adopt a harsher stance toward the Reich, as already described, to prepare the ground for a military putsch. To carry out this planned putsch, the collaboration of at least a portion of those in command of the army was indispensable. Is the suspicion to be entirely dismissed that what Hossbach accentuated in his Note was in order to prejudice those in the army command against Hitler and his policy? It was after all high treason, also against the country, that the conspirators contemplated and later also put into effect. Could the Note which Hossbach drafted for Beck have perhaps been intended as an alibi and justification for such plans? Halder, Beck's successor as Chief of the General Staff and close colleague, was 'de-Nazified' on the grounds that 'Halder's conduct in 1938 constituted consummated high treason'.

Irrespective of this, however, when studiously perused, the remarks Hitler would have made, according to Hossbach, in essence turn on the strategic problem of Czechoslovakia. Hitler probably saw Austria in the light of its German population's great liking for him and his party as the lesser problem, insofar as it is not plausible that he will have meant that Austria would have to be 'crushed'. Czechoslovakia, on the other hand, in view of her alliances with France and the Soviet Union (the Little Entente with Poland and Yugoslavia was also still in force), represented a grave threat to the Reich. A head of state is entitled to his due that in the narrowest circle of his military or foreign policy advisers he would express considerations of the possibilities of neutralizing such a danger or of taking a suitable opportunity to eliminate it. He would have exposed himself to weighty reproaches if he had neglected this.

Another important indication of the clearly minor significance of what was said – from Hitler's point of view – is his reply to Hossbach's attempt, as the latter repeatedly maintained, to persuade Hitler to take note of the Protocol (that had been handwritten from memory). Hitler refused to do so, referring to lack of time. The session will evidently have been convened, at Blomberg's wish, to discuss and solve the problems of raw material supply to the separate units of the Wehrmacht. Lower-ranking experts waited in the antechamber. As far as can be made out, the session barely produced any factual solutions, nor in fact even in any organizational respect in the sense of establishing clear competencies, which was in any case not Hitler's forte. Neither were deadlines for bringing about a specific state of armaments discussed.

Nevertheless, the situation of the foreign policy at the time of the session should not be left out. The Paris-Prague-Moscow military axis constituted a grave threat to the Reich. Britain's stance, as far as could be ascertained, was not positive regarding the Reich (as Hitler's ambassador in London, Ribbentrop, was to report a few weeks later). Poland was firmly proceeding with her policy of ethnic values, directed at de-Germanization under the protective cloak of the German-Polish pact of non-aggression, and – last but not least – the President of the United States, Roosevelt, in the so-called 'Quarantine' speech, had taken an unambiguous attitude toward Germany, with no current reason of foreign policy. One cannot fail to concede that the

German head of government had sufficient grounds to cogitate upon the 'thorn in the German side', or else the 'air force mother-ship', as a French minister designated Czechoslovakia, based on her pact policy.

Perhaps Hitler somewhat gave his oratorical steed free rein so as to extricate himself from the burdensome task of having to reach clear decisions among rival heads of department; in this case evidently as to the distribution of raw materials necessary for the armament of individual departments. It was the sort of decision Hitler eschewed. It may be particularly valid in this case where one of his most trusted followers, that is to say Göring, was himself a lobbyist.

I have depicted in detail the grave state of difficulties as to foreign policy that Germany was in when Hitler came to power. To redress them and to consolidate the Reich's position at the centre of Europe necessitated the collection of all resources in the broadest sense. Particularly essential was to motivate the leading groups in all sectors of public life. In the majority, these circles did not belong among Hitler's proven following in the internal political fight for power. They therefore had to be won over and motivated. Hitler had to achieve the step up from party demagogue to statesman. He considered the National Socialist '*Weltanschauung*' as the foundation for the motivation of all layers.

It is difficult to define what exactly is to be understood by the oft-quoted National Socialist '*Weltanschauung*', or conception of the world. I once asked a Gauleiter (second highest Nazi Party paramilitary rank, beneath the Reichsleiter) in an English internment camp this question. In some context he was talking about the 'idea' (of National Socialism), and I permitted myself the question as to just what was to be understood thereby. Slightly taken aback, at first he said I should have learned something about it at the 'Napola'. This answer revealed something of how insecure he was. I said I did have some notion of what the so-called 'idea of National Socialism' was about, but that he as Gauleiter was after all much more competent in the field than I, a minor former troop officer. Then, a little put out, he tossed me the twin concept of 'blood and soil'. My rather provocative reply that this would also entail comprehension of the world view of a black African tribe put an end to the discussion. This Gauleiter was an educated man who, in the highly unpleasant conditions in which we vegetated in the tight space of an English Nissen hut, was a thoroughly agreeable companion in fellow suffering. This negligible episode does, however, manifest how fuzzy were the notions held, even by those in high places of the Party, of what the 'National Socialist world view' actually was. In practice, National Socialism was a system upon which Hitler founded his one-man rule. The sole real component of a 'world view' in National Socialism was only the wretched racial theory with its inherent anti-Semitism.

In how confused a form perceptions were presented is demonstrated in the following episodes that I had occasion to experience. At Ilfeld, in class, the subject came under discussion when our excellent history teacher, Winkelmann, was giving justifications for Charlemagne's harsh policy in regard to the Saxons. Our class had, however, classed Charlemagne as 'the Saxon-killer'. In the end Winkelmann cunningly confuted us when in the next history class he brought along a speech Hitler had given at the Party Rally in 1935, in which Hitler defended the German Kaisers of the Middle Ages – clearly meaning Charlemagne – maintaining that in the sense of '*Volkwerdung*' (becoming one people), by unavoidably harsh measures they forcibly coerced the diverse Germanic tribes into their empire. We were very taken aback, not knowing, of course, that Hitler had indeed quite frequently and energetically supported this opinion against differing opinions such as Himmler's and Rosenberg's.[415] We were in fact convinced by our teacher's argument that history could be judged only from within the time span in which events had taken place. Barely two years later, at the Waffen-SS military academy, when again there was a discussion about 'Charlemagne the Saxon-killer', I 'made myself conspicuous', as it was called in military speech, usually meaning that it had been striking a negative attitude.

At this Waffen-SS military academy in Braunschweig there was only a weekly class of three-quarters of an hour of what was called 'world-view lessons', since military training took precedence over all else. This short class was given by someone we disrespectfully called our 'Worldview Sheikh' because of his non-military function, although he had a rank and was therefore our superior. One day he touched upon the subject of 'Charlemagne the Saxon-killer'. He may thereby have been following along the lines of the Himmlerian view of history, but I knew – from what was said at home – that the intent of the German government – Father's at any rate – was to initiate a reconciliation with France, whereby the figure of Charlemagne was to be perceived as an element of bonding and integration.[416] I countered our worldview teacher with the arguments that Winkelmann in Ilfeld had propounded. The teacher was quickly irritated and finally forbade me to speak, which as my military superior he had the right to do, but which annoyed me in my youthful – I was 19 – 'know-all' attitude.

Remembering our history teacher, during my next time away from the academy I procured myself Hitler's said speech, which was of course easily done, and presented it to the worldview teacher at his next class. This naturally made something of a fool of him to the whole auditorium. Since his classes were very boring, there was an unmistakeable aura of *Schadenfreude* (gloating over another's misfortune) in the audience.

Two days later I was summoned to report, in service dress, which meant with steel helmet and 'buckled' (i.e. with holster) to the training group commandant, who asked me, rather curtly, why I would 'express opposition' in the world-view class? I recounted the episode, to which he replied: 'Why don't you leave the man in peace!' I think he even also used the expression 'Worldview Sheikh'. Our training group commandant was an excellent seasoned veteran, who couldn't care less about the so-called 'world-view'. I followed his advice and kept my mouth shut from then on. The 'worldview' teacher was dismissed soon after, but certainly not because of this event. His successor was a highly cultivated man who lectured us on German history – it must be said, without too much ideology – and knew how to make it really come alive for us.

The starting premise of the Hitlerian concept was the consistent antagonism to Marxism in whatever form it presented itself. He countered it with Nationalism – which in those days was considered the fundament of their existence by all peoples and states in the world – extended with the addition of 'Socialism', for which he employed the notion of *Volksgemeinschaft*, which had nothing in common with the dogmatic socialism of Marxist theory, for all that undoubtedly there were 'leftist' trends in the NSDAP, which, however, were in no way organized in any form.

It is difficult to deny the sustainability of this starting point of his political battle for power, which he promised to attain by legal means. A 'National Socialism' was ideal for meeting with the approval of broader strata of the people, including the working class. Without wishing to be lost in definitions here, what was meant by 'Socialism' in National Socialism would today be expressed as 'social', to distinguish it from 'Socialism' in Marx's sense. The Communist electorate – they numbered more than five million at the time of the Reich presidential elections of 1932 – voted for the Communists out of economic necessity. For them too, a 'national Socialism' was acceptable if under its policies their condition would be improved.

Hitler conceived this concept with the gift of a visionary. He had to provide this politically substantially insecure population – insecure from the angle of national identity – with a vision. The contrast of 'national' and 'socialist' ('social') was resolved by him in the concept of *Volksgemeinschaft*, where in essence each had his or her place for the good of the community (thereby also for their own good) from which to fulfil their function. At the national level he promised the restoration of Germany's equality of rights and her defence capacity, and at the social level the resolution of the unemployment problem and the class war. The social components were to bring about the required coherence of the German people so as to put them in a position to sustain the fight for their equality of rights and to secure Germany's ever-threatened Central European situation. The experience of the First World War, when, according to the perception current at the time, the 'home front' had been shattered, here played an undoubtedly decisive role. However, here also lie the roots of the repression which made an ever stronger appearance during the Third Reich, and above all during the war. Although it was supposed to maintain the population's cohesion, in influential circles the effect was often counter-productive. A threat in the domestic sphere was added to the extremely perilous situation of the Reich in the domain of foreign politics, which has already been described, by the militant, very active German Communist Party, which, steered from Moscow, was to be regarded in the case of an emergency as definitely the extension of that imperial power.

It should additionally be noted that the social structure of the leading circles in Germany was not homogeneous. All social, religious and ideological trends were represented. However, for all groupings – with the exception of the extreme Left – the precepts 'anti-Bolshevism' and 'equality of rights' were a conceivable motivation for the Reich.

But Hitler the ideologist overburdened this generally acceptable common denominator for a national and social consensus with an ideology which he felt he had to impose upon the German people, in order – as he saw it – to extract them from the subversive influence of the 'Jewish-determined Bolshevism'. This ideology of his made claims for its acceptance to an increasing degree, penetrating deep into the domain of the private life of each and everybody. As has been said, his *Weltanschauung* was based on his racial theory. In the 'Germanic race' – whatever he perceived thereby – Hitler saw the 'positive' components, possibly with intent to give the precarious mentality of his compatriots a somewhat more solid fundament. In his view, the 'negative' side was embodied by the 'Jewish race'. By equating Bolshevism and Judaism, Hitler bridged his realistic and reasoned objective, which is to say to combat Marxism-Leninism, with his Utopian racial theory. He saw in Marxism, Jewry and Internationalization a menace to the pure-blooded and spiritual-mental substance of the German people, which he wanted to immunize against such influences. Father wrote that all his arguments, however cogent, that he propounded against Hitler's conviction that there was a world-wide Jewish Eastern-Western conspiracy against the Reich were unable to rid Hitler of this perception. It is rare if not impossible to disabuse visionaries from their visions.

He saw every deviation from the lines of his 'worldview' as deriving from this fortress mentality which had understandably arisen following the First World War, under the dictates imposed by Versailles and the impression of an indefectible fencing-in of the Reich once disarmed. Hitler considered it an internal threat which was therefore also an external hazard. In his opinion, in the First World War it had eventually led to a diminishing readiness to fight and resulted in defeat. A fortress mentality always springs from a situation of crisis, consequently a position of weakness. That there was such a state of emergency may absolutely be conceded to Hitler and his government at the time of his taking power, when he had the Communist cadres ruthlessly smashed and their officials incarcerated. The Communists were the extended arm of an imperialist and aggressive power whom it was Hitler's objective to fend off.

Few objections were raised throughout the country to the swift elimination of Communist organizations. The Weimar Republic had not succeeded in doing it; in the end, moreover, barely a tear was even shed over their party strife. After his accession to power there is no doubt that Hitler overstepped his constitutional prerogatives. Nevertheless, the Reichstag had voted for the Enabling Act in the majority, including the voices of Brüning, Theodor Heuss *et al.* A statesman would have utilized these emergency rights arising from a crisis situation with greater circumspection. The branding of Communism as the enemy could have served him as a base for attracting the diverse groupings of the common weal as a following and for uniting them. As has been said, all the social groups in Germany were prone to be won over to the cause against Bolshevism and pro the German claims for equal status – that is to say they were prepared to defend themselves against Soviet Bolshevism, with in the forefront those circles upon which Hitler had to base himself if his foreign policy were to accomplish German equal status. Even if these leading circles in the domains of the armed forces, administration, the economy and of science, not to mention the churches, did not adhere to Hitler's following from the start, they regarded him – at least at first – as a preferable alternative to Communism. Hitler must have been aware that he depended upon these leading circles of the Reich. A loyal following from the establishment elite was an indispensable necessity. In view of the pressure of the lack of time under which Hitler stood, resulting from the compulsions of foreign policy which he had not triggered, a 'substitution' of the leading groups could not be thought of.

No statesman can bring his political concepts to fruition without a following of the leading groups that – to his mind – occupy the key positions. This is especially valid in critical situations. It is tempting to remember the Great Elector Frederick William and his successors, who gave a solid structure to the framework of their state with a clear conception. They may have established the throne's authority like a '*rocher de bronze*' (brazen rock), but at the same time they charged the nobility, at that time the class constituting the bearing infrastructure of the state, with carrying out their duties – and thus binding them to their following – by filling official and military posts exclusively with representatives from that class. Their financial base was secured. In return they had to serve the monarch faithfully and, if it came to it, be prepared to die for him. To be of service to their country was the prerogative as well as the obligation of the members of their caste. This bound them to the monarch, as did a similar way of life and the same view of life. They felt themselves obligated – as did their ruler – to the supreme overriding principle of the State, i.e. the common good. They identified with the state in the person of the monarch.

This was in no way self-evident. Earlier, in the Middle Ages, the lesser nobility was in general in antagonism to the superior in the form of the *Landesfürsten* (local princes). When the first of the Hohenzollern, the Burgrave of Nuremberg, was enfeoffed with the Margraviate of Brandenburg, when he headed north he took two culverins with him, huge cannon from which correspondingly large cannonballs were fired, capable of demolishing thick walls. The nobility of Brandenburg had not exactly been idle, waiting for their new prince. To begin with, he shot to pieces the castle of the lords von Quitzow in Friesack so as to earn himself respect. As a youth I have been in the Ratskeller (council's cellar) of Königsberg in East Prussia, called '*Das Blutgericht*' (blood court of justice) because it was the site where the Great Elector had five rebels hanged who stemmed from the East Prussian nobility, led by a Herr von Kalckstein. A descendant of his sat the Abitur exam at the same time as I in 1939. Of the Kalckstein who was hanged it is said that he sported a particularly aquiline nose; his descendant was interestingly enough blessed with a similar distinctive nose. He was as good a comrade as he was a rider. Sadly, he too was killed. My intention in mentioning these relations between leading groups and their sovereign is to pinpoint their significance. Hitler's absolute powers corresponded, indeed surpassed, those of an absolute monarch in many ways, but that is precisely why he was dependent on a loyal leadership team.

But Hitler was not a statesman to follow in this tradition of the Prussian rulers, to have won the leading classes of the Reich over to share with him the commitment to the goals of foreign policy he had set, so as to join him on the fraught course he had to pursue. This was not – *nota bene* – to wring world domination, but instead a partially secure existence of the Reich in the centre of Europe. For this, the best prerequisites basically existed. The extraordinary crisis in which the Reich found itself when Hitler took over, namely the anxiety of being submerged by the Bolshevik flood, had prepared broadly based strata of society for a new beginning. This was worth setting one's sights on.

A 'Führer-Statesman' would have had to acknowledge this as a task. A condition to fulfil it was to be able to gather together all forces on the goal he had targeted. But this Führer was a visionary who had constructed for himself a world image of anti-Marxism in which he believed that only through modification of the population's *Weltanschauung* was the fight against 'Bolshevik-Judaic' internationalism to be waged. With a visionary's impatience he tried to indoctrinate the German people into his way of thought, whereby he placed himself in manifold opposition to the established groups of society, whom he needed and who were perfectly ready to align themselves with his objectives in foreign policy. Because of this impatience, and caught in the above-mentioned fortress mentality, the imposition of his worldviews was helped with the pressure exerted by means of the secret police. This is what eventually led to an uncertainty as to legal rights which, in the form it took, is in the long run untenable in a cultivated State. The danger of being arrested without the possibility of recourse to one's legal rights so as to be able to defend oneself brings about such an uncertainty as to legal rights which in the end leads to subversive activities.

Ultimately, the worst factor was the potential unpredictability of the dictator. Hitler's word was law, and he expressly laid claim to the position. Whoever names himself 'Supreme Court Lord of the German People', and in his name alone enforces a series of executions without due process, can at any time make claim to such a right. To many adherents of just those leading circles of the Reich on which he was dependent, Hitler did not transmit the feeling of security always sought regarding their circumstances and conditions of life. An uncontrolled sole ruler is from the outset no guarantor of such security, unless he submits himself to binding rules of the game that can only be postulated on the basis of a state of law.

An occurrence showing a typical example of the dictator's despotism was the totally incomprehensible dismissal of all members of the former princely houses of Germany from the Wehrmacht in 1941. True, the measure struck at a relatively small number of people. It was, however, they who in the sense of family tradition were prepared to commit entirely to Germany. The question then arose, what group of persons would be next in turn to submit to the dictator's despotism? Actions against Jews were along the same lines. Nobody guaranteed this or the other grouping that after the victorious outcome of war they would not become undesirable because of some whim of the Führer's, and submit to serious disadvantages.

In view of its intrinsic components as elements of a scale of values, the 'race theory' was not plausible and appeared as dogmatic arbitrariness. It was perfectly acknowledged that there were different races, and practising a racial policy was considered Utopian. Even in the bosom of the Waffen-SS there circulated the flippant remark about the strongly propagandized 'Northern race', according to which its main characteristics were the three great 'Bs': 'blond, blue-eyed and bird-brained'! Both the super-powers of the United States and Russia could promote ideologies effectively attracting recruits the world over, but the National Socialist racial theory repulsed all non-Nordic races. Moreover, whoever takes race and its preservation as a motto for their declared political objectives should actually take the Jewish people as the model, as is repeatedly indicated in the Old Testament. The phenomenal sense of cohesion of these people is historically unique, but also constitutes the problem. The Judaic religious tradition, despite constant persecution, spanning more than 3,000 years is the oldest in the world still 'living'.

As at the outset of the 1930s the State found itself in a situation of crisis in regard to the aggressive Communists, steered from Moscow, the German public comprehended the rigorous crackdown on the Communist Party and its operatives. Nevertheless, the events of 30 June 1934 (the aforementioned crackdown on the SA) which led to a series of executions with no due legal process were not conducive to affirming the confidence in Hitler's rule by the very circles he needed for his battle in the cause of German equality status. Looking back, Hitler's actions at this time looked ominous and, what is more, like unnecessary brutality. If Röhm or Schleicher had truly conspired with a foreign power, a trial in court would have been a great deal more convincing. They could besides at any time have been isolated by house arrest or incarceration. Churchill had the British Fascist leader Sir Oswald Mosley and his wife imprisoned for years, with no legal justification. The British system of government was in no way shattered by this illegal measure. The rescinding of constitutional personal rights is a risky undertaking because it suppresses the dissatisfaction and opposition obviously extant in every system of government under the surface, thus rendering it even more dangerous. This is especially valid when it affects strata of the community or the elite who hold responsible posts in the state's structure.

It should not be thought these are mere theoretical considerations. On two crucial points German foreign policy was secretly thwarted from within, with dire consequences. Had it not been for the activities of the State Secretary in the Auswärtiges Amt, von Weizsäcker, the Chief of the army's General Staff (Beck) and the Chief of Counterintelligence (Canaris) and their aides, who promised the British and Polish governments a military coup against Hitler if it came to war, an agreement with Poland would probably have been reached, based on the extraordinarily moderate German proposals.

At a later date, as has already been told, it was once again Weizsäcker and Canaris who deprived Hitler of the chance to turn with full force against England in the Mediterranean by dissuading Franco, behind the back of the Reich government, from placing himself on the side of Germany to take Gibraltar, whereby the British position in the Mediterranean would have been overturned, which would probably have led to Britain giving way and averted the fateful war with Russia. It is manifestly evident from the existing documents that it was only when it became unequivocally clear to Hitler that he could not count on Franco, thereby no longer keeping open the option of a decisive strike against Britain in the Mediterranean, that the definitive decision was taken to attack Russia pre-emptively. Both these acts by top officials of the Reich thwarted Hitler's policies at critical instants and brought about the fateful developments, leading to losing the war to a catastrophic degree. They are the interventions which had the gravest repercussions of the so-called resistance against Hitler.

In those days there is no doubt that the Protestant and Catholic Churches counted among the weightiest institutions in Germany. One would think that it was not too hard to acquire them as a federated partner against atheist Bolshevism. The quarrels with the Churches were, however, not conducive to gaining friends in the world for the Reich regime. At the same time both Churches certainly did not want to end up under Bolshevik overlordship. On the other hand, they also did not know what to expect from Hitler, were the dictator to remain uncontested in his absolutism.

The relations between the Churches and the regime were thus often tense. The ideologist inherent in Hitler made totalitarian demands over the souls of the population under his leadership. In this way he plunged portions of the German people – once more those of the leading classes, albeit not only them – into conflicts of conscience. As a young company commander – I was 22 at that date – I had a notable experience. In 1943 we instituted the '*Hitler Jugend*' Panzer Division. The crews were recruited from members of the *Hitler Jugend* already conscriptable who had come forward as volunteers. These men were given into the particular care of us young officers by Sepp Dietrich (who by this time was the commanding general of the '*Leibstandarte*' (Bodyguard) Panzer Corps). In all aspects of training we had to play the part of educator and leader of young people, indeed to a certain degree assume the role of father.

One day, one of my officers pointed out to me a young soldier who did not seem to be taking part in the activities with the same cheerful willingness as his comrades. He originated from Upper Silesia and had a Polish name. I had a feeling about what was going on when the young man, who gave an impression of despondency, reported to me. He soon became confident, so that when I asked what was bothering him he confessed quite openly that it was that he could not go to Mass. From the conversation that ensued it emerged that although he had joined the Waffen-SS quite voluntarily, as had the entire class, and he did not wish to be the only one to stand back, that was in fact what he would have liked to do because he had always been told that the SS were inimical to the Church. His father had been killed. His mother had seen him off with the warning: 'Preserve your faith!' It was no trouble to obtain permission from my regimental commander to send the young soldier on a motorbike to the nearest church on Sundays. It may be noted it was a French church, for at the time we were at an army training camp in France. The commander was of the same opinion as I that the youth, who was about to undergo heavy spiritual trials in what was coming in the field, should be able to exercise his faith.

Is this example not representative of the dilemma of conscience of numerous Germans? On the one hand there was the Fatherland, that found itself in a life and death battle to survive, and on the other a regime that plunged many people into conflicts of conscience because of their faith. One of our parents' best friends was Count Schönburg, 'Ernstl' as he was known. He was often and very welcome at our home as a student in the 1920s. We children were very fond of him. He was really almost one of the family. I remember well that in 1932, during the two rounds of election of the Reich's president, he foretold that sooner or later there would be a major duel to the death between the Communists and National Socialists. He believed the National Socialists would win, because the Saxon workers – he was from Saxony – were shrewd, and in the majority in favour of Hitler; and they were generally in the know of the direction things were taking. At my age of 11 I was very impressed by his expectation of an intensification of the domestic situation in Germany.

It must have been in 1935/36 when Father asked 'Ernstl' Schönburg – who was a Catholic – to make contact with Catholic circles in England so as to strive for a German-English rapprochement through them. I remember all too well my father's dismay as he related to Mother that 'Ernstl' could not see his way to a cooperation, in view of the tense relationship of the regime with the Catholic Church. Father's opinion – his sole reason for supporting Hitler – was that foreign policy had absolute precedence, even over incompatibilities in domestic policy, for in the end the very existence of the common weal depended on it. Irrespective of this, however, Schönburg became a reserve officer, and on the first day of the Polish campaign he was killed, falling for his country of whose regime he did not approve. Father was extraordinarily strongly affected by his death. Schönburg's fate is indicative of the horns of the dilemma which many Germans faced: on the one side the latent peril threatening the Reich in its Central European situation, and on the other a regime against which, for the most diverse reasons, there were great reservations. Ten first cousins of my wife were killed. They were all practising Evangelical Christians and rejected Hitler's regime.

Father proposed to Hitler to enable the Catholic Church to have access to occupied Russia. I can recall Mother's depiction exactly, because it was then the relations of the Orthodox and Catholic Churches first became clear to me, when she said: 'That was the centuries-old dream of the Catholic Church.' It need not be said that Father's urging had no results, although Hitler did at least direct that the churches closed under Stalin in the Ukraine should be reopened.

A further group – the word 'caste' could well be employed here – that was by nature of particular significance for Hitler and his policy was represented by the army leadership as a body. The loyalty of the armed forces is always of especial importance for a dictatorship, as they have the technical potential to overthrow a dictator. It fell to the generals to execute rearmament as speedily as possible so as to keep the risk phase as short as possible. The group was descended from the former imperial army. They were in a real sense conservative circles. They had succeeded in maintaining the soldiering tradition of the German army beyond the collapse of 1918 and through the confusions of the Weimar Republic. It is a particular tradition in soldiery that if called for one gave one's life for the fatherland, which has to remain the mental basis of an army if it is to fulfil its mission to protect the country from exterior aggression.

The officers of the former imperial German army in the 'Reichswehr', as it was called during the Weimar era, had formed an army of cadres which laid the foundations without which the later swift rearmament that was affected under Hitler would not have been possible. The time factor played a truly decisive role in by whom and in what form rearmament should be achieved. Overriding Röhm's concept of building up a militia force to incorporate the

SA, Hitler made the logically correct decision to opt for the Conservative body of generals and their officer corps which they had stamped with their special characteristics. It was only thus that a build-up of the army could be realized in a relatively brief time span and the 'risk phase' be kept short-lived. Hitler had to weigh the pros and cons of such a decision and bear the consequences thereof. There was, however, a reverse side to the coin of military virtues that the 'imperial' officers had preserved. 'Ancients' who were no longer suitable for a modern army given its special character by the *Volksgemeinschaft* would be defended and kept in place at least partially with arrogance and high-handedness.

It was indubitable that a basic feature of the German army was an attitude of reserve in regard to innovations, most evident when they were of a technical nature. Schlieffen, the General Staff chief, had wrestled about this with the War Ministry before the First World War in order to turn the heavy artillery into a field troop. Grandfather used to tell the story of the imperial general who had come out against the introduction of the machine gun because the unified image of the columns on the march could thereby be spoilt. Not unreasonably, after the reintroduction of general conscription in 1935, the formal uniform of the soldiers was mocked as the 'Kaiser-Wilhelm-Memorial Frock'. From my personal experience the camouflage jacket and steel helmet cover, with which every Waffen-SS soldier was equipped, had advantages for the soldier in the field that could be seen at a glance. Many German troops fell victim to the wearing of the – admittedly grey – steel helmet, which gleamed in the sun's rays. The camouflage jacket also provided some protection from rain and humidity. They were not introduced to the army, even during the war. Nowadays they are a *sine qua non* for the German Bundeswehr (Federal Defence), as well as for armies all around the world.

Returning to Hitler's relationship with the army high command, the 'risk phase' inherent in every rearmament in view of strongly armed neighbours has been exhaustively depicted. In 1938 this dangerous gap had not yet been bridged. It may be said that even the Polish war was not entered into with the proper armament. The doubts of the army command to dare to risk a war at this time are to a certain degree understandable from the military-professional point of view. However, from the angle of foreign policy it was the time factor that played the decisive role. Hitler had no choice but to render the position of the Reich in Central Europe as strong as possible as quickly as possible before potential opponents had progressed so far in their political and military preparations that they could counter the Reich, since his concept of close cooperation with both the Western powers had come to nothing. At the same time, the necessary psychological – in other words propaganda – preparations that figured prominently in the democracies should not be forgotten. The awareness of the British as to the possibility of a war with Germany had, as I have described above, progressed considerably from 1937 to 1938. Much more serious was the corresponding influence exerted on public opinion in the United States by Roosevelt, conducted intensively and systematically.

I state definitely, from what I knew at the time, that Hitler did not want a military confrontation or war over the Sudetenland issue, for what would he have gained from it? This is why he had bluffed and made a show of strength. To the outside he had played the game skilfully, with, I may add, the help of his Foreign Minister who rescued the Godesberg Conference for him (for which Hitler had emotionally thanked him). The question may, however, be asked whether Hitler had exerted the necessary effort to convince the army leadership so as to ensure their identifying with his decisions as to foreign policy.

It must not be forgotten that in 1938 the German military chiefs had experienced defeat during the First World War. The Reich had entered the First World War with the world's best army – and had lost. Now a figure unfamiliar to them and to their thought process may have been contemplating a similar confrontation with an instrument – the Wehrmacht – that had not yet reached the standard, either materially nor of training, that according to their strict criteria the generals considered essential to be in a position to carry through such a policy. The defeat of 1918 still stuck in the craw of the old imperial officers. With a certain justification they attributed the fault for losing the war to the foreign policy of the Imperial Reich. The German military was deliberately ignoring the crucial failure of its leadership in the Battle of the Marne in 1914. That loss had already heralded the loss of the war. At this point, time was running out for the 'Central Powers'. In such a situation, to conceive and conduct the Battle of Verdun as 'attrition strategy' may be designated a second seriously mistaken decision of the German military leaders in the First World War. I am not about to recapitulate their military problems in 1914-18, but merely demonstrate to what extent the attitude of the generals toward Hitler's foreign policy was influenced by their experience of the First World War. It is a well-known adage of history that most generals always prepare for the last war,[417] and that in any case it is never the fault of the military if a war is lost.

I have already mentioned that in 1925 Hitler had written in *Mein Kampf* that in modern warfare motorization would be of the greatest significance.[418] In the course of the rearmament, he carried out the creation of operationally deployable tank units. Amongst the officers of the Reichswehr he found forward-thinking supporters of the theory for surmounting the gruelling attrition-warfare of the First World War by utilizing major motorized units. He will no doubt have met with resistance on the part of Fritsch and Beck,[419] as well as from some of the generals; it was certainly discussed at our home in those days. The operational deployment of independent motorized and armoured units not dependent on infantry did come under discussion by experts, but they counted rather as outsiders and no armed power had until then been able to make up their mind about such units being employed.

As far as the European states were concerned, Hitler's motivation by anti-Bolshevism could have constituted an inducement to a broad-based support of the Reich's policies, had they guaranteed the security of a self-determined existence following a defensive action against the Bolshevik peril. A generous European Charter in this sense was no longer to be wrung from Hitler, although it became apparent during the war with Russia that all available European forces would have been necessary to resist the Soviet power underpinned by the Anglo-Saxons.

Hewel wrote on 13 October 1941: 'RAM (Reich Foreign Minister) to the F [Führer]. First thoughts about a European manifestation.'

There is a note of my father's, saying:[420]

'Berlin, 21 March 1943

'Subject: European Confederation

'I am of the opinion that, as already proposed to the Führer in my previous minutes, we should at the earliest possible date, as soon as we have scored a significant military success, proclaim the European Confederation in quite a specific form ...

'The states immediately concerned would be Germany, Italy, France, Denmark, Norway, Finland, Slovakia, Hungary, Rumania, Bulgaria, Croatia, Serbia, Greece and Spain(?). If the Führer should intend to create independent states in the parts of Europe occupied by us, these would be added to the list ...

'The establishment of a European Confederation would have the following political advantages:

1) It would dispel the fear of our friends and allies that they might all be placed under German Gauleiters as soon as peace is concluded.
2) Neutrals would be reassured that they would not be incorporated into Germany at the end of the war.

3) Italy would be relieved of their fear that powerful Germany wish to drive her into a corner.

4) If the Führer decides to set up a number of more or less independent states in certain occupied territories, which of course would remain completely in our power, it would come as a considerable reassurance to those territories and induce them to muster their forces to help us in the war.

[Points 5–7 relate to the effects of propaganda in Britain, the United States and Russia.]

8) In France and the occupied territories in general it would make all the difference to these countries' war effort in the personal and material spheres.'

At the time Father wrote this Note, Kharkov had been retaken in the counteroffensive against the advancing Russians. A military success was at hand. But a 'European Commonwealth of Nations', according to Father's concept, was nevertheless not acceptable to Hitler. On the contrary, a year later Hitler reacted in exactly the opposite way, when for the French north-western départements and Belgium he let a civilian administration take the place of the previous military administration, which inevitably sparked major fears. It is said Laval addressed Hitler in these terms:[421]

'You want to win the war so as to establish Europe, but you should establish Europe so as to win the war!'

For 24 November 1941, Hewel's diary contains the entry: 'Führer not pleased with RAM's speech.' This was the speech to the European heads of state on the occasion of the extension of the Anti-Comintern Pact. My father, as Foreign Minister, could do nothing further. He had alas been proven right in his fears of an assault on the Soviet Union.

When already within the Reich the constitutional rights had been restricted or even abrogated, it could hardly be expected of the European peoples that they would entrust their fate into the hands of the Reich and its Führer. The deportations of Jews from the occupied countries drastically presented for the European populations a picture of the danger of a later arbitrary rule by Berlin. However, it has to be stated here that the activities engaged in by high-placed officials and officers and their accomplices are indefensible. They could – possibly risking their lives – have eliminated Hitler. Not that the activities of the conspiracy in any way absolve Hitler. To employ modern terms once again, a 'manager' must thoroughly know the instrument with which he conducts his policy or his business – above all in its personnel components. This leads me to point out a further weak spot in Hitler's regime of serious, not to say fatal, consequences: Hitler had absolutely no governmental, or in contemporary terms management system other perhaps than – if it may be called a 'system' – the Ancient Roman principle *divide et impera* (divide and rule), on which basis any potential endangerment of his personal position of power was *a priori* excluded.

All the powerful figures in history have had to preoccupy themselves intensively with the problems: how to govern the construct over which I rule, and by what system can I keep the decisive instruments of authority in my hands and receive the necessary information, correct and at the right time? The exceptional problems of administration of the far-flung empire of Charlemagne under the circumstances of communication of the day may be held up as an example, along with the administrative problems of the Roman Empire. Caesar, Augustus and Diocletian, to mention but a few, were in their time highly efficient organizers and administration experts who, in the technical circumstances of the day, had the huge empire firmly in their grip. In the case of Augustus in particular, it is noteworthy to see with what clever caution and skill he got the senatorial 'elite' into his hands, thus avoiding Caesar's fate.

If one may credit Hitler with not being personally responsible for Germany's foreign policy problems, that he had found them before him so that in quite extraordinarily difficult circumstances his policies had to grapple with them, the question arises whether he dealt with the problems underpinned by taut organization, efficient mobilization of all resources and a comprehensive integral plan. Did Hitler at all times – as the fundament for his decisions – have an overview of the Reich's material situation? Did he issue unequivocally specific guidelines and set objectives? Had he constantly verified the execution of the guidelines given and the attainment of the set goals, and if necessary intervened? Did he reach his decisions following in-depth consultation with the competent persons responsible and stipulated clear responsibilities? The questions have to be answered in the negative. Hitler did not have any systematically established planning set up for the Reich's total resources, nor indeed any system at all, by which he might have regularly checked on the realization of a target plan against the existing *status quo*. There was no armaments plan (nor, correspondingly, any war plan).[422] A comprehensive plan, placing priorities or taking the Reich's potential in resources of personnel and material and the necessities of foreign policy into consideration, was lacking.

If Hitler neglected to set up integrated planning for all possibilities and necessities so as to utilize the limited resources of the Reich for armament to best advantage, that may among other things constitute proof that he evidently did not reckon with any military conflict, let alone that he purposely intended to bring one on. In any case the situation the Reich was in was exceptionally perilous, since both the USA and Soviet Russia were to be counted among its opponents. Hitler's entire concept of architectural and social luxuries such as Party buildings, motorways, the redesigning of Berlin, the KDF ('Strength through Joy') leisure organization, ships, etc. would have fallen victim to planning for the war which, if it had in the end been unavoidable, would have utilized all the resources for armament.[423]

In this context the universally held premise, that Hitler eliminated unemployment solely by means of armament, is also a cliché. Only laymen who have no idea of the organizational, staffing and material problems in an expansion of the armed forces could uphold it. Anybody minimally instructed in political economics knows that armament is not a requirement for kick-starting an economy.[424] When rearmament was introduced in 1935 by resuming general military service, there were hardly any unemployed left in Germany. Nevertheless, the motorway network project was stopped only in 1943.

The Wehrmacht embarked on the Polish war with inadequate stocks of munitions. Imagine the allegedly 'war-mongering monster' Hitler entering the war without reserve munitions. He solved the problem in a manner typical of him, by appointing one more person to be in charge. In this instance he straight away established a new ministry. Just before the commencement of operations in 1940, Fritz Todt – the motorway builder – was appointed Reich Minister for Armament and Ammunition; probably a wise decision. Todt did not, however, have the plenipotentiary powers conceded much too late to his successor Speer under the pressure of necessity.

Hitler once said to Father: 'You know, Ribbentrop, my brain starts working when difficulties arise or obstacles are in my way.' This revealing statement shows how reluctantly Hitler allowed himself to be involved in a systematic handling of problems. But planning always means systematic work beforehand and is a *sine qua non* in a modern political system. Hitler did not do his homework on this. He had no system for it.

In this context, Hewel's diary, already often quoted, is once again most illuminating. At times Hewel comments – during the war with Russia – on the sort of subjects in general upon which Hitler lectured or gave vent to lengthy criticism. We may well ask ourselves when he found the time to deal with the enormous workload with which he had burdened himself by concentrating all decision-making upon his person, without having set up a system that would have made it possible for him to do so. In the last year of the war he complained about this, saying he had been betrayed and lied to – a disqualifying admission for any top man, whatever the level. The man at the top should not permit being betrayed and lied to – not that this observation constitutes any excuse for liars and traitors.

It was a characteristic of Hitler's style of governance that he never convened sessions (of the Cabinet for instance) in which current problems of government could be discussed in depth, decisions be taken or departmental activities coordinated. Father was appointed Foreign Minister at the beginning of 1938. I have already mentioned that he took part in no session of the Reich Cabinet, because none was convened. Hitler preferred a *tête à tête*. Naturally, this 'system' caused great losses due to friction, animosity resulting in rivalry amongst the leading figures, institutions and organizations, which frequently precluded any objective decision-making. Hitler seemed to think such a strategy guaranteed his leading role; it is indisputable that he could thus play the staff one against the other if it seemed opportune to do so.

Hitler was no great coordinator, which is one of the most important duties of someone at the top; neither did he entrust the task to anyone else. Already before the war a joke circulated in government circles, in which the activities of the ministries, the highest Reich authorities and the party organizations were said to be 'NS-*Kampfspiele*' (National Socialist fighting games; these were actually sports events that took place in Nuremberg on the occasion of Reich Party Day). Hitler's Führer State was no monolithic block such as National Socialist propaganda liked to portray it. Most probably the losses due to friction in Hitler's dictatorship were no less than in the scorned democracies. Earlier in the Reich the sectionalism of the German *Länder* (an administrative subdivision, often called a 'state' in English) was spoken of. During the Third Reich one could well speak of the sectionalism of the organizations, institutions and authorities or, respectively, of their representatives.

The Hitlerian system of leadership is outlined in a statement by General Walter von Reichenau, who was not one of Hitler's opponents but who nonetheless accurately assessed the 'Führer State':

'The power is embodied in a single person – that is the reality! And when overnight something occurs to this personage or is skillfully suggested to him, there is nothing to prevent him from broadcasting it the next morning as a binding injunction. Whoever sits with him by the fireplace, irrespective of who it is, has more influence than any minister of state, let alone any of us of the military.'[425]

This could have been written by Father. He too had to fight, on a daily basis, to maintain his influence; he had 'to be there'! Reichenau was right: what do the so-called historians of today know about these realities which, as Reichenau had already quite correctly observed, 'stick to the records and memoranda, thereby as a rule masking the circumstances under which Hitler's qualified advisers had to try to obtain the decisions, in their view the right and necessary ones'?

A phenomenon of history stood at the head of the Reich. He did not, however, fulfill the step from the extraordinary propagandist of his visions to the organizing, integrative and motivating statesman who from now on, in the raw reality of foreign policy and doing the necessary detailed work, had to bring all the spiritual, intellectual and material forces of the population to concentrate on the goal of achieving a consolidated and secure position in the centre of Europe.

Did he have to pick a quarrel ideologically with everyone, instead of concentrating all anti-Bolshevik forces against the single goal, which was to fend off Marxism-Bolshevism? The answer has to be 'no'. Hitler did not comprehend the need to integrate all anti-Bolshevik forces, winning them over as his 'followers'. There were certainly many of the 'old school' mentality among them, stoutly reactionary as Reichenau calls them, who had not comprehended that Hitler's *Volksgemeinschaft* as they perceived it was the lesser evil than a Bolshevik takeover of power, which for these circles, as well as for numberless others, would certainly mean the gibbet. There is no doubt that conservative elements had often not understood the times and brought great blame onto their head. Indicative of what constitutes a motive for 'resistance' is Halder's statement:

'I may remind that the origin of what we call resistance is to be traced back to the conservative fundamental attitude of the officer corps.' [426]

The question may first of all be asked: resistance against what, whom and where? It may be pointed out that the generals made no resistance to Hitler's error in deciding to go to war against the Soviet Union, above all Halder, the Chief of Staff.

Hitler had proved he was right – contrary to most of the experts -- in two important military issues. He had enforced the institution of independently operating large motorized units and had decided against the High Command of the Army in choosing the 'Manstein Plan', which was what led to the sensational success in the West. At this point a glance will be directed at

Hitler's policies in regard to personnel. That Hitler must be given credit for having immediately recognized the advantage of the element of surprise of the 'Manstein Plan' employing a *Sichelschitt* (sickle cut), as opposed to the Army Command, makes it incomprehensible that he did not equally make full use of the designer of the plan by keeping him close by, in whatever post that may have been. While Manstein's plan was being applied, its designer was left back in Germany restructuring an army corps, and what is more (to the author's knowledge) a horse-drawn and not a motorized one. I refer to Hitler's words as uttered in the Bunker in February 1945 to Father and me: 'This Manstein is at his best operating with armies.' Had Hitler intuitively seen Manstein's strategic abilities and been afraid to have a rival close to him? Why did Hitler not later promote Manstein to Commander-in-Chief East of the Russian theatre of war? In the First World War the post was filled by the Hindenburg/ Ludendorff team. This solution guaranteed a unified and relatively 'front-line' assessment of the situation and the planning of corresponding coordinated measures. Could Hitler have feared that a Commander-in-Chief East might have been able to force him to make decisions against his will? In view of the lack of trust reigning in the relationship between Hitler and the whole body of generals, this is a perfectly reasonable presumption.

The question must again be asked: did Hitler sufficiently preoccupy himself with his military leaders so as to include them in the fresh possibilities which in his opinion – which was shown to be right – would present themselves for operationally deployed armoured battalions? Did he take the time and the trouble to get to know his 'Pappenheimers' – that is his generals – as to their qualifications and attitude and to test them by letting them talk, while on the other hand motivating them and letting them take part in the trains of thought and necessities of foreign policies?

It would have been important to convince them of the inescapability of his policy, because he could not wait for completion of rearmament. Did he convince the majority of his military leaders that he had to take the risky path, without a war, in order to establish a Central European bloc ready to defend itself, and which would maintain its hold between the world powers of the United States and Soviet Russia? Was the great demagogue able to enter into the soul of these officers – most of them ultra conservatives, to the extent that one may confidently label them as 'reactionary' in those days – and adjust to their mentality so as to convince them and win them over or to separate himself from the incorrigibles? In his memoirs, Keitel, head of the Armed Forces High Command, maintains that in March 1941 Hitler had closed his address to those destined to be in command of the Russian campaign with the words: 'I do not require the generals to understand me but I demand that they obey my orders.'[427] If these were thus formulated, they throw an awkward light on the relationship between Hitler and his generals. There can be no question of any 'motivation' in view of a military engagement about which Hitler thought that, if it did not succeed, all would anyhow be lost, let alone of a relationship of trust.

The statesman was obliged to take the conservative attitude of certain social classes into consideration if he could not dispense with the cooperation of such groups. Stalin could permit himself to cut off the heads of the Red Army at a stroke: he did it in the literal sense too! Hitler, on the contrary, could not even allow himself to get them bodily out of the way. Had Hitler correctly recognized that 'the circles which I needed for the rebuilding did not rally to me in the days of fighting', as it is said he once put it to Frau von Below? Now that he had become the all-powerful Führer of the Reich he had to mobilize everything to win them over, since he left them in their traditional leading posts in the army and administration, which – in view of the foreign policy-related time pressure – he was obliged to do. Everything had to be avoided that would have further alienated these circles. However, visionaries and prophets can never see anything but 'enemies' or 'friends' of their convictions. This may have been valid for Hitler too, making it difficult to build a basis of mutual trust with those circles who were not his ideological followers, if not actually precluding it. It was not for nothing that in the circles that took a negative view of the regime, an 'inner emigration into the army' was spoken of. It demonstrates the attitude of portions of the high-ranking officer corps toward the regime. The inconsequentiality of in effect subtracting the Wehrmacht from monitoring measures shows naivety on the one hand, while on the other that Hitler's assessment of the officer corps was positive in that he could not imagine a conspiracy as was then actually plotted. This prohibition of monitoring measures had as a consequence that the treasonable machinations that the Counterintelligence as well as the army General Staff were embroiled in since 1938 could not be prevented. They became known to the Reich leadership only out of investigations after the bomb plot of 20 July 1944. Among other things this led to the execution of Canaris and Oster. What happened before and during the war in this regard can only be guessed at, insofar as it has not been published. One need think only of Canaris's deputy, General Oster, who kept the Dutch military attaché, Sas, informed of the dates determined for the planned offensive in the West, thereby explicitly accepting responsibility for high German losses. To this day, 'Werther'[428] has not been entirely exonerated; apparently all German military planning during the Russian war was made known through him to the Soviet High Command.

Until then the army command had expressed misgivings over all of Hitler's foreign policy and military decisions. To quote Father, when general military service was announced, the army had reservations concerning thirty-six divisions that would not be acceptable to the signatory powers of the Versailles Treaty. Once the fact was accepted as such, they were suddenly not enough. I remember well how Father was laughing when he told us this. I have already mentioned Fritsch's qualms about a speedy arms build-up, now a necessity because of the dictates of foreign policy, as well as the tensions between Hitler and the army leadership during the Sudeten crisis. At that time the army had already planned a coup d'état. The generals also had substantial objections to the offensive in the West. It was only Russia that the army believed it could overthrow in only a few weeks! It is possible that here again memories of the First World War played a role.

Should the origins for the reticent, indeed negative, stance of conservative officers toward Hitler and his regime quoted by Halder not also to a certain extent be sought in the *Volksgemeinschaft* he propagandized, from which they felt a greater threat to their personal sphere of life than from Hitler's foreign policy? Should the exclusion from the field of decision-making in foreign policy have had priority over reservations in regard to foreign policy of a fundamental sort? Can it be denied that on the part of some the inducement was merely a reactionary attitude that led to the rejection of the 'Lance Corporal' and his *Volksgemeinschaft*? Kleist-Schmenzin, the scion of the old Prussian aristocracy conspiring with Churchill and Vansittart, expressed his pride in his rank by saying: 'The aristocracy has to insist on their noble ways cultivated over centuries, the feeling of lordship, the absolute conviction of being at the top, superior to others.'[429]

That other 'Little Corporal', Bonaparte, knew his generals well. In the circumstances of his days he was able to 'make' his generals himself. He could seek them out and groom them. Hitler, the 'Bohemian Lance Corporal', did not have this possibility, or at least only conditionally, in view of the predicaments of foreign policy; all the more reason for him to have occupied himself with them so as to be able to know them well and judge them. It is certain that the curtailment of citizens' rights was a weighty argument against his regime. But did not many conservatives tend toward an authoritarian rule, even if it stood under their own decisive influence?

There is no question that the German army disposed of the oldest and most efficient management system. I have already briefly mentioned the German leadership system, based on the fundamental knowledge that the highest effectiveness of deployed troops could be attained only if each soldier in his place, in the sense of the assignment of his unit, could also be capable of acting independently if required. The 'emptiness of the battlefield'[430] – as opposed to troops deployed *en masse* in the nineteenth century – demanded and imposed this contributory thinking down to the lowest rank of simple soldier. The German military system of leadership, applied from the commanders to the last grenadier, provided the most efficient framework at its disposal, in order to make sure – even under the most difficult circumstances – of the optimum deployment of the troops, which also meant with the minimum of losses. The basic troop regulations (H.Dv 300 – German Field Service Regulations) for units of the German Wehrmacht contains the noteworthy phrase: 'In a difficult situation it may be preferable to do something wrong than to do nothing.' The basic precepts of the German military code were an encouragement to the commanders of German troops of all ranks to act on their own initiative and independently.

Those in high places in politics and the economy wisely keep out of the details and restrict themselves to instituting the main issues. They oversee the progress made and retain a controlling hand. This practice keeps the man at the top out of questions of detail and protects him from being overburdened, without nevertheless relieving him from overall responsibility. In the course of time, doubtless due to having misunderstood the leader principle, Hitler took precisely the contrary road. Instead of instituting a responsible government under his leadership to execute current tasks, whom he could summon to make accountable and with whose help he might, if the need arose, have found a scapegoat, he dismissed an ever-increasing number of scapegoats and, instead of filling the many posts anew, took the reins into his own hands. In the end he even undertook the command of an army group in the distant Caucasus. It is self-evident that he could not efficiently discharge any of these functions.

De Gaulle and Franco structured their regimes, to say nothing of Stalin, who, as undisputed and absolute potentate of the Soviet Union, until 1941 was but Secretary General of the Party and occupied no fixed governmental position. As Party Secretary General he represented the highest supervisory authority; nothing more was needed, strong personality that he was, to secure his absolute power in the Soviet empire. Hitler solved problems by appointing 'special commissioners', who were most often directly answerable to him, frequently as 'Supreme Reich Authorities'; they acted on the authority of the famous (or infamous) 'Führer's Orders' without them having been introduced into a properly structured framework of organization and control. Their activities were consequently not coordinated nor subject to constant controls.

A further dramatic example of Hitler's dispositions of his staff is represented in the person of Göring. In peacetime he was saddled with functions and offices no god-like person could have carried out efficiently. Both the most important duties he was entrusted with were more than full-time jobs in themselves: as commander-in-chief of the Luftwaffe he bore the responsibility for creating a powerful air force in no time, and as the authority for the 'four-year plan' he had to make sure of the entire provision of raw materials for the Reich and the distribution thereof. It was foreseeable that both functions would moreover lead to considerable clashes of interests, as has already been shown. The aerial Battle of Britain fought in the late summer of 1940 was a warning signal and ought to have induced Hitler to preoccupy himself in depth in the evolution of the Luftwaffe and its command. At the latest following the first heavy air raids by the Allies, conclusions as to personnel should have been drawn.

If in regard to Hitler, from the angle of his style of government and personnel politics a continuity may be spoken of, this could be found in his adhesion to persons whom he believed to be loyally devoted to him, and also in his multi-track strategies for all sectors in order not to allow anyone to accumulate too much power. The prevention of groupings that may potentially have forced him to make decisions not in agreement with his concept seems to have been the fundamental principle of his 'system' of governance. It was a 'system' that, to his mind without doubt, was 'successful' until the end. Regrettably, it also constituted one of the decisive facets of Hitler's personality structure that contributed to the disaster into which he plunged Germany.

The time span of Hitler's governance may be divided into two. The first phase comprises the years from 1933 to the end of 1940. From 1941 on, a progressive alteration of his personality is observable. As Father said: 'The Führer [became] ever more rigid in his concepts.' Was the Hitler of 1942 – let alone of the later war years – the same man he was in the years to 1940? In the winter of 1939/40 it was Hitler who ordered the execution of the Manstein Plan for the campaign in the West, contrary to an ill-humoured Chief of General Staff. In 1943 *Unternehmen Zitadelle* was instituted with such lack of imagination that any cadet of some standard could have expected the German offensive against the obvious focal points. Could a Hitler who in 1940 had made the crucial decision to shift the build-up of the concentrated point of main effort (*schwerpunkt*) to the centre of the offensive front in the West still be compared to he who in 1942 splintered the forces of his army by ordering a simultaneous offensive on the Volga and in the direction of the Caucasus, finally becoming bogged down at Stalingrad, thereby offering the Russians an opportunity to strike a devastating counter-blow?

Two further decisions by Hitler should be mentioned, as illustrating examples of what can only be described as growing irrationality. One of these was to conceive the Me 262 jet fighter, already extant in principle, as a bomber aircraft, and another the institution of the so-called 'Luftwaffe Field Divisions' in which Luftwaffe ground personnel no longer needed were to be deployed for ground combat. The latter decision is possibly to be attributed to Hitler's increasing mistrust of the army, to which it was undesirable to extradite Göring's 'National Socialist' *Luftwaffen*-soldiers (*divide et impera?*). From the military point of view this institution of the Luftwaffe Field Divisions was an absurdity. The officers, NCOs and crews were totally inexperienced in warfare, nowhere close to being sufficiently trained and often not even commanded by experienced officers, which signified that the posts of command were also filled with Luftwaffe officers. These divisions were shattered when they were involved in heavy fighting. If these Luftwaffe forces had been distributed among the seasoned divisions of the army (which was general practice until the beginning of 1943) they could certainly have turned into efficient fighters. I have good grounds for what I say. Following the retaking of Kharkov, the armoured '*Leibstandarte*' Division was assigned as replacements 6,000 men who had been 'combed out' from the Luftwaffe ground personnel. These men did not volunteer for the Waffen-SS, they were simply transferred to us. The armoured regiment took in 600 men, NCOs and lower ranks. I was charged, together with some of our experienced armoured staff, to train these Luftwaffe soldiers in a few weeks into an armoured force ready for action. Looking back, I can state that this goal was achieved. As during *Unternehmen Zitadelle* I was again in command of a company, which like the other companies had been staffed with 'Luftwaffe people', I am qualified to judge the outcome. They did their duty just as faithfully and efficiently as the troops who had volunteered for the Waffen-SS. Incidentally, to this day they are still maligned – like all Waffen-SS soldiers.

I do not know the details of what had been the determinant moment for Hitler wanting to make a bomber out of the Me 262. I do, however, still remember very well how when I visited Father at his headquarters in East Prussia in the summer of 1944, he told me about it – half in despair and half resignedly – when I briefed him about the overwhelming air superiority of the Allies on the invasion front. I myself, although deep in the hinterland, had been severely wounded by a strafing enemy aircraft just before the outset of the invasion. My father said: 'The Führer wants to turn the jet fighter into a bomber aircraft!' We were now deprived of both protection from Allied carpet bombing and support from the air in ground combat. Both decisions are rationally inexplicable.

To this day the state of Hitler's health in the various phases of his government is still the subject of much speculation. I can only contribute from my own point of view what I have already reported as to his physical and mental deterioration. The role played by his personal physician, Morell, is still disputed. While on leave – she was a Red Cross nurse – my sister Bettina was cured of blood-poisoning by Professor Eppinger in Vienna. Eppinger was an internist of international renown. He was once called to Moscow to examine Stalin because of heart trouble. When Tsar Boris of Bulgaria fell gravely ill in 1944, Eppinger was consulted. He confirmed the suspicion entertained from the German side that Boris – considered a great friend of Germany's – had been poisoned. In Berlin at the time it was not excluded that members of the Italian royal family – Boris was married to a daughter of the Italian king – may have had a hand in the affair.

Mother used the occasion to ask Eppinger if he would be able to send one of his physicians to East Prussia to give my father a thorough examination. As a consequence, assistant consultant Dr Lainer turned up at Father's headquarters. I was on convalescent leave in August 1944, and met this cheerful Austrian, making friends with him in the short time we spent together. He had paid a visit to Morell in East Prussia and, as Lainer put it, 'had a quick look in Morell's medical bag'; they had spoken openly about which medication the latter would 'inject the Führer with'. Lainer had then pointed out to Mother that at the time the effects of these medicines had not been tested at all, and that the Führer's medicinal treatment was irresponsible. It should also be recounted that my wife's first husband had before the war been a patient of Morell's for many years. According to her husband's assessment, Morell was a declared opponent of Hitler and it had always been expected – my wife had married him in 1943 – that Morell would finally succeed in rendering Hitler 'harmless'. But even if Morell had purposely handled Hitler wrongly, that does not constitute any exoneration of Hitler as to his historical responsibility. History does not accept illness as an excuse for erroneous decisions or for having brought about catastrophes. As Grandfather Ribbentrop used to say: 'Whoever does not know by the age of 40 what is good for his health is beyond being helped by any doctor!'

The roots of these failures were erroneous decisions and catastrophes. What reactions are triggered of the 'greatest general of all time' by the insight into the extremely precarious situation the war had sunk to in the winter of 1941-42?

Does he gather the leading personalities around him from the military, political and financial sectors so as to mobilize all the strength of the Reich and its sphere of influence henceforth in a considered and efficient manner? Does he inspire in his staff of leaders the necessary trust in his cause so as from all sides to unleash the necessary great efforts that have to be generated for survival? Does he include the populations of Europe in the struggle against the Soviet Union – which must in any event be called a defensive battle – by giving them a clear guarantee of their national status after the war? Anything but! Hitler proceeds in the diametrically opposite direction. He dismisses his most seasoned military commanders because they took decisions in the field, having better knowledge of the situation, that were contrary to his will. Among them was Guderian, one of the creators of the German armoured corps and who – against the resistance of his superiors – had brought the 'Manstein Plan' to its overwhelming success.[431]

Instead of unburdening himself personally and concentrating entirely on the highest political and military leadership, Hitler additionally takes on the supreme command of the army and finally also of an army group, which was, according to the principles of command of the German army, a 'cardinal sin'. Never, ever, would for instance a battalion commander have at the same time been in command of a company of his battalion; he would have instead entrusted the command of the company to an NCO – which incidentally was often enough the case in war. At the banquet, mentioned before, given by Mussolini in honour of Hitler and the German delegation on the occasion of the state visit to Italy in 1938 (when Mother, who in this case was the 'First Lady' of Germany, was seated next to Mussolini), both heads of state among other subjects discussed the respective organization of their supreme military commands. Upon her return, Mother had said that Hitler's formulations had not been convincing, adding that: 'He himself seemed, however, none too pleased with his solution!' This intuitive observation on the part of a woman who may unquestionably be seen as 'favourably inclined' toward Hitler at that time, and who had no clue as to military organization, is illuminating.

Hitler's weaknesses, which were analysed above, now began to take effect ever more fatefully. Hitler interferes ever more in details; nevertheless, he is ever less successful. His failure as political and military 'Führer' brings the radical ideologist in him into the arena. Only then is the 'Jewish star' introduced and deportations begun. Hitler balks at every one of the peace feelers that his Foreign Minister repeatedly proposes. All he now does is flail around, insofar as he still can. He is now painting his negative image to an ever-increasing degree, which nowadays so often obscures the view of the coerciveness which his – that is to say Germany's – policies were exposed to at the outset of his taking over the government.

It must have been quite early on – in my opinion at the latest in November 1941 – that the realization dawned on Hitler that the attack on Russia was a crucial mistake. The crisis on the Eastern Front at the onset of winter, the spontaneous entries in Hewel's diary about the ambience in the Führer's headquarters in December 1941, the impulsive cry on receipt of the news of the Japanese attack on Pearl Harbor ('Germany is saved now!'; when Mother told me about it she put her hand over her mouth again, a gesture that signified her horror) – all these indices testify to the profound shock that the obviously erroneous estimation of Russia strength, and of the environmental conditions under which the German army had to wage the war in Russia, caused to Hitler. He appeared less and less in public, already not at all at mass gatherings – with the cogent argument of not wanting to expose his audiences to a possible air attack – but he also did not see the troops at the front any more. Only once, in January 1943, did he do so, flying for a brief visit to see Manstein in the southern sector, an occasion when it must be admitted that from his point of view he was quite right to mistrust his officers. They conspired against his life and found a suitable opportunity to load brandy bottles full of explosives into his airplane, that only by chance did not explode.

Militarily again and again he staked all on a single throw. In 1943 *Unternehmen Zitadelle* burned out the armoured divisions only recently refurbished, that were then bitterly lacking in countering the 1943 Soviet summer offensive. The Ardennes Offensive (Battle of the Bulge) in December 1944, in view of the ratio of forces and the situation of supplies, was an irresponsible gamble. As regimental adjutant of the armoured regiment of the right-wing division I had a detailed insight into the preparations, and as battalion commander experienced at first-hand the hopeless inferiority in men and matériel – not least the lack of air support – that to my mind from the outset did not give the offensive the slightest chance. Even the early successes that could be achieved by surprise in the southern attack area did not make any difference. The fact that this operation was executed in the West, in view of the concurrent march on Berlin of the Red Army for the final offensive, in massively superior numbers, underlines how unreal Hitler's perceptions of the operative goals were.

The German people, let this here be firmly stated, were the main victims of the Hitler regime. From the beginning of the 1930s, slowly and with reservations – before 1933 he had never obtained an absolute majority – they had preferred him to the Communists, and therefore to Bolshevism. In view of the failure of the Weimar Republic and the Treaty of Versailles, the German people no longer had a third alternative. The much-abused German people had thereby reached a decision of historical dimensions, if one pictures what consequences a Bolshevik Germany would have had for Europe and the world.

In this way a calamity for Germany is indissolubly linked to Hitler, comparable only to the Thirty Years' War. A true statesman ought to seek every means of averting such a fate as struck the German people. To say it clearly and explicitly, Hitler cannot be forgiven, let alone rehabilitated. Whether the taboo applied today in Germany to his personage is of benefit in the sense of a historical 'coming-to-terms' may with good reason be doubted.

However, the sober, historical conclusion from Hitler's twelve-year domination is the ascertainment that to cede absolute and uncontrolled power to only one person simply represents too great a risk. An exchange with controlling bodies in whatever form is essential in order to avoid erroneous decisions or indeed despotism, not to mention the possible effects of health problems. The political acumen of Rome is a source of admiration in that they were aware of the institution of 'dictator' as an efficient way of dealing with existence-threatening situations. This office was entrusted to the dictator by Rome for one year only, not least because it was known that once a sole ruler is established it is extraordinarily difficult to get rid of him. It should at the same time not be overlooked that in Rome this institution was the creation of a more or less homogeneous leading class, against which, at least in Republican Rome, a dictator did not have the slightest chance. Think of Caesar's fate! The so-called Third Reich did not have a homogeneous leading class which could at an earlier stage have forced Hitler to abandon or at least to modify his policies. And yet, if like Hegel one sees in historical figures the instruments of the world's Spirit that utilizes them for its purposes, which remain concealed from us, it was Hitler who forced Bolshevism with its imprint of Stalin to enter the arena. Stalin could do naught else but 'fetch the chestnuts out of the fire' for the great Western power, the United States. That is, however, precisely what Stalin wanted to avoid.

I allow myself a chuckle and concede in my mind, slightly arrogantly, when German historians such as for instance Andreas Hillgruber speak of Hitler's *Stufenplan* (stage-by-stage plan) to achieve world domination, thereby making a fairy story out of the most recent German past, to say nothing of the ridiculous 'puppetries' of their contemporary successors. In those days I was aware from the beginning of the fatal weakness of the German position. It is the only premise from which to understand Hitler's policies.

From a certain point on, Hitler offered the Germans an alternative to Bolshevism as a solution to the overwhelming problems with which Germany was faced. That was his role in the history of the world. The 'vortex of combined circumstances', to quote once again from Dostoyevsky's *The Possessed*, is what brought him to power. As I see it, the taboo under which Hitler is put today is incomprehensible. Hitler is, again according to his self-conception, responsible for a disaster that struck the people of Germany. This is absolutely factually ascertainable and permits no grotesque exaggerations nor mistaken or indeed ridiculous accounts that furthermore are often apt to be harmful to the interests of the country and to blur Hitler's responsibilities.

Father

'*Ein Unglück für den Toten, daß ihn der Feind
überlebte und seine Geschichte schrieb.*'
(free translation from German: 'It is a misfortune for the dead man,
that the enemy survived him and wrote his story.')
Friedrich von Schiller, *Geschichte des Dreißigjährigen Krieges*
(History of the Thirty Years' War)

Who was this Foreign Minister really, this Ribbentrop, who by his appointment as '*Reichsaussenminister*' at the beginning of 1938 officially became Hitler's top foreign affairs adviser? It meant that he stepped into a post into which in the foregoing years he had grown to an increasing degree. However, at no time was he exclusively Hitler's only interlocutor in matters of foreign affairs, it being well known that Hitler did not let himself be bound to departmental responsibilities. There is on the other hand no doubt that for long intervals my father had Hitler's ear regarding German foreign policy, thereby exerting influence on the formulation of a foreign policy which, as he expressed it during the Nuremberg Trials, 'was determined by another'. This points to Hitler. Father was not attempting in this way to disclaim his responsibility in German foreign policy when testifying at the victors' tribunal – he explicitly took it on at the trial; he was instead expressing his regret that his opinions and conclusions had not prevailed at later phases of German policies.

In his major speech to the Reichstag after the campaign in the West, only after thanking the generals did Hitler give thanks to the man who had executed his instructions in regard to foreign policy. Father was awarded the War Merit Cross First Class (*Kriegsverdienstkreuz 1. Klasse*), a decoration for non-combatants affiliated to the Wehrmacht; in my regiment, for example, the regimental engineer received the award. For Father, knowing the circumstances, it was almost somewhat offensive, which may have been the objective! In his well-known speech to the Reichstag of 30 January 1939, Hitler had still said that: 'It was in the first place the correct as well as bold evaluations and exceptional conduct in every detail of the problems of foreign affairs on the part of the party member von Ribbentrop that in the momentous times behind us constituted for me the greatest assistance in carrying out these aspects of my policies.' From the outset of their collaboration, a considerable degree of volatility characterized the relations between the two men. Common successes on the one hand, divergent points of view on the other and of course intrigues from all sides; this all fostered an ever 'fluctuating mood' between them. Hitler was entirely amenable to intrigue; it was the cause of the disturbances in the chequered relations between him and my father. In the end, however, the basic differences of opinion as to the policy in regard to Russia had been the reason for the gradual overshadowing of the relationship.

Nonetheless, Father had given German foreign policy significant impulses. The major issue of an agreement with England was Hitler's and Father's grand objective, but thanks to Father's influence, Hitler was then also open to achieving a lasting understanding with France. Father was the initiator of the Anti-Comintern Pact which brought Germany out of years-long isolation. It was Father who finally induced Hitler, who initially resisted, to conclude the treaty with the Soviet Union, whereby Germany's encirclement, which was close to being completed, was broken through and the Reich's position decisively improved. Note that he saw in it the prerequisite for putting the Eastern European problems on the path to negotiation, that is for them to be peaceably solved.

Who was this man, who went from a comfortable livelihood as an independent and successful self-made businessman, to enter into politics, uniting his destiny with an extraordinary historical phenomenon – take him as you will – and then to end at the gallows? *'Von der Parteien Haß und Gunst verzerrt, schwankt sein Charakterbild in der Geschichte!'* ('Distorted by the parties of hatred and goodwill, the depiction of his character sways in history!') Historians and biographers are fond of placing this famous quotation from Schiller at the head of accounts of historically disputed personalities. It would be very wrong of me to begin my description of Father's political impact and the depiction of his personality with this quotation. In the history written about Hitler's foreign policy, the image of his Foreign Minister is completely distorted beyond recognition by hatred and vilification. Of the 'favour' that in Schiller stands next to 'hatred' – even in the sense of a half-way truthful description of the role Father played – there is not the slightest trace. With regard to Joachim von Ribbentrop, therefore, a lesser known dictum by the Chinese sage Confucius is more apt at the head of a record: 'Where all praise, you have to check, where all condemn, you have to check!'

The judgements passed today on Hitler's Foreign Minister contain just about every negative feature that can be thought of. It makes one wonder how a man supposed to have been so stupid, conceited, pompous, arrogant, cowardly, weak, dishonest, insincere, ambitious, pretentious, tactless, characterless and finally, according to Joachim Fest, so 'bigoted', managed in a short time after the First World War to build up a prestigious mercantile firm – the first and largest of its field – in Germany, without, mind you, the financial support of his father-in-law Henkell. One should very particularly ask oneself how this man, with the features quoted that were attributed to him, was capable of making himself a circle of friends, at home and abroad in a few years after 1920, that was later the exact prerequisite and the stepping-stone for his entry into the sphere of high politics. It is worth noting and should be borne in mind that the most prominent of those foreign friends were the ones who were loyal to him through war and execution. In 1948, in not very pleasant French imprisonment, I was able to enjoy their helpfulness. These friends, at home and abroad, of our father's were the starting point of his political career.

It will therefore initially have to be investigated which characteristics constituted Ribbentrop's personality, to ask subsequently who it actually was who attributed these bad qualities to him, and, above all, for what reason? We shall have to ask the famous question impressed by the Roman Consul Lucius Cassius upon the Roman judges: '*Cui bono?*' ('to whose benefit?'). Why was Father maligned, and still maligned to this day? Light will be thrown on the underlying background reasons for such a campaign and the people behind it will be identified.

'Where all condemn, you have to check!' To begin with, the condemning judgement on Ribbentrop resounds from all the circles that played a role in the so-called 'Third Reich', whatever their political conviction, whether Hitler's supporters or opponents: they all condemn Hitler's Foreign Minister, albeit, as will be seen, out of very differing motives. The much-adopted practice may once again be mentioned here, according to which historians, biographers and memoirists simply draw from one another or, in other words, are mere plagiarists,[432] giving the others as sources. A glance at the index of sources and the Notes and comments – footnotes – in the relevant writing shows this distinctly. In this way identical wrong depictions, calumnies, errors and misunderstandings are constantly repeated and finally assumed to be the truth by the reader. 'Through long enough usage, out of lies there will come no truths, but facts',[433] as a man of great experience stated. I shall give instances of this. Only very few people had any personal knowledge, in view of Hitler's work style which was not to hold any sessions, enabling them to appraise what role Father had in fact played in consultations with Hitler. They have all long been dead. Besides, discussions between Hitler and my father often took place when they were alone.

So who was this Ribbentrop, as a person and of course as a politician, who, before he was 40, entered the maelstrom of high politics that was to be his destiny? Who was he and where did he come from, when in January 1933 he was taken hold of by politics and never released?

The Road into Politics

Since, among all the rest, our family name too has become the object of polemic, I shall start at the beginning. I no longer remember how the genealogical tree of the Ribbentrop family – or Ribbentrup as it was in the Middle Ages – came into the hands of us children, my sister Bettina's and mine. I must have been about 10. I was a *Sextaner* – in those days that was a pupil in the first year of secondary school, at the time when a German *gymnasium* still aspired to inculcate as broad as possible a general education into its pupils – when our class teacher, Dr Lüders, gave us the assignment to find out something about the origins of our family name. I must have either forgotten about this project or our parents, whom I could have asked, were away. In any case, when my turn came to say something about our family name, I was up in front of the class with embarrassingly empty hands. Lüders helped me out of my awkward position, saying: 'Your origins must be from Westphalia: an ending in "trop" to your name is a sure indication of that.'

Father, whom I naturally asked about this straight away, briskly confirmed my teacher's assumptions; it turned out that he had shortly before been with Mother at the 'Ribbentrup', as the lovely 400-acre farm in the vicinity of Bad Salzuflen is still known. He had been offered the chance to buy it. It was a fine property with boundaries, situated in the Lippe district. Father's decision at the time not to buy the farm was without doubt the right one from a financial angle, for we were on the brink of the world-wide Great Depression. Father's careful dispositions permitted us to survive the bad years well, although I still distinctly remember the measures taken at home to save money. During the war the farm came on to the market again. However, Father thought that, as Minister, he could not buy land while there was a war on.

The farm is mentioned for the first time in the register of Herford Abbey at the end of the twelfth century under the name of 'Ricbrachtinctorpe'. A 'Heinrich de Ricbrachtinctorpe' appears in the oldest deeds. It cannot, however, be traced as genealogical evidence that this is a direct ancestor. In about 1300 the original four farms were united into a single possession as what was called a '*Meierhof*' (a farm occupied by an administrator, the Meier).

In the sixteenth century we were known as 'Meyer zu Ribbentrup'. Our grandfather Richard told us – his grandchildren – that our forefathers had always been 'freemen' and not 'bondsmen', as was then often the case. Our French governess put the family tree up on the wall of our nursery, saying that such a family tradition signified we had a duty to accomplish something of value – just now the obligation, against which there was no appeal, of a prompt and proper execution of our homework.

There was an interesting figure among our ancestors: Friedrich von Ribbentrop. The work he did for the Prussian state still has relevance to the present day. It was he who instituted the Prussian High Chamber of Audit, precursor to the Reich/Federal Court of Auditors. In the framework of the army reforms of 1806, he founded the military officialdom; in other words, he devised the 'paymaster'. A friendship was formed with Blücher when Friedrich intervened following the 1813 Battle of Katzbach, when disorder arose among the young Prussian troops, which he quelled energetically and harshly. Blücher made him Chief of Administration of the occupied regions in France. In this function he had to recover art works plundered by Napoleon. His opposite number on the French side was the well-known Director of the Louvre, Dominique Denon. The chivalry with which he carried out his task is shown in a letter he wrote to Denon before leaving Paris to return to Prussia. Among other things the letter says: '[H]owever unpleasant for you too our professional relations may have been, you have but increased my personal esteem for a scholar to have made whose acquaintance I consider myself lucky.'[434] In his letter of thanks in reply, Denon says: 'Between people who esteem one another, professional relations elicit a personal connection and from that in turn friendship ensues.'[435] It was also this ancestor who traced the Brandenburg Gate Quadriga (a chariot drawn by four horses) in Paris and arranged for its return to Berlin.[436]

Another forefather may be mentioned, not only because he was a gallant officer – as artillery captain in the storming of the Düppeler entrenchments in the German-Danish War of 1864 he received the very seldom awarded order Pour le Mérite – but because we became his adopted descendants. As battery commander in the Guard Artillery Brigade, Karl Barthold Siegmund Ribbentrop received this order, as beautiful as it is an honour, a reward, as stated in the award proposal, for the great sang-froid, prudence and resoluteness he evinced in leading his battery in the storming of the Düppeler entrenchments, which was the turning point of the war. He wrote in all modesty to his wife:

'I hold the Order – the highest of our military decorations – in such high esteem that I would certainly not have awarded it to myself and can over the graciousness of my King only think with shame of all my brave companions who certainly deserved the award more than I.'

The brother of our grandfather Ribbentrop was awarded the Pour le Mérite as Lieutenant General and Division Commander in the First World War and, while briefly giving out division daily orders, transmitted to his division that he received the award for the bravery of the division.

The captain who distinguished himself at the Düppeler entrenchments later became a general and was ennobled. It is from this that the two crossed gun barrels feature on our coat of arms. He played a substantial part in the further evolution of the Prussian-German artillery. Frederick III, as he later became as Kaiser, is said to have addressed him with the words: 'Well, Ribbentrop, your name will one of these days not be unforgotten by history!' These words, albeit not referring to the courageous general and in their inverse meaning, became true for his adoptive grandson, my father. Father was adopted by a daughter of the general in 1925. What hateful and vilifying things have been hurled at this adoption – which by the way was not at all an unusual practice. A statement of Goebbels' about Father is peddled around: 'He bought his title of nobility and acquired his fortune by marriage.'

General Karl von Ribbentrop had a son and a daughter. The son did not have any children. He promised his father the general on the latter's deathbed to maintain the noble line of the family through adoption of a family member – there were no descendants of Friedrich von Ribbentrop the army commissionary. The general's son thus approached Grandfather Richard before the First World War and proposed to adopt him. As will be seen however, Richard, a wilful man, rejected his cousin's proposal. He suggested that instead Grandfather's eldest son, Lothar – Father's brother – be adopted. As, however, both brothers were already living in Canada, nothing came of this before the First World War.

Lothar died of pulmonary tuberculosis in Switzerland shortly after the war, in 1919. Father too came back to Germany from Turkey in 1919. Inflation was in full spate and the family's members were plagued by worries other than possible adoptions. When there had been a general consolidation of the conditions, the thought of adoption was brought up again by the general's son, Siegfried von Ribbentrop. He had, however, meanwhile adopted the daughter his wife had brought in from a previous marriage. It was therefore agreed that Siegfried's sister, the general's daughter, should adopt Father. Our esteemed aunt, Tante Gertrud, lived in Naumburg, where our grandparents too lived. She had not been blessed with worldly goods, was not married and the inflation had devalued her savings so that in any case Father was supporting her. He naturally continued to do so after the adoption; through the adoption he was legally bound to support her (which Goebbels evidently did not grasp). Furthermore, Tante Gertrud had quite properly notified the *Adelsgenossenschaft* (nobility cooperative) about the adoption, as was then customary.

It should also be mentioned here that Siegfried and his sister Gertrud respected their father's wish that the family's hereditary nobiliary particle 'von' should be handed on to a branch of the family, members of whom had distinguished themselves on the battlefield. Three generations – my great-grandfather, grandfather and father – had been awarded the Iron Cross First Class in the respective wars of 1870-71 and 1914-18. That the leading classes of those days were prepared to commit themselves for their country, and if required to lay down their life for it, then still played an important part, and up to the last war significantly counteracted the materialism concomitant with the meteoric evolution of technology.

A curious family trait should not be overlooked, as it is connected to an indirect forefather with the not unknown first name of Adolf. During the 1848 Revolution, this Adolf von Ribbentrop, as Prussian government councillor, went over to the insurgents and, following the quelling of the revolution, fled to France, where he joined the circle round Karl Marx, who also lived there as an immigrant. Arnold Ruge, a Radical Democrat, at the time wrote to Max Duncker, who was like himself a member of the Frankfurt National Assembly, the '*Paulskirche*' (St Paul's Church in Frankfurt am Main is a church with important political symbolism in Germany), saying: '[T]here was in the beginning in his [Marx's] crowd an acquaintance of his whom I still frequent, a Herr v. Ribbentrop.' What Duncker, who at the time in Paris, together with Marx, was publishing the German-French yearbooks, proceeds to say in his letter is amusing:

'I now have to overcome this [Marx School] if I felt like taking on the yoke. But just at the moment we are already sufficiently unpopular and Marx particularly the object of loathing for the French because of his cynicism and crude insolence. He is of the opinion that this whole culture of the present existence of France has to be demolished, and since at the start the new humanity could only be raw and inhuman he immediately takes on these virtues. French *ouvriers* [workers] are infinitely more humane than this humanist *ab inhumanitate* [out of inhumanity].'[437]

This is a noteworthy judgement of Marx, which history has bloodily confirmed. I shall restrict myself to describing these three ancestors. To a certain extent they reflect the Prussian history of the last 200 years. It may incidentally be mentioned that another forefather signed the Peace of Westphalia in lieu of Count von Lippe in 1648.

They say that as a youth and a young man, Father was 'beloved of the gods'; they had endowed him with multiple talents. He was exceptionally musical, had perfect pitch and at the age of 13 entertained the idea of becoming a violinist, having played the violin on the occasion of a concert in Metz, where he was a great success. In his memoir sketches Father writes about his mother and his love of music:

'She was highly musical, as was my father, and she played the piano wonderfully. She would play for me hour after hour whilst I sat spellbound in a corner and could have listened for ever. My mother, in her love for me and willingness was touchingly prepared to respond to my endless requests that she should play for me.'

Self-modesty and the desperate risk constituted by undertaking an artistic career without the certainty that he would be a great performer caused him, while he was still at school, to renege on the idea of embarking upon a course as an artist. A pupil of the famous violinist Joachim taught Father the violin, and had pronounced the verdict that Father had 'great talent', but left it in doubt whether it would suffice for the 'breakthrough to stardom' as they say today. Music moved Father profoundly. It must have been in 1934 when I was allowed to accompany my parents to a concert by the Berlin Philharmonic. In Hitler's presence, Wilhelm Furtwängler conducted Beethoven's Ninth Symphony, with the then famous Bruno Kittel Choir. This performance was especially notable in that it represented Furtwängler's reconciliation with the regime. As I heard at the time, the bad blood will have been caused by Furtwängler's intervention on behalf of Hindemith and the latter's Jewish secretary.

Thanks to our piano teacher Fräulein Munding I went to the concert well prepared. Even for me, a 13-year-old boy who was far from having inherited Father's feeling for music, the performance was a tremendous experience. After the concert my parents treated me to dinner in Berlin's renowned Horcher restaurant. Father was quiet and absorbed in his thoughts, and suddenly turned to Mother to say: 'Do you not get the feeling that he [he meant Beethoven] was a man struggling with a great problem?' Mother, who did not have such an intense relation to music – she was a 'visual' person –

seeing the turmoil Father was in, responded with tenderness. I took in what Father said, albeit at my age unable fully to comprehend it, but the depiction of the artist in his 'struggle' in the execution and perfection of his work was for me henceforth a given and was often a help to find the way to access a work of art, especially when at first glance or first hearing it seemed austere. Father's musicality – as is so often the case – went hand in hand with an extraordinary gift for languages. He spoke faultless French and English, the latter in fact, as I was told, without an accent.

He must have radiated extraordinary charm too as a young man. Grandfather once told us with a chuckle how in Arosa once upon a time Father had fallen in love with a particularly attractive young Englishwoman, who was however a few years older than Father, who was then 15. She too had obviously found the youth not lacking attraction, so that Grandfather had 'stepped in' to put a halt to the affair. Thereupon Father, furious, had climbed the 'Hörnli' (an 'elbow macaroni'-shaped rock outcrop in Arosa) – in those days no easy undertaking – all alone, under the banner 'Serves my parents right if …'.

Father spent the greatest and most important part of his young years abroad. When Grandfather Ribbentrop took voluntary retirement, he moved to Arosa. Our grandmother had died of tuberculosis. Up until the outbreak of war in 1914, Father lived in Switzerland, France, England, the States and Canada. He came back during the war (in a Dutch steamer's coal bunker), fought in Russia and France, and in 1918, after being wounded a second time, became adjutant to the German military plenipotentiary in Turkey. When he returned to Germany in 1919 he could almost have been said to be a German 'expatriate'. It has been proven from experience that these Germans are particularly attached to their native country.

If Father writes somewhere that as children, for him and his brother their father was 'more the strict master than a loving father', then the relationship of the father with the two brothers had altered fundamentally while they grew up. My mother and grandfather were certainly the two people Father was closest to in his life, indeed they were arguably the only two people in whom he had absolute trust, although the influence both of them exerted on him was anything but unlimited – as will alas be seen. A depiction of Father's personality would therefore be incomplete if I did not again bring in his father, our Grandfather Richard. For both the boys as they grew up he was the open-minded, highly cultured, totally impartial mentor, who above all things gave them an acute perception of current politics, already at that time from a standpoint of criticality of imperial foreign policy. Later on Grandfather was my mentor too, albeit not with the same intensity as our grandparents lived in Naumburg. When I was asked to give an impromptu little speech at his 75th birthday, I was able to bail myself out by describing him as our 'living encyclopaedia'.

His main interest lay in his country's destiny. This does not mean he was – in the demeaning sense it is given in the jargon of today – a nationalist, which in the usage of those days was someone whose patriotism placed his native country above all others. He was able to subject personages, customary practices and institutions of his country to sharp criticism and would without compunction compare it to other countries, even if it were to the detriment of his own. He had a mortal hatred of brash 'Hooray Henry Patriotism'. In this sense, he was critical of the Kaiser. When we visited the Berlin Arsenal one day, he pointed out a picture to us: it depicted the scene when at the Battle of Fehrbellin, Froben, Master of the Horse to the Elector, asked the Elector to exchange horses with him because he thought the monarch was in too great a peril on his white steed. Froben is said to have been killed during the battle while he was riding the Great Elector's horse. As a little boy this preparedness of Froben's to die for his country, embodied by the person of the suzerain, made a lasting impression on me. Nowadays the sacrificial death of Froben is said to be a myth. It may be so. Goethe referred to such myths, bringing them to life, when he said about the example of Mucius Scaevola: 'If the Romans had the greatness to invent such stories, shall we not, at least, have the greatness to believe them?'[438] Thus did the prevalent attitude reigning at home quite naturally and without pathos inculcate into us children to be prepared to give one's all for our country, meaning, if necessary, one's life too. A well-known engraving hung in Grandfather's study, showing Frederick the Great, after defeat in the Battle of Kolin, sitting on the trunk of a tree. Grandfather's comment was unforgettable, that the quality of a troop is shown exactly at the moment of defeat. I was to experience the significance of these words myself in impressive fashion on the day of capitulation in 1945. I shall recount it in another place.

Frederick the Great was represented in the Hall of Fame by the famous painting showing how he gave his generals leave to depart before the Battle of Leuthen, which was the outcome of a desperate situation, as he was about to attack the enemy against all the rules of the art of war for he had no other way out but to let himself be buried in front of his batteries. If Father writes in the legacy of his writings that 'Frederick the Great was Hitler's model', a greater contrast cannot be imagined. Not one of his generals abandoned the king, although he assured them that he would hold it against nobody if they did not wish to share the risk of a battle with a force nearly three times superior.

Hitler, on the contrary, had not managed to have a sustainable relationship of confidence with his generals that was unshakeable even when the fault was his own.

Grandfather held Frederick's achievement in the highest esteem as the absolutely decisive element that brought about Prussia's later rise to a great power, without forgetting Frederick's father, who, incidentally, despite his characterization as the 'soldier king', never waged a war. He also unreservedly endorsed the attribute of 'the Great' to Frederick, taking the whole personality into consideration. On the other hand, he considered it unforgiveable that Frederick's foreign policy had eventually brought about the aggressive coalition against Prussia of the three Great Powers, Russia, Austria and France. The king should at all costs have averted this constellation. This was why Grandfather was aware of the dire state of the Reich's foreign policies. His criticisms stemmed from the experience of the First World War and the absolutely maximum priority incumbent upon German policy at all costs to avoid a similar coalition against the Reich. This was the core problem of German foreign policy. It was Grandfather's censure of Frederick the Great on this issue that made me realize the importance of always bearing in mind that prominent and successful personalities, particularly when they are publicly acknowledged as such, should always be critically appraised in their conduct of affairs. Mother well knew why at that particular time she so often quoted the Latin adage '*nil admirari*' ('admire nothing').

Grandfather reproached Frederick that, for the sake of a few sharp-tongued *bon mots* about the 'ladies' Elisabeth of Russia and the Marquise de Pompadour at the French court, he had played into the hands of Austrian State Chancellor Count Kaunitz in the latter's efforts to bring about a superior coalition against Prussia. Just like Father, Grandfather perceived how the problems of anti-German coalitions were ever-present. The feeling that a latent danger lurked of an encirclement of the Reich – a concept from the First World War – existed everywhere. I wish to add here to Frederick's nasty *bon mots* about the Russian and French ladies that Mother always held it ill-advised when the wife of the American president, Anna Eleanor Roosevelt, was the butt of attacks on her femininity. It was well known that she was no beauty – mostly because of her somewhat toothy look – and the target thus set up for them was naturally exploited to the full by the caricaturists. In this way, Mother argued, Eleanor Roosevelt was attacked as a woman and not only as a politician. A woman could not, even in her subconscious, remain indifferent to such treatment, and consequently fuel was unnecessarily poured onto the anti-German fire already kindled by Roosevelt. Mother used Grandfather's criticism of Frederick the Great to support her premise with Father, but he had no influence over German domestic propaganda, since he was constantly obliged throughout his time in office to fight with Goebbels over influencing foreign policy, because as so often, Hitler could not be persuaded to establish clear-cut situations.

These discussions with Grandfather about the era of Frederick the Great and other stages of German history clearly demonstrate the place of top priority held in Grandfather's thinking by foreign policies. He had already passed these categories of thought down to his sons when they were still children, for Father had completely absorbed them. In their opinion, the location of Germany in the centre of Europe, in an era of Nationalism and global power politics, necessitated the subordination of public life – in its broadest sense – to the demands of foreign policy. The unfortunate outcome of the First World War, with the ensuing Versailles Treaty, the military threat from all directions against a Germany disarmed and, lastly and most decisively, the danger to Germany and Europe from the Soviet Union were ultimately the crucial factors for their change of direction toward Hitler. Domestic policy – that is first of all the solution of the 'social question' – to their mind had to create the prerequisites to render the German people ready for defence against external dangers. In the state of affairs of the time, Father and Grandfather saw in Hitler the sole chance of righting the desperate situation the Reich's foreign policy was in. It was only from this point of view that Father had placed himself at the disposal of Hitler.

All his life, Grandfather could not be persuaded to make compromises. That was doubtless also the reason why he did not make a success of his career, for he had been said to excel. He owed to it to have been appointed adjutant to the commanding general in Metz. However, if something did not suit him, he quickly discarded it and stayed out of it, glowering. He lacked the minimum tolerance for compromise necessary in every organization of any size so as to have one's opinion prevail and not to crumble before encountering any opposition. The manner in which he finally requested his discharge is typical. As has been said, his predominant interest was in foreign policy. Following Bismarck's dismissal and the concomitant estrangement of Russia, Grandfather adopted an increasingly critical attitude toward German foreign policy and, as we knew him, would surely not have made any bones about it. Added to this there were, as Father writes, from his post as adjutant of the Metz Army Corps, insights into the military policy for personnel that will not have met with his entire approval.[439] Lastly, Grandfather's distance from Kaiser Wilhelm II will most probably have increased, caused not exclusively by objective concerns in regard to the latter's policies but also his rejection of the Kaiser's style. Thus in his discharge application Grandfather added 'with no right to wear uniform', which at that time was unheard of. The right to wear uniform after discharge was denied only in cases of dishonourable conduct. He will no doubt have wished to express his dissatisfaction thereby. It goes without saying that he received his discharge with the right to wear uniform.

It is worth recording a further incident I experienced with my grandfather. It played a part in a very difficult stage of my life and I have had every reason to keep it in memory: in one of my history books I came across the practice applied under exceptional circumstances of releasing prisoners of war in exchange for their word of honour that they would no longer fight as soldiers. This custom derived from a time when the waging of war was still largely a matter handled by the soldiery and before what is nowadays called the 'home front', which has to place all that is necessary for a war at disposal, played the decisive role. 'Total war' had not then yet been invented. I asked Grandfather whether it might be possible to be obliged to keep to a word of honour given in this sense, since according to one's own code of honour one's duty was to one's own country only. I went even further in my query: was it not a duty to break one's word of honour, so as to be able to fight for one's country again? Grandfather looked at me in astonishment – I thought myself at my age of 13 or 14 rather clever – and then he answered very calmly but emphatically: 'You are trusted, you pledge your honour, and that you can do only once.' At that time I could not foresee that I would one day have occasion very well to recall Grandfather's words. At Christmas 1947 I was an inmate in an English internment camp – it could perhaps be called a concentration camp – and requested a week's leave for the Holy Days, upon my word of honour to return, and I was granted it. I went back to the camp at the end of my leave, albeit in the particular situation I was in I had to reckon with all thinkable eventualities. Sure enough, promptly after my return I was handed over to the French.

When we talked to Grandfather about Alsace-Lorraine – we knew that he had been in the Metz garrison for a long time – all he said, cuttingly, which once again left us speechless, was: 'The Alsatian Lorrainians are always dissatisfied with the nation to which they just then belong.' He furthermore told us Bismarck had not wanted to annex Alsace-Lorraine,[440] but that because of the strongholds of Metz and Strasbourg the military had insisted on it. Our grade teacher Lüders told us the same. Father's endeavours and his influence on Hitler led to Hitler's enlightened relinquishing of Alsace-Lorraine. He thought thereby to have averted a possible obstacle to a German-French understanding.

I have already described how shortly before his death Grandfather had said to Mother: 'If he [Hitler] wants to lose the war, all he needs to do is to go to war with the Russians!' Grandfather chose the right moment to say farewell to this Earth. He died on the first day of the fateful year of 1941. He was spared having to live through Hitler himself bringing about the 'nightmare' of a war on two fronts, to avoid which had always been the decisive motto in all political discussions between my father and my grandfather. Long before Father did so, Grandfather had seen in Hitler the sole alternative to Communism in Germany.

I have spoken of my grandfather in such detail because he was without doubt the personality which exerted a prevalent influence on Father's youth. The capacity to think quite objectively and pragmatically, combined with a great love of his country, were important qualities that Grandfather handed down to his son on the path of life. Father had acquired his world-wide overview – beyond the often narrow confinement of circumstances in Germany before 1914 – through his long sojourn abroad and overseas before and after the First World War.

I have already posed the question whether Grandfather's influence over Father would have been sufficient – had he lived long enough – to instigate Father to enforce his resignation, which he had offered Hitler at the outset of the Russian war. Under reference to the 'Hess affair', which was taken in the public view as a negative symptom for the German position, Hitler had restrained Father from resigning. Such a resignation of the Foreign Minister following shortly after would have further reinforced the unfavourable impression given. Father submitted to the argument and withdrew his resignation. His decisive mistake! At the time, however, he believed he had to act thus in the common good. Besides, Father was conscious of Grandfather's incapacity to make compromises and had once, at the onset of his political career, said with a smile: 'If I had Grandfather's mentality I would for one thing not have gone in for politics at all, and if I had, would very soon have been out again!' Mother's and Grandfather's combined efforts might nevertheless have succeeded in persuading Father to push his resignation through, especially in view of his personal credibility and that of German policy. In 1943, at a severely deteriorated state of the war, Mother observed: 'If he had only listened to me he could now be recalled as a signal to the Russians!' Whether Hitler would in fact have 'recalled' him must be placed in doubt; at that point Hitler was no longer thinking along such subtle lines, nor was he in the least prepared to attempt a diplomatic solution. A window in time was open for Father for the duration of just a year – from the beginning of the war with Russia until the summer of 1942 – when his resignation could have helped without causing the German position greater detriment nor exposing himself to the reproach of being a rat abandoning a sinking ship, one that he wanted at all costs to avoid, as he once said to me later.

Father wrote more about the time in Metz:

'If in later life I felt myself particularly in tune with the world of French culture, it is traceable back also to these early impressions [in Metz], that were to be reinforced later due to a lengthier sojourn, together with my brother, at the Grenoble Higher School of Commerce. Our knowledge of the French language was then perfected.'

The ensuing years in Arosa ranked for Grandfather and the two brothers amid the happiest of their life. With Grandfather as brakeman, Father steering, and two Englishmen, they must for a time have manned one of the fastest bobsleighs in Switzerland. Before the First World War, the English and Canadians predominated over sporting life in Switzerland. This resulted in our family making personal contacts, especially with a Canadian family – Father recalled: 'We youngsters both had particularly congenial feelings for a Canadian woman and this contributed to our going to spend many years on the other side of the Atlantic.' Father again:

'When we talked about our own future with our father it was clear to us that we would never be soldiers. Both my brother and I felt a very strong urge for far places.

… In 1909 – when I was just sixteen – English friends of ours invited my brother and me to a stay in London. We wanted to perfect our knowledge of English at a school in London so as to prepare ourselves for a career in business. We lived in the house of a well known English doctor in South Kensington and stayed there for nearly a year. Never shall I forget the touching care with which Dr Grandage – who was killed in WWI – and his sister surrounded us two brothers … When I was in London again in 1920 after the Great War, staying at the little Brown's Hotel, the city was still as familiar to me as if I had just left it.'

Father and his brother Lothar did then go to Canada. The 'great wide world' must in those days have held a special attraction for enterprising young Germans, perhaps as a result of the somewhat narrow and fossilized social relations that reigned in Germany then. Father writes that: '[W]e [i.e. he and his brother] enormously liked the laid-back attitude of the English.' At first he worked in a bank, then joined a building enterprise, when in the construction of the National Transcontinental railway he 'got to know all the hardship and roughness of Canadian pioneering life'. He also experienced 'the Canadian virgin forest in its size and beauty, as well, however, in its formidableness'.

A case of kidney tuberculosis caused by infected milk, resulted – as has been mentioned – in removal of a kidney. When after his recovery he returned from Germany, facilitated by an influential New Yorker family, Father initially worked in New York for a few months as a daily reporter for a few newspapers: '[T]his profession, perhaps the most exciting of all, provided me with an insight into the American psyche with all its passion for action, novelty and sensationalism.' He considered this one of the most interesting memories of the time he spent in the States.

On the invitation of a friend he eventually went back to Ottawa, to try to set himself up as an independent entrepreneur. Also of interest is his realization of the structure and system of the British Empire. He was able to garner these observations through the opportunity given him by a friend's father, the Canadian Lord Chief Justice, to frequent Rideau Hall, the Governor General's residence. Father's notes about the time he spent in the USA and Canada were published under the title *Zwischen London und Moskau* (Between London and Moscow). A short excerpt is interesting, included here:

'The social life of the Canadian capital had a particular charm of its own. It centred round Rideau Hall, the Governor General's residence, master of which was the Duke of Connaught, brother of Edward VII at the time an especially worthy representative of the British Crown. The Duchess was a German princess, Margarete of Prussia, daughter of our 'Red Prince' of the [18]70 war. I was taken to Rideau Hall by a friend's father, Canada's Lord High Justice. I spent many agreeable hours in the home of this English aristocrat the Governor and his wife, who was particularly kind to me as a German, as well as their beautiful daughter Patricia, later Lady Patricia Ramsay. My violin too occasionally gave a good performance. I saw the aged Duke again at a later date during my time as ambassador in London. He was then in his eighties and yet remembered in a very friendly way a number of little episodes we had experienced in common from those days.

'Ottawa society, revolving round Government House consisted of the families of the government officials, Ministers, judges, officers and leading personalities from the business world. All prominent families from the whole country were invited to the receptions and festivities at Rideau Hall.

'In those days, as a young man, I already noted with admiration in what a clever way, while leaving her dominions their complete independence, England comprehends how nevertheless – and actually only through the person of the governor general – to keep them closely bound to the mother country on all issues. From the renowned Lord Strathcona of the Hudson Bay Co. on, to this day a number of the leading successful Canadian families, old or new, are bound to the British throne through a peerage or a knighthood. Business interests in many fields are also closely intra-connected with England and other dominions. This was the reason for the proclamation in Ottawa in 1932 of the new major Imperial Economic Conference (Ottawa Conference) …

'Neither the First nor the Second World Wars were popular in Canada, nevertheless English politics succeeded in that the sons of Canadians unhesitatingly enlisted in both. This was also the case in the other Dominions. This strong cohesion of the Commonwealth is the great achievement of the British royal house and one of the secrets of the British imperial system which, in its organic growth, built on the experience of many generations, is a *chef d'oeuvre par excellence* of organization and of the art of governance.'

From discussions with my parents, which were naturally particularly intense during our time in London, some of the structures of British society were, however, known to me from an early age. In this way, before we moved to London I knew that a peer's title is inherited by the eldest son only, whose brothers often have another name. The formal principle of equality of birth, which has often played such a role on the Continent, therefore does not exist. My parents also did not omit to point out that in Britain, snobbishness, in the sense of class distinction, is often more marked there than it is for us, but and consequently not so much publicized. The consistent 'shuffling' of peers – encouraged by the government per se – saw to a constant regeneration.

In the First World War Father served as an officer of the Torgau Hussars, and in 1917, after being wounded and suffering illnesses he was awarded the Iron Cross First Class, and posted to Turkey in the spring of 1918 as adjutant to the German military plenipotentiary. After some adventures which led him as far afield as Odessa, in 1919 he finally reached Germany again via Italy and was transferred to the War Ministry. This is how he described the early time he spent in Germany again after the end of the war:

'One day I had to present myself before General von Seeckt, whom I knew already from Constantinople, and was to travel to Versailles with him. This did not come to pass. When we received the text of the Treaty in Berlin, I read it through in one night and then threw it away, in the sacred conviction that there could not be any German government that would sign such a thing. Foreign Minister Count v. Brockdorff-Rantzau resigned but it was still signed, notwithstanding.

'Had I still wavered as to whether I should remain an active soldier, the question was thus decided. I left the army and became a businessman again. To go into business was an easy decision to make, as in the years I had spent in English-speaking countries I had acquired fundamental business knowledge. However, at first I encountered greater difficulties than I had expected. In Germany, in the commercial field a former *Hussar Oberleutnant* (Lieutenant) apparently did not inspire confidence, nor was there less mistrust of American experience in business life.

'Nevertheless, in the early summer of 1919 I found an ideal field of activity in the Berlin branch of an old-established Bremen firm of cotton importers. I had not been scared off by the difficulties I encountered at first, they had instead reinforced my resolution. I was in fact soon able to be granted full powers by the owners of the firm and, when I had succeeded in bringing off certain favourable transactions, I earned the increasing confidence of my bosses, who in my regard, in true Hanseatic manner demonstrated great generosity.

'This was of special importance for me, for my Canadian capital had been lost and, at the onset of the burgeoning times of inflation, as a result of a heavy Swiss debt incurred for my brother's illness, my father was in a serious financial situation. I was able to help him, in fact to save his house in Naumburg. Of course, this meant that all of my early earnings evaporated, but the moving affection of my father, who never forgot this, was the greatest thanks I could have …

'In 1920, I was asked in my work to choose between Bremen and Berlin. My father-in-law Henkell's [cotton] firm had made me the offer of a partnership in their representation in Berlin to replace their representative who had died. I chose Berlin, at the same time venturing to start my own import–export business, making use of the connections I had already established in diverse European countries, principally England and France. I was able to realize my plan in a few years and to make good success of it. By the mid-1920s my import–export business was one of the largest of its kind.'

Father's description should be complemented a little. The firm my father joined had among other agencies the representation of the Henkell firm in Berlin. To be noted is that these company representatives were independent businessmen. Their owners had excellent contacts with their clientele, so that relations with the firm represented were absolutely reciprocal. It was only after the Second World War that sales organizations were converted to employing salaried representatives. These agents did not represent the Henkell firm alone, but also other most diverse enterprises of their sector. The owners were therefore businessmen independent of the firms represented. It is only because of the defamation of my father – I have already quoted Goebbels before – that it was stated as a fact: Father was in consequence in no way dependent on his father-in-law!

To go back to Father's further career in business, he wished, as has been said, to make use of the experience he had acquired abroad and have his own import-export firm. The starting point was a recommendation Grandfather Henkell gave him, upon which Father went to Reims. In the First World War Grandfather Henkell had been of assistance to a French business friend in Reims, whom he knew through his winery, when the latter got into serious trouble with the German occupation authorities, being suspected of spying. Grandfather had vouched for him and was in consequence well regarded in Reims.

Father succeeded right away in obtaining the agency for Germany of one of the foremost champagne producers of those days, namely the firm of Pommery. It developed into a long-lasting friendship between him and the owners, the Polignac family. The Marquis de Polignac had helped me to find a lawyer in Paris when I was in most uncomfortable conditions as a prisoner of war of the French. For Father's part, he had successfully intervened on behalf of a Polignac family member who was in difficulties with the German occupation authorities over possession of undeclared hunting firearms.

Shortly thereafter Father obtained the sole representation for Germany of the famous Johnnie Walker whisky brand. The company's owner, Sir Alexander Walker, also kept faith with our family after the war, when he unhesitatingly provided my mother and me, waiving repayment, with the means for payment of a French lawyer who was to defend my rights as prisoner before the French judiciary. There followed a series of renowned foreign brands of spirits who gave Father's firm representation for Germany, so that he was soon able to name the firm 'Impegroma', which stood for '*Imp*-ort and *e*-xport of *gro*- sser-*ma* –rken' (major brands).

In the Anglo-Saxon countries personal defamation of political opponents has a much longer tradition than it has with us. As is the case for all expertise, in this field too subtleness and great refinement were frequently exercised. During the 1936 Royal crisis, for example, an English newspaper that was on the side of Edward VIII printed a photograph of his brother the Duke of York when, on the run from reporters, he was just disappearing, sleeves flying, through his front door. The caption was: 'The Duke of York in a hurry!' As in the case of the king's abdication the Duke of York was in line for succession to the throne, the photograph and caption insinuated that the Duke was in a hurry to be king. The expression goes back to Benjamin Disraeli, who attacked his political party opponent, the aged Prime Minister William Ewart Gladstone, labelling him 'an old man in a hurry', implying that because he was old he wanted, quickly, to do something of historical significance. As far as I know, at issue was the Home Rule Bill for Ireland. In this way, English newspapers, who were stirring up antagonism against Father's efforts to bring about German-British cooperation, found the attribute for him of 'the champagne-selling diplomat'. It was also adopted in Germany by interested circles and belonged for a while among the standard stock of formulations demeaning Father. It is the sort of thing that always, at the outset of a major political career, has an effect on an easy target. They preferentially point the finger at such as have not taken the smooth path of a career, the most likely being a Party post and the Civil Service. It is curious, nonetheless, that persons – whether in Germany or abroad – purporting to be convinced democrats should feel they have to mock Father's business activities. It would be most amusing to scrutinize the origins and course of the career of our German government ministers, among whom there was just recently a minister for foreign affairs fawned over by the media who, other than a taxi driver's permit, had neither a secondary school nor so much as a professional qualification. In the attempt by some to diminish Father's status because of his firm's field of activity, he was in the best of company. Stresemann was attacked by his political opponents for having compiled a doctorate thesis on the importance of the Berlin bottled beer industry.[441]

Joachim von Ribbentrop can be designated as a successful businessman. His success enabled my parents to enjoy a comfortable lifestyle for the circumstances of the time. Grandfather Henkell's lawyer, who had advised Grandfather in legal matters along his profitable entrepreneurial path, once said to us that Father had been one of the few to comprehend the inflation that began in the early 1920s. These were the years when, outside of business affairs, he made the friends and acquaintances who were the basis for his later entry into politics. His business partners in France and England belonged in those circles from which the leading political personalities were also recruited. Thereby Father had connections in England and France who could be bridges to German politics. Thanks to his personality, however, he also found doors opening for him in Berlin. Here I must touch upon one more defamatory calumny concerning Father's position in the Berlin of the 1920s, for it claims that twice he was not accepted, or that he was 'blackballed' in the ballot, for admittance to the Union Club, that then held a place of political importance in Berlin. According to information from the Club Secretary of long standing, Herr von Beaulieu, Father was a member of the Union Club from 10 August 1928 by decision of the acceptance committee.[442]

From the interest in politics he had acquired from Grandfather – for instance, during the First World War he had written articles from Turkey for the then very well-known Berlin *Vossische Zeitung* – he found the way to approach political personalities, on both the German side as well as the diplomatic corps accredited to Berlin. His leaning politically was toward Stresemann, whom he also knew. I recollect furthermore – this is in connection with the 'Good morning' that we as well-behaved children had to say and which we downright disliked having to do – greeting a series of foreign diplomats: among others British ambassador Edgar Vincent d'Abernon, Brazilian ambassador Quintana and French ambassador Pierre de Margerie, who was particularly friendly to us children. It is to be said again that it was precisely these connections to political circles that induced Hitler to ask Father in 1933 to sound out the possibilities of exercising Hitler's foreign policies in the countries of the West.

Whoever is in a position to see through the fog of targeted calumnies cannot fail to acknowledge that Father's career, his talents, international connections and, finally, his success personally and in business, were a good basis for involvement in the foreign policy sector. True, anyone who considers that the best training to become a German diplomat is that of a Prussian assessor and administrative lawyer – as far as possible as member of a student fraternity – may not be of the same opinion. Added thereto, Father was an excellent sportsman. He rode, could shoot with accuracy, especially with a shotgun – a particularly important accomplishment in England for knotting or reinforcing contacts – and played tennis and golf. His lifestyle corresponded to that of the political circles, above all in England and France. I have already mentioned his exceptional gift for languages. I find myself obliged to write of these qualities in every form that my father possessed so as to demonstrate how distortedly his career and his importance are depicted today, triggered by the targeted calumnies in the interest of his enemies. They are slanders that were then taken up by scribblers out of convenience and opportunism and, from being repeated, gradually became 'the truth'. There is no recourse for those still stricken today – that is such as our family. An insertion here of an interesting example from history: the name 'Lucrezia Borgia' is unwittingly associated by most people with daggers, poison, murder and debauchery. If it is looked up in the *Brockhaus Encyclopedia*, the following will be found: 'Her evil repute lingering over the centuries came about through calumny.' If – ever subject to an angle of objectivity – Father possessed the optimum qualifications to be entrusted with foreign affairs, it was precisely these attributes which constituted his aptitude for it, namely talent, personality, career, experience abroad, connections, circle of friends, origins as well as lifestyle and attitudes, that represented major handicaps for him to evolve with success in Hitler's regime and system, and to enable his concept of foreign policy to prevail.

In the 1920s he still perceived the prospects and entertained the hope – certainly not least from his acquaintance with Stresemann – of seeing in time the Reich's claim for equality of rights restored to a course of negotiation by means of a parliamentary German government. Now he had to become increasingly aware that the claim would not be conceded to the Weimar Republic's governments. Added to this was the acknowledgement of a Communist threat domestically, as also of one externally from the Soviets. In the growing German Communist Party the Soviet Union possessed an ever stronger Trojan Horse. The economic crisis, with its army of millions of unemployed, was the ideally fertile ground for radical solutions, from wherever they came.

At a later date Mother told me one day that on the occasion of the Young Plan referendum, Father had declared for the first time that he had decided to take up a position against adoption of the plan, which fixed the amount of German reparation debts and their settlement. I have already mentioned that the last instalment had been due a few years earlier. Moreover, the Young Plan lacked the so-called 'Transfer Clause'[443] of the foregoing Dawes Plan, according to which payment due could be suspended when the necessary foreign currency was not available. Following an acceptance of the Young Plan, the Reich could therefore possibly be exposed to suffer measures of coercion.

At this time Father was fully aware that the 'social question' had to be resolved if Germans wanted to tackle the problems of foreign policy – above all to be relieved from the greatest pressures of the Versailles Treaty terms. As things stood, such a resolution could come about only either under Communist auspices or through Hitler! His slogan at the time addressed to his foreign friends was: 'Give Brüning a chance, or else we shall have Hitler or Communism!'

Father's stance to Hitler and his regime was determined exclusively from the point of view of foreign policy. It was up to the Party to guarantee the cohesion of the German people; this was in his view, after the experience of the First World War and the 'Weimar' days, the crucial prerequisite so as to attain the 'Revision Notes' (of the Treaty of Versailles) which would provide the Reich, in its position in the middle, with the indispensable means for defence necessary to be capable of repulsing the aggressive Soviet Bolshevism. This point of view of Father's as to the cruciality of the issue should be borne in mind when the retrospective question is asked why he 'cooperated' with Hitler's regime. The disaster of the First World War, the deprivation of the Reich of its rights by the Treaty of Versailles and finally the threat of Bolshevization – with its unforeseeable consequences for the whole of Europe – permitted it to justify the utilization of extraordinary means to counter these risks, at least in the interior. However, never did Father place himself beyond the bounds of the *Rechtsstaat* (state under the rule of law).

When I was a boy not yet 11 years old I had a friend, Heinz Körner – killed in 1941 – whose father was a Supreme Court Councillor. This judge was a practising devout Evangelist Christian, as far as I could tell at that time, utterly upright, and as he was described to me by my friend a patriot, albeit anything but a National Socialist. I have already said that we youngsters were of course perfectly cognizant of the events of the First World War, foremost of the Battle of the Marne, Germany's fateful battle. We were therefore aware of how calamitously the Kaiser and his Chief of Staff, the 'younger Moltke', had failed when they sent the pitiable Lieutenant Colonel Hentsch[444] to the forces of the army's right wing and left the decision to him whether there should be an advance against Paris, which lay not far in front of the armies, or whether, due to a localized crisis, a retreat should be effected.

At the time my friend told me that his father had said that if he had known of Lieutenant Colonel Hentsch's mission and had had the opportunity, he would have had him shot. Körner the elder, judge at the Berlin Court of Appeal, was a man of strong convictions! It had then preoccupied me greatly, because it was the attitude of a strict and upright jurist and devout *pater familias*. Execute an innocent man, to avert harm to the fatherland? A person who was guilty only because of destiny and with no personal perpetration? Whoever did not live through it cannot imagine to what extent the catastrophe of 1918 and the desperate situation of the Reich was universally uppermost and the ambience was propitious to a readiness to accept extraordinary measures and circumstances.

Joachim von Ribbentrop may be reproached that after 1933 he concerned himself too little with the domestic affairs of Germany. Mother, however, once said to me that shortly after Hitler formed a government, in the realization of which as has been seen Father had taken part, he will, in view of any illegal occurrences, have had spontaneous doubts about whether they were right. His concern was, however, ultimately for foreign policy issues. He was utterly convinced that to change horses in mid-stream, i.e. replace Hitler, in the perilously needy situation the Reich found itself, was out of the question; it would in his view have led sooner or later to a Bolshevization of Central Europe, irrespective of the matter of who could overthrow Hitler, going against the prevailing opinions of the population. There was nothing to be done but to brave out the risk phase of Hitler and his regime: anything else was at present something to leave until later to worry about. During the war this dilemma Father was in became much more marked. To remove Hitler would set the seal on defeat in the form postulated by Roosevelt and Churchill of 'unconditional surrender', with the incursion of the Soviets into Central Europe. Who, today, can imagine the desperate predicament faced in those days by many good Germans: their own country in a life-or-death battle, led by a dictator and his regime which did not appear acceptable to them?

My father had entered politics as a 'Johnny-come-lately', as it is called nowadays when someone has not had to tread the slow, hard path of Party hierarchy. Coming as he was from a different background, he was not inured in and steeled to the infighting of the Party for influence and power. The quarrelling, intrigues, factional struggles and fractionizing were unknown to him. He lacked the opportunity to get to know those under Hitler's influence – who were reciprocally influencing him as well – to assess their character and estimate their weight. These people at the head of the regime, with whom he had to cooperate, were foreign to him as to their origins and mentality. He had come into favour with the Führer 'from the top', and many envied him his position and influence. Goebbels' aspiration, as was said then, was to occupy the post of Foreign Minister himself. He had gone to Geneva with the German delegation to the League of Nations in 1933 and had perhaps been encouraged to a certain degree by Hitler to entertain hopes of an appointment at some time. As he entered into politics my father had no access to the world with which he was now connected, which was personified by Hitler and the leading Party figures.

Whoever wishes to deal in politics has to be influential. In a democracy, for a start the leading players are independent of the electorate. Of greater importance is the delegate from the local association who will vote in the Party

Rally, thereby determining who the actors are to be. In a dictatorship this is the dictator, which is particularly valid in the case of a manic power-grasping sole ruler such as was Hitler. Whoever wishes in consequence to exert any influence in a dictatorship must have the dictator's ear, or else will have no opportunity to realize his political objectives. His conduct has to be submitted to this goal or he must otherwise withdraw from politics – to this extent Father had to be in tune with the spirit of those times. There is an additional circumstance in connection with this problem area: Father fought with Hitler over the so-called world-view aspect of National Socialism. He once said to me: 'With whom, abroad, if you think about it, should I discuss foreign policy issues? All our foreign interlocutors belong in groups whose toes we are treading on.' It is perfectly reasonable that a foreign minister should wish to exercise his politics free as far as possible from ideological constraints. In this case there was no other way open to Father but to disclose his 'open flank', meaning to expose himself to the reproach that he was 'betraying' the National Socialist world-view, a whispered rumour of propaganda targeting him, among other things, as upholding a pro-Russian policy. It was after all not only the Jewish question that was a grave burden on German foreign policy. Father spoke of a further 'great power' that was placed on the side of Germany's opponents – among the 'world-view' opponents were ranged the socialists, liberals, capitalists, freemasons, monarchists, some races, representatives of certain artistic movements and not least the churches, Rotary Clubs and many more. All of these increased the number of enemies of the Reich in its already desperate position of isolation.

Wherever it was appropriate, Bolshevism reckoned with the internationality of the proletariat, thereby representing a principle that could ensure its popularity all over the world with the corresponding classes. If Stalin was now pursuing a policy of classic power-play, he found a convenient cover in this principle. The National Socialist racial theory, above all through its inherent value-components, constituted major problems for foreign policy, restricting gravely the Reich's field of play in this field.

The ideology of liberty and prosperity, eschewing colonialism, that Roosevelt broadcast in the American sense of mission, could also be assured of broadly diffused international resonance, especially in the Third World, albeit equally in the liberal, socialist and intellectual circles of Europe. Father, however, as a foreign affairs politician, could not seek interlocutors abroad along the principles of National Socialism. There is no doubt that this vulnerable flank was constantly targeted, particularly when the war situation deteriorated and increasingly geared Hitler towards the world-view motivation of his Russian war.

It is tempting to think of the famous correspondence between Bismarck (during his time as delegate to the Frankfurt Bundestag) and the Prussian General Leopold von Gerlach, an adviser to King Friedrich Wilhelm IV. Bismarck had been invited to Paris by the Prussian delegate there on the occasion of an industrial exhibition, when he made the acquaintance of Napoleon III, perhaps also seeking a meeting but in any case not avoiding one. He was castigated for this by the royal court and its extremely conservative faction, to which Gerlach too belonged. The reason was that Napoleon III's legitimacy was disputed and the conclusion drawn therefrom that no politics could be conducted with him. Bismarck's impressive arguments set down in this correspondence are still worth reading today from the angle of a foreign policy free of ideology. In 1860, Bismarck apparently formulated it that 'one cannot play chess if 16 of the 64 squares are forbidden from the beginning'.[445] This can be transferred to the period treated now to query how many 'squares' were out of bounds or at least very difficult to access for German foreign policy, for ideological reasons, on the global chess board. True, with his 'Russian policy' Father had disregarded these world-view hurdles, in the sense of a genuine *Realpolitik*. Ideology can, if necessary, constitute a weapon in a foreign-political conflict. For example, today the call for 'democratization' is raised every time it is expedient but it must not impose limitations on the flexibility of one's own political options. United States governments, for instance, have never shied away from cooperating with dictators when the purposes of their foreign policy were served, in the first place with Stalin. Roosevelt and Stalin were in agreement in applying the ideologies at their disposal, in the sense of an imperialist policy in the broadest sense.

Father did not come from the same stable as the old Party comrades, which for Hitler was an important factor. Hitler's loyalty to old comrades-at-arms often bordered upon the inexplicable. Father formulated it thus:[446]

> 'Adolf Hitler's loyalty toward those who had once done something for him sometimes bordered on the unbelievable. On the other hand, he could be inexplicably mistrustful. He was only too prone to come under influence, yea believe in tittle-tattle, from persons who knew how to hoodwink him cleverly, which brought out the less appealing sides of his character. He was also capable of purposely wounding people.'

Whoever wanted to exert influence had to adjust to the style of the times, and it was Hitler who determined this style. In 1933, Father was placed *à la suite* of the SS, meaning he was given an honorary rank, initially as Standartenführer, entitling him to wear uniform. The rank was bestowed by Hitler, or at least with his assent. The idea was to reinforce Father's position – as an outsider – within the Party and in a way to assimilate him outwardly; he thereby was able, on corresponding occasions, to appear in uniform, conforming to the style of the day. Mention could be made, without reiterating the comparison between Bismarck and my father – which Hitler once made in a quite definite context and which is thereafter quoted (with relish, and naturally with intent to disparage) – that Bismarck had for example been posted *à la suite* of the Pasewalker cuirassiers so as to be able to appear in uniform on appropriate occasions. It is not only from this image, which Franz von Lenbach has repeatedly immortalized – but who painted the Chancellor in civilian clothes just as often – that the appellation of 'Iron Chancellor' derives, which Bismarck with his sensitive constitution was anything but.

Every epoch has its style, as is today easily observed when eminent politicians go about in an open shirt and baker's boy cap, appearing thus clad at the races or the opera. The introduction of the uniform for the staff of the Auswärtiges Amt should also be seen from this point of view. It was supposed to facilitate their work in this 'uniformed' state and to proclaim the independence of the Amt from any state- or party-controlled organization. The problem of the firm consolidation of the Auswärtiges Amt in Hitler's eyes arose for Father from the moment he became the chief of this office. Under Neurath, the Amt had remained conservative, that is had not become National Socialist. Hitler let Neurath do as he liked, but, as so often manipulating multiple tracks, he made Father his close foreign policy adviser while at the same time permitting the foreign policy activities of the Party and Alfred Rosenberg to continue. His aversion to the Amt remained, however, also after Father's appointment, and consequently henceforth constituted a crippling open flank for Father's position – always concurrently having an impact on policy – that was favourable to his opponents. In connection with the Scheliha spying affair – he had passed information in Warsaw to a Russian in return for remuneration – Goebbels stressed: 'What is to be expected from a ministry in which the country's traitors are constantly coming and going freely!' Hitler's dislike of the Amt was made use of for intrigues, whereby specific employees were frequently targeted. Although in such cases Father stood by his staff loyally, it was often sufficient to ensure that, to Hitler, the insinuations were enough to be effective.

Karlfried Count Dürckheim was part of the '*Dienststelle Ribbentrop*'. He had been recommended to Father by Hess, although he was not entirely 'Aryan'. Father had not hesitated to employ Dürckheim, because of his knowlefge of British affairs. In 1941 he sent him to Japan on an official mission, not least to get him out of the line of fire of the intensifying anti-Semitism in Germany. For the duration of the war his salary in East Asia was paid by the Auswärtiges Amt upon Father's instructions.[447] Dürckheim was once interviewed on television as a contemporary witness,[448] when he made a noteworthy statement: 'Ribbentrop never let anybody down!'[449]

In different circumstances it could well have been risking his neck. As is known, the deputy chief of counterintelligence, General Oster, had regularly been passing on the dates of the attacks planned in the Western campaign to the Dutch military attaché, Sas.[450] The fact in itself was known through German telephone surveillance, without the source having been localized. This is how it came about that counterintelligence directed its suspicions against Mme von Steengracht. This could have had fatal consequences for her and her husband, who was an employee of Father's.[451] When he gave Father his word of honour that the suspicion was groundless, Father stood up for him one hundred per cent. General Oster, a pastor's son, would have had no compunction about attributing the worst blame to the innocent so as to save himself and conceal his betrayal of military secrets.[452]

If in his diaries, Goebbels maintains that my father had no friends in the regime, and one can hardly contradict him, it is worth asking why he was not able to form a friendly relationship, or at least one not so tense, with some of his colleagues in the Cabinet or in the highest echelons of the Reich. It must first of all be borne in mind that Hitler himself did not really see cordial relations among colleagues in a favourable light. I do not wish to judge for myself to what extent he went a step further to keep them apart as far as possible, and possibly even consciously created tensions among them, but from what I have heard it is perfectly credible. The fact alone, already mentioned, that in Father's days Cabinet sessions were no longer held speaks for the hypothesis. Speculation remains if he should not have been able to make friends among the leading figures of the regime, in the sense of 'variable majorities' as it is termed in parliamentary language, so as to safeguard and even bolster his influence, and to further his goal of pushing through his aims in foreign policy.

Personalities who could have been considered as being effective in this sense were Göring, Goebbels, Himmler and Hess. From the outset of his political activity, Father had had good relations with Blomberg, from the latter's appointment as Special Envoy for Disarmament. However, Father's post as

Foreign Minister coincided with Blomberg's dismissal. There was no further close or even so much as a personal relationship with any leading figure in the Wehrmacht. Tensions between foreign affairs and the army leadership are virtually a classic theme in history; one need think here only of Blücher's 'pen-pushers', as he called diplomats, or of the murky relations between Bismarck and Moltke the Elder before Paris in 1871. Nevertheless, the total lack of contact between Father and Generals Keitel and Jodl, as well as with Raeder, is food for thought.

The negative attitude of the original army chief (Beck) to Hitler's policies should not be overlooked, which already in 1938 had led to conspiring with the potential opponent, which certainly did not construe a relation of confidence with the foreign affairs department, which, at this point in time – unavoidably– considered a certain audacity in decisions of foreign policy as a necessity. This was in contrast to 1941, when the Foreign Minister did everything in his power to avert war with Russia whilst the military underestimated the risk and made a fatal error.[453] During the war I had occasion a few times to be present with Father at a short lecture on the situation by the liaison officer of the OKW (High Command of the Wehrmacht) to the Auswärtiges Amt, Colonel von Geldern. The Foreign Minister could not have been worse briefed as to the military situation. It was not ill-meant by Colonel von Geldern, but was part of Hitler's system of keeping departments separate so as to be able to come down on either side as arbiter. Father's entourage mockingly referred to the information received by the Foreign Minister about the military situation as the 'expanded Wehrmacht report'. These minor supplementations to the actual Wehrmacht report consisted of a few negligible details handed out to the press by the OKW.

I would have wished that my father had overridden Hitler's 'system' in that he had tried to form some personal contact at least with Keitel or Jodl, so as to be more or less in the picture – even were it 'from the back door' – as to the true military situation. It is, however, doubtful whether it could have been achieved. I point to Schnurre's perception of avoidance of a war with Russia expressed to Generals Keitel, Jodl and Warlimont, and the fruitless outcome of his efforts. It was hardly feasible to establish a tolerable rapport with Göring or Goebbels; the necessary artfulness for this was not an ingredient in Father's personality structure. To form a coalition with people such as Göring or Goebbels would have necessitated also to a certain degree delivering oneself into their hands. This left Hess and Himmler. Hess was already considered a misfit, and his position with Hitler as not a particularly strong one. Hess once wrote a letter to Father in which he complained that 'Madame your wife shops in Jewish stores'; such stores were neither singled out nor was shopping there forbidden. It indicated reservations as to Father. It is possible that Hess in his view wrote the letter with 'good intentions' – there is no doubt he was not prone to intrigue. In any case it is evidence how meticulously and critically from the Party's side the conduct of the elders was observed and occasionally criticized, being at any time fertile ground for intrigue.

This left Himmler. For a time, in the framework of the circumstances, Father had normal relations with him, until from the outset of the war an 'enmity to the death', as Father expressed it, gradually developed. He finally reckoned with the worst from Himmler.[454] Initially, Himmler took pains with the new Minister for Foreign Affairs. It should be added to this that Himmler was the big loser in the so-called Fritsch crisis. The outcome of the affair is well known. Fritsch evidently did not behave very cleverly towards Hitler, which increasingly irritated the latter. I shall not resurrect here the story of the Blomberg-Fritsch crisis. Only to be noted is that in this case it is confirmed that it was not a question of a planned intrigue on Hitler's part. Hitler had exchanged the Brauchitsch-Halder pair for Fritsch-Beck for himself. He therefore had no need to take the whole problematic domestic and foreign politics 'affair' upon himself for the purpose.[455] Nonetheless, Himmler was affected insofar as Hitler held it against him that the SD (Security Service) and Gestapo had acted most inefficiently, erroneously informing Hitler and thereby putting him in a difficult situation. Mother told me at the time that Himmler had complained bitterly to Göring that he himself was now the scapegoat. It was also in this context that she said that Hitler never appointed Fritsch Commander in Chief of the army because he did not 'fully cooperate' in the creation of major motorized formations.[456] This is how Hitler will have expressed it to Father. In any case, when Fritsch was then transferred to 'Chief' of an artillery regiment he seemed completely rehabilitated to the outside.

In this situation Himmler sought allies wherever he could find them. Himmler impressed Father at first as being most down-to-earth. Father clearly saw Himmler's efforts to create a convincing elite through the incorporation of old elites, including such as the aristocracy. The potential of the foreign intelligence service of the SS could have been of use. There were also potent grounds not to cut oneself off from Himmler's approaches, who was more needed to be reckoned with, preferably as an ally rather than an opponent. The Auswärtiges Amt, of which Hitler was not fond and which was ill-disposed toward Father, the 'outsider', did not constitute a reliable base for him. When barely six weeks had passed since Father had taken over the Amt, a dynamic of foreign policy set in that for more than three years – until the beginning of the Russian war – made for a highly tense atmosphere in foreign affairs, such as is rarely seen in modern history. It allowed Father no leeway of time to get to know, one by one, the staff of his Amt personally, let alone to institute a reshuffle or even so much as a reorganization. Himmler's attempts to acquire influence over foreign policy, not least through the so-called '*Polizeiattachés*' he placed in the German missions abroad, among other effects swiftly led to estrangement. Later, in the so-called 'Luther affair', Himmler tried to have Father overthrown.[457]

Joachim von Ribbentrop may be reproached with not having counteracted Hitler's game of playing the departments and their chiefs against one another by seeking a dialogue with the leading figures of the regime, even when they were his rivals or opponents. However, in the end it was but two important decisions that could have been influenced if he had. In the first, Father could have sought support to avert the attack on Russia and the declaration of war on the United States. It is extremely doubtful whether it would have been feasible to recruit 'combat comrades' against Hitler in this sense. Göring's intervention, described by Schnurre, to attempt to persuade Hitler to maintain a sustainable relationship with the Soviet Union speaks for itself. If allies had been found, it would have been most improbable that they could have been incited to cooperate in a common cause. Moreover, since it was not supported by the military, it is certain the venture would have failed. For the second, he would have needed all conceivable 'allies' to achieve Hitler's agreement to put out peace feelers toward the Soviets. It would finally have made sense to have a picture reflecting the true realities of the state and the dimensions of German resources rather than to have to rely on data provided by Hitler.

The information received through the liaison officer to the OKW – as has been said – was unworthy of the acting Foreign Minister. This was the reason why in 1944 he sent an employee from the earliest days, Gottfriedsen, to the front of the invasion so as to be briefed on the actual state of the military situation. Picture this: the Foreign Minister is obliged to send – almost unofficially – an employee to the front so as to obtain realistic information about the military situation. Gottfriedsen had also visited me before Caen, and I have no doubt whatsoever about the relative military strength ratio, in particular as to the absolute Allied air superiority. The shot that had gone through my back from a strafing aircraft vividly underscored my perception. Gottfriedsen's information, and my own descriptions which I passed to Father shortly after on the occasion of convalescent leave, were expressed in a memorandum from Father to Hitler in which once again he urged immediate negotiations for peace.

One would be glad to have retrospectively ascertained the disloyalty necessary for Father, for him to establish contact with the persons concerned, behind Hitler's back, which would have given him access to all important internal information. When Father was appointed Foreign Minister, Grandmother Henkell, who was very fond of him, made him a present of a gold cigarette case (which I still have) with the date engraved, and made the wish 'I hope he is a Talleyrand!' Father used to say of himself 'I am no Talleyrand!', as he did not wish to be seen as such because of Talleyrand's dubious human qualities. Irrespective of this, there was unfortunately nobody in Germany who could have played the role of a Talleyrand, who, regardless of his personal ruthlessness, as the descendant of one of France's oldest families – and moreover enjoying indestructible esteem from all sides as a figurehead of the Revolution – saw through all the revolutionary turmoil and military conflicts, time and again occupying the highest offices of state.

Father was loyal to Hitler. For Father, that was not merely a question of decency; it was also for reasons of state, in the sense that it would have inevitably had devastating repercussions on German policies if he were to broadcast to the outside the various differences of opinion he had with Hitler, or had even indulged in intrigue. The image of determination and unity in the state leadership was indispensable to demonstrate a strength – that had not yet materialized to any great extent and was consequently part of the game of poker to be played – so as to be able to achieve Germany's needs in a peaceful manner. Father's loyalty also consisted in firmly giving Hitler his opinions privately, as well as defending them against him. Since his discussions with Hitler on subjects requiring significant decisions were conducted on a one-to-one basis – as was Hitler's way – they mostly had no witnesses. This gave Hitler the opportunity – and I have no reason to doubt that he took advantage of it – to use his Foreign Minister's putative opinions and judgement as arguments to third parties, of which the latter was completely unaware. Father writes:[458]

'I have also been reproached with having been weak in my handling of Hitler. He for his part called me his "most difficult subordinate",[459] because I always very calmly set forth my point of view, frequently contrary to his, even when he believed he had convinced me.'

However, for just those reasons of state Father was obliged to stand loyally by Hitler in the latter's final decisions. When they had been reached by Hitler despite Father's contrary opinion, the minister had no choice but to accept them out of loyalty so as not to cause damage to the Reich, unless he resigned. As the resignation of a foreign minister is nevertheless a high-grade political issue, from this point of view too Father was not entirely master of his decision. The decisive element in forming a judgement of Father's role lies in Hitler's way of working. He convened no Cabinet session from which the positions taken up by the participants were officially minuted. His increasing touchiness often made for a discussion to take place in a *tête-à-tête*, especially when something had to be effected against his will. The criticism of Father's observers at this time – even those with the best intentions – always runs along the lines that he did not stand by his opinion vis à vis Hitler: that he was a 'yes-man'. There is very little to support this, in fact quite the contrary. Goebbels – as already mentioned – criticizes Father's 'inflexibility' toward Hitler. Hewel notes – as has been said – the 'tug-o'-war' between Father and Hitler over the latter's wish to respond to Roosevelt's speech with a speech in reply, finally recording what Hitler had said to him: 'I would not like to have to work under your chief for as much as three weeks!' It will have to be admitted, as I record these instances, that they do not point to 'bondage' on Father's part toward Hitler, as is today maintained by many sides.

Dr Werner Best,[460] the Reich Plenipotentiary for Denmark, whose post was under the Auswärtiges Amt as Denmark had remained officially a sovereign state, also mentions Ribbentrop's 'subservience' toward Hitler, 'particularly at the beginning of the war'. At that time, Best hardly knew my father at all, except for a very brief professional contact years earlier that had concerned suspicion of a colleague in the Ribbentrop *Dienststelle*. In this first meeting with him, Best describes Father as 'generous, comprehending, controlled, dexterous and likeable'. What Best said later is purely based on hearsay, that is to say the calumnies spread about by Weizsäcker and the conspirators. According to his own account, while he was working in Denmark he had seen Father just five times. In every other aspect he speaks of him in positive terms. He stresses that Father always maintained a 'judicious' policy for the Reich toward Denmark. He concedes Father demonstrated 'personal courage', for example by refuting claims harmful to German foreign policy put forward by other departments. His verdict of 'subservience' consequently relies mainly on hearsay, and since he enjoyed an amiable relation with Weizsäcker, this will most probably have been his source.

Best explicitly mentions an occasion when Father defended him, against whom from Himmler's side an intrigue was plotted, to Hitler. He mentions another submission of Father's to Hitler on 19 September 1943, recorded in the law papers of the Copenhagen court, in which Father opposed the deportations of Jews ordered by Hitler and demanded a review of the order.[461] Best quotes an interesting example of the relations among the highest leadership of the Reich in 1944. On 19 September 1944, by order of Hitler – engineered by Himmler – the Danish police force was to be dissolved and partially incarcerated. Reich Plenipotentiary Best was specifically to be excluded from being informed, as his opinion was known. Best vehemently protested to Father, and has this to say:

> 'R. was genuinely outraged by what had happened. He had already intervened with Hitler, and had received the information that the action to be taken had resulted out of military grounds and was therefore no concern of his or mine. The prohibition of informing me had been ordered because "with me everything came to light". R. had already replied with a submission to Hitler in which he vigorously came to my defence in the accusation of treason … The text of the submission is to be found in the court papers of my Copenhagen trial; it is couched – carefully expressed – in pragmatically very energetic and courageous terms, above all in view of the general state of relations between R. and Hitler.
>
> 'He promised me every assistance in the settlement of the matter with the Danish police. He indeed kept this promise, as up until the spring of 1945 he strongly urged the reinstatement of the interned Danish policemen …
>
> 'This is how my last encounter with R. ended – as had the first – with a positive impression: the impression of his insight, good will, personal sympathy for and intervention on the side of an unjustly attacked employee. The experience also showed that R. – even when he made the effort – could no longer assert himself with Hitler.'[462]

I have given these examples so as to clarify the conditions under which Father had to attempt to conduct a halfway viable sensible foreign policy. It was up to him to decide, on every occasion that came up, when an occurrence was important enough to have another tussle with Hitler. In the course of the war in Russia, his first concern was to obtain Hitler's assent to putting out feelers for peace in the direction of the Russians. All else was secondary to this. However, without Hitler's acquiescence the attempt would have been fruitless and, as things stood in 1943–45, could have instead done more harm than good. In view of Hitler's mental state, Father had to avoid the appearance of being once again a troublemaker if he insisted on issues of lesser significance. It is understandable that Best or others may have been disappointed if Father did not succeed in putting through their proposals, however much Father himself may have been on their side. Best does, however, repeatedly say that Father tenaciously supported Best's views vis à vis Hitler.[463]

I have already mentioned that relations between Father and Hitler – that from the start had not been free of tensions – rapidly worsened when the war with Russia broke out. In the spring of 1942 matters came to a head. On this Father writes:

> 'In spring 1942 there arose a serious disagreement between Hitler and myself. The external cause of our dispute was at first inconsequential … the argument that broke out over it became ever more aggravated on both sides and eventually extended … to our opposing conceptions on the Jewish and other questions of *Weltanschauung*. This caused the cup to overflow: I heatedly asked to be let go and it was willingly granted.
>
> 'Adolf Hitler was in such a state of irritation as I had never seen before. As I prepared to leave the room he sharply rebuked me for ever bringing up objections, which was a crime against his health. The way in which he hurled this grave reproach at me shook me profoundly and made me at that moment fear the worst for him. I searched for words to calm him. The Führer begged me never to demand my departure again, and I gave my word of honour that I would not make such a demand while the war lasted.'[464]

Hitler's accusation that Father's constant contradiction would be injurious to Hitler's health is already a fatal indication of the mental and physical state of collapse in which Hitler found himself – which I myself was horrified to witness in February 1945 – but he was evidently still very good at acting, since he made such an impression on Father as to make him retract his resignation. Ribbentrop the 'patriot' – in the somewhat old-fashioned sense – lacked the callousness in personal matters which had become the style of the day. When Mother told me that when Hitler had made that scene with him, Father had retracted his resignation, once again she made that gesture – now one of desperation – of putting her hand over her mouth, and she blurted out, 'He now no longer has a chance of having his way!', meaning making contact with the Russians. Father nevertheless tried again and again to persuade Hitler of the necessity for it.

In the attitude of today, what a British historian calls 'correctness' may perhaps also be designated as 'old-fashioned', in that it could sometimes be regarded as ridiculous. Father had given the employee who handled his finances, Gottfriedsen,[465] a general order couched as follows:

'[T]hat my financial affairs during my holding office as Reich Foreign Minister be so structured as to ensure that after my demise neither the capital at disposal of my family be touched nor any increase of capital take place (with the exception of the ... one and only donation).'

In critical phases of German foreign policy Father was always prepared to submit to the requirements of the situation and if necessary to step back, as is proven by the following occurrences. In August 1936 in Bayreuth, Hitler had appointed him State Secretary in the Auswärtiges Amt following the death of Bernhard Wilhelm von Bülow. Father then asked Hitler to cancel the appointment as he was of the opinion that he could provide a more important service as ambassador in London. 'When I asked the Führer to send me to London', was how he wrote a report of the matter at the end of 1937, laying the foundations of his role as ambassador.[466]

It is obviously necessary to feel a substantial sense of duty toward an issue if one turns down the influential position of State Secretary in Berlin in Hitler's close proximity, and instead tries to clarify a fundamental question of German policy (i.e., an alliance with England) from an outpost far away from direct contact with the Führer. Father was perfectly aware in this that his mission would more probably fail than succeed. What politician willingly takes such a risk?

The second occurrence which allows clear insight into Father's preparedness to disregard his own person is his proposal, in August 1939, not to send himself – the Foreign Minister who had fought for months for an arrangement with the Soviet Union – to Moscow, but Hermann Göring instead. Father considered reaching an agreement with the Soviet Union as unconditionally essential for two reasons: firstly, in order to prevent a definitive encirclement of the Reich, which English policy had been working on for months by the well-known sending of a French-British military mission to Moscow; secondly, because he saw in a German-Soviet *rapprochement* a potential peaceful solution to the Danzig problem. These were the grounds for Father's view that negotiations in Moscow absolutely had to succeed. He was worried that his activities, which had brought about the Anti-Comintern Pact, might possibly have a negative effect on the negotiations. At the time Hitler had decided that Father should lead the negotiations. These negotiations in Moscow and the German-Russian agreement achieved thereby represented the culmination of his political activity in foreign relations. He was nevertheless prepared to renounce the glory of having achieved such an agreement for the sake of avoiding an endangerment of its successful conclusion, which he held as vital for the Reich.

It revolves upon me to show how conscientiously Father thus acted. The tussle for position and influence was a factual necessity if one wanted to have a say in anything. It is possible to have divergent views as to whether Father always proceeded expediently in defending his influence over foreign policy. Whether it made any sense to want to hold on to his position must remain anyone's guess, but it must be credited to him that for as long as he considered it the right thing, he had the right and the duty to assert his conception and his insights. In all sytems of government this has to be fought for.

Up to this point Father had no experience in the leadership of a large number of organized employees, let alone of a huge and chaotic government agency. He would at any rate have needed a capable and loyal state secretary who would have directed the department in the weighty policy decisions to be made, in alignment with Father's wishes and thus protecting his back. It was, however, that very state secretary who, in collusion with Kordt, the temporary chief of the minister's office, not only obstructed Father's policies but behind his back, for conspiratorial political reasons, calumniated and defamed him personally. The question arises whether Father did not in fact too easily facilitate these people to wreak their malice under his very eyes.

In his basic personality structure Joachim von Ribbentrop was a lone wolf, eschewing any sort of conformism. Indeed, timewise he was very reluctant to commit himself – which often made things difficult for Mother, as for instance she could never be sure at what time a meal could be served. Outside the private domain, this had negative consequences. Whoever has been a manager knows the importance of punctuality. If the boss does not keep to fixed or predetermined times, it has an undermining effect, aside from the fact that the subordinate feels disregarded. Father has been charged with frequently having kept employees of the Amt waiting. I do not wish to pass judgement on this personally; all I know is that he often showed a lack of sense of time in family rendezvous.

He also left the direction of the morning sessions of executive meetings to his state secretary, which gave the latter a god-sent opportunity to influence the top men of the Amt, in this way recruiting them to oppose the Minister, as well as German policy. The direction of the Ministry was left to a state secretary who, behind the back of the government, adjured a potential opponent to 'stick to his guns' – in other words he was one who, unbeknownst to his own government, stealthily undermined negotiations being conducted by that government. It is easy to see that this bode no good for the Minister. To have turned a blind eye to such a state of affairs was, looking back, with no doubt a serious omission of Father's. It also explains why he had no backing from his home base, and of course there was none at all after the war was lost. Hasso von Etzdorf, a professional diplomat and during the war a party to the conspiracy, once said to me on the subject: 'Your father was badly treated.'[467]

Motivation of German diplomats in the sense of German policy could only be inspired directly by the Foreign Minister. Circular decrees sent to German diplomatic missions could have little effect if, behind the Minister's back, they were repudiated by his state secretary, who had known the German diplomats for years. It seems Father exercised too little the capacity of his personality or persuasive powers to win people over to his side within the Auswärtiges Amt. As Herr von Etzdorf put it to the the English historian David Irving: 'He [my father] could look at you so nicely, unfortunately he rarely did!'[468] Father himself – if he were still in a position to do so – would have retorted: 'I no longer had time for it.' That is certainly a valid argument if one thinks back to the lightning speed with which world political dynamics evolved right after his taking office. Nevertheless, this deficiency of personal contact and the lack of motivation arising from it laid the groundwork for the defamation and slandering of the Minister in his own department. For the clique in the Amt who operated the campaign against him, however, as we have seen, the decisive factor rested on high politics and had nothing to do with the Minister's personality.

Father had not grown grey in war in the internal trench warfare of everyday domestic politics, placing loyal staff whom he knew in key positions of the Auswärtiges Amt, which was common practice. The loyalty of employees in leading posts is an inescapable prerequisite for the man at the top to succeed. This is especially valid in times of crisis and risk. There is no doubt that Father gave this point of view too little consideration; he could have been reinforced by having recourse to his employees from the Ribbentrop *Dienststelle*.

Naturally, he was aware of the 'conservative' mentality of many echelons of the Auswärtiges Amt; they were in the majority no partisans of Hitler's. Basically, he did not really care. Yet he proceeded on the assumption that especially in these circles, loyalty to one's country superseded a liking or dislike of Hitler's regime. He assumed that even in cases of a difference of opinion they would not counteract the policy of the government, which as things stood would have disastrous repercussions.

Every person is born with a particular physical and mental capacity, which he or she can make the best of with energy and a will of iron. To be able to wind down or have any distraction are essential aids in enduring stress over such a length of time as Hitler's Foreign Minister had to undergo from 1938 to 1941. In this Father suffered from two serious built-in handicaps: he slept badly and had difficulty 'switching off'. Poor sleep was a problem for Father for as long as I can remember, long before he was involved with politics. He told me once that even as 'a young fellow' he slept badly. Now, under the burden of responsibilities, this inherent condition was naturally aggravated. It is said that Johanna von Bismarck once told a guest at breakfast: 'We hated the whole night!' It seems that under certain circumstances Bismarck had trouble sleeping; it is experienced by everybody who has weighty responsibility to bear. True, he had made the rather flippant remark to Friedrich-Wilhelm IV, when during the revolutionary days the queen had brought to Bismarck's notice that the king had not slept for days: 'A king must always be able to sleep.' However, Herr von Bismarck himself was not the Minister who bore the responsibility. There is no doubt that a problem with sleep is most wearying.

Father's willpower also dominated his ability to relax. This handicap may have had something to do with his sleep problems. Perhaps somewhere he also lacked a small dose of fatalism. It is certain that one can only make the best of life if one is completely committed to something and prepared to cope with the highs and lows that are always part of it. On the other hand, a little fatalism allows there to be enough distance from one's own commitment so as not to stand or fall with it and to cultivate some serenity, so as to be able to monitor one's strengths. But fatalism was not a word in Father's vocabulary.

After he became Foreign Minister and the problems to be faced burdened him more intensively, he gradually became more withdrawn and monosyllabic towards us children. I never held it against him as I was aware of the load he had to bear. It did, however, begin to affect our parents' active social life and contacts with their friends. Ever more rarely did we see the familiar faces of their friends who had frequented our home since our childhood. The absence of a year and a half in London contributed to this. The foreign policy dynamics that set in when Father was appointed Foreign Minister led to their formerly intensive private socializing with friends switching into almost complete abeyance. Father no longer had enough time for it. It is possible that some acquaintances and friends did not understand, or indeed took it as arrogance. It is understandable that from that angle their Jewish friends should have been particularly sensitive. They for their part kept away, which from my personal experience after the war, when circumstances were reversed, I can well comprehend. Additionally, some of the old friends had reservations about the regime or were hostile toward it, which to some degree hindered the earlier enjoyable and amusing social intercourse they had. Our parents were aware of this censorious attitude. They gave their assistance, or tried to, when they were asked for it. One of the few who remembered this after the war was the renowned artist Olaf Gulbransson. Before 1933 he had caricatured Hitler and his party in the satirical magazine *Simplicissimus*. When he was in trouble about this after Hitler came to power, Father spoke directly to Hitler about it, appealing to the 'artist' in him, whereupon the latter without hesitation saw to it that Gulbransson was left in peace. After the war Gulbransson made his gratitude to Father's friendship known in diverse ways. Incidentally, our parents did not pay court to the official policy in regard to art with their 'modern' pictures: paintings by Nolde, Séraphine Louis, Vivin, Lhote, Chagall and others stayed hanging on the walls of our private quarters. Through her friendship with the painter Lenk, Mother came across pictures and portraits by Dix which – the portraits in particular – she found beautiful. She wanted him to paint our younger siblings. What came of this? To my amusement, in an Otto Dix exhibition at the Vence Maeght Foundation there was a large notice, saying: 'During the war the German Foreign Minister wanted Dix to paint his portrait, but the latter refused.' You can make of that whatever one wishes!

There was, however, an occasion – they were not as frequent as I would have liked – when Father was in a good mood and relaxed: that was the duck shoot on the River Oder, when in the summer of 1938 the two of us alone went from Sonnenburg near Bad Freienwalde and drove to Kienitz by the Oder so as to be in a hide on a deserted island of reeds in the evening. Father, who was an excellent shot, enjoyed the suspense of the ducks' fly-over and the peace and quiet of the Oder landscape. He grew up with hunting and nature. His grandfather's estate, Hertwig an der Mulde, must have been a hunter's paradise. I know the feelings Father enjoyed in those hours spent by the Oder. A shoot of wild birds with a shotgun is hardly equalled as an occupation, to think of other things and momentarily forget about 'business'. When the ducks fly over in the evening, as the day slowly fades, is an instant of extraordinary charm, especially on the banks of the Oder under the high arch of the evening sky. The interchange between the elegiac surroundings and the keenness excited by the flight of the flock is an unsurpassable experience for those who combine a love of nature and of hunting. Ducks – an elegant yet natural wild bird – are not an easy target, and shooting them requires accurate marksmanship and concentration. Father was delighted when, next to him, I bagged a few with a clean shot. He preoccupied himself with familiarization with weapons and introducing me to the shoot. I have never forgotten the rule I was inoculated with from the start: 'There is no discussion about who shot what, all that matters is that every piece of game killed is found.' Here the 'Minister' became my father again, a father who gave me friendly advice, a father who shared my happiness and taught me how to work a dog, which was very important among reeds higher than a man. For me these hours were wonderful; unfortunately there weren't many of them.

In 1945 there was a Russian bridgehead at Kienitz by the Oder. Father, who visited the front with Colonel von Geldern from time to time – it was barely an hour away from Berlin by car – had joined in an attack that was to break through the bridgehead once more. Geldern will have accepted, suspecting that Father wished to be killed in action. He writes that at one point, while Father and he were in the car, they were made aware by an infantryman that they were right in front of a Russian anti-tank gun emplacement. Geldern said to Father that they were racing towards Russia at 80km an hour; he could not be responsible for Father falling into Russian hands. To this Father answered, laughing, that in that case Geldern might have to shoot him. Father went to have a look at the front-line troops on the Oder with Geldern on various occasions. In a note, Geldern explicitly contradicts the pronouncement made after the war – in addition to all the other negative characteristics attributed to my father – that the Foreign Minister was a coward. Geldern underlines the good impression made by Father's excursions to the front, since at the time no other member of the government visited the troops or appeared before the population of the Oder.[469] I am duty bound, in view of the flood of calumnies poured to this day over my father, to state such self-evident truths.

One of the staff of the Auswärtiges Amt whom Father had found already in place was the chief of the legal department, Friedrich Gaus. It was his job to draft the treaties between the Reich and other countries. Father briefed him in many strictly confidential matters. Gaus was not liked in the Amt because of his opportunism and unstable character. Father had obligatorily trusted in him, insofar as Gaus had to be informed of many aspects and considerations in order to draw up a treaty. In this way, in due course he became a close collaborator of Father's. Gaus had a particular problem in the Third Reich because his wife was Jewish. Despite this fact, Father appointed him Undersecretary of State and later instigated Hitler to award him the Golden Party Badge and to give him an autographed photograph with a dedication – which was unquestionably unusual for those days.[470]

At the opening of the Nuremberg trials, Father counted on Gaus's knowledge of a number of facts that could have exonerated him, and thus also German policies, in the sense of the indictment. He was to be bitterly disappointed. Gaus placed himself as principal witness at the disposition of the prosecution. It is now recognized as a fact that Robert M. Kempner, once a German government cadre, who emigrated to the United States in 1933 for racial reasons and was one of those representing the prosecution at

Nuremberg, made Gaus available for support of the prosecution under threat of delivery into the hands of the Soviet Union.[471] In a statutory declaration submitted by the prosecution authority, Gaus had stated:

'The German political leadership saw in the Japanese attack on Pearl Harbor on 7 December 1941 the first step in the realization of the idea of founding a Greater German Reich. For this Reich was not to rule over Europe alone, but was to be the absolute decisive factor for its control over world affairs.'[472]

In this instance, out of his hatred – understandable in an emigrant – Kempner had again been over-reacting when he forced Gaus to make this nonsensical declaration. However, once again the questionability of the Nuremberg proceedings in historical research is demonstrated when it is considered that in the winter of 1941/42 the situation of the German Wehrmacht was desperate, which had called forth from Hitler the exclamation already mentioned: 'Germany is saved now!'

Much too late, Father had transferred State Secretary v. Weizsäcker as ambassador to the Vatican and replaced him in the post with an assistant from the '*Dienststelle* Ribbentrop'. Before his execution, Father had learned nothing further about Weizsäcker's conspiracy with the British government or his activities in Spain which had deprived the Reich of the opportunity to take Gibraltar.

Thus the extraordinarily difficult situation Ribbentrop was in acquires an outline. He was head of a department he was not familiar with, which, for personal reasons as well as due to internal politics, had its reservations about him, not to say was actually spurning him. The government establishment of which he was a part was foreign to him, and regarded him – for whatever reasons – as an antagonist or even as an opponent. He was attached to a head of government who was not willing to pre-plan nor debate weighty political decisions with a government committee so as to have them systematically initiated, and who conducted discussions in private, whereby he split up his leading aides, namely his ministers, instead of coordinating them (there was finally a considerable number thereof whom Hitler directly subordinated to himself). Finally, Father had a state secretary at his back who in crucial phases undermined the Reich's policies by collaborating with potential opponents, under the cloak of a systematic diffusion of false representations of the persona of his Minister and his judgements as to foreign policy.

This brings up the question of why under such circumstances Joachim von Ribbentrop did not resign. From today's point of view it is a justified query. I have already told of the pronouncement expressed with the object of denigrating him, that he was dependent on my mother.[473] I can only repeat once more that he was unfortunately not, in the sense of any greater influence Mother may have exerted upon his personal decisions. At the outbreak of the war with Russia, Mother had virtually urged him to resign, not only because he had advised against a pre-emptive strike on Russia but also, as she argued, for the sake of the credibility of German policy.

It will of course to some extent have played a role for Father in a deteriorating situation to be the captive of his honour and have to come through the problems. Somebody who at that time had a perception of Hitler and his policies as being the destiny of Germany, as well as of one's self, perhaps felt it would be wrong to withdraw. There is a resonance of emotionalism which is not comprehensible to us as third parties used to consider politics as a cool business matter. There is no question that Hitler was in a position to present himself as a phenomenon of Fate, and as such was also regarded by broad portions of the nation. He did not reciprocate the personal loyalty of his Foreign Minister. Father considered it beneath his dignity to abandon his loyalty when he appeared before the tribunal of the victors in Nuremberg. I do not feel myself bound to this. Hitler waived Father's conception of foreign policy, whose cornerstone was the relations with Russia, and plunged into staking all on a pre-emptive war with Russia. This is how it may validly be designated, even when taking into account that there were indications that Stalin too no longer felt himself bound by the pact of non-aggression. Irrespective of this, militarily the offensive remained a gamble and, since it was launched with almost no political groundwork, was a fiasco of foreign policy. It is my opinion that I have the right to condemn Hitler for this error.

An attitude we held in our family was expressed in our motto '*Ni nalaten*' ('Do not give up'). Father explained it to me when I was about 8 or 9 and he showed me our family tree, on which the motto appeared. This instruction to be tough in the pursuance of goals, to have endurance through difficulties and steadfastness in setbacks was an element of our upbringing by our parents in those years when one is marked for the rest of one's life. I had occasion in my later life to gauge the significance of having these characteristics.

The fascination of high politics will of course up to certain time have contributed, which grips every active politician. No man undertakes a job that is trying and thankless in the upshot without being driven by a great passion, even more so somebody who does not need it, from their personal circumstances.

This also goes for the alleged ambition, which is so often criticized. If there were no ambition as incentive for a driving force of the psyche, mankind would probably still be living in trees. Ambition signifies being prepared to perform just as well without equivalent material remuneration. An excessive or even morbid ambition may exist, which is counter-productive, but in general it is usually only losers who rail against ambition.

Just as Hitler acted with growing rigidity and inflexibility in military matters, in the same way did he operate – or rather, no longer operate – and deal with foreign affairs. Thus the strengths of the Minister for Foreign Affairs were also neutralized and blocked. Father was temperamentally a man of action. Once a concept had grown out of analysis of a situation, he proceeded to its realization, if necessary with dogged determination. The way Mother put it was: 'He was a cavalry man, he charged obstacles.' At the same time the merchant in him well knew that the necessity to compromise was always arising.

Father's propensity to get to grips with problems and, in the absence of other possibilities, to take risks, as well as securing the activities of foreign policy by having alternative solutions available, his negotiating skills and his preparedness to come to a compromise if necessary, were all qualities that complemented Hitler's personality structure, which was hardly ideal for the diplomatic 'game'. This complementary relationship between the two men fell apart after the war with Russia broke out, as did also their personal relations. There was an unmistakeable resentment on the part of the 'infallible' visionary towards his Foreign Minister, who, resulting from the considerations of sober business politics, had warned him against initiating a pre-emptive war with Russia, advice which – there is no doubt that Hitler had to acknowledge as early as October 1941 – had been proved right.

Let it be made quite clear: Father did not remain in the Amt for fear of some sort of personal reprisals. He had no reason to expect any, or at any rate not as long as he was not implicated in the conspiracy, of whose activities he had no idea. Moreover, even if he should have expected personal repercussions if he were to resign, it would not have restrained him from leaving.

During convalescent leave following my fourth wound I was able to visit Father for two or three days in East Prussia. Albeit until then he had always been a slightly distant figure of respect for me, those days we had together were characterized by great intimacy and personal contact. I recall a noteworthy little episode that took place between us. After breakfast one morning when we were alone together, he was handed cuttings from the foreign press. Suddenly he pushed one across the table, saying: 'Will you believe this is possible?' It was an announcement the international press had borrowed from the Russians. It reported on the systematic murder of Jewish prisoners in a German internment camp in Poland that had been taken by the Russians. I just laughed, and answered almost reproachfully, without giving a moment's thought to such a possibility: 'But, Father, this is again the hacked-off hands of children in Belgium of the First World War.' It was part of the basic training of the entire Wehrmacht to label inimical propaganda material such as pamphlets as 'enemy propaganda' and hand it in to a superior. A lesson had been learned from Allied defamatory propaganda diffused during the First World War One. In this sense the troops were completely clear as to its nature and hence in general little influenced by it. Father was visibly relieved to agree with my spontaneous reaction.

It sounds unbelievable nowadays when chief functionaries of the Hitler regime claim to have known nothing of serious issues such as extermination of Jews. It is hard, in our epoch where nothing stays confidential or secret, to comprehend the isolation of the separate government representatives in Hitler's 'system'. The complete disintegration – as willed by Hitler – of the work of governance had fostered this situation. The concentration camps and what went on in them was Himmler's exclusive domain. They represented major economic complexes that were at his disposal only. For this reason alone he allowed no insight into the cards he held. No Cabinet sessions took place in which questions might have been asked. The total disintegration of the echelons of government was Hitler's basic aim. One need but think of the internment of the Danish police force, which had been kept secret from Best, the Reich plenipotentiary, and his chief, the Foreign Minister.

The successful attempt to keep extermination of Jews strictly secret is proof of the concern taken by those responsible not to call up an adverse reaction from the population of Germany if what was happening became known; even within government, knowledge of the killings was a secret. An internal investigation conducted by SS Sturmbannführer and Judge Konrad Morgen during the war led to the initiation of a judicial inquiry against Adolf Eichmann, Rudolf Höß, Oswald Pohl and others, as well as to the outcome that the circle of those in the know was restricted to a few hundred persons.[474] The existential persecution of Jews instituted in the war went against the ethical maxims of the German people. The extent to which it was undertaken was not known. However, the visible facts (wearing of the yellow Star of David, deportations, etc.) were sufficient to undermine confidence in the leadership and its moral legitimacy, and consequently had an adverse effect on the war effort. On the other hand, the population was aware that in view of the massive threat posed by Russia and of the ultimatum from Roosevelt and Churchill for 'unconditional surrender', they had to fight for survival. For many Germans – precisely those in posts of responsibility – a frightful dichotomy! Under these circumstances, to malign the entire German people as Hitler's 'willing helpers', to apply, that is, *Sippenhaft* (kin liability) unto the third degree and farther, will perhaps also one day turn out to be a grave error. The declaration by former Federal President Richard von Weizsäcker that 'everyone could have known of it' is incomprehensible,[475] especially as at Nuremberg his defence of his father, who was State Secretary of the Auswärtiges Amt until 1943, was based on the argument that his father had known nothing of it. Deportations are today always identified with killings, but in those days that was not evident.

During Hitler's governance Joachim von Ribbentrop was a stranger to the German Jewish policy. In the relevant Holocaust literature it is therefore attributed to him that he did not condone the persecution of Jews, nor that he was an initiator therein; neither is any collusion of his in their ensuing killings by the National Socialist regime insinuated. This is accurate. For reasons of his career and upbringing, as in many a case, on the whole he distanced himself from the ideological radicalness of those totalitarian days. In his memoirs he accurately records that although he did see that there were problems with the Jews in Germany, he had been openly outspoken against the anti-Jewish laws, were it only because of the repercussions on foreign policy. He urged Hitler – in his own words – for an 'evolutionary development in the Jewish question'. In a time when because of the ongoing problems of life in a non-Jewish environment, Jews demanded the establishment of a Jewish state, this may not seem out of the ordinary. Nonetheless, at no time did Father's opinions get through decisively to Hitler, in fact during the war they were progressively less successful. Hitler was always convinced that it was in effect British and American Jewry that had constituted the driving force behind the war on Germany.

Father was not of this opinion. To his mind, the hostile policy of the Third Reich directed against Jews added an additional major power as ally to the considerable list of opponents. He considered this a given fact; not a decisive one, but a factor among many. The power factor of Jewish organizations existed and had significance. These organizations were still to be reckoned with, both as opponents as well as allies, but their effects were manageable. It was also the pre-condition with which at the end of 1939 the British War Cabinet debated the earlier and present influence Jews had in America, as well as their possible usefulness for the British war effort.

As head of department of the Auswärtiges Amt during the war, Father knew about the concentration of Jews in camps. In certain single cases – such as Italy

– he also demanded that allies concur with the proceeding. It corresponded to the impression there was that the Jews of Europe were consciously aiming at the defeat of Germany. In view of the overt fundamentals of National Social policies, such an enmity was understandable. However, Chaim Weizmann (later the first President of Israel) had offered the British government to bring European Jewry into the war against Germany,[476] whereby admittedly he clearly overestimated his own influence and/or the potential of the World Zionist Organization. Basically, for the British government it was not a matter of reprisals for any anti-Semitic policy, actually not even to help save lives. There are many examples of this.

The persecutions of Jews from 1941 on have to be seen as the ideologist Hitler having run amok, having acknowledged that he would founder politically and militarily. His terrible declaration – twice quoted by Hewel in his diary for 1941 – 'If Barbarossa fails, it is all over anyway', shows that he had burned all his bridges, so he was indifferent to how his actions would turn out. His personality allowed him no feasible way out of the catastrophe. It was in this way that he ran amok during the war, including against his own people – there is no other way to describe the senseless struggle after the successful Allied invasion of France. The visionary had turned into an egocentric power maniac who, with open eyes, led his people to its doom.

When I visited Father in August 1944, the outcome of the reversal of fortune had long become reality. Upon my asking him about Hitler's perceptions of the way to turn the situation around, Father pointed me in the direction of what Hitler had said to him concerning the employment of new weapons ('wonder-weapons'), which were soon to be expected.[477]

He gave me a lengthy memorandum addressed to Hitler to read, which he was about to send him. It analyzed the current political and military situation the Reich found itself in, also taking into account the situation of supplies. He concluded that the war could no longer be won, and once again requested to be empowered to initiate peace talks. I, by reason of my painful experiences in the heavy fighting at the front, could only urge Father to express the crushing superiority of the Allies in the most emphatic terms. It was to my mind a cheering thought that he could corner the increasingly reluctant Hitler using Hitler's own words. Father put the memorandum under the heading of a quotation from Hitler's book *Mein Kampf*:

'It is the business of diplomacy to see to it, not that a people falls heroically, but that it is preserved practically. Every road leading to this is, therefore, suitable, and its evasion must be marked as criminal neglect of duty.'[478]

At the time, the clear-headed, materialistic analysis of the state Germany was in that Father put to paper no longer greatly impressed me. The situation at the fronts from which I had come were even more desperate. When on the way back from East Prussia via Berlin to join my division in the West, I saw my mother once more and we talked about the paper. Naturally I wanted to know right away whether, as Father intended, the memorandum had elicited a positive reaction from Hitler. With profound resignation, Mother told me that according to Hewel, Hitler, enraged, had thrown it across the room, saying: 'To want to investigate the preparedness of the Russians to negotiate is the same as touching a red-hot oven to see if it is burning!' As has been said, Father had based his request on detailed justifications. Hitler was, however, no longer accessible to listen to an argument, as he no longer admitted to his own earlier rationale either. Anyway, for some time now he had eschewed relying on diplomacy, which might have averted – in the terrible way in which it finally came about – the fate of doom.

In the further course of the war Father had but two alternatives. He could force his resignation, thereby risking earning the image of a rat abandoning the sinking ship, or he could turn into a treacherous assassin and shoot Hitler. The death of the tyrant was the sole chance to get rid of Hitler and bring about a ceasefire. Father would on no account become a 'rat', and had not been born to be an assassin.

To sum up Father's main maxims and convictions in foreign policy, the following points must be made:

1. To the full extent and out of conviction, he stood by Hitler's 'Western policy', i.e. the objective of coming to an arrangement with Britain, a policy which had always also been Father's. He complemented the concept with the inclusion of France as a condition for an agreement with Britain. The choice was overall decidedly of opting for the West.
2. Regarding the reluctance of the two 'Western' powers, Father had cautiously tried to break through the Reich's isolation by the conclusion of the Anti-Comintern Pact without obstructing the arrangement desired with Britain.
3. He had ascertained Britain's covert anti-German policy in 1937, and at the beginning of 1938 had clearly and unequivocally stated to Hitler that in the new order of Eastern Europe the antagonism of Britain 'to the point of war' had to be taken into account.

4. As it became manifest that no arrangement with Poland in the sense of setting up an anti-Communist bloc was to be reached, since Poland had opted for the opposing side, thus placing herself on the side of Britain and, indirectly, America, he had proposed a 180 degree turn-about of German policy to a pro-Russian line and pushed it through to Hitler. In that way he could achieve the strongest foreign policy grouping for the Reich since Bismarck.

5. Father saw his Russian policy as focused on the long term and was prepared for tough negotiation with Stalin. He wanted to accept the Russian concessions, so as to come to a lasting agreement. Father saw in a Continental bloc comprising good relations with the Soviet Union the sole possibility of ending the war and securing the Reich in the long run.

6. In this sense he attempted to restrain Hitler from a pre-emptive strike against the Soviet Union, to avoid a war on two fronts. His advising against a declaration of war on the USA was along the same line.

7. Finally, he had perceived and consistently represented to Hitler the necessity, in view of the military power balance, to try to initiate peace talks with Russia.

After 1940, Father's concepts of foreign policy could no longer be realized, as Hitler no longer followed suit with them. To this extent the question or reproach is justified as to why he did not hand in his resignation. I have tried above to give a reply. Father's concept failed with Hitler. For that reason he ascended the victors' gibbet. He accepted it in the sense of a 'higher justice'. In his last letter to our mother he wrote:

'[T]he Führer and his people have failed. Millions have fallen. The Reich is destroyed and our people are prostrated. Is it therefore – not because of the Nuremberg verdict pronounced by foreign judges – but in the sense of a higher justice that I too should fall? I ... shall face all that is to come standing upright, as is due from me to the past of my family and my own as German Foreign Minister.'

He does not deserve to be maligned and vilified, to the present day, in a way that makes a mockery of historical facts. To Father, Hitler was Germany's destiny personified, for better or worse. There is no doubt he was under the impression that he was at the mercy of this destiny and did not evade it, albeit after 1941 he basically knew that despite all the attempts he made there was no longer any possibility that he would influence the fateful course of doom that destiny would take. By 1932 he had, for a multitude of reasons, finally made a bond with Hitler, whose *Realpolitik* plans, at the outset of his becoming Chancellor, had been quite modestly directed to a consolidation of Germany's position. What anyone wanted to do from now on in view of the looming disaster for Germany was something they would have to come to terms with in their conscience. Those who tried to stage a coup d'état were not the worst; nor were those who submitted to Hitler's leadership and carried on with the fight against the Allies from their positions to the full. None of these courses led out of the destiny, whose name was 'Hitler', of the Germans, but that destiny was by no means solely homemade. Only whoever understands this will also be able to understand Joachim von Ribbentrop's decision.

The so-called 'legal process' of the Allies' conduct of the post-war trials can contribute nothing to finding the historical truth. I shall in consequence not occupy myself with the Nuremberg trials; among objective professionals of law and historians, the opinion has prevailed that they were not a proper procedure in the sense of the Western concept of legality. What is to be gleaned for history from the Nuremberg trials is largely insignificant if gauged by the yardstick of serious historical research. How unjust the procedure against my father was in the sense of any traditional legislation has to be clearly seen. I have outlined the major developments that led to the Second World War, and there cannot be any doubt – at least for an objective observer – that the blame for its outbreak cannot be attributed to Germany alone. Although the Allies were perfectly aware of this, from before its installation they accordingly manipulated the Nuremberg Statute so that any debate of this issue – that is, the core question – was excluded. Robert H. Jackson, Associate Justice of the United States Supreme Court in 1945, formerly United States Attorney General, at the time the 'strong man' at the Nuremberg trials, feared things could otherwise go wrong:

> 'The Germans will certainly accuse all three of our European Allies of adopting policies which forced them to war. The reason I say that is that captured documents of the Foreign Office that I have examined all come down to the claim "We have no way out; we must fight; we are encircled; we are being strangled to death." Now, if the question comes up, what is a judge to do about it? I would say, before one is judged guilty of being an aggressor ... but say we will hear his case.'[479]

The German Foreign Minister was successfully prevented from declaring his motives at Nuremburg. The Allies gave themselves the right of the 'law of nations' to take the life of the Foreign Minister of their opponent, the basis for which was nothing other than the primitive right of the victor. A legal status awarded *a posteriori*, that definitively cut the rights of the accused, that accredited the identity of legislators, prosecutors and judges, and besides numerous minor offences against legal decency even offended against the tenet of the general validity of laws – it was applied uniquely to German foreign policy – cannot provide the basis for a correct process of justice. A law or, as it was called in Nuremberg, a 'statute' *a priori* retroactive mooted to be valid legal grounds for a condemnation, makes a mockery of any judicial concept of the West. To condemn Father for having conducted a war of aggression against Poland in the presence of Soviet judges, when the Soviet Union had also attacked Poland, blatantly proves the injustice of this so-called litigation.

Upon conclusion of presentation of the evidence, prior to the verdict, I was brought to Nuremberg for a few days and confined to a cell in the witness wing, to be able to talk to my father for about ten minutes every day through a netting, with guards on either side. Actually, we were both aware of what the verdict would be; not because Father was guilty in the court's sense, but because the court had been so structured as to make unequivocally sure that the process taken was directed to capital punishment. After pronouncement of the verdict, which, as we both expected, was a death sentence, I was not given an opportunity to say goodbye to my father. After my visit to Nuremberg and the talks I had there, I made a note for myself of the names of the accused who, in view of the conduct of the trial, could expect a death sentence. My prediction was absolutely right.

If he was not 'eliminated', as he used to say about the probable death sentence, Father wanted to write his memoirs. I asked him if he did so expressly to bring out his divergences of view from Hitler's. My main thought about this was of his efforts to avert the war with the Soviet Union. As I have already said, I was aware of these disputes from the start. However, during the trial, Father had consciously refused to expose his disparities with Hitler before the tribunal of the victors. In one of his last letters to Mother (dated 5 October 1946) he wrote:

> 'I did not want at this trial to speak about my grave disputes with Adolf Hitler. The German people would then rightly say: "What sort of a man is that who was Adolf Hitler's Foreign Minister and now turns against him for selfish reasons, before a foreign law court?" You must understand

this, however hard it is for us both and the children. But without the respect of decent Germans and above all without self-respect I could not have gone on living nor wanted to live.'

Today I am grateful that in his defence Father did not take the 'low road' against Hitler. When we talked he regretted the generally spineless attitude that had been noticeable at Nuremberg. Father and I had brief chats with great warmth of feeling, which we both kept free of tension, conscious as we were of submitting to an ineluctable fate. I must not omit what Dr Werner Best stated in conclusion to Nuremberg: 'At these last months of his life R. gave an impression of absolute dignity … He is also said to have stepped under the gallows keeping the same stance.'

I shall close the description of my father with a formulation by Theodor Fontane, the nineteenth-century German poet and novelist:

'The dead can no longer defend themselves. They therefore all the more deserve justice.'

Painful Aftermath

'If I wished to do you harm
I would wish you a famous father!'

Chinese proverb

Anyone who has followed the course of my life from 1933 until 1945 will understand how apt the above quotation is in regard to me, not to mention the phase of my life that began on 8 May 1945. It will, however, perhaps become clear after reading about it that a destiny – that of having a father with a well-known name is definitely one from which there is no escape – also has two sides, one negative but also a positive one. In any case, from 1934 our name represented an incremental personal challenge as the post Father held became better known and of greater importance.

My sister Bettina and I were introduced to these personal family circumstances when, some time at the beginning of 1934, we were rather formally summoned by our parents, who informed us that Father was about to undertake an official position. This signified for Bettina and me that we had at all times to behave correctly and politely, indeed with restraint. We had to expect not the slightest prerogatives to derive from Father's position: on the contrary, it entailed only duties deriving from it. The lecture can be imagined. Suddenly I was no longer merely an ordinary pupil of the well-known Arndt-Gymnasium (grammar school) in Berlin-Dahlem – as were more than 500 others; it meant that if anything 'happened' – usually something slightly reproachful – what I heard was: 'You ought to be an example because of your father's status!' This justifiable wish of our parents, which also comprised the expectation that one would try to accomplish something outstanding, became a motivation that was to remain a determining factor in my life under the most diverse conditions. When an evidently highly placed American questioner asked Mother whether she had been 'loyal to Hitler', she replied: 'I was loyal to my husband.' From time to time I am asked about my motives for returning to duty again and again during the last stages of the war, despite my various injuries. Loyalty to my parents, who had after all brought us into this world, categorically required such behaviour, not least towards one's comrades-at-arms. '*Sippenhaft*' (kin liability), in the true meaning of the word, also signifies that one is liable for the family's reputation and in consequence also responsible for it. One would wish that many a scion of a prominent family were to take it to heart.

It was at this early stage that 'kin liability' in its true sense began for me. If I depict certain personal experiences in what follows, it is not because I give my destiny any particular significance. Millions in other countries have been exposed to the hazards I encountered. I had the unlikely good luck to be among those who came through the war alive.

A reader who is interested only in Hitler's foreign policy may at this point put this book away without compunction. However, the account of some personal experiences may also to a certain degree legitimize me and permit me to judge the historical epoch during which they befell me, without bias and – as I believe – reasonably objectively, as well as in some cases not quite 'in the spirit of today'! I leave it to the reader to decide whether the perceived duties give me the right to do so.

'Kin liability' is maybe as old as the history of man. Its earliest form was the blood feud. The affected member of the kinship was liable, without having been individually guilty. Nowadays 'kin liability' appears in the most diverse forms, beginning with physical annihilation and reaching the subtle forms of discrimination, defamation, disregard, social disadvantage or even just the lack of casualness and naturalness when concerned with members of a kin whose family name was once prominent in the public's awareness. As may perhaps be imagined, I had plenty of opportunity to experience the diversification of the contemporary *Sippenhaft* and was able to witness examples of impressive human noble-mindedness prevailing over these prejudices.

I first escaped a physical end being put to my earthly existence – which because of my name was not entirely excluded – by being taken prisoner by the Americans south of the Danube. The American General Patton was in command here, of whom it was said he had given the order that capitulating German military formations – as well as refugees from the Russian side who wished to be interned by the Americans – were to be taken in and not handed back to the Russians: a normal practice of the Americans and British. In my case, my 'kin liability' would probably have been fatal at the hands of the Russians.

While I was fulfilling my Reich's Labour service duties in the summer of 1939, I had a minor opportunity to shed, once and for all, the stigma of the 'well-known figure' – for the duration of my work at least. At roll-call one morning, a volunteer was sought for the job of shovelling out the latrine. Nobody was eager to come forward for this duty, extremely unappetizing in the early heat of May, and nor was I. Then a day's special leave was promised, which set off a trigger in my train of thought and made me realize it gave me a chance to counter all prejudices. This is how, to the astonishment of the entire labour service division, I volunteered for the task, and from this moment on had won, meaning that all prejudices against the Minister's little boy were done away with. One day a worker from another division asked me: 'You have that Ribbentrop with you, what's he like?' While my comrades roared with laughter, I replied: 'Actually, he isn't half as bad as we thought!'

At London's Westminster School I was naturally from the beginning a 'political animal' in miniature. Father had just been appointed Ambassador to the Court of St James – the official designation of his post. When I started school – I was 15 years old – it was covered by the entire press corps, with photographs and commentary.

While I was in the military, at the 1939 Christmas Eve celebration in barracks my group leader, an NCO, considerably under the influence of drink, admitted to me that he had been instructed by the company chief to drill me mercilessly until the 'water boiled in his a***' if I did not do as I was told. Well, the problem did not arise.

At the Waffen-SS military academy in Braunschweig, a 'well-known figure' was blatantly discriminated against. The best of each year's class was preferred for promotion, meaning he obtained officer's rank before any other participant in the training course. Later, in the internment camp, I came across my training course commander of that time again, who showed me once more that the finger had been pointed at the 'well-known figure', in a negative sense, when he said: 'I can tell you this now, you were the best of the whole year's class, but we really could not make it known.' I was in complete agreement with him!

As a 'well-known figure' in the garb of the paternal position, one stood always between Scylla and Charybdis. On the one hand, one was supposed to have a modest and reticent demeanour so as not to allow the impression to permeate that you laid claim to any preferential treatment or privileges because of your father's position. On the other hand, one wanted to go one's own way, in the hope of success and also of being able to take advantage of an opportunity if it presented itself, always risking that any success or recognition could be reduced by the envious to being due to your father's position rather than to your performance. This is how in the spring of 1940 I heard that the SS officer candidates for a post of commander were to be drafted to the *Junkerschule* (military academy) for the coming training course. My friend Wedel and I were worried this might mean we would miss the expected deployment to the West. Although we would also have liked to become officers soon, we considered it indispensable to have garnered some previous experience of warfare so as to be able to lead war-experienced soldiers. Since we all started out from the assumption that an offensive was soon to be launched in the West – what Hitler had said upon a visit he made on Father's birthday on 30 April 1940 confirmed the impression we had – we naturally wanted to take part in the campaign, particularly as we had no prior experience at the front. It should also not be overlooked that for Wedel and myself, in view of the fact that our fathers' position in the limelight in the regime (Wedel's father was Chief of Police in Potsdam), it was important to give a good example and not to spare ourselves. Today I am often asked whether Father could not have saved me from being drafted to the front. It might, if he had really wanted it, have been possible for him to do so. But Father had not even tried, and I would not for all the world have wanted it. In our day, 'political correctness' signified simply that it goes without saying that offering one's life and limb for one's country is self-evident, irrespective of domestic politics. I have already mentioned my wife's ten cousins who were killed. Himmler's appearance at a little reception given for Father's birthday on 30 April 1940 gave me the opportunity to clarify the matter. Therefore, behaving all correctly and smartly turned out, I went up to Himmler and told him about my concern that I would be sent to the military academy before having previously had the opportunity to obtain experience at the front; I appended the request that we should please be given the opportunity to do so. Curtly and with no sign of understanding – we were not trying to get out of it, but on the contrary to be called up – Himmler replied: 'You will do as you are ordered!' There is no doubt he was formally in the right, but a little comprehension of our wish to be able to prove ourselves before we were made officers might have been expected. But then Himmler had never been a soldier.

In the afternoon of 9 May 1940, there was another alarm. Was it the real thing this time? The alarm had been given several times during the winter months. They may well have been deceptive manoeuvres, as German telephone surveillance had ascertained that the assault dates had regularly been transmitted to The Hague by the Dutch military attaché. The information, as has been said here, was to be traced back to Colonel Oster's as yet unknown traitorous activities. I was hopeful, as it seemed that the danger of being unable to take part in the campaign because of the transfer to the military academy may have been averted. As we marched off, however, the order came:

'Officer candidates to remain and will be marched to the military academy in Braunschweig.' Our worst fear was realized.

However, true to our family motto '*Ni nalaten*' in the sense of tenacity in the pursuit of one's goals, I was not ready to give up. If I wanted a chance to rescind the standing order and take part in the campaign, I had to be ruthless. I was determined to try everything. A few weeks earlier, I chanced to make the acquaintance of the regimental adjutant in a tavern, when he sat at our table, jovially chatting to us ordinary soldiers without knowing us. As our quarters were near the regiment's staff quarters in the little town of Ahlen, I went there on the off chance and happened to run into this adjutant who, of course, asked me what I was doing there. To my terse reply that I wanted to join the campaign he laughed and, understanding completely, told me: 'Wait here, I'll ask the commander!' He reappeared a few minutes later and said: 'The commander will take you along with him [against the explicit order from Berlin] if your father agrees, in case something happens to you.' He wanted, though, to hear it from my father himself.

The ambassadors of Holland, Belgium and Luxembourg were expected at the Auswärtiges Amt to receive the declarations of war. They were consequently extremely busy, and an employee of Father's thought it proper to turn down the adjutant's telephone call, saying that the Herr Reichsmininster could give no orders to the SS, which the regiment's adjutant had to take as a refusal. I was, however, able to get Father on the telephone. He told me briefly that of course he agreed, if I wanted to join the campaign, except that he could not give the order!

I needed nothing more. I arranged for a taxi at three in the morning – whose driver was a sturdy woman – and went after the regiment. By chance, at dawn, on a street corner in Lüdinghausen, I came across Felix, the regimental commander, who asked me: 'Where did you spring from again?' But he gave up and took me with him. That morning at the crossing of the Rhine at Rees I was with the company again, still worried I might be caught and sent back to the academy. A few days later I received my baptism of fire. We had embarked upon the breakthrough to Vlissingen and had reached the Woensdrecht isthmus in our rapid progress. We saw gunners on motorcycles coming to stop on a dam, and a few moments later we – the three runners that is – stood amongst the motorcycles, engines running; the drivers had not dismounted, but the gunners proceeded along the dam.

We were suddenly under heavy fire from a well-camouflaged bunker some 50 metres away. We jumped from the crown of the dam to its left side, but were fired on there too, and then tried to find shelter on the right side, where, however, the barrage of infantry fire even intensified. I called out: 'Onto the dam!' The two others followed me. We pressed ourselves down into a rut as flat as we could on the gravel. I was lying next to a sidecar motorcycle whose driver had been shot down, but the motor was running at full throttle and minutes later I was totally deaf. The machine-gun fire from the bunker 50 metres in front of us, which controlled the dam, hit the metal of the sidecar just above my head with a horrible clanging. I knew perfectly well it was but a matter of time before a bullet would pierce my steel helmet, which could not resist it, would penetrate my skull and then, as we ordinary soldiers said, I would have 'gone for a Burton'! In our exhilaration of the charge we had literally crashed onto the enemy, who had let us and the *Kradschütze* motorcyclist gunners approach as close as possible before opening fire.

I have to admit to having thought that this is what you get from having wanted at all costs to be in the war! It soon transpired that both my runner comrades had been killed (the place was finally cleared by the French). Why were they both killed, whereas I had only a minor splinter injury to the shoulder? We had after all been lying close together, cheek by jowl. I could not guess at the time how often the question would come back to me in the five years that ensued.

Himmler resented my taking part in the Western campaign, as well as Father's role in it. All the same, it had been the decision of the regiment commander, who had deliberately ignored an order from Berlin. In his opinion young officer candidates ought to have taken part in battle at the front before they became officers. My punishment followed later, when the time came for commissioning upon graduating from the military academy. The best of the graduates were allowed to choose which division they wished to be transferred to. Naturally, I chose the SS panzer division that my regiment's commander, Felix Steiner, had newly set up, known as the '*Wiking*', comprising volunteers from Belgium, Holland, Denmark, Norway, Sweden and Finland to join in the fight against Bolshevism. Following the start of the Russia campaign it quickly became an elite division. However, due to Himmler's explicit order my wish was not to be realized and I was transferred instead to a combat group in Norway (which was in no way combat-ready); in those days it was in effect a disciplinary transfer. That was small-minded of Himmler. Himmler's less than respectful nickname in the Waffen-SS, *Reichsheini*, deriving from his first name and his title of *Reichsführer SS*, reflects the distance between Himmler and the troops. I was to feel the effects of this. A somewhat flippant remark of mine, which was of course promptly reported, may have had something to do with it. A friend of mine (a Waffen-SS officer) was getting married. For this he had to produce two guarantors for the bride and fill in a questionnaire about her. Among other things it was asked whether she was too fond of finery and cosmetics. I had said to this, probably too loudly, that if one day the entry to this was a 'No' in regard to my intended, I would not have her. I was at that time of the same mind as the Prussian king, who is said to have declared: 'I am always happy when my female subjects dress up prettily: it makes it easier for my male subjects to stay faithful!'

In September 1941 I was severely wounded in Karelia. After a stay of months in hospital, I happened by accident to bump into Sepp Dietrich, the *Leibstandarte* commander, who took me under his wing and transferred me to a newly formed column of tanks. It was only then, at the beginning of 1942, that three divisions of Waffen-SS received any tanks at all. As Himmler would not take on Sepp Dietrich, I became a panzer man and remained one to the end of the war, when I was once again an infantryman as there were no tanks left and some of us, still in our black uniforms, fought the Russians to the last.

I have given some descriptions of my experiences in the fighting. From 1942 on we began, somewhat self-mockingly, to speak of the 'poor man's war' which – in view of the enemy's superiority – we were waging in all sectors. It is particularly applicable to the fighting after the Allied landing in Normandy on 6 June 1944.

In 1944, in the West, it had filtered down to the troops that Rommel wanted to have the tank divisions positioned at the coast, arising from the correct conclusion that due to absolute Allied air supremacy the tanks coming from the hinterland would not reach where the landing took place in time to throw the enemy back into the sea.

During a reconnaissance of the road between our quarters near Bernay to Honfleur at the Seine estuary, in view of dispositions for defence works that could only be described as ridiculous, our division commander had drily declared: 'Gentlemen, it is quite obvious that they are coming!' On our way to Honfleur, low-flying Allied fighters flew over us, unmolested by the Luftwaffe that was far back inland. At the time we hardly took them seriously, but I was soon enough to make my acquaintance with this lethal menace from the air.

At the beginning of June 1944, on the Route Nationale highway from Evreux to Lisieux deep in France's interior, sudden bursts of machine-gun fire flew about my ears and those of my driver as we were coming back from a night-time manoeuvre. I turned round to see an enemy fighter plane 50 metres behind us, shooting with all its guns. Instinctively, I put my head between my knees (this is what saved me) and shouted: 'Halt! A strafer!' Then I was hit between the shoulder-blades and was paralysed, blood spurting out of the exit wound in my neck near the carotid artery.

I managed to roll out of the vehicle, and called out to the driver: 'Pull me into the ditch, he's coming back!' The driver was able to drag me into the ditch, although the fighter plane attacked twice more and left our vehicle in flames. The ammunition from his guns missed my head by a hair's breadth and clattered against the paving. I was now lying on my back, paraplegic, the carotid presumably hit. It really looked like this was the end. I was not even in a state of shock – perhaps after being wounded a number of times, like a shot-peppered hare, it does not recur. It was always expected that at some point one would get it in the neck, and obviously this was it! Very upset, the driver was trying to press a gauze pad onto my throat, which was not really of much use. I awaited the gradual loss of consciousness from blood loss, asked the driver to transmit my farewell to the company, and for the favour if he had a chance, to tell my mother exactly what had happened. It was all over now.

However, apparently it was not! Shortly after, I felt a pricking in my right big toe, like when a foot had 'gone to sleep' and comes awake again. Suddenly, sensation and mobility returned. I was able to stand up and go back to the vehicle, and told the driver to try to start the engine, which he managed to do. The *VW Kübelwagen* were, you see, extremely difficult to burn.

I was taken to the Luftwaffe hospital in Bernay, near our quarters. The surgeon who dealt with my wound just shook his head at my narrow escape and said: 'If the strafer had flown a millimetre to the left he would have hit the spine from behind and the carotid from in front and no divinity would have got you to the operating table in time.' In hunters' parlance, they call this a *Krellschuß* (a spine-grazing shot). Adding to my luck, no major vessel in my lung was hit, when again there would have been no saving me if it had been. In the Eastern Westphalian homeland of our origin, it would be said about such a stroke of luck that 'the dear Khod [God] cares for the stupid!'.

Next day, 4 June 1944, the chancellor of the Paris embassy appeared in a 'wood gas car' with news to tell my parents. He told me that according to the latest information, the Allied invasion was to take place on 5 June. When he said goodbye on the morning of 5 June, to drive back to Paris, I said to him, laughing, that on the fifth again nothing had happened, which he countered curtly with the perfectly apt remark that 'the fifth is not yet past'. And indeed the Allies did arrive on the night of 5/6 June. Rommel, who was commander of Army Group B and responsible for us, was back in Germany celebrating a birthday with his family.

The 12th SS Panzer Division hurled themselves against the Allied forces – admittedly with some inexplicable delay on the part of *OB* (C in C) West. For weeks they prevented Montgomery from breaking through in spite of his grotesque superiority in men and matériel. Only when the Americans in the western sector of the invasion front succeeded in a breakthrough did the German front in the eastern sector also collapse, by reason of unrealistic orders to hold position that came from the Führer's headquarters. The British general Michael Reynolds has written about the 1st and 12th SS Panzer Divisions in the I SS-Panzer Corps: '[T]hey would be a strange mixture of leaders, hardened … in the crucible of the Eastern Front, and fanatical young soldiers … they were remarkable soldiers – the like of which we may never see again.'[480]

When the invasion began, the senior consultant of the Bernay Luftwaffe hospital wanted to have me relocated to Germany as he would soon be needing every available bed. But I wanted for all the world to stay with my company. I had trained the men, led them from day one and was very attached to them. So I left the hospital and drove after my company, which led to me being reported as a 'deserter' by the senior consultant.

In August I was given convalescence leave because of the after-effects of jaundice. I have told of the meeting with Father and his memorandum to Hitler in which he belaboured the latter with one of his own own statements: 'It is the business of diplomacy to see to it, that a people be kept alive, and not fall heroically.'

The Battle of the Bulge (in German *Die Ardennenoffensive*) ensued in December, to my mind irresponsibly staking everything on its outcome. As regimental adjutant of the panzer regiment of the right-wing division, I was in a position to judge. Yet again, dear God was on the side of the 'stupid' ones! The Americans, who were preparing for an offensive from Aachen to the Rhine, threw every available means at us, in particular their artillery. What they offered us in the way of artillery fire from the first days of the offensive put everything we had previously undergone in the shade. One of our battalions was stuck in the heaviest of artillery fire. While standing on the back of his tank, I had to give fresh instructions to the commander. He said: 'It's too "windy" out there, you had best come in to the tank.' I had not yet quite closed the hatch, when a grenade exploded on the rear of the tank. The impact fuse could not do the tank much damage, but I would have been mincemeat if I had disappeared inside it but a second later. As it was, all I got was a splinter in the face from the grenade, a most uncomfortable and painful wound. I had to disregard it and continue leading the battalion. The commander, whose care

I had to thank for saving my life, was killed shortly after in execution of the order I had transmitted. He was a hardened bachelor and had been unaffected by Himmler's written threat that he would not be promoted if he was not married by a certain time. Marriage was a bone of contention for Himmler. The commander had been ordered back from leave because of the Ardennes offensive. He reported to the regimental command post, beaming, with the words: 'Ribbentrop, I have found the right woman, now I'm getting married!' His happiness was visible. He was dead a few days later.

We no longer queried what happened. We could not possibly influence the fatal evolution of circumstances, we had to restrict ourselves to preventing senseless things happening in our scope. To abandon the troops, which would mean leaving our comrades high and dry, was not to be thought of for an instant.

On the way East in March 1945 I had been to Berlin to say goodbye to my father. Before seeking him out at the Wilhelmstrasse (where the Foreign Ministry building was), I had another minor experience in Berlin whose grotesque dimension hardly bears recounting. In the weeks on troop training grounds I had made friends with an actress of the Berlin Staatstheater. To say goodbye to her, I met her in the Ufa film studio in Grunewald. She was being filmed there with Heinrich George, whom I met then. The film, as I remember it, was set in the seventeenth or eighteenth century. In March 1945 the filming work went on as if it was peacetime, whilst the Russians were standing ready at the Oder for the final attack on Berlin. It was a weird situation, and turned to absurdity when the air raid sirens sounded. In the most beautiful weather, together with George and the other actors of the company, in their costumes, we were standing in front of the studio watching waves of hundreds of four-engined bombers as they flew above us to sow death and destruction somewhere. I remembered at that moment that I had heard George was very fond of a good cognac. We still had a bottle in the car, saved for a special occasion. This was one such – what other special occasion could any of us poor soldiers expect, who were about to come up against yet another hopelessly superior strength. I asked my adjutant to fetch the bottle from the car. George was already beaming at the promised treat. The adjutant came back, waving the bottle still swaddled in straw as he came up to George, when it slipped out of the casing and smashed to the ground! This 'disaster' was the absolute peak of a truly surrealist scene. George, who was corpulent, was still trying, with our help and bewailing the loss of the cognac, to get his massive body on his knees so as to dip his fingers into the little pools of cognac and lick them, and meanwhile the deep drone of the American bombers still sounded over our heads.

On this day Father and I talked together for the last time as free men. The next time we saw each other was a year and a half later, just before the verdict was pronounced at Nuremberg. As I have said, I was not allowed to see him again before the execution to bid him goodbye. We sat opposite one another in his study – which, surprisingly, still survived, albeit much battered. He said there was going to be terrible starvation. He would remain in Berlin. After a pause, he looked long at me, obviously profoundly moved, and said slowly: 'It was a great opportunity for Germany!' Then he said it again. Unspoken in the air was the sequel, 'if I had been listened to!' I knew only too well what he meant: the war on two fronts – the attack on Russia– should have been avoided. We hugged for the last time.

Another minor occurrence is worth mentioning briefly. In the last position we had to defend I had set up my command post in a forest keeper's hut. When in the last days of April, after a tour of the positions, I arrived there again I found twenty or thirty youths of the *Hitlerjugend* mustered in front of the hut. The adjutant reported that the youths were allocated to us as reinforcement from the Mountain Riflemen, to whom we were subordinated. The little huddle was 'armed' with a few old carbines and a couple of anti-tank weapons, while the uniforms and equipment were correspondingly inadequate. I instructed the adjutant to send the youths to the supply company, where they could make themselves useful in the field kitchen and elsewhere. At the same time he was to tell the chief of the supply company to send me up front some of the men who would be replacing the boys. But my Hitler youths then began to moan that they were not there to peel potatoes but to fight. I was deeply touched: we were a few days from capitulating. However, there was no way they could be deployed at the front line. I had to point out to them in a few curt military words that if they truly wanted to be soldiers it would be a good thing if they began by taking the foremost precept as being to obey.

A day or two later Hitler was dead. He meant nothing to me any more. I had not been surprised by his instruction to remove the stripes from the seasoned divisions of the Waffen-SS because the men could not fulfil the unrealistic standards required for the Ardennes and Spring Awakening (German '*Plattensee*') operations, nor had it bothered me unduly since, as I have already told, I had seen the sorry state he was in at the beginning of February in Berlin. Nevertheless, on receipt of the news of Hitler's death we let off a short volley from all weapons. In the dense woods it would hardly have touched a single Russian, and was not meant as a final salute to Hitler.

On this day of 1 May 1945 we were thinking of the enormous numbers of our comrades who had given their life for their country: the highest of sacrifices at all times and for all nations. An attitude of defiance may also have played a part, against an ineluctable fate, similar to that supposed to have been used by Napoleon's Old Guard general Cambronne, made famous by his expletive 'Merde!' ('Shit') in reply to a summons to surrender in the face of the final collapse of the emperor's rule at the Battle of Waterloo.

The final hours of the war reserved yet another magnificent experience for me: the ceasefire had been ordered for 00:00 hrs on the night from 7 to 8 May 1945. The war was over! I had been ordered, with my battalion, to meet up once again with the division, which already stood at the line of demarcation between the Russians and Americans. I therefore gave the companies the order to vacate their positions at midnight, under some minor pretext of rearguard safety measures, and by forced march to get to the few supply vehicles we had left, commandeered for the transport of troops. It was important to hand the troops over to the Americans as quickly as possible. I sent them on to march out from the mustering point as soon as they arrived, for the Russian would probably push forward to the line of demarcation come the morning. When the last company had passed the departure point, I waited for the last military backups that were to leave their positions only after a time lag, so as to simulate a complement of men. When they too had set out, I stayed there with the driver and the dispatcher for a moment more in the starry night, my thoughts occupied with what lay ahead for my men and myself. From the outset of the invasion we had not thought about the war we had lost, for we did not believe we would live to see the end. Henceforth, however, it was a question of dealing with what was of greatest urgency. Very soon these thoughts were at the back of my mind again. As always when the situation seems without hope, it matters to deal with the immediate, which meant saving the men who had been entrusted to me from being taken prisoner by the Russians and to hand them over to the Americans. The greatest hurry was imperative.

I then drove after the companies, having ascertained that for the time being all was quiet on the Russian side, and soon caught up with them. I could not believe my eyes and ears: the companies were marching in perfect alignment, officers at the head, singing, towards imprisonment! For a second I let the overwhelming impression overcome me, and then I gave the order for an immediate forced march.

The great touchstone for a troop's morale is at the moment of defeat. These soldiers could say of themselves that despite their young age they went to their imprisonment with the dignity and serenity of elite soldiers. It was best expressed when, three years later in the French Cherchemidi military prison in Paris, my fellow prisoner Dr Karl Epting,[481] who had been incarcerated for a long time in a dark cell, with shaven head and on a diet of bread and water because he had defied a drunken warder, said to me: 'Ribbentrop, they can treat us basely but they cannot debase us!'[482]

This famous quotation from Schiller goes for the treatment the Waffen-SS received at the hands of the state and the public, and still do to this day. Nonetheless, politicians who experienced wartime made *amende honorable* to the soldiers of the Waffen-SS, as did Konrad Adenauer (the first Chancellor of West Germany) in a letter addressed to Waffen-SS Colonel General Paul Hausser,[483] or Kurt Schumacher (West Germany's first Leader of the Opposition) to a foreign journalist. The excellent discipline of my troop in the face of definitive defeat made it possible for the whole company to be taken over to the Americans, thus rescuing them from imprisonment by the Russians.

Because of my father's position, the division commander considered me particularly vulnerable and made out for me a military passbook under another name, with the rank of serviceman. When a few days later all the Waffen-SS officers and sergeants were deported to an unknown destination, he gave me permission to stay behind as it was quite possible they were to be delivered to the Russians. In the course of the slowly proceeding organization of the internment camp, we other members of the Waffen-SS now had army officers as our superiors.

A while later we heard that our deported comrades had not been handed over to the Russians. I therefore decided to go to the Americans and give myself up, abandoning my disguise, as it may constitute a risk for those of my men who were still with me. I presented myself to our company leader, an army captain, and revealed myself with the explanation of my wish to go over to the Americans. To be sure, I requested that my false papers in his possession would be destroyed so that the regimental comrade who had signed them would not get into trouble. The same would apply to the men of my regiment with whom I had been under disguise. Although the captain gave his promise, he did not do it. He took me to the German general who supervised the diverse detention camps for the Americans, a certain General von Bünau. He was sitting with his staff at a coffee table in an orchard of his quarters, did not acknowledge me, left me standing some distance away and, without saying a word, handed me over to the American military police whom he had called in. I did not deserve such unworthy treatment, as I had taken action to rid myself of the disguise and had not asked for it. A captain of his staff, painfully eager to please, demanded both the military policemen to arrest me and handed them my false papers. I sent the general warm wishes, saying that his conduct was unworthy of a German officer.

At the military police I was interrogated by a friendly first lieutenant. We were seated facing one another when he suddenly asked me why I was not standing to attention with my hands along my trouser seams, as did all German officers, including generals? He accepted my reply – 'because I would not have had prisoner American officers stand to attention' – with a laugh. There was after all no army regulation regarding how to behave with dignity as a prisoner after a war was lost.

I was then taken to a former German work camp where the Waffen-SS officers were incarcerated. At the entrance a giant of a sergeant of the military police and the lieutenant officer of the guard descended upon 'van Ribbentrop's son' and plundered my person down to my underwear. The two of them shared the 'booty' – my silver cigarette case, epaulettes, decorations, etc. I was sitting on a cot in a small guard room, wearing only my underpants, with a GI in front of me, sweating under his helmet, the barrel of his machine gun in my navel. It was not a pleasant feeling: these fellows were often trigger-happy, as certain tragic occurrences in the earlier camps had shown. (The American guard posts had fun from time to time simply shooting into the camps.)

Now I got dressed again and enquired to have my epaulettes back. I had noticed that my indifference to his loutishness had shaken the young rogue, which is what he was basically. He refused to return this 'war booty' taken from a defenceless prisoner. I told him he could keep them; German officers were recognizable even without epaulettes. When he asked what they were to be recognized by, I answered angrily: 'For instance that they would not rob a prisoner.' The lieutenant, named as I remember Berry or Clerry or some such, who belonged to the so-called 'Rainbow' division, yelled for the guard, at the head of which an old sergeant – with studied coolness – appeared, wearing the 'Blue rifle', an American combat infantryman's badge, in fact with oak leaves, whilst Berry had nothing to show. 'Berry' advised the guard that 'van Ribbentrop's son' had accused the Americans of theft. It was a delight to see the contemptuous expression on the face of the aged sergeant, who without a word left the guard room, visibly displaying his displeasure at the conduct of his lieutenant. In the evening the old warrior – as he had proved he was – brought my rucksack to the empty cell in which 'Berry' had me shut to punish me, with the remark – charged with meaning – that he hoped there was not too much missing. That was the first time I experienced the extremes that I was to encounter often as a prisoner of the Americans: on the one hand naïve brutality, with unconventional humaneness on the other.

Although what I had experienced at the hands of General von Bünau was in some way of an abstract nature, since I did not know him and had never seen him before, I would soon have a similar experience of a highly personal nature. I was taken from Innsbruck back to Salzburg to a camp into which some 3,000 prisoners of diverse provenance were squeezed. The Americans did not set foot in it, leaving us to our own devices. After a few days I happened to meet five gentlemen from the Auswärtiges Amt, all of whom I knew well. They were housed in another shack from mine. After dark one of them came up to me to ask if I would stay away from them so that they should not be compromised through me, as he put it. I was rather stunned, and, without a word, turned away.

As it happened, some days later the Yanks put together a work commando of about 300 men which included the five from the Auswärtiges Amt as well as myself. We were housed in nearby Golling, in a former German prisoner of war camp, and were to be occupied with some sort of work for an American battery under the command of a burly first lieutenant. This American must somewhere have obscurely heard something about the Geneva Convention, because he arranged for one of the five shacks to be designated for officers, as according to international regulations imprisoned officers should be housed separately from the troops.

As the five German diplomats were not officers, they were put in the shacks with the ordinary soldiers. They argued that they belonged to a 'higher service' and consequently belonged with the officers – which offered no advantages, whether in regard to the accommodation nor the provisioning, and which, moreover, did not correspond to Geneva Convention regulations. The American first lieutenant could not care less where these people were housed, so they were distributed among the three rooms of the officers' shack. I was thereupon prompted to explain to my 'prefect', a bearded admiral, that if one of those five was to be lodged in our room, I would go to the Americans to ask to be housed in a soldiers' shack. When he found out why, which was that I did not want to impose upon the gentlemen to have to share living space with me, he laughed and assured me he would not let any one of them into his room. The navy had preserved its camaraderie, which was brought forth by sharing very close living quarters, and continued beyond and after the catastrophe of Germany's defeat. Two years later, in another camp, one of the five gentlemen sought me out to present his most formal apologies. Herr v. 'S.' was Austrian, a bearer of the Party's so-called Blood Order, conferred for bodily injuries received by the bearer in the course of fighting days. 'S.' had been incarcerated by the Austrian Fascist government in Wöllersdorf concentration camp and tortured, he told me, among other forms by being made to stand in a very narrow cell with water up to the knees for days on end.

In the meantime, after an odyssey through various camps and prisons, I ended up in Dachau, where approximately 10,000–15,000 internees were gathered under American supervision. One day the German camp chief, a prisoner himself, had me brought to see him, when he told me – having enjoined me to the strictest secrecy – that I had cropped up on the Allied list of war criminals. He showed me the entry: 'Pillaging in Harcourt'. This was indeed the place where my company had been quartered for a few weeks before the Allied invasion of Normandy.

The German camp chief offered to supply me with forged liberation papers and sufficient money, and have me taken to Munich's main train station. In most cases departure from the camp was effected in the fire engine. Albeit I was not charged with murder, because of my name I had no chance of a fair hearing in a war trial. I thanked him heartily for his comradeship in my regard, but asked for time to think it over. The camp chief had at his disposal the means he had offered me because, for the sake of convenience, the Americans let the war criminal documents in part be perused by prisoners. It was in this way possible for the German camp administration to obtain the entire 'war criminals' lists, which were kept safe under the floorboards of the camp's administration shack. Fresh issues were continually appearing. My name had come up as recently as in a list dating to late 1946.

In all situations during the war and my imprisonment, I had no trouble sleeping, but in this case I spent a sleepless night. The camp chief's proposal signified in essence that I would go undercover and adopt an entirely new identity. I could only trace the cause for my suddenly appearing as a 'war criminal' in 1946 to a social evening, a gathering of my company on 1 May 1944; it was a correct assumption, as was later to be proved. This is what happened that evening. Harcourt in Normandy, a small village of some 300 inhabitants, had a little village green in the centre, where the church also stood. By necessity the green was also the site of the company's roll-call and muster – the village was so small there was no other possibility. At dark on 1 May 1944, a May bonfire was lit, to be jumped through, accompanied by singing, as is usually done to entertain 17 to 18-year-old youths. At some point in the evening my company sergeant reported to me that a *Rottenführer* (lance corporal) had got blind drunk, gone on the rampage in the church, broken some windows of village houses and had now disappeared. Thereupon I put an end to the evening. The man had just been transferred to us from heavy fighting in Russia and was inclined to be undisciplined, wherefore he had not been promoted, and I had been told by my commanding officer to improve his behaviour by taking appropriate measures. In this I was successful, making him maintenance sergeant responsible for the motor pool; it was not an easy job and he carried it out splendidly. On this convivial evening he had somewhat gone overboard, and had he not unfortunately landed in the church nobody would have taken exception after the damage had been paid for.

Next day the damage was revealed. In the church the man had stumbled against a plaster candle stand, which fell over and broke. He had broken a window in the pub and taken a rocking chair away with him, which was found in the street; in a little garden he had kidnapped a rabbit from its hutch, which was caught in good condition in his quarters and safely returned to its owner, as was the rocking chair. Finally, the high point of his 'outrages', was that the man had passed a house in the village street, against whose outer wall a ladder led up to a first floor window. I learnt this only from the investigating judge in Paris, Capitaine Garat, suppressing his laughter, who said that my man had climbed the ladder and at the top had huffed and hawed into the open window, whereupon Monsieur 'X' and Mademoiselle 'Y', with no clothes on, had had to flee, as was now documented. This is anyway how Capitaine Garat, with a smile, presented it to me.

My first visit was to the priest, to present my excuses and, of course, to assess the cost of paying for the repairs. The second was to the mayor, an aged general confined to a wheelchair. I am not at all sure he understood the reason for my coming to him, for he recounted to me – as he did every time I saw him – that it was he who prevented the Germans from taking Verdun in 1916. It goes without saying that the other damages were also paid for. Furthermore, a detailed report was drawn up indicting the man, by order of the company commander, which could possibly have led to a court-martial. More could hardly have been done. By 1948, when I was finally handed over to the French, the incident had become the 'pillaging and partial destruction of the village and church of Harcourt' – thus the Americans delivered me to the French.

I had thus become a 'war criminal'. My examination was undertaken by Mr Howard, a Jew from Frankfurt, who spoke accent-free German. The prisoners considered him to be particularly sharp. When a letter-smuggling was exposed, he had greeted me with the words: 'So you want to step into your father's footsteps do you?' (Father's execution dated back just a few weeks.) It is best not to react at all to such rudeness, or in any case merely do so haughtily.

I was fetched before him again for interrogation. When I entered his room this time, he said: 'Don't I know you?' I laughed, and said: 'Yes, from that letter smuggling!' I had been caught getting a letter to my mother 'out' without being censored, with the help of a friend. Howard then asked me whether I had been given the leave I had applied for. When I answered 'of course not!' he proposed I should write my mother a letter, as long as I wanted. He would see to sending it off without being censored. He kept his word too.

He then began to make notes about my military career, beginning with the question what rank I had entered the army with. My answer was rather provocative, that unlike his President's sons I did not join the army starting out automatically with the rank of colonel. I had been a mere foot soldier and had taken part in the Western campaign as such, when I had been wounded. When we spoke further about my various wounds, he shook his head and said: 'You really didn't have to go through that.' Only now did the question come: 'What reason are you here for now?' When he ascertained that the French wanted me handed over, he spoke disparagingly of them and announced that he would prevent me from being delivered to them. In my presence he rang up the chief of the War Crimes Commission, a colonel, and argued with him that 'van Ribbentrop's son ... is obviously a much nicer man than his father' and such a hand-over should be prevented. Naturally, Howard could not obstruct my transference to the French for very long: this much was clear to me. At that point I had to ask myself the momentous question which was to determine my fate for many years, namely whether I wanted to disappear into 'freedom' or run the risk of being imprisoned for a long time, since I could not count on being treated with anything approaching a halfway legally permissible procedure. At the turn of 1946/47 it was not at all clear what would happen in general to us internees; we could maybe be held for years. I did now have a chance to escape this. Just in case, the camp chief gave me the forged release papers. One set was in the name of a Sergeant Wilke, signed by the American colonel and stamped, furthermore a letter of recommendation to all American services to be of assistance to me if necessary. I was also provided with another whole set of blank papers. I have them in my possession to this day.

I was then indeed handed over to the French and was driven, together with a bunch of fellow-sufferers, on a very cold day – it was January 1947 – in an open truck to Reutlingen, to a French war criminals' camp. It was under the command of a French captain, who behaved impeccably to us.

I was very soon transferred from the camp to Reutlingen prison, whence a few days later two decent French gendarmes took me to the former Germersheim German military prison on the Rhine, which was now serving the same purpose for the French. As the two gendarmes had not thought of the fact that the Germersheim railway bridge had not yet been restored to use, we had to walk a long distance to a ferry, a trek that for me, being not fit and in a debilitated condition from undernourishment and lack of exercise, was very trying, to the extent that the kind-hearted gendarmes carried my luggage for me. Whereas in Reutlingen we were decently treated, by contrast in Germersheim the treatment was more abusive. One evening a cohort of French officers, with their wives in evening dress, had the cell door opened so as to take a look at me, which was the ultimate insult and demonstrates their level. That we twenty-five officers were almost naked due to the heat, as the cells had been locked, evidently did not bother the 'ladies' in the least. However, what well-qualified officer gets a post as prison minion in an occupied area?

In Dachau (see page 94) I had heard nothing further from the Canadians regarding the shooting of a prisoner. In Germersheim, however, after a few days I was fetched by a Canadian officer and taken via Heidelberg prison to Minden to the military penal facility that went under the code name 'Tomato'. There yet another Canadian officer took over, who again said nothing about the site nor the date of the alleged incident until it really became too much for me and I told him I was entirely at his mercy – that was perfectly clear to me; he could have me killed at any moment, I could do nothing to prevent it. Bearing this in mind, I added that from this instant I would answer no more questions until a lawyer I was to appoint had received the indictment, stating the circumstances of the alleged incident. It is unnecessary to say that this information was never transmitted to me or my lawyer. I was instead kept in Fischbeck the whole summer of 1947, in the 'murder cage', without being questioned, until finally, as I have said, I turned to my former headmaster at Westminster School.

I have already recounted how my request to the headmaster to do something for me resulted in my being handed to the French, and in fact to the charge of 'pillaging and destroying the church and village of Harcourt', or in other words because of a kidnapped rabbit, a rocking chair (both having been returned), a broken candle stand and a window (both paid for), not forgetting the fright caused to the mystery Monsieur and Mademoiselle!

Looking back, the decision I took to see the business through was correct. I had committed no crime. The minor damage, which always occasionally happens with all troops in the world, had all been paid for. I had moreover presented my excuses. A report had been issued against the guilty party. There was therefore objectively no reproach against me. But in those days this was immaterial. On the other hand, if I had gone undercover I would to this day not have been able to live freely. But there was still a major risk, and there certainly were moments in the next year or two when I thought back as to whether I had taken the right decision.

A few weeks later I was moved again, this time to Hamburg-Fischbeck, the location of a British 'war criminals' camp' in a former German barracks. Our welcome was appalling. A British army captain by the name of Carter received our group, first of all by indiscriminately striking the prisoners with a substantial truncheon. He then ordered us to march off at the double, and under continued beating we went to the parade ground. He had meanwhile smashed a prisoner's nose. Carter was a repulsive creature, red haired, a typical 'brutal colonial'! I was at the back of the little column and would not let myself be hustled, which made him constantly kick my backside while hitting me on the head and back with his truncheon. Well, I'm a tough guy and survived the process without undue damage – I was wearing a thick winter anorak. To be fair it must also be said that the complaint of one of the released prisoners, addressed to the British Labour MP Victor Gollancz – who was Jewish – motivated his visit to the camp and led to Carter's dismissal. His successor, also a captain, was a correct and affable person.

As after the war 'ugly Americans' or 'hateful Germans' were spoken of, it should not be overlooked that there was an equivalent British type, the 'brutal colonial', who simply kicked the heels of the natives in India or wherever if they did not get out of the way fast enough. Carter was one of those. He was visible in the dead of night with his red moustache on his red face! His sort exists all over the world. In this case too the question is what well-qualified officer would become compound officer in a prisoners' camp?

If by any chance one was enmeshed in such a war-criminal's machinery, great care had to be taken. We were at their mercy. My statement that I would say nothing more until the indictment was presented was punished with incarceration in the 'murder cage' mentioned above, for months on end, with no interrogation. There ensued the hand-over to the French already recounted. This is how I landed in Wittlich penitentiary in January 1948. The administration was already back in German hands. The 'correctional staff' sometimes could not quite distinguish between the rogues and the military interned by the French, and this had sometimes to be made quite clear to them. But both prisoner chaplains showed themselves to be most helpful owing to the fact that they had fully grasped the difference. The Evangelical pastor, a kind elderly man, once put a tiny wrapped piece of butter, stealthily – it was of course prohibited – on my bunk. The Catholic priest was a bright little fellow. He asked me, speaking between clenched teeth, whether my mother knew where I was. I was to have a piece of paper with her address ready for his next visit, and he would let her know straight away. And he did it too!

About three weeks later, near the end of January 1948, eight prisoners from Wittlich, chained together two by two, were taken by rail to Paris. The gendarmerie officer who was in charge of the transport with a few gendarmes was sentient enough to remove my handcuffs during the night, as they were obviously too small for my hands and cut deep into my flesh. At the Gare du Nord we stood around on the platform for a long time as the '*Grüne Minna*' ('Black Maria') did not arrive. I noticed that none of the passers-by called out anything rude to us.

Our arrival at Cherchemidi prison was once again an astounding experience. As it was a military prison, the 'delivery' was overseen by an officer. He was the equivalent of the 'ugly American' or 'hateful German', looking like a caricature of Napoleon III, sporting the same Van Dyke beard on his jaundiced face. His complexion indicated a probable bilious or liver complaint, and he behaved accordingly. I was singled out again and taken to his office, where with the help of several warders I was frisked and eventually stood in front of his desk stark naked. He was not even bothered that from time to time a lady lawyer or secretary had to come in. In the end my belongings were piled into one big and one small heap. I would be allowed to take the small one with me to my cell, while the bigger was to go into store. I was duly to sign for it in a book. This I refused to do, as I had not been correctly treated, uttering an angry '*Je ne signe pas!*' The diminutive French officer became so furious he almost had a stroke. His outbreaks of rage always culminated with the words: '*On va te mettre au cachot!*' (which roughly translates as 'take him to the dungeon'). I remained obdurate. Thereupon, clothed once more and carrying no luggage, I was shut in a cell with windows but no window panes, which was most uncomfortable as at the time the temperature in Paris was several degrees below freezing. I crouched in a corner of the cell, hugging my knees, to expose as little as possible outer surface of my body to the cold – an old soldier's habit. A judicial officer appeared in the course of the next day, apparently supposed to be the alternate prison governor. He instructed a piece of cardboard to be put in the pane of the broken window and I was given two – albeit very thin – blankets.

Next morning another prison lackey appeared in my cell, one whom the prisoners called '*La Pipe*' because he always went around with a pipe in his mouth. He was of the harassing kind and, as was to emerge, understandably little loved by the prisoners. In my case he behaved with the utmost politeness, took me to the store room and told me to examine my luggage and inform him what items should stay in storage. He then very accurately entered them in his book. Evidently my refusal to sign had hit a bull's eye with the prison bureaucrats. I did not need to have been a prisoner for many years to know how to use the opportunity to let various little things, unlawful per se, such as patience cards, penknife etc., get back to the cell with me. '*La Pipe*' asked me if I would sign now. With the amicable remark '*Maintenant c'est correct, je vais signer!*' ('Now it's OK, I will sign'), I signed the inventory.

I was now put in a 'normal' cell. It consisted of the following: width 1.30m; length 2.30m; furnishings: three straw sacks, two stools, an ancient washbasin, a repellent jug of water and, finally, the most important, a tiny bucket with a lid in which to relieve oneself. The bucket was emptied into the yard early in the morning and in the afternoon. There were three of us in the cell; we literally could not hide anything from one another! Both my cell-mates were interesting people: one had been governor of a Danzig bank of issue, a member of the Reichsbank's directorate, international currency expert and commissioner for the Banque de France during the German occupation. After his discharge he was Finance Minister of a German Federal Land. A highly cultivated personage, he could once in a while be amusing. The other was a counter intelligence officer, apparently inconspicuous – as are all the clever members of that profession – widely travelled, mostly in Spanish/French areas, kindly and companionable: an especially pleasant cell-mate. Every morning the bald pates of both gentlemen looked like crumble topping, so much had they been bitten, because they gleamed and attracted bugs. They had me, as the youngest, lying in the middle, which I accepted (my feet between their heads, their feet at my head).

The Reichsbank man was most interesting. He elaborated thoughts about a currency reform that was still in the future in Germany. His summing up was always: 'Ribbentrop, it is the same for a currency as for butter: if there is too much of it, the price falls!' He made it clear that he attributed a major role to the dollar. When I happened to come across him again many years later – he was again active in the banking business, as by then I was too – he said to me: 'What did I tell you then in Cherchemidi about the dollar? Now the same has become our problem!' I learned a lot from him and it was never boring in that awful cell, to which the counterintelligence officer's stories also contributed a lot, about the agents' games with the Allies and the *Résistance*. If one kept one's eyes and ears open and managed to get the older men talking, there was always an interlocutor to talk to in a profitable dialogue. I had realized long ago that it was worthwhile to find one's way about a totally different world from the ideal of soldierly comradeship one had lived in for so many years.

To my pleasure, in Cherchemidi I again met Dr Epting, whom I had known in other prisoner camps. Conversations with him touched on all possible fields of knowledge, often being great fun.[484] One day he said: 'You need a lawyer, else you will be made sausage-meat of.' But where was I to find a lawyer? He suggested that I ask the Marquis de Polignac to recommend one. Polignac was a very old friend of my father's from days long before Father went in for politics. Polignac duly recommended a Maître Sauerwein, who immediately came to see me in prison and told me he would charge a hundred pounds sterling in cash as his fee. In reply to a relevant letter from me, Mother was confident she could find the money. Her own finances were completely blocked, but Mother was going to ask a Dutch relative by marriage whom Father had freed from a concentration camp and whose court martial he had prevented, and she was quite assured of success. It is well known that in 1945 courts martial could easily become very rough. However, this person did not seem to value his self or indeed his life very highly, because he summarily refused Mother's request. She therefore turned to another very old friend of Father's in England, the proprietor of the Johnnie Walker Whisky Company. Sir Alexander Walker unhesitatingly put the cash at her disposal, with the explicit proviso that he did not want to be repaid.

I did have some slight qualms whether Sauerwein was the right choice, for I knew that his father, Jules Sauerwein, had been a leading-article writer in the 1920s and 1930s as renowned as he was hostile to Germany. Epting correctly countered that for that very reason my lawyer would be all the more free to take all the steps necessary in my interest. Furthermore, the Polignac name still carried substantial weight and Sauerwein – in those days still an up and coming 'fashionable' lawyer – would certainly not want to disgrace himself. Meanwhile I had been brought before the investigating judge for examination. Capitaine Garat was very correct and, in view of the ridiculous accusations, apparently felt uneasy. He did, however, inform me that he had now to get the statements from Harcourt.

Mother had meantime addressed François-Poncet, asking him to intervene. I deduced from something Garat said that François-Poncet had indeed written to the Paris judicial authority, although he did not let me see the letter. I do not know if it had any effect. It did not look as if for the time being it had, for Garat explained that he had to await the report of an inhabitant who had meanwhile emigrated to the African bush. It would take a long time to find him and get a statement from him. Sauerwein, on the other hand, categorically assured me that I had no indictment to expect as the accusations were ridiculous, but the *juge d'État* (state judge) would not quash the procedure since he feared to be attacked in the press because of my name. As Sauerwein had no further steps to propose taking, the outlook was grim, for the summer recess of law courts which began in mid-July and lasted three months was rapidly approaching.

It would therefore be October or even perhaps November before there was the chance of anything moving in my case and there was no purpose in taking steps in that sense.

Grandfather Henkell was fond of citing an adage that one should be good friends with a good doctor, a good banker and a good lawyer, but that one should have the good ideas oneself! I therefore racked my brain to think what could be done for me to get out of prison before the judicial recess. It was known from time to time that one or another fellow prisoner – mostly elderly or gravely ill – had been released in what was called *liberté provisoire* against a bail caution, which signified that they were granted provisional freedom under conditions, without the procedure being officially closed. It occurred to me one night that this could be the solution for the prosecutor. He could claim that the investigation process was underway. I might thereby have the possibility of free movement, at least in the French zone. Admittedly, I gave no special chances to my ideas but it could not make things worse if the attempt should not meet with success.

I therefore asked Sauerwein to come and see me in Cherchemidi. He sent a young assistant, to whom I told my thoughts, undoubtedly recklessly, maintaining that the necessary money for bail would surely somehow or other be obtained, not that I had the slightest inkling whence it would come. The lawyer wanted me to give him an address in the French zone where, after *liberté provisoire* had been granted, I could if necessary be found when I was released. All I knew was that a cousin of Mother's had a vineyard in the Mainz neighbourhood. The little village where it lay was always known in the family just as 'Bischheim' (in Hessian, 'Bischem'). I therefore gave the name of the Schultz family in Bischheim and was duly released to go there – and this was the most noteworthy – without a deposit for bail. In fact the village was called Gau-Bischhofsheim. The French judiciary had not even troubled to check the address. It was further proof of the 'gravity' of the alleged accusations against me.

It was disclosed to me on 7 July 1948 that under reserve of *liberté provisoire* I would be released from prison the next day and 'shoved off' to Germany. I need hardly say that I had little sleep in the night of 7/8 July 1948. Was it really possible that after three years and two months I would regain my freedom, could take my fate back into my own hands and would once more be able to go wherever I wanted? Having been so long a prisoner, one had become rather sceptical – it was all happening with such speed.

On the morning of 8 July, the '*Grüne Minna*' – as Berliners called the green prisoners' transport vehicle – carried us to the prefecture's 'deportation' department. Besides myself there was a Waffen-SS private who had spent years in Cherchemidi without being informed to what the honour was due. There was great commotion in the strictly guarded space, where a motley crowd of crooks awaited their transportation to countries all over the world. In the end we Germans were the only ones left, as our express train to Strasbourg departed Paris at the dead of night. A gendarme accompanied us until we boarded the train to Germany in Strasbourg. We were terribly hungry, for the prison had not provided us with any victuals for the trip.

When we travelled over the bridge on the Rhine at Kehl – very slowly, as it had been only provisionally repaired – we gasped with relief: it seemed we had really made it, we were back in Germany. The brilliant sunshine of the day suddenly appeared even brighter to us. But the suspense lasted to the very last moment for we were not really in Germany, at least not what we always used to call it.

In Kehl's still almost completely demolished station our papers were of course scrupulously examined, with the result that the gendarmes in control informed us two Germans that we could go no further. I was told, baldly, that because of my name – 'here we go again', I thought to myself – the chief of the local Sûreté (the French criminal investigative bureau) had first to give his approval; my companion lived in the Saar (German, Saargebiet), so he could not travel there through the French occupied zone and had to go back and make his way through French territory. However, the Sûreté chief would be there only the next day, as on that day there were no more rail departures for Germany. My pointing out that I had my impeccable release, or rather deportation, papers was of no use; we were told to find ourselves a nook anywhere in the ruins of the station and await the next morning. Had there in the meanwhile been a hitch? A helpless prisoner with no will of his own, who can have but the slightest effect on his destiny, will always feel under threat from dark, indiscernible powers.

All we could do was find ourselves the least draughty little corner affording some shelter from possible rain showers. The best thing to do in such situations is to keep busy with something, so I took my 'Theory of Business Management' manual out of my bundle of books, which had in the meantime become a properly weighty load, and got to work.

A short while later the gendarmes fetched me to the Sûreté chief's office, which had been set up for him in a shack. The gendarmes of the station guard also congregated there, about eight of them, curious to see what was now about to happen. The 'chief', who had been found somewhere, did offer me a chair, whereupon he narrated in detail to his ever-more-darkly glowering audience how the nasty Germans had prodded and pinched him and all that he had had to endure from them. When at last he paused and looked around for applause, I merely asked curtly, in French for the gendarmes to understand, if he did not think I would be able to tell exactly the same story about my imprisonment? He immediately replied, this time in accent-free German: 'Of course I believe you!' After he had furthermore assured me that on the next morning I could travel onward on the first train, he disappeared.

Then, something unexpected happened. The oldest-serving gendarme, a fellow built like a wardrobe, trotted up to me with that particular rapid little regulation tread, stood to attention, and asked in the best correct manner whether he and his mates could invite the 'Capitaine' to dinner. I thanked him most affably but pointed out that I had a companion with me whom I could not leave alone. Naturally, my companion was also invited, was the friendly reply. A draisine (light auxiliary rail vehicle) driven by one of the gendarmes pulled up, which took us to a specially engineered track in the next village where the gendarmes were quartered and had set up their 'mess'. Both of us were then treated to all imaginable delicacies – or so it appeared to us at least – naturally accompanied, in the good habitual French way, by wine.

When we had returned to the station in the draisine after a plentiful dinner, in an adjoining room we found two camp beds made up with white sheets, on which we hardly dared to lie down, used as we were to sleeping on filthy straw sacks for so many years. It had been a long time since we slept as well as we did that night. There is no doubt the unaccustomed wine imbibed will have contributed to it, but so did the feeling that all would be settled on the morrow. So too will the unexpected comradely gesture those ordinary gendarmes spontaneously demonstrated have helped.

The next morning, after a full breakfast in the gendarmes' mess to which we were once more invited – and we were what is more liberally provisioned for the journey ahead – I said goodbye to my companion, who had to travel in the opposite direction, back to France. When I boarded the train that was now really to take me to 'freedom', the gendarmes stood in line to bid me farewell; I shook hands with every one of them and while they called out '*Bonne chance, mon Capitaine!*', the train was set in motion. I waved back to the gendarmes for as long as I could see them. A word spoken at the right time, which one should always have the courage to speak, had triggered a charming reaction. My memory of these gendarmes from Kehl has remained unaltered in spite of the many years that have elapsed, whilst the many unfriendly incidents of imprisonment are gradually fading away!

I had one more magnificently humane experience in connection with what occurred at Harcourt. My lawyer, the attorney Dr Grimm, well known in Hamburg, advised me to collect as many sworn statements as possible from members of my company who had taken part in the celebration of 1 May 1944. I agreed, under condition that it would be left to me to decide if and when such statements were to be introduced in an eventual court case. The reason was that according to the juridical practices of the Allied war criminals' tribunals, witnesses for the defence were often simply arrested and also indicted. I wanted my men to be spared this. My men naturally knew all about these practices of the Allies and the risk they ran if they put their statements to paper. Nevertheless, all those who could be reached placed themselves as witnesses at the disposal of the defence. What a splendid example of true comradeship in a time when, after the defeat, all formal bonds had been loosed and there was no longer any obligation on anybody. In this context Mother's old English governess must be brought to mind, the good 'Petty' whom I have already mentioned. She had written from Sheffield with penetrating questions to the court in Paris!

Freedom

I did not need to have more than five years of war and more than three of imprisonment behind me in order not to be so hard-nosed that once I was in Germany to go directly to where my family was in the British zone, thus contravening the condition of permission to remain only in the French zone of occupation. Border control between the British and French zones was dealt with by the expedient of hiding in the express train's toilet. I had a delightful welcome from Uncle and Aunt Schniewind, who had already taken Mother and my little siblings in. They made my step out into freedom as easy as possible, as did the family of Mother's cousin, Fritz-Rudi Schultz, in Gau-Bischhofsheim, alias 'Bischem', where I had been ordered to go. From the start he and his family took me to their heart in the nicest possible way. The weeks spent in his vineyards, where in glorious weather I tried my hand at some weeding to loosen my limbs, which had become rather stiff, are among my first happy post-war memories. This pleasant stay in 'Bischem' was over all too soon when I was notified from Mainz by the Sûreté of the official calling-off of the investigation. After all the rigours I had undergone, I found the formulation in the court's decision for termination in my case, that 'Capitaine von Ribbentrop's' conduct had been absolutely correct, an irony of fate.

Uncle and Aunt Schniewind and the Schultz family stood by me in the most selfless and familial way, as I now, like millions of others submitting to a similar fate after the war, took my first steps into another, a new world. Such family fidelity was not a self-evident matter of course. This was soon to manifest itself. I was to experience the most aggravating example of kin liability (*Sippenhaft*) only now after I was liberated from prison, inflicted by my own family, combined once again with an exceptionally positive humane experience. I must give here in detail what happened, out of gratitude to the person who at the time placed himself at our disposition – my mother's, Uncle and Aunt Schniewind's and mine – in the most generous manner: the alas long-deceased Dr Franz Rosenfeld.

As attorney in Mannheim, Rosenfeld had looked after my grandfather Henkell's extremely profitable business career. It was also he who drew up the will of my grandfather, who died in 1929. According to the testament, I had the right one day to join the Henkell firm. In 1938 Rosenfeld emigrated to Basel, where he became a highly esteemed notary. (He was for many years legal adviser to the German Embassy.) As a result of the death of my uncle, Stefan Karl, killed in the Western campaign, the Henkell & Co. company partnerships had to be restructured. Mother and her Schniewind sister were henceforth partners of the Henkell firm in Wiesbaden founded by their father. In this new order, my mother had the right to nominate one of her three sons at an appropriate time as a managing partner. Mother nominated me. My mother's cousin, Otto Henkell, the sole general partner, objected to this, as did the legal representatives of another cousin and a female Henkell cousin. At that time both the latter cousins were under age and consequently did not take part in their guardians' opposition. Their argument was that my family name was so bad for business that it was out of the question that anybody bearing it should become a managing partner. The fact that even supposedly superior personalities, however intelligent, could not escape the predominant spirit of the age was amusingly demonstrated by the well-known banker Hermann Josef Abs. He was connected with the family for many years and a friend of my grandfather. He had therefore long been chairman of the company and a family adviser. He too, giving evidence as a witness, made it known in writing that he adhered to *Sippenhaft* in that as bearing the name of Ribbentrop I was not tolerable for the firm. The *Sippenhaft* principle was quite openly stated in this case and represented in law by a society to which the well-known member of the resistance, Fabian von Schlabrendorff, also belonged. Does it read correctly nowadays? Did the so-called resistance not wish to restore the rule of law? In his book *Offiziere gegen Hitler*, he expounded the thesis that a heavy defeat would have had to be inflicted on the German Wehrmacht in order to bring about Hitler's overthrow.[485]

The counter-example to the jurist and lawyer Schlabrendorff was also given by a lawyer. When Rosenfeld heard of our difficulties with the family, he made it known to us through an acquaintance that he was at the disposal of my mother and I. It reached the point of the relatives provoking a legal action on our part, wherein Uncle and Aunt Schniewind selflessly joined forces. Rosenfeld exerted a decisive influence on the tactics of litigation for our side, which led to a successful outcome for our charge. When he was asked by Otto Henkell how come he, being a Jew, had taken our side, Rosenfeld gave the magnificent retort: 'Herr Henkell, I am a lawyer, which means that I advocate the law!' One may well ask whether Rosenfeld and Schlabrendorff are equal 'advocates of the law' in the eyes of Our Lord.

A friend convinced me to stay away from the family clique and go to work for him. The business opportunity he made available to me constituted a greater challenge for me than I could have imagined. I shall ever be grateful to him.

This description of diverse minor experiences of mine, as a 'well-known' figure, is in no way a lamenting railing against the fate of having a well-known name, and is intended instead only to show the difficulties that those with a famous name may encounter, which in my case dated to well before 1945.

I also want to state that I do not wish I had missed out on any instant of my life, and this also goes for the worst circumstances and dangers. It is they that have made me what I am today and gave me a certain inner distance from life's perils. What does having had a 'full life' really mean? A full life signifies an exceptional breadth of more profound – not to say existentially mental, intellectual and perceptional – experiences and lessons learned that was granted to one. To this the ultimate peril belongs, namely to do, despite one's natural fear, what has to be done. To overcome this fear when it is imperative represents a further human fundamental experience of the very first order. It comprises an atavistic element. Nowadays courage is counted as a negligible, secondary virtue, an extraordinarily outstanding stupidity of our times.

All sort of deprivations such as hunger, thirst, cold, exhaustion and pain belong among these fundamental experiences. So does the realization of one's own limits of achievement and, possibly, of going beyond them when there is nothing left but the will to endure. Comradeship received and rendered under the most threatening circumstances crowns the series of great experiences, as well as, let it not be forgotten, the moment of 'victory' – whatever each understands by this at any given time – among others in battle, which is always a matter of life or death; and finally, to submit body and soul to an idea – for instance to a God or the idea of one's fatherland or something held by each to be of value to which the whole person is duty bound to dedicate their self. Whoever was not given the opportunity of such an experience in whatever form, to my mind lacks something in a 'full life'. Nothing alters this ascertainment, even when a subsequent somewhat melancholy realization dawns upon one that it is evidently no longer that country of mine to which I had given my commitment; a country in which those citizens are defamed as 'murderers' who are or were at any rate ready to give up their life for their homeland. They can not, or could not, in general judge the politics, let alone influence them, but they were prepared for the eventuality of having to sacrifice their life for their country. This tendency to defamation when at the same time, from the other side, engagement for the common good is postulated, can be designated only as exceptionally stupid. To have experienced total defeat, the complete loss of rights it entails, represents an awesome extension, a complementing of my life's experiences. I may mention in passing that preservation of dignity in the face of a national misfortune does not necessarily seem to be the strongest aspect of my countrymen.

Irrespective of which insights and outlooks into the world's activities were granted to me from my early youth, I may call myself a 'witness of the times' in a phase of political compression of events seldom encountered in the history of the world. Against this, what do the personal difficulties, adversities and imperilments signify, to which one was inevitably – *nota bene*, at any time – exposed and from time to time still is today?

As I come to the close of this manuscript I have reached the end of the 87th year of my life. As is pointed out from time to time in a friendly or tactful way, the rest of my life can henceforth be 'overviewed'. In the sense of what stands above, to quote from Horst Wolfram Geissler's book *Der liebe Augustin*: I may say – possibly slightly exaggerating – I have been greatly smiled upon in my life!

Notes

1. To this I do however have to say that when I was with the troops in the East I did not hear of any instance where a prisoner political Commissar had been executed by shooting.
2. Father stated in a Note: 'The Führer became very agitated and abruptly cut me short.'
3. *cf* Goldhagen, Daniel J.: *Hitler's willing executioners: ordinary Germans and the Holocaust*, London, 1996.
4. Thus formulated by Fyodor M. Dostoyevsky in his novel *The Possessed*.
5. Reference is made to an article by Maurice Druon, Perpetual Secretary of the Académie Française, in *Le Figaro*, 30 August 1999.
6. Quoted from Haffner, Sebastian: *Von Bismarck zu Hitler*, Munich, 1989, p.61 (English edition: *Germany's self-destruction: Germany from Bismarck to Hitler*, London, 1989); and Gall, Lothar: *Bismarck*, Berlin, 1995, p.517 (English edition: *Bismarck: The White Revolutionary*, London, 1986).
7. Froment-Meurice, Henri: *Vu du Quai – Memoirs 1945–1983*, Paris, 1998, p.660.
8. The attack on the French navy in Oran in 1940 should be brought to mind, after the conclusion of the campaign in the West. In allusion to such preventive action in peacetime such as the attack by the British navy against Napoleon's in 1807, the verb-notion 'to Copenhagen' was coined.
9. See Ferguson, Niall: *The Pity of War*, London, 1998.
10. After the end of the war, ridiculous representations appeared in the memoirs written then, as to whether it was my father's own wish to go to London or whether, on the contrary, Hitler had 'fobbed him off as compensation', in addition and further to the negative assumptions that were made in regard to the stories of the duration of the ambassadorship. In a personal report addressed to Hitler in 1937/38, my father states: 'When I asked the Führer to have me sent to London …' He would hardly have written in these terms if he had wished to become or to remain State Secretary, or if against his will Hitler appointed him to London, as Reinhard Spitzy and Paul Schmidt maintain (See the latter's book *Statist auf diplomatischer Bühne* [*A Bystander on the Diplomatic Stage*] *1923–1945*, Erlebnisse des Chefdolmetschers im Auswärtigen Amt mit den Staatsmännern Europas, Bonn, 1949; English edition: *Hitler's Interpreter*, London, 1951). In his book *So haben wir das Reich*

verspielt. Bekenntnisse eines Illegalen, Munich, 1986, p.95 (English edition: *How we squandered the Reich*, Wilby, 1999), Spitzy says: '... immediately following the Olympiad, after having organized diplomatic receptions on a large scale, he [Ribbentrop] approached Hitler in order to request the post of Secretary of State. Hitler however took Neurath's side in his assumption. Ribbentrop had been "fobbed off" with the post of ambassador to London.' The appointment had however already been announced during the Olympic Games. When distorting the truth, as Spitzy does yet again on this point, it would be advisable to be more accurately informed about generally known facts, irrespective of the fact that before the announcement the Agrément (official approval) too was to be negotiated.

11. Striefler, Christian: *Kampf um die Macht*. Kommunisten und Nationalsozialisten am Ende der Weimarer Republik, Frankfurt/Main, 1993.

12. At this time the Red Army had already been on stand-by for years, in order to take best advantage of political developments for an advance westward. *Cf* Musial, Bogdan: *Kampfplatz Deutschland*, Berlin, 2008, p.389.

13. In the First World War, during his command post in Turkey, my father had written articles for a well-known newspaper of those days, the *Vossische Zeitung*.

14. The position of Foreign Secretary of State had also been newly freed to be occupied since the death of the incumbent State Secretary Bernhard Wilhelm von Bülow.

15. Eden, Anthony: Memoirs – *Facing the Dictators*, London, 1962, p.509. In this context, also interesting is Ferguson, Niall: *The Pity of War*, on the subject of British policies before the First World War.

16. Reventlow, Graf Ernst zu: *Deutschlands auswärtige Politik 1888–1914*, Berlin, 1916 (1918), p.XVIII. In this sense, see also Ferguson, Niall: *The Pity of War*.

17. See Musial, Bogdan, *op. cit.*

18. See also Kordt, Erich: *Nicht aus den Akten*, Stuttgart, 1950, p.70.

19. According to an unpublished memorandum by Hermann von Raumer, Hitler's words were 'Ribbentrop, ... have England brought in to the Anti-Comintern Pact: that would fulfil my dearest wish.' Here *cf* Michalka, Wolfgang: *Ribbentrop und die deutsche Weltpolitik 1933–1940*, Munich, 1980, p.155.

20. *cf* Hitler's speech to the Reichstag of 28 April 1939: 'This desire for Anglo-German friendship and cooperation conforms not merely to sentiments which result from the racial origins of our two peoples, but also to my realisation of the importance for the whole of mankind of the existence of the British Empire.

'I have never left room for any doubt of my belief that the existence of this empire is an inestimable factor of value for the whole of human cultural and economic life …

'Now there is no doubt that the Anglo-Saxon people have accomplished immeasurable colonising work in the world. For this work I have a sincere admiration. The thought of destroying this labour appeared and still appears to me, seen from a higher human point of view, as nothing but the effluence of human wanton destructiveness.' *The British War Bluebook. Extract from Speech by Herr Hitler to the Reichstag on April 28, 1939*, http://avalon.law. yale.edu/wwii/blbk21.asp.

21. *Cf* Harrison, Ted: 'Alter Kämpfer im Widerstand: Graf Helldorff, die NS-Bewegung und die Opposition gegen Hitler', in *Vierteljahrshefte für Zeitgeschichte*, 45, 1997/3, pp.385–423.

22. On Ribbentrop's involvement in the negotiations, *cf* Michalka, Wolfgang: *op. cit.*, p.30 *et seq.*, and Ribbentrop, Joachim von: *Zwischen London und Moskau, Erinnerungen und letzte Aufzeichnungen* [trans., Between London and Moscow, Memories and final Notes], Leoni, 1953, p.36 *et seq.*

23. Wilhelm Keppler (1882–1960) joined forces with the NSDAP in 1927, and in 1931 founded the 'Keppler-Kreis' (Keppler Circle), later the 'Freundeskreis des Reichsführer SS' (Circle of Friends of the Reichsführer SS). In 1933 he became a member of the Reichstag and Commissioner for Economic Questions in the Chancellery of the Reich. From 1938 on he was State Secretary for Special Duties in the Auswärtiges Amt.

24. Joachim Fest, in his well-known biography of Hitler, mentions only a little of the 18 January 1933 meeting – reporting the content thereof erroneously – as he describes it as having been a 'breakthrough' and that Oskar von Hindenburg had taken part. *Cf* Fest, Joachim: *Hitler*, London, 1974, p.360 f.

25. Ribbentrop, J. v.: *op. cit.*, p.40 *et seq.*

26. 'Prussians' in this context is understood to mean the Conservatives, that is the *Deutschnationale Partei* (German National People's Party).

27. Handwritten reports of this sort are kept in the Hoover Archive.

28. This declaration was delivered by the USA, France, Britain and Italy on 11 December 1932 in the framework of the Disarmament Conference there; *cf* Scheil, Stefan: *Fünf plus Zwei*, Die europäischen Nationalstaaten, die Weltmächte und die vereinte Entfesselung des Zweiten Weltkriegs, Berlin, 2003, p.166.

29. See e.g. the article in *Le Figaro* of 30 August 1999 by Maurice Druon, Perpetual Secretary of the Académie Française, as well as statements by the French minister Chevènement on the French TV channel France 2: 'Basically [Germany] is still always dreaming of the Holy Roman Empire German Nation and has not yet recovered from the derailment that National Socialism has been in her history.' Quoted in *Die Welt*, 23 May 2000; see

also 'Hitler-Vergleich: Mitterands Angst vor den Deutschen' in *Die Welt*, 11 September 2009; and 'Wie Thatcher die deutsche Einheit verhindern wollte' in: *Die Welt*, 15 September 2009.

30. Scheil, Stefan: *op. cit.*, p.118, footnote 26; Willms, Johannes: *Nationalismus ohne Nation*, p.495.

31. Froment-Meurice, H.: *op. cit.*, p.289.

32. *Welt am Sonntag*, 13 November 1994. The well-known American political scientist Samuel Huntington in *The Clash of Civilizations and the Remaking of World Order*, in German translation, Munich, 1996, p.208. Incidentally, the notion of 'partnership in leadership' stems from George Bush Senior.

33. Churchill, Winston: *Memoirs of the Second World War*, vol. I: *The Gathering Storm*, London, 1949, p.187.

34. *Cf* Lord Robert Vansittart on 6 September 1940 on the instructions to the British envoy in Stockholm: 'The German Reich and the Reich idea have been a curse of the world for 75 years ... The enemy is the German Reich and not merely Nazism, and those who have not learned this lesson have learned nothing whatsoever.' Quoted from Allen, Martin: *Himmler's Secret War*, London, 2005, p.85 f.

35. *cf* Ribbentrop, J. v.: *op. cit.*, p.45.

36. The final instalment of the Reparations would have been due in 1988.

37. IMT (Trial of the Major War Criminals before the International Military Tribunal), vol. XVII, pp.551–55; see also Kranzbühler, Otto: *Rückblick auf Nürnberg*, pamphlet, Hamburg, 1949, p.21 *et seq.* Kranzbühler was counsel for the defence of Admiral of the Fleet Dönitz at the first Nürnberg trial.

38. Protocol of the main trial of 5 July 1946, Afternoon session, IMT, vol. XVII, p.552.

39. Thus in the lecture by Professor Hans Mommsen, given in the Düsseldorf Rotary Club on 28 January 1988. This is all the more puzzling because the Saint Germain and Trianon Treaties made largely similar stipulations.

40. Keynes, John M.: *The economic consequences of the peace*, New York, 1920, p.145.

41. Quoted from Vansittart, Robert: *The Mist Procession. The Autobiography of Lord Vansittart*, London, 1958, p.300; see also Paxton, Robert: *Europe in the twentieth Century*, San Diego. 1985, p.45; and Weber, Eugen: *Action Française – Royalism and Reaction in Twentieth-Century France*, Stanford University, 1962, p.121.

42. See statements by Supreme Army Command Chief Kurt Freiherr von Hammerstein-Equord, of 27 February 1932, quoted from Meinck, Gerhard: *Hitler und die deutsche Aufrüstung 1933–1937*, Wiesbaden, 1959, p.195, Note 88.

43. He was Hans Heinrich Dieckhoff, later (1937–38) German ambassador to the United States.

44. On 12 November 1918 the German-Austrian National Assembly declared Austria as part of the German Republic. There followed on 12 March 1919 a renewed announcement of union. Article 88 of the Saint-Germain-en-Laye Treaty stipulated the prohibition of the union without the approval of the Council of the League of Nations. Source: http://aeiou.iicm.tugraz.at/aeiou.encyclop.a/a586894.htm.

45. *Cf* Bogdan Musial's description of corresponding Politbüro sessions at the beginning of the 1930s, *op. cit.*

46. Büchmann, Georg: *Geflügelte Worte*, Munich, 2001, p.416, mentions *The Times*'s military correspondent Colonel Charles Repington as originator (*The Times*, 13 August 1914).

47. Quoted from Uhle-Wettler, Franz: *Das Versailler Diktat*, Kiel, 1999, p.155.

48. Reply of the allied and associated powers to the observations of the German delegation on the conditions of peace, London, 1919, Part V, p. 22.

49. Quoted from Benoist-Méchin, Jacques: *Jahre der Zwietracht 1919–1925*, Geschichte der deutschen Militärmacht 1918–1946, Oldenburg, 1965, p.354.

50. Meinck, G.: *op. cit.*, pp.36, 199, Note 70; Schwendemann, Karl: *Abrüstung und Sicherheit*, vol. II, p.454.

51. *Cf* Uhle-Wettler, Franz: *op. cit.*, p.66.

52. Meinck, G.: *op. cit.*, pp.19, 196, Note 6, Krupp-Prozeß, Vert.-Dok.-Buch-Krupp 2b, p.25 *et seq.*, in Krupp-105.

53. Quoted from Meinck, G.: *op. cit.*, pp.19, 196, Note 7, Krupp-Prozeß, Vert.-Dok.-Buch-Krupp 2b, p.10 *et seq.*, in Krupp-104.

54. Meinck, G.: *op. cit.*, pp.15, 195, Note 88. Chancellor Brüning confirmed the Polish plans for an attack; *cf* Brüning, Heinrich: 'Ein Brief', in *Deutsche Rundschau* 70, July 1947, pp.1–22.

55. *Cf* Meinck, G.: *op. cit.*, p.13; resp. p.194, Note 78; Polish General Staff archive, p.112 *et seq.*

56. DGFP (Documents on German Foreign Policy), Series C, vol. I, Doc. Nos 83, 120, 180; Meinck, G.: *op. cit.*, p.18 *et seq.* and p.196, Note 5; Roos, Hans: 'Die "Präventivkriegspläne" Pilsudskis von 1933', in *Vierteljahreshefte für Zeitgeschichte* 3/1955, p.344 *et seq.*; Rönnefarth, Helmuth/Euler Heinrich (publ.): Vertrags-Ploetz. Konferenzen und Verträge (Pt II, vol. 4: Neueste Zeit 1914–1959), Würzburg 1959, p.125. *Cf* also Scheil, Stefan: *Logik der Mächte*, Berlin, 1999, pp.100–04.

57. *Cf* Vansittart, Robert: *op. cit.*, p.412.

58. *Cf* also Meinck, G.: *op. cit.*, p.19.

59. Vertrags-Ploetz: Part II, vol. 4, p.119; 'Der große Ploetz', 1991, p.863.

60. Vertrags-Ploetz: Part II, vol. 4, p.119.

61. In the Bad Aibling detention camp the plank bed underneath mine was occupied by a Chief Prosecutor named Hattingen. In Paris he belonged to

Ernst Jünger's circle – who spoke of Hattingen as his 'dear friend' in a letter addressed to me – and told of a then written text by Jünger, entitled 'Der Friede' (The Peace). A few years ago I asked Jünger to be so kind as to let me have the text, with which request he promptly complied, writing among other things: 'Your father had at that time invited some writers to Fuschl, with myself among them as well as Sieburg, because he had in mind to set up a sort of brain-trust. Each of us was among other things to have privileged access to contact the Auswärtiges Amt by telephone so as to be able to choose a post as correspondent abroad – of which I did not avail myself.' Father wished to make use of Jünger's affinity with the French cultural milieu, in the sense of activating German-French understanding. It was alas in vain. An interesting example of the stance of outright denial held by a portion of the intellectuals.

62. Schwerin von Krosigk, Lutz Count: *Es geschah in Deutschland*, Stuttgart, 1951, pp.121-22.
63. Churchill, W.: *op. cit.*, p.88.
64. *Cf* Plehwe, Friedrich-Karl von: *Reichskanzler Kurt von Schleicher*, Esslingen, 1983, p.300.
65. *Cf* the Hitler Interviews in *Le Matin* (Paris), 22 November 1933; *Daily Mail* (London), 5 August 1934.
66. 10 to 14-year-old youths were enrolled in the 'Deutsches Jungvolk' of the Hitler Youth organization.
67. Ribbentrop, J. v.: *op. cit.*, p.51.
68. Ribbentrop, J. v.: *op. cit.*, p.51.
69. *Cf* the book '*The Revolver Republic*' by *The Times* journalist George E.R. Gedye, London, 1930.
70. Hitler, Adolf: *Mein Kampf*, New York, 1941, p.944: 'The demand for the re-establishment of the frontiers of the year 1914 is political nonsense of such a degree and consequences as to look like a crime.'
71. *Cf* Vansittart, R.: *op. cit.*, p.412.
72. Ambassador Dr Paul Karl Schmidt (retd) (Press): *Ribbentrops Reise nach Warschau Ende Januar 1939*, Hamburg, 1963, p.6; drafted for the Auswärtiges Amt (Bonn), MS in the possession of this author.
73. See also Colvin, Ian: *Master Spy*, New York, 1952 (First edition London, 1951, under the title *Chief of Intelligence*).
74. *Cf* Charmley, John: *Churchill, the End of Glory*, Suffolk, 1993, p.444.
75. Reinhard Spitzy was my father's secretary until 1938. He planned to marry a young English society lady and therefore, according to the rules of those days, had to leave the diplomatic corps. It was surmised at the time that on the part of the lady the relationship had come about for reasons to do with the British Intelligence Service, because she broke it off when Spitzy left the Corps.

76. Ribbentrop, J. v.: *op. cit.*, p.52 *et seq.*

77. Ribbentrop, J. v.: *op. cit.*, p.56 *et seq.*

78. Meinck, G.: *op. cit.*, pp.70, 208, Note 238; Loosli-Usteri, Carl: *Geschichte der Konferenz für die Herabsetzung und die Begrenzung der Rüstungen 1932-1934*, Ein politischer Weltspiegel, Zürich, 1949, p.643.

79. Meinck, G.: *op. cit.*, p.60 *et seq.*

80. Meinck, G.: *op. cit.*, pp.69, 208, Note 235; Loosli-Usteri, Carl: *Geschichte der Konferenz für die Herabsetzung und die Begrenzung der Rüstungen 1932-1934*, p.679.

81. Meinck, G.: *op. cit.*, p.71 *et seq.*; Berichte des Auswärtigen Amtes über den Besuch Edens, in DGFP, Series C, vol. II, Docs Nos 270 and 271, dated 20 February 1934.

82. Wheeler-Bennett, John W.: *Documents on International Affairs 1934*, London, 1935, p.384.

83. François-Poncet, André: *Als Botschafter in Berlin 1931–1938*, Mainz, 1949, p.178.

84. RGBl 1934 Part II dated 26 March 1934; DGFP, Series C, vol. II, Doc. No. 378.

85. See DGFP, Series C, vol. II, Doc. No. 402, Aufzeichnung des Außenministers (written account by Foreign Minister) v. Neurath, dated 16 April 1934.

86. The German air force was supposed to be allowed to reach 30 per cent of the forces of all her neighbours but no more than 50 per cent of the French air force. DGFP, Series C, vol. II, Doc. No. 399; see also Meinck, G. *op. cit.*, pp.81, 211, Note 283; Wheeler-Bennett, John: *Documents on International Affairs*, Oxford, 1929, p.384.

87. On 18 May 1925, Stresemann declared in the Reichstag: 'There is nobody in Germany who could admit that the borders drawn in the East in flagrant contradiction to the peoples' right to self-determination is an everlastingly unalterable fact.'

88. François-Poncet: *op. cit.*, p.178.

89. On how correct this observation was, *cf* Duppler, Jörg/Groß, Gerhard P. (publ.): *Kriegsende 1918*, Ereignis, Wirkung, Nachwirkung, Munich, 1999, p.57.

90. Ribbentrop, J. v.: *op. cit.*, p.60.

91. Meinck, G.: *op. cit.*, p.76 *et seq.*, plus p.210, N. 267; Herriot, Édouard: *Jadis*, vol. 2, D'une guerre à l'autre 1914–1936, Paris, 1952, p.399.

92. Memo for the Führer of 3 April 1935. Louis Lochner Papers, Hoover Library, accession # XXo31 – 9.12. Box # 1

93. This was Leni Riefenstahl's film *Triumph of the Will*.

94. Herbert Hoover Archives, Louis Lochner Papers, Hoover Library, accession # XX031 – 9.12. Box # 1 (the words set in italics are handwritten insertions of my father).

95. The rapid eradication of unemployment was not achieved through rearmament but through a taxation policy that offered attractions and, above all, the reawakening of confidence in the general state of affairs, which triggered investments in the economy. Among other references, *cf* here Reinhardt, Fritz (publ.: Ralf Wittrich): *Die Beseitigung der Arbeitslosigkeit im Dritten Reich. Das Sofortprogramm 1933/34*, Straelen, 2006.

96. As to what extent Germany's armament was in effect overestimated, insofar as the exaggeration did not serve the purpose of propaganda, see Klein, Burton: *Germany's Economic Preparations for War*, Harvard, 1959.

97. Ribbentrop, J. v.: *op. cit.*, p.61.

98. Ribbentrop, J. v.: *op. cit.*, p.62.

99. Fest, Joachim: *op. cit.*, p.492.

100. A purely marginal remark: in his biography of Hitler, among other things Fest often mentions Hermann Rauschning. Rauschning (1887–1982), intermittently a politician of the NSDAP; after the NSDAP's electoral victory in Danzig in 1933, among his other posts was President of the Danzig Senate. His purported *Gespräche mit Hitler* (trans., Discussions with Hitler) (Zürich, 1940. First edition, London, 1939, under the title *Hitler Speaks. A Series of Political Conversations with Adolf Hitler on his Real Aims*) were convincingly unmasked as forgeries by the Swiss teacher and historian Wolfgang Hänel in 1983/84. In Issue 30 of 19 July 1985 of the weekly *Die Zeit*, it is written that 'In Joachim Fest's biography of Hitler alone, Rauschning's spurious discussions and statements are quoted more than fifty times.'

101. Ribbentrop, J. v.: *op. cit.*, p 64.

102. Expression used in the famous 'Blood and Iron' speech to the Prussian Landtag during the constitutional conflict regarding the aggrandisement of the army.

103. *Cf* the text of the Crowe Memorandum in HMSO, British Documents on the Origins of the War, Vol. III The Testing of the Entente 1904-6, pp.397 *et seq*, 421.

104. Erhard Milch (1892–1972), State Secretary of the Reich Aviation Ministry (RLM) from 1933–45; at the same time Inspector General of the Luftwaffe; after the suicide of Ernst Udet in November 1941, he was his successor as Luftzeugmeister (LZM) in charge of logistics until July 1944.

105. Irving, David: *Churchill*, Munich, 1990, p.71, Notes 2 und 3 (English edition: *Churchill's War*, Indianapolis, 1987).

106. Ribbentrop, J. v.: *op. cit.*, p.67 *et seq*.

107. Ribbentrop, J. v.: *op. cit.*, p.70 *et seq*.

108. *Cf*. Scheil, Stefan: *Fünf plus Zwei*, p.172.

109. Ribbentrop, J. v.: *op. cit.*, p.79.

110. Ribbentrop, J. v.: *op. cit.*, p.77 *et seq*.

111. Klein, Burton, *op. cit.*, p.17: 'Up to the time of the German reoccupation of the Rhineland in the Spring of 1936, rearmament was largely a myth.'
112. Ribbentrop, J. v.: *op. cit.*, p.78.
113. Ribbentrop, J. v.: *op. cit.*, p.83.
114. Ribbentrop, J. v.: *op. cit.*, p.85 *et seq.*
115. Hoover-Archives, Louis Lochner Papers, Hoover Library, accession # XX031 – 9.12. Box #1.
116. The ostensible cause of the conflict between Prussia and France in 1870 that led to the German-French War of 1870/71 was the intention of the Spanish Cortes to offer the Spanish throne to a member of the House of Hohenzollern-Sigmaringen.
117. Ribbentrop, J. v.: *op. cit.*, p.88.
118. Ribbentrop, J. v.: *op. cit.*, p.89.
119. Ribbentrop, J. v.: *op. cit.*, p.89 *et seq.*
120. Ribbentrop, J. v.: *op. cit.*, p.90 *et seq.*
121. Ribbentrop, J. v.: *op. cit.*, pp.91–93.
122. Michalka, W.: *op. cit.*, p.154 *et seq*; Ribbentrop, Annelies von: *Die Kriegsschuld des Widerstandes*, Leoni am Starnberger, see 1974, p.16 *et seq.*
123. Ribbentrop, J. v.: *op. cit.*, p.94 *et seq.*
124. Ribbentrop, J. v.: *op. cit.*, p.96 *et seq.*
125. Vansittart, Robert: *The Mist Procession*, p.525 *et seq.*
126. In the film *Un Taxi Mauve* (1977) with Fred Astaire, Charlotte Rampling and Philippe Noiret.
127. Father once recounted that Hitler had expressed a very negative opinion of a beautiful blonde lady of the diplomatic world of Berlin. When Father asked him why he had this opinion, Hitler had answered that she had conceived her children in a tipsy haze of champagne. Father was perfectly aware what other Berlin society 'beautiful blonde lady' had unleashed this little intrigue.
128. This is a reference to a quotation attributed to Mark Twain: 'Never argue with a fool; onlookers may not be able to tell the difference.'
129. Abbreviated as MP.
130. See the books by Monsignor Karl Morgenschweis, the prison chaplain in the American war criminals prison in Landsberg, where the executions were carried out; Morgenschweis, Karl: *Strafgefangener Nr. 9469 Pater Rupert Mayer S. J.*, Munich, 1968.
131. In the then famous literary magazine *The Strand*, Vol. XCII., in March 1937 (No. 555, pp.511/519) an unusually long article about my father appeared, headed 'Hitler's Man of Strength, A Character Study of Herr von Ribbentrop, The New German Ambassador to Britain', wherein is also stated that 'He is unmistakably one of the most attractive spokesmen of a regime … handsomely endowed both mentally and physically … He represents modern Germany to the world in its most attractive light.'

132. One more particularly wicked blow from Spitzy, R., *op. cit.*, p.99, for he was from personal experience perfectly aware of my parents' position in London society. The high esteem in which what is called 'success in high society' is held by such, as in this instance, as Spitzy, reveals the mentality of the slanderers! Just as an example, here is a letter from the American writer Jason Lindsay to Mme Marianne Steltzer in Bonn dated 15 May 1991, in which he says: 'Before the second War, I was in London and was fortunate enough to be on Herr Ribbentrop's invitation list when he was Ambassador here. An invitation to the German Embassy during his tenure was the most sought after and most highly prized in London. My good friend Prince George (later Duke of Kent) never turned down an invitation from Ribbentrop and it had been through Prince George that I had been introduced to Ribbentrop. I thought he had great charisma and he was certainly a superb host.'

133. Joseph Chamberlain (1836–1914) was an influential British politician in the nineteenth century and the father of the later British Prime Minister Arthur Neville Chamberlain.

134. Quoted from *New York Times*, 11 February 1902.

135. It is the case here of an orally delivered objection within inter-state relations.

136. For instance the shelling of a German battleship which caused lives to be lost.

137. From US General Albert Wedemeyer: *Wedemeyer Reports!*, New York, 1958, quoted in Nevins, Allan: *Henry White, Thirty Years of American Diplomacy*, New York, 1930.

138. 'Report on the Coronation and then present situation', dated 21 May 1937; drawn up on the occasion of the coronation of George VI. Printed in: DGFP, Series C, vol. VI, Doc. No. 380.

139. IMT, vol. VIII, p.205.

140. Approximately the view of Friedman, George: 'Russian Economic Failure invites a New Stalinism', in: *International Herald Tribune*, 11 September 1998.

141. Ribbentrop, J. v.: *op. cit.*, p.112.

142. Ribbentrop, J. v.: *op. cit.*, p.113.

143. The hotel was the Kaiserin Elisabeth in Feldafing, which was highy rated before the war.

144. The historian Andreas Hillgruber, for instance, represented the theory of Hitler's 'stage-by-stage plan' as steps to attain world hegemony. (*Hitlers Strategie, Politik und Kriegsführung 1940–1941*, 1965, dissertation).

145. The 'mother-ship' term derives from the French Minister for Air, Pierre Cot.

146. Quotation from Schiller's *Wallenstein*.

147. Main Report (A 5522); mentioned in DGFP, Series D, vol. I, Doc. No. 93 as 'Not found'. To trace it, see Thompson, Laurence: *The Greatest Treason*

– *The untold Story of Munich*, New York, 1968, in: Ribbentrop, A. v.: *op. cit.*, p.59 *et seq.*

148. Federal Archives PA/AA, R 28 895a (BRAM); reproduced in: Ribbentrop, A. v.: *op. cit.*, pp.61–74; quoted from the original carbon copy from the Foreign Office (in free translation): 'The document was produced at the Nuremberg Trials and for a long time later said to be lost [see data under DGFP, Series D, vol. I, Doc. No. 93] and was allegedly … traced only in the Acts of the British Foreign Office. It is consequently not quoted in the archives of the DGFP. The document is in the possession of the Auswärtiges Amt's Political Archive only since 1994.]

149. The word 'heroic' was added subsequently.

150. Emphasis in bold by the author.

151. IMT, vol. XXXIX, Doc. No. 075-TC, pp.91–98 (pp.94–98), and DGFP, Series D, vol. I, Doc. No. 93.

152. Emphasis in bold by the author.

153. Underlinings in this list were marked as 'underlined by hand' in the IMT-Source.

154. Papen and Spitzy have constructed out of the phrases *in italics* a 'Memorandum for the Führer': Papen in his book *Der Wahrheit eine Gasse* (Munich, 1952), p.423 (English edition: *Memoirs*, London, 1952, p.375), Spitzy reproducing it in his book *So haben wir das Reich verspielt* on page 222 (English edition: *How we squandered the Reich*). At the places mentioned it is couched as follows:

    German Embassy London, 2.1.1938

    Note for the Führer

    Outwardly, continued understanding with England. Quiet but determined establishment of alliances a g a i n s t England. Only in this manner can we meet England, whether it be for a settlement someday or in conflict.

    Ribbentrop

    Spitzy evidently simply copied Papen's falsification without checking: typical of him! Furthermore, he presents the layout of the Note differently from Papen.

155. Compare the interpreter Schmidt's assertion as to Ribbentrop's alleged disappointment at being posted to London whereas he wished to be Foreign Minister. Schmidt, Paul: *Statist auf diplomatischer Bühne*, Bonn, 1949, p.331 *et seq.* In his book *Memoirs*, p.375, Papen too asserts: 'Ribbentrop was resisting the idea of going to London.' How revealing these examples are of the 'love of the truth' of Messrs Papen, Schmidt (interpreter) and Spitzy!

156. Marked as 'underlined by hand' in the IMT-Source.

157. There is a copy of the transcript of the document in the Auswärtiges Amt's Political Archive. It is of interest that it can clearly be seen that the last word of the document has been tampered with, whether on the original of the

transcript or the copy itself. The expression 'enemies' is without any doubt not part of Father's vocabulary, in fact neither in its formulation nor from the sense of the context.

158. IMT, vol. XXXIX, Doc. No. 075-TC; DGFP, Series D, vol. I, Doc. No. 93.

159. Ribbentrop, J. v.: *op. cit.*, p.113 *et seq.*

160. Documents of the German Institute for Foreign Policy Research, Berlin 1942: Ribbentrop, J. v., *Der Freiheitskampf Europas*, p.9 *et seq.*

161. In Höhne, Heinz: *Die Machtergreifung. Deutschlands Weg in die Hitler-Diktatur*, Hamburg, 1983, p.247.

162. Papen, Franz von, *op. cit.*, p.423 (German edition).

163. Letter from Papen to my mother, 17 June 1953.

164. Spitzy, R.: *op. cit.*, pp.133, 146, 190, 228.

165. Maria von Ebner-Eschenbach coined the clever aphorism (trans. from the German): 'To defend oneself against calumny is either unnecessary or pointless!' Here however, as has been seen, it is a case of hard political facts of long, great and momentous effect that have to be taken into consideration. To enter into other personal small-minded calumnies of my father I consider to be beneath my dignity.

166. Quoted from Walter Hewel: Tagebuch (trans., Diary), 8 September 1941 (in the author's possession).

167. Ribbentrop, J. v.: *Zwischen London und Moskau, Erinnerungen und letzte Aufzeichnungen*, p.113.

168. Report from the German Embassy, London, dated 28 December 1937, and the accompanying Conclusions, dated 2 January 1938.

169. Ribbentrop, J. v.: *Zwischen London und Moskau*, p.124 *et seq.*

170. On the Blomberg-Fritsch-crisis *cf* Janßen, K.-H./Tobias, F.: *Der Sturz der Generäle*, Munich, 1994, *passim*.

171. Ribbentrop, J. v.: *Zwischen London und Moskau*, p.113.

172. Beham, Mira: *Kriegstrommeln*, Medien, Krieg und Politik, Munich, 1996, p.28 *et seq.*

173. Henderson, Nevile: *Failure of a Mission. Berlin 1937–1939*, London, 1940, p.140.

174. DBFP, Third Series, Vol. I, Doc. No. 232.

175. *cf* IMT, Vol. XI, p.436 *et seq.*

176. Author's italics.

177. Letter from the lecturer Gabriele Blod to the author, dated 18 February 1993.

178. Notification from the envoy Dr Paul Karl Schmidt, Head of the Auswärtiges Amt's Press and Information department, to the author.

179. DGFP, Series D, vol. II, Doc. No. 221, 30 May 1938. The formulation is an intensification of the one proposed by Keitel: see DGFP, Series D, vol. II, Doc. No. 175 (Encl.), 20 May 1938: 'It is *not* [author's italics] my intention

... Czechoslovakia ... in the immediate future without provocation.' Hitler expressly reserved for himself the initiative for when there would be a politically favourable point in time.

180. Not to be mistaken for the interpreter of the same name.

181. Orally communicated to the author by Dr Paul Schmidt.

182. *cf* Ribbentrop, A. von: *op. cit.*, *passim*.

183. Colvin, Ian: *Vansittart in Office*, London, 1965, p.210 *et seq.* A detailed account of Kleist-Schmenzin's activities is to be found in Ribbentrop, A. v.: *op. cit.*, pp.126–39.

184. DBFP, Third Series, Vol. II, p.687 *et seq.*

185. Count Stauffenberg, a severely disabled officer, took this road. He is owed our esteem. In my opinion it is not due to the conspirators of 1938–40.

186. Colvin, Ian: *Master Spy*, p.72.

187. Dokumente der Deutschen Politik und Geschichte, Vol. 4., p.447; *cf* also Ribbentrop, A. v.: *Deutsch-Englische Geheim-Verbindungen*, Tübingen, 1967, pp.126–28.

188. Kordt, Erich: *Wahn und Wirklichkeit*, Stuttgart, 1948, p.131, Footnote 1.

189. Rothfels, Hans: *The German opposition to Hitler. An Assessment*, London, 1961, p.61.

190. Adamthwaite, Anthony: *The Lost Peace–International Relations in Europe 1918–1939*, Basingstoke, 1981.

191. Ribbentrop, J. v.: *Zwischen London und Moskau*, pp.154–59; *cf* 100 Documents on the Origin of the War, Docs Nos 15 (197) and 16 (198).

192. 100 Documents on the Origin of the War, Berlin, 1939, Docs Nos 17 (200) and 18 (201); on this *cf* also Ribbentrop, J. v.: *Zwischen London und Moskau*, p.158 *et seq.*

193. Author's italics.

194. DBFP, Third Series, Vol. V, Doc. No. 364, Letter from Sir Nevile Henderson (Berlin) to Viscount Halifax (C 6799/54/18).

195. Beck, Joseph: *Dernier Rapport*, Politique Polonaise 1926–1939, Paris, 1951, p.188.

196. Schnurre, Karl: *Aus einem bewegten Leben-Heiteres und Ernstes*, Bad Godesberg, 1987 (in the possession of the author).

197. Quoted from Schmidt, P. (Press): *Ribbentrops Reise nach Warschau Ende Januar 1939*, p.2.

198. Schmidt, P. (Press): *op. cit.*, p.7.

199. DBFP, Third Series, Vol. III, Doc. No. 285.

200. Ribbentrop, J. v.: *Zwischen London und Moskau*, p.88.

201. *cf* DGFP, Series D, vol. IV, Doc. No. 356.

202. *cf* DGFP, Series D, vol. IV, Doc. No. 370 (see here also Footnote 1 of the document on p.471) and Doc. No. 383; Schmidt, P. (Press): *op. cit.*, pp.15-16; Schmidt, P. (Interpreter): *Statist auf diplomatischer Bühne*, pp.423-24.

203. Letter from Phipps to Sargent dated 12 December 1938.

204. Noël, Léon: *L'agression Allemande contre la* Pologne (The German Aggression against Poland), Paris, 1946 (German edition: *Der deutsche Angriff auf Polen*, Berlin, 1948, p.246).

205. Quoted from Schmidt, P. (Press): *op. cit.*, p.51 *et seq.*

206. Łukasiewicz, Juliusz: *Diplomat in Paris 1936–1939*, New York-London, 1970, p.152; Report addressed to the Minister of Foreign Affairs in Warsaw, No. 1/F-58., Political Report No. XL/3., Paris, December 17, 1938, Secret.

207. Łukasiewicz, Juliusz: *op. cit.*, p.156.

208. Łukasiewicz, J., *op. cit.*, p.159.

209. See Schmidt, P. (Press): *op. cit.*, p.52.

210. *cf* Schmidt, P. (Press): *op. cit.*, p.7.

211. Ribbentrop, J. v.: *op. cit.*, p.160.

212. Quoted from Schmidt, P. (Press): *op. cit.*, p.26.

213. Schmidt, P. (Press): *op. cit.*, p.64 *et seq.*

214. Schmidt, P. (Press): *op. cit.*, p.67.

215. Schmidt, P. (Press): *op. cit.*, p.69 *et seq.*

216. Quoted from Noël, L.: *op. cit.*, p.265. In the same sense Noël also quotes Robert Coulondre, the French ambassador in Berlin; ibid, p.266.

217. Quoted from the Auswärtiges Amt (ed.): The German White Paper – Full Text of the Polish documents, New York, 1940, Doc. No. 4.

218. He was in Warsaw on 25 January.

219. Ribbentrop, J. v.: *op. cit.*, p.166.

220. Schmidt, P. (Press): *op. cit.*, pp.80 *et seq.* and 93 *et seq.*; see also Auswärtiges Amt (ed.): The German White Paper – Full Text of the Polish documents, New York, 1940, Docs No. 4 and 9.

221. Tansill, Charles: *Back Door to War. The Roosevelt Foreign Policy 1933-1941*, Chicago, 1952, p.555. Bullitt as well as Kennedy later did not want to remember any such directive from Roosevelt in messages to Tansill (*cf* ibid.); Millis, Walter: *The Forrestal Diaries*, London, 1952, maintains the contrary.

222. The German White Paper – Full text of the Polish documents, Auswärtiges Amt (ed.), New York, 1940, Ninth Document, Report from Łukasiewicz of February 1939.

223. Millis, Walter: *op. cit.*, p.129.

224. The German White Paper – Full text of the Polish documents, Auswärtiges Amt (ed.), New York, 1940, Doc. No. 6.

225. I remember a minor episode in connection with Count Potocki and his wife, with admittedly no diplomatic consequences, rather the contrary. The couple came to a luncheon at our house in Dahlem, it must have been January 1935; I remember them as cheerful, elegant people. After lunch the gentlemen smoked cigars that with a little 'bang' turned into a sort of broom, while the Countess, with a little cry spat a chocolate into an ashtray.

For the entertainment of the family New Year's festivities a few days earlier, my sister Bettina equipped Father's cigars with tiny percussion caps and enriched Mother's confectionary with a few pepper chocolates. As always, when the mood is anyway cheerful – and it was that at the Potockis' visit – such little incidents enhance it even more.

226. According to the entry in Henry L. Stimson's diary for 25 November 1941, the question is posed 'how we [the USA] should maneuver them [the Japanese] into the position of firing the first shot without allowing too much danger to ourselves'. Printed in: Hearings before the Joint Committee on the Investigation of the Pearl Harbor Attack, 79th Congress, 2nd Session, P.11, p.5,433. The question whether in the case of the United States entering the war Roosevelt approvingly accepted an attack on Pearl Harbor, or had indeed provoked it, is to this day the object of intensive discussion among historians. Particularly critical of Roosevelt is: Morgenstern, George, *Pearl Harbor – The story of the secret war*, 1947; Toland, John, *Infamy: Pearl Harbor and Its Aftermath*, 1986; Bavendamm, Dirk, *Roosevelts Krieg 1937-45 und das Rätsel von Pearl Harbor*, 1993; and finally Stinnett, Robert B., *Day of Deceit. The Truth about FDR and Pearl Harbour*, 2000.

227. Ribbentrop, *op. cit.*, p.169, statement of Undersecretary Richard Austen Butler in the House of Commons on 19 October 1939.

228. *cf* Scheil, Stefan: *Fünf plus Zwei*, p.57 *et seq.*; Rydz-Smigly: 'Believe me, that the Polish mobilization was not merely a demonstration. We were ready for war.'

229. Ribbentrop, J. v.: *op. cit.*, p.160; see also Tansill, Charles: *op. cit.*; Fish, Hamilton: *FDR. The Other Side of the Coin*, New York, 1976.

230. Schmidt, P. (Press): *op. cit.*, pp.78–80.

231. Among professionals the military concept of the 'deployment area' contains an offensive component. Schmidt was not a military man. The concept is here meant in the sense of an Eastern European military zone against the Soviet Union.

232. Nadolny, Rudolf: *Mein Beitrag*, Wiesbaden, 1955, p.167.

233. Ribbentrop, J. v.: *op. cit.*, p.148; see also DGFP, Series D, vol. IV, Doc. No. 168.

234. Ribbentrop, J. v.: *op. cit.*, pp.149-51.

235. See Goebbels' diary entry dated 13 March 1939 in: *Der Spiegel*, No. 29/1992, p.122; Irving, David: *Goebbels: Mastermind of the Third Reich*, London, 1996.

236. Thus in Schwerin von Krosigk: *op. cit.*, p.237, as well as Weizsäcker, Ernst von: *Erinnerungen*, Munich, 1950, Spitzy and others.

237. DBFP, Third Series, Vol. V, Doc. No. 365.

238. Ribbentrop, J. v.: *op. cit.*, p.151 *et seq.*; see also Auswärtiges Amt (ed.): Documents on the events preceding the outbreak of the war, New York, 1940, Doc. No. 259.

239. Fish, Hamilton: *op. cit.* (German edition: *Der zerbrochene Mythos*, Tübingen, 1982, p.69 *et seq.*); Wirsing, Giselher: *Der maßlose Kontinent*, Jena, 1942, p.238 *et seq.*

240. DBFP, Third Series, Vol. IV, Doc. Nos 247 and 232, see also No. 230.

241. Schnurre, K.: *op cit.*.

242. Schnurre, K.: *op. cit.*

243. *cf* Schwendemann, Heinrich: *Stalins Fehlkalkül*, Die deutsch-sowjetischen Beziehungen 1939–1941, in *Tel Aviver Jahrbuch für deutsche Geschichte* XXIV/1995, p.10.

244. Ribbentrop, J. v.: *op. cit.*, p.171 *et seq.*

245. DGFP, Series D, Vol. VI, Doc. No. 583.

246. Schnurre, K.: *op. cit.*

247. DGFP, Series D, Vol. VI, Doc. No. 729 dated 27 July 1939.

248. Schnurre, K.: *op. cit.*, and DGFP, Series D, Vol. VI, Doc. No. 729 dated 27 July 1939.

249. DGFP, Series D, Vol. VI, Doc. No. 760.

250. Ribbentrop, J. v.: *op. cit.*, p.47.

251. *cf* Auswärtiges Amt (ed.): Documents on the events preceding the outbreak of the war, Doc. No. 446. The Polish government threatened: 'the Polish Government will consider as an aggressive act any possible intervention of the Government of the Reich which may endanger these rights and interests [in Danzig].'

252. DGFP, Series D, Vol. VII, Doc. No. 56.

253. Telegram from Hitler to Stalin dated 20 August 1939. DGFP, Series D, Vol. VII, Doc. No. 142.

254. DGFP, Series D, Vol. VII, Doc. No. 159.

255. Ribbentrop, J. v.: *op. cit.*, p.177.

256. The 'Fuschlturm' (tower) was subordinated to administration by the Finance Ministry of the Reich, destined as the seat of the current Reich Foreign Minister when Hitler was residing on the Obersalzberg. The owner had been arrested following the *Anschluß*. Contrary to what is every so often erroneously asserted, there was never any personal interest from our father in the ownership of the property. The proprietor had moreover not been dispossessed. He had, however, found himself in dire financial difficulties at the time of the Anschluss. The source of these slanders appears to be Vansittart (*cf* his pamphlet 'Black Record', 1941). Furthermore, Father had given instructions to the Legation Councillor Gottfriedsen, competent for the strict separation of the official sphere from the private, that upon termination of Father's political activity his fortune should not exceed what

it was at the outset, with the exception of both endowments – '*Grundsätzliche Anordnung des Reichsaußenministers*' (Basic Order of the Reich Foreign Minister), 'Westfalen' (Westphalia), 23 October 1941. ['Westfalen': code name for the RAM billet.]

257. Ribbentrop, J. v.: *op. cit.*, p.178 *et seq.*

258. On 3 and 7 August 1939, Schulenburg was still sceptical about an agreement between the Reich and the USSR; *cf* DGFP, Series D, vol. VI, Docs No. 766 and 779.

259. Ribbentrop, J. v.: *op. cit.*, p.184 *et seq.*

260. 100 Documents on the Origins of the War (publ. Auswärtiges Amt, 1939), Doc. No. 15 (197) – 16 (198).

261. Below, Nicolaus von: *Als Hitlers Adjutant 1937 – 45*, Mainz, 1980, pp.187–88 (English edition: *At Hitler's side. The Memoirs of Hitler's Luftwaffe Adjutant 1937-1945*, Barnsley, 2001).

262. *cf* Scheil, Stefan: *op. cit.*, p.70 *et seq.*

263. Dahlerus, Birger: *Der letzte Versuch*, München, 1948, p.110 (English edition: *The Last Attempt*, London, 1945).

264. DBFP, Third Series, Vol. VII, Doc. No. 546.

265. DBFP, Third Series, Vol. VII, Note 4 to Doc. No. 546.

266. Kordt, Erich: *Nicht aus den Akten*, p.278.

267. In his endeavours to present his significance as a resistance fighter, Spitzy confirms these cogitations expressly when he writes on p.300, *op cit.*, 'A second solution would have been … to allow a revolt of the German army to break out, preparation for which London … had already got wind of.'

268. The German White Paper – Full Text of the Polish documents, New York, 1940, Doc. No. 11 of 29 March 1939.

269. Colvin, Ian: *op. cit.*, p.72.

270. DBFP, Third Series, Vol. IV, Doc. No. 118, pp.120–22, Report from Henderson to Halifax, 18 February 1939.

271. Ribbentrop, J. v.: *op. cit.*, p.160.

272. Bonnet, Georges: *Les fils de la mémoire* (Edition in German: *Vor der Katastrophe.* Erinnerungen des französischen Außenministers 1938–1939, Cologne, 1951, pp.307-09.)

273. Trials of War Criminals before the Nuernberg Military Tribunals, Vol. XII 'The Ministries Case', p.347.

274. Best, Sigismund Payne: *The Venlo Incident*, London, 1950, p.7; Roth, Heinz: *Widerstand im Dritten Reich*, Odenhausen, 1976, p.240.

275. *Cf* FAZ, 5 April 1952.

276. Morand, Paul: *Journal inutile*, mémoires, vol. 2, p.403.

277. Feiling, Keith: *The Life of Neville Chamberlain*, London, 1946, p.418.

278. This notion has passed into general usage with the meaning of an 'ideal solution' to a problem.

279. FAZ dated 15 April 1970, p.2.

280. Documents on the events preceding the outbreak of the war, Doc. No. 208: Record of the discussion between the German Foreign Minister and the Polish ambassador Joseph Lipski, 26 March 1939.

281. The German White Paper – Full Text of the Polish documents, New York, 1940, Doc. No. 11: Report of the Polish ambassador in Paris, Łukasiewicz, addressed to the Polish Foreign Minister Beck dated 29 March 1939 concerning a conversation with the US ambassador in Paris, Bullitt.

282. Cf for the rest Ribbentrop, J. v.: *op. cit.*, pp.186–204, here pp.186-87.

283. Below, Nicolaus von: *op. cit.*, p.187 *et seq.*

284. In her book on Albert Speer, Gitta Sereny's judgement on Below's memoirs is: 'I consider Below's book to be a unique document, for here a man, an uncomplicated one actually, but absolutely honest, makes a serious attempt to work things out.'; *cf* Sereny, Gitta: *Das Ringen mit der Wahrheit*, Munich, 1995, p.139 (English edition: *Albert Speer: His battle with Truth*, London, 1996).

285. Ribbentrop, J. v.: *op. cit.*, pp.188–90.

286. British War Blue Book, Doc. No. 74.

287. Ribbentrop, J. v.: *op. cit.*, p.191.

288. Ribbentrop, J. v.: *op. cit.*, pp.191–93; *see* also British War Blue Book, Doc. No. 78.

289. Ambassador Sir Howard Kennard to Foreign Secretary Halifax, Warsaw, 30 August 1939; as in the official British original documentation HMSO, Miscellaneous No. 9 (1939), Documents concerning German-Polish Relations and the outbreak of hostilities between Great Britain and Germany on September 3, 1939, Doc. No. 84: 'I am, of course, expressing no views to the Polish Government, nor am I communicating to them Herr Hitler's reply till I receive instructions which I trust will be without delay.'

290. Even the conspirator Dr Paul Schmidt (not to be confused with the chief of the Auswärtiges Amt's Press Department of the same name) says in his book *Statist auf diplomatischer Bühne* on p.459: 'Ribbentrop read the proposals out loud to Henderson in German [Henderson spoke German fluently], without however, as has often been maintained since, being in any particular hurry. On the contrary he elucidated certain points.'

291. Ribbentrop, J. v.: *op. cit.*, pp.195-97; Chamberlain noted in his diary under the date of 10 September 1939: 'I believe he [Hitler] did seriously contemplate an agreement with us, and that he worked seriously at proposals (subsequently broadcast).'; from Feiling, K.: *op. cit.*, p.416 *et seq.*

292. Ribbentrop/Hitler proposals (through Dahlerus) to Henderson in: Documents on the events preceding the outbreak of the war, Doc. No. 466.

293. IMT, vol. XVII, Proceedings, 28 June 1946, Morning session; p.193 *et seq.* Stated in the Nuremberg trials by the head of the ministry department at the time Hans Fritzsche.

294. HMSO, Miscellaneous No. 9. (1939), Documents concerning German-Polish Relations and the outbreak of hostilities between Great Britain and Germany on September 3, 1939, Doc. No. 96.

295. *Cf* Documents on the events preceding the outbreak of the war, Doc. No. 469.

296. *Cf* Statement by Birger Dahlerus in the Nuremberg trials from: IMT, Vol. IX, Proceedings, Morning session of 19 March 1946, p.470.

297. Feiling, Keith: *op. cit.*, p.416 *et seq.*

298. Ribbentrop, J. v.: *op. cit.*, pp.197-203.

299. Ribbentrop, J. v.: *op. cit.*, p.203.

300. *Cf* Musial, Bogdan: *op. cit.*

301. See primarily Schustereit, Hartmut: *Vabanque. Hitlers Angriff auf die Sowjetunion* (Hitler's attack on the Soviet Union), Herford, 1988; as also Klein, Burton: *op. cit.*

302. Kunert, Dirk: *Ein Weltkrieg wird programmiert* (A World War is programmed), Kiel, 1984, pp.31, 309, footnote 9; Wilson quoted by Dulles, Foster Rhea: *America's Rise to World Power, 1898–1954*, New York, 1955 (1963), p.115.

303. Tansill, Ch.: *op. cit.*, p.35 *et seq.* and footnote 42; Wheeler-Bennett, John: *Documents on International Affairs – 1933*, London, 1934, p.209.

304. Quoted from: Peace and War, United States Foreign Policy, 1931-1941, Index No. 14, President Roosevelt to the Secretary of State, May 6, 1933, Washington, 1943.

305. Had Eisenhower not employed the term 'Crusade in Europe' for his Memoirs? *Cf* Eisenhower, Dwight D.: *Crusade in Europe*, New York 1948.

306. *Cf* amongst others Morgenstern, George: *Pearl Harbor – The story of the secret war*, New York, 1947.

307. Memorandum of a conversation between Secretary Hull and the French Ambassador (Georges Bonnet), March 18, 1937. 500. A 19/70, MS, Department of State quoted from Tansill, Charles: *Back Door to War*, p.327 *et seq.* and p.328, footnote 2.

308. Tansill, Ch.: *op. cit*, p.328 and *ib.* footnote 4, Norman H. Davis to Secretary Hull, London, April 10, 1937. 740.00/143, Confidential file, MS, Department of State.

309. German White Paper – Full text of the Polish documents, New York, 1940, Doc. No. 9.

310. *100 Documents on the Origin of the War*, Berlin, 1939, p.109.

311. English: 'It is hard not to write satire.' (Juvenal)

312. See the President's Memorandum to the Director of the Franklin D. Roosevelt Library, Washington, 16 July 1943, in which he determines the

treatment of the written legacy he would leave and where he specifies his wish to 'select those which are never to be made public'.

313. 'Novus ordo seclorum' alludes to Verse 5 of the 4th Eclogue of the Latin poet Virgil: *Magnus ab integro saeclorum nascitur ordo* (The great order of the ages is born afresh). Charles Thomson, the designer of the Great Seal of the United States (published for the first time in 1782), wrote that these words were to herald the onset of a new American Age.

314. Eden, Anthony: *Memoirs – Facing the Dictators* (Book Two: Responsibility), p.509.

315. Tansill, Ch.: *op. cit.*, p.514 and *ib.* footnote 17, Ambassador Kennedy to Secretary Hull, London, April 4, 1939. 740.00/736, *Confidential file*, MS, Department of State.

316. Charmley, John: *Churchill, The End of Glory*, Suffolk, 1993, pp.438, 685, footnote 55; Reynolds, D.: *The Creation of the Anglo-American Alliance 1937-41*, p.156.

317. Charmley, J.: *op. cit.*, pp.437, 685, footnote 47, PRO Prem. 3/486/1, fos 299-35, for the various drafts; Cadogan Diary, 11 November 1940, p.335; Reynolds, ibid., pp.150-51.

318. Charmley, J.: *op. cit.*, pp.437, 685, footnote 49; Cadogan Diary, p.335.

319. Charmley, J.: *op. cit.*, pp.443, 686, footnote 16; Ponting, C.: *1940 – Myth and Reality*, p.212.

320. Charmley, J.: *op. cit.*, pp.443, 686, footnote 18; Reynolds, D.: *The Creation of the Anglo-American Alliance 1937-41*, pp.164-65; Dobson, A.P.: *US Wartime Aid to Britain 1940-46*, p.29.

321. Charmley, J.: *op. cit.*, pp.438, 685, footnote 59; Taylor: *Beaverbrook – Beaverbrook to Churchill, 26 December 1940*, p.439.

322. *Cf* FAZ, 31 July 2006, p.3; see also *Stars and Stripes*, 12 January 2007: 'U.K. makes final payment to U.S. for post-WWII reconstruction'.

323. Charmley, J.: *op. cit.*, p.444.

324. Charmley, J.: *op. cit.*, pp.438, 685, footnote 53; Reynolds, D.: *The Creation of the Anglo-American Alliance*, p.154, also footnote 58; Kimball, W.F. (ed.): *Churchill & Roosevelt – The Complete Correspondence*, vol. I, p.120.

325. *Cf* Morgenstern, G.: *op. cit.* (German edition: *Pearl Harbor 1941 – Eine amerikanische Katastrophe*, Munich, 1998, p.131).

326. *Cf* Morgenstern, G.: *op. cit.*; Tansill, Ch.: *op. cit.*

327. Tansill, Ch.: *op. cit.*, p.651 *et seq.*

328. *Cf* Scheil, Stefan: *Fünf plus Zwei*, p.486 *et seq.* and footnote 180; Nicolson, Harold: *Harold Nicolson's Diaries and Letters*, 2 vols, p.104. Scheil convincingly points out that Lothian knew the German conditions, considered them reasonable and transmitted them to London.

329. On 21 November 1942, the American writer Henry Miller wrote to the British writer Lawrence Durrell that 'Churchill announces that he is not

giving the Empire away (sic). That didn't meet with such a warm reception over here. We want the English to give their bloody Empire away, doesn't he know that, the old pfoof?' Quoted from: *The Durrell–Miller Letters, 1935-80*, New York, 1988, p.157.

330. *The Times*, 2 January 1993.

331. A unification of the European countries under German leadership had long been planned in case there would be no agreement with England. My father insisted on this also during later stages of the war, as for instance in the record 'Regarding European Confederation of States' dated 21 March 1943. Werner Best on Ribbentrop; in Matlok, Siegfried (publ.), *Dänemark in Hitlers Hand*, Husum, 1988, p.202.

332. Cassell (publ.): *The Testament of Adolf Hitler*, London, 1961, p.63.

333. As said to me by my father in August 1944.

334. *Cf* Andreas Hillgruber, Stufentheorie' zur Weltherrschaft (Stage theory (Harmony)) in *Hitlers Strategie, Politik und Kriegsführung 1940-1941*, p.22 *et seq.* and p.207 *et seq.*

335. Schustereit, Hartmut: *op. cit.*, pp.13-20.

336. Mueller-Hillebrand, Burkhart: *Das Heer 1933-1945* (The Army), Vol. II. *Die Blitzfeldzüge 1939–1941*, Frankfurt/M., 1956, p.63 *et seq.*

337. Schustereit, H.: *op. cit.*, p.21 *et seq.*

338. Wagner, Gerhard (publ.): *Lagevorträge des Oberbefehlshabers der Kriegsmarine vor Hitler 1939–1945* (Situation Conferences of the Commander-in-Chief of the German Navy to Hitler), Munich, 1972, p.104.

339. Wagner, G. (publ.): *op. cit.*, p.106

340. Schustereit, H.: *op. cit.*

341. Wagner, Gerhard (publ.): *op. cit.*; Situation Conference of 6 September 1940, *op cit.*, p.136; *cf* also Rahn, Werner: *Kriegstagebuch der Seekriegsleitung* [KTB SKL] *1939–1945* (War Diaries of the Maritime Warfare Command), 68 vols, reprint 1988; here: KTB SKL, A, vol. 13, p.69.

342. See also Schustereit, H.: *op. cit.*

343. Quoted from KTB SKL, A, Vol. 13, p.197. Attacks on London's city precincts were thus prohibited to the Luftwaffe. A telegram with the following content is delivered by Göring: 'It is to be announced without delay which crews have bombed the area of London exempt from bombing. The Luftwaffe Commander-in-Chief reserves the right to punish those in question himself.' From Zentner, Christian: *Der zweite Weltkrieg*, p.64.

344. Wagner, G. (publ.): *op. cit.*, p.148.

345. Wagner, G. (publ.): *op. cit.*, p.149.

346. Wagner, G. (publ.): *op. cit.*, p.166.

347. Wagner, G. (publ.): *op. cit.*, p.172.

348. Quoted from Scheil, Stefan: *1940/41 Die Eskalation des Zweiten Weltkriegs*, Munich. 2005, pp.67, 463, footnote 42; Halder, Franz: *Kriegstagebuch*, II.

349. DGFP, 1962, Series D, Vol. IX, Doc. 129.

350. Detwiler, Donald S.: *Hitler, Franco und Gibraltar*, Wiesbaden, 1962, pp.25, 148, Note 18; from Peers, E. Allison: *Spain in Eclipse*, and Hoare, Sir Samuel: *Complacent Dictator*.

351. Josef Müller (1898–1979) was a delegate of the Bavarian People's Party (Bayerische Volkspartei) in the Weimar Republic, and at the time of National Socialism a member of the Catholic Resistance against Hitler. After 1945 he was the first chairman of the CSU (Christian Social Union).

352. Colvin, Ian: *op. cit.*, p.149.

353. Serrano Súñer, Ramón: *Zwischen Hendaye und Gibraltar* (Between Hendaye and Gibraltar), Zürich, 1948, pp.168, 240.

354. Maser, Werner (publ.): *Keitel, Wilhelm – Mein Leben*, Berlin, 1998, p.313.

355. Serrano Súñer, R.: *op. cit.*, p.192.

356. Churchill, W.: *The Second World War* (Vol. II: Their Finest Hour), London, 1949–54, pp.460, 469.

357. Alfred Seidl was the attorney for the defence of Rudolf Hess at the Nuremberg trials, and among other posts was Bavarian State Justice Minister.

358. Walter Hewel's Diary, (1941).

359. Wagner, G. (publ.) *op. cit.*, p.143 *et seq.*

360. Keitel, W.: *op. cit.*, p.313.

361. Study by General Erich Marcks, Chief of Staff of the 19th Army that guarded in the East in case of a military confrontation with the Soviet Union.

362. Uhle-Wettler, Franz: *Alfred von Tirpitz in seiner Zeit* (Alfred von Tirpitz in his day), Hamburg, 1998, p.147.

363. *Cf*, among other works, Bereshkov, Valentin M.: *Ich war Stalins Dolmetscher* (I was Stalin's interpreter), Munich, 1991, p.290.

364. As per Roland von zur Mühlen, also present; *cf* Scheil, Stefan: *Eskalation*, p.520, N.77.

365. For the rest *cf* Walter Hewel's diary for 29 and 30 May as well as 8, 13 and 20 June 1941.

366. *Cf* Keitel, W.: *op. cit.*, p.290.

367. *Cf* on this: Schnurre, K.: *op. cit.*

368. This is stressed above all by Stefan Scheil; *cf Eskalation*, p.170 *et seq.*

369. Schnurre, K.: *op. cit.*

370. Ribbentrop, J. v.: *op. cit.*, p.237.

371. Schnurre, K.: *op. cit.*

372. Speaking in private, Schnurre mentioned General Walter Warlimont as another person taking part in the conversation.

373. This was the French general and statesman Marquis Armand Augustin Louis de Caulaincourt, Duke of Vicenza (1773–1827). He advised Napoleon against a war with Russia.

374. Hewel, W.: Tagebuch (Diary) for 28 April 1941.

375. Seidl, Alfred: *Die Beziehungen zwischen Deutschland und der Sowjetunion* (The relations between Germany and the Soviet Union) 1939–1941, 251 Dokumente, *Schulenburgs Niederlegung über den Verlauf des Gespräches mit Hitler* (Schulenburg's account of the course of the discussion with Hitler), Doc. No. 231, p.379.

376. *Cf* Reschin, Leonid: *Feldmarschall im Kreuzverhör* (Field Marshal in cross-questioning), Berlin, 1996, p.233 *et seq.*

377. Communicated by former delegate Dr Paul Schmidt-Carell to the author.

378. Ribbentrop, J. v., *op. cit.*, S. 248.

379. Hewel, W.: Tagebuch (Diary) 1941, entry dated 20 June: Risk: 'a locked door'.

380. *Cf* Allen, Martin: *The Hitler/Hess deception: British Intelligence's Best-Kept Secret of the Second World War*, London, 2003, (German edition: *Churchills Friedensfalle* (Churchill's Peace Trap), Stegen, 2003).

381. DGFP, Series D, Vol. VIII, Doc. No. 663, p.871.

382. At the Navy Commander in Chief's Situation Conference with Hitler on 27 December 1940, Hitler said to Raeder: 'In general, however, in view of the present political developments (Russia's refusal to be involved in Balkan affairs) the last Continental opponent has to be eradicated.' From Wagner, G.: *op. cit.*, p.174; Ribbentrop, J. v.: *op. cit.*, p.239 *et seq.*

383. *Cf* Schustereit, Hartmut: *op. cit.*, p.100 *et seq.*

384. Suvorov, Viktor: *Stalins verhinderter Erstschlag*, Selent, 2000.

385. Ribbentrop, J. v.: *op. cit.*, p.206 *et seq.*

386. Communication from Delegate K. Schnurre to the author.

387. Ribbentrop, J. v.: *op. cit.*, p.208.

388. DGFP, Series D, Vol. XI, Doc. No. 176, p.296 *et seq.*; publ. in Seidl, Alfred: *op. cit.*, p.236, Doc. No. 171, as in Ribbentrop, J. v.: *op. cit.*, p.230 *et seq.*

389. Ribbentrop, J. v.: *op. cit.*, p.231.

390. Wagner, G. (publ.): *op. cit.*; Conference dated 26 September 1940.

391. *Cf* Scheil, Stefan: *Eskalation*, p.131.

392. Ribbentrop, J. v.: *op. cit*, p.235 *et seq.*

393. Hewel, W.: Tagebuch (Diary) (1941).

394. Beard, Charles A.: *President Roosevelt and the Coming of the War, 1941: Appearances and Realities*, New Haven, 1948, p.105.

395. *Cf* Ribbentrop, J. v.: *op. cit.*, p.249 *et seq.*

396. Ribbentrop, J. v.: *op. cit.*, p.262 *et seq.*

397. Ribbentrop, J. v.: *op. cit.*, p.264 *et seq.*

398. At Cannae in southern Italy Hannibal defeated a numerically greatly superior Roman army – whose forces against him had been deeply massed in the centre – by weakening his army in the centre and attacking the Roman flank in a pincer movement, finally enveloping and annihilating them.

399. Particularly unpleasant is Schmückle, a lieutenant colonel in his day, and press aide to Defence Minister Strauss, and also Philipp von Boeselager and others.

400. In post-war literature General Hubert Lanz is represented as a brave man who opposed senseless orders to hold a position. At that time the Panzer Corps under his orders was unaware of such an attitude. As late as 14 February 1943, radio message No. 624 was sent to the SS-Panzer Corps General Command which read 'Panzer Corps according to Führer's order holding present position on the Kharkov eastern front to the last man. sgd Lanz.' Thereon see also Romedio G. Count Thun-Hohenstein in Poeppel, Hans/W.-K. Prinz von Preußen/Hase, K.-G. von (eds): *Die Soldaten der Wehrmacht* (The Wehrmacht Soldiers), Munich, 1998, p.107.

401. Meyer, Kurt: *Grenadiere*, München, 1956, p.172 (English edition: *Grenadiers: The story of Waffen-SS General Kurt 'Panzer' Meyer*, Mechanicsburg, 2005).

402. A Russian 7.62cm cannon was called 'Crash-Bang' ('*Ratsch-Bum*' in German) because when it fired, first the sharp bang of the shot was heard, like a 'crash', and only then the dull thud of the cannon thunder. It was the Russian weapon that we tank people feared the most.

403. This culvert is shown in the ZDF film mentioned below about the Prokhorovka tank battle, albeit in a different context.

404. To return again to the allegedly better arming and equipment of the Waffen-SS divisions: the Panther units for *Unternehmen Zitadelle* remained reserved for the army; the Waffen-SS divisions acquired Panther units only later.

405. In a ZDF film about the battle at Prokhorovka, a Russian tank commander describes both shots.

406. This too is mentioned in the ZDF film by a Russian tank officer who had taken part in the action. The Grenadiers, who were positioned to our right at the secure railway embankment, were able to observe what went on. One of them wrote to me after the war: 'All four of us saw exactly what happened ... all four could not understand what was going on. I also watched your carousel around the T-34, which was earlier. We had a good laugh about how you outwitted them ... I saw how you drove ahead in your P-IVs [Panzer IV] and that they were shot out one after another, not without scoring richly against the attackers. All at once I saw how a P-IV suddenly joined in with the Russians. It drove fully in with their attack in the direction of the anti-tank ditch, while firing all the time in the direction of its comrades. Until suddenly the penny dropped and I realized that "mad dog" was firing one fatal shot after another at his new friends. The Russians absolutely did not catch on.' (Letters from former Technical Sergeant Wilhelm Rogmann [Freiberg i. Sa.] dated 7 January 1991 and 3 February 1991.)

407. My radio operator Bergner's diary was placed at my disposal only in July 2001 by his brother. In the war Bergner himself was later taken out of a tank, gravely wounded, and carried onto an armoured ambulance which received a direct hit immediately afterwards, to which Bergner too fell victim. For 12 July 1943 he writes: 'General tank alarm. Immediate attack necessary ... With our 7 tanks remaining in the past days from the initial 22. We drive fast to the rise where the infantry is shooting off violet flare cartridges in such numbers that we have to assume a major tank attack is underway. And suddenly, there they are. A T-34 at 20 metres next to us and then, in front of us more and more tanks, like a stampeding herd. Far and wide a rumbling, rattling, booming, dust and smoke. It was near night-fall. Did it mean the end for us all? A sudden scare ... We quickly recovered from this shock. And soon out of the mass one fell by the wayside. We fired from the shortest distance. Right in the middle of the pack of tanks we turned head to tail and fired from behind. Without attracting much attention. A few times the Russian infantrymen sitting on the tanks noticed us but it was already too late for them and my MG contributed to that. The great risk was to weave through the burnt-out tanks without being hit; also by the tanks of the other companies that for their part had taken up positions in the anti-tank ditch. Within half an hour our gunner at that time, Kurt Hoppe, had shot out 14 Russian tanks. An hour later, in the portion of the battlefield of about 500 x 1,000 metres of our unit ... more than 125 enemy tanks had been downed. At noon we drive up to the rise where the Russians wanted to catch us by surprise. But they didn't manage it. We regard ourselves as having emerged the victors over a super-power.'

408. *Cf* Klein, Burton: *op. cit.*

409. Fritz Todt (from 1940 Reich Minister of Armaments and Munitions) wanted to see that 'the issue of women's military service was not taken into consideration for the time being, out of political reasons'. See Schustereit, H: *op. cit.*, pp.27, 159, Note 72, Chef Rü, Aktenvermerk bei (Memorandum to) Reichsminister Dr Todt dated 9.1.1941, Berlin, 10 January 1941, Sheet No. 3, *ibid*.

410. See entry in Hewel's diary dated 28 May 1941.

411. *Cf* Hitler's famous speech to the Reichstag of 28 April 1939, in which he replied to a 'message' from Roosevelt who had addressed provocative 'enquiries' to the Reich government. It was a brilliant speech that he evidently had fun with! Whether it was appropriate to the diplomatic situation may be doubted; *see* Domarus, M.: *op. cit.*, p.1,148 *et sequ.*

412. Ribbentrop, J. v.: *op. cit.*, p.47 *et sequ.* and p.233.

413. Hitler, A.: *Mein Kampf*, p.958 (English edition).

414. Kluge, Dankwart: *Das Hoßbach-'Protokoll'. Die Zerstörung einer Legende*, Leoni am Starnberger See (The Destruction of a Legend, Leoni at Lake

Starnberg) 1980, p.36 *et seq.* Kluge's book moreover gives a detailed description of how the Hossbach Note came about as well as its background, and the changes the text underwent, leading to diverse versions being published.

415. It was a consistent theme of Hitler's dinner-table discourse in the war years. *Cf* Picker, Dr Henry: *The Hitler phenomenon: An intimate portrait of Hitler and his entourage*, Newton Abbot, 1974, *passim.*

416. I remember an editorial on the front page of the *Völkischer Beobachter*, the Party's official paper, entitled '*Das Erbe Karl des Großen*' ('The Heritage of Charlemagne') (author Dr Nonnenbruch).

417. Keitel, W.: *op. cit.*, p.424 *et seq.*

418. Hitler, A.: *op. cit.*, p.958.

419. See Guderian, Heinz: *Erinnerungen eines Soldaten* (A Soldier's Memories), Heidelberg, 1951, p.26 (English edition: *Panzer Leader*, New York, 1952).

420. Lipgens, Walter (ed.): *Documents on the History of European Integration*, Vol. 1, *Continental Plans for European Union 1939-1945*, Berlin, 1985, p.123 *et seq.*

421. Mazower, Mark: *Hitlers Imperium*, München 2009, p 331.

422. See Schustereit, H.: *op. cit.*, p.10 *et seq.*

423. Klein, Burton: *op. cit.*, p.24 *et seq.*

424. Reinhardt, Fritz (publ.: Ralf Wittrich): *Die Beseitigung der Arbeitslosigkeit im Dritten Reich. Das Sofortprogramm 1933/34* (The elimination of unemployment in the Third Reich. The immediacy programme).

425. Röhricht, Edgar: *Pflicht und Gewissen. Erinnerungen eines deutschen Generals 1932 bis 1944* (Duty and Conscience. Memories of a German general), Stuttgart, 1965; quoted from the note by Colonel Günther von Below (brother of the Luftwaffe adjutant Nicolaus von Below).

426. Halder's statement in the proceedings at his denazification tribunal on 15 September 1948 (BA/MA N 220/64), quoted from Hartmann, Christian: *Halder – Generalstabschef Hitlers 1938-1942*, Paderborn, 1991, p.346.

427. Keitel, W.: *op. cit.*, p.316.

428. Name of a Russian spy ring.

429. See *Der Spiegel*, 13 April 1998, p.76.

430. The concept was already current at the time of the First World War as a characteristic of the modern battlefield.

431. Guderian writes in his memoirs that the commander of the *Leibstandarte*, Sepp Dietrich, was the first to present himself to Guderian after Guderian's dismissal as commander and had vouched for Dietrich's solidarity with him against 'those up there'! See Guderian, H.: *op. cit.*, p.247.

432. See the alleged 'Note for the Führer' that Reinhard Spitzy copied from von Papen. *Cf* with p.141, Footnote 153.

433. Mann, Heinrich: *Zur Zeit von Winston Churchill* (At the time of Winston Churchill), new edition, Frankfurt, 2004.

434. Savoy, Bénédicte: *Kunstraub – Napoleons Konfiszierungen in Deutschland und die europäischen Folgen,* Vienna, 2011, pp.193, 461, Note 173; Sauvier, Charles: *Les conquêtes artistiques de la Révolution et de l'Empire*, Paris, 1902, p.159.

435. Chatelain, Jean: *Dominique Vivant Denon et le Louvre de Napoléon*, Paris, 1973, p.253.

436. See also FAZ (Frankfurter Allgemeine Zeitung) of 3 January 2004; Savoy, Bénédicte: *op. cit.*, p.163 *et seq.* and p.457, Note 49; Cullen, Michael and Kieling, Uwe: *Das Brandenburger Tor, ein deutsches Symbol*, Berlin, 1999, pp.44-45.

437. Enzensberger, Hans Magnus (publ.): *Gespräche mit Marx und Engels* (Discussion with …), Vol I, Frankfurt/Main, 1973, p.30 *et seq.*

438. Eckermann, Johann Peter: *Conversations with Goethe in the last years of his life*, Boston, 1839, p.151. Mucius Scaevola is said to have been taken, as a prisoner of the Etruscans, to the Etruscan king Porsenna who was besieging Rome. To demonstrate the courage of the Romans to the king, he burned his hand in a brazier. The king is said to have been so impressed that he abandoned the siege.

439. Grandfather used variously to mention the name of General Max von Gallwitz and his setbacks in connection with the influence – not always fortunate – of the Imperial Military Cabinet, by which Ludendorff too will no doubt have been affected. I found the confirmation in Wilhelm Keitel's memoirs: *op. cit.*, p.113.

440. Bismarck for his part is said to have stated: '… one cannot be absolved from mutilating it [a nation] and history, that great teacher of statesmen, tells us it is always regretted.' from Documents Diplomatiques Français (1871-1914), 1st Series, Vol. II, 476 (1879), quoted from Ingrim, Robert: *Bismarck selbst. Tausend Gedanken des Fürsten Otto von Bismarck* (Bismarck himself. Prince Otto von Bismarck's Thousand Thoughts), Stuttgart, 1950, p.60.

441. The exact title of the dissertation was *Das Wachstum der Berliner Flaschenbier-Industrie* (The growth of the Berlin bottled beer industry), compiled in 1900.

442. Spitzy tries yet another trick and maintains that the Club Secretary had been a Herr von Lieres, who had to inform Father of his rejection. Thereupon, when Father undertook the Auswärtiges Amt, he dismissed Lieres. As a matter of fact Lieres had misbehaved in that he defied attending a meeting of all the department employees – convened because of Father's posting – and had as a consequence been suspended.

443. *Cf* Keynes, John M.: 'The German Transfer Problem', in *Economic Journal* Vol. 39 (1929), pp.1–7; Lüke, Rolf E.: *Von der Stabilisierung zur Krise* (From

stabilization to crisis), Basle Centre for Economic and Financial Research (publ.), Series B, No. 3, Zürich, 1958, p.56 *et seq.*

444. When in May 1940 it was thought to halt General Guderian, who with his armoured Corps had broken through to the coast of the Channel, because of a threatening flank movement, he had rejected the order, couched in the words: 'I cannot make any good use here of a Hentsch mission.'

445. Quoted from Haffner, Sebastian: *Von Bismarck zu Hitler,* p.65; see also Steinberg, Jonathan: *Bismarck: A life*, ch.5, New York, 2011.

446. Ribbentrop, J. v.: *op. cit.*, p.47.

447. Information from the then competent chief of the Press and Information Department of the Auswärtiges Amt Delegate Dr Paul Schmidt to the author.

448. The video tape of the interview is in my possession.

449. After the war I tried in vain to contact Dürckheim through a close collaborator of his whom I knew well. Apparently meditation and East Asian serenity, which Dürckheim exercised as therapy, are no protection against the fear of 'politically correct' contact!

450. See the book *Les avertissements qui venaient de Berlin* (The warnings that came from Berlin) by the Belgian historian Jean Vanwelkenhuyzen, Paris, 1982, pp.22 and 365, Note 28.

451. Confirmed by the Steengrachts' son to the author.

452. Spitzy mentions the intention to incriminate Baroness Steengracht so as to trip up Steengracht as a 'Ribbentrop acolyte'. He does, however, take judicious care not to mention the betrayal of the dates for the outbreak of the Western campaign as incitement in connection with it. *Cf.* Spitzy, R.: *op. cit.*, p.408.

453. *Cf* Magenheimer, H.: *Entscheidungskampf 1941* (Decisive Battle 1941).

454. I have referred here to the notes of Colonel von Geldern in my possession.

455. Janssen, K.-H., and Tobias, F.: *Der Sturz der Generäle* (The overthrow of the generals).

456. Schall-Riaucour, Heidemarie Gräfin von: *Generaloberst Franz Halder,* Beltheim, 2006, pp.142, 435.

457. Envoy Dr Paul Schmidt (Press) informed me that Himmler had wanted to launch the head of the SS foreign news agency, Walter Schellenberg, as state secretary in the Auswärtiges Amt. Himmler's major 'Luther intrigue' against Father had been the result of Father's refusal to accede to Himmler's wish.

458. Ribbentrop, J. v.: *op. cit.*, p.46.

459. See also Junge, Traudl: *Hitler's Last Secretary*, New York, 2011, p.66. Junge writes that Hewel retorted to a joking observation Hitler made to him, that Hewel was after all 'no diplomat! More of a giant diplomatic cowboy!', saying: 'If I weren't a diplomat I couldn't stand between you and Ribbentrop, my

Führer.' Hitler had to acknowledge the truth of this, for he knew what a difficult character the Foreign Minister was.

460. Matlok, S. (ed.): *Dänemark in Hitlers Hand* (Denmark in Hitler's hands. Report by the Reich Plenipotentiary), pp.140, 202.

461. We have unfortunately been unable to obtain a copy of the entry, or even permission of access for inspection.

462. Matlok, S. (ed.), *op. cit.*, p.146 *et seq.*

463. After the war, Dr Werner Best was initially condemned to death by the Copenhagen municipal court, the sentence then commuted by the court of appeal to five years' imprisonment, and was finally released as early as 29 August 1951.

464. Ribbentrop, J. v.: *op. cit.*, p. 256.

465. Counsellor Gottfriedsen orally reconfirmed this instruction to the author.

466. This formulation, directly addressed to Hitler, contradicts the contentions advanced for example by the interpreter Schmidt and by Spitzy that Father wanted to be State Secretary but had instead been fobbed off to London by Hitler.

467. On the occasion of a dinner at friends of the family in Bergisch-Gladbach.

468. A note of a talk with David Irving about Herr von Etzdorf at the author's home.

469. From Colonel von Geldern's notes.

470. Information transmitted to the author by the envoy and head of the Press Department Dr Paul Schmidt.

471. Confirmation in writing to the author through Otto Kranzbühler, the defendant of High Admiral Dönitz at the Nuremberg trials.

472. See: 'Es stand in der "WELT"' ('It was published in *Die Welt*'), in *Die Welt*, 31 January 1993, and '*Die Zeit*'/*Online-Politik*.

473. As maintained by R. Spitzy.

474. *Cf.* Konrad Morgen's declaration in: IMT, Vol. XLII, p.559 *et seq.* In addition: Hoffmann, Hans: *Hast Du diese Tötungen befohlen?* (Did you order the killings?), Bad Harzburg, 1997.

475. Federal Press Office, Bulletin 52/S. 441: Speech of 8 May 1995 on the occasion of the 50th Anniversary of the end of the Second World War.

476. See *The Times*, 5 September 1939, as well as the *London Jewish Chronicle*, 8 September 1939.

477. In the winter of 1943/44 in Staff quarters it was discussed that in the foreseeable future weapons of mass destruction would be at disposal against the British Isles. They were evidently rumours spread by propaganda with the object of hindering the invasion plans of the Allies.

478. Hitler, A.: *op. cit.*, p.897.

479. Quoted from Scheil, Stefan: *Fünf plus Zwei* (Five plus Two), p.304 and footnote 177; Jackson, Robert H. (ed.): *International Conference on Military Trials, A documentary record of negotiations*, Washington, 1949, p.306.

480. Reynolds, Michael: *Steel Inferno*, New York, 1998, pp.16, 353.

481. Karl Epting was for many years the head of the Paris German Culture Institute. During his time in Cherchemidi he published *Aus dem Cherchemidi. Pariser Aufzeichnungen 1947-1949* (From the Cherchemidi. Parisian Notes 1947–1949), Bonn, 1953.

482. Ref. to: Schiller, F. v.: Maria Stuart, I, 2; V.

483. Letter dated 17 December 1952.

484. An amusing fellow-inmate had said that the Allied prisons and internment camps were as well known to the German intelligentsia as the good hotels and restaurants were to globetrotters.

485. Schlabrendorff, Fabian von: *Revolt against Hitler – The personal account*, London, 1948, from Ribbentrop, J. v.: *op. cit.*, p.270.

Index